Hugo Grotius on the Law of War

Despite its significant influence on international law, international relations, natural law and political thought in general, Grotius's *Law of War and Peace* has been virtually unavailable for many decades.

Stephen C. Neff's edited and annotated version of the text rectifies this situation. Containing the substantive portion of the classic text, but shorn of extraneous material, this edition of one of the classic works of Western legal and political thought is intended for students and teachers in four primary areas: history of international law; history of political thought; history of international relations; and history of philosophy.

Stephen C. Neff is a reader in public international law at the School of Law, University of Edinburgh. His subject area is the history of public international law.

Hugo Grotius
On the Law of War and Peace

Edited and annotated by
STEPHEN C. NEFF

CAMBRIDGE
UNIVERSITY PRESS

CAMBRIDGE UNIVERSITY PRESS
Cambridge, New York, Melbourne, Madrid, Cape Town,
Singapore, São Paulo, Delhi, Mexico City

Cambridge University Press
The Edinburgh Building, Cambridge CB2 8RU, UK

Published in the United States of America by Cambridge University Press, New York

www.cambridge.org
Information on this title: www.cambridge.org/9780521197786

First published 2012

Printed and Bound in the United Kingdom by the MPG Books Group

A catalogue record for this publication is available from the British Library

Library of Congress Cataloguing in Publication data
Grotius, Hugo, 1583–1645.
[De jure belli ac pacis libri tres. English.]
Hugo Grotius on the law of war and peace / Hugo Grotius ; edited by Stephen C. Neff.
    p.   cm.
Includes index.
ISBN 978-0-521-19778-6 (hardback)
1. International law – Early works to 1800.   2. War (International law) – Early works to 1800.
3. Natural law – Early works to 1800.   I. Neff, Stephen C.   II. Title.
KZ2093.A3J8813   2012
341.6 – dc23   2012021560

ISBN 978-0-521-19778-6 Hardback
ISBN 978-0-521-12812-4 Paperback

For Nancy, once again (and always)

Contents

BOOK III

Preface

Apart from the late Hugo Grotius, I am grateful to a number of people for assistance of various kinds in bringing this project to fruition. Finola O'Sullivan, from Cambridge University Press, was both supportive from the start, and patient at the end – a most welcome combination. For heroic labours at the word-processor, my greatest thanks go to Marie Armah-Kwantreng. Professor John Cairns and Dr Paul Duplessis, of the University of Edinburgh School of Law, kindly assisted with some Latin translation. For excellent work in editing, proof-reading, and general criticism (fortunately constructive), I am in deepest debt to Ashley Theunissen. For a splendid job of copy-editing, my heartiest thanks go to Kate Ollerenshaw.

Abbreviations

Aquinas, *Treatise on Law*	Thomas Aquinas, *The Treatise on Law* [being *Summa Theologiae*, I–II, QQ. 90–7], edited and translated by R. J. Henle (University of Notre Dame Press, 1993)
Aquinas, *Political Writings*	Thomas Aquinas, *Political Writings*, edited and translated by R. W. Dyson (Cambridge University Press, 2002)
Articles on State Responsibility (2001)	International Law Commission, Articles on State Responsibility (2001), in Malcolm D. Evans (ed.), *Blackstone's International Law Documents* (Oxford University Press, 10th edn, 2011), at pp. 556–64
Consolato del Mare	*Consulate of the Sea and Related Documents*, edited by Stanley S. Jados (University of Alabama Press, 1975)
Digest	*The Digest of Justinian*, translated by Alan Watson (Philadelphia, PA: University of Pennsylvania Press, 1998), 2 vols.
Hague Rules	Hague Rules on Land Warfare, Hague Convention IV, 18 October 1907, 205 *Consolidated Treaty Series* 277
Protocol I of 1977	Protocol I Additional to the Geneva Conventions of 1949, 8 June 1977, 1125 *UN Treaty Series* 3
Suárez, *Treatise on Laws*	Francisco Suárez, *A Treatise on Laws and God the Lawgiver*, in *Selections from Three Works of Francisco Suárez*, translated by Gwladys L. Williams, Ammi Brown, and John Waldron (Oxford: Clarendon Press, 1944 [1612])
Vienna Convention on the Law of Treaties	Vienna Convention on the Law of Treaties, 23 May 1969, 1155 *UN Treaty Series* 331

Introduction

Hugo Grotius's *On the Law of War and Peace* could be described as a stately circumnavigation of the juridical world. Like Tolstoy's later novel of similar name, it provides a teeming, sprawling overview of the richness of life – legal life, of course, in the case of Grotius. Unlike Tolstoy's novel (unfortunately), Grotius's treatise is excruciatingly pedantic. Grotius may have been a towering intellect, but he is no one's candidate for a great stylist. His substantive message comes perilously close to being drowned in a veritable torrent of intimidating – and often tedious – displays of classical and biblical learning. In this respect, the remorseless humanist maestro shows no mercy to his benumbed and beleaguered readers. In short, as a writer, he was his own worst enemy.

It is important, however, to rescue Grotius from his own shortcomings, as he had so much of substance to say – to our time as well as to his own. To that end, this edition of his great treatise ruthlessly prunes the dense overgrowth of classical and biblical display, to allow the substantive ideas of Grotius to be absorbed in straightforward (or at least relatively straightforward) form by modern readers. When the text is stripped of its vast array of baroque scholastic ornament, the present-day reader can discern a remarkable mind at work. It is a mind that soars high, but also burrows deep. It expounds the loftiest and most abstract general principles – but also applies them in the nooks and crannies of everyday life.

In large part – but far from entirely – this great work (duly shorn) can speak for itself. But copious notes are provided for the assistance of readers in the many instances in which Grotius's point is not fully or clearly expounded in the text. For more general guidance, the following introductory remarks should prove helpful.

A life in turbulent times

Hugh de Groot (invariably Latinised to 'Hugo Grotius') was born in Delft in the Northern Netherlands on 10 April 1583 to a prominent family.[1] At the time,

---

[1] The leading English-language biography of Grotius is still W. S. M. Knight, *The Life and Works of Hugo Grotius* (London: Sweet and Maxwell, 1925). The present biographical sketch relies strongly on it.

the Dutch War of Independence (from Spain) was in full swing. His father, Jan de Groot, was a staunch Protestant who held various posts in the city government and who was also friendly with a number of prominent people in the intellectual world. Grotius senior received a doctorate in law from the University of Leiden, which had been established in 1575 for the purpose of providing training in the latest humanist learning for the leaders of the new country. He also served as curator (or chief administrative officer) for the University, and later as counsellor to the Count of Hohenlohe. The family of Hugo's mother included persons active in trading with the East Indies, and later in the operation of the Dutch East India Company (which would have use for Grotius's legal knowledge).

Young Hugo very soon proved himself a child prodigy matched by few in the historical record. (In the 1920s, he even received the posthumous honour of tying for second place in a retrospective assessment of the IQs of three hundred noted geniuses in world history.)[2] By the age of eight, he was composing Latin verse. A legend grew up that he gave an early demonstration of advocacy skills by converting his mother from the Catholic faith to Protestantism.

At the tender age of eleven, he enrolled in the Law Faculty at the University of Leiden. Amongst his fellow students was Frederick Henry of Nassau, the future stadtholder of the Netherlands. Although he was enrolled in the Law Faculty, Grotius's actual studies were in the liberal arts. He was placed in the particular care of Joseph Justus Scaliger, a prominent historian, classical scholar, and anti-Jesuit polemicist. During his period at Leiden (which lasted for three years), he continued to compose poetry. He is also said to have been something of an art critic and (later) an admirer of Rubens.

His first exposure to public service came in 1598 (at age fifteen), when he formed part of a Dutch diplomatic mission to King Henry IV of France. The purpose of the mission was to persuade Henry to continue his support of the Dutch insurgency against Spain. Grotius had no official role, but went as the protégé of Johan van Oldenbarnevelt, the most prominent civilian political leader of the Netherlands (since the assassination of William the Silent in 1584). These remonstrations proved unsuccessful, as Henry proceeded to make a separate peace with Spain (the Treaty of Vervins of 2 May 1598). For young Grotius, the journey marked the start of his role as protégé and loyal supporter of Oldenbarnevelt – a relationship which continued, at some considerable cost to himself, up to Oldenbarnevelt's death.

The journey to France was momentous for Grotius in another way, and more relevant to his future fame. He enrolled at the University of Orléans for a

---

[2] See Catherine Morris Cox, *Genetic Studies of Genius: The Early Mental Traits of Three Hundred Geniuses* (Stanford University Press, 1926), at pp. 153–5, 161–2. In this assessment, Grotius tied for second place with the German polymath Gottfried Leibniz. First place (for the record) went to the German literary giant Wolfgang von Goethe.

doctorate in law. It is interesting that the one year that he spent there was the only period of formal law study in his life. It clearly made a very great impression on him.

On his return to the Netherlands, Grotius was admitted to the bar for the province of Holland (the largest and most prominent of the United Provinces of the Netherlands). Immediately thereafter, he was admitted to the bar of the High Council of the two provinces of Holland and Zeeland. His first important literary work was an edition, in 1599, of the *Satyricon* by the fifth-century classical author Martianus Capella (sometimes called *On the Seven Disciplines*, with reference to the *trivium* and *quadrivium* of medieval liberal arts education). The following year, he published an edition of *Phenomena*, an astronomical work in verse by Aratus, a Hellenistic Greek poet of the third century BC.

Scientific concerns occupied Grotius's attention at this stage of his life in other ways too, in the form of service under his father's friend Simon Stevin. Stevin was a multifaceted person – entrepreneur, social reformer, and political writer, as well as mathematician and scientist. In mathematics, he is remembered as the inventor of modern decimal notation. He was also interested in hydrostatics and formulated the theory of the inclined plane, as well as the concept of the parallelogram of forces, which became a mainstay of the study of physics. He wrote a handbook on nautical science for mariners, for which young Grotius supplied the introduction. In 1600, Grotius assisted with one of Stevin's more ambitious projects: a land ship, i.e., a wind-propelled vehicle for land travel. A prototype of the craft was actually built, carrying twenty-eight persons on a trial journey of fourteen leagues in two hours. This triumph elicited a further three poems from Stevin's assistant.

In 1601, Grotius published his first major original poetic work, 'Adamus Exul', on the biblical story of Adam and Eve. This poem proved widely popular and brought his name before the general public for the first time (he was not yet twenty). Two years later, he received his first continuous government employment, as historiographer of the United Provinces. In this, his chief task was the preparation of an official history of the War of Independence, which was still raging. It was largely complete by 1611, but was only published posthumously, in 1657, as *Annales et Historiae de Rebus Belgicis*. He made a more immediate, if rather modest, contribution to the Dutch cause, in the form of a poem 'Prosopopoeia', all of eleven lines long, on the protracted Spanish siege of Ostend (1601–4).

His serious legal work appears to have begun in 1604, when he was employed by the Dutch East India Company to present its case in a controversy arising from the capture of some Portuguese ships in the Indian Ocean by Dutch vessels. At that time, Portugal claimed a monopoly on Indian Ocean trading, insisting that ships involved in trade could only do so if they carried a licence (or '*carteza*') issued by the Portuguese government. The Dutch resisted this – to the point of using armed force to capture Portuguese ships. Grotius's task was to defend the legality of these seizures, essentially on the basis that the

Dutch were protecting their basic natural-law right to trade with other states without molestation by third parties (i.e., Portugal). Central to this thesis was the position that the claimed Portuguese monopoly on East Indies trading was invalid.

In pursuance of this assigned task, Grotius drafted what was, for all intents and purposes, a detailed and systematic treatise, in the period 1604–5, which he entitled *De Indis*. For those who seek to follow the evolution of Grotius's legal and political thought, this is an essential text. It went unpublished – save for one chapter – during Grotius's lifetime. It only reached the general public in 1868, when it was discovered and published by the Dutch publisher Martinus Nijhoff under the title *De Iure Praedae* (*On the Law of Prize and Booty*).[3]

In 1607 came his first important appointment: as Advocate-General of the Fisc of the three provinces of Holland, Zeeland, and Friesland, apparently on the basis of his reputation as a legal advocate. The task involved the zealous guardianship of the rights of the Count of Holland in the three provinces. In 1608, he married a woman from a prominent Zeeland family. The union appears to have been a happy one, producing three sons and three daughters. That same year, Grotius published 'Christus Patiens', a verse tragedy on the death of Christ, in five acts. (It was translated into English in 1640.) Two years later, he published his first historical work, *De Antiquitate Republicae Batavicae*, a patriotic (and largely speculative) pre-history of the Dutch people.

At this time, he became involved in diplomatic negotiations with Spain for a truce in the War of Independence. Grotius himself was of the war party, pressing for the continuation of the armed struggle; but he nonetheless played a role in the truce discussions, again on the subject of freedom of the seas and freedom of trade. This time, the object was to contest Spain's claim to trading monopolies in the East and West Indies. These negotiations were the occasion for the publication, in March 1609, of the one chapter of *De Indis* that appeared during Grotius's lifetime. It took the form of a short book entitled *Mare Liberum* (*Freedom of the Seas*), in which the core argument against Portugal's monopoly claim was discussed and refuted.[4] In the event, a twelve-year truce with Spain was successfully concluded the following month.

The arguments of *Freedom of the Seas* did not go unchallenged. A principal opponent was William Welwood of the University of St Andrews in Scotland, who was a professor first of mathematics and then of civil law. In 1613, Welwood published *An Abridgement of All Sea Laws*, which contained a chapter asserting (on the authority of the fourteenth-century lawyer Bartolus of Sassoferrato) that coastal states possessed sovereignty over the seas for at least one hundred

---

[3] For an English translation, see Hugo Grotius, *Commentary on the Law of Prize and Booty*, translated by Gwladys Williams (Oxford: Clarendon Press, 1950).

[4] For an English translation, see Hugo Grotius, *Freedom of the Sea; or, The Right Which Belongs to the Dutch to Take Part in the East Indian Trade*, translated by Ralph van Deman Magoffin (New York: Oxford University Press, 1916).

miles offshore. Welwood agreed with Grotius, though, that the high seas beyond
that limit were free to all and not subject to the sovereignty of any state. Grotius
wrote a response to Welwood, *In Defence of Chapter V of Mare Liberum* – but
it went unpublished until 1872.[5] A more famous attack on Grotius's thesis was
published by John Selden, though only much later (in 1635), in a work entitled
Mare Clausum seu de Dominio Maris. By that time, Grotius had little interest in
the subject, so did not trouble to reply.

Grotius's short book was put to further use soon after publication, in opposition to yet another monopoly claimant. The government of England, during
the reign of James I, was claiming exclusive rights to fisheries off the shores of
England. In 1610, a Dutch diplomatic embassy was sent to England in 1610,
armed with Grotius's *Freedom of the Seas*, with a view to arriving at a settlement of the question. They were at least partially successful, in that James I was
induced to postpone, for an indefinite period, the execution of his proclamation.

In 1613, Grotius became Pensionary of Rotterdam, which was basically the
chief administrative position in the city council. One of his tasks in this new
post was to revisit the vexed question of trading monopolies – this time as a
defender. The Dutch were now being accused of illegal monopolistic practices
by other governments, particularly that of England. The grievance concerned
treaties that the Dutch had entered into with various local rulers in the East
Indies, which provided that trade was to be exclusively with the Dutch.

In connexion with this dispute, Grotius travelled to England in 1613 with a
diplomatic mission. He defended his country against the accusations, arguing
that the native rulers were within their rights to enter into such agreements.
His previous arguments, against Portugal, Spain, and England, had been that
monopolies could not be imposed from 'outside', as it were, by unilateral fiat.
Monopoly arrangements founded on treaties, freely consented to by both parties, were (in Grotius's view) entirely different.[6]

It appears that, during his time in England, Grotius attempted to entice that
country into re-entering the hostilities over the independence of the Netherlands on the Dutch side. England had made a separate peace with Spain in 1604 –
and the Netherlands itself was even at peace with Spain at the time, following the
conclusion of a nine-year truce agreement in 1609. Specifically, Grotius offered
the English government £4 million in gold if it would mount an attack on Spain
in the Philippines. In return, the Dutch would assist the English in expelling
the Spanish from the West Indies. These interesting offers were, however,
declined.

During this period, the religious controversies were brewing which were to
change Grotius's life very drastically. In 1603, Jacob Arminius was appointed
Professor of Theology at the University of Leiden (with Grotius's father, as

---

[5] For the texts of these works, see David Armitage (ed.), *The Free Sea* (Indianapolis:
Liberty Fund, 2004).
[6] A matter touched on in *On the Law of War and Peace*. See pp. 103 below.

University Curator, on the selection committee). His 'Arminian' doctrine (as it came to be known) was, briefly, a departure from the teaching of John Calvin. Where Calvin had taught that God had the sole and exclusive choice as to who was amongst the elect and who was not, Arminius contended that God, in effect, only determined eligibility for membership of the elect. A person designated by God had the power to 'refuse' the divine gift by devoting himself or herself to a life of wickedness. Grotius was never an Arminian himself, nor was he much concerned with theology at this stage of his life. But he vigorously supported his patron Oldenbarnevelt in pressing for toleration of Arminius's views.

The controversy came to a climax after the conversion of the principal military leader of the country, Maurice of Nassau, to the anti-Arminian cause. In 1619, the Synod of Dort condemned the teachings of Arminius. Oldenbarnevelt, now in disgrace, made an attempt to raise an armed force against Maurice but was apprehended, tried for treason, convicted, and put to death. Grotius could easily have followed him, as a prominent supporter. But he was fortunate in receiving only a sentence of life imprisonment in the Castle of Loevestein.

The period of captivity was not an unfruitful one for our cerebral hero. He put his enforced leisure to work composing, in Dutch verse, a treatise *On the Truth of the Christian Religion*, his first major foray into the subject of theology. He also drafted a private textbook for the assistance of his sons in their study of Dutch law. Then in 1621, two years into his term of imprisonment, he managed to escape. It was commonly said that he was smuggled out of captivity in – all too appropriately – a crate of books. (The crate is on display in the Riijksmuseum in Amsterdam to the present day.)

After the escape from Loevestein, Grotius made his way to France, where he was fortunate to receive a modest pension from King Louis XIII (although payment of it proved to be inconveniently irregular). Nearly the whole of his remaining life would be spent outside his native Netherlands. But his homeland links were not entirely severed. He remained in the good graces of the Dutch East India Company for his past services to them. He also retained his friendship, from student days, with Maurice of Nassau's brother, Frederick Henry, who became stadtholder himself on his brother's death in 1625.

The year 1622 saw the publication of *On the Truth of the Christian Religion*. But Grotius's principal project in these first years abroad was the writing of his famous treatise *On the Law of War and Peace*, on which his principal modern fame rests. He began working on it in late 1622 and published it in Paris in 1625, in Latin, as *De Iure Belli ac Pacis*, with an effusive dedication to King Louis XIII. The book was an immediate success in some quarters at least, most notably in Protestant countries and France. It was paid the compliment of being pirated in Frankfurt the year after it came out. Somewhat less welcome was the placement, that same year, of Book III of the treatise onto the Catholic Church's Index of Forbidden Books (where it remained until 1896). Nevertheless, it found some admiring readers among prelates high in Church circles.

In 1631, finances became a problem, with the halting of his pension from the French government. This was apparently at the instigation of Cardinal Richelieu, who had taken a dislike to Grotius. That year, he made a visit to the Netherlands. He remained there for about six months but found the atmosphere to be hostile. There were even warrants issued for his arrest, although they were not executed. He managed to put his time in the country to good use. The legal textbook that he had written for his sons during his imprisonment was published, as *The Jurisprudence of Holland*.[7] In addition, a second edition of *On the Law of War and Peace* came out in Amsterdam in December 1631. A so-called third edition came out shortly afterwards, by a different publisher; but Grotius denounced it as unauthorised and full of errors.

He departed the Netherlands for Hamburg in 1632, where he remained for two difficult years. It was there that his connexion with Sweden began. Grotius already stood in high repute in that country, with King Gustavus Adolphus said to have been a great admirer of his famous treatise. It was even claimed that he carried a copy of it with him throughout his military campaigns in Germany during the Thirty Years' War. Be that as it may, the king expressed a wish to have the illustrious author in his service.

Gustavus himself would not be the one to bring that about, however, as he was killed in 1632 in the Battle of Lützen (near Leipzig). Fortunately for Grotius, the king's wish was known to Swedish Chancellor Axel Oxenstierna, the effective ruler of the country after Gustavus's death. Oxenstierna summoned Grotius from Hamburg to Frankfurt for a meeting in February 1633, which resulted in an offer of employment as Sweden's ambassador to France, although the distractions of the war prevented Grotius from taking up the position immediately. He eventually arrived in Paris early in 1635, where he remained until nearly the end of his life.[8] It was a highly important post, since Sweden and France were, at the time, co-operating against the Habsburgs in the Thirty Years' War.

Grotius was not, however, a notable success in this position. Although friendly with King Louis XIII, he was disliked by Richelieu, the real power in the land. He failed in his first important task, which was to persuade France to declare war against the Holy Roman Empire and thereby enter the Thirty Years' War fully and officially (instead of supporting Sweden from behind the scenes). Oxenstierna had to go to Paris to plead the Swedish case himself, finally eliciting the desired French declaration of war in March 1636.[9] Grotius's ambassadorial

---

[7] For an English translation of this work, see Hugo Grotius, *The Jurisprudence of Holland*, vol. 1, translated by R. W. Lee (Oxford: Clarendon Press, 1926). A second volume (published in 1936) is a commentary.

[8] For an informative account of this final period of Grotius's life, see R. Warden Lee, 'Grotius – The Last Phase, 1635–45' (1945) 31 *Transactions of the Grotius Society* 193–215.

[9] See Geoffrey Parker, *The Thirty Years' War* (London: Routledge and Kegan Paul, 1984), at pp. 144–8.

life was also made uncomfortable by factions at the Swedish court which, out of jealousy, worked actively to undermine his position. He constantly complained of not being kept sufficiently informed of the policies that he was meant to be executing, and of arrears in the payment of his salary and expenses. His hopes of playing a part in the peace negotiations in Westphalia also went unrealised.

On the positive side, his diplomatic duties appear to have left him with substantial spare time, since his written output during this last phase of his life was very large. It included an anthology of Greek epigrams, as well as a history of the Goths and Vandals, which was published posthumously in 1665 as *Historia Gothorum Vandalorum et Langobardorum*. His most prominent work in this period was in the area of theology. In this connexion, it is worth noting, if only briefly, that his theological work was, in many respects, more modern in outlook than his legal and political writings. He was a major pioneer of modern biblical scholarship, in which the Bible is treated in its historical context. His purpose in taking this controversial approach was to help promote the reunion of the Christian churches, on the basis of an agreed interpretation of the Bible arrived at through historical and critical study, rather than through the lens of pre-existing dogmata.[10] It was in this spirit that he wrote a set of *Annotationes* on the Old and New Testaments (which were only published in full in 1679, after his death). Also of note was a treatise on the Antichrist, written in 1640, which argued against the idea (widespread in Protestant circles at the time) that the pope was the Antichrist. Not surprisingly, these writings made him many enemies in zealous Protestant circles.

Grotius did not neglect his major secular work, since he oversaw the publication of a fourth edition of *On the Law of War and Peace* in 1642 (with which he was dissatisfied, as it contained many errors). It differed from the previous ones in including, for the first time, some illustrations from medieval, and even modern, history, to accompany the copious biblical and classical references already present. He also made a brief, and rather unfortunate, foray into anthropology, in a short work on the origin of the American Indian peoples. In it, he argued for a Norwegian origin of the North American peoples, and for a Chinese and East Indian origin for the South Americans. His reputation, clearly, does not rest on this work. His thesis was strongly criticised – and strongly defended by Grotius too, in an ill-tempered polemic.

In 1645, his ambassadorial services were terminated, ostensibly because the relations between Sweden and France were now being placed in the hands of the two countries' respective representatives at the Westphalia peace negotiations. Grotius apparently sought to obtain employment from the English government, although this initiative did not bear fruit. Instead, he then travelled to Sweden to discuss further service for that government. He went by way of the Netherlands

---

[10] Jonathan I. Israel, *Radical Enlightenment: Philosophy and the Making of Modernity 1650–1750* (Oxford University Press, 2001), at p. 447.

for his final, and brief, visit to his native land. It was a happy parting, as he was received with great honour in Rotterdam and Amsterdam.

On arrival in Sweden, he was again treated with honour – only to find, to his dismay, that any further work for the government would have to be in Sweden, where the climate was not to his liking. He was therefore at rather a loose end when he set sail for Lübeck. He failed to arrive there, however, as his ship was wrecked in a storm off the north coast of Germany. Grotius survived the disaster, but not for long. He was taken to Rostock, where he died on 26 August 1645, at the age of sixty-two. Legend has it that his final words were: 'By undertaking many things, I have accomplished nothing.' His body was taken to his native town of Delft and buried in the Niewe Kirche. The following year, the fifth and final edition of his famous treatise came out, albeit with no significant changes from the previous one.

The intellectual world of Hugo Grotius

One of the intriguing things about Grotius is the extent to which he stands so delicately poised between the Middle Ages and modernity. On the side of modernity, his literary education was in the humanist mode, which entailed the application of critical historical methods to the study of classical and biblical texts. The era he lived in, however, is now most commonly seen (if only through the benefit of hindsight) as one in which much of the inheritance of the past was being ostentatiously cast off and new intellectual worlds boldly explored. In this connexion, it may be noted that Grotius was a contemporary of three of the foremost pioneers of this new modern world: Francis Bacon (1561–1626), the English Lord Chancellor, essayist, and scientific visionary; René Descartes (1596–1650), the founder of modern philosophy and noted mathematician; and Galileo (1564–1642), the seminal figure in modern physics and astronomy.

To some extent, Grotius was a participant in this intellectual ferment. It was noted above that he had some contact with the early stages of what came to be called the Scientific Revolution, in the form of his work with Simon Stevin. We know, in addition, that he was acquainted with Descartes's *Discourse on Method*, published in 1637. He had some awareness of Galileo's legal problems, if not of the substance of his scientific ideas. In the mid 1630s, shortly after arriving in Paris for his diplomatic duties, he sought to provide some assistance to the beleaguered Galileo, by urging friends in the Netherlands to offer him employment in Amsterdam to remove him from the clutches of the Church – a mission of mercy that did not bear fruit.[11] Grotius also had some familiarity with the early writing of Thomas Hobbes.[12]

---

[11] Lee, 'Grotius', at 206.
[12] Johann Sommerville, 'Lofty Science and Local Politics', in Tom Sorell (ed.), *The Cambridge Companion to Hobbes* (Cambridge University Press, 1996), pp. 246–73, at 247.

On the whole, though, Grotius is to be ranked amongst the conservatives of his time, rather than the modernisers. Instead of breaking radically with the past, in the manner of Bacon, Descartes, Galileo, or Hobbes, he sought to take the best knowledge of the past and to make it relevant to the conditions of the modern world. For present purposes, it will be helpful to take particular note of two aspects of his general intellectual armoury: first, of the three major intellectual traditions with which he worked and, second, of the general contours of his legal universe.

A triple inheritance

Three of the foremost systems of thought in the European tradition constituted Grotius's principal intellectual inheritance: Roman law, Aristotelian philosophy, and natural law. It should immediately be noted that all three of these were ultimately legacies not even of the medieval world, but of the ancient one. This reverence for the ancient past was a key indication that Grotius's basic intellectual bent was humanistic.

Loyalty to Aristotelian philosophy was perhaps the most conspicuous sign of Grotius as a conservative rather than an innovator. For the one feature that markedly distinguished such contemporary modernisers as Bacon, Galileo, and Descartes (and Hobbes later on) was their explicit – and even contemptuous – repudiation of the venerable sage of Stagira. Grotius, in contrast, hailed Aristotle (in the Prologue of his book) as holding 'the foremost place' amongst philosophers. The influence of Aristotle is immediately apparent in Grotius's discussion (p. 26) of the two basic kinds of justice, labelled 'expletive' and 'attributive' (though Aristotle called them 'commutative' and 'distributive'). Aristotle's presence is also apparent in Grotius's political philosophy, as will be pointed out below.

The second major heritage of Grotius was Roman law. So deeply was most of European scholarship in thrall to Roman law in Grotius's time (and for long before and long after as well) that it was well-nigh impossible for any legal writer to avoid thinking in terms of that received framework. In this, Grotius was no exception. Considerations of Roman law are most apparent in his discussions of the acquisition and extinction of title to property, as well as in his expositions of promises and contracts in Book II. On the laws of war, the phenomenon of postliminy (Chapter 9 of Book III) is drawn practically entirely from Roman law. Perhaps most significant of all – though not very apparent on the surface – is the influence of Roman law on his treatment of the nature of political sovereignty, discussed below.

Finally, and most of all, there was natural law, which, even in Grotius's time, had the distinction (perhaps a dubious one) of having the lengthiest and most continuous intellectual pedigree of any major element of Western European thought.[13] It pre-dated Christianity by several centuries, going back at least to

---

[13] For a broad survey of at least a major part of the history of natural-law thought, see Clarence J. Glacken, *Traces on the Rhodian Shore: Nature and Culture in Western*

the writings of various Greek philosophers of the fifth and fourth centuries BC. Most outstandingly, though, natural law formed a major component of the writing of the Stoic philosophers of the Hellenistic period. From there, it won acceptance from the Christian Church, under whose auspices it was preserved, and enriched, in the Middle Ages. Grotius is sometimes regarded, quite wrongly, as a pioneer of natural-law thought. In fact, he was the heir of a very long tradition, as will be explained further below.

Two major points about this triple intellectual heritage should be noted. The first is that none of these three streams of thought was of Christian origin. It is true that Christianity embraced all three, to varying extents, in its capacious grasp. Roman law, for example, was put to some use in the development of the canon law of the Catholic Church. Aristotelian philosophy was an important inspiration for the writing of Thomas Aquinas in the thirteenth century, and of his many followers.[14] And natural law received the approbation of a host of scholastic writers and theologians in the Middle Ages. Nevertheless, all three of these systems of thought were fundamentally secular in character. We must therefore withhold from Grotius any praise (which he has sometimes been accorded) of being a leading 'securaliser' of medieval religious thought (in particular of natural law).

The second major point about this triple heritage is that Grotius would be of little interest if he were *only* a legatee of the traditions of the past. On the contrary, if he was a respectful heir, he could also be a critical one; and his esteem for received wisdom fell well short of slavishness. He repeatedly showed his willingness to depart from his models when he believed them to be in error. Regarding Aristotle, for example, immediately after according him the foremost place amongst philosophers, Grotius lost no time in regretting that the Master's pre-eminence had degenerated into a tyranny – and also in pointedly announcing (p. 14) that he (Grotius) would reserve to himself 'the same liberty which [Aristotle], in his devotion to truth, allowed himself with respect to his teachers'. He felt similarly free to reject the rules of Roman law whenever they conflicted with his conclusions about natural law. Here, his humanistic training showed through, with its perception of Roman law as 'merely' the law of a particular society in a particular era.

Despite these various caveats, however, the conclusion must stand that Grotius was fundamentally a conservative – nearer to being the last of the medieval writers than the first of the moderns. There was nothing in him of the self-conscious rebel, in the manner of Bacon or Descartes. Although he stood ever prepared to purge his three intellectual heritages of errors and

Thought from Ancient Times to the End of the Eighteenth Century (Berkeley: University of California Press, 1967).

[14] For a stimulating history of the impact of Aristotelianism in medieval Europe, see Richard E. Rubenstein, *Aristotle's Children: How Christians, Muslims, and Jews Rediscovered Ancient Wisdom and Illuminated the Middle Ages* (Orlando, FL: Harvest, 2003).

misunderstandings, his fundamental goal was, in the final analysis, to clarify and systematise, not to overthrow.

An overview of Grotius's legal universe

A quick summary of the legal universe in which Grotius operated is in order. At the highest or broadest level was a divide between law and ethics. Law, broadly speaking, concerns what persons owe to other persons. By extension, it deals with rights and obligations, which are enforceable (at least potentially) by magistrates or courts of law or in exceptional cases by means of self-help. Ethics – or 'the law of love', as Grotius sometimes called it – is a rather broader field, encompassing actions which enhance the quality of life of one's fellow humans, or the harmoniousness of social life generally. Ethical obligations (unless they are at the same time rules of law) are left to be enforced by God in the life hereafter, rather than by human agents on earth.

The realm of law then falls into two major divisions: natural law and positive, or 'volitional', law. Natural law is eternal and unchangeable, founded on reason and on the nature of things. Positive, or volitional, law is an expression not of reason but of will. Positive law, in turn, comes in two kinds: human, and divine. As the names imply, human laws are enacted by people, while divine law comprises the commands of God. Natural law either commands or forbids various things, while leaving a range of matters in between these two extremes – i.e., as neither mandatory nor prohibited. It is in this middle region that human law is free to operate.

Human laws are then divided into three groups: laws applicable to the whole of a state; laws applicable to entities which are smaller than states; and laws applicable to entities that are larger than states. Laws of states are known as civil law – with the civil law *par excellence* being, of course, that of Rome (i.e., the *ius civile*). Entities smaller than states are provinces, cities, and the like. They will have various local laws dealing with, say, market regulation, liability to public service, and the like. By entities larger than states is meant the international community. Laws applicable to this larger community comprise the law of nations, about which more will be said below.

With these broad introductory remarks in mind, we may proceed to say a bit more about the three great contributions made by Grotius in *On the Law of War and Peace*: in the areas of natural law, of political theory, and of international law.

Grotius the natural lawyer

A very large portion of the treatise – some 40 per cent – comprises an extended treatment of natural law. For it was one of the primary purposes of *On the Law of War and Peace* to provide a systematic exposition of that subject. The detailed exposition of natural law in the main body of the text appears, however, almost by stealth, when Grotius begins discussing the second of his three just

causes of war, which is a response to 'an injury to that which belongs to us'.
(The first just cause of war is defence against an impending injury, and the
third is punishment for past misdeeds.) In order to have a full appreciation of
this second class of just war, it is necessary, in Grotius's opinion, to have a clear
idea of exactly what it is that 'belongs to us', and why. Basically, what belongs to
us falls into two broad categories: property rights, and benefits of obligations
owed to us by others.

For the most part, Grotius's exposition of natural law can speak for itself.
For the full appreciation of that exposition, however, it is well to provide some
background on two particular points: the rationalist tradition of natural law
(the one to which Grotius subscribed) and the nature of rights in natural law.

The rationalist view of natural law

There are, broadly speaking, three different streams of thought to which the
label 'natural law' could be, and has been, attached. The first of these could be
called the voluntarist position. It regards natural law as being of divine origin.
Its content comprises commands issued by God to the human race at large.
The second stream of thought could be called the organicist. It regards natural
law as, in essence, the species character, or biological nature, of the creature
now labelled as *homo sapiens* – as well as, by extension, the biological features
of other animals as well. Natural law, on this view, is regarded, basically, as
instinct, 'hard-wired' in some way into each and every member of the human
race – or 'written in the hearts of men', as was often said.

The third stream of natural-law thought may be termed the rationalist one.
It regards natural law as being basically a hypothetico-deductive system, in the
nature of a mathematical system, in which conclusions are arrived at logically,
by an objective process of reasoning from basic axioms or first principles. This
approach to natural law was relatively late in arising, receiving its first major
exposition from Thomas Aquinas in the thirteenth century.[15] It then underwent
something of a renaissance with the revival of interest in Thomist thought in
Catholic circles in the sixteenth century, reaching its apogee with the writing of
the Spanish Jesuit writer Francisco Suárez (1548–1617).[16]

Grotius was squarely within the rationalist tradition. Some of its more salient
features may be briefly noted here, as they find reflection – but not always a
very explicit exposition – in his treatise. Two of its most important features
should be particularly borne in mind. The first is that natural law speaks only
to rational beings, i.e., to humankind. That is to say, the rationalist tradition
rejected the idea, inherited from Roman law, of natural law as applicable to the
whole of the animal world, including humans.[17] (This was an early expression
of the organicist view of natural law mentioned above.) Natural law, to the
rationalists, was a law about social relations between people.

---

[15] See generally Aquinas, *Treatise on Law*, at pp. 235–74.
[16] On Suárez, see generally Suárez, *Treatise on Laws*.   [17] See *Digest* 1.1.3 (Ulpian).

The second principal feature of the rationalist tradition was the idea that the content of natural law arises out of reason itself, independently of will. That natural law is not a product of *human* will is obvious enough. Less obvious is that it is not a product of *divine* will either. The content of natural law is no more changeable by God than are the laws of mathematics. Indeed, as Grotius famously pointed out in the Prologue (p. 4), even if there were no such thing as God, there would still be natural law precisely as we now have it. Grotius has sometimes been hailed as an innovator by virtue of his articulation of this point – as the person who 'secularised' natural-law thought by cutting it loose from theology. Such a view is simply incorrect. Grotius was merely reiterating a long-held tenet of the rationalist stream of natural-law thought extending back to Aquinas.

To the adherents of the rationalist tradition, the lure of mathematics, as the most rational and indubitable of all the sciences, was difficult to resist. And Grotius was among the non-resisters. His treatise, though, is a far cry from being an exercise in rigorous mathematical demonstration (along the lines of Spinoza's *Ethics*). But in one respect, the mathematical spirit is apparent. That is, that, just as mathematics deals with eternal truths, so does natural law – with the immediate consequence that there is no need for topical or contemporary illustrations. Examples of natural law in action can come from any era of history and any culture. Grotius took advantage of this by loftily forswearing, at the outset, any intention to comment on contemporary events. '[J]ust as mathematicians treat their figures as abstracted from bodies', Grotius averred in the Prologue (p. 19), 'so in treating law I have withdrawn my mind from every particular fact'.

It should not be thought, however, that Grotius provided no illustrations of his various assertions about natural law. On the contrary, he practically drowns his hapless reader in a torrent of them. But practically all of his illustrations are from classical and biblical sources, rather from contemporary (or anything resembling contemporary) history. Only with the publication of the fourth edition of the treatise, in 1642, did he relent even slightly from this self-abnegation. The principal area in which contemporary matters are discussed is the law of neutrality – and only because, in Grotius's candid confession, there was a paucity of classical material on that particular topic.

In sum, Grotius should be regarded as a thoroughgoing conservative in his treatment of natural law generally. The value of the book in this regard, therefore, lies in the way in which it provides a wide-ranging summation of natural-law thought across the board, rather than in any major innovations. Even if he was no innovator, however, he was certainly not without influence. The major natural-law writers of the following centuries took Grotius as their starting point – probably in large part because most of these writers were Protestant, like Grotius, and hence loath to appeal too overtly to medieval Catholic traditions. In all events, if Grotius is to be seen as an innovator, it is to other areas of his thought that we must look.

On rights

Great care must be taken to refrain from equating natural *law* with natural *rights*. To be sure, the rationalist natural-law tradition that Grotius inherited from the Middle Ages did recognise certain important inherent rights of persons – most outstandingly the right of self-preservation. For the most part, however, Grotius deals with rights in very different terms.

To appreciate Grotius's conception of rights, it should be noted that the term may be employed in either of two basic ways, a broad and a narrow. The broad meaning refers to what might be called 'free-standing' or inherent rights – prerogatives possessed by each person independently of any other person. This is the usage typically employed in modern civil-libertarian discourse, with reference to freedom of speech, freedom of religion, and the like. The narrow meaning refers, more specifically, to the ability to obtain something from someone else, or to perform some kind of task. An example is the right of a creditor to receive due payment from a debtor; or the right of a person to cross over the land of another at will. Rights in this narrow sense, in other words, concern entitlements vis-à-vis some other person, with respect to some identifiable transaction or relationship. Rights in the narrow sense are therefore intimately connected with duties – when one person (such as a creditor) has a right, some other person (i.e., a debtor) must be under a corresponding duty.[18]

For the overwhelming part, Grotius's conception of rights is the narrow kind. But we can go further than this and say that, in the natural-law tradition in which Grotius thought and wrote, duties were more fundamental than rights. The single fundamental principle of natural law, in Grotius's view – inherited from the writings of Plato and Aristotle on justice – is the obligation to give to others what is due to them. This fundamental obligation gives rise, in turn, to a right on the part of those others to compel the performance of the duty in the event of recalcitrance on the part of the person subject to it. This 'right' to compel the performance of obligations is in fact the basis of Grotius's principal category of just war (p. 82).

Grotius did not actually speak in terms of rights. Instead, he spoke of 'faculties', by which he meant, basically, the power to perform some act or to achieve some end (p. 24). For example, making a will and thereby disposing of one's property after death is a faculty. The ability of a creditor to compel his debtor to pay him money that is owed is also a faculty. In sum, rights are many and varied in the legal universe of Hugo Grotius – but they are, for the overwhelming part,

---

[18] This two-fold classification of rights essentially replicates what the American legal philosopher Wesley Hohfeld would later call 'rights' and 'privileges' – with rights being what are here termed rights in the narrow sense, and privileges being rights in the broader, civil-libertarian sense. See Wesley Newcomb Hohfeld, *Fundamental Legal Conceptions as Applied in Judicial Reasoning*, edited by David Campbell and Philip Thomas (Aldershot: Ashgate, 2001), at pp. 75–80.

the epiphenomena of the duties of others, rather than free-standing inherent rights of the modern civil-libertarian kind.

Grotius the political theorist

The political-theory discussion forms only a very modest portion of Grotius's compendious treatise (in the order of one-tenth), although it has attracted much attention. In this area too, his discussion in the book can largely speak for itself. But some background remarks may be helpful.

In the area of political theory, natural law was of little (if any) relevance to Grotius. In the political sphere, we are in the realm of free human choice. Natural law was a pre-political system of norms, governing relations between persons in a 'state of nature' rather than in an organised political community. For the intellectual backdrop of Grotius's political ideas, we need to look to the other two streams of his heritage: Aristotelian thought, and Roman law. The more salient elements of these will be pointed out presently.

Grotius did not present (or pretend to present) a comprehensive political theory in his treatise. His concern was chiefly with sovereignty – or, more strictly, with what Grotius termed 'sovereign power' or 'sovereign authority'. His discussion is therefore, not surprisingly, strongly legalistic. Two principal expressions were employed in connexion with sovereignty: *summa potestas* and *imperium*. *Summa potestas* was a medieval concept, meaning basically that the political authority in question was not legally subject to the will of any superior, i.e., was under no legal obligation to execute the commands of another. It was consequently the highest power in the land, possessing (crucially) the power to legislate. *Imperium* was a Roman-law concept, referring to the right to exercise coercive power in the enforcement of laws. It was therefore, in essence, executive power. Both of these concepts are to be distinguished from *dominium* – also from Roman law – which referred to absolute ownership of property in private law.

Three major aspects of sovereignty are discussed in the book: the basic nature of sovereignty; the question of resistance by subjects against sovereigns; and the question of resistance against usurpers of sovereignty. A few words on each of these (but especially the first) are in order.

The nature of sovereignty

The exposition of sovereignty, like that of natural law, makes a somewhat furtive appearance in Grotius's text. Its relevance derives from one of the basic principles of medieval just-war theory: that of *auctoritas*. This states, in brief, that war can only be waged justly if, *inter alia*, it is done with the permission of the relevant authority, i.e., of the political superior of the person waging the conflict. In the case of a person who has no political superior – i.e., a sovereign – the sovereign can (and must necessarily) self-authorise the resort to armed force. But, in any case, it then becomes necessary to determine, in Grotius's words, 'what sovereignty (*summa potestas*) is, and who hold it' (p. 49).

Grotius contends, in clear allegiance to the Aristotelian view, that the people as a whole are the ultimate sovereigns – with the immediate consequence that 'a people can select the form of government which it wishes' (p. 52). He further makes clear that the decision as to the form of government is a matter of free choice on the people's part. His writing, in short, gives no shred of support to theories of the divine right of kings. The acceptance of this basic principle might incline a reader to place Grotius amongst the radical democratic writers, or amongst the social-contract theorists. Great caution, however, is in order on both of these counts.

Regarding Grotius as a supporter of democracy, it should be appreciated that he goes no further than to credit the people with being the ultimate *source* of sovereignty. He does not contend that the people actually *exercise* that sovereignty. He therefore makes a careful distinction between sovereignty as such, and the exercise of that sovereignty. The exercise of the sovereignty is commonly entrusted to a government of some kind, typically to a king. A people, as Grotius explained, when making itself subject to a king, 'retains its sovereignty over itself, although this must now be exercised not by the body, but by the head' (p. 173). As will be explained below, Grotius did not hold that there was a general right on the part of a people to recover their sovereignty from a ruler who acted oppressively.

Regarding Grotius's connexion to social-contract theory, it is important to avoid confusing the two distinct phenomena of contract and conveyance. In brief, contract refers to a commitment to do something in the future (e.g., to repay a debt, to deliver goods, to perform some task, and so forth). Conveyance refers to the actual performance of a specific kind of act, i.e., the transfer of legal title to something from one party to another. A conveyance may be effectuated in exchange for money, in which case it is a sale. But it may also take the form of a gratuitous transfer. Or it may fall between these two, with legal title to the object being transferred without any *explicit quid pro quo*, but nonetheless on a general hope or expectation of receiving, at some point, a favour of some kind in return.

A contract, it is true, may consist of a commitment to convey legal title to some object at some future point, and perhaps subject to the occurrence of certain conditions. But it still remains the case that there is a conceptual distinction – particularly to a lawyer – between a commitment to convey something in the future, and the actual *act* of conveying something in the present. In the example just posited, the conveyance of the property, when it occurred, would constitute the performance (or discharge) of the contract.

The principal model for this conveyance – as opposed to contract – perspective was one that Grotius must surely have had in mind: that of ancient Rome. It was held in Roman law that the legislative prerogative of the emperor originated from a transfer by the Roman people of its residual sovereign power onto the emperors, beginning with Augustus in the first century BC. It was believed that this transfer of power was effectuated by a statute known as the *lex Regia*, adopted by the people in their political assembly.[19]

This reputed *lex Regia* was, in all probability, fiction rather than fact. But it was a most useful fiction, particularly to lawyers, in that it explained, with the utmost clarity and efficiency, how sovereignty could be transferred from one holder to another. Grotius's position, in line with this Roman-law theory, was that, in the typical case, an originally sovereign people transfers the exercise of that sovereignty to a ruling body of some kind. Furthermore, that sovereignty, once so transferred, is gone, in the manner of property sold or given away.

Several points about this basic theory may be pointed out, which Grotius does not deal with very forthrightly. Most outstandingly, the question of what authority is actually exercised by a given sovereign in a given case can only be determined empirically – by considering the actual terms of the particular conveyance of powers. This is to say, that in a given transfer of sovereignty, certain rights or powers might be withheld by the grantors (i.e., by the people), or certain conditions imposed onto the grantee. This point was appreciated by Grotius, and formed the basis of some qualifications to the basic thesis (discussed below) that there is no right of revolt on the part of the people.

Even if there can be no absolute general rule as to how much power, or what sort of power, people decide to transfer to their rulers, or subject to what conditions, Grotius nevertheless makes it clear that, in the majority of cases, the people choose to transfer the right of exercise of the *whole* of their sovereign powers to a ruler, without retaining anything for themselves. What is transferred, however, is not – at least in the usual case – absolute 'ownership' of the sovereign rights. Instead, what is given to the ruler is a usufructuary right to exercise sovereignty. This betrays, yet again, Grotius's allegiance to the thought categories of Roman law. A usufructuary, briefly, possesses only a right to *use* or exercise the sovereign power. He is therefore a kind of tenant of the sovereign powers rather than an absolute owner. The 'tenant' or usufructuary typically possesses a tenancy that extends indefinitely through time and is heritable – but it is, strictly speaking, a right to use or to exercise sovereignty, with ultimate ownership still lying in the hands of the people.

It only remains to mention several limitations which Grotius places onto sovereignty as such, and onto its transfer and exercise. The lawyer within him (never far from the surface) appreciates that, by the nature of things – i.e., according to natural law – a people cannot transfer to a ruler powers which they themselves did not possess originally. As a consequence, a sovereign cannot have, or be given, a right to kill his subjects because the people never had a right of self-killing (i.e., of suicide) to begin with.

More generally, Grotius held that sovereigns must necessarily be subject to three highly important limitations – not because the people withheld certain

---

[19] See Justinian, *Institutes*, 1.3.4; and *Digest* 1.4.1 (Ulpian).

attributes of sovereignty at the time of transfer, but rather because sovereignty *as such* is subject to these limitations. The first of these is that sovereigns are subject to natural law. Second, they are subject to divine law. And finally, they are subject to international law (as explained below). It is therefore fair to place Grotius amongst the staunch opponents of governmental absolutism.

Resistance by subjects to sovereigns

Those who seek in Grotius an intellectual ancestor of Locke or Jefferson, as a supporter of a right of revolution against tyrannical rule, must look in vain. He did not posit the existence of a general right to rebel against duly constituted rulers. On this point, the distinction between contract and conveyance is particularly relevant. The transfer of power was in the nature of a conveyance – meaning that, once the power was conveyed, it was gone, like property sold or given to a new owner. There was therefore, in Grotius's eyes, no *inherent* power on the part of the people to re-take sovereignty that was given to another. He emphatically rejected the *general* proposition that 'it is permissible for the people to restrain and punish kings, whenever they make a bad use of their power' (p. 51).

There were, however, some caveats to this basic opposition to a right of rebellion against tyranny. One is that, in certain cases, passive disobedience to wicked rulers is allowed – and even required. In particular, if a ruler were to command his subjects to commit violations of natural law, then the subjects can and should refuse to comply. But Grotius very carefully explains that this does *not* mean that there is any limitation on the right of the king to govern. Rather, it means that there is an entirely separate duty on the part of ordinary citizens to refrain from violations of natural law (p. 55) – and also (for what it is worth) a separate natural-law duty on the part of the ruler to refrain from issuing such wicked commands. Note that, in this view of things, it is duties rather than rights which are fundamental, for both rulers and subjects.

In addition, there were seven other significant caveats to the general principle of no right of rebellion. These generally relate to special terms or conditions that might have been included in the original transfer of power to the ruler. Grotius carefully enumerated seven of these in Sections 8–14 of Chapter 4 of Book I. As this part of the text is very straightforward, there is no need for an exposition here. The reader may turn to p. 72 for the discussion.

On obedience to usurpers of power

It is obvious that the principle which precluded a general right of resistance to legitimate sovereigns – the fact of an earlier voluntary conveyance of sovereign powers – cannot apply to usurpers. For usurpers, by definition, are persons to whom the people have *not* previously transferred any of their sovereign rights. In the terminology of private law, usurpers are mere trespassers and not owners. Consistently with his views as outlined above, Grotius therefore allows considerably more latitude to people to resist usurpers. Here too, though, he can hardly be classed as a zealous revolutionary. He cautioned that, even when an illegitimate ruler is in power, considerations of social harmony might well militate, as a practical matter, in favour of obedience to the usurper's commands. In all events, Grotius's discussion of this subject is both clear and brief. So readers may turn directly to it (p. 74).

Grotius the international lawyer

It was noted above that sovereigns, according to Grotius, are subject to international law. Regarding Grotius's conception of international law, some background information is necessary. Most fundamentally, it should be appreciated that, in Grotius's opinion, two quite distinct bodies of law regulate the relations between states: natural law, and what he usually called the 'law of nations' (*ius gentium*). Natural law, it will be recalled, was a body of eternal and unchangeable principles. Here, it is only necessary to stress that this body of law was binding on *all* human beings – subjects and rulers alike. Natural law was not, therefore, a body of international law *specifically*.

It was otherwise with the law of nations, or *ius gentium*, which (as noted above) was seen as a man-made body of law. It was applicable to states as such and *not* to private parties. As it differs in some important ways from what we now regard as international law, a few words about it are in order.

What Grotius meant by the 'law of nations'

It was noted above that the category of laws wider in scope than national laws was divided by Grotius into two sub-groups: the Roman-law *ius gentium*, and the volitional law of nations. The second of these approximates to what is now referred to as international law. More specifically, the volitional law of nations approximates to what is now known as customary international law, meaning a law which arises out of tacit agreement between the various states of the world. When first introducing the concept, in the Prologue (p. 5), Grotius characterises it as a body of law 'between all states', which looks to promote the advantage 'not of particular states, but of the great society of states'. The Roman-law *ius gentium*, in contrast, is not really international law in this sense, because it does not arise out of agreement between states. Rather, it arises out of separate unilateral enactments by states – with the contents of those unilateral enactments 'matching up' with one another. This Roman-law concept will be referred to as the '*ius gentium* proper', although Grotius did not employ this precise turn of phrase himself.

Although the *ius gentium* proper and the volitional law of nations are distinct from one another in principle (as just explained), in practice they are often difficult to distinguish. The reason is that they share two very crucial features.

The first is that both are applicable universally, i.e., to all (or nearly all) states. The second is that both of them are bodies of *man-made* law – and, as such, both of them are quite distinct from natural law, whose basis is reason. The basis of both the *ius gentium* proper and the volitional law of nations is human will.

These two key shared features of the *ius gentium* proper and the volitional law of nations make for an unfortunate imprecision in terminology on Grotius's part. He frequently employs the general expression 'law of nations' (*ius gentium*), without expressly saying whether he is referring to the *ius gentium* proper, or to the volitional law of nations, or to both. The reader therefore needs to be aware of this potential ambiguity. As a general measure of guidance, it may be said that frequently, the expression 'law of nations' will refer to *both* the *ius gentium* proper and the volitional law of nations. The effect, then, is that the general expression 'law of nations' becomes, for Grotius, an umbrella term, a generic category of law of which there are two species: the *ius gentium* proper, and the volitional law of nations.

It is annoying that Grotius never deals very squarely with this terminological ambiguity. Perhaps the most forthright expression of the distinction between these two kinds of law occurs in Chapter 1 of Book III (p. 330), where he notes, though only in passing, that 'the term law of nations (*ius gentium*) includes both what is approved by separate nations without mutual obligation [i.e., the *ius gentium* proper] and what contains a mutual obligation in itself [i.e., the volitional law of nations]'. His best discussion of the distinction – and it is extremely brief – occurs in the first section of Chapter 8 of Book II (p. 159), where he contrasts the Roman-law concept of the law of nations (the *ius gentium* proper) with 'that law of nations with which we are concerned'. The Roman-law concept (or *ius gentium* proper), he goes on to say, 'is not international law strictly speaking (*ius illud gentium*), for it does not affect the mutual society of nations in relation to one another; it affects only each particular people in a state of peace'. But he says hardly anything more, proceeding instead to his immediate subject, the acquisition of title to various kinds of property.

Things are not helped by Grotius's use of a variety of different expressions such as: 'law of nature and nations' (*iurae naturae gentiumque*); 'volitional universal law' (*lege gentium voluntaria*); 'international law strictly speaking' (*ius illud gentium*); 'common law of nations' (*iure gentium communi*); 'universal common law' (*iure gentium nonnunquam*); 'universal customary law' (*ius gentium ex communi*); or 'strict law of nations' (*ius externum gentium* or *iure gentium externo*).

The crucial point to bear in mind here is that, for Grotius, the fundamental divide in law is between the law of nature on the one hand, and the generic law of nations on the other. The distinction *within* the generic law of nations between the *ius gentium* proper and the volitional law of nations is of comparatively little moment for practical purposes. A few words on that fundamental dichotomy – between natural law and the generic law of nations – are therefore in order.

The dichotomy between natural law and the law of nations

It is particularly unfortunate (and decidedly odd) that the distinction between
the law of nature and the generic law of nations received so little explicit
discussion by Grotius, because it constitutes his foremost contribution to the
development of international legal thought. There was an element of historical
accident in this.

For one thing, Grotius was not the first to articulate the basic dichotomy
between the law of nature and the law of nations. That honour belongs to
Isidore of Seville, as far back as the seventh century.[20] More importantly and
more recently, the subject had been given a thorough airing, in the generation
just before Grotius, by the Spanish Jesuit scholar Francisco Suárez. Moreover,
Suárez's treatment of the subject must be said to be, on every count, superior to
that of Grotius.[21] Nevertheless, it was Grotius's treatment which attracted the
greater attention of later writers, probably (as speculated above) because the
great majority of international-law writers in the generations following Grotius
were Protestants.

A further element of historical accident to Grotius's reputation in international law arose over the century and a half or so following *On the Law of
War and Peace*. In that period, international-law writers divided into two broad
camps, which came to be labelled the 'naturalists' and the 'Grotians'. The defining feature of the naturalists, whose most conspicuous figure was the German
scholar Samuel Pufendorf, was the belief that legal relations between states were
governed exclusively by natural law. That is to say, they rejected the very idea of
a separate, man-made law of nations.[22] They did accept that treaties concluded
between states were legally binding – but only in the sense that contracts are
legally binding in private law. The law governing treaties as such, the naturalists
insisted, is part of natural law and is consequently not man-made.[23]

The Grotians (sometimes labelled 'eclectics'), in contrast, endorsed a dualistic
view of international law. That is to say, international law, to the Grotians,
came in two distinct varieties noted above: the eternal and unchangeable law of
nature, and the man-made, or volitional, law of nations, which, by its nature, was
subject to enactment, alteration, and repeal at the will of the various sovereigns

[20] See Isidore of Seville, *Etymologies*, edited and translated by Stephen A. Barney,
W. J. Lewis, J. A. Beach, and Oliver Berghof (Cambridge University Press, 2006
[c. AD 630]), at pp. 117–18.
[21] See Suárez, *Treatise on Laws*, at pp. 325–33, 341–4. On Suárez, see generally Brian
Tierney, 'Vitoria and Suárez on Ius Gentium, Natural Law, and Custom', in Amanda
Perreau-Saussine and James Bernard Murphy (eds.) *The Nature of Customary Law:
Legal, Historical and Philosophical Perspectives* (Cambridge University Press, 2007),
pp. 101–24, at 114–24.
[22] F. H. Hinsley, *Sovereignty* (Cambridge University Press, 2nd edn, 1986), at pp. 184–6.
[23] See Samuel Pufendorf, *On the Law of Nature and Nations*, translated by C. H. and
W. A. Oldfather (Oxford: Clarendon Press, 1934 [1672]) at pp. 226–9.

of the world. (The *ius gentium* proper faded gradually from consideration in this period.) Conspicuous later figures in this Grotian, or dualist, camp included the German scholar Christian Wolff and the Swiss diplomat and writer Emmerich de Vattel.[24]

In the longer run, the Grotian school of international lawyers came to prevail over the naturalists. But there also came to be an important shift of emphasis *within* the Grotian camp. Grotius himself, and many of his early followers, had been primarily interested in the law of nature, and only secondarily in the law of nations. But over time, writers in the Grotian tradition came to accord ever more attention to the man-made (or volitional) law of nations, and ever less to the law of nature. This tendency reached its fullest fruit in the nineteenth century, when the positivist school of international lawyers went so far as to deny outright the existence of natural law as part of international law – relegating it to, at best, a sort of ethical or philosophical commentary on international law. In the positivist view, international law was wholly a creature of human will.

It is deeply ironic to see nineteenth-century positivist lawyers looking back to Grotius as their forebear – and even crowning him as the 'father of international law'[25] – given that Grotius himself had been far more concerned to expound the law of nature than the law of nations. He even said at one point (p. 32) that there is actually comparatively little law – apart from natural law – that is truly common to the whole world. He would have been deeply shocked to learn that later writers who were outright non-believers in the law of nature would regard him as a precursor.[26]

For all of this, however, Grotius does deserve credit for assisting in the process of uncoupling natural law from international law – a process which, in the long run, enabled international law to grow into the discipline that we know today. If Grotius was far more a midwife than a father, more a facilitator than an innovator, his impact on later writers has been nonetheless substantial for that. Against considerable odds, this pious and dutiful heir to the great traditions of the ancient and medieval past managed to play a modest and memorable role in the transition to our modern world.[27]

STEPHEN C. NEFF

[24] On Vattel, see generally Vincent Chetail and Peter Haggenmacher (eds.), *Vattel's International Law in a XXIst Century Perspective* (Leiden: Martinus Nijhoff, 2011); and Emmanuelle Jouannet, *Vattel and the Emergence of Classic International Law*, translated by Gina Bellande and Robert Howse (Oxford: Hart, 2010).

[25] See, for example, Hamilton Vreeland, Jr, *Hugo Grotius: The Father of the Modern Science of International Law* (New York: Oxford University Press, 1917)

[26] See, for example, John Westlake, *International Law*, vol. 1 (Cambridge University Press, 2nd edn, 1910), at pp. 12–13.

[27] For an appreciative survey of Grotius's modern legacy, see Hersch Lauterpacht, 'The Grotian Tradition in International Law' (1946) 23 *British Year Book of International Law* 1–53.

Note on the text

The first edition of *On the Law of War and Peace* was issued in Paris in 1625, in Latin (as *De Iure Belli ac Pacis*), in three slightly varying versions. Only modest changes were made in the subsequent editions. Most of these were made for the second edition, published in Amsterdam in 1631. The most notable of the changes made was the placing of an increased emphasis on the innate sociability of humans, in contrast to a more individualistic emphasis in the first edition.[1] The third edition, of 1632, contained no significant changes (and was condemned by Grotius as unauthorised). For the fourth edition of 1642, some material was added relevant to contemporary events. The fifth and final (posthumous) edition of 1646 made no substantive changes from the fourth one.[2]

This present text comes from the fifth edition. The English translation is that of Francis W. Kelsey, first done for Oxford University Press in an edition dated 1925.[3] (In fact, it was published several years later than that. The backdating was probably done to provide the appearance of a three-hundredth anniversary edition.)

It must be confessed that much bibliographic labour remains to be done on this text. A definitive Latin version, correcting Grotius's many errors in references, has been published in the Netherlands in 1993, edited by Robert Feenstra, C. E. Persenaire and E. Arps-de Wilde.[4] This is an updated version of a work first done in 1939. Grotius scholars will be forever in the debt of Professor Feenstra and his associates. What is needed – but appears not to be

---

[1] Richard Tuck, *The Rights of War and Peace: Political Thought and the International Order from Grotius to Kant* (Oxford University Press, 1999), at pp. 96–7, 101–2.

[2] For useful information on the publishing history of the book, see Jesse S. Reeves, 'The First Edition of Grotius's De Jure Belli ac Pacis, 1625' (1925) 19 *American Journal of International Law,* 12–22; and Jesse S. Reeves, 'Grotius, De Jure Belli ac Pacis: A Bilbiographic Account' (1925) 19 *American Journal of International Law,* at 251–62.

[3] Hugo Grotius, *On the Law of War and Peace,* translated by Francis W. Kelsey (Oxford University Press, 1925).

[4] Hugo Grotius, *De Iure Belli ac Pacis Libri Tres: in quibus ius naturae et gentium item iuris publici praecipua explicantur,* edited by B. J. A. de Kanter-van Hettinga Tromp; additional annotations by R. Feenstra, C. E. Persenaire, and E. Arps-de Wilde (Aalen: Scientia Verlag, 1993).

on the horizon – is a comprehensive modern English translation from this 1993 Latin edition.

Making Grotius readable requires a liberal brandishing of the editorial pen. Even the international-law scholar Hersch Lauterpacht, a great admirer of Grotius, pronounced the book to be 'no longer a readable work for the purposes of current instruction'.[5] Speaking of the book in its unabridged form, this is, if anything, a significant understatement. The beleaguered reader can easily harbour the suspicion that Grotius must have intended the book to be as difficult as possible to read. This edition is a determined, and long-overdue, effort to rescue Grotius from the consequences of his own ornately pedantic writing style.

The guiding policy behind the editing has been ruthlessly to prune the vast amounts of illustrative material from classical literature and from classical and biblical history. In terms of sheer bulk, this has resulted in the excision of something like two-thirds of the original text. It should be emphasised that this drastic reduction in the bulk of the work is readily justified by the very stance on natural law endorsed by Grotius himself. In the rationalist view, the content of natural law is discerned (at least ideally) by reason, in the manner of, say, a mathematical proposition, and not by appeal to authority. Consequently, the vast ocean of illustrations that Grotius gives for his ideas are just that – illustrations, rather than authorities. For that reason, they are omitted here, as they massively intrude on the reading of the substantive portions of the text. Also, they are, in a disturbing number of cases, only doubtfully on point.

The principal exception to this policy of omitting merely illustrative material concerns references to Roman law (chiefly to Justinian's *Digest* but occasionally to other sources). The reason is that these can be said to approximate to actual sources of authority, so they have been left in (save where they are not really on point). References are in the standard form of Roman legal reference, to book, chapter, and section.

Occasionally, some illustrative material has been left in, when (as is very rare) it actually helps to elucidate an idea that Grotius himself does not express very clearly, or when the illustration provided is particularly succinct or vivid. The result is to give the reader a fair flavour of Grotius's general style.

At the same time, the editorial policy has been to include, as nearly as feasible, the whole of Grotius's substantive text. Only in three areas has there been some marginal trimming of substantive material. The first is in Chapter 2 of Book I, where Grotius shows his prowess as a theologian by proving the compatibility of warfare (i.e., of just warfare) with the New Testament, by way of exegesis of a host of passages from the Gospels. This has been omitted, although the immediately following material, on the attitude of the early Christian Church to warfare, has been included. Second, the exposition of inheritance, in Chapter 7 of Book II, has been trimmed down. Much remains in – perhaps

---

[5] Hersch Lauterpacht, 'The Grotian Tradition in International Law' (1946) 23 *British Yearbook of International Law*, 1–53, at 18.

even all too much, as this is one of the most tedious parts of the book. Third, the material on alluvial deposits in rivers, in Chapter 8 of Book II, has been trimmed down. Most readers (it is confidently supposed) will agree that quite enough is left in on that less-than-scintillating topic. Otherwise, an occasional illustration of a point has been left out when it is too convoluted to be of any real value. But the guiding policy has been to leave out nothing of substance.

Notes which contain only references derive from Grotius himself – corrected where necessary in the instances in which they were erroneous in some way. Notes containing explanatory text are nearly all by the editor. In a very small number of instances, Grotius had a textual footnote which was worth retaining. These few instances are clearly identified as such, with Grotius's note given in quotation marks.

On some occasions, it has been possible to avoid recourse to an editorial note by making a slight alteration to the text in the interest of greater clarity. Only fractions of individual sentences have been altered in this manner. These slight alterations are marked by square brackets.

Only in one place in the entire text does Grotius give any extended attention to contemporary state practice in international law. This is in a long footnote in Chapter 1 of Book III, on the subject of neutrality (p. 329). The reason for this anomaly, as Grotius explains, was a dearth of material from his beloved classical and biblical sources on the subject. The footnote is by far the longest in the book and has been relegated to Appendix 1.

References to biblical sources are given in the standard way, by book, chapter and verse. References to classical sources are given in the manner traditional to classicists, of book and chapter, or chapter and section. This enables the source to be located by curious readers in any language or translation. Where sources cited are within edited works, a short-form citation is given in the notes. Readers can consult the table of abbreviations at the beginning for the full references, as well as for full citations to treaties that are referred to in the notes.

The titles of the sections within the chapters have been slightly trimmed down. They have sometimes been slightly amended to give a more accurate indication of the content of the section in question.

In the interest of attractiveness to the reader's eye, ellipsis marks are omitted from the beginnings and ends of paragraphs, but employed to indicate deleted material within paragraphs.

When the expression 'law of nations' appears, it is a translation of '*ius gentium*' from the original text. Sometimes, Grotius employed alternative expressions. In those cases, the original Latin is given in brackets in the text, alongside the English translation.

In the interest of enabling readers to employ the text as they would a modern treatise, Appendix 2 provides an alternate Table of Contents. The Table of Contents at the beginning is that of the 1925 edition noted above (with only slight amendment).

Prologue to the three books On the Law of War and Peace

The municipal law of Rome and of other states has been treated by many, who have undertaken to elucidate it by means of commentaries or to reduce it to a convenient digest. That body of law, however, which is concerned with the mutual relations among states or rulers of states (*inter populos plures aut populorum*), whether derived from nature, or established by divine ordinances, or having its origin in custom (*moribus*) and tacit agreement,[1] few have touched upon. Up to the present time, no one has treated it in a comprehensive and systematic manner; yet the welfare of mankind demands that this task be accomplished.

Such a work is all the more necessary because, in our day as in former times, there is no lack of men who view this branch of law with contempt as having no reality outside of an empty name. On the lips of men quite generally is the saying... that, in the case of a king or imperial city,[2] nothing is unjust which is expedient. Of like implication is the statement that, for those whom fortune favours, might makes right, and that the administration of a state cannot be carried on without injustice.

Furthermore, the controversies which arise between peoples or kings generally have Mars as their arbiter. That war is irreconcilable with all law is a view held not alone by the ignorant populace; expressions are often let slip by well-informed and thoughtful men which lend countenance to such a view. Nothing is more common than the assertion of antagonism between law and arms.

Since our discussion concerning law will have been undertaken in vain if there is no law, in order to open the way for a favourable reception of our work and at the same time to fortify it against attacks, this very serious error must be briefly refuted. In order that we may not be obliged to deal with a crowd of opponents, let us assign to them a pleader.

---

[1] By 'custom' should probably be understood the *ius gentium* proper; and by 'tacit agreement' the volitional law of nations. But Grotius is not explicit on this point. See the Introduction on these two concepts.

[2] By 'imperial city' is meant, basically, a self-governing, independent city or city-state, such as emerged in the Holy Roman Empire (in northern Italy) from the eleventh century.

Carneades,[3] then, having undertaken to hold a brief against justice, in particular against that phase of justice with which we are concerned, was able to muster no argument stronger than this, that, for reasons of expediency, men imposed upon themselves laws, which vary according to customs, and among the same peoples often undergo changes as times change; moreover that there is no law of nature, because all creatures, men as well as animals, are impelled by nature toward ends advantageous to themselves; that, consequently, there is no justice; or, if such there be, it is supreme folly, since one does violence to his own interests if he consults the advantage of others.

What the philosopher here says . . . must not for one moment be admitted. Man is, to be sure, an animal, but an animal of a superior kind, much farther removed from all other animals than the different kinds of animals are from one another. [E]vidence on this point may be found in the many traits peculiar to the human species. But among the traits characteristic of man is an impelling desire for society, that is, for the social life – not of any and every sort, but peaceful, and organised according to the measure of his intelligence, with those who are of his own kind; this social trend the Stoics called 'sociableness'.[4] Stated as a universal truth, therefore, the assertion that every animal is impelled by nature to seek only its own good cannot be conceded.[5]

Some of the other animals, in fact, do in a way restrain the [appetite] for that which is good for themselves alone, to the advantage, now of their offspring, now of other animals of the same species. This aspect of their behaviour has its origin, we believe, in some extrinsic intelligent principle,[6] because, with regard to other actions which involve no more difficulty than those referred to, a like degree of intelligence is not manifest in them. The same thing must be said of children. In children, even before their training has begun, some disposition to do good to others appears; . . . thus sympathy for others comes

---

[3] Carneades of Cyrene, active in the second century BC, was the leading figure of the sceptical school of philosophers in Hellenistic Greece. He was a popular lecturer but left no writings of his own. The core belief of scepticism was a denial of the possibility of attaining knowledge with absolute certainty. More specifically, the sceptics disbelieved in natural law and in the existence of universal moral principles, holding instead that all law was of merely human creation. The sceptical view-point is presented in Cicero's *Republic*, by the character Lucius Furius Philus.

[4] The Stoics, from the third century BC onwards, were the foremost expositors in the classical world of natural law. A part of their doctrine was a monistic outlook, in which the universe was seen, in basically organic terms, as a single gigantic organism, with all parts interconnected into a coherent whole. In political and social terms, this outlook took the form of a belief that the whole of human society formed, fundamentally, a single moral community.

[5] This passage shows Grotius's commitment to the belief in a fundamental principle of traditional natural-law thought: the inherent sociability of the human species.

[6] I.e., to some, the law of nature was imposed from outside, and then implanted in humans as a kind of instinct. On this view, the property of sociability would therefore not be something that humans devised for themselves by their own initiative.

out spontaneously at that age. The mature man in fact has knowledge which prompts him to similar actions under similar conditions, together with an impelling desire for society, for the gratification of which he alone among animals possesses a special instrument, speech. He has also been endowed with the faculty of knowing and of acting in accordance with general principles. Whatever accords with that faculty is not common to all animals, but peculiar to the nature of man.[7]

This maintenance of the social order, which we have roughly sketched, and which is consonant with human intelligence, is the source of law properly so called.[8] To this sphere of law belong the abstaining from that which is another's, the restoration to another of anything of his which we may have, together with any gain which we may have received from it; the obligation to fulfil promises, the making good of a loss incurred through our fault, and the inflicting of penalties upon men according to their deserts.

From this signification of the word law, there has flowed another and more extended meaning. Since over other animals, man has the advantage of possessing not only a strong bent towards social life, of which we have spoken, but also a power of discrimination which enables him to decide what things are agreeable or harmful (as to both things present and things to come), and what can lead to either alternative; in such things it is meet for the nature of man, within the limitations of human intelligence, to follow the direction of a well-tempered judgement, being neither led astray by fear or the allurement of immediate pleasure, nor carried away by rash impulse. Whatever is clearly at variance with such judgement is understood to be contrary also to the law of nature, that is, to the nature of man.

To this exercise of judgement belongs, moreover, the rational allotment to each man, or to each social group, of those things which are properly theirs, in such a way as to give the preference now to him who is more wise over the less wise, now to a kinsman rather than to a stranger, now to a poor man rather than to a man of means, as the conduct of each or the nature of the thing suggests. Long ago, the view came to be held by many, that this discriminating allotment is a part of law, properly and strictly so called. [N]evertheless law, properly defined, has a far different nature, because its essence lies in leaving to another that which belongs to him, or in fulfilling our obligations to him.[9]

---

[7] A key feature of the rationalist stream of natural-law thought, to which Grotius adhered, is that humans are fundamentally distinct from all other animals, by virtue of their possession of reason – with reason also forming the basis of natural law.

[8] The rationalist approach to natural law held that law in the proper sense is applicable only to humans. Consequently, laws of nature, such as the 'laws' of physics or biology, applicable to inanimate objects or to non-human creatures, cannot be regarded as laws in the proper sense.

[9] In other words, the central feature of natural law is the principle of due fulfillment of obligations. It is therefore an error to regard the natural law of Grotius as being fundamentally a law of rights.

What we have been saying would have a degree of validity even if we should concede that which cannot be conceded without the utmost wickedness: that there is no God, or that the affairs of men are of no concern to Him. The very opposite of this view has been implanted in us partly by reason, partly by unbroken tradition, and confirmed by many proofs as well as by miracles attested by all ages. Hence it follows that we must without exception render obedience to God as our Creator, to Whom we owe all that we are and have; especially since, in manifold ways, He has shown Himself supremely good and supremely powerful, so that, to those who obey Him, He is able to give supremely great rewards, even rewards that are eternal, since He Himself is eternal. We ought, moreover, to believe that He has willed to give rewards, and all the more should we cherish such a belief if He has so promised in plain words; that He has done this, we Christians believe, convinced by the indubitable assurance of testimonies.

Herein, then, is another source of law besides the source in nature, that is, the free will of God,[10] to which beyond all cavil our reason tells us we must render obedience. But the law of nature of which we have spoken, comprising alike that which relates to the social life of man and that which is so called in a larger sense, proceeding as it does from the essential traits implanted in man,[11] can nevertheless rightly be attributed to God, because of His having willed that such traits exist in us.[12]

There is an additional consideration in that, by means of the laws which He has given, God has made those fundamental traits more manifest, even to those who possess feebler reasoning powers; and He has forbidden us to yield to impulses drawing us in opposite directions – affecting now our own interest, now the interest of others – in an effort to control more effectively our more violent impulses and to restrain them within proper limits.

But sacred history, besides enjoining rules of conduct, in no slight degree reinforces man's inclination towards sociableness by teaching that all men are sprung from the same first parents. In this sense, we can rightly affirm also that . . . a blood-relationship has been established among us by nature; consequently, it is wrong for a man to set a snare for a fellow-man. Among mankind generally, one's parents are as it were divinities, and to them is owed an obedience which, if not unlimited, is nevertheless of an altogether special kind.

---

[10] The commands of God, emanating from God's free will, comprise divine law – a category of law quite distinct from natural law.

[11] It is conceded that natural law 'so called in a larger sense' arises from 'the essential traits implanted in man', i.e., from biological features of the human species. But natural law properly speaking is, for Grotius, a law whose basis is reason, not instinct.

[12] Because the existence of natural law itself must ultimately be attributed to the will of God, there cannot, strictly speaking, be a total separation of natural law from divine law. These two categories of law are therefore distinct not in their ultimate origin (since both are the creations of God), but rather in the means by which their contents are discerned by humans. The content of natural law is known by means of the human intellect, while divine law can only be known by revelation.

Again, since it is a rule of the law of nature to abide by pacts[13] (for it was necessary that among men there be some method of obligating themselves one to another, and no other natural method can be imagined), out of this source the bodies of municipal law have arisen. For those who had associated themselves with some group, or had subjected themselves to a man or to men, had either expressly promised, or from the nature of the transaction must be understood impliedly to have promised, that they would conform to that which should have been determined, in the one case by the majority, in the other by those upon whom authority had been conferred.[14]

What is said, therefore, in accordance with the view not only of Carneades but also of others, that

> Expediency is, as it were, the mother
> Of what is just and fair,[15]

is not true, if we wish to speak accurately. For the very nature of man, which, even if we had no lack of anything, would lead us into the mutual relations of society, is the mother of the law of nature. But the mother of municipal law is that obligation which arises from mutual consent; and since this obligation derives its force from the law of nature, nature may be considered, so to say, the great-grandmother of municipal law.

The law of nature nevertheless has the reinforcement of expediency; for the Author of nature willed that, as individuals, we should be weak, and should lack many things needed in order to live properly, to the end that we might be the more constrained to cultivate the social life. But expediency afforded an opportunity also for municipal law, since that kind of association of which we have spoken, and subjection to authority, have their roots in expediency. From this, it follows that those who prescribe laws for others, in so doing, are accustomed to have, or ought to have, some advantage in view.

But just as the laws of each state have in view the advantage of that state, so by mutual consent it has become possible that certain laws should originate as between all states, or a great many states; and it is apparent that the laws thus originating had in view the advantage, not of particular states, but of the great society of states. And this is what is called the [volitional] law of nations, whenever we distinguish that term from the law of nature.[16]

---

[13] For the full treatment of this subject, see p. 202 below.

[14] This passage indicates Grotius's commitment to the idea that human political authority derives, ultimately, from the consent of the governed. To this extent, Grotius is fairly grouped amongst social-contract theorists. For Grotius's fuller exposition of the source and nature of sovereignty, see p. 50 below.

[15] Horace, *Satires*, I.3.98.

[16] This is Grotius's first reference to the volitional law of nations, and to the distinction between it and natural law. Natural law is rooted, ultimately, in transcendental principles of right and wrong, instilled into the human psyche (or else discoverable by reason). The volitional law of nations is rooted in expediency – though

This division of law Carneades passed over altogether. For he divided all law into the law of nature and the law of particular countries. Nevertheless if undertaking to treat of the body of law which is maintained between states . . . he would surely have been obliged to make mention of this law.

Wrongly, moreover, does Carneades ridicule justice as folly. For since, by his own admission, the national who in his own country obeys its laws is not foolish, even though, out of regard for that law, he may be obliged to forgo certain things advantageous for himself, so that nation is not foolish which does not press its own advantage to the point of disregarding the laws common to nations. The reason in either case is the same. For just as the national, who violates the law of his country in order to obtain an immediate advantage, breaks down that by which the advantages of himself and his posterity are for all future time assured, so the state which transgresses the laws of nature and of nations (*iura naturae gentiumque*) cuts away also the bulwarks which safeguard its own future peace. Even if no advantage were to be contemplated from the keeping of the law, it would be a mark of wisdom, not of folly, to allow ourselves to be drawn towards that to which we feel that our nature leads.

Wherefore, in general, it is by no means true that

> You must confess that laws were framed
> From fear of the unjust,[17]

a thought which, in Plato, someone explains thus, that laws were invented from fear of receiving injury, and that men are constrained by a kind of force to cultivate justice.[18] For that relates only to the institutions and laws which have been devised to facilitate the enforcement of right; as when many persons, in themselves weak, in order that they might not be overwhelmed by the more powerful, leagued themselves together to establish tribunals and by combined force to maintain these, that as a united whole they might prevail against those with whom as individuals they could not cope.[19]

And in this sense, we may readily admit also the truth of the saying that right is that which is acceptable to the stronger; so that we may understand that law fails of its outward effect unless it has a sanction behind it.[20]

Nevertheless law, even though without a sanction, is not entirely void of effect. For justice brings peace of conscience, while injustice causes torments

---

expediency must be understood to mean that which is expedient for 'the great society of states' in general, rather than for the interests of individual states.

[17] Horace, *Satires*, I.3.111.   [18] Plato, *The Republic*, II.358–62; and *Gorgias*, 482–4.

[19] It is conceded that some laws are made by humans specifically for the purpose of coercing wicked persons into behaving lawfully. But these are laws which are ancillary or procedural in character rather than substantive – i.e., laws which institute enforcement mechanisms. The substantive law which is being enforced, in contrast, is (according to Grotius) natural law, which is not man-made.

[20] I.e., a sanction (meaning punishment meted out to law-breakers) is essential for the limited – though admittedly important – purpose of giving 'outward effect' to laws. But it is not a definitional component of law as such.

and anguish…in the breast of tyrants. Justice is approved, and injustice condemned, by the common agreement of good men. But, most important of all, in God injustice finds an enemy, justice a protector. He reserves His judgements for the life after this, yet in such a way that He often causes their effects to become manifest even in this life, as history teaches by numerous examples.

Many hold… that the standard of justice which they insist upon in the case of individuals within the state is inapplicable to a nation or the ruler of a nation. The reason for the error lies in this, first of all, that in respect to law, they have in view nothing except the advantage which accrues from it, such advantage being apparent in the case of citizens who, taken singly, are powerless to protect themselves. But great states, since they seem to contain in themselves all things required for the adequate protection of life, seem not to have need of that virtue which looks toward the outside, and is called justice.

But, not to repeat what I have said, that law is not founded on expediency alone, there is no state so powerful that it may not sometime need the help of others outside itself, either for purposes of trade, or even to ward off the forces of many foreign nations united against it. In consequence, we see that even the most powerful peoples and sovereigns seek alliances, which are quite devoid of significance according to the point of view of those who confine law within the boundaries of states. Most true is the saying, that all things are uncertain the moment men depart from law.

If no association of men can be maintained without law,… surely also that association which binds together the human race, or binds many nations together, has need of law. This was perceived by him who said that shameful deeds ought not to be committed even for the sake of one's country.[21]

Least of all should that be admitted which some people imagine, that in war all laws are in abeyance. On the contrary, war ought not to be undertaken except for the enforcement of rights;[22] when once undertaken, it should be carried on only within the bounds of law and good faith.[23] … For judgements are efficacious against those who feel that they are too weak to resist; against those who are equally strong, or think that they are, wars are undertaken. But in order that wars may be justified, they must be carried on with not less scrupulousness than judicial processes are wont to be.

Let the laws be silent, then, in the midst of arms, but only the laws of the state, those that the courts are concerned with, that are adapted only to a state of peace; not those other laws, which are of perpetual validity and suited to all times.[24]

---

[21] Cicero, *On Duties*, I.159.
[22] This is a capsule statement of just-war doctrine. For more extended treatment of the subject, see p. 81 below.
[23] For the detailed treatment of the law on the conduct of war, see p. 325 below.
[24] The reference is to a famous – and much misunderstood – passage of Cicero, in which it was stated that 'when swords are drawn the laws fall silent'. Cicero, *Pro Milo*, IV.10. Some have interpreted this to mean that, between belligerents in wartime, no law is in force. In fact, Cicero made the remark in the context of asserting a right of

The ancient Romans . . . were slow in undertaking war, and permitted themselves no licence in that matter, because they held the view that a war ought not to be waged except when free from reproach.

The historians in many a passage reveal how great in war is the influence of the consciousness that one has justice on his side; they often attribute victory chiefly to this cause. Hence the proverbs, that a soldier's strength is broken or increased by his cause; that he who has taken up arms unjustly rarely comes back in safety; that hope is the comrade of a good cause; and others of the same purport.

No one ought to be disturbed, furthermore, by the successful outcome of unjust enterprises. For it is enough that the fairness of the cause exerts a certain influence, even a strong influence upon actions, although the effect of that influence, as happens in human affairs, is often nullified by the interference of other causes. Even for winning friendships, of which for many reasons nations as well as individuals have need, a reputation for having undertaken war not rashly nor unjustly, and of having waged it in a manner above reproach, is exceedingly efficacious. No one readily allies himself with those in whom he believes that there is only a slight regard for law, for the right, and for good faith.

Fully convinced by the considerations which I have advanced, that there is a common law among nations, which is valid alike for war and in war, I have had many and weighty reasons for undertaking to write upon this subject. Throughout the Christian world, I observed a lack of restraint in relation to war, such as even barbarous races should be ashamed of; I observed that men rush to arms for slight causes, or no cause at all, and that when arms have once been taken up there is no longer any respect for law, divine or human; it is as if, in accordance with a general decree, frenzy had openly been let loose for the committing of all crimes.[25]

Confronted with such utter ruthlessness, many men, who are the very furthest from being bad men, have come to the point of forbidding all use of arms to the Christian, whose rule of conduct above everything else comprises the duty of loving all men. . . . [T]heir purpose, as I take it, is [that] when things have gone in one direction, to force them in the opposite direction, as we are accustomed to do, that they may come back to a true middle ground. But the very effort of pressing too hard in the opposite direction is often so far from being helpful

individual self-defence against an assailant, making the point that, in such an emergency, it is not possible to mobilise the normal forces of the state against the criminal. It is therefore necessary for the law to allow self-help in such an emergency. Cicero was making no reference to war between states. Grotius therefore rightly points out that the laws which are silent, in Cicero's statement, are the ordinary civil laws applicable *within* a state (i.e., the law forbidding forcible self-help by individuals) and not the law of nature, which is of permanent and eternal validity, even between enemy belligerents in time of war.

[25] It will be recalled that these words were written as the Thirty Years' War was raging.

that it does harm, because in such arguments the detection of what is extreme is easy, and results in weakening the influence of other statements which are well within the bounds of truth. For both extremes, therefore, a remedy must be found, that men may not believe either that nothing is allowable, or that everything is.

At the same time, through devotion to study in private life, I have wished – as the only course now open to me, undeservedly forced out from my native land, which had been graced by so many of my labours – to contribute somewhat to the philosophy of the law, which previously, in public service, I practised with the utmost degree of probity of which I was capable. Many heretofore have purposed to give to this subject a well-ordered presentation; no one has succeeded. And in fact, such a result cannot be accomplished unless – a point which until now has not been sufficiently kept in view – those elements which come from positive law[26] are properly separated from those which arise from nature. For the principles of the law of nature, since they are always the same, can easily be brought into a systematic form;[27] but the elements of positive law, since they often undergo change and are different in different places, are outside the domain of systematic treatment, just as other notions of particular things are.

If now, those who have consecrated themselves to true justice should undertake to treat the parts of the natural and unchangeable philosophy of law, after having removed all that has its origin in the free will of man; if one, for example, should treat legislation, another taxation, another the administration of justice, another the determination of motives, another the proving of facts, then by assembling all these parts a body of jurisprudence could be made up.

What procedure we think should be followed we have shown by deed rather than by words in this work, which treats by far the noblest part of jurisprudence.

In the first book, having by way of introduction spoken of the origin of law, we have examined the general question, whether there is any such thing as a just war; then, in order to determine the differences between public war and private war, we found it necessary to explain the nature of sovereignty – what nations, what kings possess complete sovereignty; who possess sovereignty only in part, who with right of alienation, who otherwise; then it was necessary to speak also concerning the duty of subjects to their superiors.

The second book, having for its object to set forth all the causes from which war can arise, undertakes to explain fully what things are held in common, what may be owned in severalty; what rights persons have over persons, what obligation arises from ownership; what is the rule governing royal successions; what right is established by a pact or a contract; what is the force of treaties of

---

[26] I.e., man-made law.

[27] The second major purpose of this work (along with an exposition of international law relating to war) is announced: the systematic exposition of natural law. This occurs in Chapters 2–21 of Book II.

alliance; what of an oath private or public, and how it is necessary to interpret these; what is due in reparation for damage done; in what the inviolability of ambassadors consists; what law controls the burial of the dead; and what is the nature of punishments.

The third book has for its subject, first, what is permissible in war. Having distinguished that which is done with impunity, or even that which among foreign peoples is defended as lawful, from that which actually is free from fault, it proceeds to the different kinds of peace, and all compacts relating to war.

The undertaking seemed to me all the more worthwhile because, as I have said, no one has dealt with the subject-matter as a whole, and those who have treated portions of it have done so in a way to leave much to the labours of others. Of the ancient philosophers nothing in this field remains; either of the Greeks . . . or – what was especially to be desired – of those who gave their allegiance to the young Christianity. Even the books of the ancient Romans on fetial law[28] have transmitted to us nothing of themselves except the title. Those who have made collections of the cases which are called 'cases of conscience' have merely written chapters on war, promises, oaths, and reprisals, just as on other subjects.

I have seen also special books on the law of war, some by theologians, as Franciscus de Vitoria,[29] Henry of Gorkum,[30] [Wilelmus Mahiae];[31] others by doctors of law, as John Lupus,[32] Franciscus Arias,[33] Giovanni da Legnano,[34]

---

[28] This was the law and procedure relating to declarations of war.

[29] Francisco de Vitoria (c. 1480–1546) was a Spanish Dominican who taught theology at the University of Salamanca. His most noted works were compiled from lectures given there. Three of these are referred to by Grotius in this treatise: *On Civil Power* (1528), *On the American Indians* (1539), and *On the Law of War* (1539). They are available in Vitoria, *Political Writings*, edited by Anthony Pagden and Jeremy Lawrance (Cambridge University Press, 1991).

[30] Henry of Gorkum (c. 1386–1431) was a noted Thomist writer who taught philosophy at the University of Cologne and apparently founded a school of his own in Cologne. He later became a canon of the Basilica of St Ursula and pro-chancellor of the University of Cologne.

[31] Wilelmus Mahiae, a highly obscure figure, was the author of a book entitled *Libellus de Bello Justo et Liceto*, published in Antwerp in 1514.

[32] John Lupus, or Juan López (d. 1496), was a now obscure Spanish writer who travelled to Italy, where he became vicar of the Archbishop of Siena, the future Pope Pius III (who reigned for twenty-seven days in 1503). Lupus wrote a book entitled *De Bello et Bellatoribus*.

[33] Franciscus Arias de Valderas was a native of Spain and member (c. 1530) of the Spanish College at Bologna. In 1533, in Rome, he published a book entitled *De Bello et Eius Iustitia*.

[34] John of Legnano (c. 1320–83) was a distinguished doctor of civil and canon law at the University of Bologna. His principal contribution to international law was the treatise *Tractatus de Bello, de Represaliis et du Duello* (c. 1360). An English translation was published by Oxford University Press in 1917.

Martinus Laudensis.[35] All of these, however, have said next to nothing upon a most fertile subject. [M]ost of them have done their work without system, and in such a way as to intermingle and utterly confuse what belongs to the law of nature, to divine law, to the law of nations, to civil law, and to the body of law which is found in the canons.

What all these writers especially lacked [was] the illumination of history.... [Attempts in this direction were made] by Balthazar Ayala[36] and, still more fully, by Alberico Gentili.[37] Knowing that others can derive profit from Gentili's painstaking, as I acknowledge that I have, I leave it to his readers to pass judgement on the shortcomings of his work as regards method of exposition, arrangement of matter, delimitation of inquiries, and distinctions between the various kinds of law. This only I shall say, that in treating controversial questions, it is his frequent practice to base his conclusions on a few examples, which are not in all cases worthy of approval, or even to follow the opinions of modern jurists, formulated in arguments of which not a few were accommodated to the special interests of clients, not to the nature of that which is equitable and upright.

The causes which determine the characterisation of a war as lawful or unlawful Ayala did not touch upon. Gentili outlined certain general classes, in the manner which seemed to him best; but he did not so much as refer to many topics which have come up in notable and frequent controversies.

We have taken all pains that nothing of this sort escape us; and we have also indicated the sources from which conclusions are drawn, whence it would be an easy matter to verify them, even if any point has been omitted by us. It remains to explain briefly with what helps, and with what care, I have attacked this task.

First of all, I have made it my concern to refer the proofs of things touching the law of nature to certain fundamental conceptions which are beyond question, so

---

[35] Martinus Garatus (d. 1443, sometimes called Laudensis, or Martin of Lodi, after his birthplace of Lodi) was a professor of law in the fifteenth century, at the Universities of Pavia and Siena. He wrote a treatise on war, and also one of the earliest works on the law of treaties.

[36] Balthasar de Ayala (1548–84), from the Southern Netherlands, served as judge advocate general to the Spanish armies in the Netherlands during the Dutch War of Independence. He was the author of *On the Law of War and on the Duties Connected with War and on Military Discipline* (1581). An English translation was published by the Carnegie Institution of Washington in 1912.

[37] Alberico Gentili (1552–1608) was an Italian Protestant lawyer whose principal career was in England, as Professor of Civil Law at the University of Oxford. His book *On the Law of War* (1598) was an important contribution to international law (with an English translation in 1933 by the Clarendon Press). He also did works on diplomatic law (*De Legationibus* in 1582, with an English translation by the Carnegie Endowment for International Peace in 1924), on various aspects of prize law (published posthumously as *Hispanicae Advocationis* in 1613, with an English translation by Oxford University Press in 1921) and a historical study of *The Wars of the Romans* in 1599 (with an English translation by Oxford University Press in 2011).

that no one can deny them without doing violence to himself. For the principles
of that law, if only you pay strict heed to them, are in themselves manifest and
clear, almost as evident as are those things which we perceive by the external
senses; and the senses do not err if the organs of perception are properly formed
and if the other conditions requisite to perception are present.

In order to prove the existence of this law of nature, I have, furthermore,
availed myself of the testimony of philosophers, historians, poets, finally also
of orators. Not that confidence is to be reposed in them without discrimination; for they were accustomed to serve the interests of their sect, their subject, or their cause. But when many at different times, and in different places,
affirm the same thing as certain, that ought to be referred to a universal cause;
and this cause, in the lines of inquiry which we are following, must be either a
correct conclusion drawn from the principles of nature, or common consent.
The former points to the law of nature; the latter, to the law of nations (*ius
gentium*).

The distinction between these kinds of law is not to be drawn from the
testimonies themselves (for writers everywhere confuse the terms law of nature
and law of nations), but from the character of the matter. For whatever cannot
be deduced from certain principles by a sure process of reasoning, and yet is
clearly observed everywhere, must have its origin in the free will of man.[38]

These two kinds of law, therefore, I have always particularly sought to distinguish from each other, and from municipal law. Furthermore, in the law of
nations, I have distinguished between that which is truly and in all respects
law, and that which produces merely a kind of outward effect simulating that
primitive law.[39]

With no less pains we have separated those things which are strictly and
properly legal, out of which the obligation of restitution arises, from those
things which are called legal because any other classification of them conflicts
with some other stated rule of right reason [such as moral obligations]. In
regard to this distinction of law, we have already said something above.[40]

Among the philosophers, Aristotle deservedly holds the foremost place,
whether you take into account his order of treatment, or the subtlety of his
distinctions, or the weight of his reasons. Would that this pre-eminence had

---

[38] Natural law is, in a hypothetico-deductive manner, 'deduced from certain principles
by a sure process of reasoning'. In contrast to this is law which is 'clearly observed
everywhere', which is most clearly the *ius gentium* proper, law adopted by each state
in the world as a matter of its own independent choice.

[39] This probably refers to the distinction between two possible effects that the law of
nations can have. First, things which are permissible according to natural law can be
made either mandatory or forbidden by the law of nations. Second, there are things
which natural law itself commands or forbids, but for which the law of nations
provides no punishment in the event of disobedience. This second group of acts will
have only the outward appearance of true lawfulness.

[40] See p. 3 above.

not, for some centuries back, been turned into a tyranny, so that Truth, to whom Aristotle devoted faithful service, was by no instrumentality more repressed than by Aristotle's name!

For my part, both here and elsewhere I avail myself of the liberty of the early Christians, who had sworn allegiance to the sect of no one of the philosophers, not because they were in agreement with those who said that nothing can be known – than which nothing is more foolish – but because they thought that there was no philosophic sect whose vision had encompassed all truth, and none which had not perceived some aspect of truth. Thus they believed that to gather up into a whole the truth which was scattered among the different philosophers and dispersed among the sects, was in reality to establish a body of teaching truly Christian.

Among other things – to mention in passing a point not foreign to my subject – it seems to me that, not without reason, some of the Platonists and early Christians departed from the teachings of Aristotle in this, that he considered the very nature of virtue as a mean in passions and actions.[41] That principle, once adopted, led him to unite distinct virtues, as generosity and frugality, into one; to assign to truth extremes between which, on any fair premise, there is no possible co-ordination, boastfulness, and dissimulation; and to apply the designation of vice to certain things which either do not exist, or are not in themselves vices, such as contempt for pleasure and for honours, and freedom from anger against men.[42]

That this basic principle,[43] when broadly stated, is unsound, becomes clear even from the case of justice. For, being unable to find in passions and acts resulting therefrom the too much and the too little opposed to that virtue, Aristotle sought each extreme in the things themselves with which justice is concerned. Now in the first place, this is simply to leap from one class of things over into another class, a fault which he rightly censures in others. . . . [F]or a

---

[41] See Aristotle, *The Nicomachean Ethics*, II.6.

[42] The point (not very clearly expressed) is that Grotius disagrees with Aristotle's view of virtue as a medium between extremes. According to Grotius, this rigid view of virtue often had the perverse effect of compelling Aristotle artificially to contrive two extremes between which to encase (so to speak) any virtue – and that sometimes the two extremes actually had little real relation to one another. Instead of searching for extremes and means, the proper method, in Grotius's view, is to analyse acts and attitudes in their own right, according to the principles of natural law. Moreover, Grotius maintains, it is sometimes the case that extreme attitudes are actually virtuous (or at least are not vices), e.g., contempt for pleasure and honours, or a stout refusal to become angry at others even in situations where most persons would do so. Another example is the virtue of justice, as Grotius immediately goes on to explain. Grotius is actually not being very fair to Aristotle here. Aristotle did recognise that some characteristics, such as spite, shamelessness, and envy, are evil per se, so that his general theory of virtue as a mean between extremes would not apply to them. See *ibid*.

[43] I.e., Aristotle's view of virtue as a mean between extremes.

person to accept less than belongs to him may in fact, under unusual conditions, constitute a fault, in view of that which, according to the circumstances, he owes to himself and to those dependent on him; but in any case the act cannot be at variance with justice, the essence of which lies in abstaining from that which belongs to another.[44]

By equally faulty reasoning, Aristotle tries to make out that adultery committed in a burst of passion, or a murder due to anger, is not properly an injustice.[45] [The true position is that] injustice has no other essential quality than the unlawful seizure of that which belongs to another; and it does not matter whether injustice arises from avarice, from lust, from anger, or from ill-advised compassion; or from an overmastering desire to achieve eminence, out of which instances of the gravest injustice constantly arise. For to disparage such incitements, with the sole purpose in view that human society may not receive injury, is in truth the concern of justice.[46]

To return to the point whence I started, the truth is that some virtues do tend to keep passions under control; but that is not because such control is a proper and essential characteristic of every virtue. Rather, it is because right reason, which virtue everywhere follows, in some things prescribes the pursuing of a middle course, in others stimulates to the utmost degree. We cannot, for example, worship God too much; for superstition errs not by worshipping God too much, but by worshipping in a perverse way. Neither can we too much seek after the blessings that shall abide for ever, nor fear too much the everlasting evils, nor have too great hatred for sin.

Our purpose is to make much account of Aristotle, but reserving in regard to him the same liberty which he, in his devotion to truth, allowed himself with respect to his teachers.

---

[44] The contention is that the virtue of justice illustrates with particular clarity the error of Aristotle's view of virtue. To be extremely just is clearly better than to fall mid-way between justice and injustice. Aristotle attempted to avoid this problem (Grotius asserts) by shifting the focus away from justice itself, and concentrating instead on the material goods that are at stake in a dispute to which justice is to be brought to bear. The party acts justly, on Aristotle's argument, when he accepts a quantity of the disputed goods which is midway between the two possible extremes (i.e., between the one extreme of receiving nothing at all and the other extreme of receiving everything). Grotius is critical of this approach of focusing on the subject-matter of a dispute rather than on the virtue of justice as such. According to Grotius, the just solution is not to divide the property between the claimants, but rather to grant the whole of it to one party (the true owner) and none of it to the other.

[45] Aristotle, *The Nicomachean Ethics*, V.6. Aristotle made a distinction, which Grotius rejects, between an unjust *act* and an unjust *person*. A person who is personally just might nonetheless commit an unjust act out of passion, such as murder or adultery – but the person would not thereby cease to be personally just. Grotius rejects the whole concept of a just person, holding instead that injustice is entirely a feature of conduct.

[46] It is asserted that justice is a strictly objective matter – in essence, scrupulously refraining from infringing the rights of others. The motives behind such infringements ('incitements', as Grotius calls them) are irrelevant.

History in relation to our subject is useful in two ways: it supplies both illustrations and judgements. The illustrations have greater weight in proportion as they are taken from better times and better peoples; thus we have preferred ancient examples, Greek and Roman, to the rest. And judgements are not to be slighted, especially when they are in agreement with one another; for by such statements the existence of the law of nature, as we have said, is in a measure proved, and by no other means, in fact, is it possible to establish the law of nations.[47]

The views of poets and of orators do not have so great weight; and we make frequent use of them not so much for the purpose of gaining acceptance by that means for our argument, as of adding, from their words, some embellishment to that which we wished to say.

I frequently appeal to the authority of the books which men inspired by God have either written or approved, nevertheless with a distinction between the Old Testament and the New. There are some who urge that the Old Testament sets forth the law of nature. Without doubt they are in error, for many of its rules come from the free will of God. And yet this is never in conflict with the true law of nature; and up to this point the Old Testament can be used as a source of the law of nature, provided we carefully distinguish between the law of God, which God sometimes executes through men, and the law of men in their relations with one another.[48]

This error we have, so far as possible, avoided, and also another opposed to it, which supposes that, after the coming of the New Testament, the Old Testament in this respect was no longer of use. We believe the contrary, partly for the reasons which we have already given, partly because the character of the New Testament is such that, in its teachings respecting the moral virtues, it enjoins the same as the Old Testament or even enjoins greater precepts. In this way, we see that the early Christian writers used the witnesses of the Old Testament.

The Hebrew writers, moreover, most of all those who have thoroughly understood the speech and customs of their people, are able to contribute not a little to our understanding of the thought of the books which belong to the Old Testament.

The New Testament I use in order to explain – and this cannot be learned from any other source – what is permissible to Christians. This, however – contrary to the practice of most men – I have distinguished from the law of

---

[47] This is the first indication – made almost in passing – of the important point, that the volitional law of nations can only be discerned by empirical means, by actually surveying the practices of states. Notice the contrast made (though not very emphatically) with the law of nature. In the case of the law of nature, history provides merely the *proof* – i.e., the evidence. But the law *itself* (i.e., the content of the law) derives from reason. In the case of the volitional law of nations, in contrast, history plays an importantly different role: it actually *establishes* the rules of this body of law.

[48] 'The law of men in their relations with one another' is natural law, which should be carefully distinguished from divine law.

nature, considering it as certain that, in that most holy law, a greater degree of moral perfection is enjoined upon us than the law of nature, alone and by itself, would require.[49] And nevertheless I have not omitted to note the things that are recommended to us rather than enjoined, that we may know that, while the turning aside from what has been enjoined is wrong and involves the risk of punishment, a striving for the highest excellence implies a noble purpose and will not fail of its reward.[50]

The authentic synodical canons are collections embodying the general principles of divine law as applied to cases which come up. [T]hey either show what the divine law enjoins, or urge us to that which God would fain persuade. And this truly is the mission of the Christian Church, to transmit those things which were transmitted to it by God, and in the way in which they were transmitted.

Furthermore, customs which were current, or were considered praiseworthy, among the early Christians and those who rose to the measure of so great a name, deservedly have the force of canons.

Next after these comes the authority of those who, each in his own time, have been distinguished among Christians for their piety and learning, and have not been charged with any serious error; for what these declare with great positiveness, and as if definitely ascertained, ought to have no slight weight for the interpretation of passages in Holy Writ which seem obscure. Their authority is the greater the more there are of them in agreement, and as we approach nearer to the times of pristine purity, when neither desire for domination nor any conspiracy of interests had as yet been able to corrupt the primitive truth.

The Schoolmen,[51] who succeeded these writers, often show how strong they are in natural ability. But their lot was cast in an unhappy age, which was ignorant of the liberal arts; wherefore it is less to be wondered at if, among many things worthy of praise, there are also some things which we should

[49] The distinction is between morality and natural law – with morality guided by the New Testament and natural law by reason. Some later positivists claim Grotius as a precursor on this basis. It should be noted, though, that Grotius is only asserting that morality goes beyond natural law in its demands. He is not claiming (as later positivists inclined to do) that law and morality have no intrinsic relation at all to one another. Grotius's view is better characterised as holding natural law to be a sort of sub-category of morality. It comprises the rules that are necessary for harmonious human sociability, and which give rise to enforceable obligations. It is not concerned (as moral rules are) with ensuring the saving of the soul in the after-life.

[50] I.e., natural law may be said to be negative in character, in that it imposes obligations onto persons and exposes them to punishments for infractions. Morality is positive, in that it carries the promise of the reward of eternal life. By obeying natural law, a person provides against punishment on earth. By obeying divine law (or morality), he or she obtains salvation of the soul.

[51] The scholastic philosophers of the Middle Ages. Foremost amongst these was Thomas Aquinas (1225–74), the leading figure in the rationalist school of natural-law thought, to which Grotius belonged. Francisco Suárez (1548–1617), the Spanish Jesuit writer, was another important figure in this tradition.

receive with indulgence. Nevertheless, when the Schoolmen agree on a point of morals, it rarely happens that they are wrong, since they are especially keen in seeing what may be open to criticism in the statements of others. And yet in the very ardour of their defence of themselves against opposing views, they furnish a praiseworthy example of moderation; they contend with one another by means of arguments – not, in accordance with the practice which has lately begun to disgrace the calling of letters, with personal abuse, base offspring of a spirit lacking self-mastery.

Of those who profess knowledge of the Roman law there are three classes.

The first consists of those whose work appears in the Pandects,[52] the Codes of Theodosius and Justinian,[53] and the Imperial Constitutions called Novellae.[54]

To the second class belong the successors of Irnerius,[55] that is Accursius,[56] Bartolus,[57] and so many other names of those who long ruled the bar.

The third class comprises those who have combined the study of classical literature with that of law.[58]

To the first class, I attribute great weight. For they frequently give the very best reasons in order to establish what belongs to the law of nature, and they often furnish evidence in favour of this law and of the law of nations. Nevertheless

---

[52] The Pandects (from a Greek expression meaning 'complete law') refers to what was called the *usus modernus Pandectarum*, which was the modernised form of Roman law taught in European universities in the fourteenth and fifteenth centuries. This form of Roman law was heavily influenced by the canon law of the Catholic Church.

[53] The Code of Theodosius (named for Roman Emperor Theodosius II) was promulgated in AD 438. It was a collection of imperial enactments over the previous century (since the reign of Emperor Constantine). The Code of Justinian, or *Corpus Iuris Civilis*, in contrast, purported to be a complete codification of Roman law, in three parts: the *Institutes*, a short textbook summary of Roman law (AD 533); the *Digest*, a collection of extracts from legal writers covering basically the whole of Roman law (AD 533); and the *Codex* (AD 529), which was a collection of imperial enactments from the second century AD.

[54] The *Novellae* were laws newly promulgated by Justinian after the publication of the *Corpus Iuris* in 529–33.

[55] Irnerius (c. 1050–c. 1130), originally a grammarian, was traditionally regarded as the founder of the famous school of Roman-law scholars at the University of Bologna in the eleventh century.

[56] Accursius (1185–1263), from Florence, was one of the foremost Roman-law scholars of the Middle Ages. His chief monument was the *Glossa Ordinaria* (or Standard Gloss), which was a massive commentary on Justinian's *Corpus Iuris*, and the principal basis for the medieval study of Roman law.

[57] Bartolus of Sassoferrato (c.1313–57) was one of the most eminent legal scholars of the fourteenth century, learned in many branches of law, including Roman law and the constitutional law of the Holy Roman Empire.

[58] This third group are the humanists, who saw Roman law not as a kind of disembodied statement of the general principles of law – i.e., as a codification of natural law – but instead as the product of a particular society in a particular historical context. An early figure in this tradition was the Italian Alciatus (Andrea Alciato, 1492–1550), who taught at the University of Bourges in France.

they, no less than the others, often confuse these terms, frequently calling that the law of nations which is only the law of certain peoples, and that, too, not as established by assent, but perchance taken over through imitation of others or by pure accident.[59] But those provisions which really belong to the law of nations they often treat, without distinction or discrimination, along with those which belong to the Roman law.... We have... endeavoured to distinguish these matters from each other.[60]

The second class, paying no heed to the divine law or to ancient history, sought to adjust all controversies of kings and peoples by application of the laws of the Romans, with occasional use of the canons. But in the case of these men also, the unfortunate condition of their times was frequently a handicap which prevented their complete understanding of those laws, though, for the rest, they were skilful enough in tracing out the nature of that which is fair and good. The result is that, while they are often very successful in establishing the basis of law, they are at the same time bad interpreters of existing law. But they are to be listened to with the utmost attention when they bear witness to the existence of the usage which constitutes the law of nations in our day.

The masters of the third class, who confine themselves within the limits of the Roman law and deal either not at all, or only slightly, with the common law of nations (*ius illud commune*) are of hardly any use in relation to our subject. They combine the subtlety of the Schoolmen with a knowledge of laws and of canons.

The French have tried rather to introduce history into their study of laws. Among them Bodin[61] and Hotman[62] have gained a great name, the former by an extensive treatise, the latter by separate questions; their statements and lines of reasoning will frequently supply us with material in searching out the truth.

In my work as a whole, I have, above all else, aimed at three things: to make the reasons for my conclusions as evident as possible; to set forth in a definite

[59] The distinction made – though only by implication – is between the volitional law of nations and the *ius gentium* proper. The volitional law of nations is a law between nations created by actual (even if only tacit) agreement amongst the nations. The *ius gentium* comprises those domestic laws of various states which resemble one another and which therefore have a wide field of application – but which are created by each state individually as a matter of its own free will. The rules of this *ius gentium* therefore resemble one another, in Grotius's words, 'through imitation of others or by pure accident', rather than by 'assent' (i.e., agreement with other states).

[60] Grotius is announcing his determination not to confuse or conflate the three different bodies of law to which he has just referred: the volitional law of nations, the *ius gentium* proper, and Roman law.

[61] Jean Bodin (c.1530–96) was a French lawyer and champion of royal prerogatives, in opposition to local and feudal vested interests. He is chiefly famous for his exposition on sovereignty in *The Six Books on the Commonwealth* (1576).

[62] François Hotman (1524–90) was a French lawyer who was chiefly known for his opposition to the use of Roman law and canon law in France, in favour of a native French legal tradition (including the use of the vernacular rather than Latin in legal actions). He was a Protestant and spent the later part of his life in Switzerland.

order the matters which needed to be treated; and to distinguish clearly between things which seemed to be the same and were not.

I have refrained from discussing topics which belong to another subject, such as those that teach what may be advantageous in practice.[63] For such topics have their own special field, that of politics, which Aristotle rightly treats by itself, without introducing extraneous matter into it.[64] ... In some places, nevertheless, I have made mention of that which is expedient, but only in passing, and in order to distinguish it more clearly from what is lawful.

If anyone thinks that I have had in view any controversies of our own times, either those that have arisen or those which can be foreseen as likely to arise, he will do me an injustice. With all truthfulness I aver that, just as mathematicians treat their figures as abstracted from bodies, so in treating law I have withdrawn my mind from every particular fact.

As regards manner of expression, I wished not to disgust the reader, whose interests I continually had in mind, by adding prolixity of words to the multiplicity of matters needing to be treated. I have therefore followed, so far as I could, a mode of speaking at the same time concise and suitable for exposition,[65] in order that those who deal with public affairs may have, as it were, in a single view both the kinds of controversies which are wont to arise and the principles by reference to which they may be decided. These points being known, it will be easy to adapt one's argument to the matter at issue, and expand it at one's pleasure.

I have now and then quoted the very words of ancient writers, where they seemed to carry weight or to have unusual charm of expression.

I beg and adjure all those into whose hands this work shall come, that they assume towards me the same liberty which I have assumed in passing upon the opinions and writings of others. They who shall find me in error will not be more quick to advise me than I to avail myself of their advice.

And now if anything has here been said by me inconsistent with piety, with good morals, with Holy Writ, with the concord of the Christian Church, or with any aspect of truth, let it be as if unsaid.

---

[63] This is a disclaimer of any intention of taking a utilitarian or consequentialist approach, i.e., explaining the content of a body of law in terms of the effects that it produces. Grotius's concern is to expound the content of law – whether natural law or the volitional law of nations – without regard to the material consequences that flow from obedience to that law.

[64] See generally Aristotle, *Politics*.   [65] This is a remarkably disingenuous claim.

Book I
On the Law of War and Peace

1

What is war? What is law?

1. Scope of the treatise

Controversies among those who are not held together by a common bond of municipal law are related either to times of war or to times of peace. Such controversies may arise among those who have not yet united to form a nation, and those who belong to different nations, both private persons and kings; also those who have the same body of rights that kings have, whether members of a ruling aristocracy, or free peoples.

War, however, is undertaken in order to secure peace; and there is no controversy which may not give rise to war. In undertaking to treat the law of war, therefore, it will be in order to treat such controversies, of any and every kind, as are likely to arise. War itself will finally conduct us to peace as its ultimate goal.

2. Definition of war, and origin of the word

As we set out to treat the law of war, then, we ought to see what is war, which we are treating, and what is the law which forms the subject of our investigation. Cicero defined war as a contending by force.[1] A usage has gained currency, however, which designates by the word not a contest but a condition; thus war is the condition of those contending by force, viewed simply as such.[2] This general definition includes all the classes of wars which it will hereafter be necessary to discuss. For I do not exclude private war, since in fact it is more

---

[1] Cicero, *On Duties*, I.34. Cicero (106–43 BC) was a prominent Roman who had several important careers: as a philosopher, as a renowned orator and legal advocate, and as a practising politician. He was put to death in the course of the civil strife accompanying the end of the Roman Republic.

[2] Later international lawyers would refer to this as a state of war. Sometimes this 'condition', as Grotius calls it, was called war in the legal sense, in contrast to war in the material sense, which referred to the physical clashing of opposing forces. War in the legal sense (or a state of war) is, more specifically, a legal condition in which it is regarded as lawful for the opposing sides to employ armed force against one another.

ancient than public war and has, incontestably, the same nature as public war; wherefore both should be designated by one and the same term.

If, to be sure, the term 'war' is at times limited to public war, that implies no objection to our view, since it is perfectly certain that the name of a genus is often applied in a particular way to a species, especially a species that is more prominent.

I do not include justice in my definition because this very question forms a part of our investigation, whether there can be a just war, and what kind of a war is just; and a subject which is under investigation ought to be distinguished from the object towards which the investigation is directed.

3. Law divided into rectorial law and equatorial law

In giving to our treatise the title 'The Law of War', we mean first of all, as already stated, to inquire whether any war can be just, and then, what is just in war. For law, in our use of the term, here means nothing else than what is just, and that, too, rather in a negative than in an affirmative sense, that being lawful which is not unjust. Now that is unjust which is in conflict with the nature of society of beings endowed with reason.

Moreover, just as there is one form of social relationship without inequality, as that between brothers, or citizens, or friends, or allies; another with inequality . . . as that between father and children, master and slave, king and subjects, God and men; so there is one type of that which is lawful applying to those who live on an equality, and another type applying to him who rules and him who is ruled, in their relative positions. The latter type, if I mistake not, we shall properly call rectorial law; the former, equatorial law.[3]

4. Division of rights into faculties and aptitudes

There is another meaning of law viewed as a body of rights, different from the one just defined but growing out of it, which has reference to the person.[4] In this sense, a right becomes a moral quality of a person, making it possible [for the person] to have or to do something lawfully. Such a right attaches to a person, even if sometimes it may follow a thing, as in the case of servitudes over lands, which are called real rights, in contrast with other rights purely personal;[5] not

---

[3] For an application of rectorial law, see p. 313 below.

[4] Equatorial law and rectorial law are, broadly, both concerned with obligations of individuals – in the one case with obligations owed to equals (such as the obligation of a debtor to a creditor), and in the other case with obligations owed by inferiors to superiors (such as subjects to sovereigns). Grotius explains that law can also be seen in terms of the rights of individuals, as he proceeds to explain.

[5] A real right is, basically, a right over property of some kind – the most obvious example being ownership of a plot of land. It confers the right to occupy and use the property in question, as well as the right to exclude other persons at large from the property. A personal right, in contrast, is not attached to a piece of identifiable

because such [real] rights do not also attach to a person, but because they do not attach to any other person than the one who is entitled to a certain thing.[6]

When the moral quality is perfect we call it *facultas*, 'faculty',[7] when it is not perfect, *aptitudo*, 'aptitude'.[8] To the former, in the range of natural things, 'act' (*actus*) corresponds; to the latter, 'potency' (*potentia*).[9]

5. Faculties divided into powers, property rights, and contractual rights

A legal right (*facultas*) is called by the jurists the right to one's own. [A]fter this, we shall call it a legal right properly or strictly so called. Under it are included

property. Nor is it exercisable against the world at large, but only against particular persons who are under some kind of obligation to the right-holder. An example is the right of a creditor to be repaid by his debtor.

A servitude, of the kind referred to, is a sub-species of real right. It is a right to exercise certain powers associated with ownership, but over property owned by another. An example is a right of way (or right of passage) over land belonging to someone else. Grotius has in mind here what was called, in Roman law, a praedial servitude, meaning a servitude which was designed to benefit a piece of property rather than a person as such – i.e., a servitude that belonged to a person only in his capacity as the owner of some property. In the example of the right of way, the land subject to the right of way was called the servient *praedia*. The land to which the right of way led was called the dominant *praedia*. The dominant *praedia* 'follows the thing', in the sense that it belongs automatically to whoever happens, at any given time, to own the land to which the right of way runs. The dominant *praedia* therefore belongs to its owner in his capacity as owner of that land, but not otherwise.

[6]   Even a right which 'follows a thing' (i.e., a praedial servitude) is actually personal in a certain sense, Grotius explains. It does belong to a person – though only so long as the person possesses the dominant *praedia* (the 'certain thing' referred to).

[7]   A faculty is, in essence, a right in the fullest sense of the term. That is, it is not merely a legal entitlement to do, or receive, or enjoy something, but also a power to compel others to respect that right. An obvious example is the right of a creditor to compel his debtor to pay him by taking him to court. By a 'perfect' quality is meant one which a court of law will enforce. It is therefore clear that a faculty is, virtually by definition, a perfect right.

[8]   An aptitude, in contrast to a faculty, is an imperfect right, i.e., one which cannot be enforced by way of a legal action in a court of law. It is therefore in the nature of a moral claim or expectation. An example is the expectation of a person who has diligently cared for an aged man of receiving a legacy in the man's will. As will be seen in due course, an imperfect right is not a mere nullity because it is potentially enforceable by various self-help means, though not by suits in a court. For Grotius's discussion of this subject, see p. 144 below. For the application of the concept of aptitude to the holding of public office, see p. 253 below.

[9]   By 'act' is apparently meant the bringing of something to fruition or completion, such as a creditor's bringing about the payment of his debt by suing his debtor. By 'potency' is apparently meant potential, or the possibility that something may be brought to fruition. For example, a person, by caring for a testator, creates a more or less realistic possibility of being given a legacy.

power, now over oneself, which is called freedom, now over others, as that of the father [over children] (*patria potestas*) and that of the master over slaves; ownership, either absolute, or less than absolute, as usufruct[10] and the right of pledge;[11] and contractual rights, to which on the opposite side contractual obligations correspond.

6. Division of legal rights into private and public

Legal rights, again, are of two kinds: private, which are concerned with the interest of individuals; and public, which are superior to private rights, since they are exercised by the community over its members and [over] the property of its members, for the sake of the common good. Thus the power of the king has under it both the power of the father and that of the master.[12] [T]hus, again, for the common good, the king has a right of property over the possessions of individuals greater than that of the individual owners;[13] thus each citizen is under a greater pecuniary obligation to the state, for the meeting of public needs, than to a private creditor.[14]

8. On expletive justice and attributive justice

Legal rights are the concern of expletive justice (*iustitia expletrix*), which is entitled to the name of justice properly or strictly so called. . . . [Aristotle] aptly termed it 'restorative' justice.[15] Aptitudes are the concern of attributive justice

---

[10] Usufruct is a concept from Roman law, referring basically to the right to the fruits of some property, without ownership of the property itself. An example would be a right to pick apples annually from an apple tree on a neighbour's land. The neighbour owns the tree itself; but the person with the right to the apples possesses a usufructuary right. Such a right is an example of a servitude.

[11] Pledge refers to the passing of possession of property, usually to a creditor, for retention pending the discharging of some obligation by the pledgor, such as repayment of a debt. Pledge gives the holder only a right of retention, not of sale.

[12] That is, the king possesses power over the persons of his subjects, comparable to the *patria potestas* of a father over children; and he also possesses *dominium* over the territory of his kingdom, comparable to ownership of land by a private party.

[13] In other words, a king is a sort of ultimate owner of all of the land in his kingdom – even of land which is in private ownership. Ordinarily, this royal right of ultimate ownership lies dormant. But in a condition of general emergency, the king can activate his right and take the property from the private owner in the interest of protecting the community at large, of which the king is the supreme protector. This is the right of eminent domain.

[14] In severely practical terms, the effect is that, when a person is on the edge of insolvency, and owes money both to a private party (as a debt) and to the state (as a tax), the state is the preferred creditor and is entitled to be paid first. The private creditor is left with whatever remains.

[15] See Aristotle, *The Nicomachean Ethics*, V.4. Aristotle also refers to it as 'commutative' justice. The essence of it is the obligation of a person to render to another person that which he owes to that person. The most obvious form of this kind of justice is

(*iustitia attributrix*). This Aristotle called 'distributive' justice.[16] It is associated with those virtues which have as their purpose to do good to others, as generosity, compassion, and foresight in matters of government.[17]

Aristotle says also that expletive justice is expressed by a simple proportion, which he calls 'arithmetical',[18] attributive justice, by a proportion involving comparison, which he calls 'geometrical',[19] this having the name of a proportion only among mathematicians.[20] Such proportions are often applicable, but not always so. [A]nd in fact expletive justice differs essentially from attributive justice not in a relation expressed by such a proportion but in the [subject] matter with which it is concerned, as we have already said.[21] Thus a partnership agreement is carried out according to a proportion based on comparison; and if only one person can be found who is fitted for a public position, the award will be made to him on the basis of a simple proportion only.[22]

the duty of a debtor to make due payment to his creditor, as agreed in the original loan agreement. More broadly, any duty to perform a contractual obligation to another party falls under this heading. Grotius points out that this kind of justice extends further than contractual obligations. For example, a person might find an object belonging to another, which that other has lost or misplaced. The finder has an obligation to return it to the owner. In such a case, there is no contract in existence. But it is still a case of commutative justice in action – or, in Grotius's term, expletive justice.

16 See Aristotle, *The Nicomachean Ethics*, V.3.

17 This is the branch of justice which governs the conferring of discretionary benefits onto persons – as opposed to the discharging of legal obligations, which is the realm of commutative (or expletive) justice. Distributive justice is therefore relevant, most obviously, to situations in which a superior grants rewards to inferiors. It dictates that such rewards should be made on the basis of merit or desert of some kind and not randomly or on the basis of some kind of personal favouritism. Distributive justice, in other words, is broadly the form of justice associated with good governance. Potential beneficiaries have a moral claim to have the rewards distributed in a fair and equitable fashion – but, as this is a moral claim rather than a strictly legal one (i.e., one which is not enforceable by action in court), it must be classed as an aptitude rather than as a faculty.

18 By 'arithmetical' is basically meant that the principle of equality is the dominant consideration. As Aristotle explains, commutative justice treats the parties themselves as being equal and focuses on the nature of the transaction between them. If one party has gained more than the other from the transaction, the function of commutative (or restorative) justice is to rectify that imbalance and to restore the parties to a position of parity.

19 By 'geometrical' is meant that there is to be some kind of apportionment of rewards or resources that will be made on a basis other than strict equality between the parties. The apportionment will, instead, be made on the basis of some kind of merit or desert.

20 Aristotle, *The Nicomachean Ethics*, V.3.

21 I.e., expletive justice deals with faculties (or true legal rights), and attributive justice with aptitudes (or moral claims and expectations).

22 The point is that partnership agreements are matters of contract between private parties, so that the shares of partners are a matter of expletive justice – even if the shares of partners are not precisely equal (i.e., 'arithmetical') but instead are

Not more true, again, is that which some say, that attributive justice is concerned with public property, while expletive justice is concerned with private property. On the contrary, if a man wishes to give a legacy from property belonging to him, he acts in conformity with attributive justice; and the state which pays back, from public funds, what a citizen has advanced for the public interest, is discharging the function of expletive justice.

9. Law as divided into the law of nature and volitional law

There is a third meaning of the word law: . . . as statute, whenever this word is taken in the broadest sense as a rule of moral actions imposing obligation to [do] what is right. We have need of [a legally binding] obligation; for counsels and instructions of every sort, which enjoin what is honourable indeed but do not impose an obligation, do not come under the term statute or law. Permission, again, is not, strictly speaking, an operation of law, but a negation of operation,[23] except in so far as it obligates another not to put any hindrance in the way of him to whom permission is given.[24] We said, moreover, 'imposing obligation to [do] what is right', not merely to [do] what is lawful, because law in our use of the term here stands related to the matter not only of justice, as we have set it forth, but also of other virtues. [Consequently] that which [is] in accordance with this law [used in this] broader sense is called just.

The best division of law thus conceived is found in Aristotle, that is, into natural law and volitional law, to which he applies the term statutory.[25]

10. Definition of the law of nature

The law of nature is a dictate of right reason, which points out that an act, according as it is or is not in conformity with rational nature, has in it a quality

unequal, being in proportion to the differing investments made by the various partners. Similarly, the distribution of public offices is a matter of merit and therefore is in the sphere of attributive justice. But there is no division by proportion – one person receives the office, to the complete exclusion of all others.

[23] By 'negation of operation' is meant the absence of rule of law prohibiting the action which is being permitted.

[24] A mere permission (or option) can be regarded as a rule of law in a certain limited sense. A permission does not either compel or prohibit the exercise of the permission by the holder. In that sense, it cannot be regarded as law. It does, however, prohibit third parties from interfering with the exercise of the permission. So to that extent, it can be considered as a law.

[25] Aristotle, *The Nicomachean Ethics*, V.10. Actually, Aristotle, in the passage cited, does not contrast natural law and positive (or 'volitional') law, but rather justice and equity. Justice is basically the application of law, which is promulgated in general terms – and which, as a consequence, risks being inappropriate in certain particular situations. Equity involves the correction of the law by taking due account of the special facts of a given case at hand.

of moral baseness or moral necessity; and that, in consequence, such an act is either forbidden or enjoined by the author of nature, God.[26]

The acts in regard to which such a dictate exists are, in themselves, either obligatory or not permissible, and so it is understood that necessarily they are enjoined or forbidden by God. In this characteristic, the law of nature differs not only from human law, but also from volitional divine law; for volitional divine law does not enjoin or forbid those things which in themselves and by their own nature are obligatory or not permissible, but by forbidding things it makes them unlawful, and by commanding things it makes them obligatory.[27]

For the understanding of the law of nature, again, we must note that certain things are said to be according to this law not in a proper sense but – as the Schoolmen love to say – by reduction, the law of nature not being in conflict with them; just as we said above that things are called just which are free from injustice. Sometimes, also, by misuse of the term, things which reason declares are honourable, or better than their opposites, are said to be [in accordance with] the law of nature, although not obligatory.[28]

It is necessary to understand, further, that the law of nature deals not only with things which are outside the domain of the human will, but with many things also which result from an act of the human will.[29] Thus ownership, such as now obtains, was introduced by the will of man; but, once introduced, the law of nature points out that it is wrong for me, against your will, to take away that which is subject to your ownership.[30]

The law of nature, again, is unchangeable – even in the sense that it cannot be changed by God. Measureless as is the power of God, nevertheless, it can be said that there are certain things over which that power does not extend; for things of which this is said are spoken only, having no sense corresponding with

[26] It is conceded, as it was in the Prologue (p. 4), that God is the ultimate author of natural law. But this is really only in the rather general sense that God is the author or creator of everything. Grotius is correctly regarded as being in the rationalist tradition of natural law (as is evident at p. 4 of the Prologue) because he does not hold natural law to consist of *arbitrary* commands by God. This is clear from the contrast that Grotius immediately goes on to make between natural law and what he calls the 'volitional divine law'.

[27] This succinct statement captures the essential distinction between the rationalist and the voluntarist approaches to natural law.

[28] In other words, some things are said, wrongly, to be 'according to' natural law simply because they are allowed by natural law, or because they are morally praiseworthy (without being obligatory). But natural law properly understood (according to Grotius) is comprised wholly of commands and prohibitions, i.e., of things which are either mandatory or forbidden.

[29] Since natural law is the law of reason, it is independent of human will, just as the truths of mathematics are independent of the human will. Grotius cautions that this view, though apparently reasonable, is mistaken.

[30] The point is that natural law can, so to speak, attach itself to matters of purely human creation, such as rights of property.

reality and being mutually contradictory.[31] Just as even God, then, cannot cause that two times two should not make four, so He cannot cause that that which is intrinsically evil be not evil.[32]

This is what Aristotle means when he says: 'Some things are thought of as bad the moment they are named.'[33] For just as the being of things, from the time that they begin to exist, and in the manner in which they exist, is not dependent on anything else, so also the properties, which of necessity characterise that being. [S]uch a property is the badness of certain acts, when judged by the standard of a nature endowed with sound reason. Thus God Himself suffers Himself to be judged according to this standard.[34]

Sometimes nevertheless it happens that, in the acts in regard to which the law of nature has ordained something, an appearance of change deceives the unwary, although in fact the law of nature, being unchangeable, undergoes no change; but the thing, in regard to which the law of nature has ordained, undergoes change. For example, if a creditor gives a receipt for that which I owe him, I am no longer bound to pay him, not because the law of nature has ceased to enjoin upon me that I must pay what I owe, but because that which I was owing has ceased to be owed.... So if God should command that anyone be slain, or that the property of anyone be carried off, homicide or theft – words connoting moral wrong – will not [thereby] become permissible; it will not be a case of homicide or theft, because the deed is done by authority of the Supreme Lord of life and property.[35]

---

[31] The power of God does not extend to violations of the laws of logic. If a proposition (something that is 'spoken only') is internally, or logically, self-contradictory, then God is powerless to render it otherwise.

[32] This paragraph is perhaps the strongest statement in the book of Grotius's adherence to the rationalist wing of natural-law thought.

[33] Aristotle, *The Nicomachean Ethics*, II.6. Aristotle was not, in fact, discussing the power of God over logical propositions in this passage. He was making a somewhat different point: that certain actions or passions are intrinsically bad (such as spite, envy, or murder), and that it can accordingly make no sense to speak of moderation in these things as being good.

[34] For Biblical support of this thesis, Grotius cites: *Genesis*, 18:25; *Isaiah* 5:3; *Ezekiel*, 18:25; *Jeremiah*, 2:9; *Micah*, 6:2; and *Romans*, 2:6 and 3:6.

[35] There are several possible interpretations of this interesting passage. One is that homicide that is commanded by God ceases to count as homicide on that ground alone. Alternatively, it might be an assertion that divine law overrides natural law in the event of a clash between them, so that the character of the act as homicide is not, strictly speaking, altered but merely becomes irrelevant. A third possible reading is that Grotius is asserting that God has a perspective on events far broader than humans have, so that God is able to discern justifications which are not apparent to mere humans. If, therefore, God commands what *appears* to be homicide from the human perspective, the truth is that some factor is present – known only to God – which takes the action out of the category of homicide. On the first of these interpretations, God actually alters the character of the act itself. On the second, He

Furthermore, some things belong to the law of nature not [throughout history] but as a result of a particular combination of circumstances. Thus the use of things in common was in accordance with the law of nature [prior to the introduction of] ownership by individuals [and not after that]; and the right to use force in obtaining one's own existed before [the civil] laws [of political societies] were promulgated [and not afterwards].

11. Whether instinct constitutes another kind of law

The distinction, which appears in the books of Roman law, between an unchangeable law common to animals and man, which the Roman legal writers call the law of nature in a more restricted sense, and a law peculiar to man, which they frequently call the law of nations (*ius gentium*),[36] is of hardly any value. For, strictly speaking, only a being that applies general principles is capable of law.[37]

If, however, a sense of justice is sometimes attributed to brute creatures, that is done without proper grounds, in consequence of observing in them a shadow or trace of reason. But whether an act, in regard to which the law of nature has pronounced, is common to us and other animals, as the rearing of offspring, or peculiar to us, as the worship of God, has no bearing whatever on the nature of the law.

12. How the content of the law of nature is proved

In two ways, men are wont to prove that something is according to the law of nature, from that which is antecedent and from that which is consequent. Of the two lines of proof, the former is more subtle, the latter more familiar. Proof *a priori* consists in demonstrating the necessary agreement or disagreement of anything with a rational and social nature; proof *a posteriori*, in concluding, if not with absolute assurance, at least with every probability, that that is according to the law of nature which is believed to be such among all nations, or among all those that are more advanced in civilisation. For an effect that

---

leaves the nature of the act as it was, but holds it to be inapplicable to the situation at hand. On the third, the act never had the character of homicide to begin with.

[36] The reference is to the distinction made in Roman law between natural law and the *ius gentium*. Natural law was presented as a law common to all living creatures, human and animal alike. See *Digest*, 1.1.3 (Ulpian). The *ius gentium* was stated to be that portion of natural law which applies to the human species in particular. See *Digest*, 1.1.4 (Ulpian). See also Justinian, *Institutes*, 1.2 and 1.2.2.

[37] A distinctive tenet of the rationalist tradition of natural-law thought was its rejection of the Roman-law view of the law of nature as applicable to all living creatures. Rationalist writers (such as Grotius) insisted instead that natural law has no application to animals, but applies only to rational beings (to 'a being that applies general principles'), i.e., to humans.

is universal demands a universal cause; and the cause of such an opinion can hardly be anything else than the feeling which is called the common sense of mankind.

13. Division of volitional law into human and divine

We have said that another kind of law is volitional law, which has its origin in the will. Volitional law is either human or divine.

14. Human law as divided into municipal law and the law of nations

We begin with human law, because that is familiar to the greater number. Human law, then, is either municipal law, or broader in scope than municipal law, or more restricted than municipal law. Municipal law is that which emanates from the civil power. The civil power is that which bears sway over the state. The state is a complete association of free men, joined together for the enjoyment of rights and for their common interest.

The law which is narrower in scope than municipal law, and does not come from the civil power, although subject to it, is of varied character. It comprises the commands of a father, of a master, and all other commands of a similar character.

The law which is broader in scope than municipal law is the law of nations; that is the law which has received its obligatory force from the will of all nations, or of many nations.[38] I added 'of many nations' for the reason that, outside of the sphere of the law of nature, which is also frequently called the law of nations,[39] there is hardly any law common to all nations. Not infrequently, in fact, in one part of the world there is a law of nations which is not such elsewhere, as we shall at the proper time set forth in connexion with captivity and postliminy.[40] The proof for the law of nations is similar to that for unwritten municipal law; it is found in unbroken custom and the testimony of those who are skilled in it.

15. Divine law as either universal or as peculiar to a single people

What volitional divine law is, we may well understand from the meaning of the words. It is, of course, that law which has its origin in the divine will; and by

---

[38] It is not clear whether the reference is to the *ius gentium* proper or to the volitional law of nations. There is no need, in the particular context, to distinguish them because the point being made is that man-made law exists which is 'broader in scope than municipal law'. Both the *ius gentium* proper and the volitional law of nations have that feature.

[39] Although the law of nature may be 'frequently called the law of nations', Grotius is firmly of the view that this is erroneous.

[40] For the discussion of captivity, see p. 368 below. For the discussion of postliminy, see p. 376 below.

this origin, it is distinguished from the law of nature, which also, as we have said, may be called divine. In the consideration of volitional divine law, . . . God does not will a thing because it is lawful, but that a thing [becomes] lawful – that is obligatory – because God willed it.

This law, moreover, was given either to the human race, or to a single people. To the human race, we find that the law was thrice given by God: immediately after the creation of man; a second time in the renewal of human kind after the Flood; lastly, in the more exalted renewal, through Christ.

These three bodies of divine law are beyond doubt binding upon all men, so far as they have become adequately known to men.

2

Whether it is ever lawful to wage war

1. Whether war is in conflict with the law of nature

Having seen what the sources of law are, let us come to the first and most
general question, which is this: whether any war is lawful, or whether it is ever
permissible to war. This question, as also the others which will follow, must first
be taken up from the point of view of the law of nature.

Marcus Tullius Cicero, . . . following Stoic writings, learnedly argues that there
are certain first principles of nature – 'first according to nature', as the Greeks
phrased it – and certain other principles which are later manifest but which
are to have the preference over those first principles. He calls first principles
of nature those in accordance with which every animal from the moment of
its birth has regard for itself and is impelled to preserve itself, to have zealous
consideration for its own condition and for those things which tend to preserve
it, and also shrinks from destruction and things which appear likely to cause
destruction. Hence also it happens, he says, that there is no one who, if the
choice were presented to him, would not prefer to have all the parts of his body
in proper order and whole rather than dwarfed or deformed; and that it is one's
first duty to keep oneself in the condition which nature gave to him, then to
hold to those things which are in conformity with nature and reject those things
that are contrary thereto.

But after these things have received due consideration [Cicero continues],
there follows a notion of the conformity of things with reason, which is superior to the body. Now this conformity, in which moral goodness becomes the
paramount object, ought to be accounted of higher import than the things to
which alone instinct first directed itself, because the first principles of nature
commend us to right reason, and right reason ought to be more dear to us than
those things through whose instrumentality we have been brought to it.[1]

Since this is true, and [even] without other demonstration would easily
receive the assent of all who are endowed with sound judgement, it follows that,

---

[1] The rationalist view of natural law held reason, and not instinct, to be the basis of
   natural law – even if instinct happens to reinforce or replicate reason, as it sometimes
   does.

in investigating the law of nature, it is necessary first to see what is consistent with those fundamental principles of nature, and then to come to that which, though of later origin, is nevertheless more worthy – that which ought not only to be grasped, if it appear, but to be sought out by every effort.

According to the diversity of the matter, that which we call moral goodness at times consists of a point, so to speak, so that if you depart from it even the least possible distance, you turn aside in the direction of wrong-doing. [A]t times it has a wider range, so that an act may be praiseworthy if performed; yet, if it be omitted altogether or performed in some other way, no blame would attach, the distinction being generally without an intermediate stage, like the transition from being to not-being.[2] Between things opposed in a different way, however, as white and black, a mean may be found either by effecting a combination of the two or by finding an intermediate between them.

It is with this latter class of actions that both divine and human laws are wont to concern themselves, in order that those acts which were in themselves merely praiseworthy might become also obligatory. But we said above, in discussing the law of nature, that the question is this, whether an act can be performed without injustice; and injustice is understood to be that which is utterly repugnant to a rational and social nature.[3]

In the first principles of nature, there is nothing which is opposed to war; rather, all points are in its favour.[4] The end and aim of war being the preservation of life and limb, and the keeping or acquiring of things useful to life, war is in perfect accord with those first principles of nature. If, in order to achieve these ends, it is necessary to use force, no inconsistency with the first principles of nature is involved, since nature has given to each animal strength sufficient for self-defence and self-assistance.

---

[2] In other words, the judgement about the act in question is strictly a binary one – performance being praiseworthy and omission being blameless – with no gradations or half-way judgements of any kind between the two categories.

[3] An important point is made about the natural law and its contrast with human and divine law. Human and divine law are distinctive in that both of them are products of conscious will (that of God in the one case, and of a human legislator in the other), so that these two types of law can 'come and go' by being enacted and repealed at will. Natural law, in contrast, is eternal and unchangeable, even by God himself. Moreover, human and divine law can go beyond natural law, at least in some cases. For example, a given act might be merely permissible under natural law (i.e., with no sanction applied in the event of non-performance). But the act could be made obligatory by either human or divine law, with a sanction imposed upon violators.

Another important difference is that human and divine law are capable of dealing with nuances and fine distinctions, in the sense that they can make judgements about matters which are not merely 'black and white', but in which there is continuous gradation from the one extreme to the other. Natural law, in contrast, deals with things that are mandatory at the one extreme, and prohibited at the other. Things in between are not, strictly speaking, the concern of natural law. See p. 29 above.

[4] It is apparent that Grotius is speaking only of *just* wars, to the exclusion of unjust ones.

Right reason, moreover, and the nature of society, which must be studied in the second place and are of even greater importance, do not prohibit all use of force, but only that use of force which is in conflict with society, that is, which attempts to take away the rights of another. For society has in view this object, that through community of resource and effort, each individual be safeguarded in the possession of what belongs to him.

It is easy to understand that this consideration would hold even if private ownership (as we now call it) had not been introduced; for life, limbs, and liberty would in that case be the possessions belonging to each; and no attack could be made upon these by another without injustice. Under such conditions, the first one taking possession would have the right to use things not claimed and to consume them up to the limit of his needs; and any one depriving him of that right would commit an unjust act.[5] But now that private ownership has by law or usage assumed a definite form, the matter is much easier to understand.

It is not . . . contrary to the nature of society to look out for oneself and advance one's own interests, provided the rights of others are not infringed. [C]onsequently the use of force which does not violate the rights of others is not unjust.

3. General agreement that war is not in conflict with the law of nature

Our thesis is proved also by the general agreement of all nations, and especially among the wise. Well known is the passage of Cicero in regard to force used in the defence of life, in which he bears witness to nature herself:

> There is this law which is not written, but born with us; which we have not learned, have not received, have not read, but which we have caught up, have sucked in, yes have wrung out from nature herself; a law – regarding which we have not been instructed, but in accord with which we have been made; to which we have not been trained, but with which we are imbued – the law that if our life has been placed in jeopardy by any snare, or violence, or weapons either of brigands or of enemies, every possible means of securing safety is morally right.[6]

The jurist Gaius says: 'Natural reason permits defence of oneself against danger';[7] the jurist Florentinus, 'In accordance with this law it comes about that whatever each may have done in defence of his person he is thought to have

---

[5] A legally protected right of possession and use is distinguished from true legal ownership. The former was present even in the first, or most primitive, stage of the state of nature. The latter came at a second stage of the state of nature.

[6] Cicero, *Pro Milone*, IV.10.

[7] *Digest*, 9.2.4 (Gaius). Gaius was a Roman jurist of the second century AD. His *Institutes* (a general handbook on law) is the lone text of the classical period of Roman law which survives in anything approaching its entirety. In addition to this text, Gaius features prominently in Justinian's *Digest*.

done lawfully'.[8] So obvious is the fairness of this principle that, even among brutes which, as we have said, have not the substance of legal rights but only a shadowy appearance of them, we may distinguish between the use of force which attempts an injury and that which wards it off.

4. Whether war is in conflict with the law of nations

It is sufficiently well established, therefore, that not all wars are at variance with the law of nature; and this may also be said to be true of the law of nations.

That wars, moreover, are not condemned by the volitional law of nations, histories, and the laws and customs of all peoples fully teach us. Rather, Hermogenianus said that wars were introduced by the law of nations;[9] but I think that this statement ought to be understood as having a meaning slightly different from that ordinarily given to it, namely, that a definite formality in the conduct of war was introduced by the law of nations, and that particular effects follow wars waged in accordance with such formality under the law of nations. Hence arises the distinction, which we shall have to make use of later, between a war which, according to the law of nations, is formally declared and is called legal, that is a complete war; and a war not formally declared, which nevertheless does not on that account cease to be a legal war, that is according to [natural] law. For as regards other wars, provided the cause be just, the law of nations does not indeed lend them support, but it does not oppose them, as will be explained more fully later.[10]

5. Whether war is in conflict with the divine volitional law before the time of the Gospel

A greater difficulty presents itself in connexion with the divine volitional law. Let no one at this point raise the objection that the law of nature is unchangeable, and that, in consequence, nothing can be established by God which is contrary to it. For this holds true in respect to those things which the law of nature forbids or enjoins, but not in respect to the things which by the law of nature are permissible only. Things of the latter class, since they do not properly belong

---

[8] *Digest*, 1.1.3 (Florentinus). Florentinus was a Roman jurist who appears to have been active in the second century AD.
[9] *Digest*, 1.1.5 (Hermogenianus). Hermogenianus was a Roman legal writer about whom hardly anything is known. He was probably active in the third century AD.
[10] As will be discussed later (at p. 344 below), the law of nations determines the lawfulness of a war on the basis of certain formalities, chiefly the issuing of a declaration of war. Natural law, in contrast, determines the lawfulness of a war on the basis of substantive criteria, set out at p. 81 below. The rights of belligerents are somewhat different in these two bodies of law. See p. 338 below for a fuller exploration of this point.

to the sphere of the law of nature but are outside that sphere, can be [either] forbidden [or] enjoined [by divine law].

[The biblical] prohibition in regard to the shedding of blood has no wider application than the commandment, 'Thou shalt not kill'; but this commandment, it is clear, has not proved to be an obstacle either to capital punishment or to wars. The latter rule of law then, as well as the former, had in view not so much the ordaining of something new as the declaration and repetition of a rule of the law of nature which had been effaced by degenerate usage. Hence these words are to be taken in a sense which conveys the idea of a moral fault, just as by the word 'homicide' we understand not the slaying of a man in general, but a premeditated murder of an innocent man. What follows in regard to the shedding of blood in turn seems to me to contain not a statement of a bare fact, but a provision of law.

I explain the matter thus. According to nature, it is not unfair that each suffer to the full extent of the evil he has committed, in accordance with the principle which is called the law of Radamanthus.[11]

In those first times, however, either on account of the scarcity of men or because criminals were few in number and so there was less need of an example, that which seemed to be permitted by nature God repressed by a command. He desired that contact and intercourse with a murderer be avoided, but that life be not taken from him.

But since already before the Flood, in the period of the giants, a general orgy of murders had prevailed, in the renewal of the human race after the Flood God judged that severer measures must be taken . . . and having done away with the mildness of the former age, He Himself permitted that the man who had killed a murderer should be innocent – a measure which nature declared was not unfair. Afterward, when courts were established, for very weighty reasons this permission was restricted to judges alone. Nevertheless, a trace of the older customs remained in the right of the next of kin of a murdered man; this right was recognised even after the law of Moses.

In favour of our interpretation, we have the great authority of Abraham, who . . . took up arms against the four kings, obviously in the belief that his action was not in conflict with that law.[12] In like manner also, Moses ordered that the Amalekites, who were attacking the people, be resisted by force of arms. [H]e made use, as we see, of the law of nature, for it does not appear that God

---

[11] Radamanthus, the mythological son of Zeus and Europa, ruled Elysium, the after-life paradise of Greek mythology. He was the Greek exemplar of justice, deciding (along with his brothers Minos and Aeacus) the fate of persons after death. According to Virgil, he presided over Tartarus, punishing the wicked for their sins. In all events, the implication here is that Radamanthus's decisions were based strictly on the moral merit of the persons concerned, without any element of sentiment or mercy.

[12] See *Genesis*, 14:8–16. The four kings had abducted Abraham's nephew Lot, along with his property.

had been specifically consulted in regard to this act.[13] Furthermore, it is clear that capital punishment was already applied not only to murderers but also to other criminals, and not merely among foreign peoples but among the favoured recipients of the holy teaching.[14]

Beyond doubt, interpretation of the divine will, with the help of natural reason, had proceeded from like to like, so that it seemed not unfair to apply to others who were guilty of exceptional crimes the penalty which had been appointed for the murderer. For there are certain things which are rated of equal value with life, as reputation, maidenly chastity, and conjugal fidelity; and things without which life cannot be safe, such as respect for the governing power which maintains the social order. Those who attack these things seem no better than murderers.

9. The position of the early Christians on the lawfulness of war

[T]hose who oppose wars are wont to bring forward several sayings of the early Christians in regard to which I have three things to say. In the first place, any inference based upon these sayings represents nothing more than the private opinion of certain individuals, not the opinion of the churches publicly expressed. Further, the authors of the sayings referred to are for the most part men who like to follow a road different from that of others and to set forth a teaching on some point in rather a lofty strain. Such are Origen[15] and Tertullian;[16] and these writers are, in fact, not self-consistent. For Origen says that bees were given by God as an example to show 'how wars, if ever there should arise a necessity for them, should be waged in a just and orderly manner among men';[17] and the same Tertullian, who elsewhere seems to be less in favour of capital punishment, said: 'No one denies that it is a good thing when the guilty are punished.'[18]

In regard to military service Tertullian hesitates. For in his book *On Idolatry*, he says: 'The question is raised whether the faithful can turn to military service,

[13] See *Exodus*, 17:8–10; and *Deuteronomy*, 25:17–18. The Amalekites had apparently instigated hostilities by attacking the Israelites.

[14] Grotius cites the story of Tamar, who was ordered to be put to death by her father-in-law for engaging in prostitution. See *Genesis*, 38:24.

[15] Origen was a highly eminent Christian philosopher and theologian who wrote in the third century AD. He appears to have been from Egypt, but he lived in Caesarea in Palestine during his active writing career. His output was gigantic, but very little of it survives.

[16] Tertullian (Quintus Septimius Florens Tertullianus) was one of the most prominent of the Church fathers. He was from Carthage and lived in the late second and early third centuries AD. He is most famous today for being the first systematic expositor of the theological doctrine of the Trinity, although Grotius's interest is in his views on war.

[17] Origen, *Against Celsus*, IV.52.   [18] Tertullian, *De Spectaculis*, 19.

and whether the military can be admitted to the faith';[19] and in this connexion, he seems inclined to a view adverse to military service. But in the book *On the Soldier's Chaplet,* having presented some considerations adverse to military service, he immediately distinguishes those who were enrolled in military service before baptism from those who enlisted after they were baptised.... He recognised the fact ... that the latter class remained in military service after baptism;[20] but this they would by no means have done if they had understood that military service had been forbidden by Christ – no more than the soothsayers, the magicians, and other practisers of forbidden arts were permitted to remain in the practice of their art after baptism.[21]

My second observation is that Christians have often disapproved or avoided military service on account of the condition of the times, which hardly permitted them to engage in such service without committing certain acts in conflict with Christian law.... Tertullian [in this vein] urges against the military service of his day. In the book *On Idolatry,* he says: 'Incompatible are the oath of allegiance to God and that to man, the standard of Christ and the standard of the Devil.'[22] [T]he reason is that soldiers were bidden to take oath in the name of the gods of the nations, as Jupiter, Mars, and other divinities.

[W]e [also] note that the Christians of the earliest time were fired by so great zeal to attain to the most excellent things that they often interpreted divine counsels as commands.... [I]n respect to the taking of an oath [for example], ... most of the early Christians disapprove without making any exception.... In like manner Lactantius declares that the just man, such as he wishes the Christian to be, will not engage in war; but at the same time and in the same way he declares that the just man will not travel on the sea.[23] How many of the early writers try to dissuade Christians from second marriages? All the things recommended are praiseworthy, excellent and in a high degree pleasing to God. [B]ut they are not exacted of us by the required observance of any law.

In order to establish our case, first, on our side there is no lack of writers, and very early writers, too, who hold the opinion that both capital punishment and war, the legitimacy of which depends on the justification of capital punishment, may be lawfully resorted to by Christians.

[19] Tertullian, *On Idolatry,* 19.
[20] Tertullian, *The Soldier's Chaplet,* 11. Grotius's presentation of Tertullian's position is not quite accurate. Tertullian did hold that serving soldiers could *become* Christians after their entry into service. But he went on to emphasise that continuation in military service after baptism would be well-nigh impossible for a good Christian.
[21] Tertullian, *On Idolatry,* 9.   [22] *Ibid.,* 19.
[23] Lactantius, *Divine Institutes,* VI.20.16. Lactantius (Lucius Caecilius Firmianus Lactantius), from North Africa, was an early Christian writer of the third and fourth centuries. He was an adviser to Constantine I, the first Roman emperor to favour Christianity, and also a teacher of rhetoric.

But let us leave the expressions of opinion by individuals and come to the authoritative public practice of the [C]hurch, which ought to be of very great weight. I say, then, that men engaged in military service have never been refused baptism, or excommunicated from the Church. [N]evertheless such action ought to have been taken, and would have been taken, if military service had been irreconcilable with the provisions of the New Covenant. . . . Furthermore, there were some soldiers who, having suffered tortures and death for Christ, received from the Church the same honour as the other martyrs. . . . From all this it is clear what opinion the body of Christians held in regard to military service, even before there were Christian emperors.

It ought not to seem strange if, in those times, Christians did not willingly take part in criminal proceedings, since very frequently judgement was to be passed upon Christians themselves. There is the further consideration that, in respect to other matters also, the Roman laws were harsher than accorded with Christian lenience.

And at that time among so many bishops, of whom a number had passed through the most cruel sufferings for their religion, we do not read that there was a single one who, by arousing fear of the wrath of God, sought to deter either Constantine from inflicting the death penalty and engaging in war, or Christians from military service; this, too, in face of the fact that a great many of the bishops were very alert guardians of discipline, and not at all disposed to hold back any suggestion regarding the duty either of the emperors or of other persons. Such a bishop, in the time of Theodosius,[24] was Ambrose,[25] who in . . . his work *On Duties* says, 'Bravery, which by means of war defends one's native land from barbarians, or at home protects the weak, or safeguards one's associates from brigands, is complete justice'.[26] This argument seems to me to be of so great force that I do not need to add anything to it.

Nevertheless I am not unmindful of the fact that frequently bishops and Christian people, by interposing their supplications, have averted punishments, and death penalties especially; also that the custom had been introduced that they who had taken refuge in a church, should not be given up except under a pledge that their lives would be spared, and that about Easter time those who were being kept in prison on account of their crimes should be set free. But he who will take the pains to weigh all the facts cited, and others like them,

[24] Roman Emperor Theodosius I reigned from AD 379 to 395, the last person to rule over both the Eastern and Western parts of the Empire. He is best remembered for his policy of suppression of all forms of pagan worship in the Empire.
[25] St Ambrose (c. AD 337–97) was one of the most prominent early fathers of the Catholic Church. From a prominent Roman family, he served as Bishop of Milan. In a particularly dramatic incident, he barred Roman Emperor Theodosius I from entering church, for massacring some three thousand people in Thessalonika in 390 in the course of suppressing a rebellion (later readmitting him after the doing of penance).
[26] Ambrose of Milan, *On Duties*, 1.27.

will find that these are the manifestations of Christian goodness which seizes every opportunity to show mercy, not of a spirit that condemns all judicial proceedings involving the death penalty. Hence such kindnesses, and even intercessions, were restricted by various exceptions arising from both place and time.

It was [admittedly] forbidden to admit to the clerical profession those who, after baptism, had taken office as magistrates or had assumed military responsibilities.... Candidates for [holy] orders, as we know, were chosen not from among Christians of any and every sort, but only from among those who had presented an example of the most correct life.... [T]hose who were set aside for the sacred office were not to allow themselves to be distracted by any outside responsibility or daily task. For this reason, [it was] ordered [by canon law] that no bishop, priest or deacon should administer secular interests [and] that they should not become involved in public administration.

3

Distinction between public and private war; explanation of sovereignty (*summi imperii*)

1. Division of war into public and private

The first and most essential division of war is that into public war, private war, and mixed war. A public war is that which is waged by him who has lawful authority to wage it; a private war, that which is waged by one who has not the lawful authority;[1] and a mixed war is that which is on one side public, on the other side private. Let us deal first with private war, as the more ancient.

That private wars in some cases may be waged lawfully, so far as the law of nature is concerned, is, I think, sufficiently clear from what was said above, when we showed that the use of force to ward off injury is not in conflict with the law of nature.[2] But possibly some may think that, after public tribunals had been established, private wars were not permissible. For although public tribunals are the creation not of nature but of man, it is, nevertheless, much more consistent with moral standards, and more conducive to the peace of individuals, that a matter be judicially investigated by one who has no personal interest in it, than that individuals, too often having only their own interests in view, should seek by their own hands to obtain that which they consider right; wherefore equity and reason given to us by nature declare that so praiseworthy an institution should have the fullest support. Says Paul the Jurist, 'Individuals must not be permitted to do that which the magistrate can do in the name of the state, in order that there may be no occasion for raising a greater disturbance'.[3]

The laws term it a use of force 'when an individual tries to enforce his claim to what he thinks is due him without having recourse to a judge'.[4]

---

[1] Meaning a resort to forcible self-help by a private party on his own initiative.
[2] See p. 36 above.
[3] *Digest*, 50.17.176 (Paul). Paul the Jurist (Iulius Paulus), who lived in the third century AD, was one of the most prolific of Roman legal writers. Though no treatise of his survives, he is amply represented in the *Digest*.
[4] *Digest*, 4.2.13 (Callistratus).

2. Whether all private war is impermissible

It is surely beyond doubt that the licence which was prevalent before the establishment of courts has been greatly restricted. Nevertheless, there are circumstances under which such licence even now holds good, that is, undoubtedly,
where judicial procedure ceases to be available. For the law which forbids a
man to seek to recover his own otherwise than through judicial process is ordinarily understood as applicable only where judicial process has been possible.
Now judicial procedure [sometimes] ceases to be available either temporarily
or continuously. It ceases to be available temporarily when one cannot wait to
refer a matter to a judge without certain danger or loss. It ceases to be available
continuously either in law or in fact: in law, if one finds himself in places without
inhabitants, as on the sea, in a wilderness, or on vacant islands, or in any other
places where there is no state; in fact, if those who are subject to jurisdiction do
not heed the judge, or if the judge has openly refused to take cognisance.

It seems clear that this ordinance,[5] which makes so careful a distinction,
not only assures impunity but also explains the law of nature, and that it is
not founded upon a special divine mandate, but grounded in common equity.
Hence, we see, other nations also followed it. Well known is the provision of
the Twelve Tables,[6] undoubtedly taken from the ancient Attic law: 'If a theft has
been committed at night, and anyone has killed the thief, be it that the thief
was rightly slain.' Thus by the laws of all peoples known to us, the person who
in peril of his life has by means of arms defended himself against an assailant is
adjudged innocent. An agreement so manifest furnishes in itself the proof that
in it there is nothing in conflict with the law of nature.

3. On the permissibility of private war according to the law of the Gospel

Among the early Christians, there was no lack of those who did not indeed
disapprove of public war, but who thought that, in the case of an individual,
self-defence was forbidden. . . . [Augustine,[7] for example,] declares: 'The idea of
killing men in order not to be killed by them is not acceptable to me, unless,
perchance, in the case of a soldier or of a public functionary acting not for
himself but on behalf of others, in the exercise of a lawful authority.'[8]

---

[5] I.e., this rule of natural law which permits forcible self-help only when there is no
possibility of a judicial remedy.
[6] The Twelve Tables are the oldest written Roman law, dating from the mid fifth
century BC. Only fragments survive.
[7] Augustine was the famous philosopher and theologian of the late fourth and early
fifth centuries AD. He served as Bishop of Hippo in North Africa. The core of the
Catholic Church's position on war was developed by him.
[8] Augustine, Letter 47 (To Publicola), 5.

The contrary opinion, that no such degree of forbearance is required, is certainly more common, and also seems to me more true. For in the Gospel we are bidden to love our neighbour as ourselves, not above ourselves; further, if a like evil threatens, we are not forbidden to look out for ourselves in preference to others.

Perhaps someone may press the point and say: 'Even if I may be able to give the preference to my own advantage over the advantage of my neighbour, this would not hold in the case of unequal advantages; wherefore I ought rather to give up my life than to suffer that my assailant fall into eternal damnation.'[9] But the answer may be made that, in many cases, even the man who is attacked has need of time for repentance, or probably thinks he has; and the assailant also may have time for repentance before death. Further, from the point of view of morals, it is not clear that that ought to be accounted a danger into which a man has thrown himself, and from which he can extricate himself.

The opinions which are cited from the Christian writers seem in part to embody counsel and exhortation to a lofty purpose rather than a rigid rule; in part they are the personal views of the writers themselves, and do not reflect opinions shared by the whole Church. In fact in the most ancient canons, which are called Apostolic, only he is cut off from the communion who in a quarrel has killed his opponent with the first blow 'on account of the excess of passion'.

4. Division of public war into formal and less formal

Public war is either formal, according to the law of nations, or less formal.[10] The word 'formal' I use here as equivalent to 'legal' (*iustum*) in the sense in which we speak of a legal will (*iustum testamentum*) as distinguished from codicils, and a legal marriage as distinguished from the union of slaves (*contubernium*).[11] This

---

[9] The suggestion is that all persons, including the assailant, should have a fair opportunity to repent of their sins prior to death, and that it would accordingly be wrong to deny him that opportunity by summarily killing him, even in self-defence.

[10] It should be appreciated that the concern is with the justice of resorting to war according to the law of *nations*, rather than the law of *nature*. According to the law of nature, a war is just if it falls into any of the three *substantive* categories stated on p. 81. According to the law of nations, a war is regarded, by the general agreement of states, as just if two sets of *formal* conditions are satisfied (as Grotius explains in this section). It was remiss of Grotius not to make this important distinction more prominently than he does here.

[11] A codicil, in Roman law, was an informal will – a set of instructions as to the disposition of a person's property after his death. It was informal in that it did not require the various formalities which attended the making of a will (such as the presence of seven witnesses). In early Roman law, codicils were regarded as mere requests and were not legally binding; but later law (from Augustus onward) made them legally binding. Similarly, unions between slave couples were not regarded as lawful marriages in Roman law; but they did have some legal effects (such as acting as a bar to a later marriage by one of the parties after emancipation).

does not mean that it is not permissible for any one to make codicils who may desire to do so, or for a slave to have a woman living with him (*in contubernio*); but it does mean that, from the point of view of the civil law, the formal will and the formal marriage have certain peculiar effects.[12] It is useful to note this distinction; for many, having a wrong understanding of the word 'legal' (*iustum*) in such a connexion, think that all wars, to which the adjective 'legal' (*iusta*) is inapplicable, are under condemnation as inconsistent with justice or not permissible.[13]

In order that a war may be formal, according to the law of nations, two conditions are requisite: first, that on both sides it be waged under the authority of the one who holds the sovereign power in the state; then, that certain formalities be observed, which we shall discuss later in the proper connexion.[14] Since both conditions are conjointly requisite, one without the other does not suffice.

A less formal public war may lack the formalities referred to, may be waged against private persons, and on the authority of any public official. And surely if the matter be viewed without reference to the laws of particular states,[15] it would seem that every public official has the right to wage war for the protection of the people entrusted to his charge, and also in order to maintain his jurisdiction if assailed by force. But because the whole state is endangered by war, provision has been made by the laws of almost every state that war may be waged only under the authority of him who holds the sovereign power in the state.

But as all statements, no matter how general, are to be interpreted in the light of justice, so also is this law. For in the first place, it cannot be doubted that it is permissible for a public official, who has proper authority over a district, through his subordinates to restrain by force a few that are disobedient,

---

[12] In Roman civil law, formal wills and formal marriages had a greater range of legal effects than their informal counterparts, codicils and slave unions, did. For example, the appointment of an heir (meaning a successor to the whole of the decedent's rights and liabilities) could be made only by will and not by codicil.

[13] The need for a correct understanding of the word 'legal' is emphasised. In the present context, 'legal' refers to the satisfying of *formal* requirements (such as the procedure for making a will or concluding a marriage). Grotius cautions that it should not be concluded that, if the formalities are not present, no legal effects follow. The true position is that *some* legal effects do follow, even if these are fewer in number or importance than the ones that would have followed if the formalities had been observed. Much the same is true in the case of war, as will be explained in more detail later (see p. 344 below). A war that is formally declared is 'legal' from the standpoint of the law of *nations*. But a war that is not formally declared may nonetheless be lawful from the standpoint of the law of *nature*. The difference is that, in a war that is lawful according to the law of nations, the belligerents have a greater latitude in the capture of enemy property than they do under the law of nature.

[14] These 'certain formalities' refer to the public declaration of the war and the observance of the laws of war.

[15] I.e., from the standpoint of natural law.

whenever there is no need of larger forces for the purpose, and danger does not threaten the state.

Again, if the danger is so pressing that time does not permit consultation with him who has the supreme authority in the state, in that case also necessity will make an exception. Of such a justification Lucius Pinarius, who was in command of the garrison at Enna, in Sicily, availed himself. Having learned with certainty that the people of the town were planning to revolt to the Carthaginians, he had them massacred, and so held possession of Enna.[16] When no such necessity was present, Franciscus de Vitoria presumed to ascribe to citizens of towns the right to carry on war in order to redress wrongs which the king had neglected to prosecute;[17] but his view is deservedly rejected by others.

5. On public war waged by the authority of a subordinate public official

The jurists . . . are by no means agreed regarding the circumstances under which minor public officials may have the right to inaugurate a movement of arms, or whether such a war should be called a public war. The affirmative view is held by some, the negative by others.

Truly, if we use the word public as including whatever is done by the authority of an official, there is no doubt that such wars are public, and consequently those who under conditions of this sort oppose public officials expose themselves to the punishment awaiting men that stubbornly resist their superiors. But if the word public is understood in a higher sense as characterising that which is done with due formality, as beyond question this word often is, such wars are not public, for the reason that both the decision of the sovereign power and other conditions are necessary for the fulfilment of the legal requirements involved. And I am not affected by the consideration that, even in disturbances of the kind under consideration, men who resist authority are ordinarily deprived of their property,[18] which may even be turned over to the soldiers. For such occurrences are not so peculiar to formal war that they may not also take place under other conditions.

This situation, moreover, may arise, whereby in an empire having a wide extent of territory, subordinate authorities may have a delegated power of beginning war. If such a situation does arise, we are to consider that the war is actually being waged by virtue of the sovereign authority; for he who vests another with the right to do anything is himself regarded as doer of it.

---

[16] This incident occurred in 214 BC, during the Second Punic War.

[17] Vitoria, *On the Law of War*, 9.

[18] The reference is to an important feature of just wars: that persons unjustly waging war may have their property taken from them in the course of the conflict, with full legal title passing to the captors. For further discussion of this point, see p. 359 below.

A more controverted question is whether, in case such an authorisation has not been given, the presumption that such an authorisation is intended will be sufficient. The affirmative view ought not, I think, to be conceded. For it is not enough to consider what under such conditions would be acceptable to him who holds the sovereign power if he could be consulted; the real point to be considered is, what he would wish to have done without consulting him in a matter admitting delay, or of doubtful expediency, if a general law covering the case were to be passed. For although, in a particular instance, a consideration influencing the decision of the head of the state may seem, if examined from a particular point of view, to be inapplicable; yet, generally speaking, the consideration arising from the desire to avoid danger does not cease to apply. The general consideration cannot have its proper weight if every public official takes the decision of such questions into his own hands.

Cato[19] wished to have Julius Caesar delivered up to the Germans because he had made war on them; but I believe that he had in mind not so much the question of right as a desire to free the city from the fear of a prospective master.[20] The Germans, in fact, had helped the Gauls, who were enemies of the Roman people, and consequently they had no reason to complain that a wrong had been done to them, provided the Roman people had a just cause for making war on the Gauls. But Caesar ought to have been satisfied with driving the Germans out of Gaul, the province which had been assigned to him; he ought not to have carried war against them into their own territory without first consulting the Roman people, especially since there was no imminent danger from that source. The Germans therefore did not have the right to demand that Caesar be surrendered to them, but the Roman people had the right to punish him. [21]

Marcus Tullius Cicero defended the action of Octavius and of Decimus Brutus in taking up arms against Antony on their own initiative.[22] And yet, even if it

---

[19] The Younger Cato (Marcus Porcius Cato of Utica, 95–46 BC) was from a prominent Roman family and was active in Roman politics in the late Republican period. He was a staunch enemy of Julius Caesar, to the point of committing suicide rather than accepting a pardon from him.

[20] I.e., Cato's concern was not primarily with Caesar's waging of an unjust war against the Germans, but rather with the fear that Caesar was becoming dangerously powerful in Rome itself.

[21] That is, Caesar could possibly be justly punished by the Roman people for waging war against the Germans in excess of authority granted to him, in Roman law. But that would be an offence only against Rome itself, not against the Germans. Another way of putting it would be to say that, even if Caesar's war against the Germans violated Roman domestic law, it did not violate international law regarding the resort to war.

[22] This was in the civil wars in Rome in the first century BC in the wake of the assassination of Julius Caesar. Octavius was the future Emperor Augustus. Decimus Brutus was one of the chief instigators of the assassination of Julius Caesar (but was not the famous Marcus Iunius Brutus who was also part of that conspiracy). Octavius and Decimus Brutus were opposed to one another, but they shared a

were settled that Antony deserved to be treated as an enemy, they ought to have waited for the decision of the senate and the Roman people as to whether it was in the public interest to overlook the action of Antony or to avenge it; to come to terms of peace, or rush to arms. No one, in fact, is compelled to avail himself of a right of which the use frequently involves the risk of loss. Again, even if Antony were adjudged a public enemy, it was for the senate and the Roman people to decide to whom they would prefer that the conduct of the war should be entrusted. Thus, when Cassius requested auxiliary troops of the Rhodians in accordance with the treaty, they answered that they would send the forces if the Roman senate should so direct.

This illustration – and there are many others – may serve to remind us that we are not to receive with approval everything which authors, no matter how famous, may tell us; they are under the influence often of their times, often of their feelings, and they fit 'their measuring-rule to the stone'. Wherefore in these matters, we must make every effort to use a discriminating judgement and not allow ourselves rashly to seize upon something as a precedent which can be exculpated rather than praised. In the use of such a method vicious errors are commonly committed.

Since, then, it has been said that a public war ought not to be waged except by the authority of him who holds the sovereign power, for the understanding both of this subject and of questions relating to formal war, and consequently for the understanding of many other questions, it will be necessary to understand what sovereignty is, and who hold it. This inquiry is all the more necessary because learned men of our own age, treating the matter from the point of view of usage under present conditions rather than from that of the truth, have added greatly to the complexity of the subject, which in itself was far from simple.

6. In what the civil power consists

The moral faculty of governing a state, which is ordinarily designated by the term civil power, is described by Thucydides[23] as having three characteristics. He speaks of a state, which truly is a state, as 'having its own laws, courts, and public officials'.[24]

---

mutual opposition to Mark Antony. Decimus Brutus was killed in 42 BC, while travelling to Macedonia to join the forces of Marcus Brutus and Gaius Cassius.

[23] Thucydides was a renowned Greek historian of the late fifth and early fourth centuries BC, justly famous for his account of the Peloponnesian War, in which he himself took part. His lack of success as a commander, on the Athenian side, led to his exile for some twenty years.

[24] Thucydides, *The Peloponnesian War*, V.18. Grotius's characterisation of Thucydides's account is not very accurate. Thucydides is quoting the text of the Peace of Nicias, concluded between Athens and Sparta in 421 BC. One of the provisions was that the citizens of Delphi 'shall be governed by their own laws, taxed by their own state, and judged by their own judges . . . according to the custom of the place'. This does not

Aristotle distinguishes three parts in the government of a state: deliberation in regard to matters of common interest; the choice of officials; and the administration of justice.[25] [T]he first... refers [to] deliberation in regard to war, peace, the making and abrogation of treaties, and legislation. To this he adds, further, deliberation in regard to the death penalty, exile, confiscation of property, and proceedings in cases of extortion, that is, as I interpret the passage, the administration of justice in criminal cases, since previously in treating the administration of justice he has dealt with cases involving the interests of individuals only.

Now if one wishes to make an exact division, he will find it possible to easily include everything relating to civil power in such a way that there will be nothing omitted and nothing superfluous. For he who governs a state governs it in part through his own agency, in part through others. He governs through his own agency by devoting his attention either to general interests or to particular interests. In devoting himself to general interests, he concerns himself with framing and abrogating laws respecting religious matters (so far as the care of religious matters belongs to the state) as well as secular.[26]

The particular interests, with which he who governs concerns himself, are either exclusively public interests, or private interests which have a relation to public interests. Exclusively public interests are either actions, as the making of peace, of war, and of treaties; or things, such as taxes, and other things of a like nature, wherein the right of eminent domain, which the state has over citizens and over the property of citizens for public use, is included.

Private interests [as here understood] are controversies between individuals the termination of which by public authority is important for the tranquillity of the state.

The affairs that are administered through others are administered either through public officials, or through other responsible agents, among whom ambassadors are included. In these things, then, the civil power consists.

7. On sovereignty (*summa potestas*)

That power is called sovereign whose actions are not subject to the legal control of another, so that they cannot be rendered void by the operation of another human will.[27] When I say 'of another', I exclude from consideration him who

purport to be a sweeping statement about the nature of civil power in general, as Grotius appears to suggest.
[25] Aristotle, *Politics*, IV.4. In the passage cited, Aristotle actually set out eight elements of a state. The designation of these three in particular as governmental is a characterisation made by Grotius, not by Aristotle. Also, Aristotle does not actually go into the detail concerning the deliberative element which Grotius sets out.
[26] Aristotle, *The Nicomachean Ethics*, VI.8.
[27] This is, in substance, the conception of sovereignty that had been advanced by Bodin in the previous century.

exercises the sovereign power, who has the right to change his determinations; I exclude also his successor, who enjoys the same right, and therefore has the same power, not a different power. Let us, then, see who is the subject of sovereignty.

The subject of a power is either common or special. Just as the body is a common, the eye a special subject of the power of sight, so the state, which we have defined above as a perfect association, is the common subject of sovereignty.

We exclude from consideration, therefore, the peoples who have passed under the sway of another people, such as the peoples of the Roman provinces. For such peoples are not in themselves a state, in the sense in which we are now using the term, but the inferior members of a great state, just as slaves are members of a household. Again, it happens that several peoples may have the same head, while nevertheless each of them in itself forms a perfect association. While in the case of the natural body, there cannot be one head belonging to several bodies, this does not hold also in the case of a moral body. In the case of a moral body the same person, viewed from different relations, may be the head of several distinct bodies. [28] A clear proof of this may be found in the fact that, on the extinction of the reigning house, the right of government reverts to each people separately.

It may also happen that several states are bound together by confederation, and form a kind of system, . . . while nevertheless the different members do not cease in each case to retain the status of a perfect state.[29]

It may be granted, then, that the common subject of sovereignty is the state, understood as we have already indicated.

8. Whether sovereignty always resides in the people

At this point first of all, the opinion of those must be rejected who hold that everywhere and without exception sovereignty resides in the people, so that it is permissible for the people to restrain and punish kings whenever they make a bad use of their power. How many evils this opinion has given rise to, and can even now give rise to if it sinks deep into men's minds, no wise person fails to see. We refute it by means of the following arguments.

To every man it is permitted to enslave himself to any one he pleases for private ownership, as is evident both from the Hebraic and from the Roman Law.[30] Why, then, would it not be permitted to a people having legal competence to submit itself to some one person, or to several persons, in such a way as plainly to transfer to him the legal right to govern, retaining no vestige of that right for

---

[28] An example would be England and Scotland in the period 1603–1707, when both kingdoms shared a common monarch, but remained entirely separate political entities (a 'union of crowns', as it is commonly termed).

[29] The clearest historical example is the German Confederation of 1815–66.

[30] Regarding the Hebraic law, see *Exodus*, 21:2–6. Regarding Roman law, see Justinian, *Institutes*, 1.3.4.

itself? And you should not say that such a presumption is not admissible; for we are not trying to ascertain what the presumption should be in case of doubt, but what can legally be done. It is idle, too, to bring up the inconveniences which result, or may result, from such a procedure; for no matter what form of government you may devise, you will never be free from difficulties and dangers.

Just as, in fact, there are many ways of living, one being better than another, and out of so many ways of living each is free to select that which he prefers, so also a people can select the form of government which it wishes; and the extent of its legal right in the matter is not to be measured by the superior excellence of this or that form of government, in regard to which different men hold different views, but by its free choice.[31]

In truth, it is possible to find not a few causes which may impel a people wholly to renounce the right to govern itself and to vest this in another, as, for example, if a people threatened with destruction cannot induce any one to defend it on any other condition; again, if a people pinched by want can in no other way obtain the supplies needed to sustain life.... It may happen, again, that the head of a house possessing great estates may be unwilling under any other conditions to allow permanent residents to come upon his lands; or that the owner of a great number of slaves may set them free upon condition that they submit to his authority and pay him taxes. For these supposed cases we do not lack concrete examples.

Further, as Aristotle said that some men are by nature slaves, that is, are suited to slavery,[32] so there are some peoples so constituted that they understand better how to be ruled than to rule.... Some, again, cannot fail to be impressed by the example of nations which for a number of centuries have lived happily enough under a form of government clearly monarchical.... For these and similar reasons, then, it not only can happen, but actually does happen, that men make themselves subject to the rule and power of another.

Just as private property can be acquired by means of a war that is lawful (*iustum*), according to our use of the term above, so by the same means public authority, or the right of governing, can be acquired, quite independently of any other source. What has been said, again, must not be understood as limited to the maintenance of the rule of a monarch, when that is the type of government concerned; for the same right and the same course of reasoning hold good in the case of an aristocracy which governs with the exclusion of the common

---

[31] Note that Grotius accepts the view that, in many cases, the will of the people is the ultimate source or origin of sovereign power. What he insists is that this does not imply a continuing right on the part of the people to reverse a prior decision to transfer its sovereignty to a ruler. He also points out below, in Section 13, that there are cases in which sovereign power does not originate in a grant from the people (such as the case of conquest).

[32] Aristotle, *Politics*, I.5.

people. What shall I say of this fact, that no republic has ever been found to be so democratic that in it there were not some persons, either very poor people or foreigners, also women and youths, who were excluded from public deliberations?

Some peoples, moreover, have under their sway other peoples as subject to them as if they obeyed kings.

That in fact there have been kings who did not derive their power, even in a general way, from the will of the people, sacred and secular history alike bear witness.

Aristotle says that there are some kings who are vested with the same powers that in other cases the nation itself has, over itself and its possessions.[33] Thus, after the Roman emperors began to make use of a power veritably royal, it was said that to these the people had transferred all their own authority and power, even over themselves.[34]

[C]learly kings who are subject to the people are not properly called kings. . . . Aristotle declares that such kingships do not constitute a distinct type of government, because in reality they only form a part in a commonwealth controlled by an aristocracy or by the people.[35]

Furthermore, even in the case of peoples who are not permanently subject to kings, we see examples of a kind of temporary kingship which is not subject to the people. . . . Cicero declares that the dictatorship [in Rome] was invested with royal powers.[36]

The arguments which are presented on the other side are not hard to meet. For, in the first place, the assertion, that he who vests some one with authority is superior to him upon whom the authority is conferred, holds true only of a relationship the effect of which is continually dependent on the will of the constituent authority; it does not hold true of a situation brought about by an act of will, from which a compulsory relationship results, as in the case of a

---

[33] *Ibid.*, III.14.

[34] Justinian, *Institutes*, 1.3.4, which states: 'What the Emperor determines has the force of a statute, the people having conferred onto him all their authority and power by the *lex Regia*, which was passed concerning his office and authority.' See also *Digest*, 1.4.1 (Ulpian).

[35] Aristotle, *Politics*, III.14–15. Aristotle did not regard the dual kingship institution of Sparta as a true monarchy, since the powers of the Spartan kings were so limited (basically, to the commanding of the land forces in wars abroad and the performance of religious rituals). Real political power was in the hands of the Council of Elders and the ephors. This type of arrangement was therefore not a type of *monarchical* government, but instead was simply an example of an aristocratic or democratic constitution.

[36] Cicero, *Philippics*, I.1.3. The statement that the Roman institution of dictatorship was equivalent to a conferring of royal powers is basically correct. The passage that is cited from Cicero, however, merely asserts that Mark Antony abolished the office of dictator.

woman giving authority over herself to a husband, whom she must ever after obey. [37]

It is, however, not true, as is assumed, that all kings are clothed with authority by the people. This can be clearly enough understood from the illustrations given above, of the head of a house receiving strangers only under the stipulation of rendering obedience to him, and that of nations conquered in war.

Another argument men take from the saying of the philosophers, that all government was established for the benefit of those who are governed, not of those who govern; from this they think it follows that, in view of the worthiness of the end they who are governed are superior to him who governs.[38] But it is not universally true, that all government was constituted for the benefit of the governed. For some types of governing in and of themselves have in view only the advantage of him who governs; such is the exercise of power by the master, the advantage of the slaves being only extrinsic and incidental, just as the earnings of a physician bear no relation to medicine as the art of healing. Other types of governing have in view a mutual advantage, as that of marriage. Thus some imperial governments may have been constituted for the benefit of kings, as those which have been secured through victory, and yet are not on that account to be called tyrannical, since . . . tyranny, at any rate as the word is now understood, connotes injustice.[39] Some, again, may have in view as much the advantage of him who governs as of those who are governed, as when a people powerless to help itself places itself in subjection to a powerful king for its own protection.

Nevertheless I do not deny that, in the case of most states, the benefit of those who are governed is the primary consideration; and that this is true which Cicero said after Herodotus,[40] and Herodotus after Hesiod,[41] that kings

---

[37] The point is that a transfer of full authority to a sovereign which, on its terms, is final and complete, cannot later be reversed. In order for a transfer of sovereign authority to be revocable, the conditions of revocation must be established at the time that the transfer is made.

[38] The distinction, in effect, is between government *for* the people and government *by* the people.

[39] In classical political thought, a tyrant was a person who attained power by unlawful means – without regard to how wisely or humanely he exercised that power. Grotius sets out the more modern view, that a tyrant is a person who misuses powers that he possesses, without regard to how that possession came about.

[40] Herodotus, sometimes called the 'father of history', was the first important historian in Western civilisation. *The Histories*, written in the fifth century BC, are highly informative, and even more highly entertaining.

[41] Little is known of Hesiod beyond the two important works attributed to him. *Theogony*, on the origins of the gods, is a highly important source of information on Greek mythology (for the Greeks themselves as well as for us). *Works and Days* is a far different kind of work, quite possibly by a different author, on ancient agricultural life and practice. He appears to have been active in the sixth century BC.

received authority in order that men might enjoy justice.[42] But it does not on that account follow, as our opponents infer, that the peoples are superior to the kings; for guardianship was instituted for the sake of the ward, and yet guardianship includes both a right and power over the ward. Furthermore, there is nothing in the objection, which some may urge, that a guardian, in case he administers his trust badly, can be removed, and that, therefore, the same right ought to hold in the case of a king. In the case of a guardian, who has a superior, such procedure is obviously valid; but in the case of a government, because the series does not extend to infinity, it is absolutely necessary to stop with some person, or assembly, whose sins, because it has no judge superior to it, God takes into special consideration, as He himself bears witness. He either metes out punishment for them, if He deems punishment necessary, or tolerates them, for the chastisement or the testing of a people.

What we have said is in no degree invalidated by the fact that we sometimes read of people being punished on account of the sins of their kings. This happens not because the people did not punish their king, or did not restrain him, but because it connived with him in his offences, at least through silence. And yet God, even without the people, could make use of the supreme power and authority, which He has over the life and death of individuals, for the chastisement of the king, for whom it is punishment to be deprived of his subjects.

9. Whether there is always a mutual dependence between king and people

Some imagine that between king and people there is a relation of mutual dependence, so that the whole people ought to obey the king who governs well, while the king who governs badly should be made subject to the people. If they who hold this opinion should say that anything which is manifestly wrong should not be done because the king commanded it, they would be saying what is true and is acknowledged among all good men; but such a refusal implies no curtailing of power or any right to exercise authority.[43] If it had been the purpose of any people to divide the sovereign power with a king (on this point

---

[42] Cicero, *On Duties*, II.41. Herodotus, *The Histories*, I.96–8 relates the story of how Deioces became the first king of the Medes in 701 BC: by winning a reputation as an arbitrator of disputes, through his scrupulous fairness and integrity. Hesiod, *Theogony*, 81–90 states that 'heaven-favoured' rulers are upright judges who put a stop to quarrels, and who advance the public interest generally.

[43] The contention is that the right of a ruler to command and the duty of the subjects to obey are not correlative. That is, there may be cases in which, simultaneously, the ruler has the right to command and the subjects a duty to refuse to obey. An example would be the case of a sovereign who ordered his subjects to commit violations of divine or natural law. The subjects would be required to disobey the particular

something will need to be said below), surely such limits ought to have been assigned to the power of each as could easily be discerned from a difference in places, persons, or affairs.

The moral goodness or badness of an action, especially in matters relating to the state, is not suited to a division into parts; such qualities frequently are obscure, and difficult to analyse. In consequence, the utmost confusion would prevail in case the king on the one side, and the people on the other, under the pretext that an act is good or bad, should be trying to take cognisance of the same matter, each by virtue of its power. To introduce so complete disorder into its affairs has not, so far as I know, occurred to any people.

10. The distinguishing of similar words which differ in meaning

Now that the false views have been eliminated, it remains to offer some cautions which may serve to point out to us the road leading to a right decision of the question to whom, in each nation, the sovereign power belongs. The first caution is, not to allow ourselves to be led astray by the equivocal meanings of words, or by the external appearance of things. For instance, in Latin writers the words *principatus*, 'chief authority', 'principate', and *regnum*, 'kingly power', 'monarchy', are ordinarily used in contrast.

On the other hand, when the Roman emperors had come to hold absolutely unrestricted powers of government, openly and without subterfuge, they were nevertheless called 'men holding the chief authority' (*principes*). In some free states, also, emblems of royal dignity are customarily granted to those in whose hands the chief authority rests.

Again, the assembly of the estates, that is, the meeting of those who represent the people as divided into classes [i.e., the clergy, the nobility, and the 'third estate' of prominent commoners] . . . in some states at any rate serves only this purpose, that they form a greater king's council. Through it, the complaints of the people, which are often passed over without mention in the king's cabinet, reach the ear of the king, who is then free to determine what seems to him best to meet the case. In other states, such bodies have the right to pass in review the acts of the ruler, and even to enact laws by which the ruler is bound.

Many think that the distinction between sovereign power, and power that is less than sovereign, ought to be made according to the mode of conferring such power, whether by election or by succession.[44] They maintain that that alone is sovereign power which is conferred by succession, that that is not sovereign

unjust commands – but they would not thereby be dispensed from their general duty of obedience. Nor would the sovereign thereby forfeit his status as sovereign.

[44] Election does not have its modern meaning of choice exercised by some kind of democratic means. The reference is simply to any kind of original conferral or transfer of the sovereign power by voluntary act, in contrast to the acquisition of sovereign power by succession from a prior holder or by some form of force.

power which is conferred by election. But surely this cannot be universally true. For succession is not a title of power, which gives character to the power, but a continuation of a power previously existing. The legal right to govern which was founded by selection in a family is continued by succession; in consequence, succession confers only so much power as was granted by the first act of choice.

11. Distinguishing rights from the manner of possessing rights

The second caution shall be this, that the distinction must be kept in mind between a thing and the mode of its possession. This distinction holds not only for corporeal but also for incorporeal things. Just as a field is a thing, so rights of way over it for pedestrians, for cattle, and for use as a road are also things. These three rights, however, are held by some with full ownership, by others as usufruct,[45] by others still with power of temporary use. Similarly, the Roman dictator held the sovereign power by a right limited in time; but most kings, both those who are the first to be chosen and those who succeed them in lawful succession, hold it as a usufruct. Some kings, however, possess the sovereign power in full right of ownership; having acquired it in lawful war, or through the submission of a people which, to avoid greater disaster, subjected itself without any reservation.

I am unable to agree with those who declare that the dictator was not the bearer of sovereignty because his power was not perpetual. For the character of immaterial things is recognised from their effects, and legal powers which have the same effects ought to be designated by the same name. Now the dictator during his period of office performed all acts by virtue of the same legal right which a king has who possesses absolute power; and his acts could not be rendered null and void by any one. Duration, moreover, does not change the nature of a thing.

If, as we may grant, question is raised as to the prestige which is commonly called majesty, there is no doubt that this is to be found in fuller measure in him to whom the perpetual right has been given than in him upon whom a temporary right has been conferred; the manner of holding does effect prestige. I maintain, further, that the same holds true of him who is made regent of a kingdom before a king has attained...his majority, or while the king is prevented from reigning by madness or captivity. Under such conditions, regents are not subject to the people, and their power is not revocable before a time fixed by law.

We must consider as altogether different the case of those who received a power revocable at any moment, that is resting on sufferance. Such the kingship of the Vandals in Africa once was, and that of the Goths in Spain, where the people deposed their kings whenever these failed to please them. Single acts of

---

[45] On usufruct, see p. 26 above.

such rulers can be annulled by those who conferred upon them their power subject to revocation.

12. On sovereign power held absolutely

What I have said, that in some cases sovereign power is held with full proprietary right, that is in patrimony, some learned men oppose, using the argument that free men cannot be treated as property. But just as the power of the master is one thing, that of the king another, so also personal liberty is different from civil liberty, the liberty of individuals from the liberty of men in the aggregate.[46]

[W]hen a people is transferred this is not, strictly speaking, a transfer of the individuals but of the perpetual right of governing them in their totality as a people. Similarly, when a freedman is allotted to one of the children of a patron, this is not a transfer of ownership of a free man but the transfer of a right which is valid over the man.

Equally devoid of foundation is the assertion that, if a king has acquired any peoples in war, since he has not acquired them without blood and sweat of his citizens, they ought in consequence to be considered as acquired for the citizens rather than for the king.[47] For it might happen that a king had supported an army from his private means, or even from the income of the estate which came to him as holding the position of chief authority. For a king may have over such an estate only the right of usufruct, in the same way that he holds the right of ruling over the people who chose him; nevertheless the income is absolutely his own. The case is like that in the civil law, when the restitution of an inheritance has been ordered; the income is not restored, because the income is considered not as forming a part of the inheritance but as a part, rather, of the property.[48]

It can happen, then, that a king may have the sovereign power in his own right over certain peoples; in such cases, then, he can transfer it.

13. On sovereign power not held absolutely

In the case of kingships which have been conferred by the will of the people the presumption is, I grant, that it was not the will of the people to permit the king to alienate the sovereign power.

---

[46] Personal liberty refers to status as a free person, as distinct from that of a slave – i.e., it means that a person is not legally subject to the will of another private party. A person who is free in this personal sense may, however, at the same time be a member of a community that is ruled by an absolute monarch – and consequently not be free in the political, or 'civil', sense.

[47] For further discussion of legal title to property (including persons) captured in war, see p. 359 below.

[48] That is, the income, as usufruct, is regarded in law as separate property from the capital fund (i.e., from the inheritance).

14. On the holding of intermediate governmental authority absolutely

Up to this point, we have tried to show that the sovereignty must in itself be distinguished from the absolute possession of it. So true is this distinction that, in the majority of cases, the sovereignty is not held absolutely. Furthermore, in many cases intermediate governmental powers are held absolutely. In consequence, marquisates and earldoms are wont to be sold and bequeathed by will more easily than kingdoms.

15. The difference in mode of appointing regents in kingdoms

Another proof of this distinction appears in the method of safeguarding royal power when the king is prevented by age or by disease from performing his functions. In the case of monarchies which are not patrimonial, the regency passes into the hands of those to whom it is entrusted by public law or, that failing, by the consent of the people. In the case of patrimonial monarchies, the regency goes to those whom the father or near relatives have chosen.

Whether the king be, at the same time, owner of the domain in his own right as proprietor . . . or not, such ownership lies outside the realm of sovereignty and in its essence has no relation to sovereignty. Wherefore it does not constitute a separate type of sovereignty, or a different mode of possessing sovereign power.

16. On limitation of sovereignty by a promise

[S]overeignty does not cease to be such even if he who is going to exercise it makes promises – even promises touching matters of government – to his subjects or to God. I am not now speaking of the observance of the law of nature and of divine law, or of the law of nations; observance of these is binding upon all kings, even though they have made no promise.[49] I am speaking of certain rules, to which kings would not be bound without a promise.

That what I say is true becomes clear from the similarity of the case under consideration to that of the head of a household. If the head of a household promises that he will do for it something which affects the government of it, he will not on that account cease to have full authority over his household, so far as matters of the household are concerned. A husband, furthermore, is not deprived of the power conferred on him by marriage because he has promised something to his wife.

---

[49] This is an important point – that even 'absolute' sovereigns are subject to divine law, natural law, and the law of nations. 'Absolute' therefore has a technical meaning: that such a sovereign is unrestrained by his *subjects*. This thesis had previously been expounded by Bodin.

Nevertheless it must be admitted that, when such a promise is made, the sovereign power is in a way limited, whether the obligation affects only the exercise of the power, or even the power itself directly. In the former case, an act performed contrary to the promise will be unjust, for the reason that, as we shall show elsewhere, a true promise confers a legal right upon the promisee;[50] in the latter case, the act will be void on account of lack of power.[51] From this, nevertheless, it does not follow that the promisor is subject to some superior; the nullification of the act in this case results not from the interposition of a superior power but from the law itself.[52]

What if there should be added the condition that, if the king should violate his pledge, he would lose his kingship? Even under such circumstances, the power of the king will not cease to be supreme, but the mode of possessing it will be restricted by the condition, and it will resemble the sovereign power limited in time.[53]

17. The division of sovereignty

[I]t is to be observed that, while sovereignty is a unity, in itself indivisible, consisting of the parts which we have enumerated above, and including the highest degree of authority, which 'is not accountable to any one'; nevertheless a division is sometimes made into parts designated as 'potential' (*partes potentiales*) and 'subjective' (*partes subjectivas*). Thus, while the sovereignty of Rome was a unity, yet it often happened that one emperor administered the East, another the West, or even three emperors governed the whole empire in three divisions.

So, again, it may happen that a people, when choosing a king, may reserve to itself certain powers but may confer the others on the king absolutely. This does not take place, however, as we have already shown, when the king obligates himself by certain promises; it must be understood as taking place only in cases where either the division of power, of which we have spoken, is explicitly provided for, or the people, yet free, enjoins upon the future king something in the nature of a perpetual command, or an additional stipulation is made

---

[50] See the discussion at p. 186 below.

[51] The contrast, stated in modern terms, is between right and power. Once a promise is given by a sovereign, the sovereign no longer has the *right* to act contrary to it, since he is required by natural law to fulfil his promise. But he may retain the *power* to act contrary to the promise. Grotius regards it as possible that a promise could deprive the ruler of *both* the right and the power to act contrary to the commitment given.

[52] Even when the sovereign has lost both the right and the power to act contrary to a promise, Grotius denies that the beneficiaries of the promise acquire any legal remedy or right of action against the sovereign. That is, no human agency can step in to impose a punishment upon the wrong-doing sovereign. Instead, the sanction lies in the fact that any action taken in breach of the promise will be void by operation of law. Where the sovereign has retained the power to act in breach of the promise, even this sanction will not operate.

[53] I.e., in such a case, only the duration of the holding of the sovereign power is affected, not the nature or extent of that power during the period in which it is held.

from which it is understood that the king can be constrained or punished.[54] A command is, in fact, the act of one having superior authority, at least in respect to that which is commanded. To constrain is not, at any rate not in all cases, the function of a [political] superior – by nature everyone has the right to constrain a debtor; yet the act of constraining is [in principle] inconsistent with the position of an inferior. From the power of constraint, therefore, flows at least a recognition of parity, and in consequence a division of the supreme power.[55]

Against such a state of divided sovereignty – having, as it were, two heads – objections in great number are urged by many. But, as we have also said above, in matters of government, there is nothing which from every point of view is quite free from disadvantages; and a legal provision is to be judged not by what this or that man considers best, but by what accords with the will of him with whom the provision originated.[56]

18. Whether there is division of sovereignty when laws are approved by assemblies

They are greatly mistaken, however, who think that a division of sovereignty occurs when kings desire that certain acts of theirs do not have the force of law unless these are approved by a senate or some other assembly. For acts which are annulled in this way must be understood as annulled by the exercise of sovereignty on the part of the king himself, who has taken this way to protect himself in order that a measure granted under false representations might not be considered a true act of his will.[57]

---

[54] In other words, the powers of the ruler can be limited at the point of the original grant of sovereignty, by means of granting only certain powers to the ruler and withholding others, or by placing conditions, at that initial point, on the ruler's exercise of the powers granted to him. The sovereign is then the 'absolute' ruler only within the scope of the powers actually granted to him, i.e., he is not subject to the will or command of his subjects in those areas. Once the scope of the sovereign's powers have been fixed, however, any *subsequent* promises that he makes to his subjects does not diminish those powers. It merely imposes onto the sovereign a personal obligation, under natural law, to carry out the promise – and a breach of that promise does not (as noted above) give a right of action to the beneficiaries against the sovereign.

[55] The point here is that even private citizens exercise certain powers that are, broadly speaking, sovereign in character – such as the right of a creditor to 'constrain' (e.g., imprison) a debtor. Grotius advances this as an illustration of the manner in which sovereignty may be divided and shared.

[56] Questions of the scope of sovereign powers are to be resolved not according to general and abstract doctrines about sovereignty but instead, more concretely, by a determination of what the original intentions of the original grantor of sovereignty had been, in each individual case.

[57] The assertion is that the role of assemblies is not to limit or counteract the will of a sovereign, but merely to assist the sovereign in arriving at a considered conclusion as to what his true will actually is. Grotius's prior point, however, should be borne in

The case under consideration, then, resembles a will to which the clause has been added that no later will would be valid; for such a clause establishes the presumption that a later will would not express the real desire of the testator. But just as in the case of such a testamentary clause, so too the analogous declaration of the king can be nullified by an explicit order and specific expression of a later act of will.

20. True examples of mixed sovereignty

Aristotle ... wrote that there are certain types of monarchy intermediate between the full royal power, which he calls absolute monarchy ... and the kingship of the Lacedaemonians, which is merely a government by leading men.[58]

Having laid down these principles, let us discuss certain questions which frequently come up in connexion with the subject.

21. Whether sovereignty is compatible with the obligation of an unequal alliance

The first question is, whether he can possess sovereign power who is bound by an unequal alliance. By an unequal alliance I mean here not an alliance entered into between states of unequal strength.... Nor, again, do I have reference to a relation which has a temporary effect, as in the case of an enemy who is admitted to friendly terms until he pays the costs of a war, or fulfils some other condition. An unequal alliance is one which, by the very character of the treaty, gives to one of the contracting parties a permanent advantage over the other; when, for example, one party is bound to preserve the sovereignty and majesty of the other ... – that is, to put forth every effort that its sovereignty remain secure and its prestige, which is understood by the word majesty, remain unimpaired.

Characterised by a similar inequality are certain rights which to-day are known as rights of protection, defence, and patronage; also, among the Greeks, the right of the mother cities over their colonies. As Thucydides says, the colonies in respect to legal independence were on the same place as the mother cities, but they were under obligation 'to honour the mother city' and to manifest their feeling by 'the customary signs of respect'[59] – a deferential attitude, undoubtedly, and certain outward marks of honour.

mind: that it is possible that the initial grant of sovereign power was conditional upon the right of an assembly to veto the sovereign's actions. In such a case, the assembly would operate as a true limitation on the sovereign's power.

[58] Aristotle, *Politics*, III.15. The Lacedaemonian (i.e., Spartan) kingship had so little power that Aristotle did not regard it as a true monarchy. See Section 8 above.

[59] Thucydides, *The Peloponnesian War*, I.25.

We know what answer Proculus gave to the question under consideration.[60] He said that a state is independent which is not subject to the power of another, even though a stipulation may have been made in a treaty of alliance that this state shall use its good offices to maintain the dignity of another state.[61] If, therefore, a state bound by such a treaty remains independent, if it is not subject to the power of another, the conclusion follows that it retains its sovereignty.

The same conclusion, further, must be affirmed in the case of a king. The case of an independent state and that of a king, who truly is a king, are in this matter identical. Proculus adds that the stipulation referred to is made a part of a treaty in order that 'it may be understood that one state holds a position of superiority, not that it may be understood that the other state is not independent'.[62] This position of superiority we ought to consider as having reference not to power (for he had just said that the lesser state was not subject to the power of another), but to influence and prestige.[63]

Clients are under the protection of their patrons; so lesser states are by treaty placed under the protection of a state which is superior in prestige . . . .In the second book of his treatise *On Duties* Cicero, characterising the times when the Romans were more conscientious, says that with them their allies had protection, not domination.[64]

Just as private patronage in the case of individuals does not take away individual liberty, so patronage in the case of a state does not take away independence; and independence without sovereignty is inconceivable.

Contradictory, seemingly, to what we have said, is the statement which Proculus adds: 'Citizens of allied states are subject to legal proceedings among us, and if they are found guilty we punish them.'[65] In order that this statement may be understood, it is necessary to know that there are four kinds of controversies which can arise. First, if subjects of a state or of a king who is under the protection of another are charged with having violated the treaty of alliance; in the second place, if the states or kings themselves are accused of such violation; thirdly, if allies who are under the protection of the same state or king

---

[60] Proculus was a noted Roman jurist about whom little is known. But he was the leading figure of one of the two major schools of Roman lawyers who became known as the 'Proculians'. He lived in the late first century AD.

[61] *Digest*, 49.15.7.1 (Proculus).   [62] *Ibid.*

[63] Grotius proceeds to quote Proculus's statement, though not very accurately. Proculus's remarks on this subject, in full, are as follows: 'A free people is one which is not subject to the control of any other people; a *civitas foederata*, one which has either entered into friendship under an equal treaty or under a treaty [which] includes the provision that this people should with good will preserve the *maiestas* of another people. It has to be added that that other people is to be understood to be superior, not that [the federated] people is not free; and insofar as we understand our client [states] to be free, even if they are not our equals in authority, dignity or power, so also those who are bound to preserve our *maiestas* with good will are to be understood to be free.' *Ibid.*

[64] Cicero, *On Duties*, II.26–7.   [65] *Digest*, 49.15.7.2 (Proculus).

have differences among themselves; fourthly, if subjects complain that they have suffered wrongs at the hands of those to whom they are subject.

In the first case, if the offence is evident, the king or state is bound to punish the offender, or to deliver him up to the party that suffered the wrong. This holds not only in the case of unequal alliances, but also in the case of alliances made on equal terms; also, again, in the case of those who are not bound by any alliance, as we shall show elsewhere.[66] The king or state furthermore is bound to see to it that the losses are made good.[67]

In the second case, one ally has the right to compel the other ally to abide by the terms of the treaty, and also to punish him, in case he has failed to do so. But this, again, is not limited to unequal alliances. The same rule of right holds in the case of a treaty on equal terms. For in order to exact punishment from one who has committed an offence, it is sufficient that the party inflicting the punishment be not subject to the offender; but this point will be treated by us later.[68] In consequence, the same practice has arisen also between kings and states not in alliance.

In the third case, in unequal as in equal alliances, controversies are ordinarily referred to a conference of the allies who have no interest in the matter under dispute such, we read, was the practice among the Greeks, the early Latins, and the Germans; otherwise, either to arbitrators, or even to the leading member of a confederation as a common arbitrator. The latter alternative is ordinarily adopted in the case of an unequal alliance, so that controversies are settled by reference to him who has the leading place in the alliance. Even this method does not disclose an authority based on sovereign power; for kings often plead before judges appointed by themselves.

In the last case the allies have no right of intervention. This is in harmony with the statement of Aristotle, that an alliance of states differs from a single state in this, that the allies are charged with preventing the commission of wrong against any one of them, not with prevention of wrong-doing among the citizens of an allied state.[69]

Another objection is often raised, that in the histories the word 'command' is sometimes used with reference to him who holds a position of vantage in an alliance,[70] and 'obey' with reference to him who holds the inferior position. This, however, ought not to disturb us. For we are here concerned either with matters that relate to the common good of the alliance, or with the particular interest of him who in the alliance holds the position of vantage. In respect to

---

[66] There is a general natural-law duty on the part of rulers to punish miscreants.

[67] In modern international law, a breach of this duty is termed denial of justice and leads to legal liability on the part of the state at fault.

[68] See p. 271 below.   [69] Aristotle, *Politics*, III.9.

[70] By 'vantage' is meant a position of superiority in an unequal alliance, i.e., a position of superiority that is expressly agreed in the terms of the alliance itself. Grotius compares this to the situation in an equal alliance, in which there is generally one party which is dominant de facto, though not de iure.

matters of common interest, except at the time of a conference of the allies, even when there is an alliance on equal terms, he who is chosen as head of the alliance . . . ordinarily holds the command.

This right of the leading member of an alliance the Romans expressed by *imperare*, 'to command'; the Greeks, with greater self-constraint, by a word meaning 'to put in order', 'arrange'. . . . If this, then, is done by one who is only the leading member in an alliance, it is not remarkable if the same thing is done by him who in an unequal alliance has, according to the terms of the treaty, the position of vantage. Understood in this sense, the right on the part of the leading ally to hold command, that is hegemony, does not take away the independence of the others.

In matters which affect the particular interest of him who holds the position of vantage in an unequal alliance, requests are often spoken of as commands, not rightly but in accordance with the similarity of the effect produced; in like manner the prayers of kings are often said to be commands, and sick people are said to give orders to their physicians.

It is, nevertheless, true that, in the majority of cases, he who has the position of vantage in a treaty, if he is greatly superior in respect to power, gradually usurps the sovereignty properly so called. This is particularly liable to happen if the treaty is perpetual, and if it contains the right to introduce garrisons into towns. . . . When such things happen, with the result that non-resistance on the part of the weaker passes over into the right of ruling on the part of the stronger. . . . then either those who had been allies become subjects, or there is at any rate a division of sovereignty such as, according to our previous statement, may take place.

22. Whether sovereignty is compatible with the payment of tribute

There are some allies who pay a definite amount, either as reparation for wrong-doings, or as a contribution to secure protection; these are 'allies subject to tribute', as Thucydides calls them.[71] . . . I see no reason for doubting that such nations may possess sovereignty, although the confession of weakness does detract somewhat from their standing.

23. Whether sovereignty is compatible with obligations of feudal law

To many, the problem of sovereignty in relation to feudal tenure seems more difficult; it can, however, be easily solved in the light of what has been said. In discussing this type of contract, which is peculiar to the Germanic nations and

---

[71] Thucydides, *The Peloponnesian War*, I.19. In this passage, Thucydides contrasts the policies of Athens and Sparta towards their allies – with Athens requiring the payment of tribute and Sparta not.

is found only where the Germans settled, two elements need to be considered, the personal obligation, and the property right.

The personal obligation is the same whether a person by feudal law possesses the actual right of governing, or anything else even though situated in a different place.[72] Now, as such an obligation would not deprive an individual of the right of personal liberty, so it does not deprive a king or a state of sovereignty, which is political freedom.[73]

This is most clearly seen in the case of free fiefs, which are called frank-fiefs.[74] These do not consist in any property rights but in a personal obligation only. Such fiefs are, in fact, only a kind of unequal alliance, which we have been treating; of the contracting parties one engages to render service to the other, the other in turn to furnish defence and protection.

Suppose even that the service of the vassal had been promised against all men in the case of the fief now called a liege fief (formerly the term had a wider application); that in no degree lessens his right of sovereign power over his subjects[75] – not to speak of the fact that, in such a promise, there is always an unexpressed condition, provided the war be lawful, which is to be dealt with later.[76]

[72] This refers to the fact that, under feudal law, a vassal becomes a kind of ruler within his fief, by way of delegation of powers from his lord (and, ultimately, from the ruler). Grotius contends that such a right of delegated rulership, contracted out by the ruler, does not amount to a diminution of the ruler's sovereignty.

[73] Feudal arrangements were essentially contractual in character. Just as a contractual commitment by a private party is not incompatible with personal free status, so also is a feudal arrangement, entered into by a ruler, not incompatible with the holding of sovereign power.

[74] A free fief, or frank-fief, was a special kind of feudal fief. Ordinarily, a fief comprised a grant from the lord of either land or some kind of governance right (such as levying tolls or coining money) to the fief-holder or vassal, in exchange for the vassal's promise to provide military service. Free fiefs were different. They originally involved grants to ecclesiastical foundations. Instead of granting a right of property or governance rights, the lord would give only a general promise to provide protection. In place of military service, the churchmen would say prayers for the lord's soul. More broadly, a free fief came to refer to any kind of arrangement which required only 'honourable' services on the part of the fief-holder, such as military service, or the saying of prayers. Dishonourable services included such activities as menial agricultural labour.

[75] It sometimes happened that vassals took fiefs from two or more lords, with services owed to each. In such a case, a problem could arise as to which lords had first claim on the vassal's services. A liege fief was an arrangement in which the fief-holder promised to give his liege-lord priority over all other claimants. Grotius's point is that such an arrangement could not be regarded as affecting the powers of the fief-holder's sovereign, i.e., that the fief-holder continued to be subject to the full range of duties as a subject. Therefore, the liege relationship can only affect the priority of obligations among lesser lords.

[76] See p. 316 below.

So far as the property right is concerned, if one holds by feudal law, the right of governing may be lost on the extinction of a family, or even on account of certain crimes. But in the meantime, the power of the vassal does not cease to be sovereign;[77] for, as we have often said, the object is one thing, the manner of possession quite another. I see that a number of kings were placed in authority by the Romans with the stipulation that, if the royal family should become extinct, the political power should revert to them.

24. Distinction between the right of sovereignty and the exercise of the right

In the case of political power, not less than in that of private ownership, it is necessary to distinguish between the right and its exercise. . . . For a king who is an infant possesses political power but is unable to use it. A king, again, may be insane or a captive; and a king may be in foreign territory and live in such a way that freedom of action in respect to a dominion existing elsewhere is not permitted to him. In all these cases it is necessary to provide guardians, or regents.

---

[77] I.e., the delegated power held by the vassal within his fief.

4

War of subjects against superiors

1. State of the question

War may be waged by private persons against private persons, as by a traveller against a highwayman; by those who have sovereign power against those who possess like power; . . . by private persons against those who have sovereign power, but not over them, as by Abraham against the King of Babylon and his neighbours; and by those who have sovereign power against private persons who are either their subjects . . . or are not their subjects, as in the war waged by the Romans against the pirates. The question to be considered here is simply this, whether it is permissible for either private or official persons to wage war against those under whose authority they are, whether this authority be sovereign or subordinate.

First of all, the point is settled beyond controversy, that arms may be taken up against subordinates by those who are armed with the authority of the sovereign power. . . . Our question, then, is to determine what action is permissible against the sovereign power, or, against subordinates acting under the authority of the sovereign power.

Among all good men one principle at any rate is established beyond controversy, that if the authorities issue any order that is contrary to the law of nature or to the commandments of God, the order should not be carried out. . . . But if from any such cause, or under other conditions as a result of caprice on the part of him who holds the sovereign power, unjust treatment be inflicted on us, we ought to endure it rather than resist by force.[1]

2. Whether as a general rule rebellion is permitted by the law of nature

By nature, all men have the right of resisting in order to ward off injury, as we have said above.[2] But as civil society was instituted in order to maintain public

---

[1] I.e., if a subject is ordered to perpetrate a violation of natural law, then he must refuse. But if he is a victim of a violation of natural law by his sovereign, then he must suffer patiently.

[2] See p. 36 above.

tranquillity, the state forthwith acquires over us and our possessions a greater right, to the extent necessary to accomplish this end. The state, therefore, in the interest of public peace and order, can limit that common right of resistance.[3] That such was the purpose of the state we cannot doubt, since it could not in any other way achieve its end. If, in fact, the right of resistance should remain without restraint, there will no longer be a state, but only a non-social horde. . . . Hence it comes about that everywhere the majesty, that is, the prestige, whether of the state or of him who exercises the sovereign power, is safeguarded by so many laws, so many penalties; this cannot be maintained if licence to offer resistance be free to all.

If sometimes under the influence of excessive fear or anger or other passions, rulers are turned aside so that they do not enter the straight road that leads to tranquillity, this after all must be reckoned among the things that less frequently happen; and such things . . . are offset by the interposition of better things. Laws, again, count it sufficient to have in view what generally happens.

Things which happen rather infrequently ought nevertheless to be brought together under general rules; for although the principle embodied in a law may in a special case not have a specific application, yet the principle remains of general scope, and it is right that particular cases should be determined accordingly. This is better than to live without a rule, or to suffer the rule to be left to everyone's discretion.[4]

Now beyond doubt the most important element in public affairs is the constituted order of bearing rule and rendering obedience, regarding which I have spoken. This truly cannot coexist with individual licence to offer resistance.

5. On rebellion according to the practice of the early Christians

From this law of the Lord the practice of the early Christians, which is a most excellent commentary upon the law, did not depart. Although the administration of the Roman Empire was often in the hands of extremely bad men, and there was no lack of pretenders who opposed them under the pretext of rescuing the state, the Christians never associated themselves with their attempts.

---

[3] The general right to resist injury, in other words, belonged to all humans only in the state of nature, not in settled political society.

[4] I.e., laws admittedly may cause hardship in particular cases. But in general, all that can be expected of a rule of law is that it be reasonable in general, rather than in every single instance. In this case, the law prohibiting rebellion against established authorities is (according to Grotius) sensible as a general policy. Consequently, it should be adhered to, even in the exceptional cases in which it brings hardship to the subjects.

6. On the rebellion of subordinate officials against sovereign authority

In our time, there are to be met with men who possess learning, it is true, but being too much under the influence of time and place have persuaded first themselves (for so I believe), then others, that what has been said is applicable only to private individuals and not also to subordinate officials. They think that subordinate officials have the right to offer resistance to wrong-doing on the part of him who holds the supreme power; further, that these do wrong if under such conditions they do not offer resistance.

The validity of this opinion ought not to be admitted. Just as in logic, an intermediate species, from the point of view of the genus, is a species, but from the point of view of a sub-species is a genus, so subordinate officials from the point of view of officials of lower rank are persons vested with public authority, but from the point of view of those possessing higher authority are private persons. All governmental authority possessed by public officials is in fact so subordinated to the sovereign power that whatever they do contrary to the will of him who holds it is divested of authority and is, accordingly, to be considered as a private act.

7. The case of extreme and unavoidable necessity

More serious is the question whether the law of non-resistance should bind us in case of extreme and imminent peril. Even some laws of God, although stated in general terms, carry a tacit exception in case of extreme necessity. . . . This does not mean that God has not the right to oblige us to submit ourselves to certain death; it does mean that, since there are some laws of such a nature, we are not to believe that they were given with so inflexible an intent.[5] The same principle holds even more manifestly in the case of human laws.

I do not deny that, even according to human law, certain acts of a moral nature can be ordered which expose one to a sure danger of death; an example is the order not to leave one's post. We are not, however, rashly to assume that such was the purpose of him who laid down the law; and it is apparent that men would not have received so drastic a law applying to themselves and others except as constrained by extreme necessity. For laws are formulated by men and ought to be formulated with an appreciation of human frailty.

Now this law which we are discussing – the law of non-resistance – seems to draw its validity from the will of those who associate themselves together in the first place to form a civil society; from the same source, furthermore, derives

---

[5] God does have the right to command us to act in such a way as to bring certain death. Nevertheless, in doubtful cases, there is a presumption against giving so drastic an interpretation to a divine command.

the right which passes into the hands of those who govern.[6] If these men could be asked whether they purposed to impose upon all persons the obligation to prefer death rather than under any circumstances to take up arms in order to ward off the violence of those having superior authority, I do not know whether they would answer in the affirmative, unless, perhaps, with this qualification, in case resistance could not be made without a very great disturbance in the state, and without the destruction of a great many innocent people. I do not doubt that, to human law also, there can be applied what love under such circumstances would commend.[7]

Someone may say that this strict obligation, to suffer death rather than at any time to ward off any kind of wrong-doing on the part of those possessing superior authority, has its origin not in human but in divine law. It must be noted, however, that in the first instance men joined themselves together to form a civil society not by command of God, but of their own free will, being influenced by their experience of the weakness of isolated households against attack. From this origin, the civil power is derived. . . . Elsewhere, however, it is also called a divine ordinance, because God approved an institution which was beneficial to mankind. God is to be thought of as approving a human law, however, only as human and imposed after the manner of men.[8]

Barclay,[9] though a very staunch advocate of kingly authority, nevertheless comes down to this point, that he concedes to the people, and to a notable portion of the people, the right of self-defence against atrocious cruelty, despite the fact that he admits that the entire people is subject to the king. I readily understand that, in proportion as that which is preserved is of greater importance, the equity of admitting an exception to the letter of a law is increased. But on the other hand, I should hardly dare indiscriminately to condemn either

---

[6] This discussion contains one of the clearest endorsements by Grotius of the social-contract principle as the basis of political society.

[7] This reference to 'what love . . . would commend' refers, basically, to considerations of morals rather than of strict law. From the moral standpoint, it would generally be presumed that commands or laws should not have the result of leading to the death of the persons who obey them. Grotius concedes that, in general, this principle of morals should be employed in the interpretation of both divine and human law.

[8] It is apparent from this discussion that human and divine law are not so clearly distinct from one another as might be initially supposed. Laws whose immediate source is human can nevertheless be said to come indirectly or ultimately from God. This is by virtue of God's approval of the human institution of government, which has the effect of requiring subjects to obey their human rulers.

[9] William Barclay (1548–1608) was a political theorist who strongly supported monarchy as a form of government, most prominently in his book *De Regno et Regali Potestate* (1600). Originally from Scotland, but of the Catholic faith, he relocated to France, where he held various government posts. He declined an invitation from King James I of England to come to that country, since it would have been necessary for him to abjure Catholicism. In the last years of his life, he was Professor of Civil Law at the University of Angers.

individuals, or a minority which at length availed itself of the last resource of necessity in such a way as meanwhile not to abandon consideration of the common good.

Meanwhile the caution must be observed that, even in such danger, the person of the king must be spared.

Malicious false statements are not permissible even against a private individual; accordingly, in the case of a king, malicious statements even of what is true must be refrained from, for the reason that, as the author of the *Problems* which bear the name of Aristotle says: 'He who reviles the ruler works injury to the state.'[10] If, then, harm must not be done to the ruler with speech, surely much less with the hand. . . . For since the sovereign power is inevitably exposed to the hatred of many, the security of him who is charged with the exercise of it must be safeguarded in an altogether exceptional way.

We said that resistance cannot rightly be made to those who hold the sovereign power. There are certain points which we now ought to bring to the reader's attention, in order that he may not consider those guilty of disobeying this law who in reality are not guilty.

8. On war by a free people against their government

First, then, if rulers are responsible to the people, whether such power was conferred at the beginning or under a later arrangement . . . –if such rulers transgress against the laws and the state, not only can they be resisted by force, but, in case of necessity, they can be punished with death.[11]

9. On war against a king who has abdicated the sovereign power

In the second place, if a king, or any other person, has renounced his governmental authority, or manifestly has abandoned it, after that time proceedings of every kind are permissible against him as against a private person. But he is by no means to be considered as having renounced a thing who is merely too neglectful of it.

[10] In other words, the dissemination of statements that impugn public authorities should not be allowed, even if the statements are true. The reason is that such statements, even if true, are prejudicial to the maintenance of public order. Such dissemination is the essence of the English-law concept of sedition.

[11] Rulers responsible to the people are rulers who hold sovereign powers on the explicit condition that the people retain a right to dismiss them if they disapprove of their actions. A ruler who is dismissed in this fashion, and who then attempts to retain power nonetheless, can be forcibly ousted by the people as an exercise of their lawful rights. This is in contrast to rulers to whom sovereign powers had been transferred unconditionally. Their actions may not be resisted, and they cannot lawfully be overthrown by their subjects.

10. On war against a king who alienates his kingdom

In the third place, Barclay holds the opinion that, if a king alienates his kingdom, or places it in subjection to another, the kingdom is no longer his. I do not go so far. For an act of this character, if the kingship is conferred by election or by a law of succession, is null and void, and acts which are null and void do not have any effect in law. Nearer the truth, in my opinion, is the view of the jurists in regard to a usufructuary, to whose position, we have said, that of such a king is analogous; by alienating his right to a third person the usufructuary effects nothing. And the statement that the usufruct reverts to the owner of the property must be construed in accordance with the period fixed by law.[12]

If, nevertheless, a king actually does undertake to alienate his kingdom, or to place it in subjection, I have no doubt that in this case he can be resisted.[13] For the sovereign power, as we have said, is one thing; the manner of holding it is another; and a people can oppose a change in the manner of holding the sovereign power,[14] for the reason that this is not comprised in the sovereign power itself.

11. On war against a king who is the enemy of the whole people

In the fourth place, says the same Barclay, the kingdom is forfeited if a king sets out with a truly hostile intent to destroy a whole people. This I grant, for the will to govern and the will to destroy cannot coexist in the same person. The king, then, who acknowledges that he is an enemy of the whole people, by that very fact renounces his kingdom. This, it is evident, can hardly occur in the case of a king possessed of his right mind, and ruling over a single people. Of course, if a king rules over several peoples, it can happen that he may wish to have one people destroyed for the sake of another, in order that he may colonise the territory thus made vacant.

---

[12] The contention is that there is nothing wrong with a ruler alienating his authority, such as it actually is in strict law – i.e., his usufructuary right to the exercise of sovereign powers during his lifetime. According to the Roman law of usufruct, only the fruits or products of the property belong to the usufruct holder, not the property as such (e.g., the income from a fund, rather than the fund itself). In the case of a king, the sovereign power per se (i.e., the property, applying the analogy) is not affected by a ruler's alienation of his own usufructuary rights. The ruler is therefore able to transfer to someone else his own right to exercise, during his life, the powers associated with sovereignty. This does not count, in Grotius's opinion, as an alienation of the sovereignty as such.

[13] I.e., if a king actually does transfer, or attempt to transfer, the whole sovereign power per se, and not merely his own exercise of it during his lifetime, then his action can justly be resisted.

[14] Meaning a ruler's attempt to transform himself from a mere usufructuary into an absolute owner of the sovereign powers.

12. On war against a king who has violated a condition of his grant of sovereignty

Fifthly, if a kingdom be granted under the condition that, upon the commission of felony against the overlord, or the violation of a clause inserted in the grant of power, that if the king do thus and so, the subjects are released from all duty of obedience to him. In such a case also the king reverts to the position of a private person.

13. On war against a king who seeks to usurp powers not belonging to him

Sixthly, in case the sovereign power is held in part by the king, in part by the people or senate, force can lawfully be used against the king if he attempts to usurp that part of the sovereign power which does not belong to him, for the reason that this authority does not extend so far. In my opinion this principle holds, even though it has already been said that the power to make war should be reserved to the king. For this, it must be understood, refers to external war. For the rest, whoever possesses a part of the sovereign power must possess also the right to defend his part; in case such a defence is resorted to, the king may even lose his part of the sovereign power by right of war.

14. On war against a king, if liberty to resist has been reserved

Seventhly, if in the conferring of authority, it has been stated that, in a particular case, the king can be resisted, even though such an agreement does not involve the retention of a part of the authority, some natural freedom of action . . . has been reserved and exempted from the exercise of royal power. For he who alienates his own right can by agreement limit the right transferred.

15. Whether obedience should be rendered to a usurper of sovereign power

We have spoken of him who possesses, or has possessed, the right of governing. It remains to speak of the usurper of power, not after he has acquired a right through long possession or contract, but while the basis of possession remains unlawful. Now while such a usurper is in possession, the acts of government which he performs may have a binding force, arising not from a right possessed by him, for no such right exists, but from the fact that the one to whom the sovereignty actually belongs, whether people, or king, or senate, would prefer that measures promulgated by him should meanwhile have the force of law, in order to avoid the utter confusion which would result from the subversion of laws and suppression of the courts.[15]

[15] Vitoria, *On Civil Power*, 23.

In the case of measures promulgated by the usurper which are not so essential, and which have as their purpose to establish him in his unlawful possession, obedience is not to be rendered unless disobedience would involve grave danger. But whether it is permissible to use violence in overthrowing such a usurper of authority, or even to put him to death, is the question before us.

16. Resistance by force against a usurper by virtue of a right of war still continuing

In the first place, if the usurper has seized the governmental power by means of a war that is unlawful and not in accordance with the law of nations, and no agreement has been entered into afterward, and no promise has been given to him, but possession is maintained by force alone, it would seem that the right to wage war against him still remains, and whatever is permissible against any enemy is permissible against him. Just as an enemy, so also a usurper, under such conditions, can lawfully be put to death by anyone, even by an individual. 'Against men guilty of treason and against public enemies', says Tertullian, 'every man is a soldier'.[16]

Thus also, in the interest of general tranquillity, the right of enforcing public punishment against deserters from military service is granted to all.

17. Resistance by force against a usurper by virtue of a pre-existing law

I hold that the same conclusion must be accepted in the case that, prior to the usurpation, there was in existence a public law which conferred upon any man the right to kill a person who dared to do this or that which falls within its purview; who, for example, though a private individual, should have surrounded himself with a bodyguard and should have seized the citadel; who had put to death a citizen uncondemned, or without lawful judgement; or who had chosen public officials without regular elections.

18. Resistance by force against a usurper by virtue of a mandate of one possessing sovereign power

It will likewise be permissible to put a usurper to death in case the deed is explicitly authorised by the true possessor of sovereign power, whether king, or senate, or people. To these we should add also guardians of the children of kings.

---

[16] Tertullian, *Apology*, 2.

19. Why resistance to a usurper should be limited to the cases mentioned

Outside of the cases which have been considered, I cannot concede that it is permissible for a private citizen either to put down by force, or to kill, a usurper of sovereign power. For it may happen that he who holds the sovereign power by right would prefer that the usurper should be left in possession rather than that the way should be opened for dangerous and bloody conflicts, such as generally take place when those who have a strong following among the people, or friends outside the country, are treated with violence or put to death. At any rate, it is not certain that the king or the people would wish that matters should be brought to such extremities, and without their known approval the use of violence cannot be lawful.

An exceedingly weighty question it surely is, . . . which is preferable, independence or peace. It is an extremely difficult political problem, Cicero found, to determine 'whether, when one's country is oppressed by an unlawful exercise of power, every effort should be put forth to accomplish its abolition, even if the state should thereby be brought into extreme peril'.[17] Yet individuals ought not to take it upon themselves to decide a question which involves the interest of the whole people.

20. When the right of sovereignty is in dispute

Above all, in case of a controversy [over the right to sovereignty] the private individual ought not to take it upon himself to pass judgement, but should accept the fact of possession.

---

[17] Cicero, *Letters to Atticus*, IX.4.

5

Who may lawfully wage war

1. The efficient causes of war

As in other matters, so also in acts originating in the will, there are ordinarily three kinds of efficient causes[1] – principal agents, auxiliary agents, and
instruments. In war, the principal efficient cause is generally the person whose
interest is at stake – in private war, the individual; in public war, the public
power, in most cases the sovereign power. Whether war can be made by one
on behalf of others who do not make war on their own account, we shall see
elsewhere. Meanwhile we shall hold to this principle, that by nature everyone is
the defender of his own rights; that is the reason why hands were given to us.

2. The efficient causes of war are in part those who wage war on another's account, as auxiliary agents

But to render service to another, so far as we can, is not only permissible, it is
also honourable. Those who have written on the subject of duties rightly say
that nothing is more useful to a man than another man. There are, however,
various ties which bind men together and summon them to mutual aid. Thus
those who are related by kinship unite to assist one another. Neighbours, too,
and those who belong to the same state, call on one another for help. . . . But
in default of all other ties, the common bond of human nature is sufficiently
strong. Devoid of interest to man is nothing that pertains to man.

3. The efficient causes of war are those who wage war as instruments, as servants and subjects

When we use the word 'instruments' in this connexion we do not mean
'weapons' and similar things; we mean persons whose acts of will are dependent on the will of another. An instrument, as we use the term here, is a son in

---

[1] 'Efficient cause' is an expression from Aristotelian philosophy, referring to the
   immediate material cause or impetus of something (in contrast to more remote
   causes, such as the ultimate goal that is sought to be achieved by the action in
   question).

relation to his father, viewed as by nature a part, so to speak, of the father; such an instrument also is a slave in relation to his master, a part, as it were, in a legal sense. For just as a part is a part of the whole not only in the same relation that the whole sustains to the part, but also the very thing which constitutes a part pertains to the whole, so possession becomes something of the possessor.

4. Whether any one is enjoined from waging war by the law of nature

There is no doubt that, by nature, all subjects may be used for purposes of war; but certain classes are exempted by special enactment, as formerly slaves at Rome, now men in holy orders generally. Nevertheless a special enactment of this kind, as such laws generally, must be understood as subject to exception in cases of extreme necessity.

Let these general statements in regard to auxiliary agents and subjects suffice; for the special questions relating to them will be treated in the proper connexion.[2]

---

[2] See p. 319 below.

Book II
On the Law of War and Peace

1

The causes of war: first, defence of self and property

1. Justifiable causes of war

Let us proceed to the causes of war – I mean justifiable causes; for there are also other causes which influence men through regard for what is expedient and differ from those that influence men through regard for what is right.[1]

Wars that are undertaken by public authority have, it is true, in some respects a legal effect, as do judicial decisions, which we shall need to discuss later;[2] but they are not on that account more free from wrong if they are undertaken without cause.

No other just cause for undertaking war can there be excepting injury received. 'Unfairness of the opposing side occasions just wars', said... Augustine,[3] using 'unfairness' when he meant 'injury'.... In the formula used by the Roman fetial are the words, 'I call you to witness that that people is unjust and does not do what is right in making restitution'.

2. The three justifiable causes of war[4]

It is evident that the sources from which wars arise are as numerous as those from which lawsuits spring; for where judicial settlement fails, war begins.

---

[1] For the discussion of unjust causes of war, see p. 301 below.

[2] In other words, even wars which are unjust in their inception confer certain rights (now known as belligerents' rights) onto those who wage them, according to the law of nations if not the law of nature per se. An example is the right to acquire title to enemy property. See p. 359 below.

[3] Augustine, *The City of God Against the Pagans*, XIX.7.

[4] This section contains Grotius's classic statement of the just causes of war, which would be adopted virtually unanimously by later international lawyers. Two things should be noted about it. Firstly, it would appear that Grotius leaves the door open to other just causes. In practice, however, these three that are mentioned came to be regarded as a substantially complete list. Secondly, it should be noted that the causes relate to three distinct time frames: defence, relating to the pre-emptive warding off of an impending (i.e., future) attack; the obtaining of that which is owing, relating to an ongoing wrong, continuing to the present time; and punishment, relating to action in response to a past and completed wrong.

Actions, furthermore, lie either for wrongs not yet committed, or for wrongs already done.

An action lies for a wrong not yet committed in cases where a guarantee is sought against a threatened wrong, or security against an anticipated injury, or an interdict of a different sort against the use of violence. An action for a wrong committed lies where a reparation for injury, or the punishment of the wrong-doer, is sought.

Reparation is concerned either with what is or has been ours, giving rise to actions involving property interests, and certain personal actions; or with what is owed to us by contract, or in consequence of a criminal act; or by operation of law, a category to which must be referred also cases arising from implied contracts and constructive crimes. Under these subdivisions the rest of the personal actions fall. An act deserving punishment opens the way to accusation and public trial.

Authorities generally assign to wars three justifiable causes, defence,[5] recovery of property,[6] and punishment.[7]

The first cause of a justifiable war, then, is an injury not yet inflicted, which menaces either person or property.

3. War for the defence of life[8]

We said above that, if an attack by violence is made on one's person, endangering life, and no other way of escape is open, under such circumstances war is permissible, even though it involve the slaying of the assailant. As a consequence of the general acceptance of this principle we showed that in some cases a private war may be lawful.

This right of self-defence, it should be observed, has its origin directly, and chiefly, in the fact that nature commits to each his own protection, not in

---

[5] It should be noted that 'defence' is used in a general or broad sense of pre-emptive action against an *impending* injury. This is to be distinguished from the narrower concept of *individual* self-defence, which is the repelling of an *actual*, ongoing attack by an individual person, which Grotius proceeds to discuss in Sections 4–14 below. Defence in this broader sense will be referred to as 'defensive war'. Defensive war is a prerogative of states and is not relevant to individuals.

[6] 'Recovery of property', in Grotius's usage, had a broad meaning of compelling performance of an obligation which is owing, or enforcing the discharging of an obligation. It may be referred to as an 'enforcement war', although Grotius himself does not use that expression.

[7] This third category of just war could be called a 'punitive war', although Grotius does not employ that precise turn of phrase. For Grotius's discussion of punishment in general, see p. 269 below.

[8] Grotius, somewhat confusingly, has jumped topics here, to speak about the natural-law right of *individual* self-defence against actual attack. For nearly the whole of the chapter (up through Section 14), he remains on this subject. Only in Section 16 does he return to the right of *states* to wage defensive war.

the injustice or crime of the aggressor. Wherefore, even if the assailant be blameless, as for instance a soldier acting in good faith, or one who mistakes me for someone else, or one who is rendered irresponsible by madness or by sleeplessness – this, we read, has actually happened to some – the right of self-defence is not thereby taken away; it is enough that I am not under obligation to suffer what such an assailant attempts, any more than I should be if attacked by an animal belonging to another.[9]

4. On war in defence of life

It is a disputed question whether innocent persons can be cut down or trampled upon when by getting in the way they hinder the defence or flight by which alone death can be averted. That this is permissible, is maintained even by some theologians. And certainly, if we look to nature alone, in nature there is much less regard for society than concern for the preservation of the individual. But the law of love, especially as set forth in the Gospel, which puts consideration for others on a level with consideration for ourselves, clearly does not permit the injuring of the innocent even under such conditions.[10]

It has been well said by Thomas [Aquinas] – if he is rightly understood – that if a man in true self-defence kills his assailant, the slaying is not intentional.[11] The reason is not that, if no other means of safety is at hand, it is not sometimes permissible to do with set purpose that which will cause the death of the assailant; it is, rather, that in such a case the inflicting of death is not the primary intent, as it is in the case of procedure by process of law, but the only resource available at the time.[12] Even under such circumstances the person who is attacked ought to prefer to do anything possible to frighten away or weaken the assailant, rather than cause his death.

5. When war in defence of life is permissible

The danger, again, must be immediate and imminent in point of time. I admit, to be sure, that if the assailant seizes weapons in such a way that his intent to kill is manifest the crime can be forestalled; for in morals as in material things a

---

[9] It should be appreciated that, in Grotius's view, individual self-defence is not necessarily a response to a prior wrongful act. It is justifiable as a measure of self-protection without regard to whether the attack was lawful. As such, it is seen by Grotius as (in modern terminology) an exercise of the general principle of necessity. This principle of necessity justifies the commission of acts that are intrinsically unlawful, to deal with cases of serious danger. An example is the 'theft' of a fire extinguisher for the purpose of rescuing persons trapped by fire.

[10] The 'law of love' is divine law, in contrast to natural law or to man-made law.

[11] Aquinas, from *Summa Theologiae*, in *Political Writings*, pp. 263–4.

[12] This is a capsule statement of the doctrine known (somewhat confusingly) as 'double intention'.

point is not to be found which does not have a certain breadth. But those who accept fear of any sort as justifying anticipatory slaying are themselves greatly deceived, and deceive others.

Further, if a man is not planning an immediate attack, but it has been ascertained that he has formed a plot, or is preparing an ambuscade, or that he is putting poison in our way, or that he is making ready a false accusation and false evidence, and is corrupting the judicial procedure, I maintain that he cannot lawfully be killed, either if the danger can in any other way be avoided, or if it is not altogether certain that the danger cannot be otherwise avoided. Generally, in fact, the delay that will intervene affords opportunity to apply many remedies, to take advantage of many accidental occurrences; as the proverb runs, 'There's many a slip twixt cup and lip'. There are, it is true, theologians and jurists who would extend their indulgence somewhat further; but the opinion stated, which is better and safer, does not lack the support of authorities.

6. Whether defence of limb against injury is justifiable

What shall we say about the danger of injury to a part of the body? Truly the loss of a limb, especially if it is one of the principal limbs, is an extremely serious matter, and in a sense comparable to loss of life; further, we cannot be sure that injury to a part of the body will not bring danger of death. If, therefore, the injury cannot be avoided in any other way, I should think that he who is on the point of inflicting such injury can be rightly slain.

7. Whether defence of chastity is justifiable

That the same right to kill should be conceded also in defence of chastity is hardly open to question; not only the general opinion of men, but also the divine law puts chastity on a plane with life.

8. Whether it is permissible to forgo the right of defence

We said above, that while it is permissible to kill him who is making ready to kill, yet the man is more worthy of praise who prefers to be killed rather than to kill.

This principle, however, is by some conceded in such a way that an exception is made in the case of a person whose life is useful to many. But I should deem it unsafe to extend this rule, which is inconsistent with long-suffering, so as to include all those whose lives are necessary for others. And so I should think that the exception ought to be restricted to those whose duty it is to ward off violence from others, such as members of an escort on a journey, who were hired with that purpose in view, and public rulers.

9. Defence against a person useful to the state

On the other hand, it may happen that, since the life of the assailant is useful to many, he cannot be killed without wrong. And this is true, not only according to divine law, whether of the old or the new dispensation ... but also by the law of nature. For the law of nature, in so far as it has the force of a law, holds in view not only the dictates of expletive justice, as we have called it,[13] but also actions exemplifying other virtues, such as self-mastery, bravery, and prudence, as under certain circumstances not merely honourable, but even obligatory. And to such actions we are constrained by regard for others.

And I am not moved to renounce this opinion by Vázquez,[14] when he says that a ruler who maltreats an innocent man by that very act ceases to be a ruler. A statement either less true or more dangerous than that, it would be hard to make. For just as ownership, so the exercise of sovereign power is not lost by wrong-doing, unless the law so prescribe. But a law in regard to the exercise of sovereign power containing the provision that it should cease in consequence of committing a wrong against a private individual has nowhere been, and in my opinion never will be, framed; for such a law would lead to the utmost confusion.

The foundation upon which Vázquez bases this and many other conclusions is, that all exercise of sovereign power has in view the interest of those who obey, not of those who rule. Even if this should be true in general, it would not be in point here; for a thing whose usefulness is impaired only in part does not at once cease to be of use. His further statement, that the safety of the state is desired by individuals in their own interest, and in consequence every man ought to put his individual welfare above that of the whole state, is lacking in consistency. We do desire, in our own interest, that our state be safe, yet not merely for our own sake but for the sake of others as well.[15]

False, in fact, and rejected by the more sound philosophers, is the view of those who think that friendship has its origin in need alone; we are drawn to friendship spontaneously, and by our own nature. Regard for others often warns me, sometimes commands me, to put the interest of many above my own.[16]

---

[13] For the explanation of expletive justice, see p. 26 above.

[14] Fernando Vázquez de Menchaca (1512–69) taught at the University of Salamanca, and also served as an adviser to King Philip II of Spain. He wrote extensively on natural law, most notably in *Controversium* (1564). He was highly regarded by Grotius, who was influenced especially by his opposition to claims of ownership (*dominium*) over the high seas.

[15] For the full exposition of Grotius's views on sovereignty, see p. 50 above.

[16] This is a classic, and succinct, statement of the Aristotelian principle of the natural sociability of humans, in explicit contrast to theories (such as Hobbes's) which place human society on a utilitarian basis.

10. Killing to ward off a blow, avoid an indignity, or prevent an escape

There are some who think that, if a man is in imminent danger of receiving a blow or a similar injury, he has the right to prevent it by killing his enemy. For my part, if expletive justice only be considered, I raise no objection. For although death and a blow are not on the same level, yet the man who makes ready to injure me by that very act confers on me a right, a sort of actual and unlimited moral right against him, in so far as otherwise I cannot ward off the injury from myself. Furthermore, in such a case regard for others does not in itself seem to impose on us the obligation to favour the one who attempts the injury. But the law of the Gospel has made such action in self-defence altogether unpermissible; for Christ bids us submit to a blow rather than do harm to an aggressor. How much more earnestly does He forbid the slaying of an assailant in order to escape a blow!

This example warns us to beware of the [contention] that human knowledge, being not ignorant of the law of nature, does not allow anything to be permitted by natural reason which would not likewise be permitted by God, who is nature itself. For God, the creator of nature, is also able to act freely outside the realm of nature, and has the right to lay down laws for us even concerning those matters which are by nature left free and undetermined; even greater is His right to make obligatory what by nature is honourable, even though not obligatory.[17]

Since the will of God is so clearly manifest in the Gospel, strange it is that there are to be found theologians, and Christian theologians, too, who think that a man is allowed not only to kill in order to avoid a blow, but even to recover his honour, as men say, after receiving a blow, in case the assailant flees. This seems to me entirely inconsistent with both reason and religion. For honour is a recognition of superiority; but the man who endures such an injury shows that in a superior degree he possesses the virtue of long-suffering, and thus rather increases his honour than diminishes it. And it does not make any difference if some individuals of faulty judgement turn this virtue into a vice by applying to it names which they have made up; for such faulty judgements change neither the thing nor the value of the thing. The truth in this case was perceived not only by the early Christians but also by the philosophers, who said, as we have shown elsewhere, that it is characteristic of a small soul not to be able to bear an insult.

From this it is also clear that we ought not to accept with approval the opinion handed down by most authorities, that slaying in self-defence is permissible according to divine law (for I do not dispute the statement that it is permissible

---

[17] This is a warning against regarding divine law and natural law as wholly co-extensive. The truth, in Grotius's view, is that the two are compatible but not identical. Specifically, it is possible that divine law can forbid something which natural law neither forbids nor commands.

by the law of nature), even if one can escape without danger, because flight, especially in the case of a nobleman, would be disgraceful. And yet in such an act there is no disgrace; there is only a false notion of what is dishonourable, a notion deserving of contempt on the part of all true seekers after virtue and wisdom.

What I have said about a blow and flight, I wish to consider as said also about other occurrences which in reality do not in any degree affect our honour. But what if someone should spread a report about us, which, if believed, would hurt our standing in the estimation of good men? There are those who teach that such a person also can be slain. But this view is wholly erroneous, and contrary to the law of nature as well; slaying under such circumstances is not the proper means to be employed to defend one's reputation.

11. Killing in defence of property

We may now come to injuries that are attempted upon property. If we have in view expletive justice only, I shall not deny that in order to preserve property a robber can even be killed, in case of necessity. For the disparity between property and life is offset by the favourable position of the innocent party and the odious role of the robber, as we have said above. From this it follows, that if we have in view this right only, a thief fleeing with stolen property can be felled with a missile, if the property cannot otherwise be recovered.

If, furthermore, we leave divine and human law out of account,[18] regard for others, viewed as a principle of conduct, interposes no hindrance to such action, unless the stolen property is of extremely slight value and consequently worthy of no consideration. This exception is by some rightly added.

12. How far the defence of property is permitted by the law of Moses

[T]he Twelve Tables . . . forbids the killing of a thief by day, but adds the exception: unless he defend himself with a weapon. The presumption against a thief at night is, therefore, that he has defended himself with a weapon.

The presumption therefore, as I said, favours the man who has killed a thief by night. If, however, there should chance to be witnesses, through whom it can be established that the man who killed the thief was not brought into peril of life, in such a case the presumption will cease to be valid and the slayer will be held on the charge of murder. The law of the Twelve Tables further required that the man who had detected a thief, whether by day or by night, should make the fact known by shouting, undoubtedly that . . . magistrates or neighbours might if possible hasten to the place in order to give aid and to serve as witnesses. But because people are more easily brought together by day than by night, . . . the one who alleges the endangering of life at night is more readily believed.

---

[18] I.e., if we consider the question exclusively from the standpoint of natural law.

13. Killing in defence of property according to the law of the Gospel

What, now, shall we say in regard to the law of the Gospel? Does it permit the same that the law of Moses permitted? Or since it is more perfect in other respects than the law of Moses, does it also in this case demand more from us?

That the law of the Gospel demands more from us, I do not doubt. For if Christ bids that a tunic and a cloak be given up, and Paul, that an unjust loss be endured, rather than that recourse be had to a lawsuit – a contest without bloodshed – how much more do they wish that things also of greater value be relinquished rather than that a man, the image of God, sprung from the same blood with ourselves, should be killed! Wherefore, if a thing belonging to us can be saved in such a way that there seems to be no danger of causing death, it may rightly be defended; if not, then the thing should be given up, unless perchance it is of such a sort that our life and the life of our family is dependent on it and it cannot be recovered by process of law, since the thief is unknown, and also that there is some prospect that recovery will be made without slaughter.

Although to-day almost all jurists and theologians teach that we have a right to kill a man in the defence of our property, even going beyond the limits within which such an act was permitted by the law of Moses and the Roman law – as, for instance, if the thief be making off with what he has stolen – nevertheless we do not doubt that the opinion which we have just set forth was held by the early Christians.

In this matter, undoubtedly, as in many others, discipline has become relaxed with time, and little by little the interpretation of the law of the Gospel has begun to be adjusted to the customs of the age. Formerly among the clergy, conformity to the ancient practice was ordinarily kept up; but finally even the clergy have been released from censure in this matter.

14. Nature of the civil law on self-defence

The question is raised by some whether the civil law at any rate, since it contains the right of life and death, in permitting that a thief be killed by a private individual, does not at the same time free the act from all guilt. In my judgement this ought by no means to be conceded. In the first place, the law does not have the right of death over all citizens for any offence whatever, but only for offences so serious that they deserve death. Altogether worthy of approval is the opinion of Scotus, that it is not right to condemn anyone to death except for the crimes which the law of Moses punished with death, or, in addition, for crimes which, judged by a fair standard, are equally heinous. For in this so serious matter it seems possible to obtain a knowledge of the divine will, which alone gives peace of mind, from no other source than from that law, which does not with certainty appoint for the thief the penalty of death.

Furthermore, the law ought not to confer, and ordinarily does not confer, upon private individuals the right to put to death even those who have deserved death, excepting only in the case of the most atrocious crimes; otherwise the authority of the courts would have been constituted in vain.[19] Wherefore, if the law says that a thief is killed with impunity, we are to consider that it takes away a penalty but does not also confer a right.

15. When a single combat may be permissible[20]

From what we have said it is apparent that two conditions can arise under which individuals may engage in single combat without blame. The first condition is, when an assailant grants to the person attacked an opportunity to fight, though determined to kill him without combat in case he does not fight. The second is, if a king or magistrate matches against each other two criminals deserving of death; in this case it will indeed be their privilege to grasp at a hope of safety. The official who has ordered such a combat, however, would seem not to have discharged his duty properly, since, if the punishment of one seemed sufficient, it would have been better to choose by lot which one should die.

16. Concerning defence in public war

What has been said by us up to this point, concerning the right to defend oneself and one's possessions, applies chiefly, of course, to private war; yet it may be made applicable also to public war, if the difference in conditions be taken into account.[21]

In private war the right is, so to say, momentary; it ceases as soon as circumstances permit an approach to a judge. But since public wars do not arise except where there are no courts, or where courts cease to function, they are prolonged, and are continually augmented by the increment of fresh losses and injuries. Besides, in private war, self-defence is generally the only consideration; but public powers have not only the right of self-defence but also the right to exact punishment. Hence for them, it is permissible to forestall an act of violence which is not immediate, but which is seen to be threatening from a distance; not directly – for that, as we have shown, would work injustice – but indirectly, by inflicting punishment for a wrong action commenced but not yet carried through.[22]

---

[19] On the right of private parties to inflict punishments for violations of natural law, see p. 271 below.
[20] The discussion in this passage drifts somewhat away from the topic of self defence.
[21] In this section, the crucial distinction is drawn between the right of self-defence in the narrow sense (belonging to individuals) and the more extensive right of defensive war (belonging to states).
[22] The subtle, and disputable, contention is that the right of states to act pre-emptively against threats does not arise, strictly speaking, directly out of the natural-law right

17. On defensive war to weaken the power of a neighbour

Quite untenable is the position, which has been maintained by some, that according to the law of nations it is right to take up arms in order to weaken a growing power which, if it becomes too great, may be a source of danger.[23] That this consideration does enter into deliberations regarding war, I admit, but only on grounds of expediency, not of justice. Thus if a war be justifiable for other reasons, for this reason also it might be deemed far-sighted to undertake the war; that is the gist of the argument which the writers cited on this point present. But that the possibility of being attacked confers the right to attack is abhorrent to every principle of equity. Human life exists under such conditions that complete security is never guaranteed to us. For protection against uncertain fears we must rely on Divine Providence, and on a wariness free from reproach, not on force.

18. Whether defensive war is allowed to one who has given just cause for war

Not less unacceptable is the doctrine of those who hold that defence is justifiable on the part of those who have deserved that war be made upon them.[24] The reason they allege is, that few are satisfied with exacting vengeance in proportion to the injury suffered. But fear of an uncertainty cannot confer the right to resort to force. [H]ence a man charged with a crime, because he fears that his punishment may be greater than he deserves, does not, on that account, have

of self-defence per se. Its true source is the right of punishment. It could therefore be contended that Grotius actually recognised only two categories of just war rather than three: punishment and enforcement of rights (or obtaining of what is owed). Punishment, in turn, would be sub-divided, on this classification, into two kinds: punishment for past and completed wrongs, and punishment for impending wrongs. It is, however, probably more reasonable to found the right of defensive war on self-defence rather than on punishment – and consequently to regard Grotius as presenting three distinct categories of just war. Later writers generally took this view.

[23] The person cited as holding this view is Gentili, *On the Law of War*, 1.4. Gentili refers to defensive war as a war of 'expedient defence'. He refers to a war waged in self-defence properly speaking, i.e., to ward off an actual attack, as a war of 'necessary defence'.

[24] Gentili, *On the Law of War*, 1.13, is cited as advancing this erroneous view (i.e., as allowing a right of defensive war even to those who provoke an attack). It would be interesting to know whether Grotius thought that the position would be different in the case of self-defence by an *individual*, i.e., whether the individual right of self-defence is exercisable even by wrong-doers against those who exert lawful force against them, e.g., by convicted criminals against their executioners. This is not so for the right of defensive war by states, which is allowable only in face of impending wrong-doing. In this regard, then, it might be possible for a state's right of defensive war to be more restricted in scope than the individual's right of self-defence.

the right to resist by force the representatives of public authority who desire to take him.[25]

He who has done injury to another ought first to offer satisfaction to him whom he has injured, through the arbitrament of a fair-minded man. [I]f such an offer of satisfaction is rejected, then his taking up of arms will be without reproach.

---

[25] What is at stake in the present discussion is not a fear for the life of the state as such. The concern in this passage is with the fear on the part of the ruler of a state that has committed a prior wrong, that the injured state might exact greater violence against it for the wrong than the law of nature would allow. Grotius's point is that this fear, on its own, does not justify the state that committed the wrong in waging a defensive war to forestall such possible excessive action.

It is unfortunate that Grotius never spells out his views on self-defence, in the narrow sense, by states – i.e., whether he believes that the concept applies to states at all; and, if it does, whether the right is exercisable by wrong-doing states. The question, in other words, is whether Grotius believed (as Gentili did) that states possess a right of self-preservation analogous to that of individuals. Later international-law writers definitely did accord such a fundamental right to states, and it seems reasonable to suppose that Grotius would also have supported it. Modern international law accepts that states have a right of self-defence, exercisable in the face of an actual armed attack; but there continues to be uncertainty as to whether this right is exercisable against a lawful attack (such as enforcement action authorised by the UN Security Council).

2

Of things which belong to men
in common[1]

1. The division of that which is our own

Next in order among the causes of war is an injury actually received; and first, an injury to that which belongs to us. Some things belong to us by a right common to mankind, others by our individual right.

Let us begin with the right which is common to all men. This right holds good directly over a corporeal thing, or over certain actions. Corporeal things are either free from private ownership, or are the property of someone. Things not in private ownership are either such as cannot become subject to private ownership, or such as can. In order to understand the distinction fully, it will be necessary to know the origin of proprietorship, which jurists call the right of ownership.

2. The origin and development of the right of private ownership

Soon after the creation of the world, and a second time after the Flood, God conferred upon the human race a general right over things of a lower nature. . . . In consequence, each man could at once take whatever he wished for his own needs, and could consume whatever was capable of being consumed. The enjoyment of this universal right then served the purpose of private ownership; for whatever each had thus taken for his own needs another could not take from him except by an unjust act.[2]

---

[1] Here begins what is basically a gigantic diversion, extending for the next eighteen chapters, from his main theme – just causes of war – into a detailed exposition of the acquisition and scope of rights in natural law.

[2] It is important to appreciate that the reference is not to the acquisition of title to property, but rather to the acquisition of a right of possession, i.e., a right not to have one's actual physical possession disturbed by others. A full right of property differs from this, in that protection against interference is founded not on physical possession but rather on the holding of legal title. Such a full right of property only came into existence after human society had passed out of the state of nature, and had entered into politically organised communities, as explained later in this section.

This primitive state might have lasted if men had continued in great simplicity, or had lived on terms of mutual affection such as rarely appears. Of these two conditions, one, exemplified in the community of property arising from extreme simplicity, may be seen among certain tribes in America, which have lived for many generations in such a condition without inconvenience. The second, again, exemplified in the community of property arising from affection, was formerly realised among the Essenes,[3] afterward among the first Christians at Jerusalem; at the present time, also, by a goodly number who live an ascetic life.

Evidence showing the simplicity of the state of the first men who were created is to be found in their nakedness. Among them there was ignorance of vices rather than knowledge of virtue.... Men did not, however, continue to live this simple and innocent life, but turned their thoughts to various kinds of knowledge, the symbol for which was the tree of knowledge of good and evil, that is, a knowledge of the things of which it is possible to make at times a good use, at times a bad use.

The most ancient arts, agriculture and grazing, were pursued by the first brothers, not without some interchange of commodities. From the difference in pursuits arose rivalry, and even murder; and at length, since they were corrupted by contact with the wicked, there came the kind of life ascribed to the giants, that is given over to violence.... After the world had been cleansed by the Deluge, that brutish life was succeeded by a passion for pleasure, to which wine ministered; whence came also unlawful loves.

Harmony, however, was destroyed chiefly by a less ignoble vice, ambition, of which the symbol was the tower of Babel. Presently, men divided off countries, and possessed them separately. Afterward, nevertheless, there remained among neighbours a common ownership, not of flocks to be sure, but of pasture lands, because the extent of the land was so great, in proportion to the small number of men, that it sufficed without any inconvenience for the use of many.

Finally, with increase in the number of men as well as of flocks, lands everywhere began to be divided, not as previously by peoples, but by families. Wells, furthermore – a resource particularly necessary in a dry region, one well not sufficing for many – were appropriated by those who had obtained possession of them. This is what we are taught in sacred history; and it is quite in accord with what philosophers and poets . . . have said concerning the first state of ownership in common, and the distribution of property which afterward followed.

From these sources we learn what was the cause on account of which the primitive common ownership, first of movable objects, later also of immovable property, was abandoned. The reason was that men were not content to feed on

---

[3] The Essenes were a Jewish splinter group which flourished from the second century BC to the first century AD. They were said to have lived lives of voluntary poverty, and possibly to have held their property in common, as Grotius clearly believed. These features of their lives foreshadowed later Christian monasticism.

the spontaneous products of the earth, to dwell in caves, to have the body either naked or clothed with the bark of trees or skins of wild animals, but chose a more refined mode of life; this gave rise to industry, which some applied to one thing, others to another. Moreover, the gathering of the products of the soil into a common store was hindered first by the remoteness of the places to which men had made their way, then by the lack of justice and kindness; in consequence of such a lack, the proper fairness in making division was not observed, either in respect to labour or in the consumption of the fruits.

At the same time we learn how things became subject to private ownership. This happened not by a mere act of will, for one could not know what things another wished to have, in order to abstain from them – and besides several might desire the same thing – but rather by a kind of agreement, either expressed, as by a division, or implied, as by occupation. In fact, as soon as community ownership was abandoned, and as yet no division had been made, it is to be supposed that all agreed, that whatever each one had taken possession of should be his property.[4]

3. Things not subject to private ownership

Having laid down these fundamental principles, we say that the sea, viewed either as a whole or in its principal divisions, cannot become subject to private ownership. Since, however, such ownership is conceded by some in the case of individuals but not in the case of nations, we bring forward proof, first on moral grounds.

The cause which led to the abandonment of common ownership here ceases to be operative.[5] The extent of the ocean is in fact so great that it suffices for any possible use on the part of all peoples, for drawing water, for fishing, for sailing.

---

[4] The indication (not made very explicitly) is that the evolution of property-related rights evolved through three stages. The first stage had been marked by community of property, in which physical possession was protected from disturbance. In the second stage, physical possession acquired an additional significance: it conferred a full right of property onto the possessor. In other words, true property rights first evolved in this second era of the state of nature. Even in this second period, though, Grotius holds that 'no division had been made'. This means that there had been, as yet, no general parcelling out of the whole or larger part of the resources of the world amongst the global population. Property rights therefore existed in this second phase of the state of nature, but they could (as yet) only be acquired on an ad hoc basis, by means of an initial taking of physical possession. In the succeeding third stage of world history, there was a general (but not universal) 'division', or parcelling out, of the land of the world into privately owned portions. In this period, legal title was founded on receipt of the allocated shares, rather than on physical possession.

[5] It may be noted that the argument against ownership of the seas rests upon the impossibility, de facto, of satisfying the normal conditions of ownership with respect to it. It becomes apparent below, in Section 13, that Grotius concedes that it is, in fact, possible effectively to occupy certain portions of the sea.

The same thing would need to be said, too, about the air, if it were capable of any use for which the use of the land also is not required, as it is for the catching of birds. Fowling, therefore, and similar pursuits, are subject to the law laid down by him who has control over the land.

There is, furthermore, a natural reason which forbids that the sea, considered from the point of view mentioned, should become a private possession. The reason is that occupation takes place only in the case of a thing which has definite limits. . . . Liquids, on the contrary, have no limits in themselves. . . . Liquids therefore cannot be taken possession of unless they are contained in something else; as being thus contained, lakes and ponds have been taken possession of, and likewise rivers, because they are restrained by banks. But the sea is not contained by the land, since it is equal to the land, or larger; for this reason the ancients said that the land is bounded by the sea.

A division of the sea, further, is not to be imagined; for when the lands were first divided the sea was still for the greater part unknown. In consequence, no system can be conceived by which races so widely separated could have come to an agreement regarding such a division.

Those things, therefore, which were common to all men, and were not divided in the first division, no longer pass into private ownership through division, but through occupation.[6] And they are not divided until after they have become subject to private ownership.

4. How unoccupied lands become the property of individuals

Let us proceed to the things which can be made subject of private ownership, but have not yet become private property.[7] Of such sort are many places hitherto uncultivated, islands in the sea, wild animals, fish, and birds.

In this connexion, two points must be noted. Possession may be taken in two ways, either of an undivided whole, or by means of individual allotments. The first method is ordinarily employed by a people, or by the ruler of a people; the second, by individuals. Possession by individual allotments, nevertheless, is more often taken in consequence of a grant than by free occupation.

If, however, anything which has been occupied as a whole has not yet been assigned to individual owners, it ought not on that account to be considered as unoccupied property; for it remains subject to the ownership of the first

---

[6] By the 'first division' is meant the parcelling out, by agreement, of the areas of the world into privately owned plots. Anything that was not included in this process, such as the sea, can become subject to private ownership, but only by way of actual physical occupation (as had been the case in the state of nature prior to the general division of the world into private properties).

[7] I.e., the general division of the world into private estates, which took place in the third phase of world history, was not universal. Some places were left unallocated.

occupant, whether a people or a king.[8] To this class ordinarily rivers, lakes, ponds, forests, and rugged mountains belong.

5. Ownership of wild animals, fish and birds

In regard to wild animals, fish, and birds, this observation needs to be made, that whoever has control over the lands and waters can by his order prohibit any person from taking wild animals, fish or birds, and thereby acquiring them. Such an order is binding even upon foreigners, the reason being that, for the government of a people, it is morally necessary that foreigners who mingle with them even temporarily – as happens when foreigners enter a country – should conform to the institutions of that people.[9]

The principle stated is not at variance with what we often read in the Roman law, that according to the law of nature, or the law of nations, a man is free to hunt such animals. This holds true, in fact, so long as municipal law does not intervene; thus the Roman law left in their primitive condition matters concerning which different nations have established different usages. When, however, municipal law has laid down a different rule, the law of nature itself prescribes that this must be obeyed. For although municipal law cannot enjoin anything which the law of nature forbids, or forbid what the law of nature enjoins, it can nevertheless set limits to natural liberty, and forbid what by nature was permitted; thus, through exercise of the power which belongs to it, municipal law can by anticipation prevent an acquisition of ownership which by the law of nature might have been permitted.

6. The right to use the property of another in case of necessity

Now let us see whether men in general possess any right over things which have already become the property of another. Some perchance may think it strange that this question should be raised, since the right of private ownership seems completely to have absorbed the right which had its origin in a state of community of property. Such, however, is not the case. We must, in fact, consider what the intention was of those who first introduced individual ownership; and we are forced to believe that it was their intention to depart as little as possible from natural equity. For as in this sense even written laws are to be interpreted, much more should such a point of view prevail in the interpretation of usages which are not held to exact statement by the limitations of a written form.

---

[8] This refers to the continuing impact of the acquisition of property rights in the second phase of world history: when an initial physical occupation conferred full legal title, with the effect that that legal title remained with the first possessor even if physical possession was not continuous.

[9] This continues to be a basic principle of international law.

Hence it follows, first, that, in direst need, the primitive right of user revives, as if community of ownership had remained, since in respect to all human laws – the law of ownership included – supreme necessity seems to have been excepted.[10]

Hence it follows, again, that on a voyage, if provisions fail, whatever each person has ought to be contributed to the common stock. Thus, again, if fire has broken out, in order to protect a building belonging to me I can destroy a building of my neighbour. I can, furthermore, cut the ropes or nets in which my ship has been caught, if it cannot otherwise be freed. None of these rules was introduced by the civil law, but they have all come into existence through interpretations of it.

Even among the theologians, the principle has been accepted that, if a man under stress of such necessity takes from the property of another what is necessary to preserve his own life, he does not commit a theft. The reason which lies back of this principle is not, as some allege, that the owner of a thing is bound by the rule of love to give to him who lacks; it is, rather, that all things seem to have been distributed to individual owners with a benign reservation in favour of the primitive right.[11] For if those who made the original distribution had been asked what they thought about this matter, they would have given the same answer that we do. 'Necessity', says Seneca the father,[12] 'the great resource of human weakness, breaks every law',[13] meaning, of course, human law, or law constituted after the fashion of human law.

7. The requirement that the necessity be in no way avoidable

Admonitions, however, must be kept in mind, that this permission to use property belonging to another may not be carried beyond proper limits. The first is, that every effort should be made to see whether the necessity can be avoided in any other way, as, for example, by appealing to a magistrate, or even by trying through entreaties to obtain the use of the thing from the owner.

---

[10] This is an important exposition of the general principle of necessity in legal theory. See also p. 70 above. It has been given explicit recognition in modern international law in Article 25 of the Articles on State Responsibility (2001).

[11] The thesis is that the condition of necessity does not operate merely to impose a moral duty onto the owners of resources to share them. Rather, it confers a true right onto the person in distress, which he may exercise on his own initiative.

[12] The Elder Seneca (Lucius Annaeus Seneca), born about 50 BC, of whose life little is known. He wrote a history of Rome (now lost). He was the father of the more famous Younger Seneca, the eminent tragedian and Stoic philosopher. On the Younger Seneca, see p. 106 below, note 6.

[13] Elder Seneca, *Controversies*, IX.4.5. A more accurate translation is: 'Necessity is a great defence for feeble humanity'.

8. When the possessor has equal need

In the second place, this right cannot be conceded if the owner himself is under an equal necessity; for in like circumstances the position of the owner gives him the preference. 'He is not foolish', says Lactantius, 'who has not, even for his own safety, pushed a shipwrecked man from his plank, or a wounded man from his horse; for he has kept himself from the inflicting of an injury, which would be a sin; and to avoid such a sin is wisdom'.[14] Cicero had said, in his third book *On Duties*: 'Should not the wise man, therefore, if he is exhausted with hunger, take food away from another man who is of no account? By no means. For my life is no more precious to me than the possession of such a spirit that I would not harm any one for the sake of my own advantage'.[15]

9. The obligation to restore the things of another used in case of necessity

In the third place, restitution of another's property which has been used in case of necessity must be made whenever this can be done. There are some who hold a different opinion. Their plea is, that the man who has availed himself of his own right is not bound to make restitution. But it is nearer the truth to say, that the right here was not absolute, but was restricted by the burden of making restitution, where necessity allowed. Such a right is adequate to maintain natural equity against any hardship occasioned by private ownership.

10. Application of the right of necessity in the case of wars

From what has been said, we can understand how it is permissible for one who is waging a just war to take possession of a place situated in a country free from hostilities.[16] Such procedure, of course, implies these conditions, that there is not an imaginary but a real danger that the enemy will seize the place and cause irreparable damage; further, that nothing be taken except what is necessary for protection, such as the mere guarding of the place, the legal jurisdiction and revenues being left to the rightful owner; and, finally, that possession be had with the intention of restoring the place as soon as the necessity has ceased.

[14] Lactantius, *Divine Institutes*, V.17.   [15] Cicero, *On Duties*, III.29.
[16] In modern terminology, it would be said that Grotius is giving a justification for violation of the territorial sovereignty of neutral states in time of war, in exceptional cases of extreme necessity on the part of one of the belligerents. A typical illustration would be the occupation of neutral territory by the belligerent to forestall its opponent from occupying that same neutral territory and thereby gaining a military advantage. A classic example of an actual case of this was the British invasion of neutral Norway in 1940, to forestall an anticipated German invasion.

The first right then that, since the establishment of private ownership, still remains over from the old community of property, is that which we have called the right of necessity.

11. The right to use things which have become the property of another

A second right is that of innocent use. 'Why', says Cicero, 'when a man can do so without loss to himself, should he not share with another things that are useful to the recipient and can be spared without annoyance to the giver?'[17]

12. The right to the use of running water

Thus a river, viewed as a stream, is the property of the people through whose territory it flows, or of the ruler under whose sway that people is. It is permissible for the people or king to run a pier out into it, and to them all things produced in the river belong. But the same river, viewed as running water, has remained common property, so that any one may drink or draw water from it.

13. The right of passage over land and rivers

Similarly also lands, rivers, and any part of the sea that has become subject to the ownership of a people, ought to be open to those who, for legitimate reasons, have need to cross over them; as, for instance, if a people has been forced to leave its own territories and is seeking unoccupied lands, or desires to carry on commerce with a distant people, or is even seeking to recover by just war what belongs to it.[18] In such cases, the reason is the same as that stated above; it is altogether possible that ownership was introduced with the reservation of such a use, which is of advantage to the one people, and involves no detriment to the other. Consequently, it must be held that the originators of private ownership had such a reservation in view.

A noteworthy example we find in the history of Moses. When he found it necessary to pass through the territories of others, he offered first to the Idumaeans, then to the Amorites, these stipulations, that he would follow the king's highway and would not turn aside into private possessions; that if he should have need of anything belonging to them he would pay them a fair price.

---

[17] Cicero, *On Duties*, I.51. A more accurate translation has Cicero assert that 'if any assistance can be provided without detriment to oneself, it should be given even to a stranger'.

[18] Modern international law, with its insistence on the territorial sovereignty of states, does not accept the principle articulated in this passage.

When these terms were refused, for that reason he waged a just war against the Amorites.[19]

The correct view is that which lies between extremes. It holds that permission to pass ought first to be demanded; but, if it is refused, passage can be made by force.

Furthermore, no one will be justified in raising the objection that he fears the numbers of those passing through. My right is not extinguished by your fear; all the less in this case, for the reason that there are precautions which can be taken, as, for example, by arranging that troops be sent across in separate detachments; or . . . without their arms. . . . Another precaution is, for the one who grants the passage to hire suitable garrisons for his own protection, at the expense of him who makes the passage; or to see that hostages are given.[20]

Thus, again, fear of the ruler, against whom the one requesting passage is waging a lawful war, cannot be urged as a valid excuse for refusing passage. Equally inadmissible is it to say that passage could be had by another route; for any one might say the same thing, and in that way the right of passage would be altogether done away with. But it is enough if passage is demanded without evil intent, by the route which is nearest and most convenient. If he who wishes to pass is obviously commencing an unlawful war, or if he is bringing enemies of mine with him, I can refuse the passage; it would be right to meet him on his own ground, and hinder his passage.

Such passage, furthermore, ought to be conceded not only for persons but also for merchandise. No one, in fact, has the right to hinder any nation from carrying on commerce with any other nation at a distance. That such permission be accorded is in the interest of human society and does not involve loss to any one; if one fails to realise an anticipated gain, to which he is not entitled, that ought not to be accounted a real loss.

14. Whether a tax may be imposed upon merchandise passing through a country

But the question is raised, whether merchandise in transit through a country, transported across the land, or by river, or over a part of the sea which may be considered as belonging with the land, can be made subject to taxes by him who holds the sovereign power in the country. Surely equity does not permit the imposition of any burdens that have no relation to the merchandise actually in transit. Similarly, a capitation tax levied on citizens to help carry the expenses of the state cannot be collected from foreigners who pass through.

---

[19] *Deuteronomy*, 2: 26–36.
[20] Hostages are envisaged as being given voluntarily, as sureties for the good conduct of those undertaking the passage – with the hostages then to be released once the passage is completed as arranged.

If, however, expenses are incurred in furnishing protection for the merchandise, or other burdens also are increased on account of it, then a tax may be levied upon the merchandise in order to make reimbursement, provided that in determining the tax the amount actually required shall not be exceeded;[21] for upon this depends the justice of a tax as well as of tribute.

15. The right of temporary sojourn

To those who pass through a country, by water or by land, it ought to be permissible to sojourn for a time, for the sake of health, or for any other good reason; for this also finds place among the advantages which involve no detriment. . . . A natural consequence of this is that it is permissible to build a temporary hut, for example on the seashore, even if we admit that possession of the coast has been taken by a people.

16. The right of those who have been driven from their homes to reside in another country

Furthermore a permanent residence ought not to be denied to foreigners who, expelled from their homes, are seeking a refuge, provided that they submit themselves to the established government and observe any regulations which are necessary in order to avoid strifes.[22]

17. The right of possession over desert places in respect to foreigners

Again, if within the territory of a people there is any deserted and unproductive soil, this also ought to be granted to foreigners if they ask for it. [I]t is [the] right [of] foreigners . . . to take possession of such ground, for the reason that uncultivated land ought not to be considered as occupied except in respect to sovereignty, which remains unimpaired in favour of the original people.[23]

18. The right to such acts as human life requires

After the common right, which relates to things, follows the common right which relates to acts. The common right relating to acts is conceded either directly or by supposition. It is conceded directly in respect to acts indispensable

---

[21] In such a case, the 'tax' would really be more in the nature of a fee for services.

[22] The contention, in effect, is that refugees have a right of admission to states for the purpose of obtaining asylum. Modern international law does not grant such a right, although it does provide for certain standards of treatment of refugees *after* they have been admitted.

[23] The point is that the foreigners who occupy the deserted land do not thereby acquire political sovereignty over it. What the foreigners have instead is a right of settlement and not a right of annexation or of acquisition of sovereignty.

for the obtaining of the things without which life cannot be comfortably lived. Here, in fact, the same degree of necessity is not required as for taking another's property; for it is not now a question of what may be done against the will of an owner, but rather of the mode of acquiring things with the consent of those to whom they belong;[24] provided only that no obstacle be interposed by the passing of a law or by conspiracy. Such a hindrance, in fact, is at variance with the nature of society.... For we are here dealing not with things which are superfluous and ministrant to pleasures only, but with things which life requires, as food, clothing, and medicines.

19. The right to buy the things that are necessary

We affirm, therefore, that all men have the right to buy such things at a fair price, unless they are needed by the person from whom they are sought; thus in times of extreme scarcity, the sale of grain is forbidden.

Not even in circumstances of so great need, however, can foreigners, who have once been admitted to a country, be expelled; ... a common misfortune must be endured in common.[25]

20. The absence of an obligation to sell

But there is not an equally valid right obliging a man to sell what belongs to him; for everyone is free to decide what he will or will not [sell].[26]

21. The right to seek marriages in foreign countries

In this right, ... we think there is included also liberty to seek and contract marriages among neighbouring peoples; as, for example, in case a large number of men has been expelled from one place and has come to another. Although, to be sure, it is not entirely repugnant to human nature for a man to live without a woman, nevertheless this is repugnant to the nature of most men. Celibacy

[24] The 'common right relating to acts' refers basically to the right to enter into transactions with other parties – with consent on both sides – for the obtaining of things necessary to life, without interference by third parties.
[25] There has been a slight jumping of topics. Grotius is now referring to a case of a general famine in a country in which a number of foreigners are resident. There might be a temptation, in such an emergency, to expel the foreigners so that the limited supplies can be shared amongst the smaller population of nationals. Grotius holds that the foreigners cannot lawfully be expelled in such a circumstance (according to natural law).
[26] It may seem odd that Grotius posits the existence of a right to buy, while at the same time asserting that there is no correlative duty to sell. The practical effect, therefore, is that, if a third party interferes with a would-be buyer's attempt to make a purchase from a willing seller, then that third party thereby commits a wrong. If, however, the 'seller' simply refuses to sell, then no wrong is committed.

is suited only to those who possess superior endowments. Men ought not, therefore, to be cut off from the opportunity to secure wives.

The civil laws of some peoples, which deny the right of marriage to foreigners, either support their contention by this consideration, that at the time when the laws were passed there were no peoples without an abundance of women; or else they do not treat of marriages of all kinds but only of those which are regular, that is, marriages which produce certain special effects in civil law.[27]

22. The right to do those things which are permitted to foreigners in general

A common right by supposition relates to the acts which any people permits without distinction to foreigners; for if under such circumstances a single people is excluded, a wrong is done to it. Thus if foreigners are anywhere permitted to hunt, fish, snare birds, or gather pearls, to inherit by will, to sell property, and even to contract marriages in case there is no scarcity of women, such rights cannot be denied to one people alone, except on account of previous wrong-doing.

23. Such a right is limited to things permitted as it were by the law of nature

What we have said about permissible acts must be understood as applying to acts which have been permitted as deriving from the force of natural liberty, which have not been annulled by any statute law; not as applying to acts which have been permitted by favour, as an exception to the law. In the refusal of a favour, there is no injustice.

24. Whether a contract for exclusive sale to one people is permissible

I recall that the question has been raised, whether it is permissible for a people to make an agreement with another people to sell to it alone products of a certain kind, which do not grow elsewhere. I think that this is allowable, if the people which buys is prepared to sell to others at a fair price. It makes no difference, in fact, to other nations, from whom they buy what satisfies the demands of nature.[28]

---

[27] The implication is that it is permissible, under natural law, for states to confine certain legal effects of marriage to their own nationals. For example, a state might provide that property passes automatically from one spouse to another upon the death of either – while providing that that was only the case if both spouses were nationals of the state. Grotius's point is that such preference cannot, under natural law, go so far as to exclude foreigners altogether from intermarriage with nationals.

[28] In other words, a monopoly sale arrangement does not violate natural law, so long as the goods in question are *eventually* made available for general purchase. It was

It is lawful, however, for one people to [be given a preference over others] in obtaining a pecuniary advantage, especially if there is a reason; as, for instance, if the people which has obtained the concession has taken the other under its protection and on that account is incurring expense. Such an arrangement to purchase, made with the intent of which I have spoken, is not at variance with the law of nature, although in practice it is sometimes forbidden by municipal law in the public interest.[29]

generally agreed (though Grotius does not discuss the point here) that the hoarding of goods for resale in times of shortage at 'famine prices' was wrongful. In English law, this was the common-law offence of regrating. The purchase of large quantities for such purposes (i.e., the 'cornering' of a market) was the common-law offence of engrossing.

[29] It will be recalled that natural law, according to Grotius, has three basic categories of acts: things required, things forbidden, and a neutral category between, comprising acts which are allowed without being either compulsory or forbidden. Acts in that middle category can be prohibited by man-made law. A concrete example is given here.

3

Of original acquisition of things, with special reference to the sea and rivers

1. Original acquisition through division or occupation

From the view-point of individual right, a thing becomes our own through acquisition, either original or derivative. Formerly, when the human race could assemble, primary acquisition could take place also through division, as we have said.[1] [N]ow it takes place through occupation only.

2. Exclusion from consideration of other modes of acquisition

Someone may perchance say that a kind of primary right is acquired through the granting of a servitude, or the giving of a pledge.[2] To him who carefully weighs the matter, however, it will become apparent that, under such conditions, there is no new right except in form; for in essence the right was present in the proprietary right of the owner.[3]

3. Exclusion from consideration of the forming of a new property from existing materials

To the means through which acquisition may be accomplished, Paul the Jurist adds also this – which seems altogether consistent with nature – 'that we

[1] By 'division' is meant an agreed allocation.
[2] A pledge is the entrustment of possession of a good by an owner to someone else, pending the due performance of some kind of obligation on the part of the pledgor (i.e., with the pledgee entitled to retain possession of the object so long as the obligation remains unfulfilled). The point is that servitudes and pledges are not 'primary rights' – meaning that they are only, as it were, delegations to other persons by the owner of some of his pre-existing rights as owner. They therefore only involve a sharing-out of rights of ownership, and not the creation of any new rights additional to those of ownership.
[3] The point is that the pledging of property, or the granting of a servitude, does not actually create any legal right or power which did not exist already – i.e., does not create a 'primary right'. The reason is that the powers of the holder of a pledge (to have custody of property) or of a servitude (to use property in some way) were powers that the owner already had, simply by virtue of his ownership. The creation of a pledge or servitude therefore involves only a sharing-out of existing powers of ownership, rather than the creation of anything new.

have caused something to come into existence'. In nature, however, nothing is produced except from matter which previously existed. If, then, the material belonged to us, the ownership of that which is produced will continue, even though a new form is presented. If the material belonged to no one, in that case acquisition will be classed under the head of acquisition by occupation. On the other hand, if the material used was the property of another, the thing produced naturally does not belong to us alone, as will become apparent later.[4]

4. Occupation as twofold, having relation to sovereignty and to ownership

It is, then, occupation – which since those primitive times has been, and remains, the only natural and primary mode of acquisition – with which we are concerned. Now in respect to that which, in a proper sense, belongs to no one, there are two possible types of possession, sovereignty (*imperium*) and ownership (*dominium*), in so far as ownership is distinguished from sovereignty.[5] The difference between the two types is thus brought out by Seneca: 'To kings belongs the power over all things; to individuals, proprietorship.'[6] Dio [Chrysostom] makes the distinction clear in this way: 'The territory belongs to the state, but nonetheless on that account does each person in it have his own property.'[7]

Sovereignty is customarily extended over two kinds of subject matter. The one, primary, consists of persons; this alone is sometimes in itself sufficient, as in the case of an army of men, women, and children seeking new places of habitation. The other, secondary, is extended over the place, which is called territory.

---

[4] See p. 167 below.

[5] This fundamental distinction between sovereignty and ownership (*imperium* and *dominium*) is, unfortunately, not explained as clearly as it should be. Basically, ownership, or *dominium*, is a right available to private citizens, as well as to governments, entailing the right to the exclusive use of something (i.e., the right to exclude others from use) and the right to sell or will the property in question to other private parties. Sovereignty, or *imperium*, belongs only to governments and entails the right to make laws and to enforce them, by the use of force if necessary, as well as to maintain public order generally. These terms, and the distinction between them, come directly from Roman law.

[6] Seneca, *On Benefits*, VII.4.2. Lucius Annaeus Seneca (c. 4 BC – AD 65, known as the Younger Seneca) was one of the most famous literary and intellectual figures of ancient Rome. He was a famous tragedian and Stoic philosopher, as well as tutor to the future Emperor Nero. He also wrote on natural science. He fell out with his former pupil and, after being accused of involvement in a conspiracy against him, was ordered to commit suicide. This made him into a rival of Socrates as a martyr to intellectual integrity in the face of political oppression.

[7] Dio Chrysostom, 'Oration No 31, To the Rhodians', 47. Dio Chrysostom (or Dio of Prusa) was a renowned Greek orator of the first and early second centuries AD, as well as a philosopher and historian. Some eighty of his orations survive (in Latin), but none of his philosophical or historical works.

Although sovereignty and ownership are generally acquired by a single act, they are nevertheless distinct. Consequently, ownership passes not only to citizens but also to foreigners, while the sovereignty remains in the hands of him who previously held it.

5. Prohibition by law of taking possession of movable things

We said above that, in a place over which sovereignty has already been asserted, the right to acquire movable things through occupation can be prevented by the municipal law.[8] This right exists, in fact, by permission of the law of nature, not by a positive provision that such permission should always be granted; for no such provision is demanded by the requirements of human society.[9]

If someone says that there seems to be a law of nations implying such permission,[10] I shall answer that, although in some parts of the world this is, or has been, the common usage, nevertheless such usage does not have the force of an agreement between nations, but is the expression of a law received by several countries individually, which can be abrogated by each of them.[11] There are also many other practices which jurists, when they are dealing with the division of property and the acquisition of ownership, consider as belonging to the law of nations.

6. Right of ownership of property by infants and by insane persons

It must be noted, further, that, if we have in view the law of nature alone, ownership is restricted to those who are possessed of reason. But in the common interest, the law of nations introduced the provision, that both infants and insane persons should be able to acquire and retain ownership – the human race, as it were, meanwhile representing them.

Human laws indisputably have it in their province to go further than nature in regard to many points, but never to go contrary to nature. Hence this type of ownership, which by common acceptation of civilised nations has been

[8] See p. 96 above.
[9] I.e., the right to acquire property by occupation is provided for by natural law. Consequently, there is no need for it to be confirmed by positive (or man-made) law.
[10] I.e., implying that acquisition of property by occupation must be allowed.
[11] It is apparent from the context that by 'law of nations' is meant the *volitional* law of nations, which requires agreement between states. Grotius contends that there is no such agreement between states establishing a man-made rule that title to property by occupation must be allowed. It is conceded that such a rule does exist in many states. But Grotius insists that this practice does not result from an agreement between the countries of the world, as is required for a rule of the volitional law of nations. Rather, the practice results from various individual states choosing unilaterally to adopt such a rule. As a result, the rule permitting acquisition of ownership by occupation is (in Grotius's opinion) a rule of natural law only, not of the volitional law of nations.

introduced in favour of infants and those of similar condition, is limited to the first act, as the Schools say, and cannot extend to the second act; that is, it covers the right of proprietorship, but not the right of the owner himself to use what he owns. For alienation, and other acts similar thereto, by their very nature presuppose the action of a will controlled by reason, and in such persons a will subject to reason cannot exist.

7. Whether rivers can be acquired by occupation

By occupation, rivers can be acquired[12] even though neither their upper nor their lower course is included in the same territory, but they are connected with water at the upper and the lower end, or with the sea. It is sufficient that the greater part, that is that the sides, shall be enclosed by banks, and that the river by itself shall be small in extent in comparison with the land.

8. Whether a part of the sea can be acquired by occupation

In the light of the example just given, it would appear that the sea also can be acquired by him who holds the lands on both sides,[13] even though it may extend above as a bay, or above and below as a strait, provided that the part of the sea in question is not so large that, when compared with the lands on both sides, it does not seem a part of them.

The same right, further, which is conceded to a single people or king, appears to be conceded also to two or three, if they have wished to occupy jointly a sea situated between them; in this way, in fact, rivers which flow between two peoples have been jointly occupied, and then divided.

9. Ownership of a part of the sea in the countries constituting the Roman Empire

It must be admitted that, in the parts of the world that were known in connexion with the Roman Empire, from the earliest times even down to Justinian, it was not permitted by the law of nations that the sea be acquired by states through occupation, even in respect to the right to fish.[14] Heed should not be paid to those who think that when, in the Roman law, the sea is spoken of as common to all, the meaning is that the sea is the common possession of all Romans. For in the first place, the expressions are so general that they do not admit of such

---

[12] It is not explicitly specified whether the reference is to acquisition of ownership (by private parties) or of sovereignty (by states). Grotius is probably referring to both.

[13] Here too, it is not made clear whether the acquisition in question is of ownership or sovereignty. Again, Grotius is probably referring to both.

[14] Yet again, it is not made explicit whether the reference is to the acquisition of ownership or of sovereignty. From the context, it appears that ownership is intended.

restriction. . . . Ulpian said that by nature the sea lies open to all, and so belongs to all just as the air does.[15] Celsus declared that the use of the sea is common to all men.[16]

The jurists, furthermore, clearly distinguish the public possessions of a people, in which rivers, too, are included, from things that are common.[17] Thus we read in the *Institutes*: 'By the law of nature some things are common to all – the air, running water, the sea and consequently the shores of the sea. On the other hand, all rivers and harbours are public property.'[18]

Of the shores of the sea, Neratius[19] said that they are not public possessions in the sense that those things are which have become the possession of a people by inheritance, but as those things which were at first the gift of nature and have not yet become subject to the ownership of anyone, that is, not even of a people.[20] This opinion is clearly at variance with what Celsus wrote: 'I think that the seashores, over which the Roman people possesses sovereign power, are the property of the Roman people, but that the use of the sea is common to all men.'[21]

These opposing views can evidently be reconciled if we say that Neratius is speaking of the seashore in so far as its use is necessary for those sailing the sea, or passing by, while Celsus is speaking of it with reference to possession for a use unlimited in time, as for a permanent structure.[22] In the latter case,

---

[15] *Digest*, 8.4.13 (Ulpian). Ulpian (Domitius Ulpianus), a native of Tyre, was one of the most prominent of Roman lawyers, serving as the chief legal adviser to Emperor Alexander Severus in AD 224–8. His career came to an abrupt end in 228, when he was murdered by mutinous troops. He has the distinction of having more passages in the *Digest* than any other writer, accounting for nearly one-third of that entire collection.

[16] *Digest*, 43.8.3 (Celsus). P. Iuventius Celsus was the leader (with Neratius) of the Proculian school of Roman lawyers in the late first and early second centuries AD. He served as praetor (judge) and twice as consul. On Neratius, see n. 19 below.

[17] The distinction here is a subtle one. By 'public possessions of a people' is meant things which are owned (i.e., subject to *dominium*) – but owned collectively by the people as a whole. In the case of such things, foreigners can be excluded from use. This is to be contrasted to 'things which are common', which means things which may be freely used by all persons in the world because no one owns them (or has *dominium* over them), either individually or collectively, such as the oceans. It should be appreciated that when reference is made to things that are owned by a people as a whole, the concern is with ownership (or *dominium*) rather than sovereignty (or *imperium*).

[18] Justinian, *Institutes*, 2.1.1–2.

[19] Neratius Priscus was a Roman law writer who was identified as the leader (with Celsus) of the Proculian school of lawyers. Active in the second century AD, he held high political office, including the consulship. On Celsus, see n. 16 above.

[20] *Digest*, 41.1.14 (Neratius).   [21] *Digest*, 43.8.3 (Celsus).

[22] A valiant attempt is being made to interpret the Roman-law sources as being consistent, but it is not altogether persuasive. Contrary to Grotius's suggested resolution, Neratius did envisage the building of a permanent structure on the

Pomponius[23] tells us a permit was wont to be obtained from the praetor, just as a permit was required for the construction of a building in the sea, that is, in the part nearest the shore, which is reckoned as belonging to the shore.[24]

10. Acquisition of a part of the sea which is shut in by lands

Although what was just said is true, nevertheless it has resulted from established practice[25] rather than from natural reason, that the sea was not occupied, or could not lawfully be occupied, in the sense in which we have spoken.[26] A river also is public property, as we know; and yet the right to fish in a branch of a river can be acquired by an individual by occupation.[27] But even concerning the sea, Paul the Jurist said: 'If a man does have a right of property in it, he is entitled to a decree of court protecting him in his possession.'[28] [T]he reason is that the case affects a private and not a public interest, since the question at issue concerns a right of user, which is inherent in a private, not a public matter. Paul's statement without doubt refers to a small portion of the sea which is admitted into a private estate.... Of Gaius Sergius Orata, Valerius Maximus says: 'He made seas his individual possessions by shutting up waters in the inlets.'[29]

Now if a part of the sea can be added to estates of individuals, provided, of course, that it is enclosed and is so small that it can be considered a portion of an estate, and if the law of nature presents no obstacle to such procedure, why, also, may not a part of the sea enclosed by shores belong to that people, or to those peoples, to which the shores belong, provided that part of the sea, when

---

seashore. He held that, since the shore was common to all, any person had such a right, which he compared to rights obtained over wild animals when actual possession had been gained. If the building was removed, Neratius went on to explain, the place on the shore where it had stood reverted to its previous status as owned by no one. It would appear, then, that the views of Neratius and Celsus really were in conflict.

[23] Sextus Pomponius was a prolific writer on Roman law in the second century AD. No details of his career are known.

[24] *Digest*, 41.1.50 (Pomponius). The requirement for a permit was a decisive indication that the shore (and adjacent sea area) were regarded as the collective property of the Roman state and people, rather than as areas owned by no one.

[25] Footnote by Grotius: 'Such an established practice the English also utilised against the Danes.'

[26] I.e., the prohibition in, for example, Roman law against ownership of the sea or portions of it was not a rule of natural law, but instead was a rule of human creation.

[27] *Digest*, 44.3.7 (Marcion). This provision of the *Digest* establishes that, by fishing along a public riverbank for a lengthy period of time, a person can acquire the right to exclude others from fishing in that area. What is gained, then, is a legal right to exclude others from the area, i.e., a legally protected right of occupation, rather than full legal ownership.

[28] *Digest*, 47.10.14 (Paul). Grotius slightly mis-quotes the provision. What the person is said to be entitled to is a legal right to gain possession of the surrounding land.

[29] Valerius Maximus, *Memorable Doings and Sayings*, 9.1.

compared in extent with the land of the country, is not larger than an enclosed inlet of the sea compared with the size of the private estate?[30] [N]o objection can be raised on the score that the sea is not enclosed on all sides.

But many things, which were permitted by nature, universal customary law (*ius gentium ex communi*), by a kind of common understanding, has been able to prohibit. Consequently, wherever such a law is in force, and has not, by common consent, been abrogated, a portion of the sea, however small and almost enclosed by shores, cannot become subject to the ownership of any people.

11. How such possession may be taken, and how long it will last

It must also be noted that, if in any place this universal customary law in regard to the sea (*ius illud gentium de mari*) has not been accepted, or has been abrogated, from the mere fact that a people has taken possession of the land, the inference would nevertheless not be warranted that it has obtained possession of the sea also;[31] that, further, an act of the mind is not sufficient, but that there must be an outward act from which the taking of possession may be understood.[32]

But if, on the other hand, possession resulting from occupation is abandoned, the sea again comes under the law of nature, that is, it is restored to common use.

12. Possession as subject to the right of innocent passage

It is certain that one who has occupied a part of the sea cannot hinder navigation which is without weapons and of innocent intent, when such a passage cannot be prevented by land, where it is generally less necessary and more productive of damage.[33]

---

[30] Given that portions of the sea – very small portions, to be sure – can be acquired by individuals by way of occupation, it follows (according to Grotius) that collectives of individuals (i.e., states) can similarly occupy correspondingly larger portions of the seas. In each case, though, the occupation must actually be effective; and no more of the sea can be claimed than is in fact actually so occupied.

[31] The possibility is raised that there may be places in which the customary law prohibiting acquisition of possession of the seas has not been accepted or has been abrogated. In such places, the natural-law right of acquisition of possession automatically becomes applicable. But Grotius points out that mere occupation of a coastal land area does not, by itself, entail acquisition of possession of the adjacent seas

[32] The reference, made almost in passing, is to the two crucial criteria for the acquisition of ownership by occupation: an intention to effectuate an occupation (an 'act of the mind' as Grotius rather vaguely puts it); coupled with 'an outward act' which will indicate that intention to the world at large.

[33] This right of innocent passage remains a fundamental principle of the law of the sea today.

13. Whether sovereignty can be acquired over a part of the sea

It has, however, been a fairly easy matter to extend sovereignty (*imperium*) only over a part of the sea, without involving the right of ownership (*dominium*); and I do not think that any hindrance is put in the way of this by the universal customary law (*ius illud gentium*) of which I have spoken.... It seems clear, moreover, that sovereignty over a part of the sea is acquired in the same way as sovereignty elsewhere, that is, as we have said above, through the instrumentality of persons and of territory. It is gained through the instrumentality of persons if, for example, a fleet, which is an army afloat, is stationed at some point of the sea;[34] by means of territory, in so far as those who sail over the part of the sea along the coast may be constrained from the land no less than if they should be upon the land itself.[35]

14. Taxes upon those who sail upon the sea

It will not ... be contrary to the law of nature or of nations if he who has taken upon himself the burden of protecting navigation and of making it safe by

[34] The clearest example of a state stationing a fleet at sea, as 'an army afloat', is the blockading of an enemy coast or port during wartime, when a fleet of the blockading state is on continuous patrol to prevent passage to or from the blockaded area. In modern conflicts, states have sometimes declared 'exclusion zones' over portions of the high seas; but the lawfulness of these remains contentious.

[35] Parts of the sea adjacent to coasts may be 'constrained from the land' most obviously by means of fortifications on the land, which dominate areas of the sea by artillery fire. The point is that sovereignty over portions of the sea (*imperium*) is more easily acquired than ownership (*dominium*). The reason is that a state has sovereignty wherever and whenever its armed forces hold sway (in areas where no sovereign power was previously in place), even for very short periods of time, whereas acquisition of ownership by occupation requires a continuous and lasting presence. A naval fleet at sea may be said to have sovereignty over the patch of the sea on which it is sailing at any given time, and within range of its guns. Similarly, a state has sovereignty over an adjacent coast if it has artillery trained on the coastal waters in question. Notice that it is essential to this line of thinking that the artillery be *actually* in place. It is not sufficient, according to Grotius, that coastal waters *could* be covered by artillery fire *if* the government so chose.

   In the course of time, Grotius's position fell out of favour and was replaced by a general consensus that states possess, basically as a matter of *dominium*, a belt of the seas adjacent to their coasts, without the need for an actual exercise of military force. A trace of the connexion between armed force and possession of sea areas remained, however, in the thesis that the extent of a state's possession of offshore sea areas must be limited to the area that *could* be dominated from the land – i.e., a state should be entitled to a belt of territorial sea equal in width to the range of cannon shot fired from the land. Modern international law permits coastal states to claim ownership (or *dominium*) over the seas to a maximum distance of twelve nautical miles from the shore.

night-flares and marks indicating shoals shall impose a fair tax on those who sail.

15. Agreements which forbid a people to sail beyond certain bounds

Examples of treaties are to be met with in which one people binds itself to another not to sail beyond a certain limit.... Such examples, nevertheless, do not show that occupation is had of the sea or possession of the right of navigation. Peoples, just as individuals, can in fact by agreements grant in favour of one concerned not only a right which they possess in their own name but also a right which they hold in common with all men.

16. Whether a change in the course of a river involves a change of territory

When a river has changed its course, frequently strifes arise between neighbouring states over the question whether at the same time the limits of jurisdiction are changed, and whether any additions made by the river belong to those to whose territories they have been added. Disputes of this sort should be settled according to the nature and mode of acquisition.

The surveyors tell us that there are three kinds of lands: the first, divided and allotted land, which [is called] delimited, because it has limits set off by artificial boundaries;[36] the second, land allotted as a whole, or designated by measure, as by hundred-acre parcels and by acres; and [third] land having natural frontiers, which is so called . . . because it has boundaries suitable for keeping off enemies, that is, natural boundaries, as rivers and mountains. These last are called . . . 'lands under occupation', since in most cases they are lands occupied either because they are vacant, or by right of war.

In the case of the first two kinds of lands, even though a river changes its course, no change of territory is occasioned; and if anything is added by alluvial deposits, this will fall under the jurisdiction of the previous occupants.[37] In the case of lands having natural frontiers, a river by gradually changing its course changes the boundary also, and whatever the stream adds to either side becomes subject to the jurisdiction of the state to whose territory it is added; it is in fact believed that both states originally took possession of their territories with the intention that the river lying between should separate them as a natural boundary.

---

[36] See *Digest*, 41.1.16 (Florentinus).
[37] See *ibid*. In other words, in cases in which properties are marked out, rather than described with reference to natural features (such as 'land between line X and the Such and Such River'), the lands remain as marked out. A shift in the river course, or the deposit of additional land by means of alluvial silt, has no effect on the location of the defined boundaries.

17. If the bed of a river has been completely changed

What has been said will be applicable only in case the river has not changed its bed. For a river, even where it serves as a boundary between countries, is not considered to be merely where the water is, but where the water flows in a certain channel, and is confined by certain banks. Wherefore the addition or removal of particles, or such a change as leaves the former appearance of the stream substantially unchanged, permits the river to seem the same.

If, however, the appearance of the river as a whole be at the same time changed, the case will be different. As a river which has been blocked by a dam in the upper part of its course ceases to exist, and a new river is formed in the excavated channel into which its water is conducted, so if a river, abandoning its old course, has burst through in a different channel, it will not be the same as it was before, but a new river, the former river having ceased to be. In such a case, the boundary of a country would remain in the middle of the channel which had last existed, just as if the river had dried up. For it must be held that the purpose of the peoples was to accept the river as a natural boundary between them. If, then, the river had ceased to exist, in that case each would retain what he had previously possessed. In like manner, when the channel changes, the same rule ought to be observed.

In cases of doubt, however, sovereign states which border on a river must be considered as having a boundary set off by a natural frontier. Nothing, in fact, is more suitable for separating such states than a boundary which is not easily crossed. It less often happens that states have boundaries set off by an artificial line of demarcation, or designated in terms of extent; but such cases arise less frequently from primary acquisition than from a grant made by another.

18. If an entire river belongs to a single territory

Although, as we have said, in case of doubt, the jurisdiction of two states bordering on the same river extends to the middle of the stream, nevertheless it might happen, and we see that in some places it has happened, that the river as a whole belongs to the one state;[38] the reason being, of course, that jurisdiction over the opposite bank began to be exercised at a later time, after the river had already been occupied, or that the matter had been settled in such a way by agreement.

19. On things which have been abandoned

It is not out of place to remark also that primary acquisition must be conceded as possible in the case of those things which have had an owner, but have ceased

---

[38] A modern-day example is the San Juan River in Central America, which divides Nicaragua from Costa Rica, and which belongs wholly to Nicaragua.

to have one, either because they have been abandoned, or because there are no longer persons having the right of ownership over them. Such things have returned to the condition in which they originally were.

The following point, however, must at the same time be noted, that sometimes primary acquisitions by a state or by the head of a state have been so made that not only the sovereignty – in which is included the right of eminent domain, of which I have treated elsewhere[39] – but also full private ownership was first acquired in common for the state or its head; and that then a distribution was made individually to private persons, in such a way, nevertheless, that their ownership was dependent on that earlier ownership – if not in the way that the right of a vassal is dependent on the right of his lord, or the right of the permanent tenant on that of the landowner, yet in some other way that is less binding; for there are many forms of right over property, among which also is the right of one who administers a bequest for the benefit of someone else.

When, therefore, private properties distributed in the manner just described are dependent on common ownership,[40] if any property is found to lack an individual owner, it does not belong to the occupant,[41] but reverts to the community or to the higher lord. Even without such a cause, a right similar to this right of the law of nature could be conferred by a municipal statute.

---

[39] See p. 226 below.
[40] I.e., are derived from a prior original ownership, either by the sovereign or by the people in common.
[41] By 'occupant' is meant a person who takes physical possession of the property with the intention of becoming its owner by right of occupation.

4

On assumed abandonment of ownership and occupation consequent thereon; and wherein this differs from ownership by usucaption and by prescription

1. Whether ownership by usucaption or by prescription occurs between states[1]

A serious difficulty arises at this point in regard to the right of usucaption. For since this right was introduced by municipal law (time, in fact, in its own nature has no effective force; nothing is done by time, though everything is done in time) it has no place . . . in the relations between two independent states.[2] This seems to be true except in so far as a thing or an act is governed by the laws of the land. But if we admit this, a very serious inconvenience clearly follows, in that contests about kingdoms and the boundaries of kingdoms never come to an end with lapse of time. Such a condition, again, not only tends to disturb the minds of many and to occasion wars, but is also contrary to the common sense of nations.

3. The importance of presumptions of human intent[3]

What shall we say? Actions at law, which are dependent on intent, cannot indeed be inferred from a mental act alone, unless that act has been indicated

---

[1] Usucaption was a principle of Roman law, to deal with the situation in which property was transferred from one person to another, but without the formalities required by Roman law for the passage of legal title. In such cases, the recipient could nonetheless obtain good title, by continuous possession of the item for a period of one year. Essential to this process was that the original transfer had been voluntary on the part of the prior owner. Somewhat similar was the device of prescription, also from Roman law. Here, however, the acquisition by the second party occurs without the consent of the original owner. Nevertheless, the passage of time cures this defect, analogously to the case of usucaption. After the expiry of three years of continuous possession for movable property (i.e., objects) or ten years for immovable (i.e., land and things fixed to the land), the possessor acquires full legal title. Originally, prescription only gave legally protected possession (i.e., was a defence to an action for recovery by the original owner); but in later law, it gave full title.

[2] The contention is that usucaption was an institution of Roman civil law alone and not of the law of nations or of natural law.

[3] In the remainder of this chapter, the proposition is advanced that, although time *alone* cannot cure defects of legal title to property, time in combination with an

by certain outward signs. For to assign a legal effect to mere acts of the mind was not consistent with human nature, which is able to recognise such acts only from outward signs. And for this reason, purely mental acts are not subject to human laws.

Outward signs, however, do not indicate mental acts with mathematical certainty, but only with probability. For men can say something different from what they desire and feel, and can disguise their intentions by their actions. Nevertheless, the nature of human society does not allow that no effect be given to mental acts which are sufficiently indicated. And so, whatever has been sufficiently indicated is considered as true in respect to him who has indicated it. Thus, as regards words, at any rate, the difficulty is solved.

4. Such presumptions as based on acts

A thing which is thrown away is understood by the act to be abandoned, unless the circumstances of the case are such that we ought to think it was thrown aside for the moment and with the intention of recovering it later. Thus a debt is considered discharged by the return of the note. . . . Thus if anyone is the owner of a thing and knowingly treats with another who has it in possession, as if with its owner, he is deservedly considered to have abandoned his right. And there is no reason why this should not be the case also between kings and independent states.

Similarly, a higher officer who permits an inferior to do, or commands him to do, that which he cannot lawfully do unless he is freed by law, is understood to have freed him from the law.

The principle under consideration in fact has its origin not in municipal law but in the law of nature, according to which every man has the right to abandon his own; and further, in a natural presumption, in accordance with which one is believed to have wished that of which he has given sufficient indications.

5. Such presumptions as based on things not done

Under acts, moreover, consistently with moral standards, failures to act are included, considered with relation to the circumstances which ought to be taken into account. Thus he who keeps silence, when present and cognisant of

intention of abandonment by a prior owner can do so. Properly speaking, therefore, title does not pass directly from the first owner to the second one, as in the cases of usucaption and prescription. Instead, a two-phase process is posited, which has the same practical effect: the original owner abandons the property and then, in a separate act, the second party acquires title by occupation. An initial problem, to which Grotius first attends, is how to discern intention (i.e., intention of abandonment) on the basis of outward conduct.

the facts, seems to give consent. . . . Thus a thing is considered lost if the hope
of its recovery is abandoned.

For example, Ulpian says that hogs carried off by a wolf, and what we lose
in a shipwreck, cease to be ours, not immediately, but when recovery seems
impossible;[4] that is, in cases in which there is no reason why anyone should be
expected to retain the thought of ownership, when no indications of such an
intent exist. If persons had been sent to look for the property, or 'a reward' had
been offered, we should have had to judge otherwise. Thus a person who knows
that his property is in the possession of another, and during a long period makes
no claim against the possessor, unless some other reason is manifest, seems to
have pursued this course with no other thought than because he no longer
wished that object to be considered among his possessions.

Very similar to this is what appears in the establishment of a custom. For
a custom also, without regard to the laws of a state which fix a certain time
and manner for its introduction, can be introduced by a subject people in
consequence of the fact that it is tolerated by the one who holds the sovereignty.[5]
But the time within which a custom receives the effect of law is not definitely
fixed, but arbitrary, to wit, whatever length of time is sufficient to accord with
the implied consent.[6]

However, in order that silence may establish the presumption of abandonment of ownership, two conditions are requisite: [firstly] that the silence be that
of one who acts with knowledge; [and secondly, that the person act] of his own
free will. [Regarding the first of these], the failure to act on the part of one who
does not know is without legal effect. [Regarding the second], when another
apparent cause for the action appears, the inference of an act of will ceases to
be in point.

6. Length of time together with non-possession and silence as abandonment of right

That these two conditions, then, may be considered to be present, is established
by other indications, but, in the case of both, length of time is a paramount
consideration. In the first place, it can hardly happen that, with length of time,
property belonging to a man should not come to his notice, since lapse of time
offers many opportunities for such cognisance. Nevertheless, in the case of those
who are at hand, a shorter space of time suffices to establish this inference than in
the case of parties who are absent, aside from the stipulations of municipal law.
Again, fear, once inspired, is believed to endure for a time, but not indefinitely,
since length of time furnishes many opportunities for taking counsel against
the fear, either by oneself or with the help of others, and even by leaving the

---

[4] *Digest,* 41.1.44 (Ulpian).
[5] Aquinas, *Treatise on Law,* pp. 356–7; and Suárez, *Treatise on Laws,* 7.13.
[6] Suárez, *Treatise on Laws,* 7.15.

territory of the one feared; in consequence, at length a complaint may be made concerning infringement of a right, or, what is better, an appeal may be made to judges or arbitrators.

7. Time exceeding the memory of man as sufficing for such a presumption

Because a length of time exceeding the memory of man is in its essential character practically infinite, a silence for that length of time will always seem sufficient to imply abandonment of ownership, unless there are very strong reasons to the contrary. It has also been well remarked by the better jurists that time exceeding the memory of man is not the same as a century, although these two limits often are not far apart, for the reason that a hundred years ordinarily constitute the limit of human life. This period, again, generally equals three ages, or 'generations', of men.

8. Whether anyone can be assumed to abandon his right

The objection may be raised that, since men love themselves and their possessions, it ought not to be believed that they would abandon their own property; and that, in consequence, negative acts, even through a long space of time, are not sufficient to warrant the inference which I have mentioned. But again, we ought to think that good should be expected of men; and for that reason it ought not to be supposed that they have such a disposition that, out of consideration for a mere perishable thing, they would wish a fellow man to live in a continual state of sin. Without such abandonment of ownership, such a result often cannot be avoided.

In regard to the exercise of sovereign power, although generally it is greatly esteemed, we ought to know that the burdens are great, and that failure to administer them well renders a man subject to divine wrath.[7] Just as it would be a wrong thing for two persons, who claim to be guardians, to go to law at the expense of the ward in order to determine which of the two should have the right of guardianship; or . . . for the sailors with danger to the ship to struggle in order to determine which of them would best do the steering, so those are not always worthy of praise who with the greatest loss, and often with the bloodshed of innocent people, desire to decide who is to control the government of that people. . . . It is, then, to the interest of human society that governments be established on a sure basis and beyond the hazard of dispute; and all implications which point in that direction ought to be looked upon with favour.

---

[7] This paragraph seems only most distantly related to the topic of inferring intention to abandon property.

Now if those indications, which I have mentioned, should not be present, nevertheless against the presumption, according to which it is believed that each man wishes to keep his own, the other presumption has greater weight, because it is not credible that anyone in a long time should give no clear indication of what he wishes.

9. Transfer of ownership by possession exceeding the memory of man

Perhaps without improbability it can be said that this adjustment is not based on presumption alone, but that, in accordance with the volitional law of nations, the provision was introduced that possession beyond the limits of memory, not interrupted nor called in question by appeal to the courts, should absolutely transfer ownership. It is in fact credible that the nations agreed in this, since it was of the greatest importance for the preservation of the common peace.

10. Whether unborn children can in like manner be deprived of a right

At this point another, and indeed an exceedingly difficult question, arises, whether those not yet born can tacitly lose their right by such an abandonment. If we say that they cannot, the explanation just given has contributed nothing to the tranquillity of empires and estates, since most of these are held under such conditions that they ought to pass to the descendants. If we affirm that they can, it will seem strange that silence can harm those not able to speak, since in fact they do not exist; or that the act of one party should entail loss for another.

In order to solve this problem, the fact must be recognised that a person who is not yet born has no rights, just as a thing which does not exist has no attributes. If then the people, from whose will the right to rule arises, changes its will, it does no injustice to those yet unborn, since they have not yet acquired any right. Moreover, as a people can change its will openly, so it can be believed to have changed its will tacitly. If, therefore, the people has changed its will, while the right of those who may be expected to come is not yet in existence – and besides that very right has been abandoned by the parents from whom those may be born who were to possess the right in their own time – there is nothing to hinder another from occupying property under these conditions as ownerless.

We are treating of the law of nature. For as other fictions have been introduced by the civil law, so this provision may be introduced also, that meanwhile the law should defend the persons of those who do not yet exist, and should thus hinder anything from being seized to their disadvantage. Nevertheless, we should not hastily judge that such is the intent of the laws because, in such cases, private advantage is strongly opposed to public advantage.

Nothing in fact makes it impossible that such a provision should be introduced into the law of a state that a thing, which cannot be lawfully alienated by a single act, can nevertheless, in order to avoid uncertainty of ownership, be lost by neglect for a fixed period of time; and even under such a provision those born later will have the right of personal action against those guilty of neglect, or against their heirs.

11. Acquiring the right of sovereignty by long-standing possession

From what we have said, it is plain that a king can acquire a right as against a king, and an independent state as against an independent state, not only by express agreement, but also by abandonment of ownership and the occupation which follows it or assumes a new force from it. For the common saying, that 'what is not valid from the beginning cannot become valid from a subsequent act', is subject to the exception, 'unless a new cause has intervened capable in itself of producing a right'.

Similarly also, the true king of a people may lose his sovereignty and become subject to the people; and he who in reality is not a king, but only the foremost citizen, can be made king with absolute power; and the supreme authority, which was wholly in the power of either king or people, can be divided between them.

12. Whether the civil statutes concerning usucaption and prescription bind the sovereign

It is also worthwhile to investigate this question, whether a law dealing with ownership by usucaption or by prescription, and established by one who has sovereign power, can apply also to the right of sovereignty itself, and to the necessary parts of it which I have explained elsewhere. Not a few jurists, who treat of sovereignty in accordance with Roman municipal law, think that such a law does apply. But I think otherwise. For in order that anyone may be bound by a law, both power and intent, at least presumed, are requisite in the maker of the law. No one can bind himself after the manner of a law, that is after the manner of a superior.[8] Hence it is that the makers of laws have the right to change their own laws. Still, one can be bound by his own law, not directly, but by implication inasmuch as he is a member of the community, he is under an obligation imposed by natural fairness, which desires that the parts be adjusted in relation to the whole.[9]

---

[8] I.e., a person cannot impose a law onto himself. A binding law must emanate from a political superior.

[9] In other words, a person can bind himself legally not by simple pronouncement or fiat, but only by virtue of principles of general natural law which might give rise, as a

Again, the intent [that sovereignty be potentially transferred by usucaption or prescription] is not presumed to have been present, because the makers of laws are not considered as intending to include themselves, except in cases where both the subject-matter and the reason for the law are universal, as in fixing prices. But sovereignty is not of like character with other things; rather, in its exalted rank it far exceeds other things. I have not seen any civil statute treating of prescription which included sovereignty, or could be considered with probability to have intended to include it.

From these considerations, it follows that the time defined by such a statute [on prescription] is not sufficient for acquiring sovereignty or a necessary part of it, if the natural implications which we mentioned above are lacking; that so great a length of time is not required if such implications are present within the time to a sufficient degree; and, lastly, a civil statute, which forbids that property be acquired within a fixed time, does not have anything to do with matters of sovereignty.[10]

Nevertheless, in a transfer of sovereignty, the people could express its will as to the manner and time in which the sovereignty might be lost by failure to exercise it.[11] This expressed will would undoubtedly have to be followed, and could not be infringed upon even by a king possessed of sovereign power, because it applies not to the sovereignty itself but to the manner of holding it. But of this distinction I have spoken elsewhere.[12]

13. Rights ancillary to sovereignty gained and lost by usucaption or prescription

Those powers which do not belong to the nature of sovereignty, and do not have relation to it as essential parts, but can be naturally separated from it or at least shared with others, are entirely subject to such statutes of each people as have been passed concerning ownership by usucaption and by prescription. Thus we see that there are subjects who have acquired by prescription the right to judge without appeal; yet in such a way that there is always some sort of appeal from them, as by petition, or by some other means. For that anyone should be

matter of fairness or equity or good faith, to an obligation on the person's part to act in accordance with a self-made 'law'.

[10] The thesis is that a municipal law on passage of title to property by prescription will not apply to transfers of sovereignty. If the intention to transfer sovereignty be absent, then the passage of any amount of time, however long, will not effect a transfer. Conversely, if the intention to transfer sovereignty *is* present, then a short period of time by the new sovereign in actual possession can suffice to effect the transfer. In either case, the law on prescription of private property is not relevant.

[11] In other words, at the time at which sovereignty is initially conferred onto a ruler by 'the people', the condition can be added that the exercise of sovereignty will be lost by a failure to exercise it for a fixed and stated period.

[12] For the general discussion of sovereignty, see p. 50 above.

beyond the right of appeal is inconsistent with the character of a subject, and therefore this right belongs to sovereignty or to a part of it, and can be acquired in no other way than by the law of nature, to which sovereignties are subject.

14. Whether subjects are always allowed to assert their liberty

From this, it is apparent to what extent we can accept the assertion of some, that it is always permissible for subjects to regain their liberty, that is, the independence of the people, if they can. The reason given is that a sovereignty won by force can be overthrown by force, while a sovereignty which has arisen from the will of the people may be repented of, and the will may change.

In truth, sovereignties which were at first won by force may receive lawful confirmation by tacit acceptance; and the will of the people, either at the very establishment of the sovereignty, or in connexion with a later act, may be such as to confer a right which for the future is not dependent on such will.[13]

For the rest, I think it not in the least open to doubt that long indifference, such as I have described above, on the part of a king may suffice to warrant a people in recovering their freedom, on the ground of presumed abandonment of sovereign rights.

15. Whether things belonging to faculty can be lost by lapse of time[14]

There are rights which do not involve daily exercise, but an adjustment once for all when it shall be convenient, as the redeeming of a pledge by payment. Also, there are rights of free action, to which the act engaged in is not directly opposed, but is included therein as a part in the whole; an illustration would be if anyone has had an alliance with one neighbour only during a hundred years, while nevertheless it was in his power to have alliances with others also. These rights are not lost, except in consequence of a prohibition or restraint, and when obedience has been rendered thereto, with a sufficient indication of consent. Since this is in accord not only with municipal law but also with natural reason, it will properly apply also in the case of men of the highest rank.

---

[13] That is, the people may decide to confer the sovereign power absolutely onto the person who took power by force. If so, then (in Grotius's opinion) the sovereign power has been fully alienated and cannot be recovered without the sovereign's own consent or acquiescence. See p. 51 above.

[14] By faculty is meant a legal power to do something, without any obligation to do it.

5

On the original acquisition of rights over persons. Herein are treated the rights of parents, marriage, associations, and the rights over subjects and slaves

1. Rights of parents over children

A right is acquired not only over things but also over persons. Such rights have their origin primarily in generation, consent, or crime. By generation, parents acquire a right over children – both parents, I mean, the father and the mother. But if there is variance in the exercise of these rights, the right of the father is given preference on account of the superiority of sex.

2. The period of infancy, and ownership of property by infants

Moreover, in dealing with children, three periods must be distinguished. The first is that of imperfect judgement, . . . while there is lack of discretion. . . . The second is the period of mature judgement, but while the son still remains a part of the family of the parents, that is so long as he has not separated from it. . . . The third is the period after the son has withdrawn from the family.

In the first period, all the actions of children are under the control of the parents; for it is fair that he who is not able to rule himself be ruled by another. . . . But naturally no one except the parents can be found to whom such control may be committed.

Nevertheless, in this period also, a son or a daughter, according to the law of nations, is capable of ownership of property, though the exercise of the right is hindered on account of the imperfection of judgement which I have mentioned. . . . Wherefore it is not due to natural right that all the possessions of children are [the property of] their parents, but to the [municipal] laws of certain peoples, which also in this matter distinguish the father from the mother, sons not of age from those that are of age, and illegitimate children from legitimate. But nature ignores these distinctions, except as regards that supremacy of sex which I have mentioned, in case of conflict of the parents regarding the exercise of parental rights.

3. Of the period of life in the family beyond infancy

In the second period, when judgement has now matured with age, no other actions are subject to the rule of parents except those which in some way are important for the position of the family in relation to the father or the mother. It is in fact fair that the part should conform to the interest of the whole. In other actions, then, children in that period have 'power', that is, a moral faculty of action; but nevertheless, in those acts they are bound to desire always to please their parents. However, since this obligation does not arise from the moral faculty, as in the previous case, but from filial affection, respect, and gratitude, it does not make void anything done contrary to it, just as the donation of anything which has been made by the owner contrary to the rules of economy is not void.[1]

4. Concerning the right of restraining children

In both these periods, the right to govern embraces also the right to chastise, in so far as children must be forced to do their duty, or must be corrected. There will elsewhere be an opportunity of discussing what ought to be thought in regard to severer punishments.[2]

5. Concerning the right of selling children

Although the paternal authority is so attached to the person and 'character' of the father that it cannot be taken away and transferred to another, nevertheless by natural right a father can pledge his son as security, if the civil law does not prevent, and can even sell him, if it is necessary and there is available no other means of supporting him. . . . Indeed nature herself is deemed to give the right to everything without which that cannot be obtained which she demands.[3]

6. Of the period of life beyond infancy and outside of the family

In the third period, though filial affection and respect are always due, since the cause remains, yet the son is in all things 'independent' and his own master. From this, it follows that the acts of kings cannot be said to be void on this account, [simply] because they have parents [who are living].

---

[1] By 'rules of economy' is probably meant rational economic conduct. For example, a person may, in a fit of generosity, donate money to a charity which he cannot, on rational inspection, readily afford to part with. The donation would not be void on that ground.

[2] See p. 282 below.

[3] This is an application of the general natural-law principle that, if a person is required to do something, then he must necessarily be understood to possess the right to do anything which is necessary to fulfil that obligation.

7. The power of parents by the law of nature and by the municipal law

Whatever powers there are beyond those mentioned arise from volitional law, which is different in different countries.[4]

8. The right of the husband over the wife

Rights which arise over persons from consent come either from association or from subjection. The most natural association appears in marriage. However, on account of the difference in sex, the authority is not held in common, but 'the husband is the head of the wife', of course in matters relating to marriage and in matters relating to the family. The wife, in fact, becomes a member of the husband's family; and so the husband has the right to determine matters of domicile.

If any right beyond these is conceded to husbands, as in Hebraic law the right to annul vows of the wife, and among some peoples the right of selling the wife's property, such a right does not come from nature but from enactment. This subject requires us to see what the nature of marriage is.

Marriage, then, according to the law of nature, we consider [to be] such a cohabitation of a man with a woman that it places the woman under the eye of the man and under his guardianship. Such a union it is in fact possible to see even in some kinds of dumb animals. But in the case of man, as an animate being endowed with reason, there is added to this the vow by which the woman binds herself to the man.

9. Whether denial of divorce and requirement of monogamy are part of the law of nature

Nature does not seem to require anything more [beyond the vow of the woman to bind herself to the man] in order to constitute a marriage, nor indeed does the divine law seem to have demanded anything further before the spread of the Gospel.

Furthermore, the method is prescribed [in the Old Testament] for one who wishes to divorce a wife,[5] and no one is hindered from marrying a divorced woman except the one who divorced her, and the priest.[6] Nevertheless, this liberty of passing to another husband ought to be so restricted by the law of nature that confusion of offspring may not arise.

---

[4] By 'volitional law' is meant the domestic laws of various individual countries.
[5] See *Deuteronomy*, 24: 1–4, in which it is made apparent that a divorce becomes effective when a husband writes a 'certificate of divorce' and gives it to the wife.
[6] See *Leviticus*, 21:7, for the prohibition against marriage to divorced women by priests.

10. Effect of lack of consent of the parents

Now let us see what marriages are valid by the law of nature. In reaching a decision on this matter, we ought to remember that not all acts which are contrary to the law of nature are rendered invalid by it, as is apparent from the example of the extravagant gift; but only those are invalid in which the essential point is lacking to give validity to the act, or in which the fault continues in the result of the action. The essential principle, both here and in other human acts, out of which right arises, is that right which we have explained as a moral capacity for action, joined with a will sufficiently free.[7] But what freedom of will is sufficient to produce validity of action will be more conveniently discussed below, where we shall treat of promises in general.[8]

Under the moral right of action, the question here arises concerning the consent of the parents, which certain writers require as if by the law of nature for the validity of marriage. But in this they are wrong. For the arguments they offer prove nothing else than that it is in accord with the duty of children to obtain the consent of their parents. This I plainly grant, with the proviso that the wish of the parents be not manifestly unfair. For if children owe respect to their parents in all things, certainly they owe it especially in a matter which concerns the whole family, as marriage does. But from this it does not follow that the son lacks that right which is characterised as faculty or power to act.[9] For a man who takes a wife ought to be of mature age, and since he withdraws from the family, he is not subject to family rule in this matter. Moreover, the duty of proper respect alone has not the effect of rendering of no effect an act opposed to it.

Moreover, the rule established by the Romans and some other peoples, that certain marriages are void because the consent of the father is lacking, is not derived from the law of nature, but from the will of the lawgivers.

11. Marriages with the husband or wife of another, according to the law of the Gospel

Marriage with a woman who is married to another is undoubtedly void according to the law of nature, unless the former husband has divorced her; for up to the time of divorce his right over her continues. According to the law of Christ,

---

[7] That is to say, that, in general, there are two prerequisites to a legally efficacious act: the power on the part of the actor to perform the act, and a free will on the actor's part. If these two criteria are satisfied, then the act will have legal effect, even if it is contrary to natural law.

[8] See p. 191 below.

[9] As on other occasions, it is noted that legal powers (or faculties) are not co-extensive with rights and duties. In this case, the child has a *duty* (in Grotius's view) to seek the consent of his or her parents before marrying – but the child nonetheless possesses the *power* to marry, even without that consent.

his right continues until death has severed the bond. The marriage is void for this reason, that the moral faculty is lacking; this was taken away by the former marriage, and all the results are faulty.[10] The individual acts in fact involve an unlawful appropriation of that which belongs to another.

On the other hand, according to the law of Christ, a marriage with a man already married to another woman is void on account of the right which Christ gave to a virtuous woman over her husband.[11]

12. Marriages with relatives, according to the law of nature

The marriage of those who are united by blood or by relationships of marriage presents a difficult question, which not infrequently gives rise to heated discussions. For if one tries to assign definite natural causes why such marriages are unlawful – just as they are forbidden by laws or customs – he will learn from experience how difficult, if not impossible, the task is. . . . [The fact that] friendships are extended more widely by contracting marriage alliances in many places is not of so great weight that anything contrary to it would have to be considered void and unlawful. That which is less advantageous is not in fact thereby also illegal.[12]

Add a situation which may arise. This lesser advantage may be offset by another greater advantage,[13] not merely in the case of which God made an exception in the law given to the Jews, where a man has died without offspring;[14] or . . . for the purpose of keeping ancestral estates in the family; but also in many other cases, which are commonly observed, or can be imagined.

[10] In other words, the act of marriage has the legal effect of depriving the wife of the *power* to conclude a subsequent marriage (in the absence of divorce), not merely of the *right* to do so. Hence, any purported subsequent marriage will be automatically void *ab initio*.

[11] Notice the difference in treatment as between husbands and wives. A wife is barred from taking a second husband by *natural* law, as just explained. A husband, however, is barred from taking a second wife by *divine* law. In both cases, though, the effect is the same: that the purported second marriage is void.

[12] One of the explanations sometimes proffered for laws against marrying relatives is, in essence, a public-policy one: that requiring marriage outside of family circles is a device for cementing friendships with other family groups, thereby promoting social harmony generally. Grotius appreciates the sense behind such a policy, but he holds that it is not actually strong enough to account for the laws in question.

[13] In other words, the disadvantage that arises from marriage within a family – the loss of opportunity to conclude an alliance with another family – is genuine, but it can sometimes be offset by other factors.

[14] A reference to the biblical practice of a man marrying the wife of a deceased brother, if the deceased brother and the wife had been childless. The purpose was to ensure the production of offspring, even if only, so to speak, by proxy. The first son born of this union will be given the name of the deceased brother. See *Deuteronomy*, 25:5–6.

From this general principle,[15] I except the marriage of parents of any degree[16] with their descendants, the reason for the unlawfulness of which is, unless I am mistaken, quite apparent. In such a case, the husband, who by the law of marriage is the superior, cannot show such respect to his mother as nature demands, nor the daughter to her father;[17] for although the daughter in the marriage relation is inferior, nevertheless marriage itself introduces such an association that it excludes the respect belonging to the former relationship. . . . Therefore, we must not doubt that such marriages are both unlawful and void, because the fault inheres permanently in the effect.

This point ought . . . to be discussed, whether, in addition to that which, as we have already said, can be attained to by reason, there does not exist, implanted in men who have not been corrupted by evil education, a kind of [instinctive] revulsion against unions with parents or with children, especially since such unions are naturally avoided by certain dumb animals.[18]

13. Marriages within a single line of descent

Next comes the question concerning all the different degrees of marriage and of blood relationship in collateral lines, particularly those which are expressly mentioned in the eighteenth chapter of *Leviticus*.[19] For even granted that those prohibitions do not come from the pure law of nature, nevertheless they may seem, by a command of the divine will, to have passed over into that which is forbidden. In truth, this command is such that it binds not only the Jews, but rather all men. . . . Now those laws which were given to the whole human race do not seem to have been annulled by Christ, but merely those laws which separated the Jews from other nations as if by an interposed wall.

The following are the designations of [prohibited kinds of marriage by a given man, within his line of descent, according to the Jews]: . . . to use

---

[15] I.e., the general principle that marriage within a household is allowed when the important interest of producing offspring and heirs is at stake.

[16] By 'parents of any degree' is meant any lineal ancestor. This includes the immediate parents, but also grandparents, great-grandparents, and so on.

[17] I.e., a son cannot show the required degree of respect to a mother if the son is also the husband of the mother. Nor can a daughter show the necessary respect to a father if she is also the wife of that father.

[18] There is a long-standing school of thought to the effect that incest avoidance in humans is a matter of biological instinct and is therefore not of social origin. Although Grotius states that the matter 'ought . . . to be discussed', he actually fails to do so. It is nevertheless reasonably easy to surmise Grotius's opinion on the point. He was an adherent of the rationalist version of natural law, which posited a sharp distinction between humans and animals. Resemblances in behaviour between the two would therefore be regarded as merely coincidental and of no deep significance. Consequently, even if the *fact* of incest avoidance has a biological or instinctive basis, the *law* against it must be rooted, as is all of natural law, in reason.

[19] This chapter contains an extensive list of prohibited sexual relations.

the Roman terms, all grandmothers and great-grandmothers, stepmothers' mothers, great-granddaughters, stepdaughters' daughters, daughter-in-laws' daughters and mother-in-laws' mothers [meaning, in general, relationships in the first three degrees],[20] beyond which it is scarcely possible that controversy should arise, since if it could the same reckoning might go on to infinity.

14. Marriages with collateral relatives

This plain statement [prohibiting marriages in a line of descent within the third degree of relationship] seems to indicate the distinction between these and other more distant relatives. For it is forbidden to marry an aunt on the father's side; it is not, however, forbidden to marry a brother's daughter, where the degree of relationship is the same,[21] and there are to be found examples of such a marriage among the Jews. . . . The reason given by the Jews is that young men constantly visit the homes of grandfathers and grandmothers, or even live in them along with their aunts; but their access to homes of brothers is less frequent, and in these they do not have the same rights.

If we accept this explanation, which seems quite consistent with reason, we shall acknowledge that, from the time when the human race began to be numerous, the law against the marriage of relatives in the direct line and with sisters has been permanently valid, and common to mankind, since it rests on a natural sense of honour. In consequence, whatever is done contrary to this law becomes void, since the defect is permanent. The other laws nevertheless are

---

[20] Degrees of relationships within a direct line of descent are counted simply by the number of generations separating the persons in question. A father and daughter are one generation apart and therefore related in the first degree. A father and granddaughter are related in the second degree. Notice that step relatives and in-laws are treated as if they were part of the single line of descent.

[21] Degrees of relationship between any two collaterals (i.e., relatives not in the same line of descent) are determined by starting with either person and then counting the number of generations upward to the common ancestor, and then downward to the other party. A brother and sister are therefore related in the second degree (counting one generation up to the common parents and then one generation back). A 'distinction' is pointed out between the prohibition of marriages in a single line of descent and marriages with collaterals. With collaterals, the rule of prohibition within the first three degrees is not consistently followed, given that marriage by a man to a niece is permitted while marriage to an aunt is forbidden – both of these being related to the man in the third degree. From the standpoint of natural law, it would appear that these two putative marriages should be treated equally (either both allowed or both banned). The fact that one is allowed and the other not indicates that divine law, rather than natural law, governs the situation. It was God's decision to treat these two would-be unions differently, and that decision overrides considerations of natural law or the demands of logical consistency.

not on the same basis, since they contain a mode of prevention rather, which can be exercised in other ways.[22]

But it must at the same time be understood that what is forbidden by human law, if done, is not also void, unless the law has added a provision to this effect, or indicated that it will be.[23]

15. On concubinage as a type of marriage

To proceed to other topics, this observation should be made, that a certain form of concubinage is in reality a valid marriage, although it is deprived of certain effects peculiar to municipal law, or even loses certain natural effects by the hindrance of the municipal law.[24] ... [I]n the state of nature, there could be a true marriage ... if the woman was under the husband's protective care and had promised him fidelity.

16. Marriages that are unlawfully contracted

Again, if a human law forbids that marriage be contracted between certain persons, it does not therefore follow that the marriage, if in fact contracted,

[22] The point of this passage is not very clear. Grotius is suggesting that a law disallowing marriage by a man with sisters or with any females in the direct line is valid and universal, since it simply replicates 'a natural sense of honour', i.e., is in effect instinctual. Preventing marriages with various collateral relatives is justifiable, but there are other ways to achieve this than by a legal prohibition. For example, customary practices restricting free access by males to the females in question could have the same effect, in which case a formal rule would not be needed. This seems to skirt the main issue, though, which is whether a purported marriage with a collateral would be void. It would seem that, if such a marriage was held to be void, then that could only be pursuant to a rule prohibiting it.

[23] It is contended that any marriage to relatives which is prohibited by either natural law or divine law is automatically void *ab initio*, on the ground that humans lack the *power* to enter into them. The position is different, however, regarding man-made laws that prohibit marriages to relatives which natural or divine law would allow. These 'additional' man-made laws merely remove the *right* to enter into the marriages in question, not the *power* to do so.

[24] The point is that it is possible for two people to be validly married according to natural law, but without the marriage being valid according to the municipal law of the state in which they lived. For example, marriage vows may have been duly exchanged, but without the witnesses required by local municipal law being present. In such a case, the relationship would be one of valid marriage according to the one law, and concubinage according to the other. The practical effect would be that certain legal consequences of marriage which were established by the municipal law would not be present. For example, if tax privileges were given by municipal law to married persons, then the couple in question would not qualify. It is also possible that the municipal law could interfere with marital rights or duties which natural law conferred. This could occur with regard to such matters as duties of support or rights to inherit property.

will be invalid. To prohibit and to annul are in fact two different things. For a prohibition can exert its force through a penalty, whether express or arbitrary.[25] ... Often, in fact, there is greater impropriety in the [actual performance of a prohibited] act than in its results. Often, again, the inconveniences which result from annulment are greater than the improprieties themselves, or than the disadvantage of the act itself.

17. The right of the majority in associations

Besides the most natural association of marriage, there are other associations, both private and public. Public associations are formed either by a people or by peoples. All associations have this in common, however, that in those matters on account of which the association was formed, the entire membership, or the majority in the name of the entire membership, may bind the individual members.[26] In general, it must be believed that it was the wish of those who united in an association that there should be some method of conducting business.[27] But it is manifestly unfair that the majority should be ruled by the minority. Therefore, naturally, the majority has the same right as the entire body, if due exception is made of agreements and laws which prescribe the form of conducting business.[28]

18. Which opinion should prevail in case of a tie vote

If the votes are equal, no action will be taken, because there is not sufficient weight to carry a change. For this reason, where the votes for and against are equal, the accused is considered acquitted.

19. What opinions should be divided and what joined

At this point, question is usually raised in regard to the combining or separating of votes. According to the pure law of nature, that is, if no other rules have been laid down by agreement or by statute, clearly a distinction should be made between opinions that are entirely different and those of which one contains

[25] In other words, the effect of prohibiting an act might be merely to expose the actor to a criminal penalty – whilst leaving the legal effects of the act in place.
[26] Vitoria, *On Civil Power*, 14.
[27] In other words, it should be presumed that persons who form a corporate body must intend that there be some rational process by which that body can make decisions without risk of deadlock. A requirement of unanimity for decisions would clearly run that risk.
[28] I.e., it is possible that the rules of the association, established at the time of formation, might prescribe some other method of decision, such as unanimity or a majority of, say, two thirds or three quarters.

a part of the other, so that the latter ought to be combined in whatever they agree, but the former cannot be combined.

Thus, when some favour a fine of 20, others of 10, they will unite on 10 against the vote for acquittal. If, however, some vote for the death penalty, and some for banishment of the accused, these votes will not be combined, because they are different, and banishment is not included in the death penalty. But neither will those who vote for acquittal be combined with those who vote for exile, because, although they agree in not favouring the death of the accused, nevertheless this is not what the vote itself declares, and the matter is one of inference; for he who votes for banishment does not vote for acquittal.

20. Position of those who are absent

This point must also be added. If any members cannot avail themselves of their right by reason of absence or some other hindrance, their right in the meantime accrues to those present.[29]

21. What rank is to be observed among equals, even kings

The natural order of rank among members of an association is the order in which they entered it. So this order is preserved among brothers, since the first born takes precedence, and so on in succession, with disregard of all other qualities.

22. Voting in associations which are based upon property

Yet the following must be added. In the case of an association having its foundation based on property in which all do not share equally, as in an inheritance or an estate, in case one has a half, another a third, another a quarter, then not only must the order according to the amount of participation be followed, but also the votes must be counted in proportion to the shares, that is, to use a technical expression, *pro rata.* This is in accord with natural justice and was approved by the laws of the Romans also.[30]

23. The right of a state over its subjects

An association in which many fathers of families unite into a single people and state gives the greatest right to the corporate body over its members. This in fact

---

[29] The meaning seems simply to be that absent members are not counted in the determination of a majority, e.g., that a vote of a majority means a majority of those present and voting, not a majority of the whole membership.

[30] *Digest,* 2.14.8 (Ulpian).

is the most perfect society. There is no lawful act of men which does not have relation to this association either of itself or by reason of the circumstances.

24. Withdrawal of nationals from a state

Here the question is commonly raised, whether it is permissible for nationals to withdraw from their state without permission. We know that there are peoples among whom such withdrawal is not permissible, as the Muscovites; and I do not deny that a civil society can be formed on such terms, and that such a custom may receive the force of agreement.

But we are inquiring what would naturally be the rule if nothing else were agreed upon;[31] and not regarding a part of a state, but a whole state, or even the limits of a single empire. And surely, that the nationals of a state cannot depart in large bodies is quite clear from the necessity underlying its purpose, which in moral matters takes the place of law. For if such migration were permissible, the civil society could not exist.

The withdrawal of individuals, on the contrary, seems a different matter, just as it is one thing to draw water from a river, and another to conduct the stream into a canal. . . . Yet here also we must observe the rule of natural justice which the Romans followed in putting an end to private associations: that a thing should not be permitted if it is contrary to the interests of [the association].[32] . . . [I]t will be to the interest of the civil society that [a] national [does] not withdraw if a heavy debt has been contracted, unless the national is prepared to pay his share at once. Likewise if war has been undertaken because of confidence in numbers;[33] and especially if a siege threatens, unless the national is prepared to furnish an equally capable substitute to defend the state.

With the exception of these cases, it is to be believed that peoples consent to the free withdrawal of their nationals, because from granting such liberty they may experience not less advantage than other countries.

25. Exiles from a state

Thus the state has no legal claim against exiles.

26. The right, arising from consent, over an adopted child

Subjection by consent is either private or public. Private voluntary subjection can be of many kinds, as there are many kinds of authority. The noblest form is adult adoption, by which a person so gives himself to another family that he

---

[31] I.e., the question is being considered here from the standpoint of natural law.
[32] *Digest*, 17.2.65.5 (Paul).
[33] I.e., if the state has initiated a war on the assumption that a certain level of manpower will be available for prosecuting it.

is subject to it in the same way in which a son of mature age is subject to his father.[34] A father, however, cannot give his son to another in such a way that the full right of the father passes to the other, and that he himself is released from the duty of a father; for nature does not permit this. But the father can entrust his son to another, and allow him to be brought up by the other as in his place.

27. The right over slaves

The basest form of voluntary subjection is that by which a man gives himself into complete slavery, as those among the Germans who staked their liberty on the last throw of the dice.[35] . . . That is complete slavery which owes lifelong service in return for nourishment and other necessaries of life; and if the condition is thus accepted within natural limits, it contains no element of undue severity. For the lasting obligation to labour is repaid with a lasting certainty of support, which often those do not have who work for hire by the day.

28. Whether there is a right of life and death over slaves

Masters do not have the right of life and death (I am speaking of complete moral justice) over their slaves. No man can rightly kill a man unless the latter has committed a capital crime.[36] But according to the laws of some peoples, the master who has killed a slave for any reason whatsoever goes unpunished. This is the case also with kings everywhere who have the most unrestrained power.[37]

29. Concerning offspring of slaves

The question is more difficult in regard to the children of slaves. By the Roman law and by the universal customary law relating to captives, as we shall state

---

[34] This refers, in essence, to the Roman-law form of adoption known as *adrogatio*. It was a situation in which a person who was *paterfamilias* (i.e., who had no living male ancestor and who was therefore legally independent) gave up his independent status and became instead a 'son' in another family, thereby resulting in the permanent extinction of the person's own family line. *Adrogatio* was therefore, in effect, a merger of two families into one. Such a change of status could only be effectuated by an adult.

[35] Tacitus, *Germania*, 24.

[36] The contention is that even slaves are legal persons possessing at least certain basic rights. Grotius therefore rejects the concept of chattel slavery in natural law, in which slaves are regarded as mere property objects with no rights as persons.

[37] Although the killing of the slave is wrongful according to natural law, it is sometimes the case that states refrain from punishing a master who does this. Similarly, a king who is unrestrained in his acts by any man-made constraints is nonetheless still subject to natural law and therefore commits a violation of that law if he kills a person without justification. But here too, there is sometimes an absence of any human sanction or punishment for the wrongful act.

elsewhere,[38] in the case of persons of servile rank, as in the case of animals, the offspring follows the mother.[39] Nevertheless, this is not in satisfactory agreement with the law of nature, in case the father can be recognised with sufficient certainty. For since, in the case of dumb animals, the fathers no less than the mothers care for the offspring, this fact shows that the offspring is common to both. If, then, municipal law had been silent on the subject, the children would not be less likely to follow the condition of the father than that of the mother.

Let us suppose, to make the difficulty less, that both parents are in servitude, and let us see whether the children will naturally be of servile condition. Surely, if there were no other method of bringing up the children, the parents could adjudge to slavery, along with themselves, the offspring liable to be born to them, since under such conditions parents are allowed to sell children born free. But since this right derives its origin from necessity only, without such necessity the parents do not have the right to enslave their offspring to any one. Consequently, in this case, the right of masters over the children of slaves will arise from the furnishing of nourishment and other necessaries of life;[40] and so, since the children of slaves have to be supported for a long time before their work can be useful to their masters, and since the services which follow are in return for support in that period, it will not be permissible for those who are born under such an obligation to flee from slavery unless they return adequate compensation for their support.

Surely the generally approved opinion is that, if the cruelty of the master is excessive, even those slaves who have voluntarily given themselves into slavery can take counsel for their welfare by flight.

30. Different kinds of slavery

Besides the complete slavery, which we have already treated, there are also varieties of incomplete slavery, such as that which is temporary, or under a condition, or for certain purposes. Such is the state of freedmen, of those who have been promised freedom conditionally, of debtor bondsmen both voluntary and from court decree, of serfs bound to the land, of the seven year servitude among the Jews and of the other kind which lasts till the year of Jubilee, . . . and

---

[38] See p. 404 below.   [39] *Digest*, 1.5.24 (Ulpian).
[40] The allusion is to the long-standing tenet of natural law, dating from Roman times, that slavery is contrary to natural law – with the consequence that persons can be enslaved only for some just cause, such as capture in war or punishment for crime. See *Digest*, 1.5.4.1 (Florentinus). On this basis, it must be concluded that offspring of slaves are born free. In this passage, Grotius explains how this principle can be, in effect, counteracted by means of a sort of quasi-contractual arrangement between the slave-owner and the offspring, or alternatively on the basis of unjust enrichment (i.e., a duty of the slave offspring to repay the owner for expenses that he incurred in their upbringing).

finally of men hired for pay.[41] These distinctions are dependent either on laws or on agreements. Also, for reasons mentioned above, seemingly by the law of nature, incomplete slavery exists in the case of those that are born of one parent who is free while the other is a slave.

31. The right gained by consent over a people which submits

Public subjection is that condition [of] a people [which] surrenders itself to some man, or to several men, or even to another people.... There are also other degrees of subjection which are less complete, either in the manner of holding sovereign power or in the plenitude of it; the different degrees can be derived from the discussion previously given by us.[42]

32. The right over a person resulting from a crime

Subjection as a result of crime arises also without consent, whenever a person who has deserved to lose his liberty is by force brought under the power of him who has the right to exact the penalty. We shall see below who has the right to inflict punishment.[43]

In this way, individuals can be brought under private subjection; ... and also peoples can be brought into public subjection for a public crime. But there is a difference in this respect, that the servitude of a people is naturally lasting, since the succession of the parts does not prevent it from remaining one people. On the other hand, the penal servitude of individuals does not pass beyond the persons themselves, because the crime attaches to the person of the criminal. Moreover, both kinds of penal servitude, private as well as public, can be either complete or incomplete, according to the degree of the crime and punishment inflicted. Below, when we come to the results of war, there will be an opportunity to speak of slavery, both private and public, which arises from the volitional law of nations.[44]

[41] Footnote by Grotius: 'Among these, they who in England are called apprentices approach very close to the condition of slaves during the time of their training.'
[42] See p. 62 above.   [43] See p. 271 below.   [44] See p. 368 below.

6

On secondary acquisition of property by the act of man; also, alienation of sovereignty and of the attributes of sovereignty

1. What is necessary, on the part of the giver, for alienation to be valid

A thing becomes ours by secondary acquisition either through the act of man or by operation of law. After the introduction of ownership, it is of the law of nature that men, who are the owners of property, should have the right to transfer the ownership, either in whole or in part. For this right is present in the nature of ownership, at least of full ownership.

Two matters only are to be noted, the one affecting the giver, the other the receiver. In the case of the giver, a mental act of will is not sufficient, but together with it, either words or other external signs are required, because a mere mental act, as I have said elsewhere, does not meet the requirements of human society.[1]

The requirement that delivery of the property take place arises from municipal law. But because this has been received by many nations, it is improperly called a principle of universal law (*naturae societas humanae*).[2] Thus we see that, in some places, it is the custom to require a declaration in the presence of the people, or before a magistrate, and insertion in the public records; and it is quite certain that all these formalities arise from municipal law. But the act of will, which is expressed by a sign, must always be understood to be the act of a rational will.

2. What is necessary on the part of the receiver

In the case of the receiver, in turn, if we disregard the municipal law, the requirement by the law of nature is willingness to receive, accompanied by its natural sign. This willingness ordinarily follows the giving; but it can also

---

[1] See p. 116 above.
[2] By 'universal law' is meant the volitional law of nations. Even if the requirement of delivery is present in most, or even in all, countries, that would make it, at most, only the *ius gentium* in the proper sense. To be part of the volitional law of nations, it must arise out of an agreement between states, and not out of independent unilateral acts of states. Natural law does require some external sign of the donor's will, but it does not dictate any specific form which that sign must take.

precede, as, for instance, if anyone has asked that a thing be given or granted to him. It is in fact believed that the willingness continues unless a change becomes apparent.

The other conditions, which are required both for the transfer of a right and for its acceptance, and the question how both can take place, will be treated below in the chapter on promises.[3] For in these matters the method of alienation and that of promising are alike, at least by the law of nature.

3. On alienation of sovereignty

Moreover, as other things, so also sovereignty can be alienated by the one under whose control it in reality is; that is, as we have shown above,[4] by the king, if he holds the sovereignty by inheritance; otherwise by the people, but with the consent of the king, because he also has a certain right as possessor of a kind of life interest which ought not to be taken away against his will. These considerations apply to sovereignty in its entirety.

4. Alienation of sovereignty over a part of a people

In the alienation of a part of a people, there is the additional requirement that the part whose alienation is under consideration also give consent. For those who unite to form a state form a kind of perpetual and lasting association by reason of the character of those parts which are called integral. From this it follows that these parts are not so dependent on their body as are the parts of a natural body, which cannot live without the life of the body, and, therefore, may rightly be cut off for the advantage of the body.

This body of which we are treating is in fact of a different kind, since it was formed from voluntary compact. For this reason, again, the right of the whole over its parts must be measured from the original intent, which we ought not to believe was such that the body should have the right to cut off parts from itself and give them into the power of another.

5. A part of a state alienating the sovereignty over itself

Likewise in turn, it is not right for a part to withdraw from the body unless it is evident that it cannot save itself in any other way. For, as I have said above, in the case of all rules of human devising, absolute necessity seems to make an exception, and this reduces the matter to the strict law of nature.[5]

---

[3] See p. 189 below.   [4] See p. 58 above.

[5] For the discussion of the principle of necessity, see p. 96 above. In situations of necessity, human laws are dispensed with; but the law of nature continues in force. In the present context, the rules of the association (presumably prohibiting withdrawal) cease to be in effect in a state of extreme emergency.

6. The reason for the difference indicated

Hence it can be clearly enough understood why, in this respect, the right which the part has to protect itself is greater than the right of the body over the part. The part, in fact, employs the right which it had before entering the association, but not so the body.

Furthermore, no one should say that sovereignty exists in a body as in a subject, and so can be alienated by it, just as ownership can. Just as the soul, in fact, exists in bodies that are suited to it, so sovereignty resides in the corporate body as in a subject which is entirely filled, and not divisible into several bodies. But necessity, which restores a thing to the law of nature, cannot exert its force here, because in the law of nature, use indeed is included, as eating, and as keeping, which are natural acts, but not the right of alienating, because that was introduced by act of man,[6] and so by that fact the extent of its validity is measured.[7]

7. Alienation of sovereignty over an uninhabited or deserted place

Nevertheless, I see nothing to hinder a people, or even a king with the consent of the people, from alienating sovereignty over a place, that is, a part of its territory, for example, a part that is uninhabited or deserted. For because a part of the people possesses freedom of choice, so also it possesses the right of refusal; but both the whole territory and its parts are the undivided common property of the people, and therefore subject to the will of the people. If, on the other hand, the people is not allowed to alienate the sovereignty over a part of the people, as we have just said, still less can a king do so, though possessed of absolute authority, since this power is not without restrictions, as I have shown above.[8]

---

[6] This appears to contradict the assertion made above, in Section 1, that the right of alienation is a natural-law right.

[7] The basic assertion is that even the principle of necessity cannot operate to confer onto a state the right to alienate its sovereignty over a part of the state. The reason is that necessity (in Grotius's opinion) cannot give rise to a right of sale. Necessity can operate to confer a right to use something (i.e., something belonging to another) but never a right to alienate anything. This position seems difficult to reconcile with what Grotius has just said about the part of a corporate body to alienate itself in a situation of 'absolute necessity'. The distinction lies in the fact that, for the part, a situation of emergency restores the original position in natural law as it was before the formation of the state – with the result that the part of the state is now treated as if it were a whole state on its own. And a state can alienate its sovereignty over the whole of itself, as explained in Section 3 above.

[8] See p. 139 above.

8. Whether a king can lawfully alienate portions of his dominion for reasons of advantage or necessity

I cannot agree, therefore, with the jurists who add two exceptions, public advantage and necessity, to the rule concerning the inalienability of parts of a state, except with this understanding, that when the common advantage is the same, both for the corporate body and for its parts, the consent of the people and of its parts seems easily established from a silence of no long duration, but more easily still if the necessity is apparent. But when an opposing desire is manifest, either on the part of the whole state or of a part, the act must be understood to be null and void, except, as I have said, where a part has been compelled to withdraw from the corporate body.[9]

9. That infeudation and pawning are contained in alienation

Under the head of alienation is properly included infeudation with liability of forfeiture in case of felony or lack of issue; for this is a conditional alienation. Therefore we see that infeudations of kingdoms, as well as alienations, which kings have made without consulting the people, have been held void by most peoples. But we are to understand that the people [may give] its approval, whether it has assembled as a whole, as was formerly the custom among the Germans and Gauls, or has expressed its will through satisfactorily instructed delegates of integral parts. For we do also that which we do through the agency of another.

Furthermore, a part of a state cannot be given in pawn except with similar consent, and not merely for the reason that alienation customarily results from giving in pawn,[10] but also for the reason [first] that the king is under obligation to the people to exercise his sovereign authority in person, and [second, that] the whole people is likewise bound to its parts to preserve in entirety this exercise of that authority for the sake of which they united in civil society.

---

[9] I.e., parts of territory are in principle not alienable. But they can be alienated if that is in the 'public interest and necessity' of *both* the whole and the relevant part. If, however, alienation is in the 'public interest and necessity' of the whole but not of the part, or vice versa, then alienation is not allowed; and any purported alienation will be void.

[10] A pawning arrangement involves the entrustment of some property, usually by a debtor to a creditor, with a right on the creditor's part to sell the item (and pass good title to the buyer) if he chooses. This contrasts with a pledge, in which the creditor may only retain custody of the property, pending payment of the debt, but not sell it. Grotius uses the Latin word *pignoris*, which meant pledge in Roman law; but it is clear from the context that he is speaking of pawn rather than pledge.

10. Alienating inferior powers

Nothing, however, hinders the people from being able by hereditary right to bestow the inferior offices of government, since those do not at all diminish the integrity of the state as a whole, or of its sovereignty. But the king cannot do this without consulting the people, if we are to remain within the bounds of the law of nature; because a temporary right, such as that possessed by elected kings, or those succeeding to sovereignty by the law of nature, can produce no effects except those which are equally temporary.[11] Nevertheless, silence introduced by custom, as well as the express consent of the people, could have assigned this right to kings, and this we see is now the rule generally.

11. Alienation of the public domain

Also the public domain, the fruits of which have been assigned to support the burdens of government or of royal rank, cannot be alienated by kings, either in whole or in part; for in this they have no greater right than of usufruct. And I do not admit an exception if the thing is of little value; for I have no right to alienate even a small part of that which is not my own. But the consent of the people is more easily inferred from knowledge and silence in the case of small than of great matters.

   With this in mind, we can apply to the public domain what we have said above concerning the necessity and public advantage in alienating parts of the state, and with even more cogency, because here a matter of less moment is at stake. The public domain was, in fact, established for the sake of the state.

12. Need to distinguish the income arising out of public domains from the domains themselves

But many are deceived on this point, because they confuse the income from the public domains with the domains themselves.[12] Thus the right of acquiring alluvial additions ordinarily belongs to the domain, but the alluvial lands added belong to the income. The right of collecting taxes belongs to the domains, the money coming from the taxes to the income. The right of confiscation concerns the domains, the estates confiscated belong to income.

---

[11] This is an important indication of the temporal limitations on sovereignty in natural law: that acts done by a sovereign cannot have effects beyond the sovereign's own lifetime, unless accompanied by the consent of the people. Consequently, a sovereign, on his own, cannot create offices that are hereditary.

[12] The income from the domains constitutes usufruct, which is what the sovereign possesses as his own. On sovereigns as holders of usufructuary rights only, see p. 73 above.

13. Pledging of parts of the public domain

Parts of the public domain can, for good and sufficient reasons, be pledged by kings possessed of absolute power, that is, by those who have the right to levy new taxes for good and sufficient reasons.[13] For as the people is bound to pay taxes justly levied, so also it is bound to redeem property pledged for good reason. Such redemption is, in fact, a kind of tax. The public domain, moreover, is pledged to the king as a security for the obligations due from the people; and what has been pledged to me can be pledged in turn. However, what I have said thus far is valid only on the condition that no law has been enacted for the state which either has increased or diminished the power of king or people.

14. A will as a form of alienation

While we are treating of alienation, the fact should be recognised that wills also are included in this class. Though in fact a will, as other acts, can take a definite form in accordance with municipal law, nevertheless in its essential character it is related to ownership; and, if we grant that, it belongs to the law of nature. I can, in fact, alienate my property, not only absolutely but also under conditions, and not only irrevocably but also with right of recovery, even meanwhile retaining possession with unrestricted right of user. A will, however, becomes an alienation only in the event of death. Up to that time, it is recoverable, and the right of possession and enjoyment is meanwhile retained.

The fact that the right to make a will is not everywhere granted to foreigners is not due to a universal principle of law (*ex iure gentium*) but to a special statute of a particular state; and, unless I am mistaken, the restriction goes back to the time when foreigners were considered almost as enemies. In consequence, among the more civilised nations, this restriction has deservedly fallen into disuse.

---

[13] Although kings do not, under natural law, possess a *general* power to pledge parts of the public domain at will, they are allowed to do so in exceptional cases 'for good and sufficient reasons' such as safeguarding the general public welfare or dealing with emergencies.

7

On derivative acquisition of property which takes place in accordance with law; and herein, intestate succession

1. Certain unjust laws of states

Derivative acquisition, or alienation, which takes place in accordance with law, is based either on the law of nature or on volitional universal law,[1] or on a statute.

It is not our purpose to treat of the statutes of states, for that would be an endless task, and the particular disputes arising from wars are not decided in accordance with municipal law. However, attention should be called to the fact that certain laws of states are plainly unjust, such as those which confiscate in favour of the state treasury the goods of shipwrecked persons. It is, in fact, pure injustice to take away from any one his ownership of property when no adequate cause precedes.

2. Set-off

According to a law of nature, which has its origin in the very character and essence of ownership, alienation takes place in two ways, by legal compensation and by succession. Alienation by legal compensation takes place when, from one who retains my property or is in debt to me, I receive, as of equal value, something which is not yet mine but which ought to be given to me in the place of a thing belonging to me or due to me, and I am unable to obtain the thing itself.[2] For whenever expletive justice cannot acquire the [very] thing [which is owed], it tries to obtain something of equal value which, morally, is considered

---

[1] 'Volitional universal law' probably refers to either the volitional law of nations or the *ius gentium* proper.

[2] This is known as set-off: the retention of property owned by another, as compensation for the failure of that other person to discharge a legal obligation. In such a case, actual title to the property passes to the person retaining it. It is not merely a right of possession pending compensation. Rather, the retention and acquisition of title actually constitute the compensation (and thereby discharge the debtor from any further payment obligation). Set-off, as Grotius goes on to emphasise, is a self-help remedy. On set-off in Roman law, see generally *Digest*, 16.2.

the same. Moreover, the transfer of ownership in this manner is proved by the result, which is morally the best proof. In fact, I shall not be able to acquire the fulfilment of my right unless I become owner; for possession of the property will be fruitless if I cannot use it as I wish.

We know that it is forbidden, by the civil statutes at any rate, to take the law into one's own hands, so that it is called violence if any one recovers by force what is due to him; and in many places the one who has done this loses his right to the debt. Further, even if the civil law should not directly forbid such violence, the illegality of it would nevertheless be inferred from the establishment of the courts.

The right which I have mentioned will, therefore, be in force when the courts cease to act, for a continuous period. How this may take place I have explained above.[3] When the closing of the courts is of short duration, the seizing of property will in fact be lawful in the circumstances that you cannot otherwise recover your own, if perchance the debtor is absconding; but actual ownership will have to wait for the decree of the judge. This usually happens in the case of reprisals, a subject which will be treated later.[4] However, if the right is certain, but at the same time it is morally certain that enforcement of the right cannot be obtained from a judge, for the reason, for instance, that proof is lacking, the truer opinion is that, in these circumstances, the law of the courts ceases to apply and one has recourse to primitive right.[5]

3. Origin of intestate succession[6]

Aside from all positive law, intestate succession, as it is called, after ownership has been established, has its origin in natural inference as to the wishes of the deceased. Since the force of ownership was such that it could be transferred to another at the will of the owner, so also in case of . . . ownership at the time of death. [I]f anyone had given no indication of his wishes, nevertheless, since it was not credible that his intention was to yield his property after his death to the first who would take it over, the inference is that his property is to belong to the person to whom it is especially probable that the dead man had wished that it should belong. . . . In case of doubt, moreover, it is credible that each man wished what was most just and honourable. But among things of this kind, the first class includes what is actually due; and the next class, that which, though not actually due, is consistent with duty.

---

[3] See Section 2 above.   [4] See p. 338 below.
[5] I.e., recourse to self-help remedies, such as set-off, or even the forcible taking of the thing owed from the one who owes it.
[6] Intestate succession refers to rules of succession to property in the absence of a valid will.

4. Whether the property of parents is due to children according to the law of nature

The jurists discuss the question whether parents are under obligation to support their children. Some indeed think that it is sufficiently in accord with natural reason that parents should support their children, yet that there is no legal duty. I think that we ought to distinguish accurately the meanings of the word duty. This word sometimes is taken strictly for that obligation which is imposed by expletive justice; and sometimes more freely, to indicate what cannot be neglected with honour, although in this case honour does not have its origin in expletive justice but in another source.[7] We are concerned with duty in its larger sense, except when a human law intervenes.

Therefore, the one who brings a human being into existence is under a duty to look out for it as much as he can, and as much as is necessary, in those things which are essential to human life, that is, for the natural social existence for which man was born. For this reason, of course by natural instinct, the other living creatures also provide necessary nourishment for their offspring.... In consequence, the ancient jurists ascribe the bringing up of children to the law of nature, that is, to that law which reason herself enjoins upon us, while natural instinct commends it to other animals also.[8] ... Because this duty is according to nature, a mother ought to nourish her children that were begotten indiscriminately.[9]

Although it was the intent of the Roman laws that nothing should be left to children born of an illegal union, just as also the law of Solon had provided that it should not be necessary to leave anything to bastards, the canons of the Christian Church have ameliorated this severe restriction. They teach that that which is necessary for support is rightly left to all children whatsoever, or rather, ought to be left in case there is need. In this way we are to understand the common saying, that the lawful portion cannot be taken away by human laws, with the restriction, to be sure, that in that lawful portion, only the necessaries of life are included. For what is over and above the necessaries of life can be taken away without transgressing the law of nature.

Furthermore, our descendants not only of the first degree, but also of the second,[10] ought to be provided for, if there is need, and even beyond that.

5. Preference of children over parents in succession

Support is due likewise to parents. This duty has been fixed not only by laws, but also by the common proverb which bids 'to cherish in return'. ... Nevertheless, this practice is not so universal as that which we have indicated with respect to

[7] The distinction is basically between legal duty and moral duty.
[8] See Justinian, *Institutes*, 1.2; and *Digest*, 1.1.1.3 (Ulpian).
[9] *Digest*, 25.3.5.4 (Ulpian).   [10] I.e., grandchildren, as well as children.

children. For when children are born, they bring nothing with them upon which to live. Another consideration is that they have a longer time to live than their parents; consequently, just as honour and obedience are due to the parents, not to the children, so support is due to children rather than to parents.

Hence it happens that, even without the help of municipal law, the first right of succession to property falls to the children; the parents are believed to have wished to provide for them, as parts of their own body, most abundantly, not only the necessaries of life but also those resources which make it possible to spend life more pleasantly and honourably, especially after the time when the parents can no longer enjoy their property themselves.

6. The origin of vicarious succession

Because it is ordinarily the case that the father and mother provide for their children while they are alive, it is understood that grandfathers and grandmothers are not bound to furnish support. But when the parents, or either one of them, has died, it is fair that the grandfather and grandmother undertake the care of the grandsons and granddaughters, in the place of the deceased son or daughter. This, again, is extended in like manner to degrees of parentage farther removed.

7. On abdication and disinheritance

What we have thus far said about the presumption of intent is valid in case there are manifest no indications to the contrary. Among such indications the first to be mentioned is disowning, which was common among the Greeks, and disinheritance, to which the Romans frequently resorted. Yet this cutting off of a child that had not deserved death because of crimes is subject to the condition that support be provided for him, for the reason stated above.

8. Rights of illegitimate children

To the rule just stated an exception must be admitted, in case there is not satisfactory agreement as to who the father of the child is. It is true that absolute certainty is not to be found in an induction from facts. But whatever is wont to happen in the sight of people derives its own degree of certainty from evidence. And in this sense it is said that there is certainty in regard to the mother, because both men and women are available who were present at the birth and witnessed the bringing up. The same degree of certainty, however, cannot be had concerning the father.

It was necessary, therefore, to devise some method by which it might be established with probability who the father of each child was. That method is marriage, taken in its natural limits; that is, the union in which the woman is placed under the guardianship of the man. But if in a given case it is established in any other way who the father was, or if the father himself has considered it established, then by the law of nature the child concerned will have right of succession not less than any other child; and why not? For even a person of admitted foreign birth, if accepted as an adopted child, has right of succession from the presumption of the desire of the adoptive parent.

But illegitimate children also have a right even after the distinction between them and the legitimate children has been introduced by law. . . . On the other hand, it can happen, not only in accordance with law but also by agreement, that such children, just as may be the case with those born in wedlock, shall have support only, or shall be excluded, at any rate, from the principal share of the inheritance.

9. On ancestral property if there is no will and no children

When there are no children to whom the succession would naturally come, the case is less clear; and in no other matter is there greater divergence among the laws. Nevertheless, the entire range of variation can be traced to two sources. In the one case, regard is had to nearness of relationship [to the decedent]; in the other, the aim is to return the property to those from whom it came, according to the regular formula: 'The father's property to the relatives of the father, the mother's property to the relatives of the mother.'

10. Possessions recently acquired go to the nearest relatives

In the case of newly acquired possessions, . . . the duty of requiting favours ceases; it remains, then, that succession should be conferred on the person who is believed to have been most dear to the deceased. That person, moreover, is the one who is most nearly related to the deceased. . . . This duty to relatives, however, does not have its origin in expletive justice, but in 'natural fitness'.

Further, the intestate succession with which we are dealing is nothing else than a tacit will derived from inference to wishes.

What we have said of property recently acquired, that it is naturally bestowed on the nearest relatives, will also take place in the case of paternal and ancestral estates if neither the persons from whom they have come, nor their children, are alive. Under such circumstances, requital of gratitude finds no opportunity for expression.

11. Diversity of laws about succession

Although what I have said is particularly in accord with natural presumption, nevertheless according to the law of nature, it is not of the things established by necessity. Hence, in consequence of the diversity of causes influencing human choice, there arises a great variation in pacts, laws, and customs. Those who

admit succession through the right of another within certain degrees of relationship do not admit it in other degrees. Some consider the origin of the
possessions; others do not take this into consideration. There are countries
where the first-born receive more than the younger children, as is the case
among the Jews; there are others where the children are placed on an equality.

In some countries, again, account is taken only of relatives on the father's
side, in others all blood relatives receive the same as the relatives on the father's
side. Also, in some places, sex has influence, in others not; and in some places,
consideration of blood relationship is confined to the nearer degrees; elsewhere,
it has a wider range. To enumerate these diversities would be tedious, and this
is not a part of my plan.

Nevertheless, this principle should be kept in mind, that whenever there are
no quite definite indications of intent, it is to be believed that each person in
regard to his succession had in mind that which the law or custom of his people
approves. Such belief is based not only on the power of government, but also on
presumption regarding the wishes of the deceased, which has weight even with
those who possess sovereign power. For . . . those who possess sovereign power
are believed to have rendered a perfectly fair judgement in matters affecting
themselves, which they have either themselves sanctioned by laws, or approved
in custom; I mean in those matters where there is no question of any loss to
themselves.

12. The manner of succession in hereditary kingdoms

In the matter of succession to kingdoms, we ought to distinguish those kingdoms
which are held with unrestricted right of possession, and are patrimonial, from
those which derive the form of possession from the consent of the people. This is
a distinction we have treated above.[11] Kingdoms of the first class can be divided
between male and female offspring, as we see was formerly done in Egypt and
Britain.

Further, because of assumed intent in the matter of succession, adopted
children are not at a disadvantage in comparison with true children.

Furthermore, the throne will pass to those relatives of the last king who are
not connected by blood with the first king, if such a method of succession has
been adopted in those places.

13. Preference of the eldest child in indivisible hereditary kingdoms

If it is expressly stated that the kingdom shall not be divided, but no direction has
been given as to the person to whom it ought to go, the child that is the oldest,
whether male or female, will have the kingdom. . . . This principle of succession

---

[11] See p. 149 above. A patrimonial state is one in which the ruler has the right to
alienate part, or even all, of the state at will.

is to be understood as applicable unless the father has otherwise ordered. . . . But the one who has succeeded to a kingdom under such conditions will be bound to pay to the coheirs according to the valuation of their shares, if that is within the bounds of possibility.

14. Presumption of indivisibility of hereditary kingdoms

But those kingdoms which have been made hereditary by the voluntary consent of the people are handed down in succession according to the presumed will of the people. [I]t is presumed that the people desired what is most to its advantage. From this is derived the first principle, that the kingdom is indivisible; for that is of the utmost importance for protecting the kingdom and maintaining the harmony of the people. An exception is made, however, if there is law or custom to the contrary.

15. Inheritance beyond the last descendants of the first king

A second principle is that the succession is limited to those who are descended from the first king. That family, in fact, seems to have been chosen on account of its nobility; and so, when it has become extinct, the royal power reverts to the people.

16. Whether illegitimate children have succession right

The third principle is that only children who are legitimate according to the laws of the country shall be entitled to the succession. Not only are illegitimate children excluded because they are subject to scorn, since their father did not deem the mother worthy of a true marriage, and moreover because their paternity is considered less certain; whereas in kingdoms it is to the advantage of the people to have the greatest certainty possible, in order to avoid contests.

17. Preference of male descendants to females

The fourth principle is that, among those who are admitted equally to the succession, either because they are of the same degree of relationship, or because they succeed to the degree of their parents, males are given preference over females. The reason is that males are thought to be better suited than females, not only for war, but also for the other functions of government.

18. Preference for eldest male descendants

The fifth principle is that, of the male descendants, the eldest is given preference, or of the female descendants in case male descendants are lacking. It is, in fact, believed that the oldest is already, or sooner will be, of more judgement. . . . Further, because this preference of age is purely temporary, while that of sex is permanent, the prerogative of sex takes precedence over that of age.

From this, it is to be understood that, although children in some degree take the place of the parents who die before them, yet it is to be understood also that they are capable of succession only along with the others; and that among those who are capable of succession, the prerogative first of sex, and then of age, is maintained. For the quality of sex, and that of age, in so far as they are considered in this matter by the people, are so united with the person that no separation is possible.

19. Whether such a kingdom is a part of an inheritance

The question is raised whether a kingdom subject to such rules of succession is a part of an inheritance. It is nearer the truth to say that it is a kind of inheritance, but separated from . . . inheritance to . . . other possessions in the same manner as the special form of inheritance seen in certain fiefs, in subinfeudations, in rights of patronage, and in rights of special legacies requiring predelivery before the general distribution of the estate. In consequence, the kingdom may belong to the person who can be also an heir to [private] property, if he wishes, but in such a way that the kingdom can be inherited without the [private] estates and their burden.[12]

The reason is that the people is believed to have wished the succession to the kingdom to take place on the best terms possible. In fact, it makes no difference to the people whether [private] estates are inherited by the king or not [alongside the kingdom], since it did not choose the order of hereditary succession with that in view. [T]he desire of the people was that there might be something certain about the succession, that respect might be gained by prestige of family, that at the same time there might be expectation of noble qualities from birth and nurture, and that the possessor of the kingdom might care for it more deeply, and defend it more bravely, if he should expect to leave it to those whom he held in the highest regard, either on account of favours received or from affection.

20. Presumption of a customary form of succession to kingship

When, however, the custom of succession was different in fiefs and in land held allodially, if the kingdom is not a fief, or certainly was not originally a fief, even

---

[12] In Roman law, an 'heir to property' stepped completely into the legal shoes of the decedent – i.e., became entitled to the whole of the rights, but was subject also to all of the liabilities, of the decedent. Succession to a kingdom is a 'special form of inheritance' in that the successor takes only the rights and not the liabilities. Grotius points out that there is nothing to prevent a succeeding monarch from being an heir to private property in the ordinary manner, separately from his succession to the kingdom.

if afterward homage was done on behalf of it, then the succession takes place according to the law which was applicable in allodial estates at the time of its foundation.[13]

21. If the royal power is held as a fief

In the case of those kingdoms which were originally given as fiefs by one who had absolute authority, the feudal law of succession will need to be followed.

22. On cognate lineal succession

Again, frequently in kingdoms, there is a different kind of succession which is not hereditary but is called lineal. In this kind, it is not the custom to observe the right of substitution in the place of another which is called representation, but instead to hold the right of transmitting the future succession as if already conferred, since the law founds a sort of true right upon the expectation, which, of course, of itself produces nothing.[14]

Now this succession is of such a sort that the unimpaired right necessarily passes to the descendants of the first king and in a fixed order, so that the last possessor's descendants of the first degree are first called, both those living and those dead;[15] and the distinction first of sex, and then of age, is made in the case

[13] Land held allodially was, basically, land that was absolutely owned, with no feudal obligations connected with it. A fief was property of some kind (typically land) which was held conditionally on the provision of services or rents by the occupant to the grantor. The performance of the ceremony of homage was a sign of a feudal relationship, i.e., that the property in question was a fief rather than allodial land. Allodial land could be, and sometimes was, transformed into a fief, as Grotius notes. In the present context, independent kingdoms could be, and sometimes were, transformed into fiefs, most commonly into fiefs of the papacy. England, for example, was made into a fief of the papacy in 1213. Grotius holds that the rules of succession to such transformed kingdoms are those governing allodial land, since that was the original condition of the kingdom.

[14] This is not very clearly explained, and it is difficult to see the hereditary and lineal systems as really differing very importantly. Basically, in a system of hereditary succession (as just discussed), the successor to a deceased king is the person who is the heir of that king at the moment of his death. Consequently, only at that moment is the succession definitively determined; and no one is regarded as having any legal entitlement to the throne prior to that moment. 'Lineal' succession differs in that (in principle at least) a complete schedule of successions is prescribed at the outset, i.e., at the time that the sovereign power is conferred onto the first king. The successors, in a lineal arrangement, are therefore seen as having, in effect, a vested interest in the succession ('a sort of true right upon the expectation') – so that, in that sense, the future succession is regarded 'as if already conferred'. But this vested interest in succession seems to be without practical effect (i.e., it 'of itself produces nothing'). To lawyers in English-based systems, this lineal arrangement is strongly reminiscent of entailed property.

[15] The 'descendants of the first degree' are the decedent's children. If a child of the ruler does not survive but himself or herself has children who do (i.e., grandchildren of

of both the living and the dead. If the right of those who are dead proves to be the stronger, it passes to their descendants, again with like preference in respect to sex and age among those of equal degree; and the right of the dead is always transmitted unimpaired to the living, and that of the living to the dead.[16] If the last possessor has no children, the succession passes to the others who are most nearly related.

[C]ognate succession [is an arrangement] in which females and their children are not excluded, but receive a secondary place in the same line, so that the succession returns to them if males have been lacking, or descendants of males of a nearer or equal degree. The foundation of this type of succession, in so far as it differs from hereditary succession, is the hope, on the part of peoples, that the best training will be had by those who have the best-founded expectation of possessing royal power. Such are those whose parents would have had succession if they had lived.[17]

23. On agnate lineal succession

There is also another kind of lineal succession called agnate, which passes from male to male; this is commonly called the succession according to Frankish law, from the example of a very famous kingdom. In so far as agnate differs from cognate succession, it was introduced especially with the aim in view that sovereignty might not pass to foreign blood through the marriages of daughters. In both kinds of lineal succession, however, those who are related in even the most remote degree to the last possessor are admitted, provided that they are descended from the first king. There are also cases where the cognate succession is substituted in case the agnate succession fails.

24. Succession based on nearness of relationship to the first king

Other types of succession also can be introduced, either by the will of the people or by that of a ruler who holds his kingdom as a patrimonial estate, in such a way that he can alienate it. He may, for example, determine that, in every case,

---

    the decedent), then those grandchildren take the place of their deceased parent in the scheme.

[16] If anyone in the prescribed order of succession dies before taking the throne, then that person's rights pass, in their entirety, to the next person on the 'list', i.e., that next person is promoted automatically into the place of the one who has died. This same principle applies at the monarch's own death – leading, of course, to the automatic succession which is the essence of the 'lineal' system.

[17] The suggestion seems to be that an advantage of the 'lineal' system of succession is that, with the successors already identified prior to the end of any given reign, the people of the state will be in a position to ensure that those expectant successors will be given the best possible training for their future role.

those who shall be in the nearest degree related to himself shall succeed to the throne.[18]

The truer opinion is that, in case of doubt, this rule is to be followed also in the disposition of a property left to a family in trust. The rule is in fact in agreement with the Roman law, though some scholars have a different interpretation.

If the systems discussed are thoroughly understood,[19] it will be easy to settle disputes concerning the right to kingdoms which, on account of the conflicting opinions of jurists, are considered most difficult.

25. Whether a son can be disinherited in respect to succession to the throne

The first question is, whether a son can be so disinherited by his father that he shall not succeed to the throne. In this inquiry, we must distinguish alienable kingdoms, that is, kingdoms which are patrimonial, from those that are inalienable. For there is no doubt that disinheritance can take place in alienable kingdoms, since they differ in no respect from other possessions. Consequently, whatever laws or customs in respect to disinheritance are binding will be operative in this matter also.

If, on the other hand, there should be no laws or customs in effect, nevertheless by the law of nature, disinheritance will be permitted, except [for a duty to provide] bare support [to the son], or even without this exception, if the son has committed a crime deserving of death, or has otherwise grievously sinned, and, besides, has means of support.... Even more, the son will be considered as tacitly disinherited who has committed a serious crime against his father, if there are no indications that the offence has been pardoned.

In inalienable kingdoms, however, even though they are hereditary, the same rule will not hold; for while the people has indeed chosen the hereditary method of succession, it is hereditary in the sense that it is not subject to a will.[20] Still less will disinheritance hold good in lineal succession, where the throne passes on to individuals in prescribed order from the gift of the people, and without any semblance of ordinary inheritance.

[18] The reference here seems to be to a system of succession sometimes termed parentelic. It only comes into operation when a ruler dies without children. In that case, the succession is determined by going up the deceased king's line of ancestry as far as possible, to locate the living person who is directly descended from the most remote ancestor of the deceased king.

[19] Not easily achieved, on the basis of the rather cloudy accounts given here.

[20] Even in a hereditary system, the incumbent ruler does not choose his successor as an act of free will. The successor is the person who is his heir by law at the date of his death, even if the ruler would personally wish the crown to pass to someone else.

26. Whether any one can abdicate the throne for himself and his children

A similar question is, whether the throne, or the right of succession to the throne, can be abdicated. There is no doubt that a ruler can abdicate for himself; whether he can abdicate for his children is a subject of controversy. However, the matter ought to be settled by the extension of the distinction just made. For he who abdicates his right to inheritances can transfer nothing to his children. On the other hand, in lineal succession, the act of the father cannot harm children already born, because they have by law gained their own right as soon as they have begun to exist. And it cannot work harm to those yet to be born, because it cannot hinder the right from falling to them also at the proper time, as the gift of the people.

This point of view, moreover, is not inconsistent with what I have said about transmission. The power of transmission which the parents possess is, in fact, of necessity, not voluntary. Between existing children and those who are yet to come, there is this difference: those who are to come do not yet have any right, and so a right can be taken away from them by the will of the people, if it has also been yielded by the parents, whose interest it is to transmit it to their children. Here also is applicable that which we said above about abandonment of ownership.

27. Decision regarding the succession belonging neither to the king nor the people

This question, furthermore, is often raised, whether the king who is now ruling, or the people by themselves or through appointed judges, can decide concerning the succession to the throne. Both alternatives must be rejected so far as the decision is concerned, on grounds of jurisdiction. For jurisdiction belongs only to a superior, since it includes not merely the bare consideration of the person but also of the cause; and this must be examined with its attendant circumstances. But a cause of succession is not subject to the reigning king. This is apparent from the fact that the king who is now reigning cannot bind his successor by any law. Succession to sovereign power is not, in fact, included in sovereign power, and in consequence has remained in the state of nature, in which there was no jurisdiction.[21]

Nevertheless, if the right of succession is disputed, those who claim the right will act in a correct and high-minded way if they will agree upon arbitrators, a subject which will be treated later. The people, in truth, has transferred all its right of jurisdiction to the king and royal family, and it has no remnants of that

---

[21] There was 'no jurisdiction' in the state of nature because the state of nature, by definition, pre-dated the establishment of political societies. Jurisdiction is, by definition, a power attaching to government in a political society.

power so long as the former are in existence. I am speaking of a true kingdom and not of the mere possession of supreme authority.

Nevertheless, if question should arise concerning the original intention of the people, it will not be out of place for the people which now exists, and is considered identical with that which formerly existed, to express its opinion on the matter. In that case, the judgement of the people will have to be followed, unless it is quite certainly established that formerly the desire of the people was different, and that the right in question was derived from that desire.

28. Whether a son born before the father came to the throne is preferred over one born afterward

To proceed now to other questions, it holds true of every kind of succession that, in an indivisible kingdom, a son who was born before his father's accession to the throne should have the preference over a son born in the royal state. . . . [I]n a divisible kingdom, such a son will undoubtedly receive a part, as in the case of other possessions in regard to which no distinction is ever made on account of the time in which they were acquired.

Also, again, in lineal succession, as soon as a throne has been acquired, some expectation has been acquired by the children already born. If, in fact, it is assumed that other children are not born later, no one will say that those born previously ought to be excluded. In this kind of succession, a hope once established gives a right, and this right does not cease in consequence of a later act; except that in cognate succession, it is suspended in consequence of the privilege of sex.

30. Whether the son of an older son is to be given preference to a younger son

No less bitter is the contest, even with wars and single combats, over the question whether the son of an older son should be given the preference over a younger son. In lineal succession, this question presents no difficulty. For in lineal succession, the dead are considered as if living in this respect, that they may transmit their right to their children. In such a succession, therefore, the son of the first-born son will have preference without any regard to age. [A]nd in kingdoms having succession not restricted to male issue, even the daughter of the first-born will have preference; for in such kingdoms, neither age nor sex will furnish a reason for departing from the line.

In divisible hereditary kingdoms, however, such grandchildren will share in the division except in those regions where substitution in the place of another is not allowed, . . . for grandchildren were admitted late to share the inheritance with the children. In case of doubt, we ought rather to believe that the succession by substitution may take place, because it is favoured by nature, as we have stated above.

If substitution in the place of the deceased parent has been openly introduced by the civil law of the country, it will take place even if mention is made of the nearest relative in some statute. The . . . reason [is] that, when the subject-matter admits of it, the signification of words ought to be extended to the fullest possible meaning, to include not only the general but also the figurative use, in such a way that, under the term 'children', adopted children should be comprised, and, under that of 'death', civil death,[22] for the reason that the law is accustomed to use terms in this fashion. Therefore, . . . the term 'next of kin' [must be held to include those] whom the law advances to the nearest degree of relationship.[23]

31. Whether a surviving younger brother of the king is preferred over the son of an older brother

It is with the help of the same distinction that answer should be made to the question of succession between the surviving brother of the last king and the son of an older brother; excepting that, in many countries, succession to the place of the deceased is admitted among the children when it is not allowed in the collateral line. But in cases in which the right is not clear, we ought rather to incline to the view which puts the children in the place of their father because natural justice points to this point of view, that is, in respect to ancestral possessions.

32. Whether the son of a brother should be preferred to an uncle of the king

[T]he son, or even the daughter, of a deceased brother is given preference over the uncle of a king, not in lineal succession only, but also in hereditary succession, in realms where substitution in the place of the deceased is observed. This is not the case in kingdoms which, in explicit words, follow the natural order of relationship; for in these, the person will have the preference who shall have the advantage in the matter of sex or age.

---

[22] By 'civil death' is meant death pronounced by a court or magistrate, as opposed to the observed physical death of a person. Civil death may be pronounced in, for example, cases of prolonged and unexplained absences. Civil death can also refer to situations of loss of rights, as in the case of convicted criminals.
[23] I.e., must include not only the next of kin themselves but also any relatives of theirs who substitute for them after their death.

33. Whether the son of a son should have preference over the daughter of a king

[A] grandson, born of a son, takes precedence of a daughter . . . by reason of sex. [B]ut exception must be made if the question arises in a country which among the children takes account of nearness of relationship alone.[24]

34. Whether a younger grandson, born of a son, is preferred over an older grandson, born of a daughter

[A] younger grandson, issue of a son, is given preference over an older grandson who is born of a daughter. This is true in cognate succession, but not equally so in hereditary succession, unless supported by a special law. Moreover, the reason alleged, that the father of the one would have excluded the mother of the other from succession, is not sufficient; for the result would have come about from purely personal superiority, which is not capable of transmission.[25]

35. Whether a granddaughter born of an older son should be preferred to a younger son

[Some hold that] a granddaughter, born of the eldest son, would exclude a younger son from succession. This cannot be accepted for hereditary kingdoms, even if succession by substitution in the place of the deceased is admitted. [T]hat, in fact, merely makes one eligible to the succession, but among those who are eligible the prerogative of sex ought to have weight.

37. Whether the daughter of an older brother takes precedence over a younger brother

In like manner, in hereditary kingdoms the daughter of the eldest brother should be placed in the succession after the king's younger brother.

---

[24] Note that a grandson is two degrees separated from a grandparent, and a daughter only one degree from a parent.

[25] Grotius holds, as he indicated earlier, to the view that there is an inherent superiority of the male sex over the female. Therefore, if a ruler has two children, an older daughter and a younger son, the son inherits because of his 'purely personal superiority'. Grotius does not, however, hold to the view that there is a similar superiority of a line of descent traced through a male over a line traced through a female. I.e., the personal superiority of a male over a female is 'not capable of transmission'. Consequently, if the male line is to be given a preference over the female one, then there must be a special rule to that effect. Grotius holds that, in cognate-succession systems, there is such a special rule.

8

On acquisitions commonly said to be by the law of nations

1. That many rights do not truly originate in the law of nations

The order of our subject has brought us to the acquisition of property, which takes place by that law of nations that we previously called the volitional law of nations, distinct from the law of nature. Such is the acquisition made by right of war; but we shall treat of this more properly below, when the effects of war will be explained.[1]

When the Roman jurists treat of acquiring ownership of property, they enumerate many methods, which they say are according to the law of nations. If, however, anyone will examine these closely, he will find that, with the exception of the right of war, none of them have anything to do with that law of nations with which we are concerned;[2] but that they must be referred either to the law of nature – not, to be sure, in its original state, but in the state which followed the introduction of property ownership and preceded all civil law[3] – or they must be referred to the civil law itself, not alone of the Roman people but of many surrounding nations.[4]

This law of nations [of which the Roman jurists speak] is not international law strictly speaking (*ius illud gentium*), for it does not affect the mutual society of nations in relation to one another; it affects only each particular people in a state of peace.[5] For this reason, a single people can change its determination without consulting others;[6] and even this happens, that in different times and

---

[1] See p. 359 below.
[2] I.e., the volitional law of nations, arising out of agreements between states.
[3] The allusion is to the two historical stages of the state of nature – the 'original state' and 'the state which followed the introduction of property ownership'.
[4] It is apparent that Grotius sees some distinction between, on the one hand, 'the civil law . . . of many . . . nations' and, on the other hand, the *ius gentium*. It must be supposed that the difference is that the *ius gentium* is a law common not just to 'many' nations but to all (or virtually all) nations.
[5] This is one of the clearest statements by Grotius of the difference between international law properly speaking, and the *ius gentium* proper, as inherited from Roman law.
[6] I.e., it can freely alter its laws or customs.

places, a far different common custom, and therefore a different law of nations, improperly so called (*ius gentium improprie dictum*), might be introduced.

Now the first method of acquiring property, which by the Romans was ascribed to the law of nations, is the taking possession of that which belongs to no one. This method is, without doubt, in accord with the law of nature, in the state to which I referred, after the establishment of property ownership, and so long as no statute established any provision to the contrary. For property ownership can be brought about also by the civil law.

2. That fish in ponds and wild animals confined in parks are private property

First under this head, the capture of wild beasts, birds, and fish comes up for discussion. The question is by no means settled, how long these may be said to belong to no one. Nerva the son said that the fish which are in our fish-ponds belong to us, but not those in a lake; also that wild beasts which are confined in a park are our property,[7] but not those which wander at large in forests that are fenced in.[8] But fish in a private lake are no less shut in than in a fish-pond; and well-fenced forests detain wild beasts no less effectively than parks; . . . and these differ in no other respect than that one is a narrower, the other a less restricted confinement. Therefore, in our time, with greater justice the opposite opinion has prevailed, so that it is understood that we have right of ownership over wild beasts in private forests, and fish in private lakes, just as we have possession of them.

3. Wild beasts as the property of those who capture them

The Roman jurists affirm that wild animals cease to be our property as soon as they regain their natural liberty. But in all other things, ownership, which begins with possession, is not lost when possession is lost; rather, ownership gives us the right to recover possession. Besides, it makes no great difference whether another takes away our possessions from us, or they themselves escape, as a runaway slave. The truth, then, is rather that ownership is not actually lost because the wild beasts have escaped, but because of the natural inference that we have abandoned ownership on account of the difficulty of pursuit, especially since the wild creatures which belonged to us cannot be distinguished from others.

This inference, however, can be made invalid by other inferences, such as would be warranted, for example, if 'identification marks', or bells, were placed on the wild creature. [T]his, we know, has been done in the case of deer and hawks, which, when identified thereby, have been restored to their owners.

---

[7] By a park is meant something like a modern zoo.   [8] *Digest*, 41.2.3.14 (Paul).

Moreover, an actual physical possession is requisite in order to acquire owner-ship. It is ... not sufficient to have wounded an animal.[9]

4. Possession with the help of appliances

Now this physical possession of wild creatures can be acquired not only by the hands, but also by appliances, such as traps, nets, and snares, provided that two conditions are observed: first, that the appliances are in our possession; then, that the wild creature has been caught in such a way that it cannot escape. On this basis, the question of the boar caught in a snare should be decided.

5. Whether these rules are subject to alteration by human law

The principles stated will therefore be applicable if no statute has prevented. Modern jurists, in fact, are greatly mistaken who think that these rules are so bound up with the law of nature that they cannot be changed. They are not a part of the law of nature absolutely, but are such only under a certain condition, that is, if no provision has otherwise been made.... To this class belong all things which have not become the property of anyone.

6. Acquisition of possession of other things lacking an owner

In the same manner as wild animals, ... other ownerless objects are acquired. For, if we follow the law of nature alone, these also belong to the one who finds and takes possession of them.

7. To whom a treasure-trove naturally falls

Among 'ownerless objects' is also treasure-trove, that is, money the owner of which is unknown. Now that which is not known is reckoned as if it did not exist. Therefore, treasure-trove also naturally becomes the property of the finder, that is of the one who has removed it from its place of concealment and taken possession of it. Nevertheless, this natural presumption does not hinder the possibility of establishing a different rule by laws or customs.[10]

---

[9] *Digest*, 41.1.5.1 (Gaius).
[10] In English law, such a different law has been adopted, in the form of the Treasure Act 1996, which obliges finders of treasure to report their find to their local coroner. The find is then valued by an independent board of antiquities experts and offered for sale to a museum at the price determined. If a museum expresses no interest in the item, or is unable to purchase it, the owner can retain it. Treasure, for purposes of the Act, must be at least three hundred years old.

8. Roman law on islands and alluvial additions to land

Let us now come to the fluvial additions of land, to which the ancient jurists devoted many rescripts, and modern jurists even entire commentaries. The principles which they have laid down regarding this subject, however, are for the most part drawn from the established custom of certain nations, and by no means from the law of nature, though often commended through reference to that source. For most of their definitions rest on this basic principle, that not only the river banks belong to the possessors of the nearest estates, but also the river beds, as soon as these have been left dry by the river.[11] The resulting inference is that islands which are formed in the stream belong to the same owners.[12]

In the case of an overflow by a river, to be sure, the jurists do make the distinction that a slight overflow does not take away ownership, but a greater one does; with this condition, nevertheless, that, if the river should recede all at once, the estate which had been submerged would revert to its original owner by postliminy;[13] but, if the river should recede gradually, ownership would not in like manner revert, but rather would fall to the nearest landowners.[14] Now I do not deny that all these regulations might have been introduced by law, and defended on account of a certain advantage in protecting the banks; but I do not for a moment concede that they belong to the law of nature, as the jurists seem to think.

9. Natural law on islands in a river and dried out beds

For if we take into consideration that which generally happens, peoples have taken possession of lands not only with sovereignty, but also with property ownership, before the fields have been assigned to individuals. . . . Consequently, whatever was originally occupied by the people, and has not since been distributed, must be considered the property of the people [as a whole]. As an island formed in a privately owned river, or the bed of such a river that has dried out, is the property of individuals, so in the case of a public stream, both belong to the people, or to him to whom the people has granted it.

What I have said about the bed of the river should in like manner be held in regard to the bank, which is the extreme edge of the bed . . . in which the river usually flows. And such, we see, is now the usual custom. In Holland and the neighbouring regions, where in ancient times there were very frequent controversies in regard to these matters on account of the lowness of the land, the size of the rivers and the nearness of the sea, which takes up mud in one place and, by tidal changes, carries it away to another, it has always been the

[11] See *Digest*, 41.1.30.1 (Pomponius).   [12] *Digest*, 41.1.7.1 (Gaius).
[13] For a full discussion of postliminy, see p. 376 below.
[14] See *Digest*, 41.1.7.5 (Gaius); and 41.1.38 (Alfenus Varus).

established rule that islands, which were really islands, belonged to the public domain; and likewise, abandoned beds of the Rhine and Meuse, a position often confirmed by court decisions, and supported by the best of reasons.

For the Roman jurists themselves concede that an island which floats in a river, supported, let us say, by bushes, is public property.[15] [I]n fact, an island formed in a river ought to belong to the person who has a title to the river.[16] But the legal status of the river and of the bed are the same, not only from that point of view which the Roman jurists took into consideration, because the bed is covered by the river, but also from the other point of view which we mentioned above, because the river and its bed were taken possession of by the people at the same time and have not passed into private ownership.

In consequence, I do not accept, as in accord with the law of nature, the principle which [Roman lawyers] maintain, that if the fields have received definite boundaries, the island belongs to the first occupant.[17] Such an acquisition of ownership would take place only in case the river itself, and its bed along with it, had not been taken possession of by the people [as a whole]. . . . [This contrasts with] the case of an island formed in the sea, which becomes the property of the first occupant.

10. Ownership of inundated land according to the law of nature

Again, if we follow natural reason only, loss of ownership ought not to be admitted any more in the case of a greater than of a smaller flood. For though the surface of the land may be completely turned into sand, nevertheless the lower part of the ground remains solid; and though it changes its quality somewhat, it does not change its essential character, any more than the part of a field which is swallowed up by a lake, the right to which, as the Roman jurists correctly perceived, is not changed.[18] Their assertion is not in accordance with nature, that rivers perform the function of treasury officials, and take from public ownership to transfer to an individual, and from the individual to transfer to the public treasury.[19]

This opinion is not contrary to the principle which the Roman writers themselves have handed down, that what is ours does not cease to be ours except by our own act, or, again, by law.[20] But we have noted above that under acts are included also failures to act, in so far as they warrant an inference as to intention. Wherefore we grant this, that if there is a very great inundation, and there are no other indications which suggest an intention of retaining ownership, it is easily assumed that the land has been abandoned. Such an assumption

---

[15] *Digest*, 41.1.65.2 (Labeo). This was on the thesis that such a floating island was to be regarded as being part of the river itself.
[16] See *Digest* 41.1.65.4 (Labeo).   [17] *Digest*, 43.12.1.6 (Ulpian).
[18] *Digest*, 18.1.69 (Proculus); see also *Digest*, 41.1.12 (Callistratus).
[19] See *Digest*, 41.1.30.3 (Pomponius).   [20] *Digest*, 50.17.11 (Pomponius).

from the nature of the case is indefinite, on account of the variety of circumstances; and such cases should be committed to the decision of an honest man.
[C]onsequently, they are ordinarily decided by municipal law. Thus in Holland,
land is considered abandoned which has been submerged more than ten years,
if no indications of continued ownership exist. And in this case, not without
adequate reason, we have accepted a principle which the Romans rejected, that
possession may be considered as retained even by fishing, if not otherwise
possible.

But princes were accustomed to set a limit of time within which the original
possessors of the lands were obliged to drain their lands. If they did not do this,
then those who held mortgages on the lands were notified; and then again, those
who held civil jurisdiction merely, or both civil and criminal jurisdiction over
the lands. If all these delayed action, then their entire right fell to the prince;
and he either himself drained the lands and made them a part of his patrimony,
or he assigned them to others to drain, while retaining a part for himself.

11. Ownership of alluvial deposits

As regards alluvial deposits, that is, the addition of soil particle by
particle,[21] ... [i]t ought to be considered certain that such deposits ... belong
to the people [as a whole], if the people owned the river, as must be believed in
case of doubt. [O]therwise, such accretion would belong to the first occupant.

12. Alluvial deposits conceded to those whose lands have no other boundary than the river

But as the people can grant to others the right to such lands, so also it can
grant the same right to the possessors of the nearest estates. The people seems
indeed without doubt to have so granted this right in case the lands have no
boundary on that side except the natural boundary, that is, the river itself. On
this point, then, we ought not to view with contempt the painstaking of the
Roman jurists, who distinguished fields limited by natural bounds from other
fields,[22] if only we remember that, in this respect, a measured field has equal
rights with a field so bounded. For what we said above of states, when we were
treating of their acquisition,[23] likewise holds good of private lands, but with
this distinction: that, when in doubt, it is to be believed that states have natural
boundaries, since this is most in accord with the nature of a country; [but that]

---

[21] The 'alluvial deposits' referred to are islands in rivers that are newly formed from soil
washed down from upstream. These are in contrast with the 'fluvial additions to
land' referred to above (in Section 8), in which the washed-down soil builds up
along the banks of a river, thereby adding new land directly adjacent to some
landowner's existing property.

[22] *Digest*, 41.1.16 (Florentinus); and *Digest*, 43.12.1.6 (Ulpian).   [23] See p. 113 above.

private lands, on the contrary, are not supposed to have natural boundaries, but are either measured or bounded by a certain measure, because this is more consistent with the nature of private possessions.

Yet we do not deny that a people can assign its lands with the same right with which it has itself held them, that is, up to the stream itself; and if this is apparent, then it can assign the right over the alluvial deposits. This, in fact, was so decided in Holland some centuries ago in regard to the fields bordering on the Meuse and Issel, the reason being that, both in the deeds and in the tax lists, they had always been described as bordering on the river. Further, if such lands are sold, they retain their special character and the right over alluvial deposits, even though some measurement has been mentioned in the terms of sale, provided nevertheless they are not sold according to measure, but as a whole. This practice has come down to us in the Roman laws also,[24] and is now general.

13. Alluvial deposits on a bank abandoned by a river, and a part of the bed that has dried out

What I have said about alluvial deposits ought also to be held in regard to a bank abandoned by a river and a part of a river bed that has dried out; to wit, that, in the case of rivers having no owners, such parts belong not to the first occupant, but to the people [as a whole], in the case of rivers owned by the people. [But these] parts [do] belong to individuals [if the individuals] have received from the people, or from someone acting for the people, the land bordering on the river as so bounded.

14. What is to be considered alluvial deposit and what an island

Since, as we have said, the ownership of islands is subject to one law and of alluvial deposits to another,[25] disputes frequently arise in regard to the title under which that land ought to be held which, though somewhat raised, is so joined to the nearest estates that the level ground between is under water.[26] We see that this condition is common enough in our country on account of the inequality of the ground.

In this matter, customs vary. In Gelderland, all such ground that can be reached with a loaded cart is assigned to the nearest estates. . . . In the region of

---

[24] *Digest*, 19.1.13.14 (Ulpian).
[25] I.e., islands formed by alluvial deposits are publicly owned (as provided by natural law); while alluvial additions to the banks of rivers have commonly been granted to the persons owning the adjacent lands (by municipal law).
[26] The concern is with an alluvial deposit which, to the naked eye, is an island, in that it is wholly surrounded by water – but which, at the same time, is so near to a bank of the river as to afford very easy access by the nearest landowner (at the price of his becoming somewhat wet when walking from his land onto the alluvium).

Putten, such ground is similarly assigned, if a man on foot with a drawn sword can make his way to it. But it is especially in accord with the law of nature that decision in such matters be governed by the consideration whether the passage is ordinarily made by boat during the greater part of the time.

16. Alluvial deposits and the law of nature

In order to prove that the law regarding alluvial additions adopted by them is according to nature, the Roman jurists are accustomed to quote this maxim: 'It is in accord with nature that a man should acquire the advantages of anything to the disadvantages of which he is subject.' Therefore, since the river often washes away a part of my land, it is fair that I should enjoy a favour granted by it. This rule, however, is not in point, except where the advantages acquired arise from our own property. But in the case under consideration, the advantages arise from the river, which belongs to another. Again, it is in accord with nature that whatever loss there is should fall upon the owner. And finally, the fact that the jurists make an exception of measured lands shows that their proposition is not universal. I may pass over the fact that it generally happens that the river enriches some and impoverishes others.

17. That a road prevents gain by alluvial addition

Also, the assertion [in Roman law] that a public highway does not prevent gain by alluvial addition[27] has no foundation in nature,[28] unless the land is private property that has to furnish thoroughfare.[29]

18. Ownership of offspring

Another method of acquiring property, which is said to be based on universal legal principles, is through the breeding of animals. In this matter, the rule established by the Romans and some other peoples, that the ownership of the offspring is determined from the mother, is not according to nature, as I have said above, except in so far as the sire is in most cases unknown. But if the sire should be determined on satisfactory grounds, no reason can be assigned why the offspring should not in some measure belong to him. For it is

---

[27] See *Digest*, 41.1.38 (Alfenus Varus).

[28] The situation is that a landowner has land extending up to a public highway, which runs directly along a riverbank. In the case of alluvial accretion on the bank (i.e., on the opposite side of the highway from the owner's land), it was sometimes asserted that the newly formed land should belong to the owner, as if no highway was present. Grotius denies this assertion (subject to the one caveat that he gives).

[29] The reference is to the case in which the state had acquired private land by eminent domain in order to construct the road (i.e., in which, prior to the taking of the land by the state, the private property had extended all the way to the river).

certain that the offspring is a part of the father also; but whether more comes from the father or from the mother is a subject of dispute among the natural philosophers.

19. Ownership of a thing fashioned out of another's material

If anyone had fashioned a thing out of material belonging to another, [the position eventually adopted in Roman law was] that, if the material could be restored to its previous form, the owner of the material should be the possessor of the thing; but if it could not, then he who had fashioned the thing should have it.[30]

If, however, we consider the truth of nature, just as the Roman jurists also have concluded that, in the case of mingling of materials, common ownership is introduced in proportion to what each has furnished, because an adjustment could be made naturally in no other way, so when things consist of material and form, as if of parts, if the material belongs to one and the form to another,[31] it naturally follows that the ownership becomes common in proportion to the value that each has. The form in fact is a part of the substance [of the finished product], not the whole substance.[32]

20. If the material has been intentionally injured

It is not an unjust rule that those who, with fraudulent intent, expend labour on material belonging to another, should lose their labour.[33] That nevertheless is a penal enactment, and so does not come under the law of nature. Nature, in fact, does not fix penalties, nor take away ownership, on account of an offence in and of itself, although those who do wrong naturally deserve punishment.

21. Absorption of a thing of less value by one of greater worth

However, that a thing of less value should be taken over by one of greater value . . . is naturally consistent with the facts but not with right. He in fact who is the owner of one twentieth of an estate remains a part owner, as well as the one who has the nineteen twentieths. Therefore, what the Roman law has decreed in some cases, or what may be decreed in others, concerning accession on account of superiority in respect to worth,[34] is not law of nature but civil

---

[30] Justinian, *Institutes*, 2.1.25.
[31] I.e., if one party provided the physical materials and the other party shaped those materials into a finished product of some kind.
[32] For a discussion of the topic in Roman law, see *Digest*, 10.4.9.3 (Ulpian).
[33] See, for example, *Digest*, 10.4.12.3 (Paul).
[34] There were apparently some circumstances in which Roman law allowed a party with a disproportionately large share of a property to deal with that property as if it were entirely his. But Grotius provides no citation to authority for the point.

law, and has in view the transacting of business more easily. Nevertheless, the law of nature is not opposed, because statute law has the right of conferring ownership.

Yet there is scarcely any legal question regarding which there are so many divergent opinions and errors of the jurists.

22. When there is planting, sowing, or building on another's ground

In like manner, it is an established rule of law that what is planted and sown goes with the soil;[35] and the reason for this is that such things are supported by the soil. Thus a distinction is made in regard to a tree, according to whether it has put out roots. Yet the nourishment forms only a part of the thing, which was already in existence. So, just as the owner of the ground acquires a certain right over the produce from the nourishment of it, so the owner of the seed, plant, or tree does not on that account naturally lose his right. Consequently, in such cases also a common ownership is produced. The same principle is not less applicable to a house, of which the component parts are the ground and the structure. . . . [I]f the house is movable, the owner of the ground has no right over it.[36]

23. Entitlement to income from possession

In such cases of community of ownership, it is likewise not in accord with nature that one, who has in good faith become the possessor of a thing, should consider as his own all the income he has received from it.[37] . . . [H]e should merely have the right of charging for expenses incurred and useful labour expended, and on this account to deduct from the income received. Such a possessor may even retain the growing crops, if he is not otherwise repaid.

24. If possession has been obtained fraudulently

Also, it seems that the same rule [that possessors are entitled to compensation for expenses incurred by the possession] should be applied to one who has gained possession fraudulently, in case the penal law does not prevent.[38]

---

[35] Justinian, *Institutes*, 2.1.33.   [36] *Digest*, 41.1.60 (Scaevola).
[37] The reference is to the rule in Roman law to this effect. See Justinian, *Institutes*, 2.1.35.
[38] See, for example, *Digest*, 5.3.38 (Paul). Even a wrong-doer is entitled, under natural law, to fair payment for labour expended, improvements made, and the like – while at the same time remaining liable to punishment for misdeeds.

25. Actual delivery not required by natural law to transfer ownership

The last way of acquiring property that is classed under the law of nations is by actual delivery. But . . . delivery is by nature not necessary for transfer of ownership. This the Roman jurists themselves also recognise in certain cases,[39] as in donations subject to the former owner's right of use; or in the transfer of ownership to one who already has possession,[40] or to one who keeps property loaned to him; and in the case of things thrown out for distribution. Further, in some cases, ownership passes . . . before acquiring possession, as in inheritances and legacies,[41] and in gifts made to churches, holy places, or states, or for the support of the poor; and in the case of property over which a common partnership has been established.[42]

26. The application of what has thus far been said

These observations I have written down in order that he who finds the expression 'law of nations' in the Roman legal writers may not at once take as meant that right which cannot be changed, but may carefully distinguish precepts according to nature from those which are according to nature only under certain circumstances; and may distinguish, further, the laws common to many peoples separately from those which contain the bond of human society.

For the rest, this should be understood, that if by this law of nations, improperly so called (*iure gentium improprie dicto*), or even by a statute of a people, a single method of acquiring property has been introduced without distinction of citizen or foreigner, immediately thereupon foreigners acquire a right; and if the enjoyment of that right is hindered, the injury is such that it may furnish a just cause of war.

---

[39] See *Digest*, 41.1.21.1 (Pomponius).   [40] Justinian, *Institutes*, 2.1.44.
[41] *Digest*, 41.2.23 (Javolenus); and 47.2.65 (Neratius).
[42] *Digest*, 17.2.1.1 (Paul); and 17.2.2 (Gaius).

When sovereignty or ownership ceases

1. Cessation of ownership and sovereignty

I have already sufficiently explained in what manner not only private properties but also sovereign powers are originally acquired, and how they are transferred; let us now see how they are terminated.

We have already shown above, in passing, that such rights are extinguished by abandonment, for the reason that, when the desire ceases, ownership does not continue.[1] There is also another mode of extinguishment, when the subject, in whom the sovereignty or the ownership resides, is taken away before there is any transfer of ownership, either expressed or implied; such a case arises in succession to one who dies intestate. If ... a person dies without having given any indication of his will and without leaving any blood relative, all the rights which he possessed are extinguished.[2] In consequence, unless some human law prevents, his slaves will be free, and peoples that had been subject to his sway will become independent, because from their very nature, such things cannot be acquired by possession unless they voluntarily yield their liberty. Other possessions of the deceased, however, will become the property of the first one who takes possession.

2. Extinguishment of the rights of a family

The same rule is to be applied in case a family, which possessed certain rights, has become extinct.

3. Extinguishment of the rights of a people

The result is the same if a people has ceased to exist. Isocrates ... said that states are immortal;[3] that is, they can continue to exist because a people belongs to the

---

[1] For the discussion of abandonment, see p. 116 above.

[2] In most or all modern legal systems, this is not the case. The rights held by a person dying intestate will pass to someone or other, or to the state as a last resort. Grotius holds that, according to natural law, the property would belong to no one – and would thereby be subject to acquisition by anyone by way of occupation.

[3] Isocrates, *On Peace*, 120. Isocrates (436–338 BC) was a distinguished (and remarkably long-lived) Athenian writer. Although commonly regarded as an orator, he had a

class of bodies that are made up of separate members, but are comprehended under a single name, for the reason that they have 'a single essential character', as Plutarch says,[4] or a single spirit, as Paul the Jurist says.[5] Now, that spirit or 'essential character' in a people is the full and perfect union of civic life, the first product of which is sovereign power; that is the bond which binds the state together.... These artificial bodies, moreover, are clearly similar to a natural body; and a natural body, though its particles little by little are changed, does not cease to be the same if the form remains unchanged.

And so the statement of Seneca, that no one of us is the same in old age as he was in youth,[6] ought properly to be so interpreted as to be understood only of that which is material.... [Regarding artificial things] Seneca rightly [invokes the analogy of a river]: 'The [form or identity] of the river remains the same, but the water has been borne along.' Likewise also, in comparing a river to a people, Aristotle said that rivers bear the same name, though different water is always replacing that which is flowing on.[7]

But while the change in the individual members does not cause a people to cease to be what it was even for a thousand years or more, yet it cannot be denied that a people may cease to exist. The extinction of a people, moreover, may be brought about in two ways; either by the destruction of the body, or by the destruction of that form or spirit which I have mentioned.

4. Extinction takes place when the essential parts have been destroyed

A body perishes if the parts without which the body cannot exist have at the same time been destroyed, or if the corporate bond of union has been destroyed. Under the first type of destruction, we must class the engulfing of peoples by the sea, as the peoples of Atlantis mentioned by Plato;[8] ... likewise the destruction of peoples that an earthquake or a chasm in the earth has swallowed up; ... and also of those who have voluntarily destroyed themselves.

What if there are so few survivors of such a people that they cannot constitute a people? It will be possible for the ownership of the property, which the people possessed as private citizens, still to remain in their hands, but not what belonged to the people as a people. The same principle holds true also in regard to a corporation.

---

reputation as a poor public speaker. His main influence was as a pamphleteer and political theorist, most notably as a consistent spokesman for the unity of the Greek states against external foes.

[4] Plutarch, *On the Procreation of the Soul*, 25. Plutarch was not speaking of states, but rather of the human soul and also of the composition of the universe as a whole – both of these being presented as examples of the creation of unity out of diverse elements.

[5] *Digest*, 6.1.23.5 (Paul).   [6] Younger Seneca, *Epistulae Morales*, 22.
[7] Aristotle, *Politics*, III.3.   [8] See Plato, *Timaeus*, 23–5; and *Critias*, 108–21.

5. Extinguishment of rights of a people when the body of the people as a whole is broken up

The body politic of a people is broken up if, by reason of pestilence or rebellion, the citizens withdraw from the association of their own accord, or if they are so scattered by force that they cannot unite together again, as sometimes happens in wars.

6. Extinguishment of the rights of a people when the form of organisation is destroyed

A people's form of organisation is lost when its entire or full enjoyment of common rights has been taken away. In such cases, the individual citizens may also become subject to personal slavery. . . . The same thing should be said of peoples that have been reduced to the form of a province, and likewise of those that have been subjected to the sway of another people.

7. Non-extinguishment of the rights of a people by migration

If, however, a people has migrated, either of its own accord, because of famine or other misfortunes, or under compulsion, . . . the people does not cease to exist, provided the outward form . . . remains;[9] and surely a people does not cease to exist if only the walls of its city have been levelled.

8. Non-extinguishment of rights by a change of government

Furthermore, it makes no difference in what way a people is governed, whether by royal power, or by an aristocracy, or by popular government. The Roman people, in fact, is the same under kings, consuls, and emperors. Nay more, though the king rules with absolute power, the people will be the same as it was before, when it was its own master, provided that the king governs it as the head of that people and not of another. For the sovereign power, which resides in the king as the head, remains in the people as the whole body, of which the head is a part; and so when the king, if elective, has died, or the family of the king has become extinct, the sovereign power reverts to the people, as I have shown above.[10] We must, in fact, recognise that there may be several forms of a

---

9 By 'outward form' is meant the general governmental or organisational structure of the people. If the population of a country flees as a disorganised mass of individuals, without any coherent leadership, then it would be said (at least by Grotius) that the people had ceased to exist. A people is therefore, in Grotius's view, primarily an association of persons, with no necessary tie to a territory.

10 See p. 150 above.

single artificial thing, as in a legion there is one form of organisation through which it is governed, and another by means of which it fights. Thus, one form of the state is the association of law and government, another the relation to each other of those parts which rule and are ruled. The political scientist has under consideration the latter, the jurist the former. A people, by making itself subject to a king, does not cease to owe . . . money which it owed when free. For it is the same people, and it retains its ownership of all public property. [I]t even retains its sovereignty over itself, although this must now be exercised not by the body, but by the head. From this principle is derived the answer to the question sometimes actually raised, as to the place which ought to be occupied in assemblies by one who has acquired the sovereignty over a people previously free. Of course he is entitled to the same place which the people itself had occupied. Thus in the Amphictyonic Council Philip of Macedon received the place of the Phoceans.[11] In like manner a free people will take the place which had belonged to their king.

9. What becomes of such rights if peoples are joined together

Whenever two peoples are united, their rights will not be lost but will be shared in common. . . . The same principle should be applied in the case of kingdoms which are united not by treaty or by the fact merely that they have a king in common, but in a true union.

10. What becomes of such rights if a people is divided

On the contrary, it may happen that what had been a single state may be divided, either by mutual consent or by the violence of war, as the Persian Empire was divided among the successors of Alexander. When such a division takes place, several sovereignties exist in the place of one, with their respective rights over the individual parts. In such cases, whatever common property there was will have to be either administered in common, or divided pro rata.

The same reasoning must apply also in the separation of a people which occurs by mutual consent in sending out colonies. For thus also, a new people arises, possessed of its own rights. The colonists, in fact, are not sent out as slaves, but possessed of equal rights.

---

[11] In 346 BC, King Philip II of Macedon conquered the Greek city of Phocea, which was a member of an association of states known as the Amphictyonic Council, a league of states associated with the religious site of Delphi. In that Council, the Phocean position was held, in Grotius's view, by the people of Phocea collectively. After the Macedonian conquest, the position was naturally held by Philip.

11. Present possession of the rights which once belonged to the Roman Empire

Among historians and jurists, there is also the notable question, who is now the possessor of those rights which once belonged to the Roman Empire. Many hold that these now belong to the kingdom of Germany as it was formerly called, or the [Holy Roman] Empire (it makes no difference by what name you call it); and they imagine some sort of a substitution of the latter empire in the place of the former, although it is nevertheless well known that Great Germany, or Germany beyond the Rhine, was outside the territory of the Roman Empire during most of its existence.

It seems to me that a changing over or transfer ought not to be assumed, unless it is supported by sure proofs. I say, therefore, that the Roman people is the same that it formerly was, although mingled with an increment of foreigners, and that the empire has remained within it as if in the body in which it once existed and lived. For whatever the Roman people in former times could rightfully do, before the emperors ruled, it had the same right to do after each emperor had died, and so long as there was not yet a successor.[12] Besides, the election of the emperor belonged to the people, and was sometimes made by the people in person, or through the senate.

Moreover, the elections which were made by different groups of legions were not rendered valid by the right of the legions (for there could not be any sure right in an empty name) but by the approval of the people.

The fact that all the inhabitants of the Roman Empire were made Roman citizens by the constitution of Antoninus[13] is not inconsistent with this view. By that constitution, the subjects of the Roman Empire, in fact, obtained the rights which formerly the Roman colonies, municipal towns, and provinces had possessed, so that they both shared the honours and enjoyed the rights of Roman citizens. But the source of sovereign power did not reside in the other peoples in the same way as in the people of the city of Rome. This it was not in the power of the emperors to confer; they were, in fact, unable to change the mode and basis of holding the sovereign power.

The right of the Roman people was in no degree diminished by the fact that, afterward, the emperors preferred to reside in Constantinople rather than in Rome. But even then, the whole people had to ratify the election made by the part which lived in Constantinople. . . . The Roman people furthermore kept a far from unimportant survival of its right in the pre-eminence of the city, the distinction of the consulship, and other privileges. Therefore, whatever right the

---

[12] The ancient Roman Empire, in other words, was not a hereditary monarchy. Each emperor was separately elected, in his own right, by the people.

[13] This occurred in AD 212. A constitution was a general law, or statute, promulgated by the emperor (a *lex* being a law promulgated by the senate or by one of the assemblies of the people).

inhabitants of Constantinople could have had in choosing a Roman emperor was dependent on the will of the Roman people. To pass by other considerations when, contrary to the will and custom of the Roman people, the inhabitants of Constantinople had submitted to the rule of a woman, Irene, the Roman people very properly revoked its expressed or implied acceptance and independently chose an emperor and proclaimed his election by the utterance of the first citizen, that is, the bishop.[14]

This election, moreover, was personal in the case of Charlemagne and certain of his successors, who carefully distinguished the right of sovereignty which they had over the Franks and also over the Lombards from the right of sovereignty which they had over the Romans, as if this had been acquired on new grounds. Later, to be sure, the Franks were divided into the western Franks, who now possess France, and the eastern, who hold Germany or Alemania. . . . When now the eastern Franks had begun to choose their kings by election (for up to this time the succession of the Frankish kings, though implying agnate succession, had not depended so much on fixed rights as on the choice by the people),[15] the Roman people decided not to choose its own king, but to accept the king whom the Germans had elected, in order that it might have a more dependable assurance of protection. Nevertheless, it did reserve for itself a measure of right to approve or disapprove of the election, in so far as this affected the Roman people.[16]

Such approval, furthermore, was customarily proclaimed by the bishop and solemnly attested by a special coronation.[17] In consequence, the one that has been chosen as king by the seven electors who represent the whole of Germany has the right to rule the Germans in accordance with their customs; but it is by the approval of the Roman people that the same king becomes the Roman king or Roman emperor, or, as historians often style him, king of the kingdom of Italy.[18] Under that title, he holds subject to his sway all possessions that belonged to the Roman people, in so far as these have not passed under the rule of other

---

[14] The reference is to events which occurred in AD 802, when Irene (the first female Byzantine ruler) was deposed by an assembly of notables, largely out of dissatisfaction with her plans for marriage to Charlemagne. She was exiled from Constantinople and died the following year.

[15] Agnate succession means succession through the male line.

[16] The reference is to the period when Germans began to rule what became known as the Holy Roman Empire, beginning with the coronation of Otto I in 962. As Grotius points out, the emperors nonetheless continued, at least as a matter of form, to be 'elected' by the people of the City of Rome prior to their actual coronation as emperor by the pope.

[17] The bishop is the Bishop of Rome, i.e., the pope.

[18] There was actually a two-stage process involved. The first stage was the election, by the seven designated electors, of a person who thereby became, upon election, King of the Germans. The King of the Germans then traditionally travelled to the City of Rome, to be 'elected' as Roman Emperor by the people of Rome and then crowned by the pope.

peoples by treaties, or by occupation of abandoned territory, or by right of conquest.

From this, it can easily be understood also by what right, in the case of a vacancy in the Empire, the Bishop of Rome assigns investitures of fiefs of the Roman Empire. The reason is that he holds the primacy among the Roman people, who are at such a time free. The business of a corporate body is ordinarily administered in the name of that body by its leading person. . . . In fact, the principle . . . that, if the Roman Emperor is prevented from discharging the duties of his office by disease or captivity, a substitute can be appointed for him by the Roman people itself, is by no means unsound.

12. Concerning the rights of heirs

It is a clear legal principle that the person of the heir is considered the same as the person of the deceased in all that concerns the continuation of ownership of both public and private property.

13. Concerning the rights of the conqueror

In what degree the conqueror succeeds to the rights of the conquered will be discussed below, in treating the effects of war.[19]

---

[19] See p. 374 below.

10

On the obligation which arises from ownership

1. The obligation to restore the property of another to its owner

Having explained, so far as our purpose requires, the right which belongs to us over persons or over things, we must see also what obligation in consequence rests upon us. Such obligation, moreover, arises either from things which exist or from things which do not exist. Under the term things, I shall now include persons, so far as may be convenient for us.

From things which exist, there arises the obligation by which a person, who has property of mine in his possession, is bound to do what he can to restore it to my control. He is bound, I say, to do what he can; for there is no obligation to do what is impossible, or even to return the property at his own expense. The possessor is, however, under obligation to make the possession known, in order that the other may recover his own. Just as, in the state of community ownership, a certain equality had to be observed, that one might have the use of the common property as well as another, so after the introduction of property ownership, a kind of mutual arrangement was entered into between owners, that one who had another's property in his possession should restore it to the owner. If, in fact, the force of ownership had been limited to this, that property should be restored to the owner only on demand, the right of ownership would have been too weak, and the protection of property too expensive.

No consideration is here given to the question, whether a person has obtained possession of the property honestly or dishonestly; for the obligation arising from a wrong is one thing, and that from possession of property another.[1]

Now inasmuch as this obligation is binding upon all men, as if by a universal agreement, and creates a certain right for the owner of property, the result

---

[1] In other words, a person's obligation to a property owner to return property to him is the same, whether the non-owner acquired possession lawfully or not. If he came into possession unlawfully, then he is subject to criminal penalties over and above his duty to return the property. But the two legal effects are, as Grotius points out, conceptually distinct.

follows that individual agreements, as being later in point of time, are thereby restricted. This throws light on the passage of Tryphoninus:[2]

> Property stolen from me was deposited by a robber with Seius, who was ignorant of the crime of the depositor. Ought Seius to restore the property to the robber, or to me? If we take into account only the depositor and the recipient, good faith requires that the depositor receive [back] the property which he has deposited. If we consider the equity of the whole matter, which includes all the persons having an interest in the transaction, the property must be restored to me, from whom it was most wrongfully stolen.[3]

He rightly adds:

> And I agree that that is justice which gives to each man his own in such a way that it is not taken away from him in response to a more just demand of any other person.[4]

Beyond doubt, the demand of the owner is more just according to that right which we have said is as old as ownership itself. And from this is derived the following rule, which is found in the same Tryphoninus, that a person, who in ignorance has accepted his own property on deposit, is not bound to return it [to the depositor].[5]

As regards the nature of ownership, it makes no difference whether ownership arises from the universal principles of law or from the law of a particular country. Ownership, in fact, always carries with it its natural implications; and among these is the obligation on the part of every possessor to restore property to its owner. . . . Moreover, the income of the property also should be restored, after deducting expenses.

2. The obligation to restore gain made from another's property

As regards property no longer in existence, mankind has adopted this rule, that if you have been made richer through possession of my property, while I did

---

[2] Claudius Tryphoninus was a Roman jurist active in the second century AD, of whom very little is known.

[3] *Digest*, 16.3.31 (Tryphoninus).

[4] In this case, the depositor (who is a thief) is the person who is entitled, in principle, to be given 'his own', i.e., is entitled to have the thing returned to him which he had placed on deposit. This principle does not apply, however, if the return of the item would infringe the greater right of some other party (the true owner, in this case). If, however, the true owner makes no claim, then the thief is entitled, vis-à-vis his depositor, to have the thing deposited returned to him as if nothing were amiss. He would then be, of course, under an obligation himself to return the property to the true owner.

[5] The right arising from the objective fact of ownership, in other words, is held to be stronger than the duty which arises from the contract of deposit, if the two were to come into conflict.

not have possession of it, you are under obligation [to compensate me] to the extent that you have been enriched.[6] The reason is that, in the degree that you have been enriched from my property, you have more while I have less. Now property ownership was introduced for the purpose of preserving equality to this end, in fact, that each should have his own.

So great is the justice of this maxim,[7] that in accordance with it jurists decide many cases outside the narrow purview of the laws, always appealing to it as most obviously fair. A man who has placed a servant in charge of business is bound by the act of the servant, unless he has given warning that the servant should not be trusted. [B]ut even though such a warning has been given, [if] the servant has made personal gain under an [unauthorised] agreement, or [if the servant's acts have enriched] the master, action for fraud will be admissible.[8] 'The man who seeks to gain from another's loss', says Proculus, 'seems to act with fraudulent intent',[9] and in this connexion the word 'fraudulent' includes everything which is contrary to natural law and equity.

[A] wife, who has given to her husband money, which she could collect by law, is entitled to a civil action for restitution, or an action in equity for the thing purchased with the money; for . . . it cannot be denied that the husband is richer in consequence, and the question is what of his wife's property he has in his possession.[10]

If you have spent money, which my slave stole from me, thinking that it was his, I am entitled to an action for recovery against you on that account, just as if my property had come into your possession without a legal title.[11]

According to the Roman law, wards are not bound to repay loans; nevertheless an action in equity will lie if the ward has thereby become richer.[12] Again, if a debtor has pawned another's property and the creditor has sold it, the debtor

---

[6] See *Digest*, 5.3.20.6 (Ulpian).

[7] For the maxim in question, see *Digest*, 50.17.206 (Pomponius): 'By the law of nature it is fair that no one become richer by the loss and injury of another.'

[8] The action is available against any party who was enriched by the transaction – action not under the contract per se, but on the general principle of law that wealth acquired from another by unjust means should be returned. The fact that the person who contracted with the servant had been expressly warned not to do so would not preclude a claim, since the basis of the claim would be the prevention of unjust enrichment rather than an action on the contract as such.

[9] *Digest*, 14.3.17.4 (Ulpian).   [10] See *Digest*, 24.1.55 (Paul).

[11] See *Digest*, 19.1.30 (Africanus). It is clearly envisaged that the spender of the money was ignorant of the prior theft. This illustrates an important general point about infringements of the property rights of others: that good faith is generally no defence to liability.

[12] *Digest*, 13.6.3 (Ulpian). Wards lack the legal power to conclude loan agreements, so that a purported loan agreement with a ward would confer no right of repayment onto the lender. But an action to prevent unjust enrichment of the ward would still be possible.

is released, as regards his debt to the creditor, to the amount of the price received. The reason is ... that ... it is more just that the price received through the instrumentality of the debtor should profit him than bring gain to the creditor.[13] The debtor, however, will be liable to the purchaser, that he may not seek gain for himself from another's loss.[14] For even if the creditor had received from the possessor income in excess of interest, he would be under obligation to place all the excess income to the debtor's credit.[15]

Similarly, if you have had dealings with my debtor, thinking that he was in debt to another and not to me, and have borrowed money from him, this you are bound to pay to me, not because I have loaned the money to you (for such a transaction could not be consummated except between parties to an agreement), but because it is fair and right that my money, which has come into your possession, should be restored to me.[16]

---

[13] See *Digest*, 20.5.12.1 (Tryphoninus). The situation is that a debtor has somehow taken or obtained property belonging to Person X and has pawned that property to Creditor C. C has sold the property (as he is entitled to do). In a normal situation of pawn, C would keep the money received from the sale and reduce the debt owing by that amount. The question posed is whether that should be done here, in light of the fact that the debtor acted wrongfully, by pawning property that did not belong to him. Grotius holds that the debtor should be credited with the proceeds of the sale in the usual way because, if he were not, then the creditor (C) would be unjustly enriched (i.e., he would have the proceeds of the sale, plus the right to receive the whole value of the debtor's original debt).

[14] The focus now is on Person P – the one who purchased the property from C. P now possesses the property, but he does not have good title to it because X is still the true owner. P is consequently under an obligation to return the property to X – thereby putting him out of pocket by the amount that he paid for the property to C. For this reason, the debtor is obligated to make P whole. Otherwise, the debtor would be enriched (by way of the reduction of his debt to C) at the expense of P. The net result of all of this, then, is, in effect, that part (or perhaps all) of the debtor's indebtedness has been shifted from C to P, with X recovering his wayward property.

[15] C would have to pay the full proceeds of sale over to the debtor, even if it exceeded the amount of the debt, because otherwise C would be unjustly enriched. As noted, however, the debtor's good fortune would be short-lived, because he would be obligated to pay that very sum over to P.

[16] *Digest*, 12.1.32 (Celsus). This is a somewhat complicated scenario. Person A wishes to borrow money. Person B is willing to lend, but indirectly. B is already owed money by X (in the same amount), so he instructs X to discharge this loan by providing A with the desired sum (in lieu of X's repaying B in the normal fashion). B will then recoup the money from A in due course. A and X duly enter into this arrangement – but A mistakenly believes that X is indebted to Person C rather than to Person B. The question then is whether B has a legal action against A for the money, given that A did not ever contract with B (he contracted with X instead) and had no intention at any time that the money that he borrowed would be repaid to B. The answer given by Grotius, following Roman law, is that B does have an action against A for the money – not, however, on the basis of any loan contract, but rather on the general principle of preventing unjust enrichment (i.e., A would be unjustly enriched if he were to be allowed to borrow money of B's without repaying it).

The later jurists rightly extend these principles to analogous cases. For example, a man, whose goods have been sold on his non-appearance [in a court], is entitled to the money received from his property, on properly [putting in his appearance]. Another case is that of a person who has loaned money to a father for the purpose of supporting a son; [if] the father [became] insolvent, [the lender] would have the right of action against the son, when the son should have possession of his mother's property.

If the . . . rules stated have been rightly understood, it will not be difficult to reply to the questions which are commonly raised by jurists and by theologians who lay down rules for the tribunal of conscience.

3. Whether a person who has honestly come into possession of another's property is bound to make restitution, if the property has perished

In the first place, it is clear that a person who is honestly in possession of a thing does not have to make restitution if the thing has perished. In such a case, the thing itself is not in his possession; and he has not received gain from it. The dishonest possessor will be liable for his own wrongdoing in addition to accounting for the property.

4. Whether a possessor of another's property is bound to restore the income that still remains

Secondly, a possessor in good faith is bound to restore any income of the property that still remains. I speak of income from the property; for the income from the possessor's industry is not due to the property, even if it could not be obtained without the property.[17] The reason for this obligation [to restore income from the property to the property owner] arises from ownership. For the person who is the owner of a thing is likewise naturally the owner of the income derived from it.

---

[17] An example would be someone who occupied land belonging to another and who, during his period of occupation, laboured diligently to produce a crop. The whole of the crop would not be owing to the owner because an important input into the production had been the occupier's own labour. This illustrates the difficulty of determining what exactly constitutes 'income from the property'. To some extent, proceeds of sale of the crop belong to the landowner, since the crop came from his property. But the crop also derived, to some extent, from the labour of the trespasser. The proceeds of sale should therefore be shared between the two – but Grotius does not say in what proportion.

5. Whether such a possessor is likewise bound to make good the income which has been used up, if under other circumstances he would have used an equivalent

Thirdly, the possessor in good faith is bound to make restitution for the property and its income that have been used up. . . . For in that degree he is judged to be richer.

6. Whether such a possessor is bound to restore income which he neglected to collect

Fourthly, a person in possession of such property is not liable for income from it which he has neglected to collect; for he owns neither the property nor anything in place of it.[18]

7. Whether such a possessor is bound to make restitution of the property which he has given to another

Fifthly, if such a possessor has given to another a thing which was given to himself, he is not liable for it, unless he would have given the same amount in any case, if he had not had this; for in that case the sparing of his own property will be considered as a gain.[19]

8. Whether such a possessor is under obligation if he has sold a thing which he has bought

Sixthly, if such a possessor has sold property which he bought, he is not bound to make restitution except in so far as he may have sold it at a higher price.

[18] The focus on unjust enrichment explains this proposition. The possessor cannot be said to have been enriched by sums of money which he could have collected but did not. It is essential to this conclusion that the occupier be in good faith because that has the effect of making unjust enrichment the sole basis of the owner's claim against him. If the occupier was a deliberate wrong-doer, the position would be importantly different. Liability would now be on the basis not of wealth received (i.e., *actually* received) by the occupier but rather on the basis of injury suffered by the owner. In that case, the occupier would be liable for sums which he could have collected but did not (say, from tenants), since those would figure amongst the losses suffered by the owner from not being in possession of his property.

[19] In other words, if Person A receives property belonging to Person X and passes it along to Person B, then B, rather than A, is the one who is under an obligation to restore the property to X. X has an action against B for the property, but not against A because A has not been enriched by the process. Grotius points out, though, that it may be that A passed the property to B in, say, discharge of a debt that A owed to B. In that case, A has been enriched (by the discharging of his debt); and the true owner now has an action against either A or B – against A on the basis of unjust enrichment, or against B for the return of the property itself.

If he has sold property which was given to him, he is bound to restore the value, unless he has squandered the amount which he would not otherwise have wasted.[20]

9. Whether a good-faith buyer of the property of another can reserve the cost

Seventhly, another man's property, though bought in good faith, must be restored, and the price which it cost cannot be demanded back. This rule, it seems to me, ought to be qualified with the proviso, 'except in so far as the owner in all probability could not have recovered possession of his property without some expenditure', as, for example, if the property was in the hands of pirates. In such a case, then, whatever amount the owner would willingly have expended can be deducted. . . . Actual possession, in fact, especially of an object difficult to recover, can be reckoned in terms of value. In this respect, therefore, the owner is considered to have been made richer than he was after the loss of the thing.

I do not here make the requirement that the thing should have been bought with the intention of restoring it to the owner, for some say that, in such a case, there arises a right of action for services rendered, though this is denied by others. The right of action for services rendered, in fact, arises from the civil law; it contains none of those basic elements by virtue of which nature imposes an obligation.[21] But we are here trying to find out what the law of nature is.

---

[20] *Digest*, 47.2.48.7 (Ulpian); and 5.3.22 (Paul). In other words, if a person purchases an item from, say, a thief and then re-sells the item to another party for the same price, the true owner has no action against him, since he has not been enriched. If, however, the property was given to him without charge and he then sold it, then he is of course enriched to the extent of the sale proceeds; and the owner therefore has an action against him for that sum. It is curious that Grotius holds that he would not be liable if he squandered the proceeds – presumably on the understanding that he would not have been enriched by the squandering. In that event, the owner's only action would be against the purchaser, for the return of the item itself.

[21] This passage is somewhat obscure. It is pointed out that some persons contend that, when property is recovered by a non-owner for the purpose of rendering it to the owner, the recoverer has, against the owner, a 'right of action for services rendered'. Grotius concedes that this might possibly be so. But he insists that such an action is given (or not, as the case may be) by the municipal law of individual countries, and not by the law of nature. What natural law gives to the recoverer is something similar, but slightly different: an action for unjust enrichment. The difference is that the action for services rendered is valued according to the reasonable market value of the services provided, whereas the action for unjust enrichment is valued according to the benefit *actually received* by the owner in the particular case. It is likely that, in general, there would be little or no difference between these two amounts. But there is a conceptual difference between them, in that the one focuses on the effort expended by the service provider, and the other on the value actually accruing to the beneficiary.

Similar [to this is the situation in which a person] has carried on my business without regard for my interest, but for the sake of his own gain, and has incurred some expense in transacting my business. [H]e has a right of action, not indeed for what he has expended, but for the amount by which I am made richer.[22] Thus also, in fact, the owners of goods, which have been thrown overboard to lighten a ship, recover a part of the value from the others whose property was saved by the lightening.[23] The reason is that the person who has saved property that otherwise was about to perish seems in this respect to be made richer.

10. Whether purchased goods, if they belong to another, must be returned to the seller

Eighthly, the person who from one man has bought property belonging to another cannot return it to the seller, in order to recover the purchase price; for the obligation of restoring it to the owner [rather than the seller] commenced at the moment when the object came into his possession.

11. Whether a person who has in his possession property of which the owner is unknown is bound to turn it over to anyone

Ninthly, the man who has in his possession property of unknown ownership is not obliged by the law of nature to give it to the poor, although this is a very noble act; and such procedure is rightly established as a law in many places. The reason for this is that, according to the principle of ownership, no one except the owner has any right to the property. But non-existence of an owner, and not knowing who the owner is, amount to the same thing, so far as the man who does not know the owner is concerned.

12. Whether money received for a shameful cause must be restored

Tenthly, by the law of nature, whatever a person has received for a shameful cause, or for an honourable service which it was his duty to perform, does not have to be restored.[24] Yet such a rule has been introduced, not undeservedly, by certain [municipal] laws. The reason is that no one is bound to render account for property unless it belongs to another. But in the cases under consideration, the ownership passed with the consent of the former owner.

---

[22] See *Digest*, 3.5.5.5(3) (Ulpian).
[23] See *Digest*, 14.2.1 (Paul). This process of sharing losses is known in admiralty law as averaging.
[24] An example of money received for 'a shameful cause' might be income from prostitution, which was willingly paid by the client. An example of payment for an honourable service performed by obligation would be a soldier who received a payment for valour in battle.

The case will be different if there was illegality in the method of receiving the money, as, for example, by extortion. That, in fact, involves a different principle of obligation, with which I am not here concerned.

13. Whether the ownership of goods which are weighed, counted or measured changes without the consent of the owner

Let us [consider also the question of whether] the ownership of another's property can pass to us without the consent of the owner if the things are such as are ordinarily reckoned by weight, number, and measure. For it is said that things of this kind admit of substitution, that is, that they can be replaced by that which is of the same kind. Even in this case, however, such use can be made only if consent has preceded, or may be presumed from law or custom to have preceded, as in the case of a loan; or if the thing cannot be given back because it has been consumed. But such a substitution of an equivalent does not take place without consent, expressed or implied, or in the case of necessity.

11

On promises[1]

1. Whether by the law of nature a right arises from a promise

The order of our work has brought us to the obligation which arises from promises. [Some persons maintain] the opinion that, according to the law of nature, as well as the law of nations, no obligation is created by those agreements which do not contain an exchange of considerations;[2] that nevertheless, such agreements are honourably carried out if only the matter is of such a nature that it would have been honourable and consistent with some other virtue to fulfil them even without the promise.

[In support of this view, the argument is advanced] that the individual who rashly believes a person that makes a promise without any reason for it is not less at fault than the person who has made a worthless promise; then, that the fortunes of all would be greatly imperilled if men should be bound by a mere promise, which proceeds often from the love of display rather than from a purpose, or from a purpose, indeed, but a trivial and ill-considered purpose; finally, that it is just to leave something to the honesty of each person.

[This school of thought contends that, even if promises do create legal obligations, the effect is to give to the promisee a right] not [to] the thing which

---

[1] It should be appreciated (as will become apparent in this chapter) that the line between promises and contracts (the subject of the next chapter) is somewhat porous. Basically, the distinction is that, for contracts, equality between the parties is a matter of the highest concern. Promises, accordingly, come into play when there is inequality between the parties. For example, it might be agreed that A will perform a small service for B, and that B will give a very lavish reward in return. Modern observers would be inclined to see this as a contractual relationship. But to Grotius, it is a mixture of contract and promise, in light of the fact that B is committing himself to giving something to A beyond the value of what A is to give to him. The difference between these values is regarded by Grotius as a promise from B to A.

[2] The contention described (which Grotius contests) is that 'bare promises', or unilateral promises, in which one party promises something while the other promises nothing, are, in principle, not legally binding. An 'exchange of considerations' is a situation in which reciprocal promises of some kind are made.

was promised, but only what is to his interest;[3] that, for the rest, the force which agreements have they do not derive from themselves but from the contracts in which they are contained or to which they are added.

Now this opinion . . . cannot stand. For, first, it follows therefrom that agreements between kings and different peoples have no force so long as no part of such agreements has been carried out, especially in the regions where no set form of treaties or guaranteed engagements exists. Again, no reason can, in fact, be found why laws, which are a sort of common agreement of the people. . . . should be able to add the force of an obligation to agreements, while the desire of each individual striving in every way to bind himself is unable to add such force, especially in cases where the civil law offers no impediment.[4]

There is the further fact that ownership of property can be transferred by an act of will which is sufficiently manifest, as we have said above.[5] Why then, since we have equal right over our actions and over our property, may there not be transferred to a person also the right to transfer ownership (this right is less than ownership itself) or the right to do something?[6]

To these considerations, we must add the accordant opinion of wise men. For just as the jurists say, that nothing is so in accord with the law of nature as that the wish of the owner should be held valid when he desires to transfer his property to another,[7] in like manner it is said that nothing is so in harmony with the good faith of mankind as that persons should keep the agreements which they have made with one another[8] . . . Furthermore, [it] is not to be admitted . . . that we are considered to have relied on one's good faith only when action according to the agreement has commenced.

---

[3] In other words, it is contended (erroneously, according to Grotius) that the right that a promisee acquires from a 'bare promise' cannot, even on the most generous reading, be the right to have the promise performed according to its precise terms, but only to have the promise performed so far as is necessary to satisfy the promisee's actual material interest. For example, suppose that A, hearing that B's house has been damaged by storm, promises to give B £1,000 to enable repairs to be made. If, in the event, the repairs cost only £800, then the maximum claim that B could have against A, on the basis of the promise, would be for £800 rather than £1,000. Grotius, however, disagrees with this and holds that the obligation is to pay the full £1,000.

[4] It is agreed on all sides that 'laws' – meaning man-made municipal laws – can give binding effect to agreements as such, even if natural law does not do so. Grotius contends, however, that natural law does do so – i.e., that the will of an individual who is 'striving in every way to bind himself' is given force by natural law, just as natural law gives force to duly enacted municipal laws.

[5] See p. 138 above.

[6] This argument seems somewhat off-point. The assertion, in effect, is that, if a person has the right to do something (as a matter of basic personal liberty), then he should be able to transfer that right freely to another party. That may be so, but the contention seems far removed from the question of whether unilateral promises or contracts are legally binding per se.

[7] Justinian, *Institutes*, 2.1.40.   [8] *Digest*, 2.14.1 (Ulpian).

Now in order that the matter may be properly understood, we ought carefully to distinguish the three ways of speaking concerning things yet to come, which either are under our control, or, according to our expectation, soon will be.

2. That bare assertion does not create a binding obligation

The first of these three modes of speech is an assertion, setting forth a present intention concerning something in the future.[9] That this assertion may be free from fault, the true expression of the opinion held at present is required, but not the continuance of that opinion. The human mind, in fact, has not only a natural power, but also a right, to change its opinion. If there is anything wrong in the change of opinion, as at times happens, this is not inherent in the [fact of] change, but comes from the subject-matter, as, for example, because the first opinion was better.

3. That by the law of nature a promise is binding, but with no legal right gained by another

In the second mode of speech, the intention shapes itself in respect to future time, with a sufficient manifestation to show the necessity of continuance.[10] This also may be called a sort of promise, which, without regard to the civil law, is binding either absolutely or under conditions, but gives no right, properly speaking, to the second party.[11] In many cases, it happens that a moral obligation rests upon us, but no legal right is acquired by another, just as becomes apparent in the duty of having mercy and showing gratitude; similar to these is the duty of constancy or of good faith. So in the face of such a promise, the property of the one promising can be retained,[12] and the promisor cannot be compelled by the law of nature to keep faith.[13]

---

[9] An example of a 'bare assertion' is a person who communicates with a charity, praising the charity's endeavours and stating that he is minded, at a future point, to make a donation.

[10] Unfortunately, no indication is given of what sort of 'manifestation' would 'show the necessity of continuance'. Perhaps it would suffice if the promisor simply asserted verbally that he would not change his mind in the future.

[11] This is another notable instance of a case where there is a duty on one side, without a correlative right on the other.

[12] E.g., if the content of the promise was that the promisor would transfer property to the promisee.

[13] There is a subtle contrast between, on the one hand, obligations which are merely moral rather than legal and, on the other hand, obligations which are legal but not enforceable by the beneficiaries. In the one case, legal obligation is altogether absent. In the other case, legal obligation is present; but a mechanism for enforcement (i.e., for compulsion of the promisor) is lacking. In practical terms, the effect is much the same. But there is the difference that, in the case where legal obligation is present, a

4. How a second party acquires a legal right

In the third way of making a promise, such a purpose as that just mentioned is manifested by an outward sign of the intent to confer the due right upon the other party.[14] This is a perfect promise,[15] and has an effect similar to alienation of ownership. It is, in fact, an introduction either to the alienation of a thing or to the alienation of some portion of our freedom of action. To the former category belong promises to give; to the latter, promises to perform.

Naturally there can be other signs of a deliberate intent besides the formality, or whatsoever it is that the civil law requires in order to fix the rights of the parties. What is done without deliberate intent does not, as we also believe, attain to the force of an obligation. . . . As to that which is done deliberately, but without an intent to grant a corresponding right to another, we declare that a right of enforcement is not thereby naturally given to anyone, although we admit that there arises not only a question of honour, but also a kind of moral necessity.[16]

5. Need for the possession of reason on the part of the promisor

The first requisite is the use of reason; consequently the promises of madmen, idiots, and children are null and void. A different opinion should be held in regard to minors. Although it is in fact believed that minors possess a rather weak judgement, as also women, nevertheless this is not a lasting condition, and in itself it is not sufficient to destroy the force of an action.

---

self-help remedy such as set-off should be potentially available. For the discussion of set-off, see p. 144 above.

[14] This third scenario differs from the two previous ones in that an obligation is actually undertaken at the very time that the 'outward sign' is given to the promisee. This contrasts with the previous two scenarios, which concerned a statement by the 'promisor' that an obligation might be or would be undertaken in the future. For this reason, this third scenario creates a perfect obligation, while the first two do not.

[15] A perfect promise or obligation means one which confers onto the promisee a right of action by a court, by which the promisor can be compelled to carry out his promise. In the case of an imperfect promise or obligation (such as that outlined in the second scenario), the promisee has only self-help rights such as set-off, but no right to institute a legal action in the courts. The effect, then, is that, in the three scenarios which Grotius outlines, the first creates no obligation at all; the second creates an imperfect obligation; and the third creates a perfect obligation.

[16] The point is that, without an intention on the promisor's part to be legally bound, a legal obligation cannot arise, even in cases where the formalities required for concluding a contract have been performed. This heavy stress on intention (and, more generally, on subjective mental elements) was a distinctive feature of Roman law which was carried over into natural-law thought. This was in contrast to some other legal systems where the presence or absence of legal obligations is determined solely by way of objective, outward signs.

Now the time when a boy begins to employ reason cannot be absolutely fixed, but must be assumed from his daily acts, or even from what commonly happens in any region. And so among the Jews, a promise was valid which was made by a youth who had completed his thirteenth year, or by a girl who had completed her twelfth.

These, however, are the special effects of municipal law, and they therefore have nothing in common with the law of nature or the law of nations, except that it is natural that they should be observed in the places where they are in force. In consequence, if a foreigner makes an agreement with a citizen, he will be bound by the laws of the latter's country, for the reason that a person who makes a contract in any place is under the law of that place as a temporary subject.

The case will be clearly different if the agreement is made on the sea, or on a desert island, or by means of letters between those who are at a distance. For such agreements are governed by the law of nature alone, as are also the agreements of those who hold sovereign power, in so far as this affects their sovereign right.[17] For in the promises which [sovereigns] make in their private capacity, even those laws have effect which make the act void where this is to their own advantage, but not when the act is to their loss.[18]

6. Whether a promise given under a misapprehension is binding by the law of nature

The treatment of agreements based on a misapprehension is perplexing enough. It is, in fact, customary to distinguish between errors which affect the substance of the matter and those which do not; to consider whether a contract was based on fraud or not; whether the person with whom the contract was made was a party to the fraud; and whether the act was one of strict justice or only of good faith. For in view of the diversity of these cases, the writers declare some acts void and others binding, but in such a way that they may be annulled or changed at the choice of the one injured. The majority of these distinctions come from the Roman law, . . . and some of them are not entirely true or accurate.

---

[17] Agreements made on the high seas or on a desert island are governed by natural law because no state has sovereignty over those areas, so there is no municipal law to apply. The same is true for sovereigns contracting with one another (on official or public matters) – there is no sovereign above them and hence no municipal law to apply.

[18] The distinction is between contracts made by rulers in their sovereign capacity, which are governed exclusively by natural law, and contracts by sovereigns in a personal capacity, which are governed by the municipal law of the place where they were concluded (in the same manner as contracts between private parties). This latter type of contract is consequently subject to municipal laws which make contracts voidable (rather than 'void') in certain circumstances. For example, such laws typically allow the withdrawal of a promise when the promisor himself is the party that would benefit.

Now a method of ascertaining the truth according to [the law of] nature is furnished to us by the fact that, as regards the force and effect of laws, nearly every one agrees that, if [the application of] a law rests upon the presumption of a certain fact which does not actually obtain, then that law does not apply. [F]or the whole foundation for the [application of the] law is overthrown when the truth of the [assumed] fact fails. The decision [as to] when a law has been based on such a presumption must be inferred from the substance, words, and circumstances of the law.

In like manner, then, we shall say that, if a promise has been based on a certain presumption of fact which does not so obtain, by the law of nature it has no force. For the promisor did not consent to the promise except under a certain condition which, in fact, did not exist.[19]

If, however, the promisor was careless in investigating the matter, or in expressing his thought, and another has suffered loss therefrom, the promisor will be bound to make this loss good, not from the force of the promise, but by reason of the loss suffered through his fault.

On the other hand, if there was an error present indeed, but the promise was not based thereon, the action will be valid, since true consent was not lacking. But in this case also, if the person to whom the promise is made has by fraud caused the error, . . . he will have to make good whatever loss the promisor has suffered in consequence of the error. If the promise only in part was based on error, it will be valid as to the remainder.

7. Whether a promise made under the influence of fear is binding

No less involved is the discussion of that which is done under the influence of fear. For in this case also, a distinction is ordinarily made between a fear that is very great, either in its own nature or with reference to the person fearing, and a fear that is slight; between a fear that is justly and one that is unjustly occasioned; again, whether the fear was caused by the one to whom the promise is made, or by another; and also a distinction is recognised between acts that are generous and those that are burdensome. In accordance with these distinctions, some acts are said to be void, others revocable at the will of the promisor, and others entitling to entire restitution. In regard to all these cases there is a great variety of opinions.

On the whole, I accept the opinion of those who think that the person that makes a promise under the influence of fear is bound by it, if the municipal law, which can annul or diminish an obligation, is not taken into consideration.[20] For in such a case, there is a consent, not conditional, as we just now said in regard to the person in error, but absolute. As Aristotle, in fact, has rightly stated, the man who throws his property overboard because of the fear of shipwreck

---

[19] This is another indication of the central role that intention plays in natural-law theory.

[20] I.e., if only natural law is considered.

would wish to save it conditionally, if there was no danger of a shipwreck. But, considering the circumstances of the place and time, he is willing to lose his property absolutely.[21]

At the same time, this, I think, is indubitably true, that, if the person to whom the promise is made has inspired a fear, not just but unjust, even though slight, and the promise has resulted therefrom, he is bound to release the promisor, if the latter so wishes, not because the promise was without force, but on account of the damage wrongfully caused. The exception to this, which is allowed by the law of nations, I shall explain below in its proper connexion.[22]

The rule that some acts are made void on account of fear inspired by a different person from the one with whom the agreement is made, belongs to municipal law, which often makes void or revocable acts that were freely performed, but performed by a person possessed of weak judgement. Here, I wish to assume also the repetition of what I said above about the force and effect of municipal law. What effect an oath has in strengthening promises we shall discuss below.[23]

8. Whether, in order that a promise may be valid, that which is promised ought to be within the power of the promisor

In order that a promise may be valid, the subject of it ought to be either actually or potentially under the control of the promisor. In the first place, then, promises to perform an act which is in itself illegal are not valid; for no one has, and no one can have, a right to do anything that is unlawful. A promise, as I said above, takes its force from the power of the promisor, and does not extend beyond.

Again, if the thing is not at present within the power of the promisor, but may be at some future time, the validity of the promise will be in suspense; under such circumstances, the promise ought to be thought of as made on the condition that the thing should come into the power of the promisor. But if the condition under which the thing can come into the power of the promisor implies his power to obtain it, the promisor will be bound to do whatever is morally right, in order to fulfil the promise.

In this class also, ordinarily the civil law makes many promises void, which would ... be binding [under natural law].[24] Such is the promise of future marriage by a man or woman who is now married;[25] such also are not a few promises made by minors, or by children subject to parental control.

---

[21] Aristotle, *The Nicomachean Ethics*, III.1.

[22] See p. 257 below, on peace treaties between states.   [23] See p. 219 below.

[24] I.e., would be binding according to natural law.

[25] Presumably, this would therefore be understood as a promise to obtain a dissolution of the present marriage, if that were regarded as possible, or perhaps as a promise to use best efforts to obtain such a dissolution (meaning, of course, lawful efforts, to the exclusion of more robust measures such as murdering the spouse). The promise might also be understood as a conditional promise to marry the person in the event that the subsisting marriage were to terminate by some means (such as the death of the present spouse).

9. Whether by the law of nature a promise to do an illegal act is binding

At this point, the question is customarily raised, whether the promise to perform an act which by nature is morally wrong is by the law of nature valid; as if, for instance, something should be promised to a man for committing a murder.[26] In such a case, it is clear that the promise itself is criminal; for it is made to this end, that another may be induced to commit a crime. However, not everything which is done wrongfully loses the effect of a right, as is apparent in the case of an extravagant gift. But there is this difference, that when such a gift has been made, the wrongful act comes to an end; for the property is left in the hands of the recipient, without further harm. In promises made for a wrongful cause, however, the fault continues as long as the crime has not been committed; for during so long a time, the fulfilment of the promise as an allurement to crime carries a moral blemish within itself, and this comes to an end only after the crime has been committed. Hence it follows that, up to this time, the effectiveness of such a promise is in suspense, just as we said above in regard to the promising of a thing which is not in our power.[27] But when the crime has been committed, the force of the obligation, which from the beginning was not intrinsically lacking but was restrained by the accompanying wrong, is revealed.[28]

---

[26] There has already been a discussion (in Section 8) of the case of a promise 'to perform an act which is in itself illegal', i.e., the case in which the promisor promises to commit an illegal act himself. In the present discussion, the promisor is not promising to commit the illegal act himself, but instead is engaging the services of another person for an illegal end. Paying someone to perform a service for one's benefit is, of course, lawful in general. But the present issue concerns what happens when that service is an illegal act – and specifically, whether an obligation to pay the money for the performance of the illegal act is thereby created.

[27] The practical effect is that the hirer would have no legal action against the 'hit man' to compel him to carry out the crime. The 'moral blemish' of the arrangement prevents such a right of action from arising. It is interesting that Grotius regards this 'moral blemish' as expunged once the murder is actually committed. This is because the 'moral blemish' referred to is the inducing of another person to commit a crime. Once the crime has been committed, the inducement is no longer present. Grotius is taking the position that, strictly speaking, the hirer is liable only for the inducement, with the hit man liable for the actual commission of the murder.

[28] It will strike some readers as very curious that Grotius would hold that one who hires a murderer to kill someone is legally obligated to pay once the murder has been duly carried out. As Grotius put it, 'the force of the obligation' to commit the murder was not 'intrinsically lacking'. It is true, as just pointed out, that the obligation was 'restrained', in the sense that there could be no legal right to compel the commission of the crime. But once the crime is duly carried out, the hirer becomes required to perform his end of the bargain and pay the agreed fee to the hit man (i.e., the force of the obligation is then 'revealed', as Grotius puts it). It would appear that, according to Grotius, the basis of this obligation on the hirer would be the contract itself, and not the general equitable principle of unjust enrichment (i.e., the amount owed

Now if the injustice of the one to whom the promise was given has furnished the occasion for it, or if there is unfairness in the contract, the proper remedy is a different question, which we shall treat presently.[29]

10. Concerning a promise made to obtain a thing which was already due before the promise

If we look to the law of nature, what is promised for a cause already due is not on that account the less obligatory. . . . For a promise, even if made without a cause, by the law of nature would be binding. But in this case also, loss through extortion, and unfairness in the contract, will have to be made good according to the rules which are to be laid down later.[30]

11. The method of making a firm and binding promise in person

As regards the mode of making a promise, that also, as we said about the transfer of ownership, requires an external act, that is, an adequate indication of intent, for which sometimes a nod may suffice, but more often the spoken word or writing is employed.

12. Making a binding promise through the agency of others

But we may be obligated also by another, if there is no doubt concerning the intent with which we chose him as our agent, whether specifically for the

---

would be the amount that the hirer promised to pay in the contract, and not the amount by which he became better off as a result of the commission of the murder).

It should be appreciated that Grotius is speaking only of the position of the hirer, explaining why he is under an obligation under the contract. Grotius unfortunately does not address the intriguing question of the position of the hit man and what kind of rights, if any, would accrue to him. It could be argued that the hit man should have a legal action under the contract against the hirer for payment, in the ordinary manner, pursuant to the promise – with the hit man then being liable to punishment under the criminal law for his act, as an entirely separate transaction. It could also be contended that the hit man should have only an imperfect right to payment (i.e., that he would have no legal action to enforce the hirer's obligation to pay), on the ground that the due process of law should not be available for the facilitation of criminal acts. It could also be argued that the hit man should have no claim on the basis of the promise as such (because of the illegality of the arrangement), but he should be able to claim instead on the ground of unjustified enrichment, since the hirer has received the benefit which he sought and has thereby been enriched. Finally, it could be contended that the hit man obtains no right at all, on the ground that criminal conduct should not give rise to legal rights of any kind.

[29] In other words, the position is different if, say, the hit man was the one who initiated the arrangement, or if there was 'unfairness in the contract', such as a use of force to compel the hit man's assent to the arrangement, against his will.

[30] See p. 252 below.

business in hand, or under a general appointment. In the case of a general authorisation, it can happen that our agent may obligate us by acting contrary to our desires as expressed to him alone. In such a case, two acts of will must be distinguished, one by which we bind ourselves to ratify whatever our agent does in business of such a nature, and the other by which we bind him not to act except according to our directions, which are known to him but not to others. This distinction is to be noted with respect to those promises which are made on behalf of kings by ambassadors, by virtue of the power contained in their credentials, but which exceed their secret instructions.

13. On obligations incurred through the agency of ship-captains

From this we can understand also that actions associated with the transactions of ship-captains and business agents . . . come within the purview of the law of nature. In this connexion, it should be added that, by the Roman law, the provision was wrongfully introduced that shipowners should individually be wholly responsible for the acts of the captain.[31] This provision, in fact, is neither in accord with natural justice, which considers it sufficient if individuals are responsible according to their proportionate shares; nor is it advantageous for the public good. Men are deterred from engaging in commerce if they are afraid that they will be held accountable for the acts of the captain as if to any limit.

For such reasons, among the Dutch, whose commerce has greatly flourished for a long time, that law of the Romans was not formerly, and is not now, observed. On the contrary, the principle has been established that, in respect to responsibility for the acts of the captain, all the owners together are liable for no more than the value of the ship and the cargo.[32]

14. Whether the acceptance of a promise is necessary to make it binding

In order that a promise may transfer a right, the acceptance of it is no less necessary than when a transfer of ownership is made; yet in this case also, it is understood that a preceding request continues, and has the force of an acceptance.[33] And no obstacle is presented to this view by the rule of the civil

---

[31] That is, that each owner of a share of a ship should be liable for the whole of any damage caused by the captain of that ship.

[32] A twofold limit is posited to the liability of ship-owners for acts of captains: firstly, that each owner should be responsible only for a share of the damage proportionate to his own investment; and secondly, that there be a ceiling on the aggregate damages, equal to the value of the ship plus the cargo. These liability limitations are comparable to those of members (or shareholders) of a corporate body.

[33] I.e, if the promisee requested the promisor to make the promise in question, then no additional indication of acceptance is required after the actual making of the promise.

law concerning promises made to the state. Nevertheless, this consideration has led some to judge that [in general] the act of promising is alone sufficient. However, the Roman law does not say that [a] promise has full binding force before the acceptance, but [only] forbids the revocation of the promise, in order that the acceptance may be possible at any time.

This effect does not follow from the law of nature but merely from the civil law.[34] Not unlike it is the effect of the custom which the law of nations has introduced on behalf of infants and idiots. For in the interest of such persons, just as the law supplies the intent to possess the things which are sought, so it supplies also the intent to accept them.[35]

15. Whether an acceptance ought to be made known to the promisor

This question is also commonly raised, whether it is sufficient that the acceptance be signified, or whether, in fact, the acceptance ought also to be made known to the promisor before the promise attains its full effect. It is certain that a promise can be made in both ways, either thus: 'I desire that this be valid, if it be accepted'; or thus: 'I desire that this shall be valid if I shall have understood that it has been accepted.' In promises which deal with mutual obligations, the latter meaning is assumed. [B]ut in merely generous [i.e., unilateral] promises, it is better that the former meaning should be believed to be present, unless something else should appear.

16. On revocation by a promisor before acceptance

Hence it follows that, before acceptance, a promise can be revoked without injustice, since the right has not yet been transferred[36] ... Furthermore, a promise can be revoked if the person to whom it was made dies before accepting it, for the reason that the acceptance seems to have been submitted to his decision and not to that of his heirs. It is, in fact, one thing to wish to give to a man a right which will pass to his heirs, and another to wish to give directly to the heirs; for it makes a great difference upon whom the favour is conferred.[37]

---

34 Natural law allows the withdrawal of a promise at any time prior to its acceptance by the promisee. See Section 16 below.
35 It 'supplies the intent', as Grotius puts it, by conclusively presuming acceptance on their part.
36 *Digest*, 40.2.4 (Julian).
37 This exposition is rather unclear, as it seems to suggest the existence of a special rule giving the promisor an option to revoke in the event of the death of the promisee. But the logic of his argument seems to suggest, instead, that the death of the promisee automatically revokes the promise, if the promise was intended to be for his benefit only – not because of any special rule concerning that circumstance, but simply because acceptance has now become impossible. If, however, the promise was

17. Whether a promise is revoked on the death of an intermediary

A promise can be revoked also on the death of the person who has been chosen to convey orally the promisor's intent, for the reason that the obligation had been based on his words.[38] The situation is different in the case of a messenger who has not an instrumental part in the obligation, but is merely the bearer of the obligatory instrument.[39] Similarly letters, which indicate consent, can be carried by anyone.

Further, we must distinguish between the servant who has been chosen [merely] to report the promise, and the agent authorised to make the promise himself. In the former case, [a] revocation [by the promisor] will be fully binding, even if it be not known to the servant.[40] [B]ut in the second case, [such] a revocation will not be valid, because the right of promising was dependent on the will of the representative himself; and this will was without fault in promising, because lacking knowledge of the revocation.[41] So, again, in the

> intended to benefit either the decedent or his heir (in the event of his death), then the promise would remain in force upon the promisee's death – though it could still be revoked prior to acceptance by the heir. Here too, however, there is no special rule, but simply an application of the general principle, just stated by Grotius, that promises are revocable prior to acceptance.
>
> [38] *Digest*, 17.1.57 (Papinian). The situation envisaged is, apparently, one in which an agent is authorised actually to formulate the promise on behalf of the promisor. Grotius's reasoning seems questionable. The true position would seem to be that, if the agent dies before the promise is formulated and delivered, then there simply is no promise at all – and hence no cause to speak of a right of revocation.
>
> [39] In the case of an agent who is a mere courier, rather than an actual formulator of the promise, the promise is held to have been made at the time at which the promisor put the promise into words (prior to the dispatch of the courier). Consequently, the promise is in existence throughout the period of the courier's travels – and even in the event that the courier dies en route and never conveys the promise. The position then is that a promise has been made but that it cannot be accepted, since the promisee is ignorant of the existence of the promise. It is possible, however, that the promisee might learn of the existence and terms of the promise by other means – and he can then accept and thereby convert the promise into a binding obligation.
>
> [40] This seems a somewhat harsh result because it leads to the situation in which the courier duly arrives and conveys the promise to the promisee – but in which there is, in fact, no promise because of the promisor's prior revocation (unknown to both the courier and the promisee). The promisee is consequently left in a state of misapprehension. In Grotius's opinion, this awkwardness is unavoidable, since the right of a promisor to withdraw a promise prior to the acceptance of it has the higher priority.
>
> [41] *Digest*, 17.1.15 (Paul). The case, again, is one in which the agent does not merely convey the text of an existing promise, but actually formulates the promise himself, on behalf of the promisor, upon arriving at the location of the promisee. A purported revocation of the promise by the promisor whilst the agent is en route is not an actual revocation because no promise is in existence until the agent arrives at his destination and formulates and conveys the promise. The promise can only be revoked in the window of time *after* that occurs and *before* the promisee accepts.

former case a donation can be accepted after the death of the giver, as being completed on the one side, though it had been subject to revocation [prior to the death].[42] ... In the second case, the gift cannot be accepted, because it was not made, but merely ordered to be made.[43]

In case of doubt, the conclusion is that it was the intent of the person who directed the making of the promise that it be fulfilled, unless some great change has occurred, such as the death of that person. Nevertheless, there may be presumptions which suggest a different decision, and which ought to be easily admitted, so that a gift which was to be given for a worthy cause may be made.[44]

18. Whether a promise is revocable after acceptance by a proxy

Disputes are wont to arise also in regard to an acceptance given by proxy. In such cases, we must distinguish between a promise made to me about giving something to another, and a promise conveyed in the name of the person to whom the thing is to be given. If the promise has been made to me without regard to the question whether I am personally interested, ... it seems that, in accepting, by the law of nature I am given the right of effecting the transfer of the right to the other party, if he also accepts, and in such a way that, in the meantime, the promise cannot be revoked by the promisor. On the other hand, I who have received the promise may remit it. For this opinion is not inconsistent with the law of nature, and it is particularly in harmony with the wording of such a promise.[45]

---

[42] The focus is now shifted from the making of a promise to a donation of property – which, like a promise, requires acceptance by the donee in order to be legally effective. In the case in which the agent is a mere courier, bearing the news of the gift to the donee, the donor is held to have done everything in his power to transfer the property, as of the time of the dispatch of the courier, with nothing remaining to complete the transaction except the acceptance by the donee. As in the case of promises, though, the donation is revocable by the donor prior to acceptance; but this ability to withdraw ends with the donor's death. So if the donor dies whilst the courier is en route (without having revoked the gift), then the transfer of property becomes complete after the arrival of the courier and acceptance by the donee.

[43] In this second case, the gift is held not to be made from the donor's side until the agent expresses the intention to make the gift on the principal's behalf, i.e., until he arrives and informs the donee of the situation. Unfortunately for the would-be donee, the death of the principal automatically terminates the agency relationship, so that, by the time of his arrival, the agent has no power to proffer the gift. So the intended donee takes nothing.

[44] *Digest*, 40.2.4 (Julian).

[45] This situation is one in which Person A promises to Person B (Mr Grotius) that he (A) will give something to Person C. This is on the understanding that B is not an agent or servant of C but rather an altogether independent party. Grotius contends that B has the right to accept the gift, in effect on C's behalf, and thereby to impose an enforceable legal obligation onto A to effectuate the gift. But there are two

Now if the promise has been conveyed in the name of the person to whom the thing is to be given, the distinction must be made whether the one who accepts it has a special authorisation to accept it (or an authorisation so general that such an acceptance ought to be considered as included therein); or whether he has no authorisation whatever. Where such an authorisation has preceded, I do not think that we should insist on the further inquiry whether the person is his own master or not; . . . we should rather consider that, by such an acceptance, the promise is fully completed, because consent can be transmitted and indicated even by the agency of a servant. I am in fact considered to wish what I have entrusted to the will of another, if he also wishes it.[46]

When, however, there is no authorisation, if another to whom the promise was not made should with the permission of the promisor accept it, the result will be that the promisor is not permitted to revoke his promise until the person whom it concerns has accepted or refused. Yet in the meantime, the one who has accepted cannot remit the promise, for in this case he was not employed to accept a right, but merely to bind the good faith of the promisor in fulfilling the favour. And yet the situation is such that, if the promisor should revoke his promise, he would be acting contrary to good faith and not against the individual right of any one.[47]

---

caveats. The first is that C might wish to decline the gift, despite B's acceptance; and he retains a right to do this, with the effect that B's acceptance has a certain provisional character. The practical effect of B's acceptance, therefore, is to prevent A from revoking the gift prior to C's acceptance (or rejection), which he would otherwise have the right to do. The second caveat is that B has the right to release A from his promise at his own unilateral will, on the ground that the promise was made to B and not to C. In such an event, C has no entitlement to the gift.

[46] In this instance, A makes his promise to C; with B then being authorised by C to accept the promised benefit on his behalf. The promise becomes a legal obligation (owed by A to C) upon such an acceptance by B.

[47] In this scenario, Person A makes his promise to C. Now, however, B is authorised by A to accept the promise, but is not authorised by C himself to do so. (It is somewhat difficult to see how such a situation could actually arise.) B may purport to accept the promise, but this cannot amount to an acceptance by C himself; nor can B release A from the promise, as in the earlier case, since the promise was not made to or on behalf of B.

This much is clear. What is unclear is whether B's involvement has any legal significance at all. Grotius implies that it does, when he states that, once B has accepted the promise, 'the promisor is not permitted to revoke his promise until the person whom it concerns [C] has accepted or refused'. In other words, B cannot accept the promise on C's behalf; but he can perform the lesser, and still useful, service of cutting off A's general right of revocation. Grotius, however, also says – apparently inconsistently – that a revocation by A prior to acceptance by C 'is not against the individual right of anyone'. These statements are probably best reconciled on the understanding that A's duty not to revoke is owed to B and not to C. Therefore, if A does revoke (prior to C's acceptance) and fails to perform the

19. At what time a burdensome condition can be added to a promise

From what has been said, we can understand also what ought to be thought about the addition of a burdensome condition to a promise. This can, in fact, take place so long as the promise has not been completed by acceptance, nor made irrevocable by giving a pledge. Moreover, a burdensome condition to the advantage of a third party can be revoked, so long as it has not been accepted by that party.

20. How an invalid promise can be made binding

The question is also commonly discussed, how a promise, which was based on a misunderstanding, can be made valid if, after the error has been found out, the promisor wishes to keep his promise. The same question can be raised also in regard to promises which the civil law makes void because of fear, or for any other cause, if the cause has afterwards ceased to have effect.

To confirm such promises, some require merely a mental act which, joined with the previous external act, they consider sufficient to produce a binding obligation. Others, who are dissatisfied with this requirement, because an external act cannot be the sign of a mental resolve which comes later, require a new verbal promise and acceptance.

The truth rather lies between these two views. An external act is indeed required, but it is not necessarily expressed in words; for the retention of the thing promised by the person to whom the promise was made, and the abandonment of it on the part of the promisor, or some similar act, may suffice to indicate consent.

21. Whether promises without cause are void by the law of nature

In order that the civil law may not be confused with the law of nature, this statement also must not be omitted, that promises, which have no cause expressed,[48] are not by the law of nature void, any more than material gifts.

---

promise, then he does not infringe any right belonging to C. But he does not infringe any right of B either, in the sense that the non-performance of the promise is no injury to B, since the promise was not made to B. Grotius apparently takes the view that such a revocation would nonetheless be 'contrary to good faith'.

It would seem that a better interpretation would be that non-performance of the promise per se would injure neither B nor C; but that the act of revoking the promise would (arguably) be a breach of a right owed to B, and not merely an act of bad faith. B, however, would incur no material injury from that breach since the promise was not made to him.

[48] I.e., for which the donor gives no reason for making the gift.

22. Whether a person who has promised an act of another is bound by the law of nature

A person who has promised the act of another is not held accountable for the material interest involved, provided he has not omitted to do what he could on his own part to secure the action, unless the words of the promise or the nature of the business add a more strict obligation.[49]

[49] An example of 'a more strict obligation' would be a promise that the other person would actually perform the act in question, as opposed to a promise to use best efforts to induce the other person to perform.

12

On contracts

1. Of men's acts

Of the acts of men which are advantageous to other men, some are simple, others of a mixed character.

2. The kinds of simple acts

Some simple acts are merely kind, others are reciprocal. The kindnesses either are unmixed or involve a kind of mutual obligation. Unmixed kindnesses are either fulfilled in the present, or are directed to the future. A useful deed is accomplished in the present; and in regard to this, it is not necessary to speak. [W]hile it is advantageous, to be sure, it has no legal effect. Of the same character is a donation by which ownership of property is transferred, and that topic we treated above, when the matter of acquiring ownership was under consideration.[1] Not only promises to give but also promises to perform are directed toward the future; these also we have already treated.[2]

Advantageous acts which involve a mutual obligation[3] are those which dispose of property without alienation,[4] or accomplish a deed in such a way that some

---

[1] See p. 138 above.   [2] See the previous chapter.

[3] The matters discussed in this paragraph are taken from Roman law (with some modifications) and are not very comprehensible without knowledge of that background. By 'advantageous acts which involve a mutual obligation', Grotius refers, in essence, to a category of arrangements sometimes called 'real contracts' in Roman law. These are, in a manner of speaking, 'pre-packaged' or standard arrangements which are brought into legal force, or activated, by the delivery of an object by one party to the other – i.e., they do not arise merely by agreement between the parties, as in the case of contracts generally. The delivery of the object is essential. Clear examples (which Grotius immediately gives) are a 'gratuitous bailment' (called *commodatum* in Roman-law parlance) and a deposit on trust (a safe-keeping arrangement). Less clear is mandate, which (as Grotius explains) is the performance of a service. Mandate in Roman law was, however, not regarded as a 'real contract' but rather as a true contract, i.e., one in which legal obligations arose by virtue of agreement alone between the parties.

[4] I.e., things which involve transfers of possession of property, without change of legal title.

effect remains. Such in regard to things is the permission to use, which is called a gratuitous bailment; and in regard to deeds the undertaking of a costly service, or one implying obligations, which is called a mandate; one form of the mandate is the deposit in trust, which involves the expenditure of labour in guarding and keeping a thing.

3. On reciprocal acts

Reciprocal acts either separate the parties or produce a community of interests. Those acts which are separative the Roman jurists rightly divide into these classes: I give that you may give; I do that you may do; [and] I do that you may give.... [I]n accordance with nature, we shall refer all ... contracts to the three classes.

We shall say ... that, in the agreement to give that there may be giving in return, a person gives a thing directly for a thing, as in that form which is particularly called exchange of commodities. [This] is, without doubt, the most ancient form of commerce. [There is also the case of] money ... given for money, which merchants in ancient Greece called money-changing and we to-day call exchange. [O]r a thing is given for money, as in buying and selling; or the use of one thing for another thing, or the use of one thing for the use of another, or the use of a thing for money. [T]his last is called letting and hiring.... [U]nder the term 'use', we here understand not only the bare use but the use which is joined with the enjoyment of the income.

The exchanging of an act for an act [which is the second category of reciprocal acts] may [also] have innumerable forms, according to the diversity of the acts.

[The third category of reciprocal acts comprises arrangements in which the principle is that] I do, that you may give. In the one case, I do, that you may give money. [T]his, in acts of daily service, is called letting and hiring; and in the act of guaranteeing indemnity against chance losses, it is called a guarding against risk, or, in everyday speech, insurance, a form of contract which was formerly scarcely known, but is now very common. In other cases, [I do], that you may give a thing or the use of a thing.

4. Reciprocal acts that sometimes contribute to a community of interests

Acts which contribute to a community of interests bring about a sharing in activities or in things, and turn these to the common advantage; all such acts come under the head of joint undertakings. In this class is included also an association for purposes of war, as among us the frequent union of privately owned vessels against pirates or other assailants, which is now commonly called an admiral's force, and by the Greeks was named 'a sailing together' or 'a joint sailing'.

5. Acts of mixed character

Acts are of a mixed character, either in their essential elements or through the association of another act. Thus if I knowingly buy a thing at a price higher than it is worth, and give the excess in price to the seller, the act will be partly gift, partly purchase. If I promise money to a jeweller for making rings for me out of his own gold, the transaction will be partly purchase, partly hiring.[5] So in a partnership, it [sometimes] happens that one party contributes services and money, the other money only.

In a feudal contract, the granting of the fief is a kindness; but the agreement to render military service in return for protection is a contract, of the form 'I do that you may do'.[6] If, furthermore, the burden of a yearly payment is added, the transaction to that extent is blended with leasing. Also, a loan on things at sea is a mixed contract, which consists of a contract for a loan and an insurance against loss.

6. Acts that may be of mixed character only by reason of an additional act

An act becomes of mixed character by the addition of another act, as in giving security, or in putting up a pledge. For the giving of security, if you look at the transaction as between the surety and the principal debtor, is in the main a mandate; as between the creditor and the surety, who receives nothing, it seems merely an act of generosity; but because the giving of security is added to burdensome contracts, it is customarily judged a part of the same act. So the giving of a pledge seems in itself an act of generosity, by which the retention of a thing is granted; but this also derives its nature from the contract, for which it furnishes security.[7]

---

[5] I.e., it is a purchase of the jeweller's labour, and a hiring of the jeweller's gold.

[6] In theory, according to feudal law, the granting of a fief to a vassal was a unilateral gratuitous act on the part of the feudal superior. For this reason, a fief was often known as a benefice. Theoretically separate from this was the contractual arrangement of protection (by the lord) in return for services (by the vassal). In reality, however, possession of the fief was what the vassal truly desired; so that the fief was, in reality if not in theory, the 'payment' to the vassal for the furnishing of services.

[7] In an arrangement of the kind discussed, A wishes to borrow money from B; but B regards A as insufficiently creditworthy. A persuades X (who is creditworthy) to act as a surety, i.e., to promise to B that, if A should default on his repayment, then he (X) will step in and pay B the money owed. X would receive some kind of fee or other reward from A for this favour. The arrangement between A and X is one of mandate, since X is doing a service for A for a fee. Focussing narrowly on the relation of X and B, however, it appears that X is conferring a wholly gratuitous favour, since X is undertaking a potential liability to B but is receiving nothing in return from B. Grotius points out that this transaction is best viewed as a sort of single, compound

7. What acts are called contracts

Now all acts of benefit to others, except mere acts of kindness, are called contracts.[8]

8. That equality is required in contracts

The law of nature enjoins that there be equality in contracts, and in such a way that the party who receives less acquires a right of action from the inequality.

9. Equality as regards knowledge of the facts

[Regarding] acts [preceding the conclusion of a contract], consideration pertains that the person who is making a contract with anyone ought to point out to him the faults of the thing concerned in the transaction which are known to himself. This is not only prevailingly established by the civil laws[9] but is also consistent with the nature of the act. For between the contracting parties, there is a closer union than ordinarily obtains in human society.

The same thing, however, should not be said in regard to circumstances which have no direct connexion with the thing contracted for. . . . The giving of such information is, in fact, a part of one's [moral] duty, and praiseworthy, so that often it cannot be omitted without violating the rule of love. Yet such omission is not unjust, that is, it is not inconsistent with the right of the one with whom the contract is made.

In general, therefore, it is not necessary to follow the statement of . . . Cicero, that you practise concealment when, for the sake of your own gain, you wish that those, whose interest it is to know, shall be in ignorance of what you know.[10] This is applicable only when those facts are considered which are intimately connected with the subject of the transaction, as in the case of a house which is infected with pestilence, or which the magistrates have ordered to be pulled down; examples which you may find in the same passage of Cicero.

But it is not necessary that faults known to the person with whom you are dealing should be mentioned. . . . Equal knowledge on both sides, in fact, puts the contracting parties on an equal footing.[11]

(or mixed) arrangement, comprising two components (the A–X mandate, and the X–B guarantee) of differing character.

8   The exclusion of 'mere acts of kindness' is important because the effect is that there must be reciprocal benefits or obligations in a contract.

9   *Digest*, 19.1.1.1 (Ulpian).   10   Cicero, *On Duties*, III.50–7.

11   In other words, non-disclosure of the kind discussed is not, strictly speaking, wrongful per se. It is wrongful if it is the cause of ignorance on the part of the other party. So if the other party already possesses the relevant information, he can have no action for non-disclosure.

10. Equality as regards freedom of choice

Not only in the knowledge of facts but also in the freedom of choice, there ought to be a kind of equality between the contracting parties. Not indeed that any preceding fear, if justly inspired, ought to be removed, for that is outside of the contract; but that no fear should be unjustly inspired for the sake of making the contract; or, if such fear has been inspired, that it should be removed.

11. Equality in the act of making a contract

The equality demanded in the principal act of a contract is, that no more be exacted than is just. . . . In all contracts with exchange of considerations, . . . the rule should be carefully observed. And there is no reason why one should say that whatever either party has promised in excess should be considered a donation. Such is not ordinarily the intention of persons making contracts, . . . and such an intention ought not to be assumed unless it is apparent. Whatever, in fact, the parties promise or give, they should be believed to promise or give as on an equality with the thing which is about to be received, and due by reason of that equality.[12]

12. Equality in the subject of the contract

There remains equality in the subject of the contract, consisting in this, that although nothing has been concealed which ought to have been said, and no more has been exacted than was considered due, nevertheless if an inequality has been detected in the transaction, though without the fault of either party – because, for example, the fault was hidden, or because there was a mistake in the price . . . this inequality should be made good, and something should be taken from the one who has more and given to the one who has less; for, in the contract, it was proposed, or ought to have been proposed, on both sides, that each should receive the same amount.

The Roman law did not establish this rule to apply to every inequality, for it does not follow up trivial differences, since it judged that a multitude of lawsuits

---

[12] As noted in the previous chapter, there is nothing to prevent an arrangement which combines elements of contract and promise (e.g., an arrangement for the giving of a lavish reward for a small service). It is therefore always possible to characterise any arrangement in which there is inequality of benefit between the parties in that way. But Grotius insists that there is a strong presumption against interpreting an unequal arrangement in that charitable fashion. In the general case, it will be an instance of a violation of the natural-law principle that there must be equality in contracts (i.e., inequality of benefits will generally be a sign of oppression of one party by the other one, rather than a case of benevolence or generosity on the part of the disadvantaged party).

would result; but the rule is applicable in sufficiently important differences, as those which exceed one-half of the just price.

13. Equality in acts of kindness

But it is to be noted that a kind of equality is to be maintained also in contracts of beneficence, not indeed of the same degree as in contracts requiring an exchange, but in accordance with the supportive character of the transaction, in order that a person may not suffer loss from his own generosity. Therefore, a mandatary ought to be indemnified for expenses incurred and for loss which he has suffered in consequence of the mandate.[13] A bailee, too, is bound to make good a thing lost, because he is under obligation to the owner not merely on account of the thing, that is, by reason of the force of ownership, by which, as we stated above, a temporary possessor would be bound, but also by reason of the acceptance of a favour. This rule holds good except in case the thing would have completely perished also in the possession of the owner; for, in such a case the owner would have lost nothing through the bailment. The acceptor of a gratuitous deposit, on the contrary, receives nothing beyond confidence in his good faith, and so, if the thing is lost, he will not be held liable, either in respect to the thing, because it does not exist and he is not made richer by it, or by reason of the acceptance of the thing, since in accepting he did not receive a favour but conferred it.[14]

In the case of a pledge, as also of a thing that has been hired, an intermediate course ought to be followed, in order that the receiver may not be made liable

[13] A mandatary is someone who performs a service for the benefit of another. Even if the mandatary has agreed to act gratuitously, he should nonetheless be reimbursed for out-of-pocket expenses incurred. Otherwise he would actually be worse off for performing the free service.

[14] Grotius points out that bailment (or *commodatum* in Roman-law terminology) and deposit are different in character, even though each involves the entrustment of an object by an owner to another person. In the case of bailment, the owner does a favour to the bailee by giving him custody of some object *and* allowing the bailee to use that object himself before returning it. An example would be a loan of a plough by one farmer to a neighbouring farmer for the neighbour to use. With deposit, in contrast, the recipient is doing a favour to the donor. He is performing the service of safe-keeping. For example, a person embarking on a long journey might entrust valuables to a neighbour, to avoid leaving them unguarded in his house during his absence. Because of this difference, a bailee is under a stricter duty to the owner than is a depositee. A bailee is strictly liable for the loss of the object whilst it is in his care, even if there was no fault on his part (save for the marginal case in which the property would have perished even if the owner had possessed it). A depositee, in contrast, is not liable for loss. So sweeping a conclusion in the case of depositees seems misplaced, however. It would seem that a depositee should be liable to the depositor if he *deliberately* destroys the deposited property or gives it to a third party. It seems probable that Grotius would accept this caveat and that his point is that there is no liability for negligent or careless loss by a depositee.

for any and every mishap, as a [bailee or] borrower is. And yet he ought to exhibit more diligent care than one who accepts a deposit; for the acceptance of a pledge is usually without profit, but is ordinarily associated with a burdensome contract.[15]

Now all these rules are in truth in conformity with Roman law. Yet they did not have their origin in the Roman law, but in natural justice; and therefore the same legal provisions will be found among other nations also.

Having now discussed the general subject at sufficient length for our purposes, let us run over some special questions in regard to contracts.

14. In what way the price of an object ought to be estimated in a sale

The most natural measure of the value of each thing is the need of it.[16] . . . This becomes the paramount consideration in the exchange of objects among barbarous peoples. Nevertheless, this is not the only measure. For the desire of men, which controls the price of things, covets many things more than their need requires.

On the contrary, it happens that the most necessary things are of less value because of their abundance. . . . Hence it comes about that a thing is valued at the price commonly offered or given for it; and that price is not so limited that it may not have a range of variation within which more or less may be given or asked, except in cases in which the law has established a definite price.

Moreover, with respect to the current price, account is ordinarily taken of the labours and expenditure of the dealers. The price, again, is wont to change suddenly according to the abundance or scarcity of buyers, of money, and of commodities. Also, circumstances may by accident arise, on account of which a commodity may lawfully be bought or sold above or below its normal price;

---

[15] In other words, a pledge arrangement falls mid-way between bailment and deposit. A pledge is a sort of favour by the lender to the borrower (in the sense that the lender would not have lent without the pledge, so that his acceptance of the pledge is a boon to the borrower in enabling the borrower to obtain the money lent). In that sense, a pledge-holder can be said to resemble a depositee. But a pledge is, at the same time, a strictly business transaction, closely associated with the 'burdensome contract' of lending (a loan being regarded as a burdensome contract from the borrower's standpoint). It benefits the lender in giving him greater security than he would otherwise have had. To that extent, the pledge-holder resembles a bailee (although he has no right to use the property, but only to hold it). As a result, the duty of care of a pledge-holder falls between that of bailee (strict liability) and depositee (no liability, at least for negligence). Grotius is a bit vague about this halfway position, saying only that the pledge-holder would not be liable 'for any and every mishap' in the manner of a bailee. His probable meaning is that the pledge-holder would be liable for loss of the property resulting from malice or negligence on his part, but not otherwise.

[16] This is the beginning of a discussion, from the standpoint of natural law, of the problem of value in economics.

such, for example, as an expected loss, absence of profit, personal fancy, or sale or purchase, as a favour to another, of that which would not otherwise have been bought or sold. Such exceptional circumstances should be made known to the person with whom we are dealing. Also, we can take into account the loss or absence of gain which arises from deferred or anticipated payments.

15. When according to the law of nature a sale is completed and ownership transferred

It must also be noted that, in selling and purchasing, the ownership may be transferred without delivery from the very moment of the contract, and that this is the most simple form. . . . But if it has been agreed that ownership shall not pass immediately, the seller will be under obligation to give possession according to contract, and in the meantime both gain and loss in the commodity will fall to the seller.

These, then, are fictions of the civil law not universally recognised, that sale and purchase consist in guaranteeing that one may have the property and right of recovery if dispossessed; also that the property shall be at the risk of the purchaser and that the income from it shall belong to him even before ownership passes. On the contrary, many lawgivers have enacted that, up to the time of delivery, the seller should have the profit of the commodity, as well as the risk.

This rule also should be known, that if an object has been sold twice, of the two sales, [the one] that will be effective [is the one] which has included in itself immediate transfer of ownership, either by delivery or in some other way. For by this act, the essential control over the object passes from the seller, a result which is not brought about by a promise alone.

16. What monopolies are contrary to the law of nature or the law of love[17]

Not all monopolies are contrary to the law of nature. Sometimes, in fact, monopolies may be permitted by the sovereign power for a just cause and with a fixed price.

A monopoly can also be established by private persons, if only with a fair price. But those who make a compact . . . that goods may be sold at a higher price than the current range of prices, or by violence or fraud hinder a larger supply from being imported, or buy up all the goods in such a way that they sell at a price which is unfair at the time of sale, are committing a wrong, and are bound to make good the loss. If in any other way they hinder the importation of merchandise, or so buy it up that they may sell it at a price which is higher, but

---

[17] This section, while interesting, strays from the principal topic at hand, which is the natural law of contracts.

under the circumstances not unfair, they are violating the rule of love;[18] ... but, properly speaking, they do not violate the rights of another.[19]

17. How money serves as the medium of exchange

As regards money, we should know that it acquires its function naturally, not by reason of its material alone, nor by reason of a special name or form, but because it has a more general character by which it is compared either with all things, or with the things that are most necessary. Its value, if not otherwise agreed upon, must be fixed according to the time and place of payment.

[W]hatever is employed as a measure of value for other things ought to be of such a character that, in itself, it shall vary as little as possible. Such, moreover, in the class of things possessed of value, are gold, silver, and copper. For in themselves, these metals have almost the same value everywhere, and always. But just as other things of which men are in need are plentiful or rare, so likewise money made of the same material and of the same weight has now a greater value, now a less.

18. Deductions from the price of rent on account of unfruitfulness or similar misfortunes

'Renting and hiring', as Gaius rightly said, 'is very near to selling and buying, and is subject to the same rules'.[20] The price, in fact, corresponds to the rent or hire, and the ownership of the thing to the right of user. Therefore, as the loss of the property itself falls upon the owner, so by the law of nature, in the case of unfruitfulness and other misfortunes which hinder the use [of rented property], the loss is borne by the renter; and the person letting the property will not on that account have less right to the promised rental, for the reason that he himself transferred the right to use, which had that value at the time.[21]

This rule, however, can be changed both by laws and by agreement. Nevertheless, if the landlord has rented the land to another tenant while the first renter was hindered from working it, whatever he has thereby gained he will repay to the first renter, in order that he may not become richer at another's expense.

---

[18] I.e., they commit a moral wrong.

[19] In modern parlance, it would be said that Grotius is asserting that holding and exploiting a dominant position in a market is not, as such, unlawful (though it is immoral). Such actions are not unlawful, in Grotius's opinion, unless wrongful methods are employed.

[20] *Digest*, 19.2.2 (Gaius).

[21] This principle is based on the understanding that, during the time period of the rental, the renter is to be regarded, in law, as the owner.

19. How a just payment for services may be increased or diminished

In regard to a sale, I said that a thing can be sold at a higher price or bought at a lower one if it is sold or bought as a favour to the other party. . . . The same rule should be understood in regard to the renting or hiring of property or service.

If one service can be useful to more than one person, as for the undertaking of a journey [by one person on behalf of several other persons], and if the contractor has bound himself firmly to several individuals, [then, provided that the municipal] law interposes no hindrance, he will be able to demand from each the payment which he would have exacted from the one. The fact that the service will be useful to a second person also is outside the contract which was entered into with the first party, and it does not in any degree diminish the value of the service in respect to the first party.[22]

20. By what right interest is forbidden

In connexion with a *mutuum* the question is commonly raised, by what right is interest forbidden?[23] . . . [I]t is the more generally accepted opinion that interest is forbidden by the law of nature. . . . [But] the arguments advanced [in favour of such a prohibition] do not seem to be such as to require assent. . . . [I]t is not unlawful to demand a price for the use of a thing.

The argument [for a prohibition against usury] is not more convincing, that money is by its own nature unproductive.[24] For houses and other things naturally unfruitful are rendered productive by the industry of men. [A] more plausible [argument for a prohibition is] that [in the case of a loan of money], the thing is returned for the thing; that the use of the thing cannot be distinguished

---

[22] This is an illustration of a fundamental principle of contract law: that a contract between two persons, in principle, confers neither rights nor duties onto third parties. I.e., the traveller's contract with each principal is independent of his contracts with the other principals. Although Grotius does not raise the point, it seems fair to hold that the expenses undertaken in the journey must be apportioned amongst the various principals (probably in proportion to their payments to the traveller) – otherwise, the traveller will be unjustly enriched. It would be interesting to have Grotius's views on this question.

[23] *Mutuum* was one of the categories of 'real contract' in Roman law. It consisted of a transfer of goods from one party to the other, which the recipient was understood to require for consumption (such as food). In return, and in the future, the recipient would give to the donor an equivalent package of goods (though obviously not the very same goods, as those will have been consumed).

[24] This is the reflection of the common medieval view of money as being 'unproductive' in the sense that it could not be consumed; nor did it naturally reproduce itself in the manner of, say, crops or domesticated animals. Money was regarded as used productively when it was employed to facilitate exchanges of goods or services, but not when it was merely stored or hoarded.

from the thing when the use of the thing consists in using it up; and that, therefore, nothing ought to be demanded for such use.[25]

[Against this argument, it may be pointed out that] the right of repaying money or wine only after a certain time is something capable of being evaluated; for he pays less who pays later.[26]

21. What advantages do not come under the head of interest

[T]he observation should [also] be made that there are certain advantages which approach the character of interest, and commonly seem to be interest, [and which are universally agreed to be lawful.] [S]uch are agreements for making good the loss which one who lends money suffers because he misses the use of the money for a long time;[27] and likewise for the loss of gain on account of a loan, with a deduction, of course, in view of the uncertainty of expectations and of the effort which it would have been necessary to put forth.[28] So again, it is not, in fact, usury if something is demanded for the expenses of the man who lends to many and keeps cash on hand for this purpose,[29] as well as for the danger of losing the principal, in case proper security is not taken.[30]

[25] A comparison is made between a contract for the lending of money and the Roman-law contract of *mutuum*. *Mutuum*, as just noted, involved the return by the borrower to the lender of an equal quantity of goods, not a larger one. It is argued that, if loans of money are regarded as a kind of *mutuum* – but with money substituted for perishable goods – then logically, the borrower is obligated to return only the same quantity of money which he was lent, i.e., interest should not be charged.

[26] The argument is that, if someone has borrowed goods such as wine or money with a view to repayment, then the borrower derives a genuine, and quantifiable, benefit from returning the goods or the money later rather than sooner; and it is not unreasonable that he should pay a reasonable sum for that benefit.

[27] What is envisaged here is a case in which a lender suffers some kind of out-of-pocket cost by virtue of the fact that the money that he lent out to his borrower is not available to him for his own use. It was generally agreed that that out-of-pocket loss could be recovered from the borrower, over and above the repayment of the sum actually borrowed.

[28] By the same token, if the borrower has lost an opportunity to make a gain because of the unavailability of the money which he has lent out, the borrower can be compelled to compensate him for that loss (although there must necessarily be an element of uncertainty in the quantification of such a lost opportunity or, in modern parlance, loss of future earnings).

[29] In other words, borrowers can be expected to make a fair contribution to what are now called the overhead costs of the lender.

[30] It was also not regarded as usury for a lender to charge a sum to a borrower as payment for incurring a genuine risk that the money would not be repaid as agreed. In other words, usury tended, over time, to be interpreted ever more narrowly, to avoid undue interference with commerce. Basically, the position came to be that usury meant the charging of money for the mere use of money for a period of time, and absolutely nothing else. That is, that so long as the payment to the lender could

22. What the force of the civil laws is in this matter

There are, in fact, human laws which allow that a return may be agreed on for the use of money, or of anything else. Thus in Holland it has long been lawful for other persons to collect 8 per cent per annum, but for merchants to exact 12 per cent. If such laws truly keep within the natural limit of compensation for that which is, or can be, out of one's possession, they are not inconsistent with natural or divine law; but if they exceed that limit they may grant impunity, but they cannot give a right.[31]

23. What valuation ought to be put on a contract for securing against loss or insuring

A contract for securing against risk, which is called insurance, will be null and void if either of the contracting parties knew that the property in question had either arrived at its destination in safety, or had been lost. This rule is valid not only by reason of that fairness which the nature of contracts for exchange requires, but also because the particular substance of the contract is the uncertainty of the loss.[32] Moreover, the price of such insurance against risk ought to be fixed in accordance with common estimation.

24. What rule applies in the case of a partnership; wherein many kinds of partnerships are explained

In a business partnership, where the capital is made up from payments of funds, if the investments are equal, then the partners ought to have equal shares in the loss and gain; but if the investments are unequal, the division should be made proportionately. . . . The same will hold true if equal or unequal shares of work were contributed. But also money can be associated with work, or with money and work, as in the common saying: 'Like to like gives recompense, when work and funds are joined.'[33]

---

be characterised as compensation for some kind of real service or expense or assumption of risk, the transaction would be regarded as non-usurious.

[31] The meaning is that any agreement between lender and borrower for interest payments above 'the natural limit' – above a fair and reasonable rate of interest – will not expose the lender to punishment. But it will render the arrangement unenforceable, so that the lender will not have a right of action in a court for the excess amount.

[32] If the cargo has either arrived safely or been lost, there is no longer any risk to insure against – so that the subject matter of the contract has disappeared.

[33] See Plautus, *The Comedy of Asses*, 172. A more accurate translation of the line in the play is: 'A fair return has been given for a fair price, service for money.' There is no indication in the play that this was a proverbial expression. Perhaps the statement in the text was proverbial in Grotius's time, and that merely a general comparison with the line in Plautus is being noted.

Moreover, it is contrary to the nature of a partnership that one of the partners should share in the gain, when he has immunity from loss. Nevertheless, an agreement with this end in view can be made without injustice. Under such conditions, the agreement will become a mixed contract of partnership and insurance against loss, in which equality will be preserved if the one who has taken upon himself the risk of loss shall receive an equivalent increase in profit over what he would otherwise have received. In such a case, however, the risk of loss without the chance of gain ought not to be permitted, because the sharing in advantages is so essential to partnerships that a partnership cannot exist without it.

25. Concerning joint undertakings for maritime operations

In a joint undertaking of ships, the common advantage is defence against pirates; sometimes also booty.[34] Ordinarily, a valuation is placed on the ships and on their cargoes, and from this the total is reckoned, so that the losses which occur, in which the care of the wounded is included, may be borne by the owners of the ships and cargoes in proportion to the shares of the whole which they possess.

What we have said up to this point is in accordance with the law of nature.

26. No consideration, according to the law of nations, is given to an inequality which has been agreed to

In these matters, no change seems to have been made by the volitional law of nations, with the one exception that, when there has been no falsehood or concealment of what ought to have been said, an inequality in terms is considered an equality as regards external acts; . . . so among those who base their association on the law of nations alone no [liability] on . . . account [of inequality] is allowed.

[T]he advantage of introducing [this rule] is manifest: for the termination of disputes which would be without number; which, furthermore, would be interminable on account of the uncertain price of things among persons who have no common judge, and which would be unavoidable if men were allowed to withdraw from agreements on account of inequality of terms.

---

[34] Booty refers not to piratical plunder, but rather to privateering arrangements, which were commonly matters for investment by syndicates. A privateer was a ship fitted out by private parties (frequently by a partnership), which cruised, with a government licence, during wartime with a view to capturing enemy-owned property at sea. In return for their investment and risk, the owners of the privateer vessel were entitled to a share of the proceeds of any property captured – i.e., of any 'prize' taken, in the common legal parlance. That prize money is what Grotius here refers to as booty.

13

On oaths

1. How great the force of an oath

Among all peoples, and in every age, the force of an oath regarding promises, agreements, and contracts has always been very great.... Hence at no time has it failed to be believed that a severe punishment awaits perjurers. [It was sometimes believed] that even posterity might pay the penalty for the sins of ancestors, an opinion that was held only with regard to the worst crimes; and the wish also, without the act, might bring punishment on itself.

Let us now see whence the force of an oath arises, and to what point it extends.

2. Requirement of a deliberate intention

First, the statement which we made about promises and contracts, that a mind possessed of reason and a deliberate intention are requisite, is in place here.

If any one has been willing to swear but unwilling to bind himself, he is nonetheless bound, because the obligation is inseparable from the oath and is a necessary result of it.[1]

3. That the words of an oath are binding in the sense in which it is believed

But if anyone has deliberately uttered the words of an oath, yet without the intention of swearing, some writers state that he is not bound, but yet that he sins by swearing rashly. It is, however, nearer the truth to say that he is bound to make true the words which he has called God to witness. For that act, which is binding in itself, proceeded from a deliberate intention.

Nevertheless, there may be an exception in this, [when] the person taking oath should know, or should reasonably believe, that the words are understood differently by the one with whom he is dealing; for in calling to God to witness

---

[1] The requisite 'deliberate intention' means the intention to swear the oath itself. Once an oath is sworn, the swearer *ipso facto* becomes bound by its terms, even if he secretly harbours mental reservations. This point is expanded upon in the next two sections.

his words, he ought to make them true as he thinks they are understood [by the hearer].

Although in the case of other promises, a tacit condition, which absolves the promisor, is easily understood, nevertheless this ought not to be admitted in the case of an oath.

4. Whether an oath procured by means of fraud is binding[2]

From what I have said, it can be understood what ought to be thought of an oath procured by means of fraud. If it is certain that the person who took an oath believed to be true some fact which is not true, and would not have sworn if he had not believed this, the oath will not be binding. If, however, it shall be doubtful whether he would not have taken the same oath even without the erroneous supposition, he will have to stand by his words, because in an oath the greatest possible simplicity is required.

5. That the words of an oath should not be stretched

Yet the meaning of an oath ought not to be stretched beyond the usage of ordinary speech.

6. That an oath to perform an unlawful act is not binding

In order that an oath may be valid, the obligation taken ought to be lawful. Therefore, a sworn promise relating to an illegal act will have no force either by the law of nature, or by divine interdict, or even by human law.

7. That an oath is not binding which hinders a greater moral good

Furthermore, even if the thing which is promised is not unlawful, but only hinders a greater moral good, under such a condition also the oath will not be valid. [I]n truth, we are under obligation to God to advance in goodness in such a way that we have not the power to cut off from ourselves the opportunity of growth in grace.[3]

8. That an oath is not binding to perform an act which is impossible

It is not necessary to speak of impossibilities. It is, in fact, sufficiently evident that no one is bound to do that which is quite impossible.

---

[2] The logic of this discussion applies to the case of mistake, as well as of fraud.
[3] An example, relevant to a Christian of Grotius's time, might be an oath not to attend church services.

9. If an act, for which an oath has been taken, is impossible for the time being

As regards what is impossible for the time being, or in the opinion of the one who took the oath, the obligation is in suspense. Consequently, a person who has taken oath under such a supposition ought to do what he can to render his oath possible.

10. That an oath is sworn in the name of God

In regard to form, oaths differ in words, but agree in substance. An oath ought to contain this element, that God is invoked, as, for example, in this way: 'God be my witness', or 'God be my judge', two expressions which amount to the same thing. For when a superior having the right to punish is called as a witness, punishment of faithlessness is at the same time asked from him. . . . To the same category belong the ancient formulas for treaties, for which it was the custom to use sacrificial victims, as appears from *Genesis*, 15:9.[4]

11. An oath is sworn in the name of other things with respect to God

But it was also an ancient custom to swear in the name of other things or persons, either because they were invoking such things or persons to become harmful to themselves, as the sun, the earth, heaven, their ruler, or because they were demanding that they be punished in respect to such things as their heads, their children, their country, their ruler.

12. Whether an oath is binding even if one swears by false gods

But also, if anyone has sworn by false gods, the oath will be binding. For although possessed of false notions, he nevertheless has a respect for divinity under a general aspect; and so, if perjury has been committed, the true God interprets it as done to His harm.

13. Twofold effect of an oath

The chief effect of an oath is to put an end to disputes. . . . [T]he person who takes an oath is bound in two ways: first, that his words should agree with his intent; . . . and secondly, that his action should be consistent with his words. . . . The person who does wrong in regard to the first requirement is said . . . 'to swear falsely'; in the second, 'to perjure himself', a distinction which is clear enough, though these matters are wont to be confused.

---

[4] 'So the Lord said to [Abraham], "Bring me a heifer, a goat and a ram, each three years old, along with a dove and a young pigeon".'

14. Right acquired for a man and for God, or for God alone

If the matter should be such, and the words of an oath so phrased, that they may be referred not only to God but also to a man, without doubt a right will be acquired for the man from the oath itself, as if from a promise or contract.... But if either the words do not have a man in view for the conferring of a right upon him, or if they do have him in view, but if there is something which can present an obstacle to his claim, then the force of the oath will be such that the man will indeed acquire no right. [B]ut nevertheless, he who has sworn will be under obligation to God to keep his oath. An example of this occurs in the case of one who by means of an unjust fear ... [causes] a sworn promise [to be given for his benefit]. For he acquires no right, or a right which he is obliged to relinquish, because [he unlawfully caused the oath to be given].

15. Whether the giver of an oath given to a pirate or a tyrant is obligated to God

The principles stated are applicable not merely with respect to public enemies, but to any persons whatsoever. For not only the person to whom the oath is given is taken into consideration, but also God, by whom one swears; and the reference to God is sufficient to create an obligation. Therefore, we must thrust Cicero aside when he says that there is no perjury if the ransom for life, which had been agreed upon even under oath, is not paid to pirates, for the reason that a pirate is not entitled to the rights of war, but is the common enemy of mankind, with whom neither good faith nor a common oath should be kept.[5]

Although it is true that, according to the established law of nations, there is a difference between a public enemy and a pirate – that will be pointed out by us below[6] – yet the difference cannot be in point here where, even if the right of the person fails, we have to reckon with God; and for this reason an oath is called a vow. Again, that is not true which Cicero assumes, that there is no common ground of right with a robber. For Tryphoninus was right in giving the opinion that, according to the law of nations, if the true owner does not appear, a deposit must be returned to a robber.[7]

Consequently, I am not able to approve of the view held by certain persons, that one who has promised anything to a robber can discharge the promise with a momentary payment, so that it may be permissible for him to recover what he has paid. For in an oath, the words relating to God ought to be understood in the simplest manner possible[8] and so as to have effect.

---

[5] Cicero, *On Duties*, III.107.   [6] See p. 343 below.
[7] *Digest*, 16.3.31 (Tryphoninus). See p. 177 above for the discussion of this point.
[8] I.e., according to the words of the oath, interpreted in the ordinary way, without the making of fine and potentially misleading distinctions.

16. Whether an oath to a faithless person ought to be kept

The rule . . . can be approved [that] if [a] sworn promise clearly was related to
the promise of him to whom the oath was given, and . . . had been blended with
it, forming as it were a condition,[9] [and if that other promise was broken, then
the sworn promise need not be kept.] [B]ut [this result] cannot be approved
if the promises are of a different kind and without mutual relation. For in the
latter case, each must absolutely make good what he has sworn.[10]

We said above that inequality in contracts gives naturally an opportunity for
annulling or correcting them. . . . But in [that] case also, if an oath has been
added, even if nothing, or a little, is due to the person, faith will have to be kept
with God.

17. Whether an heir is obligated by an oath to God alone

[When] no right is created [by an oath] for a person, but good faith is pledged
to God, no binding obligation rests upon the heir of the man who took the oath.
For as the property passes to the heir, that is, things bought or sold among men,
so also the burdens on the property; but not in like manner other obligations,
to which a person has been subject by reason of a duty imposed by religious
feeling, gratitude, or good faith. These obligations do not, in fact, belong to
what is in a strict sense called among men a right.

18. An oath to a person that does not wish to have it kept

But also where no right is created for a person, if nevertheless the oath has in
view the advantage of some other person, and the other person does not wish
to have that advantage, the one who took the oath will not be bound. So also,
he will not be bound if the condition under which he swore to someone has
ceased, as if a magistrate should cease to be a magistrate.

19. When anything which is done contrary to an oath becomes void

The question is raised, whether anything done contrary to an oath, is merely
unlawful, or also void.[11] In this matter, I think that a distinction ought to be

---

[9] *Digest*, 12.2.39 (Julian).

[10] This indicates an important feature of an oath, distinguishing it from a contract: that
an oath is binding according to its terms, without any requirement of reciprocity, as
in the case of contracts. The equivalent in English common law is a promise under
seal, for which no consideration is required. The marginal caveat is the case in which
the oath, by its own terms, is conditional upon the good faith of the person on
whose behalf it is sworn.

[11] The question is whether the swearing of an oath deprives the swearer only of the right
to act contrary to the oath, or whether it also deprives him of the power to do so –
with the result that any acts contrary to the oath will automatically be legally void.

made. If good faith alone has been pledged, the act done contrary to the oath will be valid, as, for example, the making of a will, or a sale; but such an act will not be valid if the oath was so phrased that it contained at the same time full abdication of the right of action. These distinctions, at any rate, naturally accompany an oath. In accordance therewith, judgement should be passed on the oaths of kings, and the oaths which foreigners take to one another, since in such cases the act is not subject to the law of the place.[12]

20. Effect of the act of superiors with respect to that which a subject has sworn

Let us now see what powers are possessed by superiors, that is, by kings, fathers and masters, and also by husbands, so far as conjugal rights are concerned. The act of superiors cannot indeed bring it to pass that an oath does not have to be fulfilled, in so far as the oath was truly binding; for such fulfilment is required by both the law of nature and divine law. However, because our acts are not fully within our own power, but are related in such a way that they are dependent also on our superiors, there may be a twofold action by superiors concerning whatever is sworn, the one action directed against the person who takes the oath, the other against the person to whom the oath is given.

The person who takes the oath can be directed, either by making the oath void before it is sworn, . . . or by forbidding that the oath be fulfilled after it has been taken. For the inferior, in so far as he was inferior, could not have put himself under obligation except in so far as his act should meet the approval of his superior; for he would have no power beyond that.[13]

But an act may also result from the mingling of the rights of both parties, as if a superior should order that what an inferior has sworn in this or that case, as, for example, in consequence of fear, or from weakness of judgement, shall be valid only on the condition that it be approved by himself. Under such a condition, absolutions from oaths can be defended. Such absolutions were formerly granted by princes; but now, with the permission of the princes, by the dignitaries of the Church, in order that greater regard may be had for religious scruple.

---

[12] In these two cases, the swearers are not under the jurisdiction of the law of the place that they are in at the time of swearing – kings, because they have no mutual superior at all; and foreigners swearing to one another, because foreigners, in relations *inter se*, operate under their own national law (assuming, it appears, that the foreigners in question are from the same country). Nevertheless, the natural law on oaths, which Grotius is expounding, is applicable to these two cases.

[13] The assumption evidently is that an inferior, such as a subject or a child, lacks the capacity to make an oath to do something that is contrary to the superior's orders. Such a purported oath would therefore not, strictly speaking, be countermanded or overridden by the superior, but instead would automatically be void *ab initio*.

Furthermore, the act of the superior can be directed against the person to whom the oath is sworn by taking from him the right which he has acquired, or, if there is no right, by forbidding that he should receive anything in accordance with such an oath. This, again, by virtue of the power of sovereignty, may be done in two ways, either for a punishment or for the public advantage. However, a person who has promised something on oath to a guilty person as such, as, for example, a pirate, for this very reason cannot take away from him the promised right under the name of penalty; for then his words would be of no effect, a result which ought in every way to be avoided.[14]

Again, a human law can remove an impediment, which it had placed on acts of a certain kind, if an oath either in general terms, or in a special form, has been added. If such a case arises, the sworn act will be valid in the same way that it would naturally have been valid without human law, either by binding good faith only, or also by giving a legal right to another, according to the diverse nature of acts, which has been set forth by us elsewhere.[15]

---

[14] It might be supposed that an oath in favour of, say, a pirate can be abrogated as a means of just punishment of the pirate. Grotius denies this, on the ground that the evil character of the pirate had been known at the time of swearing and so had already (it must be presumed) been taken into account. It might be argued, though, that, if the pirate committed additional unlawful deeds *after* the oath was sworn, then the oath could be abrogated as punishment for those. Grotius seems to deny this too, as evidenced by his reference to 'a guilty person as such', which may be taken to refer to the general moral character of the pirate rather than to the commission of specific acts of piracy.

[15] The phraseology is somewhat obscure here. The case envisaged is one in which the civil law prohibits a certain act, *and* a person, in addition, swears an oath not to commit that act. It is open to the state to remove the general prohibition. But if it does so, the person's oath continues to be binding. This must be assumed to be so, provided that the text of the oath did not itself make the validity of the oath conditional upon the continuance in force of the law in question.

14

On promises, contracts, and oaths of those who hold sovereign power

1. Whether a duty of restitution applies to the acts of kings as such

The promises, contracts, and oaths of kings, and of others who like them hold the chief power in the state, present peculiar questions in regard to what is permitted to them as regards their own acts; also, what is permitted to them in relation to their subjects and in regard to their successors.

As regards the first point, the question is whether a king can restore to himself his rights in full, as he can restore those of his subjects, or can make a contract void, or can absolve himself from an oath. Bodin is of the opinion that a king who has been overreached by the fraud or deceit of another, or induced by error or fear, can be restored to his original rights for the same reasons that a subject would be restored, not only in matters which pertain to the rights of sovereignty, but also in matters which relate to his private affairs. He adds that a king is not even bound by an oath if the agreements are of a kind from which the law permits withdrawal, even though [the oaths in question] are consistent with honour; he is not, in fact, bound because he has taken oath, but because everyone is bound by just agreements, in so far as another has an interest therein.

Here also, we think that a distinction ought to be made, just as elsewhere, between the acts of a king which belong to the kingly office and those which are private. For whatever the king does in acts belonging to his kingly office should be considered in the same way as if the state did them. But as the laws made by the state itself would have no power over such acts, because the state is not superior to itself, so laws emanating from the king would not. Wherefore, restitution will not take place against . . . contracts [made by kings], for restitution arises from municipal law. No exception, then, ought to be admitted against contracts of kings which they have made in their minority.[1]

---

[1] The contention is that municipal laws providing for the voidability of contracts in certain circumstances do not apply to kings acting in their official capacities. It should be remembered, though, that rules of natural law which make contracts void or voidable do apply to rulers as well as to private parties. Also, as pointed out below, municipal laws apply to the contracts which kings conclude in their private capacities.

2. To what acts of kings the laws apply

Evidently, if a people has placed a king in power without absolute authority, but subject to certain laws, his acts contrary to those laws can be rendered void by them, either wholly or in part, because to that extent the people has preserved its own right. The acts of kings who rule with absolute power but do not hold their kingdoms as proprietary owners, [as well as] acts by which the kingdom, or a part of the kingdom, or its revenues are alienated, we have treated above; and we have shown that, by the very law of nature, such acts [of alienation] are null and void, just as if they had been performed in respect to the property of another.[2]

The private acts of a king, on the contrary, ought to be considered as acts not of the state, but of a part of the state, and therefore done with the intention that they should follow the common rule of the laws. In consequence, the laws which render some acts either void, or voidable by the injured party, will apply here also, just as if the contract had been made with that as a condition. Thus we see that certain kings have availed themselves of the aid of the laws against extortionate interest charges. Nevertheless, a king will be able to exempt from the operation of such laws his own acts, as well as the acts of others. [W]hether he intended so to do must be judged from the circumstances. If he has done so, the case will have to be judged by the bare law of nature.[3]

This should be added, that, if any law renders an act null and void, not in the interest of the doer, but for his punishment, this will have no force in regard to the acts of kings. [S]o also, other penal laws, and whatever has the force of compulsion, will not apply. For punishment and coercion can proceed only from different wills; and so, to compel, and to be compelled, require separate persons; and separate aspects of the same person do not meet the requirement.[4]

3. Whether a king is bound by his oath

A king can render an oath null in advance, just as a private person may, if by a former oath he has plainly deprived himself of the power to swear to any such thing. But after an oath has been taken, he cannot render it void, . . . because here also separate persons are required. For [an oath that] is rendered void after [being sworn] already . . . contained in itself this exception, 'unless his superior

---

[2] See p. 73 above.

[3] Sovereigns have an inherent right to grant dispensations from man-made law, either to themselves or to designated subjects. In such cases, however, the acts of the persons do not take place in a legal vacuum. They are judged according to 'the bare law of nature'.

[4] It should be remembered that coercive and punitive measures are foreign to natural law. Consequently, even though sovereigns – however absolute they may be in the sense of being unconfined by any man-made laws – are subject to natural law, they remain exempt from coercion or punishment.

should be unwilling'. But [for a king] to swear ... that [he] would be bound only if [he] should [himself] be willing is altogether ridiculous, and contrary to the nature of an oath. Although [it is possible that] from an oath of this character no right may be gained for the other party, because of some fault in himself, yet, as we have shown above, [a] person who [takes an] oath is under obligation to God.[5] This applies no less to kings than to others.

4. Whether a king is bound with reference to things which he promised without cause

It has also been shown above that promises which are complete and unconditional, and have been accepted, naturally confer a right.[6] This in like manner applies to kings no less than to others.

5. The force of law as regards the contracts of kings

[W]e said above, that the municipal law of a kingdom has no force in the agreements and contracts of kings. ... But [the] inference ought not to be conceded, that buying and selling without fixed price, letting and hiring without stated amount, and permanent right of land tenure without a written document, are valid if they are the acts of kings. The reason is that such acts are not ordinarily performed by a king as king, but by him just as by any person. So far is it from being true that the laws of the realm have no force in respect to acts of this kind, that we believe that the king is subject even to the law of the town in which he lives. ... Yet the matter stands, as we have said, only in case circumstances do not show that the king has been pleased to free his own act from the operation of that law.

6. Whether a king can be under obligation to his subjects by the law of nature or by municipal law

Almost all jurists believe that the contracts which a king enters into with his subjects are binding upon him by the law of nature only, and not by municipal

[5] This is not very clearly expressed. The basic position is that a king who makes an oath cannot afterwards dissolve it by exercising his normal sovereign power to release subjects from obligations. Just as a sovereign cannot *impose* an obligation onto himself by mere fiat, so also he cannot release himself from one, once it is in place. The reason is the same in both cases: imposing an obligation and lifting one are acts that must be done by some outside authority (or 'separate persons'); and in the case of a king, no outside authority exists.
   Grotius then advances the possibility that the human beneficiary of such an oath might somehow lose his entitlement 'because of some fault in himself'. It is not easy to see what he has in mind, and he gives no illustration. But the basic point is that the oath swearer's obligation to God remains in force.
[6] See p. 186 above.

law. This is a very obscure way of speaking. For legal writers sometimes improperly speak of a natural obligation as referring to that of which the fulfilment is by nature honourable, although not in reality due,[7] as . . . the payment of a debt from which one had been freed by a criminal penalty inflicted on the creditor, or the requiting of a favour with its like – acts . . . which [do not permit] an action to recover anything unjustly paid.[8] But sometimes the words are more properly used with reference to that which does in truth bind us, whether the other party has acquired a right therefrom, as in contracts, or has not acquired it, as in a full and firm promise.[9]

According to civil law also, a person can be said to be bound by his own act, either in this sense, that an obligation results not from the law of nature alone but [also] from the municipal law, or from both together, or in the sense that the obligation gives a right to action in a court of law. Therefore, we say that a true and proper obligation arises from a promise and contract of a king, which he has entered into with his subjects, and that this obligation confers a right upon his subjects. [S]uch is the nature of promises and contracts as we have shown above; and this holds even between God and man.[10]

Now if the acts are such as may be done by a king, but also by anyone else, municipal law will be binding in his case also; but if they are the acts of the king

---

[7] In Roman law, there was the concept of a natural obligation, in contrast to a civil obligation. The important difference was that a civil obligation could be enforced by a court action, while a natural obligation could not. The beneficiary of a civil obligation is therefore the holder of a perfect right, while the beneficiary of a natural obligation holds an imperfect right.

[8] These are examples of natural obligations in the Roman-law sense. The reference to 'a criminal penalty inflicted on the creditor' refers to a creditor who is convicted of a crime – with the penalty being the release of his debtor from the obligation to pay. Some persons assert that this must be understood as merely a matter of civil law, in which the creditor is deprived of a right to sue his debtor in court – and that, according to natural law, the debtor remains under an obligation to repay the sum lent. Grotius disagrees with this interpretation for the reason given (not very clearly) below.

[9] Sometimes, natural obligation is not understood in the Roman-law sense just given, but instead simply refers to an obligation imposed by natural law, without regard to the existence or non-existence of a civil-law remedy. This appears to be the meaning supported by Grotius.

[10] This is very obscurely put. In this paragraph, in conjunction with the next one, the basic contention seems to be that contracts concluded by kings with their subjects are binding on the kings. Contracts concluded in the king's personal capacity are enforceable like any other contract, in the civil courts of the relevant state. Contracts concluded in the king's official capacity are enforceable to a lesser extent. In the civil courts, 'the right of the creditor may be declared' (as Grotius explains in the following paragraph); but measures of enforcement cannot be ordered against the king. In modern terminology, the creditor would be said to be entitled only to declaratory relief. Consequently, the creditor's right may be said to be more than an imperfect one (of the Roman-law kind), in that he does have the right to sue in court; but it is less than a full private-law right, in that enforcement mechanisms are not available.

as king, municipal law does not apply to him . . . . [F]rom both these [categories of] acts, a legal action may arise, at least so far that the right of the creditor may be declared; but compulsion cannot follow on account of the position of the parties with whom the business is conducted. For it is not permissible for subjects to compel the one to whom they are subject. [E]quals, however, by the law of nature, have this right against equals, and superiors against inferiors even by municipal law.

7. In what way a right lawfully obtained by subjects may be taken away

This also ought to be known, that, through the agency of the king, even a right gained by subjects can be taken from them in two ways, either as a penalty, or by the force of eminent domain. But in order that this may be done by the power of eminent domain, the first requisite is public advantage; then, that compensation from the public funds be made, if possible, to the one who has lost his right.[11] Just as such a result is accomplished in other things, then, so also in respect to the right which is created by a promise or contract.

8. Whether there is a distinction here between the law of nature and municipal law

[We should not accept] the distinction . . . which some persons make, between a right gained through the force of the law of nature and a right which arises from municipal law. The right of the king is, in fact, the same over both kinds of rights, nor can the one any more than the other be taken away without cause. For when ownership or any other right has been acquired by any one in a legitimate manner, it is a provision of the law of nature that this may not be taken away from him without cause. If a king should act to the contrary, he is without doubt bound to make good the damage inflicted, because he is acting against a true right of the subject. The right of subjects, then, differs from the right of foreigners in this, that over the right of foreigners, . . . the power of eminent domain has no control. In regard to penalties we shall see below.[12] But the right of subjects is subordinate to that of eminent domain so far as the public interest may require.[13]

---

[11] These two requirements are famously echoed in the Fifth Amendment to the United States Constitution.

[12] See p. 415 below.

[13] It is regrettable that Grotius fails to explain the reason for this conclusion. The general modern view is that foreigners are subject to loss of property by eminent domain (provided that, in the process, there is no element of discrimination against foreigners per se).

9. Whether the contracts of kings are laws

From what we have said, it becomes apparent how false is the opinion which some advocate, that the contracts of kings are laws. For no one acquires a right against a king from the [municipal] laws; if therefore he revokes [laws], he does a legal injury to no one. Nevertheless, he commits a moral wrong if he pursues such a course without just cause. [Natural-law] right [by subjects against rulers], however, does arise from promises and contracts. . . . Nevertheless, some mixtures of contracts and laws are possible, as treaties made with a neighbouring king, or a contract with a farmer of the revenues which is at the same time published as a law, in so far as there are provisions in it which have to be observed by the subjects.

10. Whether the contracts of kings are binding on their heirs

Let us come now to the successors [of rulers]. In regard to these, a distinction must be made, whether they are the heirs at the same time of all the possessions, as those who inherit an hereditary kingship by will, or in default of a will; or are successors to the kingship only, as for example in consequence of a new election, or in accordance with a prescribed rule; or by a sort of imitation of ordinary inheritance, or otherwise; or whether, finally, they succeed by a mixed right. For there must be no doubt that those who are heirs of all the possessions, as well as of the kingship, are bound by the promises and contracts. The rule that the property of the deceased is subject to his personal debts also is as old as property ownership itself.

11. In what way those who succeed to the kingship only may be bound by the same contracts

But there are those who succeed to the royal power only, or to the [deceased king's] property in part and to the royal power in its entirety. The question to what extent they are obligated is one which is all the more worthy of investigation, for the reason that previously it has been confusedly handled. Now it is sufficiently clear that such successors to a kingship are not in that capacity directly, that is to say immediately, bound; they do not receive their right from the one who has last died, but from the people, whether that succession approaches more nearly to the right of ordinary inheritance, or is farther removed from it. This distinction has been treated above.[14]

---

[14] See p. 151 above. The point seems to be that, even in a hereditary kingdom, the rules of inheritance serve only the limited function of determining the *identity* of successor rulers. Succession to kingship, therefore, is not analogous to succession in Roman law, in which the decedent's rights and liabilities are preserved intact and passed along to the heir.

Such successors may be bound through an intermediary, that is through the interposition of the state. This will be understood as follows. An association, as well as an individual, has the right to bind itself by its own act, or by the act of a majority of its members. This right it can transfer, not only explicitly, but also as a natural consequence, as for example in transferring the sovereign authority. For in morals he who grants the end, grants the means which lead to the end.[15]

12. Whether those who succeed to the kingship only may be bound by the same contracts

Nevertheless, this transfer of obligations cannot go on to an unlimited extent. The unlimited power of imposing obligations is, in fact, not essential to the proper exercise of sovereignty, just as it is likewise not necessary for guardianship or trusteeship. [I]t is necessary only in so far as the nature of the power demands. . . . Nevertheless, this matter [a contract by a king] does not, as certain persons think, have to be handled according to the nature of business undertaken for others,[16] so that the act should then be considered to be ratified, if it has turned out advantageously. For it is dangerous for the state itself to reduce the ruler of the state to such straits. Therefore, it is not to be believed that the people held such an opinion when it conferred the sovereign power.[17]

Consequently, just as not all laws bind the subjects – for even in addition to laws which command something illegal,[18] there can be laws that are plainly

[15] This passage exemplifies a crucial feature of Grotius's political theory: that the actual position of rulers in any particular case is determined by the actual terms of the original transfer of sovereign rights to them. In the present context, the point is made that the people do have the power to confer onto their rulers the right to bind the state as such by their actions (since they themselves possessed that power originally). In that case, a successor ruler is bound by a prior ruler's commitment. Strictly speaking, though, the successor is only bound (in Grotius's opinion) indirectly, 'through an intermediary', i.e., the state. That is, the obligation is imposed first onto the state as such – and only as a consequence of that, onto the successor ruler when he takes office.

[16] I.e., acts done by agents on behalf of principals.

[17] The reference is to a school of thought to the effect that rulers should be regarded as concluding contracts on behalf of the state, though at their own initiative. In private law, such acts by agents are presumed to be binding on the principal (i.e., will be presumed to be ratified by the principal) if the acts benefited the principal. Some persons contended that the same rule should be applied to the question of whether contracts concluded by one king are binding on a successor. Grotius is opposed to making this analogy, at least in part because he maintains that kings ought not to be regarded as mere agents. See, however, Section 14 below, where Grotius does approve of the application of this principle in a special case.

[18] I.e., illegal in the sense of constituting violations of mandatory commands of natural law.

foolish and ridiculous – so also the contracts of rulers are binding upon subjects if they have a reasonable motive; and in case of doubt, such a motive ought to be presumed by reason of the authority of those who rule. This distinction is much better than the one commonly suggested by many writers, which is based on the slight or great injury of the outcome. In this matter, in fact, not the outcome, but the reasonable motive, ought to be kept in view.[19] If a reasonable motive is present, both the people itself will be bound, if by any chance it has commenced to be independent, and also the king's successors, as being the rulers of the people. For also in case a free people should have made a contract, the obligation would be binding upon the one who should afterward accept the sovereignty, even with the most unlimited powers.

Here also this should be added, that, if by any chance a contract should begin to lead not merely to some loss, but to the ruin of the state, so that the contract, if carried to conclusion, would have to be considered as unjust and illegal from the beginning, then it is possible not exactly to revoke it, but rather to declare that it has no further binding force,[20] as if made under a condition without which it could not have been made justly.[21]

What we have said about contracts is also to be understood in regard to the alienation of the public funds, or of anything else which, according to law, the king can alienate for the public good. Here also, a similar distinction must be maintained, whether there was a reasonable motive for giving, or otherwise alienating.

But if the contracts have to do with the alienation of the kingdom, or of a part of it, or of the royal patrimony, in so far as this has not been placed in the

[19] In other words, some persons contend that there should be an objective standard for determining when contracts of prior rulers are binding on their successors. Grotius opposes this, in favour of a subjective standard, in which all that is required is 'reasonable motive' on the part of the prior ruler.

[20] Presumably, the distinction is that, if a contract were revoked, then all acts taken pursuant to it, since its inception, would be void – with the result that any property and benefits conferred by it could be revoked and the *status quo ante* restored in full. If, on the other hand, there was merely a declaration of no further binding force, then past actions pursuant to the contract could not be disturbed. There would merely be no further performance of the contract in the future.

[21] In modern terms, this is a reference to the doctrine of the *clausula rebus sic stantibus*. This holds that all treaties should be regarded as containing in them an implicit provision (or *clausula*) to the effect that the treaty in question is to remain binding so long as no fundamental change of circumstances occurs. This contention was highly controversial in international law for many years. The present resolution, contained in the Vienna Convention on the Law of Treaties (Article 62), states fundamental changes of circumstance as a ground for termination of a treaty – but it does so as a matter of general policy, rather than on the basis of an implicit clause to that effect in the treaty itself. Although Grotius here endorses the principle of the *clausula rebus sic stantibus* with regard to contracts concluded by kings, he did not approve of its application to promises generally. See p. 248 below.

king's hands, they will not be valid, for the reason that they have been made in regard to the property of another.[22] The same will hold in limited monarchies, if the people has reserved any matter, or kind of act, from the royal power. [I]n order that such acts may be valid, the consent of the people is required, such consent being given either in person or through those who lawfully represent it.

With the help of these distinctions, it will be easy to judge whether the pleas made by those kings that have refused to pay the debts of their predecessors, whose heirs they have not been, were just or unjust.

13. What grants of kings are revocable, and what are not

This, again, which has been affirmed by many, that the grants of rulers made from generosity can always be recalled, ought not to be allowed to pass without a distinction. There are, in fact, certain gifts which a king makes at his own expense, and which have the force of an absolute grant, unless there is inserted a clause implying termination at will.[23] Such grants cannot be revoked, except in relation to subjects for the purpose of punishment, or in the public interest – in the latter case, with compensation if possible.

There are other grants which take away the binding force . . . of a law without any contract,[24] and these are revocable. The reason is that, as a law which has been annulled in regard to all people can always be re-enacted for all, so also, when a law in respect to a particular person has been annulled, it can be reinstated in regard to that person.[25] Here, in fact, no right was acquired against the author of the law.

14. Whether the rightful possessor of the throne is bound by the contracts of usurpers

Neither peoples nor rightful kings will be bound by the contracts of those who have unlawfully seized the sovereign authority. For these do not have the right

[22] See p. 223 above on this topic.
[23] These would clearly be grants of title to property of some kind, although Grotius does not so specify.
[24] I.e., dispensations from laws which are granted freely by a king (i.e., not pursuant to a contract). More specifically, the kind of dispensation spoken of places the holder outside the circle of persons to whom the laws in question apply. They are therefore not merely exemptions from enforcement of those laws.
[25] Presumably – though Grotius does not raise the point – a withdrawal of such a dispensation cannot have retroactive effect. The reason is that, during the dispensation period, the relevant law itself did not apply to the holder – so that any act done contrary to the terms of the law was not wrongful at the time of commission.

to place a binding obligation on the people. Nevertheless, they will be bound for what has been spent for their advantage, that is, in so far as they have been made richer.[26]

26 Recall that Grotius rejected the application of this principle in the general case of succession of rulers (in Section 12 above).

15

On treaties and sponsions

1. What public conventions are

[P]ublic conventions are such as can be made only by the right of a higher or lower authority of government; and in this respect they differ not only from the contracts of private persons, but also from the contracts of kings which are concerned with private affairs. However, from such private contracts . . . causes of war are wont to arise, although more frequently from public contracts. Having, therefore, sufficiently treated of compacts in general, we ought to add some details which relate to this more excellent kind of agreement.

2. Division of conventions into treaties, sponsions, and other agreements

We can divide these public conventions, which the Greeks call συνθήκας (articles of agreement), into treaties, sponsions, and other agreements.

3. The difference between treaties and sponsions

[T]reaties are made by order of the highest authority; and . . . in respect to such treaties, the people itself is liable to divine wrath if it does not keep its agreements. . . . A sponsion is made when those who do not have from the supreme authority a commission for such an act promise something which essentially affects that authority.

Moreover, just as the magistrates do not bind the people by their acts, so a minority of the people does not.

But let us see wherein those are obligated who, without the authority of a people, have promised something which is within the power of the people.[1] Someone may perhaps think that, in this case, the promisors have fulfilled their pledge if they have done their utmost to have their promise carried out

---

[1] I.e., to what extent does a sponsion bind the state on whose behalf it purported to be concluded?

in accordance with the principles which we have previously stated[2] in regard to a promise made by a third party. But in this matter, in which a contract is involved, nature desires a much stricter obligation.... [A]ccording to the civil law,... the promise to have an act ratified is... binding, so far as the promisor is concerned.[3]

5. The classification of treaties: first, treaties which establish the same rights as the law of nature

[I]t is necessary for us to make a classification [of treaties].... First, then, we shall say that some treaties establish the same rights as the law of nature, while others add something thereto. Treaties of the first class not only are wont to be made between enemies who cease from war, but formerly also they were often made, and were in some degree necessary, as between those who previously had made no compacts with each other.... In this class, I include also treaties in which provision is made that there shall be rights of hospitality and commerce on both sides, in so far as such rights come under the law of nature.

6. Treaties which add something beyond the rights of the law of nature

Conventions which add something beyond the rights based on the law of nature are either on equal or on unequal terms. Those are on equal terms which are of the same character on both sides.[4] ... Treaties of both types are made for the sake either of peace or of some alliance. Equal treaties of peace are those, for example, which are commonly arranged for the restoration of captives and of captured property, and for safety; these will be discussed below in connexion with the effects and consequences of war.[5]

---

[2] The general principle (p. 192 above) is that a promise by one person (here, the sponsion-maker) that some other person (here, the sponsion-maker's state) will do something is regarded as fulfilled if the promisor has done his best to ensure performance by that other party.

[3] That is, a sponsion, in contrast to an ordinary promise, entails more than a mere commitment on the sponsion-maker's part to use his best efforts to secure ratification by the sovereign. It entails, in addition, an absolute promise that such ratification will in fact be secured. Grotius now abruptly breaks off the discussion of sponsions for a discussion of treaties; he returns to sponsions in Section 16 below.

[4] More specifically, treaties are equal if both parties undertake the same obligations. An example is a treaty in which each state promises free admission into its territory of nationals of the other. In unequal treaties, the obligations of the two parties are not the same. For example, one state might agree to reduce customs duties for nationals of the other, in exchange for being allowed to have a military base on the other's territory.

[5] See p. 433 below.

Equal treaties of alliance have to do either with commerce, with joint action in war, or with other matters. Equal agreements in regard to commercial relations may have various ends in view, as, for example, that no import duties should be paid on either side; . . . or that no greater duties should be levied than at present; or that duties should be levied only up to a certain amount.

So also in an alliance for war, the agreement may be that equal auxiliary forces of cavalry, infantry, and ships shall be furnished, either for every war, which the Greeks call 'an offensive and defensive alliance', . . . or for protecting the boundaries only, which the Greeks call 'a defensive alliance'; or for a particular war; or against particular enemies; or against all enemies, to be sure, but with the exception of allies.

An equal treaty, as we have said, may apply also to other matters, with provisions such as these, that neither signatory shall have fortresses in the territory of the other, or defend the subjects of the other, or furnish a passage to the enemy of the other.

7. Treaties on unequal terms

From the discussion of treaties on equal terms, it may easily be understood what unequal treaties are. Unequal terms, moreover, are promised either by the party of higher rank or by the party of lower rank. Such terms are unequal on the part of the superior if he promises aid, but does not require it [in return from the other party], or promises greater aid. Unequal terms on the part of the inferior . . . are those which, as we have said, were called 'arrangements imposed by command'. Such treaties, again, are either accompanied by impairment of sovereignty, or are without such impairment.

Such treaties may be accompanied by impairment of sovereign power. . . . To this kind of treaty, there may be added a conditional surrender, excepting that such a surrender involves not an impairment but a transfer of the whole sovereign power; on this subject we have spoken elsewhere.[6]

In treaties without impairment of sovereign power the burdens are either temporary or permanent. The temporary burdens are concerned with the payment of an indemnity, the destruction of fortifications, the withdrawal from certain places; or the giving of hostages, of elephants, of ships. The permanent obligations are, for example, to recognise the sovereignty and respect the majesty of the other signatory. . . . Closely related to this is the provision that the one signatory should have as enemies and friends those whom the other signatory desires; and that a passage through his territory, or supplies, should not be given to any army with which the other is at war. Then there are the other matters of less moment – that it should not be permissible to build fortresses in certain places, or to lead an army thither, or to have ships beyond a certain number, or to build a city, or to engage in navigation, or to enlist soldiers

---

[6] See p. 51 above.

in certain places; that they should not attack the allies, nor aid enemies with provisions, nor receive persons coming from another place; and that treaties previously made with other peoples should be annulled.

Unequal treaties, moreover, are wont to be made not only between victors and vanquished, . . . but also between more powerful and less powerful peoples that have not even engaged in war with each other.

8. Treaties with those who are strangers to the true religion

A question frequently raised concerning treaties is whether they are lawfully entered into with those who are strangers to the true religion. According to the law of nature, this is in no degree a matter of doubt. For the right to enter into treaties is so common to all men that it does not admit of a distinction arising from religion. There is, however, a question in regard to the teaching of the divine law.

12. The obligation of Christians to enter a league against the enemies of Christianity

At this point, I shall add that, since all Christians are members of one body, and are bidden to share one another's sufferings and misfortunes, just as this principle applies to individuals, so also it is applicable to peoples as such, and to kings as such. For every man ought to serve Christ not only personally, but also with the power that has been entrusted to him. This, however, kings and peoples cannot do while an impious enemy is raging in arms, unless they furnish aid to one another. Such aid, again, cannot be rendered effectively unless an alliance is made for that purpose. Such a league was formerly made, and the emperor of the Holy Roman Empire was unanimously chosen as its head. To this common cause, therefore, all Christians ought to contribute men or money, according to their strength. How they can be excused from making such a contribution, I do not see, unless they are kept at home by an unavoidable war or some other equally grievous misfortune.

13. Which ally to prefer when several are at war

This question also frequently arises: [i]f several are at war, to which of two parties ought aid preferably to be given by one who is in alliance with both?[7] First, then, that is to be recalled which we previously said, that there is no

---

[7] The question concerns a state, say X, which has separate alliances with States A and B. If A is fighting against one enemy (P), and B against another enemy (Q), then which ally has the prior claim to X's assistance? The assumption, clearly, is that X's resources might not be sufficient to satisfy both claims fully.

obligation to undertake unjust wars.[8] Therefore, [whichever ally] has a just cause for war ought to have the preference. . . . The same will likewise hold if the contest is with another ally.[9]

Now if allies are engaged in war with each other for unjust causes on both sides – and this can happen – it will be necessary to refrain from aiding either party.

If, on the contrary, two allies are waging war against others, and each for a just cause,[10] aid in men and money will have to be sent to both, if this can be done, just as happens in the case of personal creditors. But if the undivided co-operation of the one who has promised is required, reason demands that preference be shown to the ally with whom the treaty is of longer standing. . . . But an exception needs to be made if the later treaty has something beyond the promise which, so to speak, contains in itself the transfer of ownership;[11] that is, some form of subjection. For so also in a sale we say that the earlier promise receives the preference, unless a later promise has transferred ownership.

14. Whether an alliance may be considered as tacitly renewed

An alliance ought not to be considered as renewed tacitly on the expiration of the time, except in consequence of acts which admit of no other interpretation. A new obligation, in fact, is not easily presumed.

15. Whether the one party may be freed by the perfidy of the other

If one party has violated a treaty of alliance, the other will be able to withdraw from it; for the individual terms of an alliance have the force of conditions.[12] . . . This, however, is true only in case there has been no agreement to the contrary; for sometimes [provision is made] that withdrawal from the league may not be permissible for a slight offence.

---

[8] I.e., that any treaty obligation to assist another party in a war actually imposes a legal obligation only to assist in the waging of just wars.

[9] If one of the allies is fighting a just war and the other not, then the aid goes to the one fighting the just war, as promised. To the one fighting an unjust war, nothing is owed. By the same token, if the two allies are fighting one another, then aid is owed to whichever side is fighting justly, with nothing owing to the unjust side.

[10] For the explanation of how a war can be just on both sides, see p. 309 below.

[11] In other words, the later promise receives priority in one exceptional case: when that later promise goes beyond being a mere contractual relationship, involving instead some kind of subjection to the other party, or some kind of transfer of sovereignty to that other party. In such a marginal case, it might be said that the later arrangement takes priority because it is (so to speak) of a higher quality than the earlier one, which was merely a contractual arrangement without any subjection or transfer of sovereignty.

[12] By 'conditions' is meant terms which are necessary prerequisites for the validity, or entry into force, of an agreement.

16. To what the signers are bound if a sponsion signed by them is rejected

Sponsions can have as many kinds of subject-matter as treaties. Sponsions and treaties, in fact, differ only in the power of the persons who make them. But in regard to sponsions, there are two questions that are commonly raised. The first question is, in case a sponsion is disapproved by the king or state, to what are the signers bound; whether they are to make good the loss, [that is] to restore matters to the state in which they were in before the sponsion; or to be surrendered in person. The first alternative seems to be in harmony with Roman civil law; the second, with equity.

Now the point which ought to be maintained above all others is that the one who holds the sovereign power is under no obligation whatsoever [as a result of the sponsion].

17. Whether a sponsion that has not been rejected is made binding through knowledge of it and through silence

A second question is whether a sponsion is binding upon the sovereign authority in consequence of the knowledge of it, [when coupled with] silence. Here the distinction should be made, first, whether the sponsion was made unconditionally, or on the condition that it should be considered as valid by the supreme authority. For this condition, if unfulfilled, makes the sponsion null and void, for the reason that conditions ought to be carried out exactly.

Then the point should be investigated whether, in addition to silence, there is anything else having a bearing on the matter. For silence, unless reinforced by some thing or act, does not supply a sufficiently probable basis for determining intent. . . . But if, in addition, there shall have been certain acts which cannot with probability be referred to any other cause, then the agreement will be understood to have been ratified.

16

On interpretation

1. How promises are outwardly binding

If we consider only the one who has promised, he is under obligation to perform, of his own free will, that to which he wished to bind himself. . . . But because internal acts are not of themselves perceivable, . . . some degree of certainty must be established, lest there should fail to be any binding obligation. [To prevent a person from freeing himself from obligations] by inventing whatever meaning he might wish, natural reason itself demands that the one to whom the promise has been made should have the right to compel the promisor to do what the correct interpretation suggests. For otherwise, the matter would have no outcome, a condition which in morals is held to be impossible.

The measure of correct interpretation is the inference of intent from the most probable indications.[1] These indications are of two kinds, words and implication; and these are considered either separately or together.

2. Words are to be understood in their ordinary sense

If there is no implication which suggests a different conclusion, words are to be understood in their natural sense, not according to the grammatical sense which comes from derivation, but according to current usage.[2]

---

[1] There are, broadly speaking, two schools of thought on interpretation of agreements. One is the subjective one, holding that the task of interpretation is, in essence, the task of determining the actual intention of the parties. The other is the objective one, in which the task of interpretation is to determine the meaning of the words used by the parties. The subjective approach searches for the meaning intended by the parties themselves. The objective approach searches for the definitions, in common practice, of the words employed by the parties. Grotius makes clear that he is an adherent of the subjective school. See Section 4 below. This is in line with the general tendency of natural-law writers to place great stress on internal states of mind. Modern international law inclines towards the objective school of thought, as evidenced by Article 31 of the Vienna Convention on the Law of Treaties. It cannot be said, however, that, even now, there has been a definitive resolution of the matter.

[2] In other words, not according to meanings given to words in the past. Grotius presumably is opposing assigning to words meanings which were already obsolete

3. Technical terms

In the case of technical terms, which the people scarcely understand, the explanation of those who are expert in the particular art will need to be utilised.

4. Ambiguous and contradictory expressions

It is necessary to resort to conjectures when the words or sentences are interpreted in different ways, that is, admit of several meanings. . . . Similarly, there is need of conjectures whenever in compacts there is an appearance of contradiction. For then interpretations are to be sought which will reconcile the different parts with one another, if this is possible. In case the contradiction is real,[3] a later agreement between the contracting parties will annul earlier agreements, since no one could at the same time have had contradictory desires.[4] Such is, in truth, the nature of acts dependent on the will, that they can be relinquished through a new act of volition, either on the one part, as in a law or a will, or conjointly, as in the case of contracts and compacts.

But at times, the conjectures themselves are so evident that they naturally suggest themselves, even against the more commonly accepted interpretation of the words.[5]

5. Conjectures from the subject-matter

[If] a thirty days' truce has been made, . . . this ought to be understood as meaning not natural days, but civil days, for that meaning is consistent with the subject-matter.[6] So the word 'to bestow' is assumed to mean 'to complete a transaction', according to the nature of the business. Similarly, the word 'arms', which sometimes means instruments of war and sometimes armed soldiers, will have to be interpreted now with the former, now with the latter meaning,

---

when the treaty was concluded, so that 'current usage' would refer to usage current at the time that the treaty was made. Applying meanings which evolved after the treaty was concluded would risk undermining the joint intention of the parties.

[3] I.e., if no possible interpretation can resolve the apparent contradiction.

[4] It should be appreciated that the case considered is one in which the same parties conclude two separate agreements, at different times, between which there is some kind of irresolvable contradiction. In such a case, the agreement concluded later in time prevails over the earlier one. See article 30(3) of the Vienna Convention on the Law of Treaties for the modern statement of this principle.

[5] In some cases, it is so clear what the parties intended by their agreement, that effect should be given to that obvious intention, even if the particular formulation of words by the parties carries, on a literal interpretation, some different meaning.

[6] By 'civil days' is meant a calculation of a time interval in which a stated number of days counts the days inclusively. For example, a time span from the fourth to the fourteenth day of some month is a span of eleven days (rather than ten) on the civil-law reckoning.

according to the subject-matter. Again, he who has promised to deliver up men ought to deliver them living, not dead, contrary to the quibble of the Plataeans.[7] [A]nd those who were commanded to deliver up their iron fulfilled the command by giving up their swords, not also their buckles, as [Paches] craftily maintained.[8] Thus, the free withdrawal from a city ought so to be understood that the journey also shall be safe, contrary to what Alexander did.[9] Finally, in a division, one-half of the ships ought to be understood of whole ships, and not as one-half of each ship cut in two, as the Romans maintained in taking advantage of Antiochus.[10] In similar cases, let the same decision be reached.

6. Conjectures from the effect

As regards the effect, especially important is the case when a word taken in its more common meaning produces an effect contrary to reason. For in the case of an ambiguous word, that meaning ought preferably to be accepted which is free from fault. In consequence, we ought not to admit the quibble of Brasidas, who, having promised that he would withdraw from the Boeotian country, denied that the land which he occupied with his army was Boeotian, as if that word

[7] The reference is to Thucydides's account of an incident in 431 BC, early in the Peloponnesian War. After an army of Thebans invaded the territory of Plataea, the Plataeans held some Theban prisoners. According to the Theban version, an agreement (ratified by oath) was reached that the Thebans would withdraw from Plataean territory in return for the release of the prisoners. The Thebans withdrew, but the Plataeans put the prisoners to death. See Thucydides, *The Peloponnesian War*, II.5–6. Grotius's account is inaccurate, however, as it does not appear that the Plataeans claimed to have to have released the prisoners. Rather, they disagreed as to what the substantive terms of the arrangement were; and they denied that any oath had been given.

[8] Paches was an Athenian commander in the Peloponnesian War. He was reported, on one occasion, to have declared to an enemy force that their lives would be spared if they surrendered their steel. The soldiers duly surrendered their arms – but Paches ordered them killed anyway, on the ground that they had retained steel brooches on their cloaks. Frontinus, *Stratagems*, IV.7.17. Grotius mis-attributes this nefarious conduct to Pericles.

[9] The reference is to an egregious breach of truce by Alexander the Great during his siege of the city of Massaga in southern Swat (in present-day Pakistan) in 327 BC. Alexander called a truce, which he then violated by ambushing the enemy forces and killing all of them. Plutarch reports this as a stain on Alexander's record, noting that he usually 'fought in accordance with the rules of war and behaved as a king should', Plutarch, *Alexander*, 59.

[10] After the defeat of Antiochus IV of the Seleucid Empire by Rome in the Syrian–Roman War of 192–189 BC, it was agreed that Rome would be allowed to take half of the Seleucid ships. It was reported that the crafty Roman commander, Q. Fabius Labeo, proceeded to cut all the Seleucid ships in half and to take half of each. Valerius Maximus, *Memorable Doings and Sayings*, VII.3.

ought to be understood of warlike possession and not of ancient boundaries; for in the former sense the compact would have been meaningless.[11]

7. Conjectures from elements that are connected, either in origin or also in place

Statements are connected either in origin or also in place. Those are connected in origin which proceed from the same will, although uttered in different places and on different occasions. [H]ence arises the need of conjecture, because in doubtful cases, the will is believed to have been consistent.

8. Conjecture drawn from reasonable motive

Among the elements which are connected in respect to place, the chief force is given to the reason for a law, which many confuse with the intent, although it is only one of the indications from which we trace the intent. Nevertheless, among conjectures, this is the strongest, if it is established with certainty that the will has been influenced by some reason as the only cause. Often, in fact, there are several reasons, and sometimes the will without reason determines itself from the power of its own freedom; and this is sufficient to produce a binding obligation.[12] Thus, a present made by reason of a wedding will not be valid if the wedding does not take place.

9. The distinction between broad and narrow meanings

Furthermore, the fact should be recognised that many words have several meanings, the one narrower, the other broader. This is the case for many reasons. One is that the name of the genus may be applied to a species; . . . likewise also in masculine nouns, which are ordinarily used as common nouns when words of common gender are wanting. Another is that the technical use of a term may give a broader meaning than the everyday use, just as the word for death is extended by the civil law to cover banishment, though it does not have this meaning in ordinary speech.

[11] Brasidas commanded an Athenian army campaigning in Boeotia in 424–423 BC, during the Peloponnesian War, with the Athenians contending that occupied territory (as it is now called) did not count as 'Boeotian country' since the Boeotians were not in effective control of it. Thucydides, *The Peloponnesian War*, III.97–9. Actually, no agreement for the evacuation of Boeotian territory had been concluded. There was only a demand on the Thebans' part for an evacuation, which was countered by the Athenians in the manner related.
[12] I.e., sometimes there is no apparent reason for a promise, but nonetheless there is a firm expression of will. In such a case, that expression of will produces a binding legal obligation.

10. Division of promises into favourable, odious, mixed, and median

At the same time, it should be noted that of promises which are made, some are favourable, some odious, some mixed, and some median. Those promises are favourable which are made on a basis of equality and promote the common advantage. The greater and more extended this advantage is, the greater the favourableness of the promise. [T]his, then, is greater in promises that contribute to peace than in those that contribute to war, greater also in promises for defence in a war that has been begun than for other causes.

Odious promises are those which impose burden on one party only, or on one party more than the other; which contain penalties in themselves which render acts null and void, and which bring about some change in previous agreements. If, again, a promise is of a mixed character, as changing former agreements, to be sure, but with a view to peace, this will be considered now favourable and now odious, as the amount of good or of change predominates, but in such a way that, other things being equal, it should preferably be considered favourable.[13]

11. The distinction between contracts of good faith and those of strict legal right

The distinction between acts of good faith and those granting a strict legal right, in so far as it is drawn from the Roman law,[14] does not belong to the law of nations. In a certain sense, however, the distinction can be applied here. [T]hus, for example, if in any countries, some acts have a certain common form, in so far as that form is unchanged, the distinction may be understood to be present in the act. But in other acts, which are in themselves indefinite in respect to form, such as a donation and a generous promise, more attention should be paid to the words.[15]

---

[13] Grotius does not define median promise. Presumably, it is one in which the favourable and the odious elements are of precisely equal weight.

[14] Roman law distinguished actions that were *stricti iuris* from those that were *bonae fidei*. In *bonae fidei* actions, considerations of good faith or equity were relevant, either for establishing a claim or for defending against one. In *stricti iuris* actions, good faith or equity (on either side) was not relevant.

[15] The reference is to Roman law, in which very specific ceremonies or rituals were often required in order to convey a full legal right to another party. In addition, though, Roman law evolved so as to give a certain (though lesser) efficacy to acts which did not satisfy the full formal or ceremonial requirements but in which there nevertheless was an intention to convey some kind of legal right. These latter are what Grotius calls 'acts of good faith'. He maintains that the law of nations does not, at least in principle, recognise this Roman-law dichotomy. But he immediately goes on to concede that, to a large extent, it actually does. In cases in which well established ceremonies are associated with certain legal acts, it can safely be assumed that the due performance of the ceremony carries with it an intention that the legal act occur, so that there is then no need to pay any close attention to the words

12. Rules in regard to interpretations

In the light of the principles stated the following rules should be observed. In agreements that are not odious, the words should be taken with their full meaning according to current usage; and, if there are several meanings, that which is broadest should be chosen, just as the masculine gender is taken for the common gender, and an indefinite expression for a universal. Thus the words, 'from which one has been ejected', will have reference even to the restoration of one who has been hindered by force from entering into possession of what belongs to him.[16]

In more favourable agreements, if the speaker knows the law or avails himself of the advice of lawyers, the words should be taken rather broadly, so as to include even a technical meaning, or a meaning imposed by law. But we should not have recourse to meanings that are plainly unsuitable unless otherwise some absurdity or the uselessness of the agreement would result. On the other hand, words are to be taken even more strictly than the proper meaning demands if such an interpretation shall be necessary in order to avoid injustice or absurdity. And even if there be no such necessity, but there is manifest fairness or advantage in the restriction, we ought to confine ourselves to the narrowest limits of the proper meaning unless circumstances persuade to the contrary.

In odious agreements, even figurative speech is sometimes admitted, in order to lighten the burden. Consequently, in the case of a donation, and in the surrender of one's right, no matter how general the words are, they are ordinarily restricted to the matters which were in all probability [actually] thought of. [On this same general thesis], the promise of auxiliary forces by one party only will be understood to be an obligation at the expense of the one who asks for them.

13. Whether under the term 'allies' future allies are included

A notable question is, whether, under the term 'allies', only those are included who were allies at the time of a treaty, or also future allies. . . . What shall we say? Indeed, there can be no doubt that, with due regard for correctness of speech,

---

actually uttered. Sometimes, however, legal acts are not closely associated with particular ceremonies; and in those cases, it is necessary to pay heed to the actual words said, in order to discern the true intention of the parties.

Grotius also points to one quasi-exception to this statement. Sometimes, states in their *national* laws have well-established ceremonies or procedures (i.e., 'a certain common form') that are understood to have, per se, certain specific legal consequences. When such ceremonies or procedures are employed in a treaty-making context, it is permissible to infer, from the presence of the ceremonies alone, that the normal legal consequences automatically follow, in international law as in domestic law. In such cases, there is therefore no need for a separate inquiry into the presence or absence of good faith or intention.

[16] I.e., ejectment should be given a broad meaning, so as to include prevention of access, in addition to its narrower meaning of expulsion.

the word 'allies' can be accepted in the narrower sense of those who were allies at the time of the treaty, and in a second and broader meaning, which is extended also to future allies. Which of the two interpretations, then, ought to have the preference will need to be inferred from the rules given above. In accordance with those rules, we say that future allies are not included [if including them would entail] the breaking of [the] treaty, which is an odious matter.

14. How a clause, that one people may not make war without the consent of the other, ought to be interpreted

As applicable to an unequal alliance, we shall present a second possibility: that is, if it has been agreed that one of the allies shall not be able to wage war without the consent of the other. . . . The expression 'to wage war' can apply to every war, both offensive and defensive. [I]n case of doubt, we shall in this connexion take it in the narrower sense [of offensive war only], that liberty may not be too greatly restricted.

16. What compacts are to be considered personal, and what real

To this topic is to be referred the question that frequently arises in regard to personal and real compacts.[17] If indeed an agreement has been made with a free people, there is no doubt that what is promised is in its nature real, because the subject is a permanent thing. Further, even if the condition of the state shall be changed into a kingdom, the treaty will continue, for the reason that, although the head has been changed, the body remains the same; and, as we have said above, the sovereignty, which is exercised through a king, does not cease to be the sovereignty of the people.[18] An exception will have to be made if it is apparent that the cause of the treaty resided in the free condition of the state;[19] such would be the case if free states had made a treaty for the purpose of protecting their freedom.

But if a compact has been made with a king, the treaty will not immediately have to be considered personal; for . . . the name of the person is for the most part inserted in a compact, not in order that the compact may become personal, but in order to show with whom it was made.[20] Now, if the addition is made to the treaty, that it shall be lasting, or that it was made for the good of the realm,

---

[17] By personal compacts are meant those that are concluded by a ruler in his personal capacity only. These bind only the ruler himself and not the state which he rules. A real compact is a compact concluded on behalf of the state as such.

[18] See the discussion at p. 172 above.

[19] I.e., the case in which the freedom of the state would be regarded as a condition, in the sense of a prerequisite to the validity of the treaty.

[20] See *Digest*, 2.14.7.8 (Ulpian).

or with the king himself and his successors, . . . or if the treaty was made for a definite time, the fact that it is real will be sufficiently apparent.[21]

Again, if the indications are evenly balanced on both sides, the result will be that favourable treaties are to be believed real, and odious treaties personal. Treaties made for the sake of peace or commerce are favourable. Treaties made for the sake of war are not all odious, as some persons think; but alliances for defence, that is, treaties for the sake of protecting each party, incline rather toward favourableness, and offensive alliances incline more toward burdensomeness. There is the further point, that in the case of a treaty which contemplates any war whatsoever, the presumption is that consideration has been had of the prudence and loyalty of the party with whom the engagement is made, as being one who clearly not only would not undertake a war unjustly, but not even rashly.[22]

To the commonly accepted statement, that associations are terminated by death, I give no place here; for this pertains to private associations and belongs to civil law.

Least of all should the argument of Bodin be admitted, that treaties do not pass to the successors of kings, for the reason that the force of an oath does not go beyond the person. It is true enough that the obligation of [an] oath can bind the person only, [but a] promise . . . can bind the heir. Furthermore, the assumption on which Bodin proceeds, that treaties are based on an oath as a kind of foundation, is not valid. The fact is that, in most cases, there is sufficient binding force in the promise itself, and that the oath is added thereto in order to secure the reinforcement of greater religious scruple.

17. A treaty with a king who has been expelled from his kingdom

A treaty entered into with a king surely continues, although the king himself or his successor has been expelled by his subjects from the kingdom. The right to the kingdom, in fact, still belongs to him, although he has lost possession.

18. Such a treaty with a usurper of a kingdom

On the contrary, there is no violation of [a] treaty [of peace] if a usurper of another's kingdom is attacked in war at the wish of the true king, or if the oppressor of a free people is attacked before an adequate approval on the part of the people is secured for the treaty. The reason is that, while such persons may have possession [of the sovereignty of the state in question], they have no legal

---

[21] The reason that the definite duration signifies that the treaty is real is that the king who concluded the treaty might die during the interval, and it would be clear that the treaty continued in force after the death.

[22] The implication is that 'any war whatsoever' would not include a war that was entered into either rashly or unjustly.

right. . . . Such elements in the treaties of a king and his successor, and similar elements, betoken a right, properly speaking; and the cause of the usurper is odious.

19. If a promise is made to the one who should do something first, and several do the thing at the same time

[I]n ancient times . . . the question [was discussed] whether a promise which had been made to the one who should first arrive at the goal would be due to each if two arrived together, or to neither. The truth is that the word 'first' is ambiguous, for it designates either the one who surpassed all or the one whom no one surpassed. But because awards for virtues are to be viewed with favour, the more just opinion is that they will together share the prize.

20. When a conjecture broadens the meaning

There is also another kind of interpretation: from conjectures outside of the meaning of the words in which the promise is contained.[23] This, again, is of two sorts, either broadening the meaning or narrowing it. Now the interpretation which broadens the meaning proceeds with greater difficulty; that which narrows the meaning proceeds more easily. For as in all other things, the absence of a single one of the causes is sufficient to prevent the result, and all causes need to concur that the effect may be produced, so also in the case of an obligation, a conjecture which extends the obligation ought not rashly to be admitted. The difficulty here is much greater than in the case of which we were speaking above, where the words admit of a rather broad interpretation, though one less generally accepted; for here we are in search of a conjecture outside of the words of the promise. Such a conjecture ought to be very certain in order to create an obligation. . . . [I]t is not always sufficient for us to affirm that the extension ought to be made in accordance with reason; for, . . . reason often moves in such a way that the will nevertheless may be a sufficient cause in itself, even without reason.[24] That such an extension,[25] then, may be rightly made, it must

---

[23] The ensuing discussion of the employment of 'conjectures' in the interpretation of agreements is fascinating, and still highly relevant today. What Grotius calls 'conjecture' now goes commonly by the label 'extrinsic evidence'. The basic issue concerns the circumstances in which evidence from outside the actual text of an agreement can be resorted to, in the interpretation of that agreement – even, as will be seen, to the point of actually contradicting the literal meaning.

[24] The fact that a broad interpretation (having the effect of extending the obligation) is more reasonable, objectively, than a narrow one is not conclusive because the basic task in treaty interpretation is to discern the actual will of the parties. And it is possible, in a given case, that the will of the parties was to depart from the course of reason.

[25] I.e., an extension of the obligation on the basis that that would be the most reasonable interpretation of the treaty.

be agreed that the reason [justifying the broad interpretation . . . was] the sole effective cause which influenced the promisor.

As an example, suppose that there is an agreement that a certain place shall not be surrounded with walls, and that this agreement was made at a time when there was no other kind of fortification. It will not be permissible to surround that place even with an earthwork, if it is fully established that the sole reason why walls were prohibited lay in the intent that the place should not be fortified.

21. Concerning the execution of a mandate in a different way

From the principles stated comes the solution of [a] famous question . . . whether the obligation of a mandate may be satisfied, not with the identical thing, but with something else equally useful, or more useful than was that which the giver of the mandate had prescribed. Such an adjustment is, in fact, permissible in case it is determined that what had been prescribed was not prescribed in a special form, but in a more general way, which made possible a different fulfilment of the conditions.

22. When a conjecture restricts the meaning

A restrictive interpretation, outside of the natural meaning of the words containing the promise, is derived either from an original defect in the intent, or from the incompatibility with the intent of a case occurring. A defect inherent in the intent is recognised from the absurdity which evidently would otherwise result, or from the cessation of the reason which alone furnished the full and effective motive for the intent, or from a defect in the subject-matter. The first case has its foundation in this principle, that no one ought to be believed to wish absurdities.

23. Conjecture may restrict the meaning by reason of the cessation of the only reason

The second case[26] is founded on the principle that, when such a reason is added, or there is agreement concerning it,[27] the content of the promise is considered not simply by itself, but only in so far as it [relates to] that reason.

24. The case of a defect in the subject-matter

The third case [in which conjecture is allowed to result in a narrowing of the obligation] is based on the consideration that it is always to be understood that

---

[26] I.e., 'the cessation of the reason which alone furnished the full and effective motive for the intent' of the promisor.
[27] I.e., when the parties actually state their reason for making the agreement, or there is no dispute as to their reason.

the subject-matter is viewed from the point of view of the speaker, even if the words have a broader meaning.[28]

25. An observation, concerning the conjectures last mentioned

In regard to the reason [underlying an agreement], it is to be noted that, under it, certain things are often included, not from the point of view of existence, but in relation to their force from the point of view of morals. When such a case arises, no restriction ought to be made.[29] Thus, if provision has been made that an army or a fleet should not be conducted to some place, it will not be possible to conduct it to that place, even without the intent of doing harm. The reason is that, in the agreement, not a certain loss but danger of any possible kind was in contemplation.

The question also is commonly raised, whether promises contain in themselves the tacit condition, 'if matters remain in their present state'.[30] To this question, a negative answer must be given, unless it is perfectly clear that the present state of affairs was included in that sole reason of which we made mention. Thus constantly in the histories, we read that ambassadors gave up their mission and returned home from the journey on which they had set out, alleging as the reason, that matters had been so changed that the entire matter or cause of the mission was at an end.[31]

26. The case of incompatibility of an agreement with the intent of the parties

The incompatibility of an actually occurring case with the intent[32] is . . . twofold; for the desire [of the parties] is inferred either from natural reason or from some other sign of intent. . . . [S]ince all contingencies can neither be foreseen nor set

---

[28] It is not very apparent why this case is given the label of 'defect in the subject-matter'.

[29] I.e., when consideration is given to the reason for the making of an agreement, there should be regard not only for the very things which the parties *actually* had in mind at the time, but also for precautions against dangers which the parties may not have actually considered. Grotius immediately provides an illustration of his point.

[30] This is another example of a purported *clausula rebus sic stantibus*. Although Grotius disapproves of the application of such a clause to promises, he approved of it in connection with the contracts of kings. See p. 229 above.

[31] Grotius (who himself served as an ambassador) clearly regards such behaviour as reprehensible.

[32] The reference is to the occurrence of a particular situation which falls outside the wording of an agreement when the parties actually intended it to be covered (or would have if they had turned their minds to the specific matter). Conversely, it could refer to a particular matter which falls within the terms of an agreement but which the parties actually preferred not to be covered. In short, the reference is to an awkward 'special case', in which the parties' actual joint intention is not reflected in the language which they employed.

forth, a degree of freedom is needed in order to make exceptions of cases which the person who has spoken would make an exception of, if he were present. Yet recourse to such a restriction of meaning should not be had rashly – that, in fact, would be to make oneself master of another's act[33] – but only on sufficient implications.

The most certain implication is if the literal meaning would in any case involve something unlawful, that is, at variance with the precepts of the law of nature, or of divine law. Of necessity, an exception must be made of such cases, since [such agreements] are not capable of imposing a legal obligation. . . . Thus a person who has promised to return a sword which he received in trust will not return it to a madman, lest he bring danger either to himself or to other innocent persons.[34] Similarly, an object received in trust will not be returned to the person who deposited it if the rightful owner demands it.[35] . . . The reason, as I have noted elsewhere, is that the force of ownership, when once introduced, is such that it is in every way unjust not to restore property to the owner, when he is known.

27. When a condition is too burdensome as regards the act[36]

A second implication will become manifest if, while the literal interpretation may not in itself involve something unlawful, the obligation, in the view of one who judges the matter fairly, shall appear to be burdensome and unbearable, whether the condition of human nature is considered in the abstract, or the person and matter under consideration are brought into comparison with the result of the act itself. Thus, a man who has lent a thing for some days will be able to demand its return within those days, if he himself is greatly in need of it; for the nature of a generous act is such that it is not to be believed that anyone has wished to obligate himself to his own great disadvantage. Thus, again, one who has promised aid to an ally will be entitled to excuse in so far as he himself needs his troops as long as he is in danger at home. Also, the exemption from taxes and tribute is to be understood as covering the usual daily and yearly requirements, not requirements imposed by extreme necessity, which a state cannot do without.

---

[33] I.e., in interpreting agreements, care must be taken to avoid altering the substance of the agreement that the parties made.

[34] This is a classic illustration of a case in which duties under natural law override normal obligations. It was first broached by Cicero, *On Duties*, III.95.

[35] On this topic, see also the discussion at p. 177 above.

[36] This interesting discussion strays somewhat from the topic of interpretation of agreements. The concern in this section is really not so much with interpretation of the meaning of agreements, as with the question of necessity as a justification for non-performance. The line between the two is by no means sharp, since it could be contended that a given agreement (or perhaps even all agreements in principle) contains a tacit provision allowing non-performance in the face of necessity.

From this, it is clear that the statement of Cicero was made too loosely, that promises without advantage to those to whom you have made them ought not to be kept, nor if they are more harmful to you than they are advantageous to the one to whom you made them.[37] For the promisor ought not to judge whether a thing will be useful to the promisee, except perhaps in the case of madness.

Furthermore, a certain [moderate] harm to the promisor is insufficient to prevent the promise from being binding. [T]he harm should be [so serious] as to require that it be considered an exception in view of the nature of the act. Thus one who has promised to work for a neighbour for some days will not be bound if the dangerous illness of his father or his son should detain him.

28–9. When the parts of a document are in conflict[38]

Of the ancient authors, Cicero laid down certain rules for the settlement of [the] question . . . as to which part of the document ought to prevail when [there is] a conflict. . . . Although these ought by no means to be disregarded, yet it seems to me that they were not arranged in their proper order. Accordingly I shall arrange them in this way:

That which permits should yield to that which [forbids]. The reason is that he who permits something seems to grant permission on the condition that nothing else hinders . . . that which is under consideration.[39]

That which is to be done at a definite time should have preference over that which can be done at any time. . . . Among agreements, . . . that should be given preference which is most specific and approaches most nearly to the subject in hand; for special provisions are ordinarily more effective than those that are general. Also in prohibitions, that which adds a penalty should be given preference over that which lacks a penalty; and that which threatens a greater penalty should have the preference over that which threatens a lesser penalty.

Then, that provision should prevail which has either the more honourable or the more expedient reasons.

Finally, that which was last said should prevail.

[T]his should be repeated from the previous discussion, that the force of sworn agreements is such that they ought to be understood according to their most generally accepted meaning; and so all restrictions that are implied, and not absolutely necessary from the nature of the case, should be rejected. If, then,

---

[37] Cicero, *On Duties*, I.32.

[38] It will be observed that Grotius's general approach is to hold that specific rules should prevail over general ones.

[39] I.e., contracting parties who agree to permit something should be understood to do so on the condition that there is not a prohibition elsewhere in their agreement against the act in question. From this, the inference is that prohibitions have, in general, a higher standing than permissions. The reasoning seems rather weak.

a sworn compact is at variance in some particular with one which has not been sworn to, preference ought to be given to the compact which has the sanctity of an oath.

30. Whether a written document is required for the validity of a contract

This question also is commonly raised, whether in a doubtful case a contract ought to be considered perfect before the written form has been completed and delivered. . . . To me it seems clear that, unless it has been otherwise agreed, we ought to believe that writing has been employed as evidence of the contract, not as part of its content.[40]

31. Interpretation of the contracts of kings according to Roman law

I shall not . . . admit the rule which has been adopted by some writers, that the contracts of kings and peoples ought to be interpreted according to Roman law so far as possible, unless it is apparent that, among certain peoples, the body of civil law has been received as the law of nations in respect to the matters which concern the law of nations. Such a presumption ought not rashly to be admitted.

---

[40] The point is that the contract, properly speaking, is the agreement between the parties. The written text is merely evidence of, or a reflection of, that agreement.

On damage caused through injury, and the obligation arising therefrom[1]

1. That fault creates the obligation to make good the loss

We have said above that there are three sources of our legal claims: pact, wrong, and statute.[2] Enough has been said about contracts. Let us come now to what is due by the law of nature in consequence of a wrong. By a wrong (*maleficium*), we here mean every fault (*culpa*), whether of commission or of omission, which is in conflict with what men ought to do, either from their common interest or by reason of a special quality. From such a fault, if damage has been caused, [then] by the law of nature an obligation arises, namely, that the damage should be made good.

2. Damage as that which conflicts with one's right taken in a strict sense

Damage [occurs] . . . when anyone has less than belongs to him, whether by a right that accrues to him from the law of nature alone, or [one that] is reinforced by the addition of a human act, as by ownership, contract, or legal enactment.[3] By nature, a man's life is his own, not indeed to destroy, but to safeguard; also his own are his body, limbs, reputation, honour, and the acts of his will. The previous part of our treatise has shown how each man, by property right and by agreements, possesses his own not only with respect to property but also with respect to the acts of others. In a similar manner, everyone acquires his particular rights from the law, because the law has the same power, or greater power, that individuals have over themselves or their property. Thus a ward has the right to demand a certain degree of diligence and care from his guardian, and likewise the state from an official; and not the state only, but also individual

---

[1] In modern terminology, this chapter would be said to be an exposition of the general law of tort or delict, from the standpoint of natural law. This is a branch of the civil law, involving compensation to victims for wrongs done. Remember that, according to Grotius, natural law has no penal provisions.

[2] A reference here, to Book II, Chapter 1, Section 2, is not really germane.

[3] It should be appreciated that by 'damage' (*damnum*) is meant, in essence, infringement of legal rights. It does not mean mere material loss on its own.

citizens, as often as the law indicates such a requirement explicitly, or by a sufficiently clear implication.

But [a legal right of action for a wrong committed does] not arise from aptitude alone, which is not properly called a right and which belongs to distributive justice; for one does not have ownership of that to which one has merely a moral claim.[4]

3. Aptitude distinguished from strict legal right

[C]are must be taken not to confuse things which are of different kinds. For [example] one who has been entrusted with the duty of appointing magistrates is under obligation to the state to choose a man who is worthy; and the state has a special right to demand this. If, therefore, the state has suffered damage from the choice of an unworthy person, the man having the responsibility of choice will be bound [to the state] to make the loss good.

[This may be contrasted with the position of a citizen of that state. Any] citizen who is not unworthy, although he has no special right to any office, nevertheless has a true right to be a candidate for an office along with others. [I]f he is hindered in the exercise of this right by force or fraud, he will be able to collect the estimated value, not of the entire thing sought, but of that uncertain damage.[5] The case will be similar if a testator has been hindered by force or fraud from willing anything to a man. For the capacity to receive a legacy is a kind of right, and in consequence it is an injury to interfere with the liberty of the testator in such a matter.

4. That damage extends also to income

Moreover, a person will be understood to have less, and therefore to have suffered loss, not only in the property itself, but also in the products which strictly belong to it, whether these have actually been gathered or not, if he might have gathered

---

[4] It will be recalled that an aptitude is, by definition, not a full legal right but something more in the nature of a hope or expectation. As such, it does not form the basis of a legal action in court. See p. 24 above.

[5] In this case of a wrongful appointment of a person to public office, the contention is that the wrong is of a different character for the state and for disappointed candidates for the office. The state possesses a faculty for the choosing of its office holders. A person who interferes with that power by choosing an unworthy person breaches the state's right and is accordingly legally liable to compensate the state for the damage caused by his interference. A disappointed candidate, in contrast, does not possess a faculty for serving in the office. He possesses only (in Grotius's parlance) an aptitude, i.e., an expectation or hope of serving, or a potential to serve – but he does possess a faculty to compete for selection. In other words, he has lost not the opportunity actually to hold the office, but only to compete for it on a fair basis. The value of that opportunity to compete should therefore be the measure of damages to which he is entitled, and not the value of actually holding the office.

them. [B]ut expenditures for the improvement of the property will need to be deducted, or expenditures necessary for gathering the fruits, in accordance with the rule which forbids us to become richer at the expense of another.

5. How the principle stated applies to the cessation of income

Also, the expectation of gain from our property will be estimated, not at its full amount, but in proportion to its nearness to completion, as the expectation of the harvest at the sowing.

6. Those who by their act cause damage primarily

Besides the one who causes damage in person and directly, others also are liable, by reason of their act or their failure to act. By an act, some are liable primarily, others secondarily. He is liable primarily who orders the act, or gives the necessary consent, or aids, or receives stolen goods, or in some other manner shares in the crime itself.

7. Those who by their act cause damage secondarily

Those are liable secondarily who give advice, praise, or approval to the act.

8. Likewise those who cause damage by inaction

Likewise, an obligation is created by failure to act, either primarily or secondarily; primarily, when one who is in strict legal duty bound to forbid the act by a command, or to render aid to one who has been injured, does not do so.

9. Those who by not doing as they ought cause damage secondarily

A person is liable secondarily who does not dissuade when he ought, or who keeps to himself a fact which he ought to make known. But in all these cases, we refer the word 'ought' to that true legal right which is the object of expletive justice, whether it arises from statute law or from a special quality.[6] For if one is under obligation according to the rule of love, by omission he will sin indeed; but he will not be held to make reparation. [F]or the source of the obligation to make good is the true right, properly speaking.

10. What kind of effective participation in the act is requisite to create such obligation

It should also be understood that all those whom we have mentioned are under obligation to make good if they have really been the cause of damage; that is, if

---

[6] On expletive justice, see p. 26 above.

they have contributed to the damage either in whole or in part. For in the case of those in the second class, who act or fail to act, and sometimes even in the case of some in the first class, it often happens that the one who has caused the damage would have been sure to cause it even without the act or neglect of the others. In such cases the others, whom I have mentioned, will not be liable.[7]

11. In what order such persons are held liable

Now those are liable in the first instance who, by command or otherwise, have impelled any one to a harmful act. When such are lacking, the perpetrator of the crime is so held. After him the others, who have caused the act, are individually liable for the whole loss, if the whole act has proceeded from them, though not from them alone.

12. Liability for resulting damage

Again, the one who is liable for an act is at the same time liable for the consequences resulting from the force of the act. In one of the *Controversies* of [the Elder] Seneca, this is illustrated by the burning of a plane tree, from which a house caught fire and burned. In this connexion, he states an opinion thus: 'Although there was a part of the damage which you did not wish to cause, you are liable for it all, just as if you had caused it intentionally. In fact, the person who defends himself on the ground of not intending wrong ought not to have willed any part of the wrong.'[8]

13. An example in homicide

Let the following serve as examples. One who unjustly takes human life is bound to pay the expenses, if any have been incurred, for doctors. He is, furthermore, bound to give to those whom the dead man was accustomed to support from a sense of duty, as parents, wife, and children, so much as that expectation of support was worth in view of the age of the person killed. . . . We are speaking of unjustifiable homicide, that is, of homicide by one who has not the right to do that from which death results. Therefore, if anyone has had the right, but has sinned against the law of love, as one who has been unwilling to flee from an attack, he will not be liable.[9]

---

[7] The justification for non-liability in this case would seem to be an absence of causation, although Grotius does not actually discuss the point.

[8] Elder Seneca, *Controversies*, V.5.

[9] The situation is one in which an innocent person is attacked, who can save himself in either of two ways: by killing the assailant in self-defence, or by fleeing. The 'law of love' requires flight. But natural law allows self-defence; so the killing in that case would be lawful, even though it was avoidable. For Grotius's main discussion of the right of individual self-defence in natural law, see p. 52 above.

14. An example of one who has used violence in a different way

One who has maimed another will in like manner be liable for the expenses, and for the estimated value of the decrease in earning power of the one who has been maimed.[10] But, as in the instance mentioned above, the life, so here the scars, are not susceptible of valuation in the case of a freeman. The same should be said of false imprisonment.[11]

15. Of the adulterer and seducer

So also, an adulterer and adulteress are bound not only to indemnify the husband for the support of the offspring, but also to repay to the legitimate children whatever loss they may suffer from the sharing of such a child in the inheritance. He who has debauched a virgin by violence or fraud is bound to pay to her the value of her diminished expectation of marriage. Furthermore, he is bound even to marry her, if by so promising he obtained the enjoyment of her person.

16. Of a thief, robber, and others

The thief and the robber are bound to restore the thing taken, together with its natural increase, and make good the resulting loss or failure to secure gain. If . . . the thing has been destroyed, they should repay not the highest, nor the lowest, but a fair valuation. In this class also those should be placed who by fraud avoid the payment of their legitimate taxes. Those are similarly liable who have caused loss by an unjust sentence, or by false accusation, or by perjured testimony.

17. Of one who has procured a promise through deceit or an unjust fear

Furthermore, one who has caused a contract or promise to be made by means of deceit or violence, or an unjust fear, is bound to free absolutely the person thus dealt with. The reason is that such persons had the right not to be deceived, not to be constrained; this right in the former case arose from the nature of the contract, in the latter case from natural liberty also. In the class with those mentioned ought to be included those who have not been willing, except for pay, to do what they were bound to do from duty.[12]

---

[10] *Digest*, 9.3.7 (Gaius).

[11] Regarding the scars, Grotius appears to be saying that an alteration of outward appearance as a result of the injury should not figure in the calculation of compensation owing. It is puzzling that Grotius sees false imprisonment as non-compensable too. It would seem that any earnings lost by virtue of the wrongful confinement should be paid by the wrong-doer.

[12] I.e., such persons are required to remit the payment that they received.

18. A promise has been motived by a just fear according to the law of nature

But one who has given cause why he ought to suffer violence, or ought to be constrained by fear, has himself to blame for it.

19. Of a fear considered just by the law of nations

But by the consent of nations, the rule has been introduced that all wars declared and waged by the authority of the sovereigns on both sides should be considered lawful as regards their external effects, of which we shall speak below;[13] and so also it follows that the fear of such a war is considered as just [with the consequence] that what has been obtained by it cannot be demanded back.[14] In this sense, the distinction . . . can be admitted, between public enemies, on the one side, with whom by the agreement of nations we have . . . many rights in common, and on the other side pirates and robbers. For if pirates and robbers have extorted anything by fear, its return can be demanded, unless an oath prevents; but such a demand cannot be made on public enemies.

20. Liability of civil authorities for loss caused by their subjects

Kings and public officials are liable for neglect if they do not employ the remedies which they can and ought to employ for the prevention of robbery and piracy.[15]

At a time when the rulers of our country had given to very many persons letters of marque and reprisal as against the enemy at sea,[16] and some of these had seized the property of friends, had abandoned their native land and were wandering about at sea without returning even when recalled, I remember that

---

[13] See p. 359 below.

[14] I.e., enemy property which is captured in such a war need not be returned, even if the war was unjust according to the law of *nature*. See p. 359 below for further discussion of this point.

[15] The meaning seems to be that rulers are 'liable for neglect' in the sense of being under a natural-law obligation to compensate persons who suffered loss because of that neglect. That is not necessarily to say, though, that those persons will actually have a right of legal action against the ruler to enforce that right. See p. 224 above on this subject.

[16] Letters of marque and reprisal were self-help licences issued by rulers to subjects, authorising the holders to employ force (in this case, on the high seas) to obtain compensation for some prior injury which they had suffered. Typically, the letters authorised the forcible taking of property from any person of the same nationality as the original wrong-doers. Persons suffering a loss of their property on this basis were then left to sue the actual wrong-doer in the courts of their mutual home state for reimbursement of those losses. The danger, as Grotius makes clear, is that holders of such letters might exceed the terms of the letter by plundering persons who were not authorised targets. Such acts, on the high seas, would then be acts of piracy. On the practice of reprisals, see p. 338 below.

I was asked whether the authorities were liable on that account, either because they had utilised the services of wicked men, or because they had not required a bond.[17] I replied that they were under no obligation except to punish the offenders as guilty, in case they could be found, or surrender them;[18] that in addition, they should see to it that the property of the freebooters should be rendered liable. For I maintained that they themselves had not been the cause of the wrongful freebootery, and that they had not had any share in it; that they had also forbidden by laws that friends should be harmed; that they had not been bound by any law to require a bond, since even without a letter of marque, they could give to all their subjects the right of plundering the enemy, as had formerly been done;[19] that such a permission was not the cause of loss inflicted on allies, since even without such a permission private persons could fit out vessels and go to sea.[20] I said that in truth it could not have been foreseen, whether the men were going to be wicked men; and that in truth we could not avoid utilising the services of wicked men, that otherwise an army cannot be collected.[21]

Kings, again, are not liable if their soldiers or sailors have injured friends contrary to orders; and this rule has been approved by witness of France and England. The liability of one for the acts of his servants without fault of his own does not belong to the law of nations, according to which this question has to be settled, but to municipal law; and that not a universal rule, but one introduced as against sailors and some other persons for particular reasons.[22]

[17] By 'bond' is meant the deposit of a sum of money with the government upon the issue of the letters of marque and reprisal, from which damages could be paid out to anyone who was wrongfully injured by the letter holders.

[18] I.e., to turn them over to someone who would punish them.

[19] Giving to all citizens the right of plundering the enemy was known as the granting of general reprisals – in contrast to special reprisals, in which only the parties injured by wrongdoers were granted the right to take self-help action to obtain compensation for their losses. For further discussion of reprisals by Grotius, see p. 338 below. The granting of general reprisals against a foreign state was, in effect, a declaration of war and was commonly treated as such.

[20] This passage appears to be an implicit endorsement of the view that a war is, by its nature, a conflict between the entire citizenry of the belligerent states. On this thesis, all citizens have a right to take such measures as the capturing of enemy-owned property, with no need for a special commission from their government.

[21] The question concerns causation or remoteness of damage. If a ruler commissions privateers to attack the enemy, and those privateers misbehave by plundering other persons as well, then the ruler (in Grotius's view) cannot be held responsible for that misconduct, which should be seen as an entirely independent act by the miscreants.

[22] The rule in modern international law is different. War crimes committed by soldiers do entail the legal responsibility of the state, even if the soldiers in question were acting contrary to orders. For a fuller discussion by Grotius of the question of liability for acts of others in natural law and the law of nations, see p. 338 below.

21. Liability for damage done by an animal or vessel without fault of the owner

This also is to be noted, that it is likewise a principle of municipal law that a slave or animal, which has caused damage or loss, is to be delivered up for punishment.[23] [B]y the law of nature, [in contrast], the owner who is not in fault is not in any degree liable. Furthermore, he is not liable [under natural law] whose ship without fault on his part has caused damage to the ship of another. Yet by the [municipal] laws of many peoples, as also by our laws, it is customary that such a loss be divided, on account of the difficulty of fixing the blame.

22. Damage to reputation and honour

But, as we have said, damage is also done to honour and reputation, as by blows, insults, abuse, calumny, derision, and other similar means. In these acts, no less than in theft and other crimes, the criminality of the act must be distinguished from its effects. For to the former, punishment corresponds, and reparation for the loss to the latter. [R]eparation is made by confession of the fault . . . and through the other means which are similar. . . . [S]uch a damage may [also] be made good with money, if the injured party so desires, because money is the common measure of useful things.

---

[23] According to something called the law of deodands, even inanimate objects could be 'guilty' of offences and delivered up for 'punishment'. An example would be a sign-board that collapsed, without fault of its owner, and injured a passer-by. The sign-board itself would be the offender. The same would be true of animals that caused injury without fault on their owners' part. Deodands were not abolished in English law until 1846. This curious branch of law seems to be based on the thesis that, ultimately, there is no such thing as a true accident. It also illustrates the obsession of natural-law writers with the principle that punishment can only be inflicted on persons when those persons are actually at fault. Natural lawyers, in other words, tended to reject the principle of vicarious liability. See p. 338 below on reprisals, in this connexion.

18

On the right of legation¹

1. Origin of the right of legation

Thus far, we have treated of rights for which we are indebted to the law of nature; we have added thereto only a few from the volitional law of nations, in so far as any addition had been made to the law of nature from that source. It remains for us to discuss the obligations that the law of nations, which we call volitional, has itself introduced. In this class, the subject of prime importance is the right of legation. Everywhere, in fact, we find mention of the sacred affairs of embassies, the inviolability of ambassadors, the law of nations which is to be observed with reference to ambassadors, divine and human law, the right of legation sacred among nations, treaties sacred with reference to nations, the alliance of the human race, and the sacredness of the persons of ambassadors.

2. Among whom the right of legation is in force

First, then, it should be understood that this law of nations, whatever it is, which we are going to treat, pertains to those representatives whom rulers with sovereign powers send to one another. For in addition to these, there are representatives of provinces, municipalities, and others, who are not governed by the law between different nations, but by municipal law.

[P]eoples who are united in an unequal alliance will possess the right of legation so long as they do not cease to be their own masters; likewise also, those that are in part subject, and in part not, will have the right of legation for that part in respect to which they are not subject. Nevertheless, kings who have been conquered in a formal war, and have been expelled from their kingdoms, along with their other royal possessions, have lost also the right of legation.

In civil wars, however, necessity sometimes opens the way for the exercise of this right, though in an irregular fashion. Such a case will arise when a people has been divided into parts so nearly equal that it is doubtful which of the two sides

---

¹ In modern terminology, an exposition of diplomatic law. This is the first topic on which Grotius's concern is principally with the volitional law of nations, rather than with natural law.

possesses sovereignty; and again, when two persons with practically equal rights are contending for the succession to the throne. Under such circumstances, a single people is considered for the time being as two peoples.[2]

Pirates and brigands, who do not constitute a state, cannot avail themselves of the law of nations.... Sometimes, nevertheless, persons of such a character obtain the right of legation on the strength of a pledge of good faith, as in ancient times fugitives in the passes of the Pyrenees.

3. Whether an embassy ought always to be admitted

Now there are two rights of ambassadors which we see are everywhere referred to the law of nations. The first is that they be admitted [into the territories of the states to which are sent]; the second, that they be free from violence.... [The first of these] ought not to be taken ... literally. The law of nations, in fact, does not enjoin that all [ambassadors] be admitted; but it does forbid the rejection of ambassadors without cause. The cause ... may arise in the case of the one who sends the ambassador, or in the case of the one who is sent, or in the reason for the sending.

But permanent legations, such as are now customary, can be rejected with the best of right; for ancient custom, to which they were unknown, teaches how unnecessary they are.

4. Self-defence against ambassadors

The question regarding the inviolability of ambassadors[3] is more difficult, and has been handled in varied fashion by the distinguished minds of this generation. We need to speak of the persons of ambassadors, then of their suite and property.

As regards their persons, some think that, by the law of nations, the persons of ambassadors are protected from unjust violence only; for their view is that the privileges of ambassadors are to be explained according to common law.[4] Others hold that violence may be done to an ambassador ... if the law of nations has been violated by him; and this is sufficiently comprehensive, for in the law of nations, the law of nature is included, so that an ambassador [could then] be punished for all crimes excepting only those which are committed against municipal law. Others restrict this right [to take action against ambassadors to

---

[2] This is a rare reference to the phenomenon of civil wars in this book – a notable omission by modern standards.

[3] Inviolability means, basically, freedom from arrest and detention by authorities of the host country. Grotius makes clear below (in Section 4) that he endorses the rather broader principle of immunity of ambassadors, in the sense of their complete exemption from the law of the state to which they are sent.

[4] I.e., some deny (wrongly in Grotius's view) that ambassadors possess any privileged status at all, and that their only 'privilege' is accordingly a higher level of concern as to possible violations of the ordinary legal rights shared by all free persons.

cases in which the ambassador has committed] crimes ... against the security of the [host] state, or the dignity of the official to whom the ambassador is sent. There are also those who think that even this right is fraught with danger; that complaints [against an ambassador's conduct] ought to be made to the one who has sent the ambassador, and the decision entrusted to him. Some, again, think that kings and peoples that have no interest in the case ought to be brought in as advisers. This may be an evidence of prudence, but it is not required by law.

The reasons which the advocates of these views severally allege lead to no definite conclusion; for [the volitional law of nations] does not certainly arise from definite reasons, as the law of nature does, but takes its form according to the will of nations. Now the nations could have made provision for ambassadors either covering all cases or with certain exceptions. For on the one side lies the advantageousness of punishment of grave offenders; on the other is the usefulness of embassies, and the ease in sending embassies is best promoted by making their safety as secure as possible.[5] The question, then, ought to be considered, to what extent have nations reached an agreement? This question cannot be answered on the basis of precedents alone; for there is a sufficient number of precedents on both sides. We must, therefore, have recourse not only to the opinions of wise men, but also to the implications.

Equity and justice, that is, the pure law of nature, allow that punishment shall be inflicted when he who has committed wrong is found. But the [volitional] law of nations makes an exception of ambassadors and of those who, like them, come under a pledge of public faith. Wherefore it is contrary to the [volitional] law of nations that ambassadors should be brought to trial; and on that account many things, which the law of nature permits, are commonly forbidden.[6]

The implications, furthermore, favour this side, for it is nearer the truth to understand special privileges in such a way that they may add something to a common right. If, now, ambassadors were protected only from unjust violence, there would be nothing great, nothing outstanding in that provision. There is the further consideration that the security of ambassadors outweighs any advantage which accrues from a punishment. For punishment can be inflicted through the one who sent the ambassador, if he so wills. If, on the contrary, he is unwilling, punishment by means of war can be exacted from him as having approved the crime.[7] Some raise the objection that it is better that one should

---

[5] The content of diplomatic law, in other words, is not deduced from fundamental principles of natural law, but instead is the product of agreement between states, arrived at on pragmatic grounds – what would now be called general public policy.

[6] Things which are merely permitted by the law of nature can be overridden by the agreement between states (i.e., by the law of nations). Things which the law of nature actually *forbids*, however, cannot be overridden, as explained at p. 96 above.

[7] In other words, if an ambassador commits offences, and his own sovereign refuses to punish him, that sovereign thereby commits an offence against the state to which the ambassador had been sent. That offence can become a cause of war between the two

be punished than that many should be involved in war. Yet, if the one who sent the ambassador approves of his act, the punishment of the ambassador will [still] not exempt us from war.[8]

On the other hand, the safety of ambassadors is placed on an extremely precarious footing if they are under obligation to render account of their acts to any other than the one by whom they are sent. For since the views of those who send the ambassadors are generally different from the views of those who receive them, and often directly opposed, it is scarcely possible that in every case something may not be said against an ambassador which shall present the appearance of a crime. And although some things are so obvious that they do not admit of doubt, yet the universal peril is sufficient to establish the justice and advantage of the universal law.

My unqualified conclusion, therefore, is that the rule has been accepted by the nations that the common custom, which makes a person who lives in foreign territory subject to that country, admits of an exception in the case of ambassadors. Ambassadors as if by a kind of fiction are considered to represent those who sent them. . . . In consequence, by a similar fiction, ambassadors were held to be outside of the limits of the country to which they were accredited. For this reason, they are not subject to the municipal law of the state within which they are living.[9] If, therefore, the crime should be such that according to all appearances it can be treated lightly, it will either need to be overlooked, or the ambassador should be ordered to leave the country. . . . If the crime should be particularly atrocious and bid fair to bring harm to the state, the ambassador should be sent back to the one who sent him, with the demand that he be punished or surrendered.

But, as we have several times remarked, all human laws have been so adjusted that, in case of dire necessity, they are not binding; and so the same rule will hold in regard to the law of the inviolability of ambassadors. Nevertheless, this extreme necessity does not warrant the infliction of punishment. . . . Such extreme necessity will be concerned . . . less with . . . punishment [than] with guarding against serious hurt, especially to the [host] state. Therefore, that an immediately threatening peril may be met, if there is no other proper recourse, ambassadors can be detained and questioned. . . . But if an ambassador should

---

countries. But in all events, the host state does not have the right to inflict punishment directly onto the ambassador himself.

[8] I.e., even if the host country inflicted punishment onto the ambassador, approval of the conduct of the ambassador by the sovereign would still (according to Grotius) be an offence against the host country – and hence still a potential justification for war.

[9] This is an implied acceptance of the principle of diplomatic immunity in its broadest sense – as immunity from the application of the law of the host country per se, and not merely as a restriction on the jurisdiction of the national courts of the host state. The 'fiction' which Grotius identifies and endorses – that 'ambassadors [are] held to be outside of the limits of the country to which they were accredited' – came to be referred to in international law as the principle of extraterritoriality.

attempt armed force, he can indeed be killed, not by way of penalty, but in natural defence.

5. Concerning persons to whom the ambassador was not sent

Now the law which I have mentioned concerning the inviolability of ambassadors[10] is to be understood as binding on the one to whom the embassy was sent. . . . This law . . . does not apply to those through whose territory ambassadors pass without receiving a safeguard. For, if they are going to, or coming from, the enemies of this people, or are planning any hostile measure, they can even be killed.

If there is no such reason, and ambassadors are mistreated, it is to be understood that not the [volitional] law of nations, which we are discussing, has been violated, but the friendship and dignity either of the one who sent or of the one who received the embassy.[11]

6. An ambassador to an enemy state in wartime

For the rest, when an embassy has been admitted, it is under the protection of the law of nations even among public enemies,[12] and still more among those who are merely unfriendly. . . . Such expressions of opinion are justified; for not only do very many matters come up in war which cannot be handled except through ambassadors, but also peace itself is hardly to be made by any other means.

7. Retaliation against ambassadors

The question is also commonly raised, whether an ambassador can be killed or mistreated by right of retaliation, if he comes from one who has committed some such act.[13] There are, to be sure, sufficiently many examples of such vengeance

---

[10] The terminology is unfortunately rather careless here, since Grotius has been arguing for something greater than mere inviolability (i.e., for exemption from the application of the law itself in the host country).

[11] I.e., the wrongful act, in law, will not be violation of diplomatic immunity per se (under the volitional law of nations), but rather a breach of general friendship and dignity (under natural law).

[12] That is, the immunity of an ambassador must be respected, even if the sending state and the host state are at war with one another.

[13] The problem here concerns a situation in which the government of, say, State A has mistreated the ambassador sent it by State B. The question is whether the officials of State B can, in retaliation, inflict a like treatment onto the ambassador sent by A to B. Grotius answers this question in the negative. So does modern international law, in which it is clearly established that justified countermeasures (as reprisals are now called) cannot take the form of infringements of diplomatic immunities. See Article 50(2) of the Articles on State Responsibility (2001).

in history; but, of course, the histories relate both just deeds and also unjust, wrathful, and violent deeds. The [volitional] law of nations safeguards not only the dignity of the one who sends, but also the safety of the one who is sent; therefore there is a tacit agreement with the latter also. Accordingly, a wrong is done [in this posited case] to the one who is sent, even if no wrong is done to the one who sent him.[14]

8. Concerning the suite of an ambassador

The suite[15] also, and the effects of ambassadors, in their own way are inviolate. . . . But these rights are sacred as accessories and, therefore, only so far as seems good to the ambassador.

If, now, members of the suite have committed a great crime, the demand can be made on the ambassador to surrender them; [but] they ought not to be taken away by force. . . . If, however, the ambassador is unwilling to surrender such members of his suite, the same course will need to be pursued as we just now mentioned in the case of an ambassador.[16]

The question whether an ambassador has jurisdiction over his own household, and whether anyone who takes refuge with him has a right of asylum in his residence, depends on the concession of him in whose domain the ambassador resides; for that right does not belong to the [volitional] law of nations.[17]

9. The movable goods of ambassadors

Again, it is the better established opinion that the movable goods of an ambassador, which in consequence are considered as attached to his person, cannot be seized as security, or in payment of debt or by order of the court, or, as some

---

[14] A retaliatory act by State B against the ambassador from State A (in our example) constitutes a wrong against the ambassador himself and not, strictly speaking, against State A as such. The reason is that the sovereign of State A merits the punishment by virtue of his prior unlawful mistreatment of the ambassador sent by State B.

[15] By suite is meant the household servants of the ambassador.

[16] I.e., the ambassador can be expelled from the host country; or a demand can be made to the ambassador's sovereign that he inflict punishment onto the wrongdoers.

[17] The position in modern international law is similar to this, but not identical. There is no right of refuge or asylum on foreign embassy properties on the part of persons (i.e., nationals of the host country) seeking to evade prosecution or mistreatment. On that point, modern law agrees with Grotius. Modern law departs from Grotius's view, however, in holding that, if the foreign ambassador *chooses* to allow persons to take refuge on the embassy property, then the inviolability of the property is not thereby lost – and that this is a matter of international law, not of the will of the host state alone. The primary remedy of the host state in such a case is a legal action against the home state of the ambassador under international law. See, for example, the *Asylum Case (Peru v. Colombia)*, 1950 ICJ Rep. 266.

claim, by the hand of the king. For an ambassador ought to be free from all compulsion – such compulsion as affects things of which he has need as well as that which touches his person – in order that he may have full security. If, then, he has contracted a debt and, as ordinarily happens, possesses no landed property in the country, payment should be demanded in a friendly way from him personally;[18] and if he refuses, then payment should be requested from the one who sent him, so that finally those methods may be employed which are customarily used in the case of debtors outside the country.[19]

10. On obligation without the right of compulsion

There is no reason for fearing that, as some think, no one can be found who would be willing to make contracts with an ambassador, if such is the ambassadorial right. For kings, who are not subject to compulsion, do not fail to have creditors.

11. Importance of the right of legation

Profane histories are full of wars undertaken on account of the ill-treatment of ambassadors.

---

[18] The obligation of debtors to pay their debts is a principle of general natural law, and not merely an enactment of the host country alone. Consequently, the ambassador's exemption from the laws of the host country does not exempt him from the payment of debts. Legal compulsion cannot be brought to bear against him, however, as Grotius explains.

[19] I.e., if the ambassador's sovereign refuses to compel him to pay the debt, then the sovereign commits a denial of justice against the creditors. This wrongful act can justify the taking of reprisals against the sovereign, or even a resort to war.

19

On the right of sepulchre[1]

1. Origin of the right of burial of the dead

The burial of the dead also is an obligation which has its origin in the [volitional] law of nations; and this, in turn, has its origin in the will. . . . Because the ancients were accustomed to refer to the gods as authors of the rights which are common to civilised men, in order that these might seem more sacred, we see that this right, as well as that of legation, is generally ascribed to the gods.

2. Whence the right arose

All do not seem to hold the same opinion regarding the cause of the introduction of the custom that bodies should be covered with earth, whether first embalmed, as among the Egyptians, or cremated, as among most of the Greeks, or buried as they are now. . . . [The simplest] explanation is that, since man surpasses the other animate beings, it has seemed an unworthy fate that other animals should feed on his body; wherefore, that this might be so far as possible avoided, burial was invented. . . . [T]he dead should not be exposed to such injuries. . . . [I]t seems foreign to the dignity of man's nature that a human body should be trodden under foot and torn to pieces. . . . Hence is it that the office of burial is said to be performed not so much for the man, that is, for the person, as for mankind, that is for human nature. . . . A natural consequence of this is that burial ought not to be denied either to private or to public enemies.

3. Whether burial is due also to public enemies

Consequently, all agree that even public enemies are entitled to burial.

4. Whether the right of burial is obligatory in the case of notorious criminals

Nevertheless, I see that there are reasons for doubt in regard to notorious malefactors. . . . We read in the histories, to be sure, that examples of those left

---

[1] Meaning the right of burial of the dead.

unburied are more frequent in civil than in foreign wars; and to-day we see that the bodies of some condemned criminals are left for a long time in the sight of the people. Nevertheless, not only statesmen but also theologians are discussing the question whether or not this custom is praiseworthy.

[W]e see that praise has been given to commanders who ordered the burial of the bodies of those that had not allowed this privilege to others.

5. On the right of burial of persons who committed suicide

Nevertheless, the fact is not unworthy of notice that, even among the Jews, the rule concerning the burial of the dead had an exception in the case of those who had committed suicide.... And this is not strange, since no other punishment can be devised against those who are beyond the reach of the death penalty.

But to return to my subject, with great unanimity, the ancients agreed that war is lawfully undertaken on account of the denial of burial.

6. Other rights that impose obligation by virtue of the law of nations[2]

There are also some other rights, which impose obligation by virtue of the volitional law of nations. Such are the right to things possessed for a long time,[3] the right of succession to one who dies intestate, and the rights which are created by a contract, no matter how unfair.[4] For although all these rights are in some degree derived from the law of nature, yet from human law they acquire a kind of support, either against the uncertainties of conjecture, or against certain exceptions which otherwise natural reason seems to suggest.

---

[2] This section is important, though it has nothing to do with the right of sepulchre, which is the subject of the chapter.

[3] This is the law of prescription, according to which a more or less lengthy period of time suffices, in itself, to discharge past wrongs. It will be recalled that, under natural law, the passage of time alone could not extinguish the right of a property owner. Intention on the owner's part was necessary. See p. 116 above.

[4] It was explained above (at p. 206) that, according to the law of nature, unfair contracts are not binding – at least not to the extent of the unfairness – because, by their nature, they involve the unjust enrichment of one party at the expense of the other. Here, it is noted that, in the volitional law of nations, the position is different.

20

On punishments

1. Definition and origin of punishment

Above, when we began to speak of the reasons for which wars are undertaken, we said that acts must be considered in two categories, according as they can be repaired or punished.[1] The former class we have already discussed.[2] There remains the latter, which concerns punishments. This we must consider all the more carefully because the lack of a clear understanding as to the origin and nature of punishment has given rise to many mistaken opinions.

Now punishment in general means an evil of suffering which is inflicted because of an evil of action. For although it is customary to assign certain tasks to persons as a punishment, yet these tasks are regarded from the point of view of their burdensomeness, and so are to be classed with sufferings. However, the inconveniences, such as exclusion from public meetings or offices, which are anywhere suffered on account of a contagious disease, or a bodily deformity, or other manifestations of uncleanness (many of these are mentioned in the Hebraic law), are not, strictly speaking, punishments, although they are called by this name on account of a certain resemblance and through a misuse of the term.

Moreover, among those things which nature itself declares are permissible and not sinful is this, that he who does evil shall suffer evil; this the philosophers call the most ancient law, and law of Radamanthus.

What we have said of punishment properly so called is summed up in this, that it is a [response to] a crime.

2. Punishment as related to expletive justice

But opinions differ as to whether punishment falls within the sphere of attributive or of expletive justice. For, on the ground that he who has committed the

---

[1] There is no mention of prevention, which is Grotius's third category of just war. Perhaps he regards defensive war as a sub-category of punitive war, as he suggested earlier. See p. 89 above.
[2] Chiefly in Chapter 17 above.

greater sin is punished more heavily, and he who has committed the lesser is punished more lightly, and that the penalty is given as it were by the whole to a part, punishments are assigned by some to the sphere of attributive justice.[3] However, this ... principle which they lay down, that attributive justice comes into play whenever an equality is established between more than two terms, we have shown to be untrue at the beginning of this work.[4] [T]hen, as regards the fact that those who have done greater injury are punished more severely, and those who have done less injury are punished more lightly, that happens only as a consequence, not because it is aimed at first and for its own sake. For first and for its own sake, a balance is aimed at between the guilt and the penalty.[5]

Nor yet do those give a better explanation who claim that expletive justice, which they commonly call commutative, is exercised in punishments. For in so doing, they consider this a business transaction, as if something were paid to the wrong-doer, in accordance with the usage of contracts. They are deceived by current speech, whereby we say that punishment is due to him who sins. This is plainly misleading. For he to whom something is properly owed has a right against another. But when we say that punishment is due to some person we mean nothing more than that it is proper for him to be punished.[6]

Nevertheless, it is true that expletive justice is exercised in penalties primarily and for its own sake, because he who punishes, that he may punish rightly, must have the right to punish; and this right arises from the crime of the guilty.[7] In this matter, therefore, there is something that approaches the nature of contracts. For just as he who sells, even if he says nothing specifically, is considered to have obligated himself to all the things which are naturally involved in a sale, so he who does wrong seems by his own will to have obligated himself to

---

[3] In saying that punishment is given 'by a whole to a part' (i.e., by a society to a member of that society), there is a suggestion that the infliction of punishment is to be likened to the parcelling out of resources by a superior to persons beneath him, which is the basic conception of attributive justice.

[4] See p. 26 above.

[5] That is, a penalty is properly apportioned not to the material damage done by the crime, but rather to the degree of guilty-mindedness or malice harboured in the actor's mind. This is another illustration of the focus of natural law on internal, rather than external, aspects of actions. The implication is that attributive justice, in contrast, focuses on the distribution of material goods in proportion to material contributions made by the various claimants, and not according to the personal virtues of the claimants.

[6] Basically, the assertion is that neither of the two forms of justice (attributive or expletive) is relevant to the question of punishment because both of those forms of justice concern the due satisfaction of rights. It makes no sense to think of a wrong-doer as having a 'right to be punished'.

[7] It is now conceded that there is an element, with punishment, of matching the punishment to the crime. This arises, however, not out of any right on the wrong-doer's part, but rather out of a proper sense of duty on the part of the party inflicting the punishment.

a penalty, because a serious crime cannot be unpunishable; hence, whoever directly wills to sin, by consequence has willed also to deserve a penalty. In this sense, the Emperors say to a person, 'You yourself have subjected yourself to this punishment'.[8]

3. Who may exact punishment according to the law of nature

[T]he subject of this right [to inflict punishment], that is the agent to whom the right is given, has not been definitely fixed by nature itself. For reason declares that the criminal may be punished. It does not, however, declare who ought to inflict the punishment, excepting so far as this, that nature makes it clear enough that it is most suitable that punishment be inflicted by one who is superior; yet not to the degree that this is shown to be altogether necessary, unless the word 'superior' is understood to imply that he who has done wrong by that very act may be considered to have made himself inferior to someone else and, as it were, to have demoted himself from the class of men into the class of beasts which are subject to man.[9]

Wherefore it follows that in any case a guilty person ought not to be punished by one equally guilty.

4. On punishment having in view some advantage among men

Another question is concerned with the purpose aimed at in punishments. What we have said thus far does at least show this, that injustice is not done to the guilty if they are punished. Nevertheless, it does not follow that they are in every case to be punished. This in fact is not true; for God and men pardon many things in many guilty persons; and for this cause they are wont to be praised.

Now, these things are true in the case of men who inflict punishment, for one man is so bound to another by ties of common blood that he ought not to do harm to another save for the sake of attaining some good. With God, the case is otherwise.... For the actions of God can be based upon the right of the Supreme Power, particularly where a man's special desert is concerned, even if they have in view no end outside themselves.... But when man punishes a man who is his equal by nature, he ought to have a definite purpose in view.

---

[8] The basic point is that liability to punishment arises ultimately out of the will of the wrong-doer himself. Moreover, it seems to be suggested that this will is that the punishment should consist of a proportionate 'payment' for the wrong committed.

[9] Ordinarily, punishments may be inflicted only by superiors onto inferiors (as by sovereigns onto subjects). If it is understood, though, that any wrong-doer, by virtue of the very act of wrong-doing itself, subjects himself to all other persons in general, then the conclusion would be that any person has the right to punish wrong-doers. Grotius endorses this line of thinking.

5. Vengeance according to the law of nature

[A] desire [simply to see a wrongdoer suffer], taken by itself, is incompatible with the faculty of reason, whose function is to govern the desires. It is, furthermore, incompatible with the law of nature, because that is the dictate of nature in so far as it is governed by reason and takes account of society; and reason forbids a man to do anything whereby another may be harmed, unless this action has some good end in view. In the bare spectacle of the suffering, even of an enemy, there is only a false and imaginary good, as in superfluous riches and many other things of the same sort. Accordingly, in this sense, vengeance among men is censured not only by Christian men of learning, but also by philosophers. . . . [I]t conflicts with nature for a man who acts against another to be sated with the other's pain, merely as pain. And so the less each man employs his reason, the more apt he is to seek vengeance. . . . From this, it is clear that man cannot rightly be punished by man merely for the sake of punishing. Let us, therefore, try to see what useful ends render punishment just.

6. The threefold advantage of punishment

We must . . . examine this question [of the purpose served by punishment] in . . . detail. We shall say then that, in the case of punishment, we must consider the advantage either of the person who does wrong, or of the person against whose interest the wrong was committed, or of other persons in general.

To the first of these three ends belongs the punishment which by the philosophers is called now 'admonition', now 'correction', and now 'exhortation'. . . . Since every action, especially one that is deliberate and repeated, produces a certain inclination towards itself, which, when developed, is called habit, for this reason the enticement must be removed as soon as possible from vices. This cannot be accomplished more successfully than by causing them to lose the flavour of sweetness by some subsequent pain.[10]

7. Who may exact punishment for the good of the wrong-doer

The punishment which serves this end is by nature permitted to any one of sound judgement who is not subject to vices of the same kind or of equal seriousness, as is apparent from reproof that is administered verbally.

However, in the case of corporal chastisement and other punishments that contain an element of compulsion, the distinction between those who may or

[10] The basic idea is that the wrong-doer must be prevented from gaining any benefit from his wrong. It is debatable whether this really falls into the category of punishment, since it is simply an application of the general principle of unjust enrichment, which (as Grotius has already explained) has a far wider application than the criminal law. See p. 178 above.

who may not apply them is not made by nature (for this could not be the case, except in so far as reason entrusts to parents in a special sense the exercise of this right over their children on account of the tie of relationship), but by the laws which have limited that common connexion of the human race to the nearest relationships for the sake of obviating quarrels. This one may see from the section of Justinian's *Code* on the right of correction of relatives, and elsewhere.[11]

This form of punishment, nevertheless, cannot be made to include the death penalty.

[Infliction of the death penalty on the ground that a criminal is beyond all possibility of redemption is highly dubious.] . . . [B]ecause the proofs of this are deceptive, charity bids us hold no man for lost without clear proof. Punishment for this purpose may in consequence only be applied upon rare occasions.

8. Who may exact punishment for the good of the victim

The advantage of him to whose disadvantage the wrong was committed consists in this, that subsequently he may not suffer any such thing from the same man or from others.[12] To secure a man who has been wronged from suffering harm at the hands of the same person is possible in three ways: first, by the removal of the wrong-doer; second, by depriving him of the power to do harm; finally, by teaching him to cease from his evil ways, which is closely allied with the reformation that we have already discussed. He who has been wronged may be secured from harm by others, not by an ordinary punishment, but by one that is public and conspicuous in the nature of an example.

Accordingly, vengeance, even if it is exacted by private individuals, is not unlawful according to the bare law of nature, that is, apart from divine and human laws and from chance circumstances, provided that it is employed for these objects and within the bounds of right. It is all the same whether vengeance is exacted by one who was injured himself or by another, since it is in harmony with nature that man should be helped by man.

But since, in our private affairs and those of our kinsmen, we are liable to partiality, as soon as numerous families were united at a common point, judges were appointed, and to them alone was given the power to avenge the injured,

---

[11] In speaking of punishment involving corporal chastisement or compulsion, reference is made to punishments which have the well-being of the criminal as their purpose ('tough love', in the modern vernacular). Punishments that have this purpose in view (whatever form they may take) may be inflicted by anyone, according to the law of nature. Human law, however, has modified this and has restricted the right of infliction of corporal punishment or compulsion to parents and certain other relatives.

[12] Notice that, in speaking of 'the good of him who has been wronged', Grotius has primarily the future in mind, i.e., safeguarding the victim from possible further wrongs at a later date.

while others are deprived of the freedom of action wherewith nature endowed them.

Nevertheless, the old natural liberty remains, especially in places where there are no courts, as, for example, on the sea. An example of this is perhaps the conduct of Julius Caesar. He, while yet a private citizen, with a hastily levied fleet pursued the pirates by whom he had been captured, sank some of their ships, and put the rest to flight. When the proconsul failed to punish the pirates who had been taken, he himself set out to sea and crucified them. The same right will exist in desert places, or where men lead a nomadic life.... Herein is the origin of the duels which the Germanic tribes employed before the Christian era and which they have not yet entirely given up.

9. Who may exact punishment for the good of society as a whole

The good of mankind in general, which was the third object of punishment, involves the same problems as those presented by the good of one who has been wronged. For in this case, the punishment may be inflicted to prevent the man who has injured one person from injuring others, which is accomplished by removing him or weakening him or restraining him, so that he cannot do harm, or by reforming him. Or the punishment may be inflicted to prevent others from being induced by a feeling of security to annoy any persons whatsoever. This is attained by the infliction of outstanding penalties, which . . . the Romans [call] *exempla*, 'examples'. These exemplary punishments are employed so that the punishment of one may cause many to fear, and that others may be frightened by the nature of the punishment.... And the possession of the right to punish for this purpose also, according to nature, may rest with any person whatever.

Nevertheless, within the state these things must be interpreted with reference to its laws.[13]

But since both the inquiry into the fact often demands great care, and the evaluation of the punishment requires much prudence and fairness, to prevent strife arising from each man claiming too much for himself, while others refuse to yield, in communities animated by a sense of right, men have agreed to select as arbiters those who they think are the best and wisest, or hope will prove to be such.

But as we just now remarked in the case of vengeance, so too in the matter of this punishment, . . . traces and survivals of primitive right persist in those places and among those persons who are subject to no fixed tribunals, and in some other exceptional cases.... Furthermore, among many peoples, the full right of punishment, even unto death, continued to be exercised by masters over their slaves and parents over their children.

From this discussion, one may understand the character of the law of nature in regard to punishments and the extent to which it still persists.

---

[13] I.e., it must be remembered that things which are permitted (but not commanded) by natural law are subject to being overridden by human laws.

12. On capital punishment and the possibility of repentance

[Some persons] attack [capital] punishment on this ground, that with the taking away of life, the opportunity for repentance is likewise removed. But they know that upright magistrates take serious account of this matter, and that no one is hurried to execution without having time to acknowledge his sins and seriously abhor them. . . . But if it should be said that a longer life would have been advantageous to a more serious reformation, one may reply that sometimes there are found those to whom may be applied fittingly the saying of Seneca: 'We shall bestow on you death, the only good thing that still awaits you',[14] as also this other remark of his, 'that they may cease to be bad men, in the only way in which this is possible for them'.[15] . . . Therefore let these things, in addition to what we have said at the opening of our work, be an answer to those who claim that punishments, whether of all kinds or merely capital punishments, are without exception prohibited for Christians.

14. On exacting of punishment by Christians

From what we have said up to this point, one may gather how unsafe it is for a Christian in a private capacity to exact punishment, especially capital punishment, from any wicked person whatsoever, either for his own or for the public good, although we have said that this is sometimes allowed by universal common law. It is, therefore, a praiseworthy custom on the part of [some] peoples [that persons] who are about to set sail [are granted] warrants, by the public authority, to destroy whatever pirates they discover on the sea; so that if the occasion offers they may be able to act as public servants and not upon their own initiative.

15. The bringing of accusation by Christians

In harmony with the foregoing is the widely current opinion, that not any and every person should be allowed to bring accusations for crimes, but that there should be certain persons upon whom this task is laid by the public authorities. The purpose is that no one may do anything toward shedding another's blood except by the necessity of his office.

16. On the seeking of the office of criminal judge by Christians

Likewise, it may be perceived from the preceding that it is by no means advisable, and not even becoming, for a man who is truly a Christian to enter of his own accord upon a public office which may have to decide upon the shedding of blood, and to think and profess that it is right that the power of life and death

---

[14] Younger Seneca, *On Anger*, I.16.   [15] *Ibid.*, I.15.

over his fellow citizens be conferred upon himself, as if he were the most exalted of them all and a sort of god among men.

17. The true legal character of the right to kill as a punishment

It is no unimportant question whether the laws of men which permit the execution of certain persons confer upon the executioners a true right even in the eyes of God, or merely freedom from retribution among men. . . . There is no doubt . . . that in certain cases the law can confer either power. And which one it does confer must be gathered partly from the substance. For if the law gives play to resentment, it gives immunity [only] from human punishment, but not from sin, as in the case of a husband who kills an adulterous wife or an adulterer. But if the law regards the danger of subsequent harm arising from deferring the punishment, it must be considered as conferring upon a private individual both right and public authority, so that he is no longer in a mere private capacity.[16]

18. Whether internal acts are punishable by men

Now let us consider this, whether all vicious actions are such as to be punishable by men. We must consider it as definitely established that they are not all of such a kind. For, in the first place, purely internal acts, even if they should come to the attention of others by some chance, as by subsequent confession, cannot be punished by men, because . . . it is not in accord with human nature that a right or an obligation should arise among men from purely internal acts. . . . However, this does not prevent internal acts, in so far as they influence external ones, from being taken into consideration, not on their own account, but in the light of the external actions which receive from them the quality of their desert.

19. Punishment of extrinsic acts which human frailty cannot avoid

In the second place, actions inevitable to human nature cannot be punished by men. For although one cannot sin except one does so of one's own will,

---

[16] The question is whether a person who kills a criminal under permission granted by a man-made law does so as a matter of true right from the standpoint of natural law, or whether natural law merely exempts the executioner from being punished himself. Grotius concludes that human laws which give 'play to resentment' have only the lesser effect of barring punishment (e.g., a law which allows the killing of an adulterous spouse or an adulterer). If, however, the human law is directed toward the worthy public policy of reducing the danger of subsequent harm that would arise if the criminal were *not* killed, then the killing can be said to have been done as a matter of true right under natural law.

nevertheless the total and perpetual abstinence from all sin is a condition that is more than human.

There are also certain actions which are not inevitable to human nature itself, but to a particular person at a particular time, because of a bodily condition which influences his mind, or because of a mature habit. Such actions are wont to be punished not so much for their own sake as on account of the guilt that precedes them, because either the remedies therefor have been neglected, or corrupt thoughts have willingly been received into the mind.[17]

20. Punishment for acts by which human society is not injured

In the third place, we are not to punish sins which neither directly nor indirectly affect human society or a fellow man. The reason is that there is no cause for not leaving such sins to be punished by God, who is most wise in perceiving them, most just in judging them, and most able to requite them. For men, therefore, to institute punishment for such acts would be clearly futile, and consequently inadequate. From this broad statement, we must except corrective punishments, the purpose of which is to improve the sinner, even although perhaps this does not concern others. And further, we are not to punish actions which are contrary to the virtues in regard to which nature rejects all compulsion, such as mercy, liberality, and gratitude.[18]

21. Whether pardon is permissible

We must next consider whether it is permissible at times to forgive or to excuse.... [I]f you understand that he who has sinned deserves punishment, that is, can be punished without injustice, it will not thereby follow that one who fails to punish him does what he ought not to do. However, if you take the view that the punishment is deserved at the hands of the wise man, that is, ought by all means to be exacted, we shall say [by way of refutation] that this does not always happen, and therefore from this point of view punishment cannot be deserved but merely permitted.[19] This, furthermore, may be true both prior to the laying down of penal law and subsequent to it.

---

[17] The reference is to wrongs that arise from bodily or mental infirmities. These are not punished 'for their own sake' (i.e., on the basis of the particular wrongful acts themselves), but only if some form of 'guilt' gave rise to the infirmity, such as 'corrupt thoughts ... willingly received into the mind', or a culpable neglect on the person's part to undergo a cure or treatment that was available to him. See also Section 31 below.

[18] These virtues, in other words, are matters of morality rather than law, so that a breach of them cannot be treated as criminal.

[19] I.e., it is not, in general, mandatory to punish crimes, but merely permissible.

22. Whether pardon is permissible prior to the establishment of penal law

Even before the establishment of the penal law, beyond doubt there may be room for punishment, because the wrong-doer is naturally in the state where punishment may be permitted. But it does not follow from this that the punishment ought to be exacted, for this depends upon the connexion between the purposes for which the punishment is instituted and the punishment itself. Consequently, if these purposes of themselves are not necessary on moral grounds, or if they are opposed by other purposes not less useful or necessary, or if the purposes set for punishment can be attained in another way, it is clear that there is nothing which strictly compels the exaction of the punishment.

Take as an example of the first case, a crime known to very few persons, the bringing of which to public notice is therefore unnecessary, or even harmful.... An example of the second case is one who pleads either his own deserts or those of his parents, which are worthy of record, to counterbalance his guilt.... An example of the third case is one who is corrected by reproof, or who has made verbal satisfaction to the injured person, so that there is now no need of punishment to attain the desired ends.

23. That pardon is not permissible in all cases

There are these three possibilities. Either the penalty is to be exacted absolutely, as in crimes of the worst type; or it is not to be exacted at all, as when the public good requires its omission; or either alternative may be possible, in which case ... clemency has freedom of judgement.

24. Whether pardon is permissible after the establishment of the penal law

There seems to be a greater difficulty with regard to pardon after the establishment of the penal law, because the lawmaker is in some way bound by his own laws. But this we have said is true in so far as the lawmaker is regarded as a member of the state,[20] not in so far as he sustains the person and authority of the state itself. For in so far as he does this, he can even suspend the whole law because it is the nature of a human law to depend upon a human will, not merely in its origin but also in its duration. However, the lawmaker should not suspend the law except for a worthy reason, otherwise he will sin against the principles of governmental justice. But just as the lawmaker can suspend the whole law, so he can suspend its obligation in respect to a particular person or fact, while in other respects the law remains in force.

---

[20] That is to say, citizens of a state are bound by the laws of the state; but the sovereign, by definition, is free to suspend the laws in appropriate cases.

But this step also is not to be taken except for a worthy reason. Although we cannot define with exactness what are worthy reasons, nevertheless we must hold that they ought to be more cogent after the institution of the law than those which were accepted before the law, because to the reasons for punishing there is added the authority of the law, which it is expedient to preserve.

25. What intrinsic causes are sufficient to cause the suspension of the law

Now the causes for freeing anyone from the punishment of the law are internal or external. An intrinsic cause occurs when the punishment, although not unlawful, is severe in comparison with the act.

26. What extrinsic causes are sufficient

An extrinsic cause for freeing anyone from the punishment of the law arises from some merit, or from some other commendatory thing, or even from a strong hope entertained for the future. This type of cause is especially effective if the reason for the law, at least in the particular instance, should cease with respect to the act in question. For although the general reason . . . is sufficient ground for maintaining the efficacy of the law, nevertheless an absence of the reason . . . in a particular instance renders it possible to suspend the law more easily and with less loss of authority. This occurs especially in the case of crimes which are committed through ignorance, even if it is not altogether excusable, or through some mental infirmity that is conquerable indeed, but only with difficulty. These things ought to be taken into especial consideration by a Christian ruler, that he may imitate God.

27. Whether the right of suspension of the law must be contained in the law as an implied exception

Now from this it is clear how far wrong [the opinion is], that the only just cause of suspending the law . . . is that with regard to which the lawmaker, if consulted, would say that it was not his intention that the law should be observed. For [this opinion fails to distinguish] between 'equity', which serves to interpret the law, and relaxation.[21] . . . However, we are so far from having to attribute every relaxation of the law, which may often be given freely or omitted, to what is properly called equity, that not even the relaxation due either to regard for others or to ruling justice can be referred thereto. For it is one thing to annul

---

[21] The assertion is that pardoning is a matter of relaxing the law (i.e., of deciding not to apply it in certain cases), not of interpreting the law. Consequently, the original intention of the legislator plays no role in decisions about pardons, as it would in questions of interpretation.

the law for a worthy or even a pressing cause, and another to declare that an act from the beginning was not embraced in the intent of the law.

Now that we have discussed exemptions from punishments, let us consider their measure.

28. The measure of punishment according to what is deserved

From what has been previously said, it appears that, in applying punishments, we must have regard to two things: that for which, and that for the sake of which. That for which is what is deserved; that for the sake of which is the advantage to come from the punishment. No one is to be punished beyond what he has deserved.

29. A consideration of the causes which lead to crime

In estimating what is deserved, we must take into consideration the compelling cause, the cause which ought to have restrained and the disposition of the person toward each. Scarcely anyone is bad for no purpose; while if anyone delights in wickedness for its own sake, he is beyond the pale of humanity. Most people are led to sin by their desires.... Now under the name of desire, I include also the impulse to avoid evil, which is very natural and consequently the most honourable of desires. Hence, unjust actions committed for the sake of avoiding death, imprisonment, pain, or extreme poverty, usually seem in great measure excusable.

But the other desires aim at some good, whether true or imaginary. True goods, apart from virtues and their actions, which do not lead to sin (for virtues harmonise with one another) are either pleasing things or the cause of pleasant things, which are called advantageous, as abundance of possessions. Imaginary but not true goods are superiority over others, apart from virtue and advantage, and revenge. And the further these depart from nature, the more shameful they become.

30. Consideration of the causes that should have restrained from sin

The general cause [of wrongdoing] is injustice. For here we are not dealing with sins of all kinds, but only with such as carry their effect beyond the criminal himself. The injustice is the greater, the heavier the loss that is brought upon another. Therefore, in order of seriousness, the first place is assigned to crimes actually carried out, and the next place to those which have proceeded to certain actions but not to the final act. Among the latter, each is more serious the farther it has proceeded. In either sort of crime, that form of injustice is prominent which disturbs the public order and therefore harms the greatest number.

Next in importance comes the injustice which affects individuals. Here, the greatest injustice is that which affects human life; the next, that affecting the family, the basis of which is marriage; and the last, that affecting desirable things severally, either by directly taking them away or through evil intent giving rise to loss.

These things may be analysed with greater precision, but we have indicated the order that God has followed in the Decalogue. For under the name of parents, who are magistrates by nature, it is right for us to understand other rulers whose authority extends over human society. There follows the forbidding of homicide; then the sanction of matrimony by the prohibition of adultery; then thefts and the bearing of false witness; and, finally, unconsummated crime.

However, ... we ought to [consider] not only the character of the crime that is actually committed, but also the character of what is likely to follow, for in the case of arson and the destruction of a dike, most serious injuries and even death in the case of many persons are to be looked for.

In addition to injustice, which we have stated as the general [source of] wrong, there is sometimes added another vice, as impiety toward one's parents, cruelty toward neighbours, and ingratitude toward benefactors, which add to the seriousness of the offence. Also the depravity appears to be greater if one sins frequently, because evil habits are worse than evil acts. From this, we may see how far the Persian custom is by nature right, which takes into consideration a man's former life along with his crime. This ought, to be sure, to have a place in the case of those who, while not otherwise prone to evil, have suddenly been carried away by some charm felt in sinning; but not in the case of those who have changed the whole character of their life. . . . Consequently, the early Christian writers, in adjusting punishments according to the Canons, very rightly desired that the crime should not be considered by itself alone, but with it the preceding and subsequent life.

But the enactment of a law against a particular crime also adds a sort of special wickedness thereto. So Augustine teaches: 'The law by its prohibition renders all crimes doubly guilty; for it is not a simple crime to do what is not only wrong but is also forbidden.'[22]

31. On the response of the sinner to incentives and deterrents

The fitness of the person, either to take into consideration deterrent causes, or to receive incentive desires, is usually considered to be the result of his bodily constitution, age, sex, education, and the immediate circumstances of the act.

---

[22] Augustine, 'On Various Questions', in *Augustine: Earlier Writings*, edited and translated by John H. S. Burleigh (London: SCM Press, 1953), at p. 377. This refers to the distinction between acts which are *mala in se* (i.e., evil in themselves, by their nature), as contrasted to acts which are *mala prohibita* (i.e., wrongful only because they are contrary to some binding command which has been issued). Augustine recognised this distinction – and went on to posit that an act may be regarded as doubly wrong if it is *mala in se* and is also prohibited by human law.

For alike children, women, and men of dull intellect and bad education, are not well able to appreciate the distinction between just and unjust, lawful and unlawful. Those too who suffer from an excess of bile are prone to anger, and those who have an excess of blood are prone to lust;[23] moreover, youth leads to the latter, while old age tends to the former.

Reflection upon a threatening evil increases fear, and pain that is fresh and not yet assuaged fires one's anger, so that they scarcely permit reason to be heard. And the crimes that arise from such impulses are deservedly less hateful than those which spring from a desire for pleasure, both because this affects one less powerfully and because it can be more easily deferred and can find for itself another object without suffering harm. . . . We must in fact absolutely adopt this point of view, that the more the judgement of a mind that can choose is restricted, and the more this restriction is due to natural causes, the less the offence that is committed. . . . Accordingly, for these reasons we must estimate the desert which punishment ought not to exceed.

32. Whether punishment may inflict a greater harm than the sinner inflicted

Further, we must hold that the teaching of the Pythagoreans that justice is 'suffering in return for suffering' – that is, the suffering of the punishment equalling the suffering of the wrongs – ought not to be taken in the sense that he who has injured another with intent and without reasons that sensibly diminish his guilt ought only to suffer the equivalent of the harm he has wrought and nothing more.

33. On proportionality in punishments

However, we must take into consideration the extent of the punishment, not only by itself but [also] in relation to the one who suffers it.[24] For the fine that will burden a poor man will not burden one who is rich; and to a man of no repute, ignominy will be a trifling harm, while for a man of consequence it will be serious. The Roman law often makes use of this kind of difference. . . . [W]e have here a simple proportion like a numerical equation, between the desert and the punishment, just as in contracts which set goods over against money,

[23] References to the theory of the four humours of the body, inherited from ancient Greek medicine and still widely held in Grotius's time. By bile is meant yellow bile or choler. The other two humours are black bile (associated with melancholy or depression) and phlegm (associated with lassitude).

[24] That is, we must consider not merely the objective severity of a punishment, but also the degree of hardship that the punishment will actually cause, for a given wrong-doer in given circumstances.

although the same goods have now more value, now less, in the same way as money.[25] . . . Such, as we have said, is the intrinsic measure of punishment.

34. Whether punishment may be mitigated on the ground of regard for others

But within the conceded limits, regard for him who is punished tends to exact the minimum penalty,[26] unless a more just regard for the greater number urges a contrary course for an extrinsic reason. This reason is sometimes the great danger from him who has sinned, but more often the need of an example. This need, moreover, usually has its origin in the general inducements to sin, which cannot be checked without sharp remedies. Of these inducements, the strongest are habit and opportunity.

35. On severity in laws and leniency in judgements

Now in passing judgements, we must aim at leniency; but in framing laws, at severity, taking due account of the time when the statutes or the judgements are made known; because the advantage derived from punishment is considered more in the generality, with which the statutes deal, while the guilt varies in individual cases.

36. The use of clemency in mitigating punishments

[W]here great and pressing grounds for punishment are lacking, we should be the more ready to mitigate the punishment.

37. What should be taken into consideration in punishments

[T]he person of him who has done the wrong is of the greatest importance in fitly judging the penalty, and the person of him who suffers the wrong sometimes is of weight in estimating the greatness of the guilt. The place of the wrongdoing usually contributes a particular degree of guilt to the injustice[27] or

---

[25] A given item will vary in the price that it will fetch, depending on the wealth of the person buying it. A wealthy person is better able than a poor one to pay a higher price. By the same token, a given wrong will correspond to varying levels of punishment, depending on the particular circumstances of the wrong-doer. Notwithstanding this variation, the underlying principle remains: that there be some kind of equivalence, or rational relation, between the wrong and the punishment.

[26] I.e., if consideration was given exclusively to the criminal himself, then the general tendency would be to impose the minimum available punishment.

[27] Presumably what is meant is that crimes are to be regarded as more wicked than usual if they are perpetrated in, say, a church or a government council chamber rather than in a tavern or on the street.

has a bearing also upon the opportunity for the deed. According as the time was long or short, it increases or restricts freedom of judgement, at times also reveals the depravity of the mind.[28] The quality of the crime has to do partly with the kinds of desires, and partly with the reasons which should have deterred from sinning. . . . The outcome must be viewed in relation to the deterrent reasons.

38. On war waged to inflict punishment

We have previously shown, and histories everywhere teach, that wars are usually begun for the purpose of exacting punishment. But very often this cause is joined with a second, the desire to make good a loss, when the same act was both wicked and involved loss;[29] and from these two characteristics two separate obligations arise.[30] However, it is quite clear that war should not be undertaken for every sort of crime. For even the vengeance of the laws, which is exercised in safety and only harms the guilty, does not follow upon every wrong.

39. Whether war may be waged to punish attempted wrongs

[It has been contended] that it is not just that anyone should be punished for a thing which he is accused merely of having wrongly desired to do. . . . [This contention], however, cannot be accepted as a universal proposition. For the will which proceeds to external acts (we have said above that internal acts are not punished by men) is usually liable to punishment. . . . On these grounds, the Romans thought that they ought to wage war with King Perseus, unless he should make amends in respect to the plans which he had formed for waging war against the Roman people, seeing that he had already gathered arms, troops, and a fleet.[31] [But the proposition may be conceded] that neither in the customs nor in the laws of any state is it provided that he who wishes his enemy to perish, assuming that he has done nothing to bring this about, is condemned to capital punishment.

But, on the other hand, not every wicked intention which has been [accompanied by some external act] gives an occasion for punishment. For if all crimes

---

[28] The reference is to the degree of planning for a crime. Crimes that are committed spontaneously, in the heat of the moment – i.e., in a short time – are regarded, in general, as less wicked than crimes which were carefully planned in advance.

[29] Again, the third type of just war, defensive, is not mentioned (but perhaps is regarded as a type of punishment).

[30] I.e., an obligation to pay compensation, and an obligation to submit to appropriate punishment.

[31] The reference is to the third Macedonian War (172–167 BC). The conflict was initiated by Rome, but allegations were put forward that King Perseus of Macedon was planning on attacking Rome. To what extent Rome actually feared an attack by Perseus is very difficult to say. In all events, Perseus was decisively defeated and brought to Rome in chains. Macedon was then divided into four republics.

that have [actually] been committed are not punished, much less are all those which have [merely] been planned and initiated.

Crimes that have only been begun are therefore not to be punished by armed force, unless the matter is serious, and has reached a point where a certain damage has already followed from such action, even if it is not yet that which was aimed at; or at least great danger has ensued, so that the punishment is joined either with a precaution against future harm, . . . or protects injured dignity, or checks a dangerous example.

40. Whether war may be waged because of violations of the law of nature

The fact must also be recognised that kings, and those who possess rights equal to those kings, have the right of demanding punishments not only on account of injuries committed against themselves or their subjects, but also on account of injuries which do not directly affect them but excessively violate the law of nature or of nations in regard to any persons whatsoever.[32] For liberty to serve the interests of human society through punishments, which originally, as we have said, rested with individuals, now after the organisation of states and courts of law is in the hands of the highest authorities, not, properly speaking, in so far as they rule over others but in so far as they are themselves subject to no one. For subjection has taken this right away from others.[33]

Truly, it is more honourable to avenge the wrongs of others rather than one's own, in the degree that, in the case of one's own wrongs, it is more to be feared that through a sense of personal suffering one may exceed the proper limit or at least prejudice his mind.[34] . . . So we do not doubt that wars are justly waged against those who act with impiety towards their parents; . . . against those who feed on human flesh . . . and against those who practise piracy. . . . Regarding such barbarians, wild beasts rather than men, one may rightly say . . . that war against them was sanctioned by nature.

---

[32] It might be supposed that this passage supports what is now called humanitarian intervention. That is not really so, however, since the primary concern here is with the punishment of the wrong-doer, rather than with the rescue of the victims, which is the chief focus of humanitarian intervention in the modern sense. For Grotius's support of humanitarian intervention in the proper sense, see p. 317 below.

[33] It is pointed out that sovereigns, unlike private citizens, have a right to inflict punishment – not, strictly speaking, because they possess any special privilege that is not available to all persons in the state of nature, but rather because sovereigns have simply retained the general, universal right to punish which was formerly held by everyone in the state of nature. Private parties, in contrast, relinquished this right when they entered into civil society. A direct implication is that sovereigns remain, in important respects, in the state of nature, whereas private citizens do not.

[34] This idea was at the heart of Augustine's original theory of just war in the fourth and fifth centuries.

Thus far we follow the opinion of Innocent,[35] and others who say that war may be waged upon those who sin against nature. The contrary view is held by ... others, who in justification of war seem to demand that he who undertakes it should have suffered injury either in his person or his state, or that he should have jurisdiction over him who is attacked. For they claim that the power of punishing is the proper effect of civil jurisdiction, while we hold that it also is derived from the law of nature; this point we discussed at the beginning of the first book.

[I]f we accept [this view], no enemy will have the right to punish another.... Nevertheless, many persons admit this right, which is confirmed also by the usage of all nations, not only after the conclusion of a war but also while the war is still going on; and not on the basis of any civil jurisdiction, but of that law of nature which existed before states were organised, and is even now enforced, in places, where men live in family groups and not in states.[36]

41. The need to distinguish the law of nature from widely current national customs

But at this point certain precautions need to be stated. First, national customs are not to be taken for the law of nature, although they have been received on reasonable grounds among many peoples.[37]

42. The need to distinguish the law of nature from the Divine law

Second, we should not hastily class with the things forbidden by nature those with regard to which this point is not sufficiently clear, and which are rather prohibited by the law of the Divine Will. In this class, we may perhaps place unions not classed as marriages and those which are called incestuous, as well as usury.

---

[35] I.e., Pope Innocent IV (Sinibaldo Fieschi), a renowned canon-law scholar of the thirteenth century, who insisted on the right of popes to punish violations of natural law wherever they might occur and whoever might commit them.

[36] An example of this in modern international law is a soldier who commits war crimes and who then is taken prisoner by the opposing side. The captors are recognised to have the right to place the offender on trial for his misdeeds, even though he is a foreigner (i.e., even though, in Grotius's terminology, there is no jurisdiction). The law which the soldier will be accused of violating is the international law of war, not the civil law of the state into whose hands he fell.

[37] Basically, those who seek to wage war for the punishment of violations of natural law must be very careful to ensure that they are not, in fact, punishing persons merely for living a different style of life (i.e., whose 'national customs' happen simply to differ from those of the war-waging state).

43. The need to distinguish between what is evident and what is not evident

Third, we should carefully distinguish between general principles, as, for example, that one must live honourably, that is according to reason, and certain principles akin to these, but so evident that they do not admit of doubt, as that one must not seize what belongs to another, and inferences. [S]uch inferences in some cases easily gain recognition, as that, for example, accepting marriage we cannot admit adultery; but in other cases are not so easily accepted, as the inference that vengeance which is satisfied with the pain of another is wicked. Here, we have almost the same thing as in mathematics, where there are certain primary notions, or notions akin to those that are primary, certain proofs which are at once recognised and admitted, and certain others which are true indeed but not evident to all.

Therefore, just as in the case of municipal laws, we excuse those who lack knowledge or understanding of the laws, so also with regard to the laws of nature, it is right to pardon those who are hampered by weakness of their powers of reasoning or deficient education. For as ignorance of the law, if it is unavoidable, cancels the sin, so also, when it is combined with a certain degree of negligence, it lessens the offence.[38]

Finally, to avoid repeating often what I have said, we must add this word of warning, that wars which are undertaken to inflict punishment are under suspicion of being unjust, unless the crimes are very atrocious and very evident, or there is some other coincident reason.

44. Whether war may be waged on account of crimes against God

Our order of treatment has brought us to the discussion of crimes which are committed against God; for there is a dispute whether war may be undertaken to avenge these.... A [strong] argument for the view which denies that such wars are just is this, that God is able to punish offences committed against Himself.

We must, however, recognise the fact that this same thing may be said about other crimes as well. For without doubt, God is able to punish these also; and yet no one disputes that they are rightly punished by men. But some will insist and say that other crimes are punished by men in so far as other men are injured or endangered thereby. But it must be noted, on the other hand, that men do not only punish the sins which directly harm others but also those which harm by

---

[38] I.e., violations of the law that occur through unavoidable ignorance of the law are to be excused. Cases in which ignorance of the law is the fruit of negligence rather than of, say, infirmity of mind are not wholly excused; but they are less wicked than violations committed deliberately.

their consequences, such as suicide, intercourse with animals, and some other things.

Moreover religion, although it is in itself [directed towards] winning the favour of God, nevertheless has also in addition important effects on human society. . . . Aristotle . . . perceived this relation, and in his *Politics*, . . . speaks thus of the king: 'For the people will be less afraid of suffering anything unlawful from their prince if they believe that he fears the gods.'[39]

Religion is of [greater use in the society of states] than in that of a single state. For in the latter, the place of religion is taken by the laws and the easy execution of the laws; while on the contrary in that larger community, the enforcement of law is very difficult, seeing that it can only be carried out by armed force, and the laws are very few. Besides, these laws themselves receive their validity chiefly from fear of the divine power; and for this reason those who sin against the law of nations are everywhere said to transgress divine law.

45. What ideas of God are most generally accepted

[There is very general agreement in human society] that God is to be honoured, to be loved, to be worshipped, and also to be obeyed. Thus Aristotle has said that he who denies that we must honour the deity or love our parents must be subdued not by arguments but by punishment;[40] in another passage, that some things are considered honourable in one place, others in another, but that everywhere it is held honourable to worship the deity.[41] Moreover, the truth of the ideas [about religion] which we have called speculative can doubtless be shown also by arguments drawn from the nature of things.

Among such arguments this is the strongest, that our senses show that some things are made, but the things which are made lead us absolutely to something that is not made. . . . [I]n every age throughout all lands, with very few exceptions, men have accepted these ideas; both those men who were too dull to wish to deceive, and others who were too wise to be deceived. This agreement in so great a variety of laws and diversity in expressions of opinions regarding other matters sufficiently reveals the tradition that has been handed down to us from the beginning of the human race and has never been conclusively refuted; and that fact of itself is sufficient to cause belief.

46. On those who do violence to these common ideas

[Therefore] those are not free from blame who repudiate these ideas, even if they are too dull-witted to be able to discover or understand positive proofs thereof, since they have guides to the right path, and the contrary view rests upon no good reasons. Since, however, we are dealing with punishments, and

---

[39] Aristotle, *Politics*, V.11.   [40] Aristotle, *Topics*, I.11.   [41] *Ibid.*, II.11.

indeed punishments inflicted by men, we must introduce distinctions among the ideas themselves and in the manner of departing from them. These ideas, that there is a divinity (I exclude the question of there being more than one), and that he has a care for the affairs of men, are in the highest degree universal, and are absolutely necessary to the establishment of religion, whether it be true or false.... [A]s though under the influence of necessity itself, these two ideas have been preserved through so many ages, among almost all the peoples of whom we have knowledge.

I think, therefore, that those who first begin to abolish these ideas may be restrained in the name of human society, to which they do violence without a defensible reason; just as they are regularly restrained in well-organised states.[42]

47. Whether other errors of religion may be punished

Other ideas [about God and religion] are not equally evident,[43] as, for example, that there are not more gods than one; that none of the things which we see is God, neither the earth, nor the sky, nor the sun, nor the air; that the earth is not from all eternity nor even its matter, but that they were made by God. Consequently, we see that the knowledge of these things has disappeared among many peoples through lapse of time, and is as it were extinct; and the more easily so because the laws gave less attention to these ideas, seeing that some religion at any rate could exist without them.

Just as those [persons] are worthy to be excused, and certainly not to be punished by men, who, not having received any law revealed by God, worship the powers of the stars or of other natural objects, or spirits, either in images or in animals or in other things, or even worship the souls of those who have been pre-eminent for their virtue and their benefactions to the human race, or certain intelligences without bodily form – especially if they themselves have not invented such cults, nor deserted for them the worship of the supreme God.... [In contrast to these] we must class with the impious rather than with the erring, those who establish with divine honours the worship of evil spirits, whom they know to be such, or of personified vices or of men whose lives were filled with crimes.[44]

---

[42] I.e., as a matter of general natural law – with the result that, even if the persons in question are not under the jurisdiction of the person who does the punishing, punishment is justifiable, just as it would be in the case of a sovereign punishing a subject for the same misdeed.

[43] I.e., ideas other than the two fundamental ones identified in the previous section: that a divinity exists, and that that divinity is concerned about the affairs of humans.

[44] These latter types are to be regarded as positively wicked – and consequently deserving of punishment – rather than as merely mistaken.

48. Wars against those who are unwilling to accept the Christian religion

What shall we say of those wars that are waged against certain peoples for the reason that they have refused to embrace the Christian religion when proffered to them? I shall not discuss here whether the religion proffered was such as it ought to be, or whether it was proffered in the manner in which it ought.[45] Let us grant that it was; then we say that two things must be taken into account.

The first is that the truth of the Christian religion, in so far as it makes a considerable addition to natural and primitive religion, cannot be proven by purely natural arguments, but rests upon the history both of the resurrection of Christ and of the miracles performed by Him and by His Apostles. This is a question of fact, proven long ago by irrefutable testimonies, and of fact already very ancient: whence it results that this doctrine cannot be deeply received in the mind of those who hear it now for the first time, unless God secretly lends His aid. This aid, when given to any persons, is not given as a reward of any work; so that, if it is denied or granted less generously to any, this occurs for reasons that are not unjust indeed but are frequently unknown to us, and hence not punishable by the judgement of man.

The second point to be considered is this, that Christ as the author of the new law desired that absolutely no one should be induced to receive His law by punishments in this life, or by fear thereof.

49. Wars against those who mistreat Christians because of their religion

Those who subject them that teach or profess Christianity to punishment for this cause certainly act against the dictates of reason itself. For there is nothing in the Christian teaching (here I am dealing with this by itself, and not with any impurities mingled therewith) which is injurious to human society; or rather, nothing which is not beneficial to it. The facts speak for themselves, and those not of the faith are obliged to recognise them. . . . Nor can we accept as an excuse for persecution that all new things are to be distrusted, especially gatherings of men. For we ought not to fear doctrines, however new, provided that they lead to all honourable things and to an exhibition of obedience to those in authority; nor should we mistrust meetings of good men, and of those who do not seek concealment unless they are forced to. . . . Those who show cruelty to such persons are themselves in the condition where they may be punished with justice.

---

[45] I.e., cases in which attempts were made to impose Christianity onto pagan peoples by harsh or oppressive means are not being considered.

50. Wars against heretics

Likewise those who oppress with punishment persons that accept the law of Christ as true, but who are in doubt or error on some points which are either outside the law or appear to have an ambiguous statement in the law and are variously explained by the early Christians, act most wickedly.

What now shall we say if the error be more serious, and one which may be easily refuted before impartial judges by sacred authority, or by the agreement of ancient writers? Here, we must take into account also the great power of habitual opinion, and the degree to which freedom of judgement is hampered by zeal for one's own sect; an evil, as Galen says, more incurable than any leprosy . . . . Remember also that the degree of guilt in this matter depends upon the method of enlightenment and other mental conditions, which it is not given to men fully to know.

51. War against those who show impiety toward the gods they believe in

More justly are those punished who are irreverent and irreligious toward the gods in whom they believe. . . . We have said also above that, whatever the divinities which are so considered may be, perjury against them is avenged by the true Divinity.

21

On the sharing of punishments

1. How punishment may pass to those who have shared in the crime

Whenever question arises in regard to the sharing of punishment, the question concerns either those who are accessories in the wrong, or other persons.

Those who are accessories in the wrong are punished not so much for another's, as for their own, misdeed. Who these are may be seen from our previous discussion of damage unjustly inflicted.[1] In fact, one comes to participation in a wrong in almost the same way as to participation in the infliction of injury.... [A]ny sort of fault may frequently be sufficient to give rise to a liability for damages inflicted.

Therefore, those who order a wicked act, or who grant to it the necessary consent, or who aid it, or who furnish asylum, or those who in any other way share in the crime itself; those who give advice, who praise, or approve; those who do not forbid such an act although bound by law properly so called to forbid it, or who do not bring aid to the injured although bound to do so by the same law; those who do not dissuade when they ought to dissuade; those who conceal the fact which they are bound by some law to make known – all these may be punished, if there is in them evil intent sufficient to deserve punishment, according to the discussion which immediately precedes.

2. Responsibility of a community or its rulers for the crime of a subject

A civil community, just as any other community, is not bound by the acts of individuals, apart from some act or neglect of its own.

Now of the ways in which those who have control over others come to participate in a crime, there are two which are especially common, and which require careful consideration: toleration and refuge. With respect to toleration, we must accept the principle that he who knows of a crime, and is able and bound to prevent it but fails to do so, himself commits a crime.

But, as we have said, to participate in a crime, a person must not only have knowledge of it but also have the opportunity to prevent it. This is what the

---

[1] See p. 254 above.

laws mean when they say that knowledge, when its punishment is ordained, is taken in the sense of toleration, so that he may be held responsible who was able to prevent a crime but did not do so; and that the knowledge to be considered here is that associated with the will, that is, knowledge is to be taken in connexion with intent. Consequently, the master is not to be held responsible in case the slave has formally claimed his freedom, or if he has treated his master with contempt;[2] for surely he is blameless who knows of an intended crime, but is unable to prevent it.[3] Thus parents are responsible for the misdeeds of their children, but only the misdeeds of those who are still under their parental authority. On the other hand, even if parents have children under their authority and otherwise could have restrained them, they will not be held responsible unless they also had knowledge. For that one person may be held responsible for the act of another, these two elements, knowledge and the failure to prevent, should be present in like degree.

3. Responsibility of a community or its rulers for refuge for wrong-doers

Let us now come to the second question, which concerns the affording a refuge against punishment. As we have said above,[4] anyone who cannot be charged with a like crime has a natural right to exact punishment. But, since the organisation of states, it is agreed that the crimes of individuals, in so far as they properly concern the community to which they belong, should be left to the states themselves and their rulers, to be punished or condoned at their discretion.

But so comprehensive a right has not been granted to states and their rulers in the case of crimes which in some way affect human society [in general], and which it is the right of other states and their rulers to follow up. . . . Much less do states and their rulers possess this full authority in the case of crimes by which another state or its ruler is in a special sense injured, and on account of which that ruler or state, for the sake of dignity or security, has the right to exact punishment, in accordance with our previous conclusions. Therefore the state in which the guilty person dwells, or its ruler, ought not to interfere with this right.[5]

---

[2] *Digest*, 9.4.4 (Paul).   [3] *Digest*, 50.17.50 (Paul); and 50.17.109 (Paul).
[4] See p. 273 above.
[5] The point is that, in the present state of the world, rulers have jurisdiction to prosecute and punish criminals only within their own territories. So if a criminal commits an injury against State A but resides in State B, then he is beyond the reach of State A's ability to inflict appropriate punishment. Moreover, State B does not possess authority to punish, since the person has committed no offence against that state. If the ruler of State B allows the miscreant to live peacefully in his territory, then he thereby interferes with the right of State A to inflict the punishment. Grotius goes on to explain how to resolve this problem.

4. Responsibility of a community or its rulers for failure to punish or surrender the guilty parties

Since as a matter of fact, states are not accustomed to permit other states to cross their borders [into other states' territories] with an armed force for the purpose of exacting punishment, and since such a course is inexpedient, it follows that the state in which he who has been found guilty dwells ought to do one of two things. When appealed to, it should either punish the guilty person as he deserves, or it should entrust him to the discretion of the party making the appeal. This latter course is surrender (*dedere*), a procedure most frequently mentioned in historical narratives.[6] But the surrendering with which we here have to do is nothing more than the entrusting of a citizen to the power of another state, for it to decide about him as it may wish. This entrusting neither confers nor takes away any right; it merely removes an impediment to the exaction of punishment.

What we have said with regard to the surrender or punishment of guilty parties applies not merely to those who have always been subjects of the state in which they are at the time found, but also to those who after having committed a crime have fled to another state for refuge.

5. On the rights of suppliants

The view just stated is not inconsistent with the much discussed rights of suppliants[7] and cases of asylum. These are in fact for the benefit of those who suffer from undeserved enmity, not those who have done something that is injurious to human society or to other men.... Accordingly, in [divine] law, places of asylum were available for those from whose hands a chance missile had slain a man,[8] and a refuge was provided also for slaves;[9] but those who had deliberately slain an innocent man, or who had disturbed the peace of the state, were not protected even by the most holy altar of God Himself.[10]

In the present and in recent generations, and in the majority of European countries, this right, which we have discussed, of demanding for punishment those who have fled beyond the frontier, has been exercised only with respect to crimes that affect the public weal or that manifest extraordinary wickedness. It has become customary mutually to ignore lesser crimes, unless some more definite agreement has been made by the terms of a treaty.

We must, however, recognise this, that robbers and pirates who have become so strong that they have made themselves formidable[11] may justly be received and [prosecuted], . . . because it is to the advantage of mankind that they should

---

[6] The modern term is extradition.

[7] By suppliants are meant approximately what are now called refugees (an expression of nineteenth-century coinage).

[8] See *Deuteronomy*, 19:1–7.   [9] See *ibid.*, 23:15.   [10] See *Exodus*, 21:14.

[11] I.e., have become so powerful that they cannot be captured or defeated by ordinary means.

be brought back from their wicked ways through confidence in their freedom from punishment, if such reform is in no other way possible; and any people or ruler may undertake to accomplish this.[12]

6. Protection of suppliants pending the hearing of their case

This, furthermore, must not be forgotten, that, during the time when the justice of their case is being investigated, suppliants are to be protected.

If the crime of which the suppliants are accused is not forbidden by the law of nature or of nations, the case must be judged according to the municipal law of their own country.[13]

7. How subjects share in the crimes of their rulers

We have seen how guilt passes to rulers from subjects, whether these are subjects of long standing, or recent.[14] Conversely, guilt will pass from the highest authority to those subject to it, if those subject to it have consented to crime [committed by that authority], or if they have done anything by order or advice of the highest authority which they could avoid doing without committing wrong. But it will be better to discuss this point later on, when we shall be investigating the duties of subjects.[15] A wrong may also be shared by both a community and individuals.

Guilt ... attaches to the individuals who have agreed to the crime, not to those who have been overmastered by the votes of others. For the punishments of individuals and of a community are different.

As a punishment [for wrongs committed by a state], individuals are reduced to slavery, ... [except for those] who had opposed the [policy of wrong-doing]. Similarly, too, a state suffers political slavery in being reduced to a province. Individuals lose their property by confiscation. In like manner, it is customary to take from a state also what belongs to it as a whole – its fortifications, naval arsenals, ships of war, arms, elephants, public treasure, and public lands.

On the other hand, it is unjust for individuals to lose their private property because of a wrong done by the community without their consent.

---

[12] This is a description of what is called, in modern terminology, universal jurisdiction, i.e., the right of any and all states to prosecute persons who are enemies of humankind in general. A difference between Grotius's concept and the modern one is that modern international law allows any state to prosecute any one guilty of piracy, while Grotius holds that the right can only be invoked against pirates 'who have become so strong that they have made themselves formidable', meaning pirates who are organised into sizeable groups in the manner of naval forces.

[13] This statement is probably made on the assumption that the act of which the suppliant is accused took place in his home country. The more general rule would be that he would be tried according to the law of wherever the alleged act took place.

[14] See Section 4 above.   [15] See p. 338 below.

8. How long the right of inflicting punishment upon a community continues

At this point, the important question arises, whether punishment may be exacted . . . for the crime of a community [at any time after the commission, however remote]. It seems that such punishment may be exacted so long as the community exists, because the same body remains, although composed of changing elements, as we have shown elsewhere. But on the contrary, it must be remembered that, in the case of a community, certain things are said to belong to it primarily and necessarily, as a public treasury, laws and the like.[16]

Into this class of things falls whatever a community deserves; for primarily this concerns individuals, as having an intelligence which the community in and of itself lacks. When, therefore, those individuals are dead through whom the community derived its desert, the desert itself lapses also; and likewise the debt of punishment which we have said cannot exist without the desert.[17]

One cannot argue that, if it is right for descendants to receive honours and rewards for the deserts of their ancestors, it is also right that they should be punished for their ancestors' sins. The character of a benefit permits its being conferred upon anyone at all without injury. [T]hat is not the case with a punishment.

9. Whether punishment may be inflicted on those not personally guilty

We have spoken of the ways in which a participation in punishment arises from a participation in guilt. It remains for us to consider whether there may still be a participation in the punishment when there is none in the guilt. To understand this matter aright, and to avoid confusing, through similarity of name, things which in reality are different, there are certain points which must be kept in mind.

10. On direct and consequential losses

In the first place, there is a difference between a loss directly inflicted and one that comes as a consequence. By a loss directly inflicted, I mean when a person loses something to which he had a special right; by a loss that comes as a consequence, when one does not have what he would otherwise have had, since the condition has ceased without which he did not have the right. Ulpian gives

---

[16]   The suggestion is that certain attributes of sovereign statehood are regarded as intrinsic features or rights of states as such, which cannot be taken away, even as punishment for wrong-doing.

[17]   In other words, the right to punish a community extends only so long as the 'desert' exists – i.e., only so long as the community deserves punishment. It deserves punishment as long as the individuals who were responsible for instituting the wrongful policy remain alive.

an illustration: 'If I have opened a well on my land, from which it results that streams that would flow through to your land are cut off', he declares that, in this case, damage has not been inflicted by a wrongful act on my part, since I have merely exercised my own right.[18]

In another place Ulpian says that there is a great difference between suffering loss and being prevented from enjoying an advantage which [someone else] had hitherto made use of.[19] Paul the Jurist also says: 'It is absurd for us to be called possessors before we have acquired something.'[20] Consequently, when the property of their parents has been confiscated, children experience some inconvenience indeed. [B]ut strictly speaking, this is not a punishment, because the property that was to be theirs would not become theirs actually unless it had been preserved by their parents to the end of life.[21]

Now, when the community is at fault through the crime of the majority, who, as we have said elsewhere, represents the personality of the community, and when, for this cause, it loses the things that we have mentioned – political liberty, fortifications, and other profitable things – the loss is felt also by the individuals who are innocent, but only in respect to such things as belonged to them not directly but through the community.

11. The distinction between the occasion of a crime and the cause of a crime

Furthermore, we must bear in mind that harm is sometimes done to a person, or some good taken away from a person, because of a fault committed by another, yet not in such a way that that fault is the proximate cause of the act, if the right behind the act is considered. . . . For as he who has gone surety for a purchaser is not, strictly speaking, bound by the purchase but by his [own] promise [of suretyship], so he who gives security for a wrong-doer is bound not [directly] by the wrong, but by his [own promise of] surety. Hence it comes about that the harm inflicted upon him who goes security is not measured by the other's wrong, but by the [burden] which he has of fulfilling his promise.

In consequence, it follows that, according to the view which we believe to be the more correct, no one may be put to death by reason of suretyship, because we hold that no one has such a right over his [own] life as to be able to take it away from himself or to bind himself to have it taken away.

---

[18] *Digest*, 39.2.24.12 (Ulpian). The point is that the neighbour has experienced a loss, but is not a victim of a wrong, since his loss was merely a consequence, de facto, of an act that was not wrongful. This situation is sometimes referred to as one of *iniuria sine damno* (i.e., material loss without wrong-doing).

[19] *Digest*, 39.2.26 (Ulpian).   [20] *Digest*, 35.2.63 (Paul).

[21] In modern terms, it would be said that the children's hope or expectation of a future receipt of property has failed to materialise, but that they have suffered no infringement of their legal rights.

What we have said regarding a man's life must be understood to apply to his limbs also; for the right has not been given to a man to deprive himself of these except in order to save the body.

A similar case arises in connexion with a right that one possesses in such a way that it is dependent upon the will of another. Such a right is one terminable at the pleasure of the grantor. . . . If something held by such a right be taken from anyone by reason of another's wrong, there is in this not properly a punishment, but the [exercise] of an antecedent right that was vested in the person who takes the thing away.

12. On punishment for another's wrong

Having drawn these distinctions, we shall say that no one who is innocent of wrong may be punished for the wrong done by another. . . . [T]he . . . reason is that an obligation to punishment arises from desert; and desert is something personal, since it has its origin in the will, than which nothing is more peculiarly ours.

14. Concerning the acts of God with regard to the children of the wicked

It is true that, in the law given to the Jews, God threatens to avenge upon descendants the iniquity of the parents;[22] but He Himself possesses the most right of ownership, both over our property and over our life, as it is His gift, which He can take away from anyone when He pleases, without any reason and at any time.

At the same time, the fact must be recognised that God does not make use of this more severe punishment except to punish crimes committed as a direct insult to Himself, such as false worship, perjury, and sacrilege. . . . However, even if God has threatened to inflict such punishment, He does not always make use of this right, especially if some remarkable virtue appears in the children of the guilty. Nevertheless, it is not permissible for men to imitate the action of God in this matter. They have not the same justification, because, as we have said before, God has a right over men's lives without regard to their guilt, but men only in consequence of deep guilt, and that too when the guilt is distinctly individual. Wherefore that same divine law forbids not only that parents be made subject to the penalty of death for the deeds of their children, but also that children should be put to death for the deeds of their parents.[23]

---

[22] *Exodus*, 20:5.

[23] *Deuteronomy*, 24:16: 'Parents are not to be put to death for their children, nor children put to death for their parents; each will die for their own sin.'

16. Denial of things which could have been had

At this point, it must be noted that, if the children of traitors have possession of, or may look forward to have possession of, something the direct right over which belongs not to them but to the people or the king, this may be taken away from them by a kind of right of ownership; the exercise of such right, however, at the same time may turn into a punishment of those who have done the wrong.[24]

17. Punishment of subjects for a wrong committed by their king

What we have said with regard to the inflicting of evil upon children because of the wrong-doings of their parents may be applied also in the case of a people that is truly subject (for a people that is not subject may be punished because of its own guilt, that is for its negligence, as we have said),[25] if the question is raised whether such a people may suffer for the crimes of its king or its rulers. At present, we are not inquiring whether the consent of the people itself is involved, or whether there has been any other act on the part of the people deserving of punishment. [W]e are concerned merely with the relation which arises from the nature of the body whose head is the king, and whose members are the other citizens.

18. Punishment of individuals for the wrong-doing of the community

[In the case of a wrong done by a community, punishment may not be inflicted] upon individuals who have not given their consent [to that wrong], that is so far as their interest as individuals is concerned.[26]

---

[24] This is an illustration of the more general principle that a person who has possession of property without having legal ownership is obliged to surrender the property to the true owner, even if he came into possession without any wrong-doing on his own part (e.g., if he obtained possession of the property by way of inheritance or gift, and even if he paid full value for it). From the possessor's standpoint, this may appear as an act of punishment; but that is not truly so. It is simply a matter of the exercise by the true owner of his own legal rights – though admittedly to the material disadvantage of the erstwhile possessor.

[25] See p. 292.

[26] See Section 7 above. The reference to 'their interest as individuals' is probably meant to indicate that persons who did not consent to the wrong may not have punishment inflicted *directly* onto them, for example by being enslaved. They might suffer indirectly, however, in their capacity as citizens. An example would be liability for contribution, as taxpayers, to a fine or tribute imposed onto the community as a result of the wrongdoing.

19. Punishment of heirs

The heir is bound to discharge other obligations,[27] but not to undergo punishment. . . . The . . . reason is that the heir represents the person of the deceased,
not in what he deserved, which is purely personal, but in his property.[28]

[27] Such as debts of the decedent.
[28] This is further evidence from Grotius that the matter is being considered from the
standpoint of Roman law, with its concept of universal succession, meaning
succession to the whole of the decedent's legal condition, which includes both assets
and obligations.

22

On unjust causes [of wars]¹

1. The distinction between justifiable and persuasive causes of wars

We said above, when we set out to treat the causes of wars, that some were justifiable, others persuasive.²

2. Wars which lack causes of either sort

There are some who rush into war without a cause of either sort.

3. Wars which have persuasive but not justifying causes

In most cases, those who go to war have persuasive causes, either with or without justifiable causes. There are some indeed who clearly ignore justifiable causes. To these, we may apply the dictum uttered by the Roman jurists, that the man is a robber who, when asked the origin of his possession, adduces none other than the fact of possession.

4. Causes which present a false appearance of justice

Others allege causes which they claim to be justifiable, but which, when examined in the light of right reason, are found to be unjust. . . . Now causes which are unjust may, up to a certain point, be recognised from the foregoing discussion of just causes.³ What is straight is in fact a guide to what is crooked. For the

---

¹ The main task of the treatise is now resumed: the discussion of the law of war and peace. The whole, or nearly the whole, of the intervening material has been, in effect, a gigantic digression on the subject of the nature of various kinds of rights and obligations.
² It will be recalled that by persuasive causes are meant causes which have an outward appearance of justice. As Grotius goes on to stress, wars which have only an outward appearance of justice, but which lack any of the three strict just causes, are unjust from the standpoint of natural law.
³ See p. 81 above.

sake of clearness, however, we proceed to mention the principal kinds of unjust causes.

5. The fear of something uncertain as a cause of war

We have said above that fear with respect to a neighbouring power is not a sufficient cause. For in order that defence may be lawful,[4] it must be necessary; and it is not necessary unless we are certain, not only regarding the power of our neighbour, but also regarding his intention; the degree of certainty required is that which is accepted in morals. Wherefore we can in no wise approve the view of those who declare that it is a just cause of war when a neighbour who is restrained by no agreement builds a fortress on his own soil, or some other fortification which may some day cause us harm. Against the fears which arise from such actions, we must resort to counter-fortifications on our own land and other similar remedies, but not to force of arms.

6. On advantage apart from necessity as a cause of war

Advantage does not confer the same right as necessity.

7. Refusal of marriage as a cause of war

So, when there is abundant opportunity for marriage, a refusal of marriage cannot furnish a cause for war.[5]

8. The desire for richer land as a cause of war

The desire to change abode, in order that by abandoning swamps and wildernesses a more fruitful soil may be acquired, does not afford a just cause for war.

9. The discovery of things previously taken over by others as a cause of war

Equally shameless is it to claim for oneself by right of discovery what is held by another, even though the occupant may be wicked, may hold wrong views

---

[4] The reference is to defensive war waged by states (one of the three kinds of just war), rather than to the natural-law right of individual self-defence.

[5] By 'refusal of marriage' is meant a state policy of refusing to foreigners a right of intermarriage with its women. This is a just cause for war, as observed earlier (on p. 102), if the foreigners are thereby effectively deprived of the opportunity of marriage. Grotius points out that such a restrictive policy is not wrongful if the foreigners have, in fact, alternate opportunities to obtain spouses.

about God, or may be dull of wit. For discovery applies to those things which belong to no one.[6]

10. When the previous occupants of a territory are insane

For the exercise of ownership, neither moral nor religious virtue, nor intellectual excellence, is a requirement;[7] except that the view seems defensible that, if there exist any peoples wholly deprived of the use of reason, these cannot have ownership, but merely for charity's sake there is due to them what is necessary to maintain life.[8] What we have said elsewhere regarding the maintenance of ownership, which the law of nations guarantees on behalf of minors and insane persons,[9] applies to those peoples with whom there exists an interchange of agreements. [B]ut such are not peoples absolutely deprived of reason, if any of this sort are to be found, which I very much doubt.[10]

The Greeks were therefore wrong in saying that the barbarians were their enemies as it were by nature, because of their differences in customs, perhaps also because the barbarians seemed to be inferior to them in intellect.[11] However, to what extent ownership may be taken away because of vicious crimes, which offend against both nature and human society, is another question, which we just now discussed when dealing with the right of punishments.[12]

11. The desire for freedom among a subject people as a cause of war

[A desire for] liberty, whether of individuals or of states . . . cannot give the right to war, just as if by nature and at all times liberty was adapted to all persons. For when liberty is said to be an attribute by nature of men and of peoples, this must be understood of the law of nature which precedes all human conditions. [T]hat is to say, that by nature no one is a slave, but not that man [can] never . . . enter [into] slavery.[13]

---

[6] Vitoria, *On the American Indians*, 1.31. This passage might be read as implying that discovery alone will confer legal title onto the discoverer, provided that no one had prior possession. That, however, is incorrect. Discovery gives only the *opportunity* to acquire title. Actual title is acquired by effective occupation, in the wake of the discovery.

[7] *Ibid.*, 1.4–24.   [8] *Ibid.*, 2.18.   [9] See p. 107 above.

[10] The view is apparently taken that any society that is capable of entering into treaties is, *ipso facto*, not in the category of 'peoples wholly deprived of the use of reason'. Grotius even doubts that any such society exists at all.

[11] For opinions of this general kind, see Aristotle, *Politics*, I.2; Plato, *The Republic*, V.470; and Isocrates, 'Panathenaicus', 42–4, 47, 59–60, 102, 163, 167, 189–90.

[12] See p. 285 above.

[13] The contention is that liberty is a right of all individuals only in the sense that, in the state of nature, prior to the formation of political societies, all persons possessed liberty. In many cases, however, that original liberty has been lost, either by

12. The desire to rule others against their will on the pretext that it is for their good, as a cause of war

Not less iniquitous is it to desire by arms to subdue other men, as if they deserved to be enslaved, and were such as the philosophers at times call slaves by nature.[14] For even if something is advantageous for anyone, the right is not forthwith conferred upon me to impose this upon him by force. For those who have the use of their reason ought to have the free choice of what is advantageous or not advantageous, unless another has acquired a certain right over them.

With infants, the case is clearly different; for since they do not have the right of exercising independence of action and of directing their own movements, nature confers the control over them upon persons who undertake it and are fitted therefor.[15]

13. The quest for universal empire by the Holy Roman Emperor as a cause of war

I should hardly trouble to add that the title which certain persons give to the Roman Emperor is absurd, as if he had the right of ruling over even the most distant and hitherto unknown peoples, were it not that Bartolus, long considered first among jurists, had dared to pronounce him a heretic who denies to the Emperor this title. . . . Nor should anyone be influenced by the arguments of Dante, by which he strives to prove that such a right belongs to the Emperor because that is advantageous for the human race.[16] The advantages which it brings are in fact offset by its disadvantages. For as a ship may attain to such a size that it cannot be steered, so also the number of inhabitants and the distance between places may be so great as not to tolerate a single government.

Again, even if we should grant that the ascription of such a right to the Emperor is advantageous, the right to rule by no means follows, since this cannot come into existence except by consent or by punishment. The Roman Emperor at present does not have this right even over all the former possessions of the Roman people; for as many of these were acquired by war, so by war they have been lost; while others by treaties, others still by abandonment, have passed under the authority of other nations or kings. Some states, too, that were once completely subject [to Roman rule], later began to be subject only in part, or merely federated on unequal terms. For all these ways either of losing or of

---

voluntary consent or by conquest. Grotius denies that there is any general natural-law right to recover such lost liberty at will.

[14] This reference is to the famous (or infamous) assertion by Aristotle that some persons are naturally suited to slavery. Aristotle, *Politics*, I.5–6.

[15] Vitoria, *On the American Indians*, 1.31. Grotius cites the wrong provision of Vitoria in his text.

[16] See generally Dante, *De Monarchia.*

modifying a right are not less valid against the Roman Emperor than against others.

14. Claim to universal empire by the Church as a cause of war

There have also been some who claimed for the Church a right over the peoples even of the hitherto unknown parts of the earth.[17] . . . Yet the right of judging possessed by the Apostles, even although it extended in its own way to earthly things, was of a heavenly nature, so to say, and not of earthly quality. [I]t was to be exercised indeed not by the sword and scourge but by the word of God enunciated in general terms and applied to particular conditions, through the revelation or denial of the signs of divine grace, according as each might deserve; in last resort even by a punishment not according to nature but from a higher source than nature, therefore emanating from God.

The question whether even kings may use armed force as a means of punishment against those who reject the Christian religion we have previously discussed, so far as is necessary for our purpose, in the chapter 'On Punishments'.[18]

15. The desire to fulfil prophecies as a cause of war

Not without reason shall I give this warning, that the hope derived from an interpretation of divine prophecies does not furnish a just cause of war. For from a comparison of modern with ancient events, I foresee the danger of great evil from this source, unless we guard against it. Apart from the fact that, without prophetic inspiration, it is hardly possible to interpret with certainty prophecies that have not yet been fulfilled, even the times set for the coming of things that are certain may be hidden from us. Finally, a prediction, unless it is a definite command of God, confers no right, since the things which God foretells He often permits to be accomplished through the agency of wicked men or base deeds.

16. The desire to obtain something not strictly owed in law as a cause of war

This principle, too, must be recognised. If a person owes a debt that is not an obligation from the point of view of strict justice, but arises from some other virtue, such as generosity, gratitude, pity or charity, this debt cannot be collected by armed force any more than in a court of law. For either procedure,

---

[17] See Vitoria, *On the American Indians*, 1.26, for a summary of such claims. Vitoria rejected these claims, as does Grotius.

[18] See p. 269 above. Recall that Pope Innocent IV, in the thirteenth century, had asserted a right of punishment over all peoples for violations of natural law, but did not assert a right of sovereignty per se.

it is not enough that the demand which is made ought to be met for a moral reason; but in addition we must possess some right to enforce it.[19] This right is at times conferred by divine and human laws even in the case of obligations that arise from other virtues; and when this happens, there arises a new cause of indebtedness, which relates to justice.[20] When this is lacking, a war undertaken on such grounds is unjust.

17. The difference between a war without a just cause and a war wrongful in other ways

It is to be observed that this often happens, that a just cause for a war may in fact exist, but that in making war, a wrong may arise from the intent of the party who engages in hostilities. This may come about either because some other thing, not in itself unlawful, in a greater degree and more effectively influences his purpose than the right itself, as, for example, an eager desire for honour, or some advantage, whether private or public, which is expected from the war considered apart from its justifiable cause. Or there may be present a manifestly unlawful desire, such as the delight of him who has pleasure in another's ill, without regard to what is good.[21]

However, when a justifiable cause is not wanting, . . . these [unlawful intentions] do indeed convict of wrong the party that makes war. [Y]et they do not render the war itself, properly speaking, unlawful.[22] Hence no restitution is due as a result of a war undertaken under such conditions.[23]

[19] Such rights fall into the category of imperfect rights – meaning rights unenforceable by legal action. A just war is, in effect, regarded as tantamount to a legal action.

[20] An example would be a case in which a subject is commanded by his sovereign to discharge what would otherwise be a merely moral obligation. By way of this command, a new obligation – this time a strictly legal one – arises. This new obligation has the same content as the moral one, but a different legal character.

[21] This is a reference to the principle of *animus* in medieval natural-law thought, according to which a war becomes unjust if waged for an improper motive, even if the party waging the war has a legal entitlement to the thing being contested.

[22] This amounts to a rejection of the medieval principle of *animus*. According to Grotius, an improper motive does not, per se, render a war unlawful, as it did in medieval just-war doctrine. Instead, the position is that the war as such is just, provided only that one or more of his three just causes is present. If such a just war is begun out of improper motives, then that is an act of personal sin or misconduct on the part of the person waging the war. For such wrongful motivation, a religious or supernatural sanction may be imposed in due course; but there is, strictly speaking, no violation of natural law.

[23] In a war which is unjust in the true sense, the unjust side must restore to their original owners any property taken. See p. 359 below.

23

On doubtful causes of war

1. On the source of the causes of doubt in moral questions

What Aristotle wrote is perfectly true, that certainty is not to be found in moral questions in the same degree as in mathematical science.[1] This comes from the fact that mathematical science completely separates forms from substance, and that the forms themselves are generally such that between two of them there is no intermediate form,[2] just as there is no mean between a straight and a curved line. In moral questions, on the contrary, even trifling circumstances alter the substance; and the forms, which are the subject of inquiry, are wont to have something intermediate, which is of such scope that it approaches now more closely to this, now to that, extreme.

Thus it comes about that, between what should be done and what it is wrong to do, there is a mean, that which is permissible;[3] and this is now closer to the former, now to the latter. Hence there often comes a moment of doubt, just as when day passes into night, or when cold water slowly becomes warm.

2. Actions contrary to the dictates of one's mind

First of all, we must hold to the principle that, even if something is in itself just, when it is done by one who, taking everything into consideration, considers it unjust, the act is vicious.[4]

Nevertheless, it often happens that the judgement presents no certainty, but is undecided. . . . [In a situation in which] one really must do one of two things, and yet is in doubt whether either is right, [a person is] allowed to choose that

---

[1] Aristotle, *Nicomachean Ethics*, I.3. Grotius mis-cites this in his text.
[2] In other words, mathematics is a subject characterised by rigorous clarity, without ambiguities and 'grey areas', unlike law or ethics.
[3] Some writers posited three gradations between things commanded and things prohibited: things preferred but not mandatory (lying nearer to the 'commanded' end of the continuum); things frowned upon but not prohibited (lying nearer to the 'prohibited' end); and, in the centre, things entirely neutral from the legal and moral standpoint. All three of these gradations share the feature of being permissible but at the same time neither mandatory nor prohibited.
[4] An act which is 'vicious' is one that is sinful from the personal standpoint of the actor even though, objectively, the act itself remains lawful.

which appears to him to be less wrong. For always, when a choice cannot be avoided, the [apparent] lesser evil assumes the aspect of the good.

3. Influence of arguments from facts on judgement

Very often in a doubtful matter, however, after some investigation, the mind does not remain neutral but is influenced to this side or that by arguments drawn from the facts, or by the opinion which it gathers from other men who express their view of the matter.... Arguments from the facts are drawn from causes, effects, and other collateral circumstances.

4. Influence of the counsel of the wise on judgement

To consider aright the arguments to which we have made reference, one must have a certain degree of experience and skill. Those who do not have such skill and experience are bound to listen to the counsels of the wise, in order that they may rightly mould their practical judgement.

5. When there is doubt on both sides

In many controversies, it may happen that strong arguments are forthcoming in support of both sides, whether drawn from the facts in the case or supported by the authority of others. When this occurs, if the matters which are in question are of slight moment, the choice may evidently be free from harm, no matter on which side it may fall. But if the question is one of great importance, such as the infliction of capital punishment, in that case, because of the great difference between the courses to be chosen, the safer is to be preferred.... And so it is better to acquit one who is guilty than to condemn one who is innocent.

6. Refraining from war in case of doubt

Now war is of the utmost importance, seeing that in consequence of war a great many sufferings usually fall upon even innocent persons. Therefore, in the midst of divergent opinions, we must lean towards peace.... There are, moreover, three methods by which disputes may be prevented from breaking out into wars.

7. First, a conference

The first method is by a conference [i.e., negotiation].

8. Second, arbitration

The second method is by agreement to arbitrate. This is applicable among those who have no common judicial authority.

9. Third, by lot

The third method is by lot.[5]

10. Single combat as a means of avoiding war

Something akin to the lot, furthermore, is single combat. [I]t does not seem necessary altogether to reject [resort to single combat] . . . if two persons, whose disputes would otherwise afflict whole peoples with very serious evils, are ready to settle their dispute by arms.

11. Significance of possession in cases of doubt

Although when the cause involves doubt, each party is bound to try to find conditions under which war may be avoided, nevertheless the party who asserts claims is under greater obligation to do this than the party who is in possession. For it is in accordance not only with the civil [law], but also with the law of nature, that when each party has a cause equally just, the case of the party having possession is the better.[6]

At this point, we must add that war cannot permissibly be waged by him who knows that he has a just cause but has not adequate proofs to convince the possessor of the injustice of his possession. [T]he reason is that [without objective proof of his right] he does not have the right to compel the other to surrender possession.

12. If neither party is in possession

In cases in which the right is in doubt, and neither party is in possession, or each holds possession in an equal measure, he is to be considered in the wrong who rejects a proposed division of the thing under dispute.

13. Whether a war may be just from the view-point of both parties

From what we have said, it is possible to reach a decision regarding the question, which has been discussed by many, whether, if we take into consideration the prime movers, a war may be considered just from the point of view of each of the opposing sides.

---

[5] No historical example is given in which this has occurred.

[6] *Digest*, 50.17.128 (Paul); and Vitoria, *On the American Indians*, 27. Notice that it is not asserted that possession, in itself, confers a superior substantive right. It is only contended that the non-possessing party has the burden of proof of establishing that the possession is wrongful. This is merely an application of the general principle that, in litigation, the plaintiff has the burden of proof. Here again, the close connection between war and litigation, in just-war thought, is apparent.

We must distinguish various interpretations of the word 'just'. Now a thing is called just either from its cause, or because of its effects; and again, if from its cause, either in the particular sense of justice, or in the general sense in which all right conduct comes under this name. Further, the particular sense may cover either that which concerns the deed, or that which concerns the doer; for sometimes the doer himself is said to act justly so long as he does not act unjustly, even if that which he does is not just.[7]

In the particular sense and with reference to the thing itself, a war cannot be just on both sides, just as a legal claim cannot; the reason is that, by the very nature of the case, [the same] moral quality cannot be given to opposites, as to doing and restraining. Yet it may actually happen that neither of the warring parties does wrong. No one acts unjustly without knowing that he is doing an unjust thing, but in this respect many are ignorant. Thus either party may justly, that is in good faith, plead his case. For both in law and in fact, many things out of which a right arises ordinarily escape the notice of men.

In the general sense, that is usually called just which is free from all blame on the part of the doer.... [M]any things are done without right and yet without guilt [on the part of the doer], because of unavoidable ignorance. An example of this is the case of those who fail to observe a law of which they are ignorant through no fault of their own, after the law itself has been promulgated and a sufficient time has elapsed for them to know of it. So it may happen in the case of legal claims also, that each party is guiltless, not only of injustice, but also of any other [personal] fault.

If we interpret the word 'just' [to mean the producing of] certain legal effects, in this sense surely it may be admitted that a war may be just from the point of view of either side. [T]his will appear from what we shall have to say later regarding a formal public war.[8] [Analogously] a judgement not rendered according to law, and possession without right, have certain legal effects.[9]

---

[7] The meaning is that, so long as a person is acting in good faith to assert his legal rights, he is not acting unjustly – even if his claim ultimately proves to be unfounded. In such a case, it could be said that the assertion of the claim was not just from the objective standpoint but that the person himself, by virtue of his good faith, could not be accused of acting unjustly, as a matter of personal conduct. In the next paragraph, Grotius applies this principle to the waging of war.

[8] A second sense is provided in which it may be said that a war can be just on both sides (the first sense being the case in which both parties act in good faith). War can be just on both sides, in this second sense, when the legal effects of war are the same for both sides – e.g., when both sides are equally exempt from punishment for acts of war committed against the other, such as killing and capturing enemy soldiers or capturing enemy property. See p. 359 below for further discussion of this point.

[9] I.e., a judgment handed down by a court, when the judge is mistaken about the law, has full legal effect, notwithstanding the error of law on the judge's part (i.e., notwithstanding its injustice). Similarly, possession, even if legally wrongful, has 'certain legal effects' such as the one pointed out above (at Section 11), of placing the burden of proof in a claim onto the non-possessing party.

Warnings not to undertake war rashly, even for just causes

1. On giving up a right in order to avoid war

Although it does not seem properly to be a part of this work, which is entitled *On the Law of War*, to inquire what other virtues [than adherence to law] enjoin or admonish with regard to war, nevertheless we must proceed to correct an error, in order to prevent anyone from thinking that, where a right has been adequately established, either war should be waged forthwith, or even that war is permissible in all [such] cases. On the contrary, it frequently happens that it is more upright and just to abandon one's right. [W]e may honourably neglect the care of our own lives in order that, to the best of our ability, we may safeguard the life and eternal salvation of another. ... Such conduct is above all becoming for Christians.

2. On giving up the right to inflict punishments in order to avoid war

There are in truth many reasons which admonish us to forgo punishments. ... [O]bserve how many things fathers pass over in their sons. ... Now whoever wishes to punish another assumes in some measure the character of a ruler, that is of a father.

At times, the circumstances of the case are such that to refrain from the exercise of one's right is not merely praiseworthy but even obligatory, by reason of the love which we owe even to men who are our enemies, whether this be viewed in itself or as the most sacred law of the Gospel demands. From that point of view, we have said that there are some persons for whose safety we ought to desire to die, even if they should restrain us, because we know that they are necessary, or extremely useful, to mankind in general. If Christ desires that some things be overlooked in order to avoid engaging in lawsuits, then in proportion as a war is more harmful than a lawsuit, the more earnestly must we believe that He desired us to pass over greater things in order to avoid going to war.

3. On giving up the right to redress wrongs in order to avoid war

Regarding punishments, it is first of all our duty, if not as men, assuredly as Christians, readily and gladly to pardon the wrongs done to us, ... This obligation to pardon rests upon us with greatest weight when either we too are conscious to ourselves of some sin, or when the sin committed against us is the result of some human and pardonable weakness, or when it is sufficiently clear that he who has wronged us is repentant.

These reasons for refraining from war have their origin in the love which we either owe to our enemies or rightly manifest toward them.

5. Rules dictated by prudence

When men weigh such matters as those mentioned, they deliberate in part regarding ends, not indeed intermediate but ultimate ends; and in part regarding the means which lead thereto. The end is always something good, or at least an avoidance of evil, which may take the place of a good. Moreover, the means which lead to this or that end are not sought for their own sake but only in so far as they lead to the ends in view. Wherefore, in deliberations, the ends must be compared with one another; and also the means which may be employed, the effective power of each for contributing to the end, must be considered. . . . For this sort of comparison there are three rules.

The first of the rules is this. If, from the moral point of view at any rate, the matter under consideration seems to have an equal effectiveness for good and for evil, it is to be chosen only if the good has somewhat more of good than the evil has of evil.[1]

The second rule is: if the good and evil, which may proceed from the matter under consideration, seem to be equal, [a resort to war] is only to be chosen if its effectiveness for good be greater than for evil.[2]

The third [rule] is: if the good and the evil seem to be unequal, and the effectiveness for these things not less unequal, then the thing is to be chosen only if its effectiveness for good is greater when compared with its effectiveness for evil than the evil itself compared with the good; or if the good is greater in comparison with the evil than the effectiveness for evil compared with that for good.[3]

---

[1] This argument is somewhat difficult to understand. It appears to concern the case in which the benefits of victory are balanced against the costs. War should be resorted to only if the anticipated benefits are greater.

[2] The concern now is with a situation in which the anticipated benefits and costs of the war are perceived to be equal. In this case, the decision as to whether actually to go to war should be determined by weighing the probability of victory against the probability of defeat. If victory is seen to be more probable, then war may be waged. This is a speculative interpretation, since Grotius gives no illustration of his point.

[3] This third rule is even more obscure than the first two. It seems now to be contemplated that there is inequality of two kinds: firstly, regarding the benefit of victory (i.e., of possession of the thing contended for), weighed against the costs incurred by war; and secondly, regarding the probability of victory weighed against

These ideas we have presented in rather studied terms; but Cicero moves toward the same goal by a more direct path when he says that we must avoid offering ourselves to dangers without cause, for nothing could be more foolish than that. [C]onsequently, in approaching dangers, we should imitate the practice of physicians, who cure by light treatments those who are not seriously ill, but are compelled to apply dangerous and doubtful remedies to more serious diseases. Wherefore he says that it is the part of a wise man, when a storm arises, to withstand it with all possible means, 'especially if you gain more good from a successful issue than evil from the risk incurred'.[4]

7. Consideration of adequacy of strength in exacting penalties

In exacting penalties, moreover, this must be observed particularly, that war is not to be waged on such a pretext against him whose forces are equal to our own. For, as in the case of a civil judge, he who wishes to avenge crimes by armed force ought to be much more powerful than the other party.

Not merely prudence, in truth, or love of one's own people, ordinarily demands that we refrain from a dangerous war, but oftentimes justice also requires it; that is, rectorial justice, which from the very nature of government binds the superior to care for his inferiors no less than it binds the inferiors to obedience.[5] From this follows the view rightly handed down by the theologians, that the king who undertakes a war for trivial reasons, or to exact unnecessary penalties, is responsible to his subjects for making good the losses which arise therefrom. For he perpetrates a crime, if not against the foe, yet against his own people, by involving them in so serious an evil on such grounds.

8. Requirement of necessity for war

Therefore, a cause for engaging in war which either may not be passed over, or ought not to be, is exceptional.

---

the probability of defeat. In effect, Grotius seems to be holding that these inequalities should be aggregated, so that a relatively low net value of the thing being fought for, if combined with a high probability of winning, could justify a resort to war. Similarly, a very high net value of the thing being fought for, if combined with a relatively low probability of victory, could also justify a resort to war. In this instance, too, the interpretation is speculative, since, again, Grotius gives no illustration of his point.

[4] Cicero, *On Duties*, I.83. Cicero's treatment of the matter does indeed seem 'more direct' than Grotius's. It suggests a general principle of proportionality – that even a war that is just in strict legal terms ought not to be waged if the collateral evil that it entails exceeds the good that a victory will bring.

[5] On rectorial justice, see p. 24 above.

9. Requirement of a most weighty cause

A second occasion to engage in war is when, after inquiring into the matter as one ought, the war is found to be in accordance with right, and at the same time – which is of the highest importance – the necessary resources are available.... Such an opportunity will be found particularly when there is hope that the matter may be settled by inspiring fear and on the strength of reputation, with little or no risk.

25

On the causes of undertaking war on behalf of others

1. War may rightfully be undertaken on behalf of subjects

In the earlier part of this work, when we dealt with those who wage war, we asserted and showed that, by the law of nature, each individual was justified in enforcing not merely his own right but also that of another.[1] The causes, therefore, which are just in relation to the person whose interest is at stake are just also in relation to those who give assistance to others. Now the first and particularly necessary concern is for subjects, either those who are subject to authority in a family, or those who are subject to a political authority. They are, in fact, as it were, a part of the ruler.

2. Refraining from war on behalf of subjects

Nevertheless, wars are not always to be waged on behalf of subjects, even though the just cause of some subject places the ruler under obligation to undertake them. Such wars are to be undertaken only when this can be done without loss to all the subjects, or to the majority of them. The duty of the ruler concerns the whole rather than parts; [although] the greater a part is, the more nearly it approaches the character of the whole.

3. Surrendering an innocent subject to avoid danger

Thus if one citizen, although innocent, is demanded by an enemy, to be made away with, there is no doubt that he may be abandoned to them if it appears that the state is by no means a match for the power of the enemy.

   [A] citizen is not [however] bound to surrender himself by law properly so called; [but] it does not follow ... that love permits him to [refuse to be surrendered]. For there are many duties which are not in the domain of justice properly speaking, but in that of affection,[2] which are not only discharged amid praise ... but cannot even be omitted without blame.

---

[1] See p. 77 above.   [2] I.e., many duties arise from morality rather than justice.

Such a duty seems quite clearly to be this, that a person should value the lives of a very large number of innocent persons above his own life.

But on the supposition that a citizen demanded by the enemy ought to surrender himself to them, there remains the question whether he may be compelled to do that to which he is morally bound. . . . We must observe, . . . that the relation of parts among themselves is one thing, and that of superiors, when they are contrasted with those subject to them, is quite another. For an equal cannot be compelled by an equal, except to perform what is owed in accordance with a right properly so called.[3] But a superior can compel an inferior to do other things also, which some virtue demands, because this is embraced in the proper right of the superior as such.[4] Thus, during a grain famine citizens may be compelled to contribute what they have to the common store. Hence in this argument of ours, it seems even more true that a citizen may be constrained [by his sovereign] to do that which regard for others requires.

4. War on behalf of allies

Next to subjects, and indeed on an equal footing with them in this respect, that they ought to be defended, are allies, in whose treaty of alliance this obligation is embraced, whether they have surrendered themselves to the guardianship and good faith of others, or have agreed to give and receive mutual assistance.

We have said elsewhere,[5] however, that such agreements cannot be stretched to include wars for which no just cause exists. . . . We may now add this principle, that not even under such conditions[6] is an ally bound to render aid if there is no hope of a successful issue. The reason is that an alliance is formed for the sake of good, and not of ill. However, an ally is to be protected even against another ally that is in alliance on the same terms, unless in the previous treaty there is some particular provision to the contrary.[7]

5. War on behalf of friends

The third cause for undertaking wars on behalf of others is obligation to friends, to whom aid has not been promised, to be sure, but yet is owed under a certain principle of friendship, if it can be rendered easily and without loss.

---

[3] If two parties are legal equals, one can compel another to perform a duty which he is under an existing legal obligation to discharge; but neither party is obligated to submit himself to the arbitrary will of the other.

[4] A political superior can compel an inferior to perform a task which is commanded by morality but not by law. Pursuant to that command, the subject becomes legally (and not merely morally) obligated to perform the task.

[5] Source not identified.   [6] I.e., not even if the ally's cause is just.

[7] This is on the assumption that, when the two allies are in conflict, one will be fighting justly and the other unjustly. The obligation is to assist the just one, whichever it may happen to be – unless that particular situation had been expressly excluded by the original treaty of alliance with the just party.

6. War on behalf of any persons whatsoever

The final and most wide-reaching cause for undertaking wars on behalf of others is the mutual tie of kinship among men, which of itself affords sufficient ground for rendering assistance. 'Men have been born to aid one another', says Seneca.[8]

7. Defence of others when there is fear for oneself

At this point the question arises, whether a man is bound to defend a man, or one people another people, from wrong. . . . [A] man [will not] be obliged to render aid [to an oppressed person] if the person oppressed cannot be delivered save by the death of the oppressor.

8. War for the defence of subjects of another power[9]

This too is a matter of controversy, whether there may be a just cause for undertaking war on behalf of the subjects of another ruler, in order to protect them from wrong at his hands. Now it is certain that, from the time when political associations were formed, each of their rulers has sought to assert some particular right over his own subjects.

If, however, the wrong [by the ruler against the subjects] is obvious, . . . the exercise of the right vested in human society is not precluded.

If, further, it should be granted that, even in extreme need, subjects cannot justifiably take up arms,[10] . . . nevertheless it will not follow that others may not take up arms on their behalf. For whenever the check imposed upon some action arises from the person concerned and not the action itself, then what is refused to one may be permitted to another on his behalf, provided that the matter is such that the one may therein be of service to the other. Thus a guardian, or some other person, goes to law on behalf of a pupil, who is personally incapable of legal action; and counsel may appear for one who is absent, even without authority. The restriction, in fact, which prevents a subject from resisting . . . [arises only] . . . from the personal condition [of the subject], which is not transferred to others.[11]

---

8 Younger Seneca, *On Anger*, I.5.
9 This is where humanitarian intervention in the modern sense of the term is considered. See also p. 285 above.
10 See p. 70 above, on this point.
11 It has already been explained (at p. 68 above) that there is no right on the part of the victims to rebel against their oppressive ruler (i.e., there is 'a check imposed' upon their freedom to rebel). This prohibition, however, arises from the relation of sovereigns to subjects – or, as Grotius puts it, the 'check' in question 'arises from the person concerned'. A prohibition against revolt by subjects cannot, by its nature, have any application to foreign rulers, who are not subjects. So the question then is whether 'the action itself' – i.e., the intervention to rescue the oppressed persons – is

We know, it is true, from both ancient and modern history, that the desire for what is another's seeks such pretexts as this for its own ends; but a right does not at once cease to exist in case it is to some extent abused by evil men.[12] Pirates, also, sail the sea; arms are carried also by brigands.[13]

9. Military alliances and mercenary service undertaken without regarding the causes of war

Again, just as military alliances, which were entered into with the intention that aid should be rendered for any sort of war without distinction of cause, are not permissible,[14] so no manner of life is more wicked than that of those who serve as soldiers for hire without regard to the cause of hostilities.... It would in truth matter little that mercenaries sell their own lives, if they did not sell also the lives of others, who are often innocent. In this respect, they are much more abominable than an executioner, in the degree that it is worse to slay without cause than with cause.[15] Warfare has no place among the useful arts. Nay, rather, it is so horrible that only the utmost necessity, or true affection,[16] can render it honourable.

10. On military service merely for the sake of pay

The same principle applies in the case of military service for pay, if this is the sole or chief aim in view.[17]

contrary to natural law. Grotius holds that it is not. So although the subjects have no right of revolt on their own behalf, foreign rulers nonetheless have a right to step in and protect them (i.e., to 'be of service' to them).

[12] Grotius shows his sensitivity to the charge that humanitarian intervention, which he is advocating, is subject to abuse – i.e., to employment as a mere pretext for the intervening party to pursue its own ends. But he insists that, notwithstanding this risk, the right does exist.

[13] Sailing the seas and carrying arms are basic rights – notwithstanding that some persons (i.e., pirates and brigands) abuse them.

[14] They are impermissible insofar as they provide that aid is to be provided in the waging of an unjust war.

[15] See Pierini Belli, *A Treatise on Military Matters and Warfare*, translated by Herbert C. Nutting (Oxford: Clarendon Press, 1936 [1563]), 2.2.4–5. Belli (1502–75) was a Piedmontese native who served as military auditor to Holy Roman Emperor Charles V. His work was largely neglected after his death. Grotius did not mention him in the Prologue amongst prior writers on legal aspects of war.

[16] By 'true affection' is meant the altruistic desire to assist persons whose rights are being infringed.

[17] There is room for doubting this proposition. The other two cases considered involved wrong-doing to other persons: fighting in unjust wars, and supplementing wages by plunder. Merely having a pecuniary motive for doing military service in a just war would seem to involve no wrong to others and therefore to be a question of morals rather than of law.

On just causes for war waged by those who are under the rule of another

1. Who is under the rule of another

We have dealt with those who are independent of any control.[1] There are others in a condition which requires them to render obedience, as sons in a household, slaves, subjects, also individual citizens considered in relation to the body politic of their state.

2. What those under the rule of another should do if they are summoned

If those under the rule of another are admitted to a deliberation, or there is given to them a free choice of going to war or remaining at peace, they should be governed by the same rules as those who, at their own discretion, take up arms for themselves or on behalf of others.

3. If those under the rule of another are ordered to go to war and should believe the cause of the war to be unjust

If those under the rule of another are ordered to take the field, as often occurs, they should altogether refrain from so doing if it is clear to them that the cause of the war is unjust.

   The civil law, which readily grants pardon to excusable crimes, is lenient to those who are under obligation to obey, but not so in respect to all things. It makes an exception in the case of those acts which display heinousness of deed or crime, which, as Cicero says, are 'of themselves atrocious and abominable';[2] or . . . deeds of evil which ought to be shunned instinctively, not in consequence of the discussions of jurists, but by a natural reaction.

---

[1] This refers basically to sovereigns, who by definition are not subject to control by superiors.
[2] See also *Digest*, 50.17.157 (Ulpian), which holds that slaves are to be pardoned for offences except where the wrong done has the 'atrocity of crime or misdeed'.

[I]f anyone is convinced that what is ordered is unjust [then he should not obey the order]. For the thing is not permissible for him so long as he is unable to get rid of that view.[3]

4. What those who are under the rule of another should do in cases of doubt

Now if one who is under the rule of another is in doubt whether a thing is permissible or not, is he to remain inactive, or obey? Very many think that he should obey; and further, that he is not hindered by the famous maxim, 'What you question, do not do', because . . . he can believe that, in a matter of doubt, he must obey his superior.

It cannot in truth be denied that this distinction of a double judgement applies in many actions.[4] The municipal law, not only of Rome but of other nations as well, under such circumstances not only grants immunity to those who obey, but also refuses to admit a civil action against them. He does the injury, they say, who orders that it be done. [T]here is then no guilt on the part of him who has to obey. The constraint of authority excuses. . . . Hence the view is widely accepted that, so far as subjects are concerned, a war may arise that is just, that is to say free from injustice on either side.

This view, however, is not free from inherent difficulty. [There is a second view, holding] . . . that whoever hesitates, when reflecting on his decision to act, ought to choose the safer course. The safer course, however, is to refrain from war.

It is no objection that . . . there is danger [arising from] disobedience. For when either course is uncertain, that which is the lesser of two evils is free from sin; for if a war is unjust there is no disobedience in avoiding it. Moreover, disobedience in things of this kind, by its very nature, is a lesser evil than manslaughter, especially than the slaughter of many innocent men.

That is not of great weight which some adduce, that if this principle should be admitted, the state would in many cases perish, the reason being that oftentimes it is not expedient that the reasons for policies should be made public. Although this may be true of persuasive causes, it is not true of justifiable causes, which ought to be clear and open and, further, should be such as may and ought to be openly set forth.

Declarations of war, in fact, as we shall shortly be saying, were wont to be made publicly, with a statement of the cause, in order that the whole human race as it were might judge of the justness of it.[5]

---

[3] Vitoria, *On the Law of War*, 22–3.
[4] The 'double judgement' refers to the fact that, in this situation, two distinct judgements are being arrived at: the judgement of the ruler that the individual should go to war; and the judgement of the individual that he is under a general duty to obey his sovereign.
[5] On declarations of war, see p. 344 below.

It seems then that [this second] view ... is absolutely to be followed, if a subject not only hesitates, but, led by more convincing arguments, leans rather to the view that the war is unjust; especially if it is a question of attacking others, not of defending one's own. Further, it is probable that even the executioner, who is going to put a condemned man to death, should know the merits of the case, either through assisting at the inquiry and the trial or from a confession of the crime, in such a degree that it is sufficiently clear to him that the criminal deserves death. This practice is observed in some places.

5. What should be done to subjects who doubt in regard to the justness of a war

Now if the minds of subjects cannot be satisfied by an explanation of the cause of a war, it will by all means be the duty of a good magistrate to impose upon them extraordinary taxes rather than military service; particularly where there will be no lack of others who will serve. For an upright king may make use not only of his subjects' good will but also of their evil purposes, just as God uses the means of the Devil and impious persons that are at hand; just as, again, he is free from blame who, under stress of poverty, takes money from a wicked usurer.[6]

Furthermore, even if there can be no doubt respecting the cause of war, still it does not seem at all right that Christians should be compelled to serve against their will. [T]he reason is that to refrain from military service, even when it is permissible to serve, is the mark of a somewhat greater holiness, which was long demanded from ecclesiastics and penitents, and recommended in many ways to other persons.

6. When it may be just for subjects to bear arms in a war that is unjust

However, I think that the case may arise in which there may be a just defence of subjects who engage in a war that is not merely doubtful but obviously unjust. For since an enemy, although waging a just war, does not have the true and perfect right of killing innocent subjects [of the unjust side], who are not

---

[6] The point being asserted is somewhat unclear. It may be contended that subjects who are not 'satisfied' by their government's justification of a war have a right to decline to do military service – although they may be assessed for an additional tax in lieu of service. The question that arises (not discussed by Grotius) is whether there might be a right to refuse to pay the taxes as well, since these are obviously for the purpose of prosecuting the war. Alternatively, Grotius may regard the refusal to do military service as wrongful, while assuming that the persons would be willing to pay a surtax instead – with governments being advised, as a pragmatic matter, to be content with this arrangement. Yet another possible interpretation is that the refusal of service is a right, and that the justification of the surtax is necessity. On this view, the surtax could be levied only in case of a genuine emergency, and not as a routine payment for avoiding military service.

responsible for the war, . . . it follows that, if it is certain that the [just] enemy comes with such a spirit that he absolutely refuses to spare the lives of hostile subjects when he can, these subjects may defend themselves by the law of nature, of which they are not deprived by the law of nations.

But even then we shall not say that the war is just on both sides; for it is not a question of the war, but of a certain and definite act.[7] This act, moreover, although done by him who in other respects has a right to make war, is unjust, and hence is justly resisted.

---

[7] The 'certain and definite act' is the act of self-defence against unlawful acts by soldiers of the just side. The reference is to acts of individual self-defence. This discussion reveals the important, and often unappreciated, fact that the natural-law right of individual self-defence is distinct from the waging of or participation in a just war.

Book III
On the Law of War and Peace

1

General rules from the law of nature regarding what is permissible in war; with a consideration of ruses and falsehood

1. The order of treatment in the discussion which follows

We have considered both those who wage war and on what grounds war may be waged. It follows that [in the following discussion] we should determine what is permissible in war, also to what extent and in what ways it is permissible. What is permissible in war is viewed either absolutely or in relation to a previous promise. It is viewed absolutely, first, from the standpoint of the law of nature, and then from that of the [volitional] law of nations.[1] Let us see, then, what is permissible by nature.

2. On things which are necessary to attain the end in view[2]

First, as we have previously said on several occasions, in a moral question, things which lead to an end receive their intrinsic value from the end itself.[3] In consequence, we are understood to have a right to those things which are necessary for the purpose of securing a right, when the necessity is understood not in terms of physical exactitude but in a moral sense. By right, I mean that which is strictly so called, denoting the power of acting in respect to society only.[4] Hence, if otherwise I cannot save my life, I may use any degree of violence to ward off him who assails it, even if he should happen to be free from wrong, as we have pointed out elsewhere.[5] The reason is that this right does not properly

---

[1] The reader is being alerted to the fact that the law on the conduct of war is going to be discussed from two different standpoints, the law of nature and the law of nations. It is accordingly necessary to be attentive as to which of these standpoints is being employed at any given time.

[2] This is a capsule statement of what is now known as the principle of military necessity.

[3] Vitoria, *On the Law of War*, 15.

[4] Laws 'strictly so called' are laws which entail rights against other human beings, i.e., laws which have an impact 'in respect to society only'. Such laws do not, therefore, create rights against God. Nor are they mere expectations or hopes about how one's fellow humans will behave. Rights in the strict sense entail the ability to compel one's fellow humans to behave in prescribed ways.

[5] See the discussion of the general principle of necessity, at p. 96 above.

arise from another's wrong, but from the right which nature grants me on my own behalf.

Furthermore, ... I can also take possession of another's property from which an imminent danger threatens me, without ... guilt [on the part of the owner]; yet not in such a way as to become its owner (for this procedure is not adapted to that end), but in order to guard it until adequate security has been given for my safety.[6] This point also we have treated elsewhere.[7] Thus I have by nature a right to seize property of mine which another is holding; and if such seizure is too difficult, I have the right to seize something else of equal value, as in the case of recovering a debt. From these causes, ownership also arises, because the equality which has been disturbed can in no other way be restored.[8]

Where, therefore, the punishment is just, all use of force necessary for the infliction of the penalty is likewise just; and everything which is a part of the penalty, as the destruction of property by fire or by other means, is certainly within the limit of that which is just and befits the crime.

3. On rights arising following the outbreak of a war

In the second place, the fact must be recognised that our right to wage war is to be regarded as arising not merely from the origin of the war but also from causes which subsequently develop; just as in lawsuits, a new right is often acquired by one party after suit has been brought. Thus, those who associate themselves with him who assails me, either as allies or subjects, confer upon me the right to protect myself against them also.

In like manner, those who join in a war that is unjust, especially if they can or ought to know that it is unjust, obligate themselves to make good the expenses and losses incurred, because through their guilt they cause the loss. Similarly, those who join in a war that has been undertaken without a cause worthy of approval draw upon themselves the desert of punishment, in a degree proportionate to the injustice which lies in their action.

4. On indirect effects of war, beyond the purpose of the doer

In the third place, it must be observed that, in addition to the right [to resort to war and to take steps to attain victory], many things follow indirectly, and

---

[6] An example would be a person's taking possession of a structure on a neighbour's property which is in a state of disrepair and which threatens to collapse onto the person at some imminent point.

[7] See p. 96 above.

[8] 'Seizing something else of equal value' to the property that is being wrongly withheld is an example of set-off. See p. 144 above. It is emphasised that such a seizure of property belonging to the wrong-doer, by way of set-off, does not amount to a mere holding of the wrong-doer's property but rather to the actual acquisition of full legal title.

beyond the purpose of the doer, for which in and of themselves a right would not exist.[9] We have explained elsewhere how this may occur in a case of self-defence. Thus, in order to obtain what is ours, if we cannot get that by itself, we have the right to accept more, subject to the obligation, nevertheless, of restoring the value of the excess. Similarly, we may bombard a ship full of pirates, or a house full of brigands, even if there are within the same ship or house a few infants, women, or other innocent persons who are thereby endangered.

But, as we have admonished upon many occasions previously, what accords with a strict interpretation of right is not always, or in all respects, permitted. Often, in fact, love for our neighbour prevents us from pressing our right to the utmost limit. Wherefore we must also beware of what happens, and what we foresee may happen, beyond our purpose, unless the good which our action has in view is much greater than the evil which is feared, or, unless the good and the evil balance, the hope of the good is much greater than the fear of the evil.[10] The decision in such matters must be left to a prudent judgement, but in such a way that, when in doubt, we should favour that course, as the more safe, which has regard for the interest of another rather than our own.

From these general rules we may learn how much is by nature permissible against an enemy.

5. Persons who furnish supplies to our enemies

But there often arises the question: what is permissible against those who are not enemies, or do not want to be called enemies,[11] but who furnish our enemies with supplies? For we know that this subject has been keenly debated in both ancient and modern times, since some champion the relentlessness of warfare and others the freedom of commercial relations.

First, we must make distinctions with reference to the things supplied. There are some things, such as weapons, which are useful only in war;[12] other things

---

[9] Vitoria, *On the Law of War*, 37. The reference, as explained presently, is basically to what is now called collateral damage to innocent parties, occurring incidentally – but foreseeably – from an attack on the actual wrong-doers.

[10] I.e., either the quantity of good to be achieved must outweigh, by a large margin, the amount of evil foreseen; or else, if the envisaged quantity of good and evil are equal, then the probability of occurrence of the good must be much higher than the envisaged probability of occurrence of the evil.

[11] These came to be called neutrals, although Grotius did not employ that particular term.

[12] In modern terminology, this is called contraband of war. More specifically, the reference is to what came to be called absolute contraband. The problem treated is that of contraband trading by neutrals, i.e., the supply of arms (and related material), as a commercial matter, by third parties not involved in the war. Some contended that this should be lawful, as a matter of freedom of trade; while others contended that such a supply, even if for purely commercial motives, makes the supplier into an ally of the belligerent who purchases the material.

which are of no use in war, as those which minister to pleasure; and others still which are of use both in time of war and at other times, as money, provisions, ships, and naval equipment.[13] Regarding the first class of things, . . . he who supplies an enemy with things necessary for warfare is on the side of the enemy.[14] Things of the second sort give rise to no complaint.

Regarding things of the third sort, useful in both war and peace, we must take into account the conditions of the war. For, if I am unable to protect myself without intercepting the goods which are being sent to the enemy, necessity, as we have elsewhere said, will give me a right to intercept such goods, but with the obligation to make restitution, unless another cause arises.[15] If, now, the enforcement of my right shall be hindered by the supplying of these things, and if he who supplied them has been in a position to know this (for example, in case I should be holding a town under siege or keeping ports under blockade, and a surrender or the conclusion of peace should already be in anticipation), then he will be liable to me for injury culpably inflicted, just as one who releases a debtor from prison or secures his escape, to my detriment. As in the case of the infliction of an injury, his goods may be seized, and ownership over them may be sought, for the purpose of recovering damages.[16]

If he who furnishes supplies has not yet caused me injury, but wished to do so, I shall have the right, through the retention of his goods, to oblige him to give security for the future, by means of hostages, by pledges, or in some other way.

If, moreover, the injustice of my enemy toward me is palpably evident, and the one who furnishes supplies to him strengthens him in a very wicked war, in that case the latter will be responsible for the injury, not only by civil law but also by criminal law, just as one would be who should deliver an obviously guilty party from a judge who is about to inflict punishment. On this ground, it will be permissible to pass upon the furnisher of supplies a sentence which

---

[13] This third category, in later terminology, would be called conditional contraband.

[14] The clear suggestion is that persons who supply absolute contraband to a belligerent are regarded as being themselves belligerents and not neutrals. In other words, the supplying of absolute contraband to a belligerent entailed forfeiture of neutral status. Later international law did not take this view. Instead, it allowed the opposing belligerent to capture and confiscate the contraband goods – but not to inflict any punishment onto the traders, who retained their status as neutrals.

[15] In other words, supplying conditional contraband to a belligerent does not entail a forfeiture of neutral status, as the supply of absolute contraband does. It only gives rise to a right of compulsory purchase of the goods by the opposing belligerent.

[16] The case of interference with a belligerent's besieging of a town actually occurred more frequently regarding towns that were besieged – or blockaded – by sea. It is pointed out that blockade-running by third parties constitutes a violation of the rights of the besieging state, giving rise to a duty to pay compensation.

suits his crime, in accordance with what we have said regarding punishments; within the limits there indicated, he may even be despoiled.[17]

For the reasons which have been stated, those who engage in war usually address public proclamations[18] to other peoples, with the object of making clear both the justice of their cause and the probable hope of enforcing their right.[19]

In this inquiry, we have referred back to the law of nature for the reason that, in historical narratives, we have been unable to find anything established by the volitional law of nations to cover such cases.

6. Ruses in war

So far as the manner of conducting operations is concerned, violence and fright-fulness are particularly suited to wars. The question is often raised, however, whether one may resort to ruses also.... [T]here is no lack of opinions which seem to [answer this question in the negative], and some of these we shall present below. The final conclusion will depend upon the answer to the question whether deceit belongs to the class of things that are always evil, in regard to which the saying is true that one must not do evil that good may come; or whether it is in the category of things which from their very nature are not at all times vicious but which may even happen to be good.

7. On deceit in a negative action[20]

It must be observed, then, that deceit is of one sort in a negative action, of another sort in a positive action.[21]

---

[17] It is asserted that, in the extreme case in which the injustice of one belligerent is 'palpably evident', the providing of contraband of war to that belligerent (or interfering with sieges or blockades of his towns) has serious consequences. For one thing, it gives rise to a liability to compensate the just side. In addition, the suppliers are subject to criminal liability and exposure to punishment, since they are, in effect, aiding and abetting the commission of crime by the unjust belligerent.

[18] Grotius has a long footnote here – the longest by far in the entire treatise – setting out information on neutrality policies of states in recent conflicts. See Appendix 1 for the text of this note.

[19] One of the most important functions served by a formal declaration of war is to give fair notice to neutrals of the dangers that they run in supplying materials to the enemy belligerent.

[20] Another digression commences here, on the subject of the making of false statements generally. Not until Section 17 is there a return to the subject of the conduct of war.

[21] By 'negative action' is meant (as becomes apparent in due course) the withholding of information that another party would wish to have. By 'positive action' is meant the putting out of false information.

8. Two categories of deceit in a positive action

Deceit which consists in a positive action, if it is exhibited in acts, is called pretence; if in words, falsehood. Some persons establish this distinction between the two terms, because they say that words are naturally the signs of thoughts, while acts are not. But the contrary is true, that words by their very nature and apart from the human will have no significance.

If now the assertion is made that the nature of man possesses superiority over that of other living creatures in this, that it can convey to others the ideas of the mind and that words were invented for this purpose, that is true. But it must be added that such conveying of thought is accomplished not by means of words alone but also by signs, as among dumb persons, whether these signs naturally have something in common with the thing signified or whether they possess significance merely by agreement. Similar to these signs are those characters which . . . do not express words formed by the tongue but objects themselves, either from some resemblance, as in the case of hieroglyphic signs, or by mere arbitrary convention, as among the Chinese.

At this point, then, we must introduce another distinction, such as we employed to remove the ambiguity in the term law of nations. For we said that the term 'law of nations' includes both what is approved by separate nations without mutual obligation and what contains a mutual obligation in itself.[22] Words, then, and signs, and the written characters we have mentioned, were invented as a means of expression under a mutual obligation. . . . This is not the case with other things. Hence it comes about that we may avail ourselves of other things, even if we foresee that another person will derive therefrom a false impression.[23] I am speaking of what is intrinsic, not of what is incidental. And so we must give an example, in which no harm follows as a consequence, or in which the harm itself, without consideration of the deceit, is permissible.

An example illustrating the latter case is found in a pretended flight, such as Joshua ordered his men to make so as to take Ai by storm,[24] and such as other

---

[22] This is perhaps Grotius's clearest recognition of the two alternate meanings of the expression 'law of nations'. See Introduction, p. xxx.

[23] Any information that is conveyed by words necessarily involves mutual agreement between the speakers, simply because language itself is the product of man-made convention (or 'mutual obligation'). The contention is that this element of mutual agreement means, by extension, that information which is conveyed by means of language carries a greater obligation to tell the truth (i.e., to act in good faith), in contrast to information which is conveyed by conduct. Consequently, deceit of the enemy by means of conduct is permissible; deceit by means of spoken or written words is not. In the modern law of war, these are known as ruses of war, which are expressly permitted by the laws of war. See Article 24 of the Hague Rules; and Article 37(2) of Protocol I of 1977.

[24] See *Joshua*, 8:3–22. Joshua hid a portion of his army to ambush the enemy, and with the other portion feigned an attack on the city of Ai, followed by a pre-planned retreat. The enemy fell into the trap. The king of Ai was taken alive, but all of his soldiers were killed.

commanders have frequently ordered. For in this instance, we regard the injury which follows as legitimate according to the justice of war. Moreover, flight itself has no significance by agreement, although an enemy may interpret it as a sign of fear; such interpretation the other party is not obliged to guard against in his use of his freedom to go hither and thither, more or less rapidly, and with this or that gesture or outward appearance. In the same category we may class the actions of those of whom we read that they made use of the weapons, standards, uniforms, and tents of their enemies.[25]

All these things are in fact of such a sort that they may be employed by anyone at his discretion, even contrary to custom; for the custom itself was introduced by the choice of individuals, not as it were by universal consent, and such a custom constrains no one.[26]

9. The second sort of deceit

Of greater difficulty is the discussion with respect to those types of deceit which, if I may so say, are in common use among men in commerce and in which falsehood in the true sense is found.

10. The use of an expression in an uncommon sense

Perhaps we may find some way of reconciling... divergent views in a wider or more strict interpretation of the meaning of falsehood.... [W]e do not understand as a falsehood what an ignorant person happens to say;[27] but we are concerned with that which is consciously uttered with a meaning that is at variance with the idea in the mind, whether in understanding or in an act of will. For ideas of the mind are what are primarily and immediately indicated by words and similar signs. [S]o he does not lie who says something untrue which he believes to be true; but he lies who says that which is indeed true but which he believes to be false. Falsity of meaning, therefore, is that which we need to exemplify the general nature of falsehood.

From this it follows that, when any term or phrase has several meanings, that is, may be understood in more than one way, either from common usage, or the practice of an art, or some figure of speech easily understood, then, if the idea

---

[25] Disguising one's own forces in the garb of the enemy has been controversial for centuries. Protocol I of 1977 prohibits the use of enemy flags and uniforms and the like 'while engaging in attacks or in order to shield, favour, protect or impede military operations' (Article 39(2)).

[26] I.e., it may be that certain ruses of war are disallowed by 'custom'. (No example is given.) But any such custom is merely a matter of the *ius gentium* proper, and not of the volitional law of nations. Consequently, acts inconsistent with such a customary practice are nonetheless lawful.

[27] I.e., we are not concerned with inadvertent false statements.

in [the] mind [of the speaker] fits one of these meanings, it is not held to be a lie, even if it is thought that he who hears it will understand it in another way. It is indeed true that the rash employment of such a mode of speech is not to be approved. It may nevertheless be justified by incidental causes, as, for instance, if thereby aid is rendered in the instruction of one who has been entrusted to our care, or in avoiding an unfair question.

On the other hand, a case may arise when it is not only not praiseworthy but even wicked to employ such a mode of speech; as when the glory of God, or the love due to our neighbour, or reverence toward a superior, or the nature of the thing in question requires that everything which is thought in the mind shall be completely revealed. Just so in the case of contracts, we said that that must be made known which the nature of the contract is understood to demand.[28]

11. Falsehood as infringement of the right of another

In order to exemplify the general idea of falsehood, it is necessary that what is spoken, or written, or indicated by signs or gestures, cannot be understood otherwise than in a sense which differs from the thought of him who uses the means of expression. Upon this broader signification, however, a stricter meaning of falsehood must be imposed, carrying some characteristic distinction. This distinction, if we regard the matter aright, at least according to the common view of nations, can be described, we think, as nothing else than a conflict with the existing and continuing right of him to whom the speech or sign is addressed; for it is sufficiently clear that no one lies to himself, however false his statement may be.

By right in this connexion, I do not mean every right without relation to the matter in question, but that which is peculiar to it and connected with it. Now that right is nothing else than the liberty of judgement which, as if by some tacit agreement, men who speak are understood to owe to those with whom they converse.[29] For this is merely that mutual obligation which men had willed to introduce at the time when they determined to make use of speech and similar signs; for without such an obligation the invention of speech would have been void of result.

We require, moreover, that this right be valid and continuing at the time the statement is made; for it may happen that the right has indeed existed, but has been taken away, or will be annulled by another right which supervenes, just as a debt is cancelled by an acceptance or by the cessation of the condition.[30] Then,

---

[28] See p. 205 above.

[29] A person who speaks is said, somewhat obscurely, to 'owe' to his listener the 'right' of 'liberty of judgement'. In plainer words, a speaker owes to his listener a duty to speak with sufficient plainness and truth to enable the listener to form a view, in his own mind, of the substance of what is on the speaker's mind when speaking.

[30] A debt can be cancelled by 'acceptance' when the creditor acknowledges that it is no longer owing. This might be because the debt was duly paid. But there can also be a

further, it is required that the right which is infringed belong to him with whom we converse, and not to another; just as in the case of contracts also, injustice arises only from the infringement of a right of the contracting parties.[31]

Moreover, the right of which we have spoken may be abrogated by the express consent of him with whom we are dealing, as when one says that he will speak falsely and the other permits it.[32] In like manner, it may be cancelled by tacit consent, or consent assumed on reasonable grounds, or by the opposition of another right which, in the common judgement of all men, is much more cogent.

The right understanding of these points will supply to us many inferences, which will be of no small help in reconciling the differences in the views which have been cited above.

12. On speaking falsehoods to infants and insane persons

The first inference is that, even if something which has a false significance is said to an infant or insane person, no blame for falsehood attaches thereto. . . . The reason is by no means far to seek. [S]ince infants and insane persons do not have liberty of judgement, it is impossible for wrong to be done them in respect to such liberty.

13. Falsehood heard by an eavesdropper

The second inference is that, so long as the person to whom the talk is addressed is not deceived, if a third party draws a false impression therefrom, there is no falsehood. There is no falsehood in relation to him to whom the utterance is directed because his liberty remains unimpaired. His case is like that of persons to whom a fable is told when they are aware of its character, or those to whom figurative language is used in irony or in hyperbole. . . . There is no falsehood, again, in respect to him who chances to hear what is said; the conversation is not being held with him; consequently, there is no obligation toward him. Indeed, if he forms for himself an opinion from what is said not to him, but to another, he has something which he can credit to himself, not to another. In fine, if, so far as he is concerned, we wish to form a correct judgement, the conversation is not a conversation, but something that may mean anything at all.

---

unilateral relinquishment by the creditor of his rights. It is cancelled by 'the cessation of the condition' if the debt was only owed subject to the occurrence or existence of some condition or state of affairs, which then ceased to operate.

[31] I.e., contracts, by their nature, confer rights and duties only onto the contracting parties, and not onto third parties, a point not made very explicitly. It is apparent from the following discussion how seriously Grotius takes the analogy between a conversation and a contract.

[32] An example would be an arrangement for the narration of a fictional tale by one person to another.

14. When the hearer wishes to be deceived

The third inference is that, whenever it is certain that he to whom the conversation is addressed will not be annoyed at the infringement of his liberty in judging, or rather will be grateful therefor, because of some advantage which will follow; . . . a falsehood in the strict sense, that is a harmful falsehood, is not perpetrated;[33] just so, a man does not commit theft who, with the presumed consent of the owner, uses up some trifling thing in order that he may thereby secure for the owner a great advantage.[34] In these matters which are so certain, a presumed wish is taken as one that is expressed. Besides, in such cases it is evident that no wrong is done to one who desires it. It seems, therefore, that he does not do wrong who comforts a sick friend by persuading him of what is not true.[35] . . . However, it is to be observed that, in this sort of falsehood, the infringement upon the judgement is of less account because it is usually confined to the moment, and the truth is revealed a little later.

15. A speaker making use of a superior right over one subject to himself

A fourth inference, akin to the foregoing, applies to the case when one who has a right that is superior to all the rights of another makes use of this right either for his own or for the public good.[36] This especially Plato seems to have had in mind when he conceded the right of saying what is false to those having authority.[37]

16. Falsehood to save an innocent life

A fifth inference may be applicable to cases where the life of an innocent person, or something else of equal importance, cannot be saved without falsehood, and another person can in no other way be diverted from the accomplishment of a wicked crime.

---

[33] An example might be a witness to a crime who falsely tells the criminal that he saw nothing, thereby increasing the criminal's chance of securing an acquittal. In such a case, Grotius contends, no 'falsehood in the strict sense' is spoken to the criminal.

[34] An example might be a person who breaks into his neighbour's house during the neighbour's absence and takes a fire extinguisher, which he uses to put out a fire in the neighbour's house.

[35] This seems doubtful, as it would appear that the sick friend's 'liberty of judgement' is being infringed.

[36] An example might be a sovereign who, in wartime, misrepresents the position and strength of the enemy forces to his subjects, in the interest of shoring up public morale and thereby enhancing the strength of the country.

[37] Plato, *The Republic*, III.389.

17. On falsehood spoken in the presence of enemies[38]

The principle which the learned generally lay down, that it is permissible to speak falsely to an enemy, goes beyond what we have just said. Accordingly, to the rule forbidding a lie, the exception [was commonly made amongst early writers allowing lies] against enemies.

[This principle does] not meet with the approval of the school of writers of recent times.... But [even the more recent writers allow] unspoken interpretations,[39] which are so repugnant to all practice that one may question whether it would not be more satisfactory to admit to certain persons the use of falsehoods in the cases we have mentioned, or in some of them (for I assume that nothing has been settled here), than so indiscriminately to exempt such interpretations from the definition of falsehood. Thus when they say 'I do not know', it may be understood as 'I do not know so as to tell you'; and when they say 'I have not', it may be understood as 'so as to give you'; and other things of this sort, which the common sense of mankind repudiates, and which, if admitted, will offer no obstacle to our saying that whoever affirms anything denies it himself, and whoever denies affirms.

It is assuredly quite true that, in general, there is no word which may not have a doubtful meaning; for all words, in addition to the significance which is called that of the first notion, have another of a second notion, and this significance varies in the different arts; moreover, words have different meanings also in metaphor and other figures of speech.

Again, I do not approve of the view of those who apply the term jokes to falsehoods which are uttered with a particularly serious expression and tone.

18. On statements containing a promise

We must, however, bear in mind that what we have said regarding falsehood is to be applied to assertions, and such indeed as injure no one but a public enemy, but not to promises. For by a promise, as we have just begun to say, a new and particular right is conferred upon him to whom the promise is made. This holds true even among enemies, without any exception arising from the hostility existing at the time. It holds true not only in the case of promises actually expressed, but also in the case of those that are implied, as we shall show in discussing the demand for a parley when we come to the part that deals with the observing of good faith in warfare.[40]

---

[38] There is now a return to the subject at hand, the permissibility of conveying falsehoods to the enemy side in wartime.

[39] I.e., unspoken qualification or conditions attached to statements. Grotius proceeds to give examples.

[40] See p. 418 below.

19. On falsehood in oaths

This also must be repeated from the portion of our foregoing discussion which dealt with the subject of oaths:[41] that whether the oath is assertive or promissory, it has the force to exclude all exceptions which might be sought in the person of him with whom we are dealing. The reason is that an oath establishes a relation not only with a man, but also with God, to whom we are bound by the oath, even if no right arises for the man. In the same place, we have furthermore stated that, in an oath, we do not, as we do in other speech, admit that interpretations [which have only a slight degree of plausibility] may be put upon words, in order to absolve us from falsehood; but we do require that the truth be spoken with the meaning which a man listening is supposed to understand in perfect good faith. Obviously, then, we must abhor the impiety of those who did not hesitate to assert that it is proper to deceive men by oaths just as boys do by means of dice.

20. On the nobility of refraining from falsehood to an enemy

We know, too, that certain types of fraud, which we have said were naturally permitted, have been rejected by some peoples and persons. But this does not happen because they view such means of deception as unjust, but because of a remarkable loftiness of mind and, in some cases, because of confidence in their strength.

21. Forcing a person to do what is right for us but not for him

To the conduct of operations, this principle also applies, that is not permissible to force or to entice anyone to anything which may not be permissible for him to do. The following may serve as examples. It is not permissible for a subject to slay his king, nor to surrender towns without public consent, nor to despoil his fellow citizens. Therefore it is not permissible to influence a subject, who remains such, to do these things. For he who gives to another cause to sin always sins himself as well. It is not enough to urge in reply that, for him who forces such a man to a crime, an act of this kind, as the killing of an enemy, is legitimate.[42] The deed it is in fact permissible for him to compass, but not in this way.[43]

---

[41] See p. 215 above.

[42] I.e., inducing another to commit a sin, in furtherance of one's war effort (i.e., just war effort) seems, at first glance, to be no worse than the outright killing of persons on the enemy side, which is clearly lawful.

[43] It is conceded that acts such as the slaying of the enemy ruler or the despoiling of enemy nationals are permissible – but only if they are done by the just side itself, on

22. On assistance voluntarily offered

The case is different when, for a thing which is permissible for him, a person avails himself of the help of one who does wrong voluntarily and not at his instigation.

its own initiative, and not if enemy subjects are induced to do them on behalf of the just side. For the treatment of assassination as a technique of war specifically, see p. 354 below.

2

How by the law of nations the goods of subjects may be held for the debt of their rulers; and therein, on reprisals

1. Persons bound by acts of others in natural law

Let us proceed to principles derived from the law of nations. These principles relate in part to war in general, and in part to a particular aspect of war. Let us begin with the general considerations. By the strict law of nature, no one is bound by another's act, except one who inherits his property; for the principle that property should be transferred with its obligations dates from the establishment of proprietary rights.[1]

The debt of the corporation, moreover, is not a debt of the individuals, ... especially if the corporation has property; for the rest the members of a corporation are bound not as individuals, but as a part of the corporate body.[2] ... Hence in the Roman Law, ... no member of a village [could] be held for the debts of other villagers; and ... no property of one person [could] be sued for the debts of others, even if public debts.

2. The position of the volitional law of nations

Although what has just been stated is true, nevertheless by the volitional law of nations, there could be introduced, and appears to have been introduced, [an exception]: for what any civil society, or its head, ought to furnish, whether for itself directly, or because it has bound itself for the debt of another – those who are subject to such a society or its head, together with their corporeal or incorporeal possessions, are held and made liable. This principle, furthermore, is the outgrowth of a certain necessity, because otherwise a great licence to cause injury would arise. [T]he reason is that, in many cases, the goods of rulers cannot so easily be seized as those of private persons, who are more numerous. This [modification of natural law] then finds place among those rights which ... have been established by civilised nations in response to the demands of usage and human needs.[3]

---

[1] Again, the Roman-law principle of universal succession is the conceptual model.
[2] *Digest*, 3.4.7.1 (Ulpian).
[3] What is envisaged is that a private citizen commits a wrong against a foreigner, with the citizen's ruler then committing the additional wrong of refusing to provide just

This principle, however, is not so in conflict with nature that it could not have been introduced by custom and tacit consent, since sureties are bound without any cause, merely by their consent.[4] It was hoped that members of the same society would be able, through mutual relations, to obtain justice from one another, and provide for their indemnification, more easily than foreigners, to whom in many places slight consideration is given. Hence the advantage derived from this obligation was common to all peoples, so that he who might now be burdened by it at another time might in turn be relieved.[5]

We see that the same right is invoked also where a state of perfect war has not yet been reached, but where nevertheless there is need of an enforcement of a right by violent means, that is, by means of an imperfect war.[6]

redress to the foreigner. In such a case, the injured foreigner could obtain from his own sovereign a licence, known appropriately as a 'letter of reprisal'. With this letter, he could proceed, in the jurisdiction of the ruler who granted it, to take property from subjects of the wrong-doing sovereign, up to the amount sufficient to compensate him for the loss that he suffered. This seems at first sight unfair, as Grotius is aware, since the victims of the reprisal are themselves entirely innocent of any wrong-doing. But there is 'a certain necessity' in allowing the practice, on the ground that an aggrieved foreigner cannot readily recoup his loss by seizing the ruler's goods. So he should be allowed to obtain compensation by seizing, instead, goods belonging to the subjects of the wrong-doing ruler – including, of course, subjects who had nothing whatever to do with the commission of the injury.

[4] It is suggested – though only in passing – that there is an alternative rationale for making the property of subjects liable to seizure for debts owed by their sovereign. That is, that the subjects could be deemed to be sureties for their ruler (or the equivalent thereof). In that event, it could be said that they lose their property by their own consent, in the manner of sureties in debt cases in private law. In fact, Grotius does not develop this idea, choosing to rely instead on 'a certain necessity' to justify subjecting subjects' property to reprisals. See, however, p. 342 below, in which Grotius does adopt the suretyship argument in the context of justifying the capture of the private property of enemy subjects in wartime. He does not explain why he relies on this argument in the one case but not the other, since both involve the taking of subjects' property because of wrongs committed by their sovereign. One difference is that reprisals, discussed here, occur in peacetime and capture of enemy property in wartime. But Grotius nowhere explains why, or whether, this difference should be seen as a fundamental one.

[5] It is pointed out that allowing reprisals against innocent subjects (in the form of loss of property) is not really as harsh as might first appear, because the innocent citizens whose property is taken should be able to obtain indemnification, through legal process, against the original wrong-doer. Being a victim of reprisals was obviously undesirable from the standpoint of the person concerned. But Grotius states that persons who are victims of reprisals at one point in time may be beneficiaries of them at others, so that a rough justice will be done.

[6] By an 'imperfect war' is meant a 'war' waged not by the society as a whole, but only by certain members of it, under government licence. More specifically, the reference is to the use of force by holders of letters of marque, which were authorisations to capture goods on the high seas belonging to persons of a designated nationality. Entitlement to be issued a letter of marque was based on a claim that the holder had

3. An example in the seizure of persons

One form of the enforcement of right regarding which I am speaking was what the Athenians called 'seizure of men'. Of this, a law of Attica said: 'If anyone die by a violent death, for his sake it shall be right for his relatives and next of kin to proceed to apprehend men, until either the penalty has been paid for the murder, or the murderers are given up. Such seizure may extend to three persons, and no more.'[7] Here we see that, for the debt of the state, which is bound to punish its subjects who have injured others, there is put under obligation a certain incorporeal right of its subjects, that is, their liberty of remaining where they wish and of doing what they wish; in consequence such subjects are temporarily in servitude, until the state does that which it is bound to do, that is, until it punishes the one who is guilty.

Similar to this right of seizure [exercised within a given society] is the right of detention of citizens of another state in which a manifest wrong has been done to a national, in order to secure [a] recovery.[8]

4. An example in the seizure of goods

Another form of the enforcement of right by violence is 'seizure of goods', or 'the taking of pledges between different peoples'. That is called by the more modern jurists the right of reprisals; by the Saxons and Angles 'withernam', and by the French, among whom such seizure is ordinarily authorised by the king, 'letters of marque'. This enforcement of right occurs, as the jurists say, where a right is denied.[9]

5. Lawfulness of seizure after a right has been denied

Seizure by violence may be understood to be warranted not only in case a judgement cannot be obtained against a criminal or a debtor within a reasonable time, but also if in a very clear case (for in a doubtful case the presumption is in favour of those who have been chosen by the state to render judgement),

suffered a prior wrong from a national of the designated 'enemy' state, which had not been redressed in the courts of that state. The object of such an imperfect war was not to subject the other state to a complete military defeat, but only to enable the letter holder to obtain property sufficient to compensate him for the wrong that he had suffered.

[7] Demosthenes, *Against Aristocrates*, 82.

[8] By 'recovery' is meant compensation for the wrong in question. It is envisaged that the wronged foreign national will kidnap some fellow subjects of the original wrong-doer and hold them as hostages pending the payment of compensation.

[9] The most important feature of this right is that it is exercised not against the actual wrong-doer, but rather against surrogates of some kind (i.e., against fellow nationals of the actual wrong-doer).

judgement has been rendered in a way manifestly contrary to law; for the authority of the judge has not the same force over foreigners as over subjects.[10]

Even among subjects, such a [wrong] decision [by a judge excusing a debtor from payment to his creditor] does not cancel a true obligation.[11] . . . There is this difference, that subjects cannot legally hinder by force the execution of a judgement even if it is unjust, or assert their rights by force against it, because of the effectiveness of the authority over them. But foreigners have the right of compulsion, which they may not use, however, so long as they can obtain what is theirs by a judgement.[12] The principle, therefore, was not introduced by nature, but has been widely accepted in practice,[13] that for such a cause the persons, or movable property, of the subjects of him who does not render justice, may be seized.

6. Whether such seizure warrants the taking of human life

That for such a cause the lives of innocent subjects are liable, has perhaps been believed among some peoples, because they supposed that every man has in himself a full right over his life, and that it was possible to transfer this to the state. That supposition, as we have elsewhere said, is by no means capable of proof, nor is it in harmony with a more sound theology.[14]

Nevertheless it may happen that those who wish by force to hinder the enforcement of a right may be killed, not intentionally but accidentally. But if this can be foreseen, . . . we ought rather to surrender the furthering of the right, in accordance with the law of love. According to this law, particularly for Christians, the life of a man ought to be of greater value than our property.

---

[10] I.e., in cases in which judges hand down judgments that are 'manifestly contrary to law', it is the duty of subjects to submit. Foreigners, however, are entitled to engage in self-help measures, such as reprisals, to rectify the injury done. The injury is termed, in modern international law, denial of justice.

[11] See *Digest*, 20.5.12.1 (Tryphoninus).

[12] The point is that the handing down of a manifestly unjust judgment by a judge does not abrogate the rights of the victimised party under natural law. It does, however – in the case of a subject – bar the aggrieved litigant from resorting to force to resist or overturn the judgment. The only possible remedy for the disappointed litigant is the possibility of set-off, if some assets of his opponent should happen to come into his hands. In contrast, a foreigner has the right of resorting to force, by way of reprisals; to obtain relief (provided of course that no judicial relief, such as an appeal to a higher court, is available to him).

[13] I.e., this right of reprisal, or forcible self-help against fellow nationals of wrong-doers, is part of either the *ius gentium* or the volitional law of nations, but not of natural law. This is one of the most important illustrations of a departure from natural law which is effectuated by human law.

[14] See p. 297 above. The right to capture the persons of fellow nationals of the wrong-doer is a right only to hold them as captives (i.e., as hostages). It cannot entail a right to kill them because those captured persons do not possess a legal right to kill themselves. As a consequence, no such right can be transferred to their captors.

7. The distinction regarding this matter between municipal law and the law of nations

In this matter, no less than in others, we must take care not to confuse the things which properly belong to the law of nations and those which are established by municipal law or treaties between peoples.[15] By the law of nations, all subjects of him who does the injury are liable to the furnishing of sureties, provided they are subjects from a permanent cause, whether native or immigrant, and not persons who are present anywhere for the purpose of travel or for a brief residence. The furnishing of pledges is treated after the manner of burdens which are imposed in order to pay the public debts, and from which those are immune who are only temporarily subject to the laws of the place. However, ambassadors are excepted by the law of nations from the number of subjects, ... and their goods also are [exempt from seizure by way of reprisal].

By the municipal law of states, however, the persons of women and children are often excepted; and in fact, even the property of those who are engaged in literary pursuits or come to carry on trade. By the law of nations, individuals possess the right of taking sureties, as at Athens, in the seizure of men. By the municipal law of many countries, this right is ordinarily sought in some cases from the supreme authority, in other cases from judges.

By the law of nations, ownership is acquired over seized goods by the mere act of seizure, up to the limit of the debt and expenditure, in such a way that the residue shall be restored.[16] By the municipal law, the parties concerned are usually summoned, and afterwards by public authority the property is sold or assigned to those who are affected. But for these and other topics, reference should be made to those who discuss the municipal codes; on this subject [see] particularly Bartolus, who has written on reprisals.[17]

A further statement I shall add, because it concerns the mollification of this law, which is in itself sufficiently rigorous. Those who, by not paying what they owe or by not furnishing satisfaction, have given occasion for the taking of sureties, by natural and divine law are bound to make good the damages to others, who for that reason have incurred a loss.

---

[15] I.e., we must not confuse the *ius gentium* proper with either of two other things: municipal or domestic laws of individual states, or the volitional law of nations. On the *ius gentium* proper, see the Introduction, at p. xxx.

[16] By 'the limit of debt and expenditure' is meant the amount of the loss incurred from the original wrongful act. This amount is the ceiling of the amount of property that can be taken by way of reprisal. Anything taken above that limit must be restored.

[17] Bartolus composed a notable treatise on reprisals in the fourteenth century. Its substance was largely replicated in John of Legnano's *Tractatus de Bello, de Represaliis et de Duello* (c. 1360).

3

On war that is lawful or public according to the law of nations; and therein, on the declaration of war

1. A public war according to the law of nations

In a previous passage,[1] we began to say that, by authors of repute, a war is often called lawful not from the cause from which it arises, nor, as is done in other cases, from the importance of its exploits, but because of certain peculiar legal consequences. Of what sort a lawful war is, however, will best be perceived from the definition of enemies given by the Roman jurists. 'Enemies are those who in the name of the state declare war, upon us, or upon whom we in the name of the state declare war; others are brigands and robbers', says Pomponius.[2]

It needs only to be noted further that we may understand that anyone who has the supreme authority in a state may take the place of the Roman people in our illustration. 'An enemy', says Cicero, 'is the one that has a state, a senate, a treasury, the agreement and concord of the citizens, and the power, if the course of events leads thereto, to conclude peace and an alliance'.[3]

2. The distinction between a people, and pirates or brigands

[A] commonwealth or state does not immediately cease to be such if it commits an injustice, even as a body; and a gathering of pirates and brigands is not a state, even if they do perhaps mutually maintain a sort of equality, without which no association can exist. The reason is that pirates and brigands are banded together for wrong-doing; the members of a state, even if at times they are not free from crime, nevertheless have been united for the enjoyment of rights, and they do render justice to foreigners. If the treatment of members of other states is not in all respects according to the law of nature, which . . . has become partly obscured among many peoples, it is at least according to agreements entered into with each state or in accordance with customs.

4. Need of sovereign power for public war

What persons have the sovereign power, we have already stated.[4] Hence it may be understood that, if any possess the sovereign power in part, they may to that extent wage a lawful war.

---

[1] See p. 45.   [2] *Digest*, 50.16.118 (Pomponius).   [3] Cicero, *Philippics*, IV.14.
[4] See p. 51 above.

5. Requirement of a declaration of war

That a war may be lawful in the sense indicated,[5] it is not enough that it be waged by sovereign powers on each side. It is also necessary . . . that it should be publicly declared, and in fact proclaimed so publicly that the notification of this declaration be made by one of the parties to the other.[6]

6. Declaration of war according to the law of nature, and of nations

To understand the foregoing passages, and others dealing with the declaration of war, we must carefully distinguish what is due according to the law of nature, what is not due by nature but is honourable, what is required by the law of nations to secure the effects peculiar to this law, and what, in addition, is derived from the particular institutions of certain peoples. In a case where either an attack is being warded off,[7] or a penalty is demanded from the very person who has done wrong, no declaration is required by the law of nature. . . . Nor more necessary, by the law of nature, is a declaration of war in case an owner wishes to seize what belongs to him.[8]

But whenever one thing is seized in place of another, or the property of a debtor is taken for his debt, and all the more if one wishes to take possession of the property of [subjects of a wrong-doing sovereign], then a demand for settlement is required, to establish the fact that it is impossible in any other way to obtain what is ours or what is owed to us. For this is not a primary right, but a secondary and vicarious right, as we have elsewhere explained.[9] Thus, . . . before

[5] I.e., in the sense that all of the required formalities have been complied with.
[6] It is not being contended that a declaration of war is necessary for a war to be just according to natural law – i.e., a declaration is not a precondition to the lawfulness of the war. The lawfulness, per se, of the war is determined by the presence or absence of one (or more) of the three just causes that Grotius set out earlier. A declaration should be regarded instead as an additional duty imposed upon the just side. Grotius goes on to explain why this additional duty is important: because a declaration of war gives rise to certain key legal effects, chiefly to the acquisition of legal title to captured property.
[7] This reference is to self-defence in the narrow sense of fending off an ongoing attack, rather than to defensive war. But see section 12 below for a treatment of this question from the standpoint of the law of nations.
[8] In effect, then, a declaration of war is required only for the remaining two categories of just war: defensive war (against a threatened wrong); and punitive war (punishing the enemy for some prior wrong).
[9] A primary right is a right against an actual wrong-doer. A secondary right is a right against a surrogate. The classic example of a secondary right in action is a reprisal, as explained at p. 338 above. But warfare is also typically the exercise of a secondary right too, since the persons against whom armed force is used (i.e., the enemy soldiers) are typically not the ones who committed the original injury which brought on the war. Another important example of secondary action is the capture and confiscation of property belonging to private parties on the enemy side. It is

the possessor of sovereign power is attacked for the debt or crime of a subject, a demand for settlement should be made, which may place him in the wrong [if he refuses to make reparation], and in consequence of which he may be held either to be causing us loss or to be himself committing a crime, according to the principles which have previously been discussed.[10]

But even in case the law of nature does not require that such a demand be made, still it is honourable and praiseworthy to make it, in order that, for instance, we may avoid giving offence, or that the wrong may be atoned for by repentance and compensation.[11]

[B]y the law of nations, a proclamation is required in all cases in order to [give rise to these secondary rights]; not, however, from both parties but from either one.[12]

7. A declaration of war is sometimes conditional, sometimes absolute

Now the declaration of war is either conditional or absolute. It is conditional when it is joined with a demand for restitution.[13] ... An absolute declaration is what is called in particular a proclamation or edict. This is made when one party either has begun hostilities ... or has himself committed crimes that call for punishment.[14]

Sometimes, indeed, an absolute declaration follows one that is conditional, although this is not necessary but superfluous.[15]

important to appreciate – although it is not clearly stated here – that these secondary effects are conferred by the law of nations, not of nature.

[10] In such a case, the sovereign becomes a guilty party in his own right if he fails to compel the subject to discharge the debt owing the foreigner. The actual debtor is guilty for his failure to pay the debt, or to pay compensation for a crime that he committed; while the sovereign is guilty of the separate offence of denial of justice, for his failure to compel the subject to do his duty. Note that the demand made of the sovereign to do justice is not a declaration of war. Once the demand is refused, the sovereign becomes a wrong-doer in his own right – and, as such, may be attacked without a declaration of war, as Grotius has just explained (i.e., an attack on the sovereign is now an exercise of a primary right and not merely of a secondary one).

[11] On the avoidance of war by acquiescence in the loss of rights, see p. 311 above.

[12] The law of nature allows dispensing with declarations of war in the cases identified. But the law of nations requires a declaration in *all* cases in which it is desired that the various secondary rights are to be exercised. A declaration is required only by one party, however, not by both.

[13] In such a case, the sovereign is being given a choice: of providing restitution, or of fighting a war. This became known as an ultimatum.

[14] It is unclear why these two circumstances are singled out for issuing an absolute declaration.

[15] In this case, an ultimatum will have been delivered, with the sovereign then refusing to provide the satisfaction demanded. That refusal, on its own, suffices to create a state of war, in Grotius's view.

Further proof of the superfluity of this formality is found in the fact that war is often declared by both parties. . . . although it is sufficient that such a declaration be made by either one party or the other.

8. Elements in declarations of war that pertain to municipal law only

To the customs and institutions of certain peoples, moreover, and not to the law of nations, belong the use of the herald's staff among the Greeks; the sacred herbs and bloody spear used first by the Aequicolae, then by the Romans, who followed their example; the renunciation of any existing friendship or alliance; the period of thirty days set after the demand for restitution; the hurling of the spear the second time; and other formalities of this sort which should not be confused with those that properly belong to the law of nations.

9. Declaration of war as encompassing subjects and allies

Furthermore, a war declared against him who holds the sovereign authority in a state is held to be declared at the same time not only upon all his subjects, but also upon all who will join him as allies in such a way as to become an accession to him.

10. Whether a declaration of war includes those who aid the enemy

If, on the conclusion of a war declared against one who holds the sovereign power, another people or king is to be attacked, because of the aid that they have furnished, a new declaration of war will have to be made in order to meet the requirements of the law of nations. For in such a case, the people or king is now not regarded as an accessory, but as a principal.[16]

11. Why a declaration of war is required

Furthermore, the reason why nations required a declaration for the kind of war which we have called lawful according to the law of nations was not that which some adduce, with the purpose that nothing should be done secretly or deceitfully, for this pertains to an exhibition of courage rather than to law, just as certain nations are said to have even appointed the date and place of battle.[17] The purpose was, rather, that the fact might be established with certainty that war was being waged not by private initiative but by the will of each of the two peoples or of their heads. From this consideration arise the peculiar effects

[16] The situation envisaged is that a third state, on its own initiative, aided the losing side in a war, but without becoming an ally.
[17] Gentili, *On the Law of* War, 2.1. Gentili also likened a declaration of war to a formal demand for redress in litigation.

which do not develop in a war against brigands, nor in a war which a king wages against his subjects.

12. The effects referred to are not found in other wars

What certain writers point out and teach by citing examples, to the effect that even in . . . wars [against brigands or rebellious subjects, property of the enemies which] is seized belongs to those who take it,[18] is indeed true, but only from one standpoint: that of the law of nature. It is not true by the volitional law of nations, since this concerns nations only, not persons who have no existence as a nation or form a part of a nation.[19]

The writers in question err in this also, that they think that a war undertaken for the defence of one's person or property does not require a declaration.[20] Such a war does require a declaration, not indeed of itself, but for the sake of those [secondary] effects of which we have begun to speak,[21] and which we shall shortly explain.

13. Whether war may be waged simultaneously with its declaration

This also is not true, that war cannot be waged at once upon being declared. . . . By the law of nations, in fact, no interval of time is required after the declaration. Nevertheless, it may happen that, from the character of the affair, by the law of nature some time may be required, as when restitution or punishment for a guilty person has been sought, and this has not been refused. In such a case, time must be granted in order that that which has been sought may be properly performed.

---

[18] See, for example, Ayala, *On the Law of War and on the Duties Connected with War and on Military Discipline*, 1.5.1.

[19] These are now called non-state actors. They are not – and cannot be – parties to the volitional law of nations, because that law, by definition, is a law between nations. Non-state actors are, however, covered by natural law.

[20] The writer cited as holding this view is Gentili, *On the Law of War*, 2.1.

[21] The statement that a declaration of war is not required 'of itself' means that a declaration is not a necessary prerequisite for the war's being a just one. As a result, force can lawfully be employed without a declaration. This is a principle of the law of nature. A declaration of war is needed, however, to trigger various 'secondary effects' of war, which are governed by the law of nations rather than the law of nature. The principal secondary effect is the right to capture enemy-owned property without limit. Enemy-owned property, according to *natural* law, can be captured only in an enforcement war, and only up to the amount which is owed to the just side. The law of nations allows more leeway, in two crucial respects that are relevant here: first, it allows capture of enemy property in a defensive war as well as an enforcement war; and second, it allows capture of enemy property without any quantitative limit. But in order to benefit from this greater latitude given by the law of nations, a declaration of war must be issued.

14. Whether a declaration of war is required in case of violation of the right of embassy

Even if the right of embassy has been violated,[22] there will not cease to be need of a declaration of war, for the sake of the effects of which I speak. However, it will be sufficient that this be made in a way in which it may be done with safety, as by means of writing, for example; for custom sanctions the use of writing for both summonses and other notices to be served in unsafe places.[23]

[22] I.e., in cases of the violation of the privileges and immunities of diplomats.
[23] The concern expressed here is that, in cases of violations of diplomatic immunities, it will be unduly risky to communicate a declaration of war to the wrong-doing side. Ordinarily, an envoy will be expected to convey the declaration; but in such a case as this one, by its nature, the declaring state would fear for the envoy's safety. Some other mode of communication, therefore, is reasonable in such a situation.

4

On the right of killing enemies in a public war, and on other violence against the person

1. The effects of a public war

[A] war declared between two peoples, or the heads of two peoples, has certain particular effects which do not arise from the nature of war itself.[1]

2. Variant meanings of the word 'permissible'

[S]ometimes that is said to be permissible which is right from every point of view and is free from reproach, even if there is something else which might more honourably be done. . . . Thus it is lawful to contract marriage; but, for a holy purpose, the chastity of celibacy is more worthy of praise. . . . Also, to marry a second time is lawful; but it is more honourable to be content with one marriage.

In another sense, however, something is said to be permissible, not because it can be done without violence to right conduct and rules of duty, but because among men it is not liable to punishment.[2] In this sense, fornication is permitted among many peoples. . . . In this sense we often see what is permitted contrasted with what is right.

3. Public war as granting impunity for certain acts

With this restriction, therefore, it is permitted to harm an enemy, both in his person and in his property;[3] that is, it is permissible not merely for him who wages war for a just cause, and who injures within that limit – a permission

---

[1] This refers to the various secondary rights and effects, to which reference was made in the previous chapter. To say that these do not 'arise from the nature of war itself' means that they are not a feature of war considered from the standpoint of the law of nature. They are products of the law of nations instead.

[2] I.e., it is not liable to punishment by human authorities.

[3] 'This restriction' refers to acts being permissible only in the lesser sense of being free of human punishment.

which we said at the beginning of this book was granted by the law of nature – but for either side indiscriminately.[4]

As a consequence, he who happens to be caught in another's territory cannot for that reason be punished as a murderer or a thief, and war cannot be waged upon him by another on the pretext of such an act.[5]

4. Why such effects have been introduced

The reason why such effects met with the approval of nations was this. To undertake to decide regarding the justice of a war between two peoples had been dangerous for other peoples, who were on this account involved in a foreign war;[6] ... Furthermore, even in a lawful war, from external indications it can hardly be adequately known what is the just limit of [defensive war], of recovering what is one's own or of inflicting punishments. [I]n consequence, it has seemed altogether preferable to leave decisions in regard to such matters to the scruples of the belligerents rather than to have recourse to the judgements of others.[7]

In addition to this effect of permissibility, that is of impunity, there is another, that of ownership,[8] which we shall discuss later.

5. Testimony regarding these effects

Moreover, that licence to injure, which we have now begun to consider, extends in the first place to persons. [I]n regard to it, there are many evidences in writers of authority.... In general, killing is called a right of war.... [By right of war is here meant not only the commission of acts which are] free ... from all blame, but [also acts which merely qualify for] immunity from punishment as I have mentioned.

---

[4] This is one of the most important theses of the book: that according to the volitional law of nations, both sides are equally entitled to commit acts of war (such as the capture of enemy property). This is in contrast to the law of nature, which permits the capture of enemy property only to the just side, and only to the amount necessary to compensate for whatever wrong the unjust side had committed.

[5] The reference is apparently to a soldier who is captured while operating in enemy territory. The soldier is not subject to the domestic criminal law of the enemy state, even though he is physically present in it.

[6] Third states become 'involved' in a foreign war if they form and act upon a judgement as to which side in the conflict is just and which is unjust.

[7] By 'the judgements of others' is meant judgements made from (as it were) the sidelines by third states, once a war was under way.

[8] One key effect of the application of the law of nations to warfare is what Grotius calls 'permissibility', meaning the entitlement of both parties to resort to war and to be treated as doing so justly – if only in the sense of not incurring punishment from humans. Another very important effect, rather cryptically referred to as 'ownership', refers (as will be seen) to the right to capture and take title to enemy private property.

6. The right to kill and injure all who are in the territory of the enemy

Furthermore, this right of doing what is permissible has a wide application. In the first place, [the right to kill and injure the enemy in war] extends not only to those who actually bear arms, or are subjects of him that stirs up the war, but in addition to all persons who are in the enemy's territory. . . . The reason is that injury may be feared from such persons also; and this is sufficient, in a prolonged and general war, to give rise to the right which we are discussing. . . . At any rate what I have said is beyond all dispute true of foreigners who enter hostile territory after a war has commenced and they are aware of it.

7. Regarding foreigners who have entered the enemy's country before the outbreak of war

[F]oreigners who have gone to a country in a period prior to the war, after the lapse of a moderate time, in which they could have departed, are apparently to be regarded as enemies[9] according to the law of nations.

8. Where injury may be inflicted upon enemies

Now those who are truly subjects of the enemy . . . may in respect to their persons be lawfully injured in any place whatsoever, according to the law of nations.[10] For when war is declared upon anyone, it is at the same time declared upon the men of his people. . . . Moreover, according to the law of nations, anyone who is an enemy may be attacked anywhere. . . . Such persons therefore may be slain with impunity in their own land, in the land of an enemy, on land under the jurisdiction of no one or on the sea.

   The fact that it is not permissible to slay or injure such persons in territory which is in a state of peace is based on a right derived not from their persons but from the right of him who exercises sovereignty there.[11] For political societies were able to agree that no violent measures should be taken against persons who are in territory at peace except by recourse to legal proceedings.[12]

---

[9] I.e., to be assimilated to nationals of the country in which they reside – with the effect that they become lawful targets of war.

[10] Grotius is speaking carelessly here; for he shortly goes on to say that an enemy cannot be killed in the territory of a neutral power. What he means (as becomes apparent) is that no legal wrong is done to the enemy national *himself* if he is slain in neutral territory.

[11] In other words, killing an enemy in the territory of a neutral state is not a wrongful act vis-à-vis the enemy himself. But it is a wrong against the neutral sovereign, as a violation of his sovereign rights over his own territory.

[12] I.e., it is a rule of the volitional law of nations that violence cannot be inflicted upon enemies in neutral territory.

Where tribunals exist, regard is had to the deserts of individuals, and that promiscuous right of inflicting injury, which we say arises as between enemies, there ceases.[13]

9. Whether the right to inflict injury extends over infants and women

But to return to the point under consideration: how far this right to inflict injury extends may be perceived from the fact that the slaughter even of infants and of women is made with impunity, and that this is included in the law of war.

10. Whether the right to inflict injury extends over captives

Not even captives are exempt from this right to inflict injury.... So far as the law of nations is concerned, the right of killing such slaves, that is, captives taken in war, is not precluded at any time, although it is restricted, now more, now less, by the laws of [individual] states.

12. Whether the right to inflict injury extends over those who have surrendered unconditionally

But you may read also that captives, whose unconditional surrender was accepted, have been put to death.... There was indeed almost a permanent custom among the Romans with respect to the commanders of the enemy, whether captured or received by surrender, that they should be put to death on the day of the Roman triumph.

13. Distinction of this right from retaliation

Sometimes historians assign the reason for the slaughter of enemies, particularly of captives or suppliants, either to retaliation, or to obstinacy in resisting; but these causes ... are plausible rather than justificatory. In fact, retaliation that is lawful, and properly so called, [can lawfully] be inflicted [only] upon the very person who has done wrong, as may be seen from what has previously been said on the sharing of punishment.[14] In war, on the contrary, what is [wrongly]

---

[13] The reference to tribunals is to tribunals of neutral states, which have jurisdiction over both belligerents when the belligerents chance to be present in the neutral state's territory. This is really, in effect, merely another way of saying that belligerents may not conduct hostilities against one another in the territory of neutral states. As noted above, this is an obligation owed by the belligerents to the neutral sovereign, not to one another.

[14] See p. 292 above. This assertion is made from the standpoint of the law of nature, which does not allow action against one person for a wrong committed by another.

called retaliation very frequently brings harm to those who are in no way to blame for that on which the issue is joined.

In truth, there is no one who holds that an obstinate devotion to one's party is worthy of punishment;...The statement holds particularly true when the party to which allegiance is maintained has been assigned by nature,[15] or chosen for an honourable reason. In fact, so far from there being any crime involved in such allegiance, it is accounted a criminal act to desert one's post....For his own advantage, therefore, each [side in a war] resorts to so extreme severity in cases in which it seems expedient; moreover, such severity is defended among men by the law of nations, of which we are now treating.[16]

14. Whether the right to inflict injury extends over hostages

This right to inflict injury [upon enemies in war] has also been exercised against hostages, not merely against those who had bound themselves, as by an agreement, but also against those who have been surrendered by others.[17]... Furthermore we must remember that even boys were commonly given as hostages;...Women also were given as hostages by the Romans,...and by the Germans, according to Tacitus.[18]

15. On killing by means of poison

However, just as the law of nations, through that form of permission which we have now explained, permits many things which are forbidden by the law of nature, so it forbids certain things which are permissible by the law of nature. If you take account only of the law of nature, in case it is permissible to kill a person, it makes no difference whether you kill him by the sword or by poison. By the law of nature, I repeat, for it is indeed more noble to kill in such a way that he who is killed may have a chance to defend himself; but this is not an obligation due to one who has deserved to die. Nevertheless, from old times,

---

[15] E.g., when loyalty is owed to the state in question from birth.
[16] The point is that the soldiers suffer from harsh measures not because they have committed any wrong – such as would justify their being punished under natural law – but rather because the law of nations simply allows such measures to be inflicted by belligerents as a normal feature of war.
[17] This statement is somewhat puzzling, since hostages 'who have been surrendered' (either by themselves or by others) would presumably have been surrendered on certain specified terms, e.g., to be held pending the performance of some act by the hostages' home state. According to what is said later (see p. 446 below), the terms of that arrangement should be regarded as binding, so that the hostage-holders would not be at liberty to kill the hostages at will. Perhaps it is envisaged that the hostages have themselves violated the terms of the arrangement in some way and that the effect of such a violation is to transform the hostages into 'ordinary' prisoners of war. See the further consideration of this subject below at p. 446.
[18] Tacitus, *Germania*, 8.

the law of nations – if not of all nations, certainly of those of the better sort – has been that it is not permissible to kill an enemy by poison.

Agreement upon this matter arose from a consideration of the common advantage, in order that the dangers of war, which had begun to be frequent, might not be too widely extended. And it is easy to believe that this agreement originated with kings, whose lives are better defended by arms than those of other men, but are less safe from poison. . . . Wherefore those who argue that it is permissible to kill an enemy by poison . . . have regard to the law of nature only. [T]hey quite overlook that which takes its rise in the will of the nations.

16. On the use of poisoned weapons or waters

Different in a degree from poisoning of this sort, and more closely allied with the use of force, is the poisoning of javelins. This is a doubling of the causes of death . . . But this also is contrary to the law of nations, not indeed of all nations, but of European nations, and of such others as attain to the higher standard of Europe.

The poisoning of springs also, though the act either is not secret or does not long remain so, is . . . not only contrary to ancestral custom but also contrary to the law of the gods. . . . It should not indeed seem remarkable if there exist some such tacit agreements among belligerents to lessen the risks of war.

17. On the pollution of waters in other ways

The rule just stated has not been established in regard to the pollution of waters without the use of poison, in such a way that one cannot drink from them. . . . This is considered to be like the diverting of a river, or cutting off the veins of a spring, which is permissible by nature and [also] by convention.

18. On use of assassins

The question is frequently discussed whether, according to the law of nations, it is permissible to kill an enemy by sending an assassin against him. In general, a distinction must be made between assassins who violate an express or tacit obligation of good faith, as subjects resorting to violence against a king, vassals against a lord, soldiers against him whom they serve, those also who have been received as suppliants or strangers or deserters, against those who have received them; and [in contrast to these], such [assassins] as are held by no bond of good faith.

Not merely by the law of nature but also by the law of nations, as we have said above, it is in fact permissible to kill an enemy in any place whatsoever;[19]

---

[19] Again, Grotius speaks carelessly. He means that no wrong is done to the individual enemy who is attacked. Attacks in neutral state territories, however, are not allowed

and it does not matter how many there are who do the deed, or who suffer.... According to the law of nations, not only those who do such deeds, but also those who instigate others to do them, are to be considered free from blame.

No one ought to be influenced by the fact that, when persons who have made such attempts are caught, they are usually subjected to refined tortures. This result does not follow because they have violated the law of nations, but because, by that same law of nations, anything is permissible as against an enemy.[20] In such cases, however, each decides upon a more severe or more lenient punishment from the point of view of his personal advantage.

Under these conditions, spies – whose sending is beyond doubt permitted by the law of nations – if caught are usually treated most severely.... Sometimes, they are treated with justice by those who clearly have a just [cause] for carrying on war. [By those without such a just cause], however, they are dealt with in accordance with that impunity which the law of war accords.[21] If any are to be found who refuse to make use of the help of spies, when it is offered to them, their refusal must be attributed to their loftiness of mind and confidence in their power to act openly, not to their view of what is just or unjust.

But a different point of view must be adopted in regard to those assassins who act treacherously. Not only do they themselves act in a manner inconsistent with the law of nations, but this holds true also of those who employ their services.[22] And yet, in other things, those who avail themselves of the aid of bad men against an enemy are thought to sin before God, but not before men; that is, they are thought not to commit wrong against the law of nations.[23] ... The reason why in this matter men have reached a conclusion different from that adopted in other cases is the same that we advanced above with regard to the use of poison. It has in view the purpose to prevent the dangers to persons of particular eminence becoming excessive.

on the separate ground that they would be offences against the neutral sovereign in question. See p. 351 above.

[20] The tortures in question are to be regarded as acts of war against enemies, and hence as exercises of the rights of belligerents. They are not acts of punishment for violations of the laws of the war.

[21] That is, if the just side in a war captures a spy, it is entitled, as a matter of justice, to punish him for wrong-doing, pursuant to the law of nature. If the unjust side captures a spy, it too is entitled to inflict punishment – but in this case, pursuant to the volitional law of nations, rather than the law of nature. The just side, then, has a true *right* to punish the spy. The unjust side only has impunity from punishment for its punishment of the spy.

[22] This is an application of the more general principle that it is wrong to induce a person to do something if it would be wrongful for the person to do the act on his own initiative.

[23] It is permissible according to the law of nations to employ 'bad men', such as ruffians or criminals, against the enemy – on the assumption that the bad men in question are not under some kind of duty of loyalty to that enemy (e.g., as nationals of the enemy state).

In a public war, therefore, or among those who have the right to declare a public war, the practice under consideration [the hiring of assassins] is not permissible. [H]owever, apart from a public war, by the same law of nations it is held to be permissible.[24] So, too, treachery towards robbers and pirates is not indeed blameless, but goes unpunished among nations by reason of hatred of those against whom it is practised.

19. Whether rape is contrary to the law of nations

You may read in many places that the raping of women in time of war is permissible, and in many others that it is not permissible. Those who sanction rape have taken into account only the injury done to the person of another, and have judged that it is not inconsistent with the law of war that everything which belongs to the enemy should be at the disposition of the victor. A better conclusion has been reached by others, who have taken into consideration not only the injury but the unrestrained lust of the act; also the fact that such acts do not contribute to safety or to punishment, and should consequently not go unpunished in war any more than in peace. The latter view is the law not of all nations, but of the better ones.

Among Christians, it is right that the view just presented shall be enforced, not only as a part of military discipline, but also as a part of the law of nations; that is, whoever forcibly violates chastity, even in war, should everywhere be subject to punishment.

---

[24] That is, treachery may be used against such persons as brigands and pirates, according to the volitional law of nations, but not against the enemy side in a war between states.

5

On devastation and pillage

1. Destruction and pillage of enemy property

[It] is not contrary to nature to despoil him whom it is honourable to kill.... Therefore, it is not strange that the law of nations has permitted the destruction and plunder of the property of enemies, the slaughter of whom it has permitted.... On almost every page of historical writings, you may find accounts of the destruction of whole cities, or the levelling of walls to the ground, the devastation of fields, and conflagrations. It must be noted furthermore that such acts are permissible also against those who have surrendered.

2. On enemy property that is sacred

Now the law of nations in itself, apart from the consideration of other obligations of which we shall speak below, does not exempt things that are sacred, that is, things dedicated to God or to the gods.... 'When places are taken by the enemy, all things cease to be sacred', says Pomponius the Jurist.[1] ... The reason is that the things which are called sacred are in fact not withdrawn from human use, but are public. [H]owever, they are called sacred from the purpose to which they are devoted. The proof of what I say is that, when any people surrenders itself to another people, or to a king, there are also at the same time surrendered the things which are called divine.

Nevertheless this is true, that, if a divinity is believed to reside in an image, it is unlawful that the image shall be defiled or destroyed by those who share such belief. On the assumption that such a belief is held, those who have committed acts of this character are sometimes accused of impiety or of contravention of the law of nations. The case is different if the enemy do not hold the same view. [S]o the Jews were not only permitted but even enjoined to destroy the idols of the Gentiles.[2]

---

[1] *Digest*, 11.7.36 (Pomponius).　　[2] *Deuteronomy*, 7:5.

3. Whether enemy property that is consecrated may be destroyed or pillaged

What we have said of sacred things should be understood of consecrated things as well;[3] for these, also, do not belong to the dead but to the living, being the possession of a people or of a family.... Nevertheless, the principle laid down must be so interpreted that the bodies of the dead are not to be mistreated, because that is contrary to the law of burials; and the law of burials, as we have shown elsewhere, was introduced by the law of nations.[4]

4. How far deceit is permissible in these matters

At this point, I shall briefly repeat, that enemy property may be seized not alone by force. [R]uses which do not involve breach of faith are held to be permissible. [P]ermissible, again, is even the inciting of another to treachery. In truth, the law of nations begins to wink at these frequent minor wrongs,[5] just as municipal laws at harlotry and usury.

---

[3] Sacred things are things that are intrinsically holy, such as cult images of deities and things that are regarded as the property of the gods, such as temples. Consecrated things are things which were not holy from the beginning, but only because holiness was conferred by human action, such as the blessing of an altar in a church.
[4] See the discussion at p. 267 of the natural-law right of sepulchre.
[5] I.e., the law of nations refrains from imposing punishments in these cases, though the acts remain wrongful according to natural law.

On the right of acquiring things taken in war

1. On the acquisition of things taken in war

Besides the impunity among men in relation to certain actions, which we have discussed up to this point, there is also another effect characteristic of public war according to the law of nations (*iure gentium proprius*). According to the law of nature, by a lawful war we acquire things which are either equal to that which, although it was owed to us, we could not otherwise obtain; or we inflict upon the guilty a loss that does not exceed an equitable measure of punishment, as has been said elsewhere.[1]

2. What the [volitional] law of nations is on this subject

By the [volitional] law of nations, not merely he who wages war for a just cause, but in a public war also,[2] anyone at all becomes owner, without limit or restriction, of what he has taken from the enemy. That is true in this sense, at any rate, that both the possessor of such booty, and those who hold their title from him, are to be protected in their possession by all nations; and such a condition one may call ownership so far as its external effects are concerned.[3]

On the authority of Aristotle also we read: 'The law is a sort of agreement, according to which things taken in war belong to those who take them.'[4] ... 'What is taken from the enemy, by the law of nations becomes at once the property of those who take it', says [Justinian]. [5] ... Aristotle said 'acquisition by war is a method according to nature'.[6]

---

[1] See p. 284 above.

[2] I.e., in an unjust war as well as in a just one, provided only that the war is waged according to the requisite formalities of a public war (i.e., that it is duly declared, and waged according to the laws of war). See the discussion of this point at p. 344 above.

[3] The distinction made is between lawfully protected possession and true ownership. See p. 116 above. But it is conceded that, in terms of mere 'external effects', there is actually no practical difference between the two.

[4] Aristotle, *Politics*, I.6.

[5] Justinian, *Institutes*, 2.1.17. (Grotius erroneously credited this passage to Gaius.)

[6] Aristotle, *Politics*, I.8. Aristotle was referring, in this passage, to acquisition by the just side in a war, i.e., in a war waged against 'such men as are by nature intended to be

3. When movable property is held to have been captured

In this inquiry in regard to war, however, the nations have agreed that he is to be understood as having captured a thing who retains it in such a way that the original possessor has lost probable expectation of regaining it, or so that the thing has escaped pursuit.... In the case of things that are movable, this principle is so extended that such things are said to have been captured when they have been brought within the borders, that is to say, the defences, of the [armed forces of the captor].

Hence it seems to follow that, on the sea, ships and other things may be considered as captured only when they have been brought into dockyards or harbours [of the captor power], or to the place where a whole fleet is stationed; for then recovery [by the original owner] begins to appear hopeless. But in the more recent law of nations, we see the doctrine introduced among European peoples that such things may be considered as captured when they have been for twenty-four hours in the power of the enemy.[7]

4. When territory is held to have been captured

Nevertheless, territory is not considered as captured at the moment it is occupied. While it is true that that part of a territory which an army has invaded in great force is temporarily possessed by it, ... still such possession is not sufficient for that effect which we are discussing,[8] for which secure possession is required.... Therefore, ... territory will [only] be regarded as captured [when it] is so surrounded by permanent fortifications that the other party will have no access to it openly unless these have first been taken.[9]

5. Concerning property which does not belong to the enemy

This also is clear: in order that something may become ours by the law of war, it must belong to the enemy. Those things which are in the enemy's possession, to be sure, in their towns, for example, or within their fortifications, but of which the owners are neither subjects of the enemy nor hostilely inclined, cannot be acquired by war.[10]

---

ruled over but refuse'. He was not contending that the two sides had an equal right to acquire property by this method. In the terminology of Grotius, it would be said that Aristotle was speaking in terms of the law of nature, and not of the volitional law of nations.

[7] In a footnote, Grotius states that England and Castile have both adopted the twenty-four hour rule, citing Gentili, *Pleas of a Spanish Advocate*, 1.3.

[8] I.e., a transfer of full ownership, or sovereignty.

[9] The distinction is between territory which is merely occupied, and territory which is conquered. The one is merely possessed de facto, while the other is actually owned.

[10] In other words, property belonging to neutral nationals is not subject to capture.

6. Concerning neutral-owned goods found in ships of the enemy

Consequently, the current statement that goods, which are found in ships of the enemy,[11] are to be considered as belonging to the enemy, should not be accepted as if it were a fixed provision of the law of nations, but as indicating a certain presumption. This presumption, however, may be overthrown by valid proofs to the contrary.[12]

In our native country of Holland formerly, in the year 1438 when war was raging with the Hanseatic towns, a decision to that effect was reached at a full session of the senate, as I have found, and from that decision the provision passed into a law.

7. Concerning property which our enemies have taken from others by war

The principle, however, is beyond dispute – if we have reference to the law of nations – that what has been taken by us from the enemy cannot be claimed by those who had possessed it before it came into the possession of our enemy.... The reason is that the law of nations, through external ownership, first made our enemy the owner, and then us.[13]

---

[11] Footnote by Grotius: 'But the ships of friends do not become prizes because they are carrying goods of the enemy, unless this happens with the consent of the owners of the ship.... In this sense I think we must interpret the laws of France, which render vessels liable to seizure because of their goods, and goods because of the ships which carry them. Such are the laws of Francis I issued in 1543;... of Henry III, issued in March, 1584;... and the Portuguese Law.... Elsewhere the [enemy-owned] goods themselves are alone liable to seizure.... Thus in the war between the Venetians and the Genoese, Greek ships were searched and any enemies who were concealed in them were removed.'

It is not specified which 'war between the Venetians and the Genoese' is referred to. There were conflicts between the two states in 1291–9, 1350–5 and 1378–81 (the War of Chioggia).

[12] According to natural law, property belonging to neutral nationals found on board an enemy ship cannot be captured. In the actual practice of European states, however, sometimes *all* goods on board enemy ships (even those belonging to neutrals) were captured. Grotius does not accept this. The furthest that he will go is to concede that, according to the volitional law of nations, there is 'a certain presumption' to the effect that any goods found on an enemy ship belong to enemy nationals (and hence are subject to capture). This is the interpretation that he places on the laws of France and Portugal identified in note 11 above. But he insists that the presumption is not conclusive, i.e., that it can be 'overthrown' by positive proof that the property in question was owned by neutrals rather than by enemies.

[13] The case discussed is one in which States A and B were first at war, with property belonging to nationals of A captured by the forces of B. Subsequently, a war ensued between States B and C, and that same property was captured by the forces of C. State B has lost ownership, and it might be contended that the original ownership of the nationals of A then revived. Grotius denies this, holding C to be the owner, with

8. To whom captured enemy property belongs

It is a more serious question, who acquires the goods of the enemy in a public and formal war: the people itself, or the individuals who are of it or within it? On this point, the more recent interpreters of the law hold very diverse opinions. The majority of them … declared – one following the other, as is usually the case – that, in the first place and by the law [of nature], things captured belong to the individuals who lay hands on them, but that they are to be assigned to the commander for distribution among the soldiers. Since this view is as widely current as it is false, we must refute it with so much the greater pains, that it may serve as an example of how little trust, in controversies of this sort, is to be placed in such authorities.

However, it is not to be doubted that, by agreement of the nations, either practice[14] may be established. … But we are inquiring what their will has been; and we say that the nations have decided that the property of enemies should stand to enemies in the same relation as ownerless property.

9. On acquisition of both possession and ownership through another

Things which are ownerless, to be sure, become the property of those who take them; but they become just as much the property of those who obtain possession of them through others as of those who take them for themselves. Consequently, not only slaves and children, but also free men, who in fishing, fowling, hunting, or gathering pearls, have given their assistance to others, at once acquire what they have taken for those persons whom they serve. … [T]he principle holds good that one may do through another what he can do himself, and that the effect is the same whether anyone acts for himself or through another.

10. The distinction between hostile acts as public or private

In our investigation, therefore, we must distinguish between acts of war that are truly of a public character, and private acts which are committed on the occasion of a public war. By private acts, a thing is sought primarily and directly for private persons; by public acts, for the people.[15]

the nationals of A still excluded. All rights of the nationals of A, in other words, were definitively lost at the point of capture of the property by the forces of B.
[14] I.e., either that captured property belongs to the actual person or persons who made the capture; or that it belongs to the government of the captors.
[15] In other words, the key to determining the ownership of captured enemy property lies in determining whether the immediate captor (the soldier) was, at the time, acting on his own behalf or on that of the state in whose service he was at the time.

11. Ownership of captured territory

Landed property is not usually taken except by a public act, upon the entry of an army and the establishment of garrisons. Thus, in the opinion of Pomponius, 'Land that has been taken from the enemy is public property', that is, as he explains in the same passage, 'it is not classed as booty', if we take the word booty in its strict sense.[16]

12. Capture of movables by a private act

But things which are movable, or are themselves capable of motion, if captured are taken either in the public service or outside of it. If they are taken outside of the public service, they become the property of the individuals who take them.

The same practice was observed with regard to men also, at the time when, in respect to the principle stated, captive men were classed with captured property.

From the same principle, it follows that, if soldiers capture anything when they are not in formation or engaged in executing an order, but when they are acting under a general right or by mere permission, this they at once acquire for themselves; for they do not make the capture in the capacity of servants. Such are the spoils seized by soldiers in free and unauthorised raids at a distance from the army – beyond ten miles the Romans used to say. . . . This sort of booty the Italians at the present day call 'raid-spoil' (*correria*), and distinguish from 'sack' (*bottino*).

13. Possible alternate provision of municipal law

But our statement that, by the law of nations, things movable or capable of motion are directly acquired by individuals, must be understood as applicable to the law of nations as unmodified by any municipal law covering the matter. Each people may in fact establish other rules valid over its citizens, and may thus forestall individual ownership; as we see is done in many places with regard to wild animals and birds. In like manner, it may also be provided by a law that goods of enemies which are discovered in our midst should become public property.

14. On things captured by a public act

With regard to those things, however, which are captured by an act of war, the situation is different. In this case, individuals represent the person of the state, and act in its stead. [H]ence through them, unless a statute otherwise

---

[16] *Digest*, 49.15.20.1 (Pomponius). Booty in the strict sense refers only to movable items, not to land.

decrees, the people obtains both possession and ownership, and transfers this to whomever it wishes.

18. On the permitting of pillaging by commanders

I now come to pillaging.[17] This was conceded to the soldiers either in the devastation of a country, or after a battle, or after the storming of a town, with permission to scatter at a given signal. . . . Sometimes, too, pillaging was permitted because it could not be prevented.

19. On the granting of the spoil to others by commanders

The practice already mentioned, that in some cases the booty, or money derived from the sale of booty, might be assigned to others than the soldiers, usually had as its purpose to make an equivalent reimbursement to those who had contributed funds for the war.[18] You may also note that public spectacles were at times produced with the money derived from the booty.

20. On division of the booty into portions

Not only in different wars are different methods employed in the disposition of booty, but in the same war booty is often diverted to different uses, after it has been divided into portions or the different kinds have been distinguished. . . . The classes into which booty may be divided are these: prisoners, herds, and flocks (which the Greeks when speaking with exactness call 'pillageable property'); money; and other movables costly or cheap.

22. On transfer of the right to booty

[B]ooty, just as other things, may be conceded by a people to others or not only after acquisition, but also prior to acquisition, in such a way that, when the capture has ensued, the claims thereby arising are immediately united in title, as the jurists say. And this concession can be made not only to specific persons,

[17] By pillaging is meant an arrangement in which each soldier is given title to whatever property he personally succeeds in capturing, even though the soldier is serving under orders and is not acting independently. This scenario is, then, an exception to the general principle, just stated, that property taken in acts of war belongs to the sovereign waging the war rather than to the individual captors.

[18] There was thought to be some element of unfairness that soldiers in the field should have the exclusive opportunity to acquire enemy property, when those who had contributed funds to the waging of the war had also aided in the capturing, albeit indirectly. To rectify this, captured property was sometimes 'nationalised', i.e., put to the benefit of the population of the warring state as a whole, rather than just to the benefit of the serving soldiery.

but also to classes; . . . or even to chance persons, after the fashion of the things thrown to the mob, which the Roman consuls made the property of those who caught them.

Furthermore, this transference of [the] right [to booty], which is brought about by a law or grant, is not always a mere gift. It sometimes represents the fulfilment of a contract; sometimes either a payment of what is owed, or a reimbursement for losses which someone has suffered, or compensation for a personal contribution to the war in money, or in service, as when allies and subjects serve either without any pay or for such pay as does not correspond with their service. It is for these reasons . . . that an assignment of the whole booty, or a part of it, has usually been made.

23. On the grant of booty to allies

Our jurists, in fact, note that, almost everywhere, the custom has been tacitly followed, that either allies or subjects who wage war without pay, at their own expense and danger, appropriate what they capture. In the case of allies, the reason is evident, for naturally one ally is bound to make good to another the losses which ensue from a joint or public enterprise. There is also the further consideration, that it is hardly customary for service to be rendered gratis. . . . Therefore it is credible that, unless some other cause should appear, as for instance pure kindness, or a preceding agreement, the hope of enriching oneself from the enemy was regarded as recompense for loss and service.[19]

24. On the grant of booty to subjects

In the case of subjects, the right to booty does not follow with equal clearness, because subjects owe their service to their state. But this reason is offset by the fact that, where not all subjects but only a part are in service, the latter are entitled to compensation from the body of the state for having contributed more service and expense than the others; and they are much more entitled to compensation for losses. In place of this clearly defined compensation, the expectation of the whole or a part of an uncertain booty is readily, and not without reason, conceded.

There are, however, certain things of so slight value that they are not worth making public property. These things everywhere by consent of the people belong to those who take them. Such under the early Roman republic were spears, javelins, firewood, fodder, water-skins, leathern money-bags, torches, and money smaller than a silver sestertius.[20]

---

[19] Perhaps the clearest example of this practice was privateering.
[20] A Roman sestertius would purchase approximately two loaves of bread, or a half-litre of wine.

Very like this concession is that which is made to sailors even when they are paid for their service. The French call this spoliation or pillage, and therein include clothing, and gold and silver under ten écus. Elsewhere, a certain part of the booty is given to the soldiers, as in Spain, where now a fifth, now a third, and again a half remains with the king, and a seventh, or at times a tenth, with the commander of the army; the rest belongs to the individual captors, with the exception of ships of war, which fall wholly to the king.

It may happen also that the division of the booty is made after account has been taken of services, dangers, and expenses, as among the Italians, where a third of a captured ship falls to the master of the victorious vessel, an equal part to those whose goods were in the ship and the same to those who engaged in the fighting.[21]

Sometimes, again, this occurs, that those who conduct a war at their own risk and expense do not receive all the spoil, but owe a part to the public authority, or to him who derives his right from the public authority. Thus among the Spaniards, when in a war ships are fitted out at private expense, part of the spoil is due to the king, and part to the highest naval authority. According to the French practice, the latter receives a tenth, and the same is customary among the Dutch; but with them, a fifth part of the booty is first deducted by the state. On land, however, it is now the general custom that, in the sack of towns, or in battle, each should have as his own what he has taken; but what is taken in raids should be the common property of those in the detachment, to be divided among themselves according to their rank.

25. The application of what has been said

As a result of these considerations, we are to know that, if within the jurisdiction of a nation that is not involved in war, a dispute arises with respect to something that has been captured in war, the thing is to be adjudged to him whose case is supported by the laws or customs of the people on whose side capture has been effected. [I]f this is impracticable, then by the common law of nations (*iure gentium communi*), the thing is to be adjudged to the people itself, provided only that it has been taken in an act of war.

Things which do not belong to the enemy, even if found among the enemy, do not become the property of the captors; for this, as we have said already, is not in accordance with the law of nature and has not been introduced by the law of nations.[22] . . . Nevertheless, if in such things the enemy enjoys any right

---

[21] *Consolato del Mare*, 288. Grotius is slightly careless here. He cited the wrong provision of the *Consolato*, and he suggests that the *Consolato* is a body of Italian law. It was actually Catalan.

[22] See p. 360 above.

which is connected with possession, as a right of pledge, restraint, or servitude, there is nothing to prevent this right being acquired by the captors.[23]

26. On things taken outside the territory of either belligerent

The question is also often raised whether things captured outside the territory of either belligerent may become the property of the captors; and this is debated with regard both to things and to persons. If we take into account the law of nations only, I think that this subject need not be considered, since we have said that an enemy may be justly slain in any place. But he who holds authority in a place may by a law of his own prohibit any such action; and if such an act is committed contrary to [this municipal] law, [the sovereign of that country] can demand satisfaction for it as for a crime. Similar to this is the ruling [in Roman law] that a wild animal caught on the land of another belongs to the captors, but access to it may be prohibited by the owner of the land.[24]

27. The right of capture as peculiar to a public war

Now this external right of acquiring things taken in war is so peculiar to a war that is public according to the law of nations that, in other wars, it finds no place. For in other wars with foreigners, property is not acquired by the violence of war but as compensation for a debt which cannot otherwise be obtained.[25] In wars between citizens, whether these be great or small, no change of ownership is made except by the authority of a judge.[26]

[23] This paragraph appears, in the Latin text, in the following section; but it logically belongs here.
[24] *Digest*, 41.1.3.1 (Gaius).
[25] The reference is to wars that are just according to the natural law (as opposed to the law of nations), in which the right to capture enemy property is limited in quantity to the amount needed to compensate the just side for whatever injury had given rise to the war. By 'external right' is meant the recognition of legal title in human courts. According to the law of nations, even an unjust belligerent acquires such 'external right' to enemy property which he captures, even though he does not acquire any title according to the law of nature. According to natural law, only the just belligerent has the right to capture and take title to enemy property, subject to the limit just mentioned.
[26] This is a rare comment on civil wars, to the effect that the right of capture of enemy property does not exist.

7

On the right over prisoners of war

1. On prisoners of war as slaves

By nature at any rate, that is, apart from a human act, or in the primitive condition of nature, no human beings are slaves. . . . In this sense, it is correct to accept what was said by the [Roman] jurists, that slavery is contrary to nature.[1] Nevertheless, as we have shown also in another connexion, it is not in conflict with natural justice that slavery should have its origin in a human act, that is, should arise from a convention or a crime.[2]

But in the law of nations, which we are discussing, now slavery has a somewhat larger place, both as regards persons and as regards effects. For if we consider persons, . . . those who surrender themselves, or promise to become slaves, are regarded as slaves. [In addition] without exception [persons] who have been captured in a formal public war become slaves from the time when they are brought within the lines. . . . And no crime is requisite, but the fate of all is the same, even of those who by their ill-fortune . . . are caught in the enemy's territory when war has suddenly broken out.

2. Descendants of persons captured in war

Not only do the prisoners of war themselves become slaves, but also their descendants for ever, that is to say those who are born of a slave mother after her enslavement.

3. What may be done to prisoners of war with impunity

Moreover, the effects of this law are unlimited. . . . There is no suffering which may not be inflicted with impunity upon such slaves, no action which they may not be ordered or forced by torture, to do, in any way whatsoever. [E]ven brutality on the part of masters towards persons of servile status is unpunishable

---

[1] *Digest*, 1.5.4.1 (Florentinus).
[2] I.e., slavery is not actually *prohibited* by the law of nature. Slavery, however, was not *instituted* by the law of nature.

except in so far as municipal law sets a limit and a penalty for brutality. . . . Also, everything that has been captured is acquired, along with the person, for the master. The slave who is himself under the power of another, says Justinian, can have nothing of his own.[3]

4. The property of captives, even if incorporeal, belongs to their master

On these grounds, the view of those who say that incorporeal rights are not acquired by the law of war is refuted, or at any rate restricted. It is true that such rights are not acquired primarily and directly, but through the medium of the person to whom they had belonged.

Nevertheless, we have to make exception of those rights which have their source in a peculiar capacity of the person and are hence inalienable, as the right of the father. For if these rights can remain, they remain with the person; if not, they are extinguished.

5. The reason why the law has thus been established

All these rights have been introduced by the law of nations, with which we are dealing, for no other reason than this: that the captors, mollified by so many advantages, might willingly refrain from recourse to the utmost degree of severity, in accordance with which they could have slain the captives, either immediately or after a delay. . . . I have said 'that they might willingly refrain'; for there is no suggestion of an agreement whereby they may be compelled to refrain, if you are considering this law of nations, but a method of persuading them by indicating the more advantageous course.[4]

For the same reason, this right is transferred to others, just as the ownership of things. Further, it has been agreed that ownership should be extended to children; the reason is that otherwise, if the captors had used their full right [of executing the captives], the children would not have been born. Whence it follows that children who were born before the catastrophe do not become slaves, unless they are themselves captured. Moreover, it has been acceptable to the nations that children should follow the status of the mother, for the reason that the unions of slaves were regulated neither by law nor by definite oversight, and consequently the father was indicated by no adequate presumption.[5] . . . [This law] represents a general custom which has grown up from a natural reason.

[3] Justinian, *Institutes*, 2.9.3.
[4] 'The more advantageous course' (for the prisoners in question) being enslavement, rather than execution.
[5] *Digest*, 1.5.24 (Ulpian). Since it was often difficult to say who was the father of any given slave, the general practice has been that children of slaves take the status of the mother.

The rights under consideration, moreover, have not been introduced by the nations in vain. This we may perceive from what happens in civil wars, in which we find that, on many occasions, captives have been killed because they could not be reduced to slavery.[6]

Whether those who have been captured become property of the people, or of individuals, must be decided by what we have said in regard to booty; for in this case the law of nations has put men in the same category as things.

6. Whether it is permissible for those who have been captured to flee

Nevertheless, as regards the belief of some theologians, that it is unlawful for those to flee who have been captured in an unlawful war, or are born of captives, unless they flee to their own people, I have myself no doubt that [this] view is erroneous. There is indeed this difference, that if captives make their escape to their own people while the war is still in progress, they attain their freedom by right of postliminy;[7] if they flee to others, or to their own people after peace has been made, they must be given up to the master who claims them.[8] But it does not follow as a consequence that a bond of conscience is laid also upon the captives. [T]here are many rights which look only to an external judgement, and such are the rights of war which we are now explaining.[9]

There is, further, no reason for anyone to raise the objection that, from the nature of ownership, such an obligation becomes binding on the mind. For I shall reply that, since there are many forms of ownership, it is possible that one may exist which is valid only in a judgement that is human and at the same time continues a condition which arises also in other kinds of rights.[10]

Not very different is the ownership of one who in accordance with the civil laws has exercised prescription in bad faith;[11] for his ownership also is protected by the civil courts.

---

[6] Presumably, they could not be reduced to slavery, at least in many cases, because the municipal law of the country in question did not provide for it (remembering that a person can become a slave only by human law, not by the law of nature). This is another indication that civil wars, in Grotius's view, were governed wholly by the municipal law of the country in question, and not by either the natural law or the volitional law of nations.

[7] On postliminy, see p. 376 below.

[8] I.e., to the enemy who obtained title to them by capture.

[9] The contention, in effect, is that the right of a master over an enslaved captive is not matched by a corresponding duty on the captive's part to submit to his new status. The same cannot be said of persons who became slaves either by agreement or as punishment for crimes committed.

[10] It is possible to have forms of ownership which are recognised only by the law of nations and not by the law of nature. The present scenario is one of these possibilities.

[11] I.e., has held or occupied property belonging to another without any claim of legal right or good faith. If the possession lasts long enough, the title to the property will pass according to civil law (Roman and Roman-based law in this case).

In the question before us, no reason can be imagined why the nations should have had in view anything else than that external restraint. For the opportunity of claiming a slave and restraining him, and further, of putting him in bonds and retaining his property, was enough to induce captors to spare captives.... [I]f they believed such a restraint [a legal prohibition against flight] at all necessary for themselves, they could have exacted an assurance or an oath [from the captive].

However, in a law which has been established not according to natural equity, but to avoid a greater evil,[12] we should not rashly adopt an interpretation which would make criminal an act otherwise permitted.[13] ... This is so because the right of captivity is of such a sort, that in another sense it is often also a wrong.... It is a right in respect to certain effects; a wrong, if we regard its intrinsic nature.[14]

Hence this also is apparent. If anyone who has been captured in an unlawful war has come into the power of the enemy, his conscience is not tainted by the crime of theft if he secretly takes away his own property, or a recompense for his toil, in case it is right that any should be furnished him over and above his keep, provided that he neither in his own name, nor in that of his state, is in any way indebted to his master, or to him whose right his master has received. And it does not matter that such flight and abstraction, when detected, are usually punished with severity.[15] For these things and many others are done by the more powerful, not because they are just, but because it is to the advantage of the more powerful to do them.

Certain canons forbid anyone to persuade a slave to desert his master's service. If you refer this to slaves who are undergoing a just punishment, or have bound themselves by a voluntary agreement, it is a just injunction. But if you refer it to those who have been captured in an unlawful war, or have been born of captives, it [should be understood only to teach] that Christians should encourage Christians to be patient rather than to engage in an action which, although permissible, might yet offend minds alien to Christianity or otherwise weak.[16] In a similar way, we may understand the admonitions of the Apostles to

---

[12] I.e., a law which is part of the law of nations rather than of natural law.

[13] The 'act otherwise permitted' refers to the right, under natural law, of an enslaved captive to escape from his or her master.

[14] I.e., the right to enslave prisoners of war is a right according to the volitional law of nature, which is only concerned with external effects. But it is not a right in its 'intrinsic nature', i.e., according to natural law.

[15] The implication is that property owned by the slave at the time of capture remains his according to natural law (though not the law of nations). So he can lawfully take that when he flees. He can also take any property that the master has entrusted to him, up to the amount sufficient to pay him for labour expended during his period of servitude (minus any debts owed to the master).

[16] It seems rather odd to suppose that slaves should refrain from exercising their natural-law right to escape, so as to avoid causing offence to non-Christians and persons of weak mind. Grotius himself does not endorse this view. He merely interprets the canon law of the Catholic Church in this manner.

slaves,[17] except that these are seen rather to demand obedience from slaves while in servitude [than to prohibit escape]. This is in accord with natural justice; for food and service have reciprocal connexion.[18]

7. Whether it is permissible for those who have been captured to resist their master

But I think that it was correctly said by the theologians to whom I have referred, that a slave cannot resist a master who is exercising that external right without violating the duty of justice.[19] Between this case and that [of escape], which we have just discussed,[20] there is a manifest difference. The external right [of the captor over the slave], which consists not only in impunity of acting but also in the protection of the courts, will be of no effect if a right to offer resistance remains on the [part of the slave]. For if it is permissible forcibly to resist a master, it will also be permissible forcibly to resist a magistrate who protects the master, [since], according to the law of nations, the magistrate should defend the master in such ownership and the enjoyment thereof. This right therefore is like that which we have elsewhere attributed to the highest authorities in each state, in saying that it is not legally nor morally permissible forcibly to resist them.

8. The law under consideration has not always existed among all nations

But the fact must further be recognised that this law of nations with regard to captives has not always been accepted, nor accepted among all nations.

9. The law under consideration does not now exist among Christians

Christians, furthermore, have as a whole agreed that those who are captured in a war which has arisen among themselves do not become slaves so as to be liable to be sold, constrained to labour, and suffer the fate of slaves in other respects. In this, they are surely right, because they have been, or should have

---

[17] For biblical instructions to slaves to give loyal service to their masters, see *Ephesians*, 6:5–9; *Colossians*, 3:22–4:1; 1 *Timothy*, 6:1–2; *Titus*, 2:9–10; and 1 *Peter*, 2:18–19.

[18] In the normal course of things, food is provided to the slave in exchange for service. This is regarded, in effect, as a kind of contract-like arrangement to which both parties should faithfully adhere. Questions of escape are, however, outside the scope of this implicit arrangement.

[19] Here too, the reference is to the normal day-to-day relations of slave to master. The slave is under a duty of due obedience, provided that the master is not exceeding his rights.

[20] I.e., between the cases of, on the one hand, normal day-to-day relations of slave and master and, on the other hand, questions of a duty not to escape.

been, better instructed in the teachings of Him who has sanctioned all charity than to be unable to be restrained from the slaughter of unfortunate men in any other way than by the concession of a lesser cruelty.... Moreover, the practice of Christians in this matter is followed also by Mohammedans among themselves.

Nevertheless, even among Christians, the custom still prevails of keeping prisoners under guard until a ransom is paid, the amount of which is decided by the victor, unless some definite agreement has been made.[21] Furthermore, the right of guarding captives is usually granted to the individuals who have taken them, except in the case of persons of high rank; for the customs of most nations (*plerarumque gentium mores*) give the right over these to the state or its head.

[21] This refers to the practice of ransoming prisoners of war, still prevalent in Grotius's time.

8

On the right to rule over the conquered

1. Acquisition of civil authority by war

It is not at all strange if he who can subject individuals to himself in personal servitude is able to subject to himself an aggregation of men – whether they formed a state, or a part of a state – in a subjection which may be purely civil, or purely personal, or mixed.

Sovereignty, furthermore, may be acquired for the victor; either such sovereignty merely as is vested in a king or other ruler; and in that case, the victor succeeds to the right of the ruler only, and nothing beyond; or such as is vested in a people, in which case the victor holds sovereignty in such a way that he can even alienate it, just as the people could. We have elsewhere said that thus it has come about that certain kingdoms were held as a patrimony.[1]

2. The loss of statehood

Even a more fundamental change may be accomplished, so that, for instance, what was a state may cease to be a state. In such cases, the state that was may become an accession of another state, as the Roman provinces did; or it may not be attached to a state, as when a king waging war at his own expense so subjects a people to himself that he wishes it to be governed not for the good of the people but above all else for that of the ruler, and this is the rule of a master, not of civil authority.

3. Mixing of the two types of authority over defeated countries

Hence we may understand the nature of that mixed authority, which I have said is in part civil and in part that of a master, that is to say, an authority in which servitude is mixed with a degree of personal liberty. Thus we read that arms have been taken from peoples; that peoples have been forbidden to have any iron except for agricultural purposes; and that other peoples have been compelled to change their language and manner of life.

---

[1] See p. 58 above.

4. Acquisition of the possessions of a people of a vanquished state

Moreover, just as the possessions which belonged to individuals are, in accordance with the law of war, acquired by those who place the owners in subjection to themselves, so also the possessions of the aggregation of individuals as a whole become the property of those who subject the aggregation to themselves, if they so wish. . . . Surrender in fact voluntarily permits what force would otherwise take. . . . Consequently, the incorporeal rights also, which had belonged to the aggregation as a whole, will become the property of the victor, in so far as he wishes.

Nor is it true . . . that only what the victor himself holds [physically] is his, [or that] a right that is incorporeal cannot be seized by force; [or] that the position of an heir and that of a conqueror are fundamentally different [on the ground that the whole of a decedent's right] passes to the former, but only [title to corporeal] property to the latter. In fact, he who is master of persons is also master of their possessions and of every right which pertains to the persons. He who is the possession of another does not possess for himself; and he who is not his own master does not have anything in his own power.[2] Furthermore, if anyone should leave to a conquered people the right to form a state, he might still take for himself certain things which had belonged to the state. It rests with him to decide what he wishes the measure of his beneficence to be.[3]

---

[2] *Digest*, 50.17.118 (Ulpian); and 48.5.22 (Ulpian).

[3] A conqueror may choose not to annex the conquered state, but instead only to take certain things from it and then to leave the people of the state on their own, to form a new state with whatever rights have been left to them.

9

On postliminy[1]

1. The origin of the word postliminy

Just as in regard to those things which are captured from the enemy, so also in regard to the right of postliminy (*postliminium*), no very sound view has been advanced by those who in more recent times have laid claim to a knowledge of the law. The subject was treated with greater painstaking by the ancient Romans, but often rather confusedly, so that the reader could not distinguish what they ascribed to the law of nations and what to the Roman civil law.

2. Where postliminy may occur

Postliminy, therefore, is a right which arises from a return to the threshold, that is, to the public boundaries. Thus Pomponius says that he who has begun to be within our fortified lines has returned by postliminy.[2] Paul the Jurist defines such a return when the captive has entered our frontier.[3]

On similar grounds, the agreement of nations [holds] that postliminy occurs if a man, or a thing of the sort in regard to which it has been decided that postliminy is possible, has come [into the territory of our friends or allies]. . . . [W]e are to understand as friends or allies not merely those with whom we are at peace, but those who take the same side in a war. Those who come to such friends . . . begin to be protected in the name of the state. It makes no difference in fact whether a man or thing has come to them or to his own people.

---

[1] In the whole of the treatise, no topic is more foreign to the modern mind than this one. In brief, postliminy refers to the treatment of captured persons or property which somehow return (or are returned) to their home state. They are then treated as if they had never been captured. That is to say, things and persons subject to this principle of postliminy automatically revert to their pre-capture status. Two concerns are particularly relevant here: escaped prisoners of war; and persons and property held by the enemy at the conclusion of the war.

[2] *Digest*, 49.15.5.1 (Pomponius).   [3] *Digest*, 49.15.19.3 (Paul).

Among those who are friends [but who are not allies in the war at hand], prisoners of war do not change their status unless by a special arrangement.[4]

3. On return of persons and recovery of things by postliminy

The later Roman jurists, ... with [great] clarity have distinguished two forms of postliminy, according as we ourselves return, or something is recovered by us.[5]

4. Whether postliminy exists in both peace and in war

We must, further, maintain ... that the right of postliminy is effective both in war and in peace.[6] ... In peace, postliminy, unless it is otherwise agreed, exists for those who have not been conquered by armed force, but caught by their ill-fortune,[7] as those who are found in the land of the enemy when war has suddenly broken out. For other captives, however, there is not postliminy in time of peace, unless this was provided for in the terms of peace.[8]

The ... explanation [for this difference in treatment] is this: that kings and peoples who undertake war wish that their reasons for so doing should be believed to be just; and that, on the other hand, those who bear arms against them are doing wrong. Now, since each party wished this to be believed, and it was not safe for those who desired to preserve peace to intervene, peoples at peace were unable to do better than to ... consider prisoners ... taken in the act of defending themselves as captured for a just reason.

But the same thing could not be said with regard to those who were caught [in hostile territory when] war had broken out; for in them no desire to injure could be imagined.[9] Nevertheless, it seemed not unfair that, while the war lasted, they should be detained in order to lessen the strength of the enemy [by preventing their return to their home country]; but when the ending of the war had been arranged, no reason could be offered for not releasing them. Consequently, this

---

[4] I.e., prisoners of war who escape to the territory of a neutral state rather than to the territory of their home state (or that of an ally in the war) do not automatically resume their former free status.
[5] *Digest*, 49.15.14 (Pomponius).　　[6] See *Digest*, 49.15.12 (Tryphoninus).
[7] See *Digest*, 49.15.5 (Pomponius).
[8] Two categories of people are treated differently. The first category comprises nationals of a belligerent who are resident in the opposing state at the time the war breaks out, and who are then detained and enslaved as enemy aliens. When peace is made at the conclusion of the war, these persons resume their former free status (unless the peace agreement provides otherwise). The other category, comprising soldiers captured during the war, are not so fortunate. They remain as slaves of their captors (again, unless the peace agreement provides otherwise).
[9] These persons who were resident in the enemy state at the outbreak of the war would have been civilians rather than soldiers and would not have been engaging in attacks against their host country. For this reason, they are entitled to more lenient treatment, regarding postliminy, than soldiers, who were actively attacking their foes.

was agreed upon, that with peace, such prisoners should always [regain] their liberty on the ground that they were innocent, by admission of the parties; but that over the [captured soldiers, each captor] should assert what he wished to be considered his right, except in so far as agreements should prescribe definite stipulations.

For the same reason, neither slaves nor things taken in war are restored with peace, unless this has been stipulated in agreements, since [they are taken by right of war]. To controvert this principle would in truth be to make wars spring up from wars.

5. Postliminy occurs upon return

A free man returns by postliminy only when he has come to his own people with the purpose of sharing their fortunes. . . . [I]t makes no difference whether a man has been recovered from the enemy by force of arms, or has escaped by a ruse. . . . It will even be sufficient if he has been voluntarily handed over by the enemy.

6. What rights a free man returning by postliminy may recover

A free man, moreover, after he has returned to his own people, not only acquires himself for himself, but also all the possessions, whether corporeal or incorporeal, which he had when the peoples were at peace. Peoples at peace accept the fact as indicating a right in the case of the man who has been set free, just the same as in the case of the prisoner, in order that they may show themselves fair to both sides.[10] Therefore the proprietorship, which he who possessed the prisoner by the law of war had over the prisoner's possessions, was not free from all limitation. [I]t could in fact cease against his will, if the prisoner should [escape and] reach his own country. Consequently, the possessor of the prisoner loses these things just as he loses the man to whom they belonged.

But what if the possessor of the prisoner has alienated the prisoner's possessions? Will he, who has his title from the [captor] be protected by the law of nations? [O]r will these things also be recovered [by the original owner]? I am speaking of the things which were [acquired by neutral nationals from the captor]. It seems clear that we must distinguish between things which are of such a kind that they may return by postliminy, and those which are not of that kind. This distinction we shall shortly explain, so that the things of the former class will seem to have been alienated with a characteristic cause and under a condition, but the latter absolutely. By alienated things, I understand also things which have been granted or acknowledged as received.

---

[10] It is generally accepted that the fact of escape and return to one's own country will operate automatically to extinguish any legal rights that existed over the escaper in the enemy state. Specifically, he will automatically lose his servile status if he was enslaved by his captors, and will not be reclaimable.

7. Restoration of rights against a free man returning by postliminy

Again, just as rights are restored to him who has returned by postliminy, so also rights are revived against him; and . . . such are held just as if he had never been in the power of the enemy.[11]

8. Whether those who surrender have the right of postliminy

To this rule in regard to free men, Paul the Jurist justly adds the following exception: 'Those who have . . . surrendered to the enemy do not possess the right of postliminy.'[12] This is doubtless for the reason that agreements with the enemy are valid by the law of nations,[13] as we shall say elsewhere, and against such agreements no right of postliminy holds. . . . Paul has [also] properly pointed out [that] there is no postliminy during the period of an armistice.[14] But Modestinus delivered the opinion that those who are given up to the enemy, that is without any agreement, return by postliminy.[15]

9. When a people may have the right of postliminy

What we have said in regard to individual persons holds true, I think, in the case of peoples also; those who were free may recover their liberty in case the power of their allies delivers them from the rule of the enemy. But if the population which formed the state has been dispersed, I think it more correct not to consider the people as the same, nor to restore their property by postliminy in accordance with the law of nations, for the reason that a people, like a ship, obviously perishes by the dissolution of its parts, since its whole nature consists in perpetual union.

10. Provisions of the municipal law on postliminy

From the preceding discussion, the nature of postliminy may be understood according to the law of nations, as regards free men. But by municipal law, that same right . . . may both be restricted by the addition of exceptions and

---

[11] See *Digest*, 49.15.12.6 (Tryphoninus). The reference is to rights such as the right of a creditor of the escaper to be repaid for a debt contracted prior to the capture.

[12] *Digest*, 49.15.17 (Paul).

[13] Surrender is understood to be a situation in which there is an agreement between the two soldiers, concerning the conditions under which the one surrendering is to be held captive in exchange for refraining from further combat.

[14] *Digest*, 49.15.19.1 (Paul).

[15] *Digest*, 49.15.4 (Modestinus). Herennius Modestinus was a student of Ulpian, active in the third century AD. He served as chief of police in Rome. He is regarded as the last writer of the classical period of Roman law.

conditions, and extended to other interests. Thus, by the Roman civil law, deserters are excluded from the number of those who return by postliminy.[16]

The right of postliminy is also in a measure limited by this provision, which we read was first established by the Athenian laws, then by those of the Romans, that the person who should be ransomed from the enemy should serve the one who ransomed him until he paid back the price. But this very provision appears to have been introduced in the interest of liberty, in order that many might not be left in the hands of the enemy because the hope of reimbursement in the sums paid as ransom had been cut off.[17] This kind of servitude is in fact mitigated in many ways by the same Roman laws; and finally by the law of Justinian, it is terminated with five years' service. On the death of the ransomed, the right of recovering the money also is extinguished,[18] just as it is held to be remitted by the contraction of marriage between the ransomer and the ransomed; and the right is lost by the prostitution of a ransomed woman.[19]

We have considered the persons who return; let us now consider the things which are recovered.

11. How slaves are recovered by postliminy

Among recoverable possessions are, first, male and female slaves, even when having been often alienated, or after manumission by the enemy. The reason is that it is not possible for one of our citizens, who is the owner of a slave, to be affected by a manumission in accordance with the law of the enemy.[20] ... But for the recovery of a slave, it is necessary that he be actually held by his former master, or that he should be easily obtainable. Therefore, although in the case of other things, it is enough for them to have been brought within the frontier, in the case of a slave this will not suffice for the right of postliminy, unless the fact [of return] is also [generally] known; for it is the view of Paul the Jurist that a slave who is in Rome, but is hidden, is not yet recovered.[21]

---

[16] *Digest,* 49.15.19.4 (Paul).

[17] This reference is to a common element of the medieval practice of ransoming prisoners of war. It was not unusual that, when Soldier A was captured by the enemy and a ransom fixed, the ransom would be paid by Person B, on A's behalf. A could then return to his home country. But A now owed it to B to perform services for him up to the value of the ransom. Here, as so often with Grotius, the underlying concern was to prevent unjust enrichment. Grotius is pointing out that the right of postliminy does not affect this obligation.

[18] I.e., the duty of the ransomed person to reimburse his ransomer does not extend to his heirs, as normal debts did in Roman law.

[19] The meaning seems to be that, if the ransomer of a female captive compels her to take up prostitution to earn the money for reimbursement of the ransom outlay, then the ransomer thereby loses his right of reimbursement as a penalty for his immoral conduct.

[20] See *Digest,* 49.15.12.9 (Tryphoninus).

[21] *Digest,* 49.15.30 (Paul). The problem concerns a soldier who is captured by the enemy along with his slave. Since the soldier himself becomes a slave of his captor, he

Just as a slave differs in the respect suggested from inanimate things, so in turn the slave differs from a free man in this, that for his recovery by postliminy, it is not required that he should come with the intention of adopting our cause. This in fact is required in the case of the man who is going to recover himself, not in the case of him who is to be recovered by another.[22]

The Roman law furthermore does not exempt runaway slaves from the operation of this law of nations. The master recovers his former right over these also, . . . the [explanation] being that [the] rule [is not] so injurious to him, who always remains a slave [while a contrary rule would be] fraught with damage for [the] master.[23]

By the Roman law, slaves who have been ransomed from the enemy become forthwith the property of the person who ransoms them; but when the price has been paid back, they are held to have been recovered.[24]

12. Whether peoples may be recovered by postliminy

We are more concerned with this question, whether peoples who were subject to a foreign rule also relapse into their former relation. This may be considered in the case that not he to whom the chief command belonged, but someone of his allies, had delivered the people from the enemy. In this case, I think we must give the same answer as in the case of slaves, unless it has been otherwise agreed in the treaty of alliance.[25]

13. Territory is recovered by postliminy

Among things recoverable [by postliminy] we have first to do with territory[26] . . . 'It is true', says Pomponius, 'that when the enemy have been

thereby loses his ownership of his slave, who now belongs to the captor as well. Suppose that the captor frees the slave; and then the soldier and his ex-slave both escape back to their home. Is the ex-slave free, by virtue of the manumission by the enemy; or does he resume his pre-capture servile status? Grotius's answer is that he resumes his prior servile status – provided that, upon the return, he is 'actually held' by the returned soldier (or is 'easily obtainable'). If the slave has returned but is in hiding from his master, there is no postliminy. There is postliminy, though, if the presence of the slave is generally known, since that makes him 'easily obtainable' by the master.

[22] For free persons, postliminy includes a mental element (an intention to associate himself with his home state) as well as a physical one (the act of returning). For a slave, as for an inanimate object, there is no mental component. The mere act of return suffices, so long as that act is publicly known.

[23] *Digest*, 49.15.19.5 (Paul).

[24] I.e., they then pass into the possession of their prior owners.

[25] If, say, a colonial area is occupied by an enemy of the mother country in war, but is then liberated by an ally of the erstwhile mother country, what is the fate of the area? Grotius's answer is that the law of postliminy applies, so that the area reverts to its former owner.

[26] The reference is to territory occupied by the enemy during war, and then recovered by the original sovereign.

expelled from the territory which they have taken the ownership of it returns to the former proprietors.'[27]

Furthermore, the enemy ought to be considered as expelled from the time when they are no longer able to approach openly.

The law regarding [rights] connected with the soil I consider to be the same as that regarding territory. Pomponius has written that consecrated and holy places, which have been captured by the enemy, if they have been freed from this misfortune, are restored to their original condition as though returned by a sort of postliminy.[28]

[For the same reason] we shall be obliged to say that the usufruct of land that has been recovered is restored.[29]

14. The distinction that was formerly observed with regard to movable things

With regard to movable things, there is a general rule . . . that they do not return by postliminy but belong with the spoil. Therefore, also, what has been acquired in trade, wherever it is found, remains the property of him who bought it, and the former owner has not the right to reclaim it if it is found among those who are at peace, or brought within the frontier.[30]

In ancient times, we see that things which were of use in war were excepted from this rule, which the nations seemed to have sanctioned, in order that the hope of recovery might render men more zealous in procuring them.[31] In those times, the institutions of very many states were organised for warfare; wherefore an agreement was easily reached in this matter. Moreover, those things . . . considered to be of use in war . . . [include] warships and transports, but not yachts and fast boats acquired for pleasure; mules, but only such as are pack animals; horses and mares, which have been broken to the bit.[32]

Arms and clothing are indeed of use in war, but they do not return by postliminy because those who lose arms or clothing in war are by no means

---

[27] *Digest*, 49.15.20.1 (Pomponius).   [28] *Digest*, 11.7.36 (Pomponius).

[29] See *Digest*, 7.4.23 (Pomponius), slightly mis-cited by Grotius.

[30] Postliminy does not apply to movable property. Therefore, if the enemy captures property belonging to Person A, the enemy thereby acquires title to it. If, later in the war, the property is captured from the enemy by B (a fellow soldier of A), then the property belongs to B, not A, i.e., the property has not reverted to its former status as owned by A. The effect, then, is that, once property is captured from A, he loses title definitively. By this same token, if the captor sells the property to a buyer in a neutral country, then the neutral buyer takes good title (i.e., he succeeds to the absolute title of the captor) – with recovery by A still excluded.

[31] This reference is probably to captured property which is sold to buyers in neutral countries. In the special case of war-related goods, the original owner has the title, by postliminy, rather than the buyer. The hope is that the original owner will then zealously set about recovering the goods from the hapless buyer.

[32] See *Digest*, 49.15.2 (Ulpian); and 49.15.2.1 (Marcellus).

deserving of favour; in fact such loss was accounted a disgrace, as is abundantly clear in the historical writings. But in this respect, it is noted, arms differ from a horse, because a horse may dash away without fault of his rider.

15. The current law with regard to movable things

But in recent times, if not previously, the distinction noted seems to have been done away with. For those who are familiar with customs generally record that movable things do not return by postliminy [even if they are war-related]; and we see in many places that this has been made a rule with regard to ships.

16. On things not needing postliminy

Things which, although seized by the enemy, have not yet been brought within his fortifications, have no need of postliminy, because by the law of nations, they have not yet changed ownership. Also, things which pirates or brigands have taken from us have no need of postliminy;[33] . . . the reason is that the law of nations does not concede to pirates or brigands the power to [acquire] the right of ownership.

19. When the right of postliminy may be enforced

In our times, however, not only among Christians but also among most Mohammedans, . . . the right of [postliminy has] disappeared, since the necessity . . . was removed by the restoration of the force of the relationship which nature has wished to prevail among men.[34] Nevertheless, that ancient law of nations could be applied if there should be an affair with a people so barbarous that without declaration or cause it should consider it lawful to treat in a hostile manner all foreigners and their possessions.

While I was writing these words, a judgement to that effect was rendered in the highest chamber at Paris. . . . The decision held that goods which had belonged to French citizens, and had been captured by the Algerians, a people accustomed in their maritime depredations to attack all others, had changed ownership by the law of war, and therefore, when recaptured by others, became the property of those who had recovered them. In the same suit, this decision was recorded, to which we just now referred, that today ships are not among the things which are recovered by postliminy.

---

[33] See *Digest*, 49.15.24 (Ulpian); and 49.15.27 (Javolenus).

[34] This passage is somewhat obscure. Perhaps it is being contended that the general law of postliminy has lost its importance because the matters covered by it are commonly dealt with in peace treaties at the conclusions of conflicts.

Cautions in regard to things which are done in an unlawful war

1. On a sense of honour forbidding what the law permits

I must retrace my steps, and must deprive those who wage war of nearly all the privileges which I seemed to grant, yet did not grant to them. For when I first set out to explain this part of the law of nations, I bore witness that many things are said to be 'lawful' or 'permissible' for the reason that they are done with impunity.[1]

3. Effect of injustice of a war

[I]f the cause of a war should be unjust, even if the war should have been undertaken in a lawful way,[2] all acts which arise therefrom are unjust from the point of view of moral injustice (*interna iniustitia*). In consequence, the persons who knowingly perform such acts, or co-operate in them, are to be considered of the number of those who cannot reach the Kingdom of Heaven without repentance. True repentance, again, if time and means are adequate, absolutely requires that he who inflicted the wrong, whether by killing, by destroying property, or by taking booty, should make good the wrong done.

4. Who are bound to make restitution for an unjust war

Furthermore, according to the principles which in general terms we have else-where set forth, those persons are bound to make restitution who have brought about the war, either by the exercise of their power, or through their advice. Their accountability concerns all those things, of course, which ordinarily fol-low in the train of war; and even unusual things, if they have ordered or advised any such thing, or have failed to prevent it when they might have done so.

---

[1] There now begins an exposition of the law of war from the standpoint of natural law, rather than of the law of nations.

[2] The reference is to a war which is unjust according to natural law, but just according to the volitional law of nations.

Thus also generals are responsible for the things which have been done while they were in command;[3] and all the soldiers that have participated in some common act, as the burning of a city, are responsible for the total damage. In the case of separate acts, each is responsible for the loss of which he was the sole cause, or at any rate was one of the causes.

5. On restoration of things taken in an unjust war

I should not think that we ought to admit [an] exception ... [for cases in which evil intent is not present]. Fault without evil intent is in fact sufficient to warrant restitution.[4] There are some who seem to think that things captured in war, even if there was not a just cause for the war, should not be restored. The reason they allege is that those who fight with one another, in entering upon war, are understood to have given these things to the captors. But no one is presumed to risk his property rashly; and war of itself is far removed from the nature of contracts.

However, in order to give to peoples that were at peace a certain rule to follow, that they might avoid being involved in war against their will, it was sufficient to introduce the idea of external ownership (*externum dominium*) of which we have spoken, which may exist along with the internal obligation (*interna obligatio*) of restitution.[5]

A not unlike case is that arising from a contract entered into without fraud, in which there is an inequality. In such a case, under the law of nations there arises a power of some sort to compel him who has made the contract to fulfil his agreements. [N]evertheless, in accordance with the duty of an upright and honourable man, he who has contracted for more than is right is nonetheless bound to reduce the transaction to an equality.

6. On restoration of captured property by later holders

[Even] he who has not inflicted the loss himself, or has inflicted loss without any fault of his own, [but merely] has in his possession a thing taken from another in an unlawful war, is under obligation to return it, because there is no

---

[3] In the modern law of war, this is the essence of the principle known as command responsibility. In modern law, however, the liability is not strict. There must be a degree of fault on the commander's part.

[4] The central concern is to prevent unjust enrichment. The fact of unjust enrichment, on its own, places the unjustly enriched party under an obligation to disgorge his or her undeserved gains, without regard to good faith or the like.

[5] The notion of 'external ownership' comes from the law of nations, as observed earlier. The 'internal obligation' comes from the law of nature. That internal obligation is in force even if there is no legal procedure whereby the property can be taken from the holder and returned to the original owner.

naturally just reason why the other should go without it – neither his consent, his deserving of evil, nor recompense.

Still, in accordance with the principles which have been elsewhere explained,[6] it will be possible, if the person who holds the thing has incurred any expense or labour, to [charge the owner an amount equal to that expense]. But if the possessor of the thing has, through no fault of his own, consumed or alienated it, he will not be held responsible except in so far as it may be held that he has been thereby enriched.[7]

---

[6] See p. 183 above.

[7] The holder of the property is, then, not required to dig into his pockets to compensate the owner. But he is required to turn over to the owner the property itself, or to disgorge any gain that he made from it.

Moderation with respect to the right of killing in a lawful war[1]

2. Who may be killed in accordance with moral justice

When it is just to kill – for this must be our starting point – in a lawful war in accordance with moral justice (*iustitia interna*)[2] and when it is not just to do so, may be understood from the explanations which were given by us in the first chapter of this book.[3] Now a person is killed either intentionally or unintentionally. No one can justly be killed intentionally, except as a just penalty or in case we are able in no other way to protect our life and property; although the killing of a man on account of transitory things, even if it is not at variance with justice in a strict sense, nevertheless is not in harmony with the law of love. However that punishment may be just, it is necessary that he who is killed shall himself have done wrong, and in a matter punishable with the penalty of death on the decision of a fair judge. But we shall here say less on this point, because we think that what needs to be known has been sufficiently set forth in the chapter on punishments.[4]

4. On killing for a fault that is intermediate between ill-fortune and deceit

But it must be observed that, between absolute wrong and unmitigated ill-fortune, a mean may often intervene which is composed, as it were, of both elements. In such a case, the action cannot be called purely that of a man having knowledge and intent, nor purely that of a man not having knowledge

---

[1] In this, and the succeeding five chapters, more than in any other part of the text, Grotius departs from concentration on law, to bring in considerations of mercy, morality and the like. He also strays from his subject of killing as a belligerent act, going into a lengthy digression on questions of fault in general. Only in Section 8 does he return to the subject of warfare.

[2] Moral justice is to be contrasted to strict right according to either natural law or the volitional law of nations.

[3] See p. 325 above.   [4] See p. 275 above.

or acting against his will. To this class of actions, . . . [the Latin label] *culpa* [may be applied].[5] In the fifth book of the *Ethics*, . . . [Aristotle] speaks as follows:

> Of those things which we do of our accord, some we do deliberately, others without premeditation. Those are said to be done deliberately which are done after a certain previous mental consideration; what is done otherwise is done without premeditation. Since, therefore, in human intercourse the inflection of injury may occur in three ways, that which proceeds from ignorance is called a mistake; as when a person has done something not against him whom he had in mind, or has done what he did not have in mind, or not in the way he thought, or not with the expected result; as if someone thought that he was striking not with this instrument, nor this man, nor for this cause, but there happened what he had not intended. An example would be if a man wished to prick, not to wound, or not to do it to this man, or not in this way.
>
> Now when the hurt is done contrary to expectation, it will be a mishap. But if the injury could have been in any way expected, or foreseen, and yet is not inflicted with evil intent, there will still be a degree of fault; for he is very near to a fault who has in himself the origin of the action, while he is unfortunate if the origin is outside of him. Whenever a person acts with full consciousness of what he does, yet not after deliberation, we must admit the presence of wrong, as in the acts which men are wont to commit under the influence of anger and similar natural or unavoidable emotions. For those who inflict injury when stirred by anger, and admit their fault, are not cleared from wrong; but yet they are not said to be unjust or wicked. But if anyone commits the same act deliberately he will rightly be styled wicked and unjust.
>
> Consequently, what is done under the influence of anger is correctly held not to have been done with premeditation. For it is not he who does something from anger, but he who has caused the anger, that started the trouble. Again, the matter in dispute is not whether the thing happened or not, but its justice; for anger arises from that which anyone thinks has been wrongfully done to him. Therefore, the question under discussion is not whether this or that has been done. . . . [T]he purpose is to discover whether what has been done has been done justly.[6]
>
> But if a man harms another by choice, he acts unjustly; and *these* are the acts of injustice which imply that the doer is an unjust man, provided that the act violates proportion or equality. Similarly, a man *is just* when he acts justly from deliberate purpose; but he *acts justly* if he merely acts voluntarily, without deliberation.[7]

---

[5] In modern usage, '*culpa*' refers basically to fault in the sense of carelessness or negligence, i.e., to situations in which the wrongful act could and should have been prevented, but in which the act was not actually intended. This contrasts with '*dolus*', a situation in which the wrong is done intentionally (or, as it is sometimes said, with malice).

[6] The point is that breach of a contract is, per se, actionable – i.e., the failure to perform is a wrongful act, without regard to the frame of mind of the defaulting party. A breach of contract, however, is not, per se, an unjust act, unless there was an intention on the defaulter's part to inflict an injury onto the other party.

[7] A person who acts in a just manner after deliberation may be said to *be* just, in addition to acting justly. A person may nonetheless act justly without deliberation –

But of the things which are not done on the spur of the moment, some are deserving of pardon, and others not. Deserving of pardon are those which are not only done by ignorant persons, but also done in consequence of their ignorance. If something is done by ignorant persons, yet not because of their ignorance, but from such a diseased mental state as goes beyond the common limits of human nature, it is not deserving of your pardon.[8]

This passage, which is truly notable and has been much used, I have rendered ... in its entirety, because in most cases it is not correctly translated and therefore not adequately understood.

[A]n example [may be given] of that which could not have been expected: the case of one who injured his father when opening a door, and of one who wounded somebody when training himself in throwing the javelin in a deserted spot. As an example of what could have been foreseen, but happens without malice, is the case of him who has thrown his javelin on a public road [and thereby injures a traveller].... [A]n example of what is done under necessity [is] the case of him who is compelled to do something by hunger or thirst; of what is done from natural emotions are cases of love, grief, fear.... [S]omething is done through ignorance when one is ignorant of a fact, as if someone should not know that a woman is married. Something is done by one who is ignorant, but not through ignorance, when one is ignorant of the law.[9] However, to be ignorant of the law is at times pardonable, at times unpardonable.[10]

6. Regarding those responsible for a war

[I]n considering those who are responsible for a war, we must distinguish between the causes of their action; for there are some causes which are not indeed just, but still are such that they may deceive persons who are by no means wicked.[11]

7. On remission of punishment

Even where justice does not demand the remission of punishment, this is nevertheless often in conformity with goodness, moderation, with high-mindedness.... An enemy therefore who wishes to observe, not what the laws of men permit, but what his duty requires, what is right from the point of

---

   i.e., by accident, as it were – but such a person cannot be said to *be* just. It may be recalled that Grotius earlier expressly rejected this Aristotelian distinction between being just and acting justly. See p. 14 above.
[8] Aristotle, *The Nicomachean Ethics*, V.8. Grotius slightly mis-cited this in his text.
[9] The effect of mistakes of fact and mistakes of law continues to cause controversy in criminal law.
[10] See *Digest*, 22.6.9.3 (Paul).
[11] Vitoria, *On the Law of War*, 59. For the discussion of plausible causes of war, see p. 301 above.

view of religion and morals, will spare the blood of his foes. [H]e will condemn no one to death, unless to save himself from death or some like evil, or because of personal crimes which have merited capital punishment. Furthermore, from humanitarian instincts, or on other worthy grounds, he will either completely pardon, or free from the penalty of death, those who have deserved such punishment.

8. Preventing the death of innocent persons

Again, with regard to the destruction of those who are killed by accident and without intent, we must hold fast to the principle which we mentioned above. It is the bidding of mercy, if not of justice, that, except for reasons that are weighty and will affect the safety of many, no action should be attempted whereby innocent persons may be threatened with destruction.[12]

9. On the sparing of children, women, and the aged

With these principles recognised, the defining of provisions to cover the more special cases will not be difficult.... In the first place, with regard to children, we have the judgement of those peoples and ages over which moral right has exerted the greatest influence.[13] ... Again, that which is always the rule in respect to children who have not attained to the use of reason is in most cases valid with regard to women. This holds good, that is, unless women have committed a crime which ought to be punished in a special manner, or unless they take the place of men.

10. Sparing those whose occupations are solely religious or concerned with letters

The same principle is in general to be applied to men whose manner of life is opposed to war.[14] ... In this class must be placed, first, those who perform religious duties. From ancient times among all nations, it has been customary that such men should abstain from the use of arms; and so in turn men refrained from violence towards them. In the same class with the priests are deservedly ranked those who have chosen a similar manner of life, as monks and novices, that is, penitents; these the canons, in accordance with natural justice, order men to spare just the same as priests. To priests and penitents, you may properly add those who direct their energies to literary pursuits, which are honourable and useful to the human race.

---

[12] The concern is with, in modern parlance, collateral damage to innocent parties by acts of war. It may be noted that the avoidance of such damage is placed in the category of moral acts or acts of grace, rather than of actual legal constraint.
[13] Vitoria, *On the Law of War*, 36.   [14] *Ibid.*, 36.

11. Sparing farmers

In the second place farmers, whom the canons also include, should be spared.

12. Sparing merchants and like persons

The canon adds merchants; and this provision is to be taken as applicable not only to those who make a temporary sojourn in hostile territory, but also to permanent subjects; for their life also is foreign to arms. Under this head are included at the same time artisans and other workmen, whose pursuits love peace, not war.

13. Sparing prisoners of war

To spare prisoners is commanded by the nature of goodness and justice.... We see that in history those are praised who, when they might have been burdened or endangered by an excessive number of prisoners, preferred to release all rather than kill them.

14. On accepting surrender with conditions attached

For the same reasons, the surrender of those who yield upon condition that their lives be spared ought not to be rejected, either in battle or in a siege.... In the case of besieged cities, the acceptance of surrender was the rule among the Romans before the battering-ram had shaken the wall.... The custom even now obtains in the case of unfortified places, before cannon fire is opened; and, in the case of more strongly fortified places, before an assault is made upon the walls.

15. Sparing those who have surrendered unconditionally

The same sense of justice bids that those be spared who yield themselves unconditionally to the victor, or who become suppliants.

16. What has been stated is true, provided that no serious crime has preceded

Against these precepts of justice and the law of nature, frequently exceptions are offered, which are by no means just; as, for example, if retaliation is required, if there is need of inspiring terror, if too determined a resistance has been offered. Yet he who recalls what has previously been said in regard to valid reasons for putting to death will easily perceive that such exceptions do not afford just grounds for an execution.

There is no danger from prisoners and those who have surrendered or desire to do so. [T]herefore, in order to warrant their execution, it is necessary that a crime shall have been previously committed, such a crime, moreover, as a just judge would hold punishable by death. [Punishment of prisoners, or a refusal to accept their surrender, is permissible] if [the prisoners] were convinced of the injustice of [their cause and yet] remained in arms; if any have injured the good name of their enemies with monstrous slanders; if they have violated their plighted word, or another right of nations, such as that of ambassadors; [or] if they were deserters.

But nature does not sanction retaliation except against those who have [personally] done wrong. It is not sufficient that, by a sort of fiction, the enemy may be conceived as forming a single body; this may be understood from our foregoing discussion on the sharing of punishments.[15]

Even the advantage, which is anticipated for the future from frightfulness, does not suffice to give the right to kill;[16] but if the right [to kill] already exists, [this] may be among the reasons for not waiving the right.

Furthermore, a quite obstinate devotion to one's own party,[17] provided only that the cause is not altogether dishonourable, does not deserve punishment, . . . Or, if such devotion is punished in any way, the penalty should not be carried so far as death; for no just judge would so decide.

17. Sparing those who are guilty, if their number is very great

Even where the crimes are such that they may seem worthy of death, it will be the part of mercy to give up something of one's full right because of the number of those involved.

18. On killing hostages

What decision according to the law of nature should be rendered in regard to hostages may be gathered from what we have said already. In former times, it was commonly believed that each person had over his own life the same right which he had over other things that come under ownership, and that this right, by tacit or expressed consent, passed from individuals to the state. It is, then,

---

[15] Enemy soldiers may be punished for war crimes only if they were personally guilty of them. Captured soldiers who are innocent of crimes may not be punished as substitutes for their guilty comrades who are still at large. In modern parlance, the contention is that what are now called belligerent reprisals are not allowed. On reprisal in general, see p. 338 above.

[16] I.e., it may be anticipated that acts of terrorism or cruelty would be expected to bring a concrete military advantage, such as inducing the enemy to surrender or agree to peace more readily than he otherwise would. Nonetheless, they are wrongful.

[17] For example, a stubborn refusal to surrender when there was clearly no reasonable hope of victory.

not to be wondered at if we read that hostages who were personally guiltless were put to death for a wrong done by their state, either as though done by their individual consent, or by the public consent in which their own was included. But now that a truer knowledge has taught us that lordship over life is reserved for God, it follows that no one by his individual consent can give to another a right over life, either his own life, or that of a fellow-citizen.

Furthermore some of the modern jurists, men not without standing, say that such agreements are valid if they are confirmed by custom. This I admit, if by right they mean mere freedom from human punishment, which in the discussion of this subject often passes under such a name. If, however, they consider that those who take the life of anyone on the justification of an agreement alone are exempt from wrong-doing, I am afraid that they are both deceived themselves and by their dangerous authority deceive others.

It is clear that, if he who comes as a hostage is, or previously was, of the number of great criminals, or has subsequently broken his pledge given in an important matter, it may be that his punishment will not be unjust.

19. All useless fighting should be avoided.

This remains to be added, that all engagements, which are of no use for obtaining a right or putting an end to a war, but have as their purpose a mere display of strength, . . . are incompatible both with the duty of a Christian and with humanity itself.[18] Consequently rulers, who must render account of the useless shedding of blood to Him in Whose name they bear the sword, should strictly forbid such combats.

---

[18] This is a capsule statement of the principle of military necessity in its restrictive aspect.

12

Moderation in laying waste and similar things

1. When devastation may be lawful

In order that anyone may be able to destroy another's property without doing wrong, it is requisite that one of these three conditions should precede: [first is a] necessity, such as should be understood to have been excepted in the first institution of ownership. An example would be that a person, in order to escape imminent danger, should cast into a river the sword of a third party, which a madman is about to use. In this case, however, we have elsewhere said that, in accordance with the better view, there remains an obligation to make good the loss.[1] [Second is] a debt arising from an inequality, it being understood that the thing destroyed is reckoned as received for that debt, since otherwise the right would not exist.[2] [Third is] a deserving of evil, for which such punishment may be an equivalent, or the measure of which is not exceeded by the punishment, for . . . equity does not suffer a whole kingdom to be laid waste because flocks have been driven off or some houses burned. These reasons, which are applicable only within proper limits, cause the absence of wrong in the destruction of another's property.

But, unless a motive of utility commends such a course, it would be foolish to injure another without securing any good for oneself. Those, therefore, that are wise are usually influenced by considerations of utility.

In fact that kind of devastation must be tolerated which compels the enemy to sue for peace in a short time. . . . Nevertheless, if you examine the matter aright, you will find that such depredations are ordinarily committed from motives of hatred rather than from considerations of prudence. It usually happens either that those [three] conditions which justify devastation are lacking, or that there are other more cogent reasons which advise against it.

---

[1] For the discussion of the general principle of necessity, see p. 70 above.

[2] The case supposed is one in which Person A becomes indebted to Person B by some kind of unconscionable means, such that A transfers money or property to B which is greater than B deserves (according to natural-law principles of justice). To destroy any property which is in excess of what B actually deserved does not amount to an injury to B. It simply rectifies the injustice done to A, and prevents B from being unjustly enriched.

2. If the area is profitable for us and out of the power of the enemy

[Devastation should be refrained from] if our occupation of fruitful ground is such that it cannot yield produce for the enemy. That is the particular point of the divine law, which ordains that wild trees be employed in making walls and military structures, but that fruit-bearing trees be preserved for purposes of food.[3] . . . Still more binding will this restriction be after a complete victory.

3. If there is good hope for a speedy victory

In the second place, what we have said will hold good even where the possession of land is in doubt: [devastation should be refrained from] if there is good hope of a speedy victory, of which the prize will be both the land and its fruits.

4. If the enemy has means of subsistence from other sources

In the third place, the same thing will happen if the enemy can have means of subsistence from another source, for instance, if the sea, or if other boundaries, shall be open. Under such conditions, therefore, it is best to leave agriculture undisturbed even along the common frontier. This we see in recent times was the arrangement for a considerable period in the war of the Netherlands against the [Holy Roman] Empire, with the payment of tribute to either party.[4]

The canons, teachers of humanity, established these practices for the imitation of all Christians, as those who ought to exercise and who profess a greater degree of humaneness than others; and so they seek to protect from the perils of war not merely the farmers, but also the animals which they use in cultivation and the seeds which they keep for sowing.

5. If the area is of no use in furnishing resources for war

In the fourth place, it happens that certain things are of such a nature that they are of no value for making or waging war. Such things reason wishes us to also spare, during the continuation of the war.

---

[3] *Deuteronomy, 20:19–20*

[4] The reference is to the Dutch War of Independence, which was in progress throughout Grotius's life. It was not definitively resolved until 1648 when, in conjunction with the Peace of Westphalia, Spain conceded independence to the Northern Netherlands (while retaining the Southern Netherlands, which approximates to present day Belgium). The payment of tribute probably refers to a practice in which the occupier of lands accepted payment from the inhabitants in lieu of destroying their crops.

6. Concerning things that are sacred

While what has been said holds true of other things of artistic value, for the reason which we have already given, there is a particular reason in the case of those things which have been devoted to sacred uses. Although such things also, as we have said elsewhere, are public in their own way, and so, according to the law of nations, are violated with impunity, nevertheless, if there is no danger from them, reverence for divine things urges that such buildings and their furnishings be preserved, particularly among those who worship the same God, in accordance with the same law, even if perhaps they disagree in respect to certain doctrines or points of ritual.

7. Concerning consecrated things

What I have said of sacred things must also be understood of consecrated things, also of structures erected in honour of the dead; for these cannot be violated without contempt for human feeling, even though the law of nations does accord impunity to the venting of anger against them. The jurists say that . . . the highest reason . . . acts in defence of religion.[5]

8 Advantages flowing from such moderation

It is, in truth, not strictly a part of our purpose to inquire at this point what is advantageous. [W]e desire rather to restrict the unrestrained licence of war to that which is permitted by nature, or to the choice of the better among the things permitted. Nevertheless, virtue itself, in low esteem in the present age, ought to forgive me if, when of itself it is despised, I cause it to be valued on account of its advantages.[6]

In the first place, then, such moderation, by preserving things which do not delay the war, deprives the enemy of a great weapon, despair. . . . There is the further consideration that, in the course of war, such moderation gives the appearance of great assurance of victory, and that clemency is of itself suited to weaken and to conciliate the spirit.

Moreover, that which has been observed by certain theologians I hold to be true, that it is the duty of the highest authorities and commanders, who wish themselves to be regarded as Christians both by God and by men, to forbid

---

[5] *Digest*, 11.7.43 (Papinian).
[6] Grotius is somewhat embarrassed to have to provide utilitarian or instrumental justifications for moral acts which ought to be performed on their own intrinsic merits.

the violent sack of cities and other similar actions. Such actions cannot take place without very serious harm to many innocent persons, and often are of little consequence for the result of the war; so that Christian goodness almost always, and bare justice very often, shrinks from them.

13

Moderation in regard to captured property

1. Limit on capture of enemy property

The capture of enemy property in a lawful war is not to be thought [to be always] devoid of wrong, or exempt from the obligation of restitution. In fact, if you consider what may justly be done, it is not permissible to take or to hold property of greater value than the equivalent of the enemy's indebtedness, with this exception, that over and above that amount one may retain things necessary for a guarantee.[1] When the danger is over, however, there should be a restoration, either of the things themselves or of their value, according to our discussion in the second chapter of Book II. What would be permitted in the case of property of persons at peace is much more permissible in regard to the property of enemies. There is, then, a certain right of seizure, without a complete right of ownership.[2]

Now since a debt may be due to us either because of an inequality of possessions,[3] or as the result of a [form of] punishment, the property of enemies may be acquired for either reason, but still with a distinction. For we have previously said that, by a debt of the former sort, not merely the property of the debtor, but also that of his subjects, according to the law of nations, is made liable, as though in the case of surety.

This right of the law of nations, indeed, we hold to be of another kind than that which exists in mere impunity or the external power of courts of law. For just as he with whom we have completed a transaction by our private consent acquires not only a legal but also a moral right to our property, so also a right is

---

[1] Vitoria, *On the Law of War*, 56. A guarantee, that is, against future wrong-doing.
[2] The discussion of this point is from the standpoint of natural law, rather than of the voluntary law of nations. That means that the right of capture of enemy property gives only a right to hold the property (pending satisfaction by the wrong-doer for his wicked acts), and does not involve a transfer of full legal title. And even a right of holding is allowed only up to the value of the loss caused by the wrong-doer. Furthermore, the voluntary law of nations allows the just war-maker to go further in this direction. See also Grotius's prior discussion of this point, at p. 359 above.
[3] By 'inequality of possessions' is meant the possession by some party of more than his due, at the expense of some other party. The injured party is entitled to have this inequality rectified.

acquired by a kind of common consent, which through a certain force contains in itself the consent of individuals, in the sense in which a law is called 'a common agreement of the state'. It is the more credible that such a basis of right was approved by nations in the kind of affair under consideration because the law of nations was introduced not only for the sake of avoiding greater evil but also to secure to each one his right.[4]

2. Whether enemy property can be held as punishment for the crime of another

But in the other form of indebtedness, which is penal, I do not see that, [even] by the consensus of the nations (*gentium*), such a right has been extended to the property of subjects. Such an obligation imposed upon the property of others is hateful, and consequently ought not to be extended further than the practice has clearly been. The advantage, furthermore, is not the same in the latter as in the former kind of indebtedness; for the former consists in goods, but the latter does not, and so its exaction can be omitted without loss.[5] . . . Therefore, the property of the subjects of enemies cannot be acquired on the ground of

---

[4] This passage sets out the justification, according to natural law, for allowing the taking of the property of enemy nationals in wartime. The thesis is that nationals are understood to 'offer' their property to their rulers, by agreeing to act as sureties for wrongs that their rulers might commit. In private law, a creditor lawfully takes – and acquires full title to – property of a surety when the principal debtor fails to pay. The same thing (according to Grotius) happens in war: the just side in a war lawfully takes the property of the enemy sovereign's sureties. Like the private creditor, the just warrior obtains full legal title to that property, and not mere exemption from punishment for the taking. The strict logic of this argument would allow it to operate only in favour of the just side in a war. But, as will become apparent, the volitional law of nations allows capture of enemy property by the unjust side as well. See p. 359 above.

[5] In the case of the taking of property as compensation for injury sustained, the injury being remedied 'consists in goods' in the sense that the injury is quantifiable in terms of money or a quantity of goods. Therefore, the taking of property of the wrong-doer by the victim is limited, under natural law, to an amount equal to the damage suffered. Punishment of a wrong-doer, in contrast, does not 'consist in goods' because, as explained in the discussion of punishment (at p. 282 above), punishment does not necessarily operate on the basis of equivalence to the material damage caused by the offence, nor is punishment compensation for such damage. Applying this reasoning to the question at hand, it would be said that, when compensation is sought for wrong-doing, it is fair to regard the subjects of a ruler as his sureties, so that their property is subject to taking. Were that not so, the victims of the wrong-doing would risk going uncompensated. This concern is inapplicable to a war waged for punishment, since injured parties are not seeking compensation. Nor is the principle of suretyship applicable in cases of criminal offences. It is confined to cases of indebtedness. Therefore, in Grotius's view, the taking of the property belonging to the enemy sovereign's subjects is not allowed in punitive wars, according to natural law.

punishment, but only that of those who have themselves done wrong. [A]mong these are included also the magistrates who fail to punish . . . crimes [committed by persons under their jurisdiction].

3. Whether debt includes indebtedness which arises in time of war

Moreover, the goods of subjects may both be seized and acquired, not only for the exaction of the original debt which gave rise to the war, but also for the exaction of indebtedness which develops subsequently; this is according to what we said at the beginning of this book.[6] In such a sense we must take what certain theologians write, that captures in war are not to be set off against the principal debt; for it is to be understood that such captures are an offset up to the point where, according to a sound judgement, satisfaction has been obtained for the loss occasioned by the war itself.

4. The obligation of humaneness not to make the fullest use of one's right

But we must keep in mind that which we have recalled elsewhere also, that the rules of love are broader than the rules of law. He who is rich will be guilty of heartlessness if, in order that he himself may exact the last penny, he deprives a needy debtor of all his small possessions; and even much more guilty if the debtor has incurred the debt by his goodness – for instance, if he has gone surety for a friend – and has used none of the money for his own advantage . . . . Nevertheless, so hard a creditor does nothing contrary to his right according to a strict interpretation. Therefore, humanity requires that we leave to them that do not share in the guilt of the war, and that have incurred no obligation in any other way than as sureties, those things which we can dispense with more easily than they, particularly if it is quite clear that they will not recover from their own state what they have lost in this way.

This also is to be observed. The right over the goods of innocent subjects has been introduced as a subsidiary means;[7] and as long as there is hope that we

---

Although Grotius does not discuss the point, the same reasoning would seem to apply to prevent capture of enemy private property, under natural law, in the third kind of just war as well: defensive war. The reason is that, here too, it is not a case of redressing a quantifiable injury.

Also unmentioned by Grotius is an important fact: that the law of nations gives a greater right to capture enemy private property than natural law does, in two respects. Firstly, in a war to obtain redress for injury, property can be taken above the level of the loss sustained from the injury. Secondly, capture of property is allowed in the other two kinds of just war as well: punitive and defensive.

[6] See p. 326 above (hardly 'the beginning of this book').

[7] Introduced, that is, by way of a kind of legal fiction, which equates subjects of a ruler with sureties in private law.

can obtain what is ours with sufficient ease from the original debtors, or from those who by not rendering justice voluntarily make themselves debtors,[8] to come to those who are free from blame, even though it is granted that this is not in conflict with our strict right,[9] nevertheless is to depart from the rule of human conduct.

Instances of such humanity are found everywhere in history, particularly in the history of Rome. Examples are when lands have been ceded to the conquered enemy on the condition that they should pass to the state, that is, that they should fall to the conquered state; or when a part of the land [of a defeated enemy] was left to the ancient possessor as a mark of respect. So you may often read that surrendered cities were not sacked, and we have said above that it is praiseworthy, and in accordance with the pious precepts of the canons, to spare not only the persons but also the property, of the tillers of the soil, subject at any rate to tribute. Upon condition of a similar tribute, immunity from war is usually granted to merchandise also.

---

[8] The reference is to denial of justice on the part of the sovereign of the debtor. A denial of justice to the creditor, through a culpable failure to compel the debtor to discharge his debt, is itself a wrong on the sovereign's part, distinct from the default of the original debtor.

[9] By 'strict right' is meant right according to the volitional law of nations.

14

Moderation in regard to prisoners of war

1. When it is permissible to take men captive, according to moral justice

In those places where custom sanctions the captivity and slavery of men, this ought to be limited primarily, if we have regard to moral justice, in the same way as in the case of property; with the result that, in fact, such acquisition may be permitted so far as the amount of either an original or derivative debt[1] allows, unless perhaps on the part of the [captured] men themselves there is some special crime which equity would suffer to be punished with loss of liberty. To this degree, then, and no further, he who wages a lawful war has a right over the captured subjects of the enemy, and this right he may legitimately transfer to others.

Furthermore in this case also, it will be the task of equity and goodness to employ those distinctions which were noted above, when we discussed the question of killing enemies.[2]

2. Treatment of slaves according to the moral power of justice

Now in the first place, it must here be noted that that right, which originates in a kind of surety on behalf of the state, can nowhere extend so widely as the right which arises [when, as a result of a crime, the criminal becomes a slave] as a penalty. Hence a certain Spartan said that he was a prisoner, not a slave;[3] for, if we regard the question properly, this general right against prisoners captured in a lawful war is equivalent to that right which masters have over those who, under constraint of poverty, have sold themselves into slavery; only the misfortune is even more to be pitied of those who have met this fate not by their own particular act, but through fault of their rulers. . . . This servitude, then, is a perpetual obligation of services for maintenance that is likewise perpetual.

---

[1] An example of a 'derivative debt' would be a denial of justice, i.e., a failure on the part of a sovereign to compel a debtor to discharge his obligation.
[2] See p. 349 above.   [3] Plutarch, *Sayings of Spartans*, Spartans to Fame Unknown, 40.

Therefore that which may be done to a slave with impunity according to the law of nations differs widely from that which natural reason permits to be done.[4] ... Seneca [stated]: 'Although against a slave all things are permissible, there are some things which the common law of living things (*commune ius animantium*) forbids to be done against a human being.'[5]

3. On killing an innocent prisoner

Therefore the right, which is called the right of life and death over the slave, causes the master to have domestic jurisdiction, which, indeed, is to be exercised with the same conscientiousness as public jurisdiction.

4. On punishment with severity

[I]n regard to minor punishments, ... as beating of slaves, we must apply fairness, and further, clemency.

5. On imposing severe tasks upon slaves

[S]ervices also are to be exacted with moderation, and the health of slaves is to receive humane consideration.

7. Whether it is permissible for slaves to attempt to escape

The question here arises, whether it is right for a person who has been made a prisoner in a just war to attempt to escape; we are not dealing with him who has deserved this penalty by his own crime, but with him who has come into such a condition by a public act. The sounder view is that it is not right, because, as we have said, by the common consent of nations (*ex conventione ut diximus gentium communi*), such a captive owes his services on behalf of his state.[6] This

---

[4] I.e., the law of nations requires more lenient and humane treatment of slaves than natural reason does. Grotius reveals his debt to the Aristotelian view of slavery, in which slavery was regarded as natural, and in which slaves were seen as mere tools or property of their masters, like beasts of burden. Aristotle, *Politics*, I.4–6. This contrasts with the Roman-law position, in which slaves had a number of legal rights, and in which slavery per se was explicitly regarded as contrary to natural law (though allowed by the *ius gentium*). See *Digest*, 1.5.4.1 (Florentinus).

[5] Younger Seneca, *De Clementia*, I.18.

[6] It will seem odd to some to contend that a captured prisoner owes services to his captor, as a form of service to his own state. After all, it is clearly in the interest of his own state that he escapes (and rejoins its armed forces). This is the view of the modern law of war. See Article 8 of the Hague Rules of 1907, which provides that prisoners may not be punished for attempting to escape. Grotius's assumption appears to be that the captured soldier was fighting on the unjust side in the war, so that his state (including himself) owes reparation to the just side for its prior wrong.

view nevertheless is not to be understood as valid in a case where intolerable cruelty imposes the necessity of escape upon the captive.

8. Whether the children of slaves are bound to the master

In another connexion, we raised the question, whether and to what extent the offspring of slaves are bound to the master by moral justice.[7] This question should not be passed over here, because it particularly concerns prisoners of war. If the parents had merited death by their own crimes, then for the preservation of their lives, the offspring which was expected of them could be bound to slavery, because otherwise these would not be born. As we have said elsewhere, parents may in fact sell their children into slavery if otherwise they would face starvation.[8]

However, children that were already born, no less than their parents, as part of the state could have been made liable for a debt of the state; but with regard to those who have not yet been born, this reason does not seem sufficient; and another appears to be required. Either the obligation in question may arise from the express consent of the parents, along with the necessity of supporting the children, and then it may exist without end; or it may arise from the mere furnishing of sustenance [by the master], in which case it exists only up to the time when [the children's] services shall have cancelled all that has been expended for them. If any further right over the children is given to their master, apparently it arises from the civil law,[9] which to masters is more generous than just.

9. What is to be done where the enslavement of prisoners of war is not customary

Among those peoples who do not avail themselves of the right of slavery which arises from war, the best course will be to exchange prisoners; the next best, to release them at a price that is not unfair.[10] What that price is cannot be set forth in exact terms; but humanity teaches that it should not be raised to the point where its payment would place the prisoner in want of the necessities of life. Such indulgence is in fact granted by the laws of certain countries to many

It might be contended that the prisoner of war owes service to his captor on the ground this is in exchange for the sparing of his life by the captor. But if that were so, then it would seem that the prisoner would owe service to the captor solely on his own behalf, not on that of his state.

[7] See p. 135 above.   [8] See p. 136 above.

[9] I.e., the municipal law of the captor's state.

[10] It will be noted that Grotius does not even consider what to us would be the obvious alternative: detention of the prisoners pending the conclusion of peace. In fact, the detaining of prisoners of war did not become a common practice until the nineteenth century.

who have fallen into debt by their own acts. In some places, the price put upon captives is fixed by agreements or by custom; as the sum of a mina among the Greeks of antiquity,[11] and at present among soldiers at a month's pay.[12]

[11] In the first century AD, a mina amounted to about one quarter of the annual earnings of an agricultural worker.

[12] Footnote by Grotius: 'In the war between the French and Spaniards in Italy, a cavalryman was ransomed for a quarter of a year's pay. But this did not include leaders of detachments or higher officers, nor those who fell into the enemy's power in a pitched battle or in the storming of a city.'

15

Moderation in the acquisition of sovereignty

1. To what extent moral justice permits sovereignty to be acquired

The equity which is required, or the humanity which is praised, in respect to individuals, is so much more required and praised in respect to peoples or parts of peoples in the degree that wrong or kindness toward a large number of persons becomes more notable. As other things may be acquired in a lawful war, so there may be acquired both the right of him who rules over a people and the right which the people itself has in the sovereign power;[1] only in so far, however, as is permitted by the measure of the penalty which arises from a crime, or of some other form of debt.[2] To these reasons should be added the avoidance of extreme danger. But this reason is very often confused with the others, although both in establishing peace and in making use of victory, it deserves particular attention for its own sake. It is possible to forgo other things from compassion; but, in case of public danger, a sense of security which exceeds the proper limit is the reverse of compassion.

4. On leaving the sovereign power to those who had held it

Another form of moderation in victory is to leave to conquered kings or peoples the sovereign power which they had held.

5. Provision for future security

Sometimes, with the concession of sovereign power [to the defeated ruler], provision is made for the security of victors [by the imposition of garrisons].

6. Provision of security by tribute and similar burdens

Often, the levying of tributes also has for an object not so much the restitution of the expenses that have been incurred as the security, in the future, of both victor

[1] Vitoria, *On the Law of War*, 59.
[2] It seems to be implied that, regarding the acquisition of sovereign rights of enemy rulers or peoples, there is no rule of the volitional law of nations allowing a victor to go beyond the constraints imposed by natural law.

and vanquished. . . . To this same problem[3] [of securing adequate assurances of security in the future] apply also the other conditions which we mentioned when discussing unequal treaties – the surrender of arms, of a fleet, of elephants, [or a commitment] not to maintain an army ready for battle nor an armed force.

7. The advantage derived from such moderation

Moreover, to leave to the vanquished their sovereign powers is not only an act of humanity, but often an act of prudence also.[4]

9. On leaving a part of the sovereignty to the conquered

If it is not safe to refrain from assuming any dominion over the conquered, the action may still be limited in such a way that a portion of the sovereign power may be left to them or to their kings. . . . We have elsewhere spoken of the ways of dividing the sovereign power.[5] To some peoples, a part of their governmental power has been left, as to former possessors a part of their lands.

10. On leaving some degree of liberty to the conquered

But when all sovereignty is taken away from the conquered with respect to their private affairs and minor public matters, it is still possible to leave to them their own laws, customs, and officials.

11. On leaving some degree of liberty in the matter of religion

A part of this indulgence is not to deprive the conquered of the exercise of their inherited religion, except by persuasion. . . . If, however, a false religion is practised by the vanquished, the victor will do right in taking steps to prevent the oppression of the true faith.

12. On treatment of the conquered with clemency

Last of all is this word of caution. Even under the fullest and, as it were, despotic sovereignty, the conquered should be treated with clemency, and in such a way that their advantage should be combined with that of the conquerors.

---

[3] I.e., the problem of securing adequate assurances of security in the future.
[4] Grotius proceeds to give many classical references; to the effect that holding onto conquered lands after a war is often more difficult than gaining them in the first place, and that moderation and justice are useful means of achieving this.
[5] See p. 60 above.

16

Moderation in regard to those things which by the law of nations have not the right of postliminy

1. On restoration of things which our enemy has taken from another in an unlawful war

We have explained above to what extent things become the property of the captors by a lawful war.[1] From such things, we must deduct those which are recovered by right of postliminy; . . . for these are regarded as not having been captured.[2]

But we said that that which was taken in an unlawful war must be restored, not only by those who took it, but also by others to whom the thing has come in any manner whatsoever. For no one, the authorities of the Roman law declare, can transfer to another more right than he himself has.[3] . . . The person who first took the thing did not have moral ownership (*dominium internum*); therefore, the person who obtains his right from him will not have it. [H]ence the second or third possessor takes an ownership which, for the sake of explanation, we call legal (*externum*), that is, an ownership which has the advantage of being everywhere protected by the authority and power of the courts. Nevertheless, if the possessor uses this advantage against him from whom the thing was taken by an act of injustice, he will not act rightly.[4]

We may here cite as pertinent the opinion which the worthy jurists gave with regard to a slave who had been captured by robbers and had afterward [been captured by] the enemy [in a war]; . . . he had been stolen, and . . . the

---

[1] See p. 359 above.   [2] On the right of postliminy generally, see p. 376 above.
[3] *Digest*, 9.4.27.1 (Gaius); and 41.1.20 (Ulpian).
[4] According to natural law, a fighter in an unjust war takes no title to property which he captures from the just side, any more than a highwayman or pirate does. Consequently, anyone to whom that property passes similarly has no legal title. The volitional law of nations, however, gives 'external ownership' even to such an unjust captor, i.e., it treats him as if he were fighting justly, with a right to take title to captured property. Only in one marginal sense is this external ownership inferior to full ownership (*dominium internum*): if the captor uses his property right against the very person from whom the property was taken. This presumably means that the true owner can recover the property if he locates it and institutes legal proceedings against the possessor – but that otherwise, the captor and his successors are regarded as having legal title.

fact that he had been in the power of the enemy [did not nullify] the right of the original owner.[5] On the basis of the law of nature, a similar opinion must also be rendered with regard to him who was captured in an unlawful war, and afterward, through an unlawful war, or from other causes, came into the power of another; for in moral justice there is no distinction between an unlawful war and brigandage.

3. Whether anything may be deducted from that which is restored

If [property captured in an unjust war] has come into any one's hands by way of trade [and is then reclaimed by the true owner], will [the buyer] be able to charge the [original owner] the price which he has paid?[6] It is consistent with what we have said elsewhere, that the possessor may charge as much as the recovery of the thing despaired of would have been worth to him who had lost it.[7] But if such an outlay may be recovered, why not also an evaluation of the labour and danger [expended in preserving the property], just as if by diving someone had recovered another's property which was lost in the sea?

4. Restoration of subject peoples or divisions of peoples to former rulers

Furthermore, just as goods are to be restored to their owner, so peoples also, and divisions of peoples, are to be restored to those who had the right of dominion over them, or even to themselves, if they had been independent prior to suffering the unjust violence.

5. When the obligation to make restoration ceases

Usually the question is raised also regarding the period of time in which the moral obligation to restore a thing may cease. But in the case of citizens under the same government, the question is answered according to their laws; . . . this may

[5] *Digest*, 49.15.27 (Javolenus). In this situation, there is a conflict between the right of the original owner and the right of the captor. In principle, the captor obtains title by virtue of the capture. But it is pointed out, on the authority of Roman law, that the original owner has the greater right because he never lost his right of ownership, i.e., the robbers who took the slave did not thereby obtain legal title to it. The true position is that, when the slave was captured in war, the captors then acquired whatever right the possessor himself had. In this case, that was no right at all because the robbers had never acquired legal title. Therefore, the original owner could claim the slave back from the captor.
[6] I.e., will the buyer be able to recover the purchase price that he paid from the true owner when the owner claimed the property back – so that the original owner would then have only the right of compulsory purchase of 'his' property?
[7] See p. 183 above.

be gathered from the language and scope of the laws by a careful examination. In the case of those, however, which are foreign in relation to one another, the question is to be answered in accordance with conjecture as to abandonment, which we have discussed elsewhere, so far as our purpose requires.[8]

6. What is to be done in a doubtful case

If, however, the lawfulness of the war is seriously open to question, the best course will be to . . . [persuade] the new possessors to accept payment and to give up what they held, and [also to persuade] the former owners to consider it more advantageous to have paid to them the value of their property than to recover it.[9]

---

[8] The obligation to return property unjustly taken lasts as long as the owner's title itself endures – i.e., forever, unless the owner is held to have abandoned the property. On abandonment under natural law, see p. 116 above.

[9] The proposal is for a somewhat rough-and-ready compromise when it is doubtful which side in the war was the just one. The effect would be to give the original owner a power of compulsory purchase from the captor. The result is that the captor is enriched by the value of the property, at the expense of the original owner – although the property itself ends up in the original owner's hands.

For a broadly similar solution to a problem of this kind, Grotius refers to Cicero, *On Duties*, II.81–2. Following the overthrow of a tyrannical government in Sicyon (in Greece) in 251 BC by a certain Aratus, the problem of competing claims to property promptly arose: between beneficiaries of the overthrown tyrants, who had held 'their' lands for up to fifty years; and the original owners, who had been exiled during the tyranny. Aratus's solution was to persuade the Ptolemaic ruler of Egypt to provide him with a large sum of money as a gift (apparently on the basis that Sicyon was a renowned arts centre and the ruler was a devoted lover of art). With this welcome largesse, Aratus was able to induce some of the claimants to settle for cash payment in return for renouncing their land claims. For this solution to work, of course, one claimant or the other, in each disputed case, would have to agree to settle for cash in place of land. Nevertheless, because of the outside gift from Egypt, no one gained or lost in terms of overall economic wealth. The solution proposed by Grotius is different, however, in that it does not envisage the arrival of an outside gift which will enable everyone to be satisfied.

17

On those who are of neither side in war[1]

1. On taking things from parties who are not at war

It might seem superfluous for us to speak of those who are not involved in war, since it is quite clear that no right of war is valid against them. But since in time of war, on the pretext of necessity, many things are done at the expense of those who are at peace, especially if they are neighbours, we must briefly repeat here what we have said elsewhere,[2] that the necessity which gives any right over another's property must be extreme; furthermore, that it is requisite that the owner himself should not be confronted with an equal necessity; that, even in case there is no doubt as to the necessity, more is not to be taken than the necessity demands. [T]hat is, if retention is sufficient, then the use of a thing is not to be assumed; if the use is sufficient, then not the consumption; if consumption is necessary, the value of the thing must then be repaid.

3. The duty of those at peace towards belligerents

On the other hand, it is the duty of those who keep out of a war to do nothing whereby he who supports a wicked cause may be rendered more powerful, or whereby the movements of him who wages a just war may be hampered, according to what we have said above.[3] In a doubtful matter, however, those at peace should show themselves impartial to either side in permitting transit, in furnishing supplies to troops, and in not assisting those under siege.[4]

---

[1] The modern term 'neutral' is not employed here, but instead the Latin '*medii*', meaning basically persons 'in between' the two belligerents.

[2] For the discussion of the principle of necessity, see p. 70 above. For the prior consideration of the rights of belligerents against neutrals, see p. 327 above.

[3] See p. 411 above.

[4] The contention is that states not participating in a war are not under a *general* duty to be truly neutral, in the sense of being scrupulously impartial to the warring sides. The primary duty of non-belligerent powers is to show partiality to the just side. Strict neutrality is only a second-best policy, to be adopted when there is doubt as to which of the belligerent parties is in the right and which is in the wrong.

It will even be of advantage [for the state at peace] to make a treaty with either party that is waging war, in order that it may be permissible to abstain from war while retaining the goodwill of either, and to render to each the common duties of humanity.[5]

[5] Agreements of this kind did in fact become common amongst European maritime powers in the period after Grotius wrote. They were not made during wars, though, as Grotius seems to suggest. Rather, they figured commonly in general friendship treaties, in provisions to the effect that, if either of the contracting states should, in the future, be at war with some third state, then the other party will be permitted to trade freely with that third party (except for contraband of war and the supplying of blockaded places).

On acts done by individuals in a public war

1. Whether it is permissible for individuals to do harm to a public enemy

What I have heretofore said applies chiefly to those who either possess the supreme command in war or are carrying out public orders. We must also consider what is permissible for an individual in war, not only according to natural and divine law, but also according to the law of nations.

In his first book *On Duties*, Cicero says that the son of the Censor Cato[1] had served in the army of the general [Popillius],[2] but that the legion in which he was serving was disbanded; nevertheless, since the youth from love of warfare remained in the army, Cato wrote to Popillius that he ought to oblige the young man to take the military oath a second time, if he wished him to remain in the army. Cato gave as a reason that after the first oath had been cancelled his son could not lawfully fight with the enemy. Cicero adds the very words of Cato from a letter to his son, in which he warns the youth to avoid engaging in battle, for the reason that it is not right for one who is not a soldier to fight with an enemy.[3]

But those are deceived who think that the principle thus stated has its origin in the law of nations. This becomes clear if you consider that, just as anyone is permitted to seize the property of an enemy, so also, as we have shown above, it is permissible to kill an enemy. For according to the law of nations, enemies are

---

[1] The reference is to the Elder Cato (Marcus Porcius Cato, 'the Censor', 234–149 BC), a famously upright figure, widely regarded as an embodiment of the traditional virtues which had made Rome great. He held a number of high offices, including the consulate (in 195 BC). He was elected as censor in 184 BC.

[2] Marcus Popillius Laenas was a Roman general and statesman active in the early second century BC. He held the consulate in 173 BC. His military activities were controversial, involving an attack, without provocation, against a tribe in northern Italy. He was put on trial *in absentia* for this conduct, although intervention by his family prevented a judgment from being rendered.

[3] Cicero, *On Duties*, I.36–7. In modern terminology, Cato would be said to have been concerned that his son would become an unlawful combatant by engaging in warfare without being a member of an organised armed force.

held to be entitled to no consideration.[4] The advice of Cato, therefore, comes from military discipline, which ... contained the provision that one who had not obeyed orders should be punished with death, even if what he had done turned out successfully.[5] But one who had fought an enemy outside the ranks and without the command of the general was understood to have disobeyed orders.... The reason why a discharged soldier cannot kill an enemy is thus stated by Plutarch: he is not bound by the military laws, by which those who are going to fight ought to be bound.[6]

If, however, we regard the law of nature and moral justice, it is apparent ... that, in a lawful war, any person is allowed to do whatever he trusts will be of advantage to the innocent party, provided he keeps within the proper limits of warfare.[7] [N]evertheless he is not allowed to make captured property his own, because nothing is due to him, unless indeed he is enforcing a legal penalty according to the common law of mankind (*communi hominum iure*).[8]

Now, a command [to attack the enemy] may be either general or particular. A general command is exemplified in the words which the [Roman] consul was accustomed to utter in the presence of the Romans in case of an uprising: 'Let those who wish the safety of the state follow me.' Individual subjects, moreover, in addition to the right of self-protection, are sometimes given the right to kill in case this is to the advantage of the state.

2. On injury to the enemy by those who are serving in the army, or fitting out ships, at their own expense

A special command may be given not only to those who receive pay, but also to those who serve at their own charges; and – a more important consideration – to those who support a part of the war with their own expenditures, such as those who fit out and maintain ships at private cost [i.e., privateers]. Such contributors, in lieu of pay, are generally allowed to hold captured

---

[4] According to the law of nations, any national of a belligerent side has an automatic right to kill enemies.

[5] *Digest*, 49.16.3.15 (Modestinus).   [6] Plutarch, *Roman Questions*, 39.

[7] This rather vague reference to keeping 'within the proper limits of warfare' implies that, even when waging a just war, certain acts are prohibited, even if they would make a material contribution to victory. Unfortunately, Grotius fails to shed any light on what these 'proper limits' are. Remember that the various kinds of 'moderation' were matters of unilateral concession or grace on the part of belligerents, or of morality, rather than of strict law.

[8] The meaning in this passage is not very clear, and no illustration is given of the point. The contention seems to be that citizens are entitled to fight on their own in a just war in which their state is involved – meaning that they are allowed to take steps that will weaken the enemy. But only soldiers in the armed forces have the right to obtain legal title to captured property. The assumption appears to be that only regular soldiers can be regarded as 'enforcing a legal penalty' in carrying on a just war.

property as their own, as we have said elsewhere.[9] How far this practice may be extended without the violation of moral justice and love, is a proper question for discussion.

Justice has regard either for the enemy or for the state itself with which an agreement is made. We have said that possession of all things, which can support war, may be taken from the enemy for the sake of security, but under the condition of making restitution.[10] Indeed, absolute ownership may be acquired in compensation for that which is due to a state waging a lawful war, either from the beginning of the war or from a later act, whether the property belongs to the hostile state or to individuals, even though the individuals themselves be guiltless. [T]he property of the guilty may be taken away and acquired by the captors as a means of imposing a penalty. Enemy goods will therefore become the property of those who are conducting at their own expense a part of the war, so far as this affects the enemy, provided that the limit which I have mentioned be not exceeded.[11] [W]hether the limit has been reached ought to be decided by a fair-minded judgement.[12]

3. What in respect to their own state is lawful for those who are serving in the army, or fitting out ships, at their own expense

As regards their own state, the arrangement with such contributors will be just, according to the standard of moral justice, if there shall be equality in the contract, that is, if the expenses and dangers shall be as great as the chance of booty. For if the expectation of booty shall be much greater, whatever shall be acquired in excess ought to be restored to the state.[13] The case is like that of

---

[9] See p. 365 above.
[10] For example, making restitution when the danger in question has passed – such as when the state from which property was taken no longer poses a threat. The holding of enemy property as security is therefore only a right of possession for the duration of the threat in question, and not an acquisition of full legal title.
[11] 'The limit' referred to is the quantity of property that is required either to compensate the wronged sovereign for actual losses (including the cost of waging the just war to obtain satisfaction), or to inflict just punishment onto the wrong-doing sovereign. It should be remembered that this limit is imposed by natural law. The volitional law of nations, in contrast, permits capture of enemy property in unlimited quantities. See p. 359 above on this point.
[12] This 'fair-minded judgement' will be arrived at by the authorities of the belligerent state itself, since there is no international tribunal available for the purpose.
[13] Vis-à-vis the enemy, the limit allowed for captures by private parties is, as just explained, the amount sufficient to compensate for wrongs, or to inflict just punishment. Vis-à-vis the entrepreneur's own state, however, the maximum is determined according to a different criterion: whatever will fairly reward the entrepreneur for the expense, labour, and danger actually undergone in his enterprise. Any amount captured above that limit should be turned over to the government.

a man who has bought at a very low price a cast of the net, which is, indeed, of uncertain value, but is easy to make and warrants the expectation of a great catch of fish.

4. What the rule of Christian love demands of such persons

Even when justice, strictly speaking, is not violated, one may sin against the duty which consists of loving others, especially the duty prescribed by the Christian law. A case of this character might arise if it should be apparent that plundering by such persons would not be especially harmful to the enemy as a whole, nor to the king, nor to those who are in fact guilty, but would harm innocent persons, and in fact to such an extent that it would plunge them into the greatest misfortunes, into which it would be the negation of mercy to cast those who are privately indebted to us. Now if to this is added the consideration that such plundering will have no notable effect in ending the war, or in weakening the public strength of the enemy, then gain acquired solely in consequence of the unhappy condition of the times ought to be considered unworthy of a just man, and especially of a Christian.

5. How a private war may be mingled with a public war

Sometimes it happens that a private war arises in connexion with a public war; as, for example, if a person has fallen among enemies and his life or property is endangered. In such cases, the rules should be observed which we have elsewhere stated in regard to the limit permissible in self-defence.[14] Public authority, again, is wont to be joined with private advantage. [A] case would be if a person who had suffered a great loss at the hands of the enemy . . . should obtain the right of collecting damage from the enemy's property. The right in that case must be defined in accordance with the principles stated above in regard to the taking of security.[15]

---

[14] This is another indication of the fact that, according to natural law, the right of individual self-defence is conceptually distinct from service in a just war (i.e., from service on behalf of one's sovereign in a case where the sovereign has been treated unjustly).

[15] The situation envisaged is one in which, during a state of war, a national of one of the belligerent states suffered losses at the hands of the enemy forces. It is possible, Grotius points out, for his sovereign to grant him an individual licence to recoup his losses by capturing enemy property. In such an event, the person has the right to take only so much property as will compensate him for his losses. And it is a good idea for the ruler to have the individual post a bond, to discourage him from going beyond this entitlement (in the way that it is a good idea for privateers to post bonds in case they commit unlawful depredations).

6. The position of a person who has done harm to the enemy without orders

But if a soldier or any other person, even in a just war, has burned houses belonging to the enemy, has devastated fields and caused losses of this character without orders; when, furthermore, there was no necessity or just cause, the theologians rightly hold that he is bound to make good the losses.[16] I am, however, justified in adding, what was omitted by them, 'when there was no just cause'; for if there is such a cause, he will perhaps be answerable to his own state, whose laws he has transgressed, but not likewise to the enemy, to whom he has done no legal wrong.

---

[16] This is an extremely important point, indicating the constraining aspect of military necessity. Just as any act which serves to advance the cause of victory is permissible in a just war (according to natural law), so, conversely, any act which does *not* contribute to victory is *not* permitted. In modern international law, this is the general principle that no 'unnecessary suffering' is permitted in armed conflict.

19

On good faith between enemies

1. On good faith with enemies in general

We have said that, in respect to character and extent, what is permissible in war is considered either absolutely or with reference to a previous promise. The first part of the subject has now been finished; there remains the latter part, which concerns the good faith of enemies with one another.[1] ... Those who are enemies do not in fact cease to be men. But all men who have attained to the use of reason are capable of possessing a right which has its origin in a promise.

From the association of reason and speech arises that binding force of a promise with which we are dealing. Because we have previously said that, in the opinion of many, lying to an enemy is either permissible, or free from wrong,[2] it must not be thought that this view can be extended with like reason to pledged faith. For the obligation to speak the truth comes from a cause which was valid before the war, and may, perhaps, in some degree, be removed by the war; but a promise in itself confers a new right.[3]

2. Whether faith should be kept with pirates and tyrants

Already in our previous discussion we have said that we ought not to accept the [contention that good faith is not owed to pirates and tyrants and the like].[4] ... Such agreements [admittedly] do not in fact share in that special community of legal obligations which the law of nations has introduced between

---

[1] Something is permitted 'absolutely' if it is allowed by the law of nature or (as the case may be) by the volitional law of nations. Such acts may, however, become prohibited on the ground that a binding promise has been made not to commit them. That situation is the one to which attention is now turned.

[2] See the discussion of this point at p. 335 above.

[3] The point is that the obligation to observe good faith towards an enemy might arise from either of two sources: general natural law (i.e., 'a cause which was valid before the war'), or the voluntary giving of a specific binding promise. In some cases, the outbreak of war nullifies natural-law obligations to observe good faith. But an actual promise made to an enemy during the conflict must nonetheless be honoured.

[4] See p. 218 above.

enemies engaged in a formal and complete war.[5] But because [the parties to these agreements] are human beings, they have a common share in the law of nature.... From this follows the consequence that the agreements must be kept [even with such persons as pirates and brigands].

3. Consideration of the fact that such persons deserve punishment

The first [point to consider] is that, as we have elsewhere explained, if we take into account the law of nature, atrocious criminals, who do not belong to any state, can be punished by any person whatsoever.[6] But those who can be punished with the loss of life can also be deprived of their property and rights.... Among the rights of such a person is the right arising from a promise. This right, therefore, can also be taken from him as a penalty.

I answer that the reasoning would hold good if one had not treated with the person in question as a malefactor; but if at any time we have treated with such a person as such, we ought to consider that we have been treating in regard to the remission of the punishment belonging to his condition. The fact is, as we have said elsewhere, that that explanation must always be assumed which prevents an act from becoming without effect.[7]

4. Concerning a promise that has been extorted through fear

Next, the objection, which I mentioned elsewhere, may be brought forward, that the person who has caused a promise to be made through fear is bound to free the promisor, for the reason that he has caused the loss unjustly; that is, by means of an action opposed to the nature both of human liberty and of an act which ought to be free.[8]

Though we admit that this is sometimes the case, yet it does not cover all promises made to brigands. For in order that the person, to whom a promise has been made, should be bound to free the promisor, it is necessary that he himself should have caused the promise by an unjust fear. If, therefore, anyone has promised a ransom in order to release a friend from captivity, he will be bound to pay; for the fear did not affect the person who came of his own free will to make the agreement.

---

[5] Conflict between law-abiding peoples and pirates does not constitute 'a formal and complete war,' which can only be waged against a state.

[6] See p. 271 above.

[7] This is rather unclearly put. The point is that, when making an agreement with, say, a pirate, with knowledge of the pirate's acts and character, we deliberately choose not to take account of that wickedness. It is therefore not open to us to repudiate the agreement later, on the ground that the person was a pirate. The position would be different if our contracting party is discovered to be a pirate only after the contract has been concluded.

[8] See the discussion on p. 256 above.

5. Concerning an oath extorted through fear

There is the further consideration that a person who has made a promise under the compulsion of an unjust fear can be obligated if the sanction of an oath has been added. For, as we have said elsewhere, a man is thereby bound not only to man but also to God; and in relation to Him, fear makes no exception.[9] Nevertheless, it is true that the heir of the promisor is not held by such a bond alone, because, according to the primitive law of ownership, those things which belong to the commercial relations of life pass to the heir but these do not include a right sought from God, as such.

This, again, must be repeated from an earlier statement, that if any one violates a sworn or unsworn pledge given to a brigand, he will not on that account be liable to punishment among other nations. For because of the hatred of brigands, the nations have decided to overlook illegal acts committed against them.[10]

6. On promises made to rebellious subjects

What shall we say regarding wars of subjects against their kings and other sovereign authorities? That subjects do not have the right to employ force, even though they have a cause which in itself is not unjust, we have shown elsewhere.[11] Sometimes even the injustice of their cause, or the baseness of their resistance, may be so great that they may be punished severely. Nevertheless, if they have been treated with as one would treat deserters or rebels, punishment cannot be inflicted contrary to a promise, as we have just stated.

In their scrupulousness the ancients held that faith must be kept even with slaves.

7. The effect of the right of eminent domain on promises made to subjects

At this point, in addition to the difficulties previously met with, a special difficulty is presented by the right of passing laws and the right of eminent domain over the property of subjects. [T]his right belongs to the state, and is exercised in its name by the one who holds supreme authority. If in fact this right covers all the possessions of subjects, why does it not cover also the right arising from a promise in war?[12] If this be conceded, it appears that all such

---

[9] See p. 218 above.
[10] In other words, the general obligation to observe agreements made with brigands is a requirement of natural law, but not of the law of nations. See p. 257 for the earlier discussion of the subject.
[11] See p. 68 above.
[12] I.e., if a sovereign has an inherent right to take a subject's property, in the name of the general public good, why does the sovereign not similarly have a right to take the

agreements will be void, and therefore there will be no hope of ending a war excepting through victory.[13]

But, on the contrary, we must note that recourse is had to the right of eminent domain, not indiscriminately, but only in so far as this is to the common advantage in a civil government, which, even when regal, is not despotic. But in most cases, it is to the common advantage that such agreements be kept.[14] . . . An additional point is that, when circumstances demand the enforcement of this right, compensation ought to be given, as will be explained later.[15]

8. On the confirmation of promises by an oath of the state

Moreover, treaties may be sanctioned by an oath taken not only by a king or a senate, but also by the state itself.

9. On promises benefiting a third person

But also a promise will be made with binding force [for the benefit of] a third person, who has not inspired fear. . . . Thus we read that, by the peace made with the Romans, Philip was deprived of the right of visiting cruelty upon those Macedonians who had revolted from him in war.[16]

> subject's power to enter into promises with the enemy? This argument appears to go to the question of preventing agreements with the enemy being made in the first place. But Grotius appears to believe that the eminent domain power would extend as well to the abrogation of existing agreements. This is probably on the thesis that the government can take from its subjects not only the power to conclude agreements, but also the duty to perform contracts already concluded. That is a doubtful proposition, though, as it would clearly involve an injustice to the other party to the contract.
>
> [13] There will be 'no hope of ending a war excepting through victory' because neither side would be willing to accept or rely on promises made by nationals of the other. This argument seems weak, since there seems to be nothing to prevent the two warring sovereigns from negotiating peace. Perhaps Grotius is contending that negotiations could not feasibly take place, since guarantees of safe conduct, truce and the like, which are necessary for the negotiating, could not be relied on. Grotius appears, however, to give no consideration to the possibility of negotiations through a neutral intermediary.
>
> [14] It is asserted that the general public benefit is the basis of the right of eminent domain. In the case of promises made to enemies, though, the general public benefit militates (according to Grotius) in favour of leaving the promises to be performed, rather than of 'nationalising' them.
>
> [15] See p. 428 below.
>
> [16] The reference is to the defeat of King Philip V of Macedon by Rome in the Second Macedonian War (200–197 BC). In modern international law, it became common to include amnesty provisions (as they were termed) in peace treaties. Their basic purpose was to deal with events in territories that had been occupied by the enemy during the war but which were then returned to the usual sovereign. It might be that, during the occupation, subjects had co-operated in varying ways with the occupying

10. How the political character of a state may be changed[17]

Further, we have shown elsewhere[18] that states of mixed character sometimes exist; and just as by agreement states may pass from one pure form into another, so they may pass also into a mixed form. Similarly, those who had been subjects may begin to hold sovereign power, or at any rate some part of it, together with the free right to defend that part by force.

11. Fear does not justify an exception in respect to a war that is formal according to the law of nations

A formal war, that is a war publicly declared on both sides, has not only other characteristics in respect to legal right but also this characteristic in particular: that all promises made in the course of the war, or for the purpose of terminating it, are valid to the extent that they cannot be made void by reason of a fear unjustly inspired, except with the consent of the party to whom the promise has been made. For just as many other things, though they may not be devoid of fault in some degree, are considered lawful according to the law of nations, so also the fear which in such a war is inspired on both sides.[19] Unless this rule had been adopted, no limit nor termination could have been fixed for such wars, which are extremely frequent. Yet it is to the interest of mankind that such bounds be set.

From this nevertheless it does not follow that the party who has extorted some such promise by an unlawful war can retain what he has received without violating the honour and duty of a good man, or even can compel the other to hold to the agreement, whether sworn to or not. For essentially and in its nature, the transaction remains unjust. This essential injustice of the action cannot be removed except through a new and absolutely free consent.[20]

12. Regarding types of fear which the law of nations prohibits

But my statement that the fear inspired by a formally declared war is considered lawful ought to be understood of such a fear as is not disapproved by the law of

---

power, for which they risked prosecution for treason after the return of the territory. An amnesty clause was designed to prevent such prosecutions from taking place, much as in the Macedonian case that Grotius cites.

[17] This section seems altogether out of place, having nothing to do with the present topic of good faith with enemies.

[18] See p. 60 above.

[19] This is another indication of a difference between the law of nature and the law of nations. According to natural law, 'a fear unjustly inspired' renders an agreement or promise void or voidable. That is not so according to the law of nations, with regard to agreements or promises made during a 'formal war'. An important caveat is given in the next section.

[20] The 'essential injustice' in question is from the standpoint of the law of nature, rather than of the law of nations.

nations.[21] For if anything has been extorted by the fear of rape, or by terrorising of any other sort which involves violation of pledged faith, it will be nearer the truth to say that the case has been brought within the scope of the law of nature; the force of the law of nations does not extend to such a fear.

13. Whether faith must be kept even with the faithless

I have previously said, in the general treatment of [oaths], that faith must be kept even with the faithless.[22]

14. Whether faith must be kept if the condition changes

At the same time, the fact should be recognised that, in two ways, one may be free from breach of faith and yet not do what was promised – if the condition ceases, and if compensation is given. The cessation of the condition does not in reality free the promisor, but the result shows that there is no obligation, since this was entered into only under the condition.[23]

To this principle we must refer the case which arises if the other party has not fulfilled what he on his part was bound to carry out. For the individual items of one and the same agreement seem to be related in respect to the two sides after the manner of a condition, as if it had been stated in this way: I will do thus and so if the other does what he has promised. . . . For this reason, whenever the intent is different, it is usually expressly stated that, if anything is done contrary to this or that provision, the [other provisions] nevertheless will remain valid.

15. Whether faith must be kept if the promisee wrongfully possesses property of the promisor

The origin of compensation I indicated elsewhere,[24] when I said that, if anything is ours or is due to us, and we cannot otherwise obtain it from him who has it or owes it to us, we can accept an equivalent amount in something else. From this, it follows the more clearly that we may keep what is in our possession, whether it be corporeal or incorporeal. Therefore, what we have promised will not have to be fulfilled if the value involved is no greater than that of our property which is wrongfully in the possession of the other.[25]

---

[21] The point is that even the voluntary law of nations does not give carte blanche to states to extort promises by means of fear. There are limits.

[22] See p. 219 above.

[23] In stating that the cessation of the condition 'does not in reality free the promisor', the meaning is that the failure of the condition does not render the promise *itself* void; it merely prevents the obligation to perform from taking effect. If the condition comes to be met, then the obligation to perform will duly arise.

[24] See p. 185 above.

[25] This is the right of set-off, discussed at p. 144 above. In the situation given here, A has promised to give something to B. B, however, has wrongfully taken possession of

16. Whether faith must be kept if the promisee has breached another contract with the promisor

The same principle will hold if the party with whom I have dealings owes as much or more under another agreement, and I am not able otherwise to secure what is due to me.[26]

17. Whether faith must be kept if the promise has injured the promisor

The same principle will have to be applied if the party who insists on the fulfilment of a promise has not carried out his part of the agreement, but has inflicted damage.

18. Whether faith must be kept when something is due from the promisee as a penalty

Finally, what is due as a penalty can be taken in lieu of what has been promised.[27]

19. Application of these principles to war

Just as in case an agreement has been made between contesting parties, while the suit is in progress, neither the action which gave rise to the suit, nor the losses and damages of the suit, can be used as an offset for what was promised; so, while a war lasts, compensation cannot be given for what originally caused the war, nor for what is customarily arranged in accordance with the laws of war among nations. For the nature of the business, that it be not void of effect, shows that the agreement was made without consideration of the controversies which led to the war. Otherwise, in fact, there would be no agreement which could not be lightly set aside.[28]

---

property belonging to A. A is therefore entitled to reduce his payment to B, pursuant to the promise, to the extent of the value of B's wrongful possession. This prevents the unjust enrichment of B at A's expense. Such a right 'trumps' the normal duty to perform a contractual obligation to the wrong-doing party.

[26] This is simply another application of the principle of set-off.

[27] Here too, the basic idea is set-off. In this case, the concern is not with the obtaining of compensation by the victim of a wrong, but instead with the infliction of a loss onto someone as punishment for some past misconduct.

[28] The reference is to a settlement agreement between opposing parties at litigation. The idea is that the settlement agreement is a free-standing arrangement, which cancels out and supersedes the plaintiff's claim. (The assumption is that there is no admission of liability on the defendant's part.) More specifically, it is not open to the plaintiff to reassert his claim, and to use the amount claimed to offset what he owes under the settlement agreement. Similarly, it is contended that arrangements between opposing sides in a war must be regarded as entirely independent of the

What, then, can be used as an offset to that which was promised? Undoubt-edly, whatever the other party owes . . . under the terms of another agreement entered into during the war; or it may be reckoned as an offset if he has caused damage during a truce or has failed to respect the inviolability of ambassadors, or has done anything else which the law of nations condemns between enemies.

Nevertheless the observation should be made that the adjustment is arranged between the same parties, and in such a way that the right of a third party is not infringed; yet so that the goods of subjects, as we have said elsewhere, are held by the law of nations to be liable for the debt which the state owes.[29]

We add this also, that it is characteristic of a noble mind to abide by treaties even after an injury has been suffered.

Almost all the questions which are wont to arise concerning the faith accorded to an enemy can be settled if we follow the rules already laid down in our discussion not only of the force of promises of all kinds, or of a special oath, or of a treaty and sponsions, but also of the rights and obligations of kings, and the interpretation of ambiguous statements.[30] Nevertheless, in order that the application of the foregoing principles may be more plain, and that our discussion may be extended to cover whatever else is in dispute, I shall not hesitate to touch on the special questions which are more common and which more generally demand attention.

dispute which gave rise to the war, so that neither party can use claims asserted in the run-up to the conflict to set off his obligations under the wartime agreement.

[29] See p. 338 above.   [30] See Chapters 11–14 above.

On the good faith of states, by which war is ended; also on the working of peace treaties, on decision by lot, on combat by agreement; on arbitration, surrender, hostages, and pledges

1. On factors which terminate a war

Understandings between enemies rest upon a promise expressed or implied. An express promise is either public or private. If public, it is imputed either to the supreme authority or to subordinate powers. That which is imputed to the supreme authority either puts an end to war or maintains its force while the war lasts.

Among the factors which terminate a war, some are looked upon as principal, others as accessory. Those are principal which themselves end the war by their own action, as treaties; or [which] refer to something else, such as the drawing of lots, the issue of combat or the decision of an arbitrator. Of the last three, the first rests on pure chance, while the other two combine chance with strength of mind or body, or with capacity of judgement.

2. The right to make peace in a monarchy

Those who have the right of initiative in conducting a war have the right to enter into treaties for the purpose of ending it. Each, in fact, is the manager of his own affairs. From this, it follows that, in a war which is public on both sides, the right to end it belongs to those who have the right to exercise supreme power. In a true monarchy, therefore, this will belong to the king, provided also the king has unrestricted power.

3. If the king is an infant, insane, a captive, or in exile

A king who is of such an age that he does not possess maturity of judgement (in some kingdoms such an age is defined by law, elsewhere it will have to be determined by a more probable estimate) or a feeble-minded king cannot make peace. The same principle will apply to a king in captivity, provided he possesses a kingly authority which had its origin in the consent of the people. It is, in fact, not credible that sovereignty was conferred by a people on such terms that it could be exercised by one who is not free. Therefore in this case also, not the undivided sovereignty indeed, but the exercise, and, as it were, the guardianship of it, will belong to the people, or to the one to whom the people has entrusted it.

Nevertheless, if a king, even in captivity, has pledged anything of his own private possessions, the pledge will be valid, in accordance with the principle set forth in what we shall state concerning private agreements.

But if a king shall be in exile, will he be able to make peace? Surely so, if it be established that he is not living under constraint; otherwise his condition will differ too little from that of a captive, for there are captives also who are loosely guarded.

4. The right of making peace in an aristocracy or a democracy

In accordance with what we have said elsewhere,[1] in aristocratic or democratic governments, the right of making treaties will belong to the majority – in the former case, the majority of the public council; in the latter, the majority of the citizens who according to custom have the right to vote. Accordingly, treaties so made will be binding even on those who have voted against them.

5. On alienation of the sovereignty, or a part of it, for the sake of peace

Let us now see what the things are which may be made subject of a treaty. Kings, such as the majority now are, are not able to alienate by treaty either the whole sovereignty or a part of it, since they hold their royal authority not as a patrimony, but as if in usufruct.[2] Even before they receive the kingship, while the people are still superior to them, such acts can be rendered entirely void for the future by a public statute, so that they cannot give rise to any obligation in the king's interest. And it is to be believed that the people have so willed. . . . In order, therefore, that the undivided sovereignty may be transferred in a valid manner, the consent of the whole people is necessary. This may be effected by the representatives of the parts which are called the estates.

In order to validly alienate any part of the sovereignty, there is need of a twofold consent, that of the whole body, and in particular the consent of that part of which the sovereignty is at stake, since without its consent it cannot be separated from the body to which it has belonged. Yet in case of extreme and in other respects unavoidable necessity, the part itself will probably transfer the sovereignty over itself in a valid manner without the consent of the whole people, because it is to be believed that that power was reserved when the body politic was formed.

---

[1] See p. 132 above.   [2] For the explanation of this thesis, see p. 57 above.

In patrimonial kingdoms, however, there is nothing to prevent a king from alienating his crown. Yet it may happen that such a king would not be able to alienate a part of the sovereignty, if indeed he has received the kingdom as his property on the condition of not dividing it. But the property described as royal may be included in the patrimony of the king in two ways, either separately, or indivisibly united with the kingdom itself. If included in the latter way, it may be transferred, but only with the transfer of the crown itself; if separately, it may be transferred separately.

But kings who do not hold their kingship in patrimony seem hardly to have been granted the right of alienating the property of the realm, unless this right plainly appears as arising from some early law, or has never been considered contrary to custom.

6. Whether the people, or his successors, are bound by a peace made by a king

We have elsewhere stated how far the people, and at the same time also the successors of the king, are bound by his promise,[3] to wit: so far as the power of creating binding obligations was included in his sovereignty. This ought neither to be given unlimited range, nor to be confined within too narrow limits, but ought to be so understood that what is based on good reason may be accepted as valid.

The case will plainly be different if a king is at the same time the absolute master of his subjects, and has received a sovereignty akin to that of a household rather than to that of a state. Such are kings who have reduced to slavery people conquered in war; or a king who does not indeed have ownership of persons but of their property, as Pharaoh in the land of Egypt, in consequence of purchase; and others, who have taken strangers into their private possession.

7. Whether in arranging peace the property of subjects can be given up for the sake of the public advantage

This question also is frequently discussed: in the effort to secure peace, what conclusion regarding the property of subjects may be adopted by kings who have no other right over the property of their subjects other than that inhering in the royal power? I have said elsewhere that the property of subjects belongs to the state under the right of eminent domain.[4] [I]n consequence, the state, or he who represents the state, can use the property of subjects, and even destroy it or alienate it, not only in case of direct need, which grants even to private citizens a measure of right over others' property,[5] but also for the sake of the public advantage; and to the public advantage, those very persons who formed

---

[3] See p. 227 above.   [4] See p. 420 above.
[5] On the general principle of necessity which is referred to here, see p. 70 above.

the body politic should be considered as desiring that private advantage should yield.

But, we must add [that], when this happens; the state is bound to make good at public expense the damage to those who lose their property; and to this public levy, the person himself who suffered the loss will contribute, if there is need. The state, furthermore, will not be relieved of this burden if perchance it is not equal to the payment at the time; but whenever the means shall be at hand, the obligation will reassert itself as if merely held in suspense.

8. Concerning property captured by the enemy in the war

I do not admit without modification the [contention] that the state ought not to take upon itself the loss already caused by a war, for the reason that the law of war permits such damages. For that law of war has reference to other peoples, as I have explained elsewhere, and in part applies to the relationships of enemies but not to those of citizens with one another.[6] Since citizens of a state are associates, it is right that they should share the common losses which are suffered by reason of their association.[7] Obviously, also, the municipal law may expressly provide that there shall be no right of action against the state for property lost in war, to the end that each individual shall defend his property with greater energy.

9. Whether there is a distinction between property acquired under the law of nations and under the municipal law

Some make a broad distinction between property which belongs to citizens by the law of nations and that which belongs to the same persons by municipal law. [I]n consequence, they grant to the king a more unrestricted right over property owned under the law of nations, even to the extent of taking it away without cause and without compensation. This distinction is wholly erroneous, for ownership, no matter from what cause it has arisen, always has effects originating in the law of nature. [C]onsequently, it cannot be taken away except as the result of causes which are inherent in ownership by its very nature, or arise from an act of the owner.[8]

---

[6] A state waging war is under no obligation to compensate the enemy for war-related losses suffered. But the question of liability of a belligerent to compensate its own citizens for losses is a separate question. See Section 7 above for the discussion.

[7] It is probably envisaged that the citizens of the belligerent state will 'share the common losses' by devising an arrangement in which all will contribute, through taxes or a similar mechanism, to a common fund which would compensate those who had lost property in war-related operations. A similar policy was suggested in the previous section, in the context of peace treaties.

[8] The contention is that, regarding private property rights, natural law acts as a constraint on both municipal law and the law of nations, in equal degree. That is to

10. A presumption of public advantage in cases of foreign-owned property

Now this doctrine, that the property of individuals should not be given up except for the public advantage, has reference to the king and his subjects. . . . The act of the king is in fact sufficient for foreigners, who make agreements with him, not only by reason of the presumption established by the dignity of his person, but also in accordance with the law of nations, which permits the property of subjects to be made liable by the act of the king.[9]

11. General rule for the interpretation of peace covenants

In the interpretation of peace covenants, the observation should be made that, as we have previously stated, the more favourable a condition is, the more broadly it is to be construed, while the further a condition is removed from a favourable point of view, the more narrow is the construction to be placed upon it.[10] If we have in view the law of nature, the most favourable condition seems to rest on this principle, that each shall obtain what belongs to him; . . . hence the interpretation of ambiguous clauses ought to be directed to the end that the party who had a just cause of war should obtain that for which he took up arms, and should likewise recover for damages and costs, but that he should not also recover anything by way of penalty, for that would arouse more hatred.

Since, however, it is not customary for the parties to arrive at peace by a confession of wrong, in treaties that interpretation should be assumed which puts the parties as far as possible on an equality with regard to the justice of the war. This is usually accomplished in one of two ways; either the possession of property, which has been disturbed by war, is adjusted in accordance with the former right of ownership; . . . or, things remain as they are (*uti possidetis*).[11]

---

say, the obligation to respect private-property rights is imposed by natural law, even if the particular property rights in question were conferred by municipal law or the law of nations. It is therefore exclusively to natural law that one must look to find limitations to the basic obligation to respect property rights.

[9] The concern is that the eminent-domain power of a ruler does not cover property belonging to foreigners within the territory. Two solutions to this problem are put forward. First, the foreigners can be regarded as parties to 'agreements' with the ruler allowing them to own property – with those agreements containing a provision allowing a taking of the property for the public good. Alternatively, it may be contended that the law of nations contains a general rule regarding foreign property owners analogous to the rule in the law of nature regarding subjects who are property owners (and who are, as such, subject to the eminent-domain powers of their ruler).

[10] See p. 243 above.

[11] Arrangements regarding property captured during the war are the same for the two sides: either both sides must return all captured property to the original owners, or else both sides retain all captured property.

12. How the understanding that things remain as they are ought to be interpreted

Of the two ways mentioned, in case of doubt the presumption is in favour of the second, because it is easier and does not introduce a change. . . . So . . . deserters will not be surrendered unless that is in the agreement. For we receive deserters by the law of war; that is, according to the law of war, we are allowed to admit and enrol on our side the one who changes allegiance. Under such an agreement, the other things [also] remain in the hands of the possessor.

In such cases, however, the word possession is understood not according to municipal law but according to the law of nature. For in wars, the fact of possession suffices, and nothing else is considered. Moreover, we have said that lands are so held if they have been enclosed by fortifications; for temporary possession, as in the case of a stationary camp, is here not to be taken into account.

Incorporeal possessions are not retained except through the things to which they belong, as the servitudes of lands, or through the persons who possess them.[12]

13. Concerning an agreement to restore all things to their pre-war condition

In the first kind of agreement, in which possession disturbed by the war is restored, we must note that the last possession, which existed before the war, is meant; nevertheless with the understanding that private persons who have been dispossessed may institute legal proceedings either by possessory action or by a claim for damages.[13]

14. Concerning those who gave up their freedom voluntarily

But if any free people has, of its own will, yielded to one of the belligerents, restitution [an agreement to restore pre-war conditions] will not be applicable to it; for restitution applies only to those things which are accomplished by force or fear, or in other ways through deceit permissible only against an enemy.

---

[12] Some servitudes are 'attached' to property, such as a right of way to a particular adjacent property. If the property in favour of which the servitude is held passed to the opposing side by way of capture or conquest, then so does the servitude. If, however, the servitude had been for the benefit of a person (and not attached to any particular land), such as a right to gather wood, then that servitude can only pass to the opposing belligerent if the holder of the servitude transferred nationality.

[13] This proviso deals with the case in which a private property owner, prior to the outbreak of the war, had been wrongfully dispossessed of his property, with the trespasser being in possession when the war broke out. The contention is that the return of things to their pre-war condition must be understood in such a way that the dispossessed owner is not deprived of his right of action against the trespasser.

15. Whether damages caused by the war itself are considered as remitted

If no other agreement has been made, in every peace it ought to be considered settled that there shall be no liability on account of the damages which have been caused by the war. This is to be understood also as to damages suffered by private persons; for such damages also are the result of war. In case of doubt, it is presumed that the belligerents intended to make such an agreement that neither would be condemned as guilty of injustice.

16. Concerning what was owed to individuals before the war

Nevertheless, we ought not to consider that debts, which were owed to individuals at the outbreak of war, have been cancelled. For cancellations of debts are not obtained by the law of war, but their collection has only been hindered by the war. When, therefore, the hindrance has been removed, they retain their full force.[14]

17. Concerning punishments which were due before the war

The . . . principle [that rights and duties existing prior to the war are revived] does not apply to the right to inflict punishment. For this right, in so far as it concerns kings or peoples, ought to be considered as held in abeyance, from fear that the peace will not be a perfect peace if it leaves the old causes for war.[15]

18. Concerning the right of private persons to inflict punishments

As to the right of private persons to inflict punishment, the reason is not so strong for thinking that it should be held in abeyance, because it can be

---

[14] The concern is with debts owed by nationals of one of the belligerent states to nationals of the other. During the war, the payment of these debts would generally have been prohibited, on the ground that the transfer of funds to the enemy state could work to enhance the enemy's strength in the struggle. The debt would be regarded as having been seized or captured by the debtor's state only if the debt had been entirely cancelled. Grotius explains that this is not the position. War merely acts to postpone payment of the debt, not to cancel it. So the obligation to repay revives when peace is made.

[15] By 'right to inflict punishment' is meant the right of one of the belligerent rulers to inflict a punishment onto a subject of the other one. It is apparently assumed that the claimed right to inflict the punishment had been one of the issues that gave rise to the war. In such a case, it should be presumed that the peace treaty abrogated the right to punishment, on the ground that the very purpose of a peace treaty is to eliminate all disputes that led to the war. On this reasoning, if the right to punish had been unrelated to the war (e.g., if it had been a matter of punishing the person for a violation of the ordinary criminal law), then presumably the punishment could proceed once peace had been restored.

enforced through the courts without war. Nevertheless, since this right is not so clearly ours as that which arises from inequality,[16] and punishments always cause hatred, a slight extension of the scope of the words will suffice to suggest that this right also may be understood to have been given up.

19. Concerning a right which was publicly alleged before the war

What I have said, that a right which existed before the war ought not easily to be considered annulled, should be firmly maintained with respect to the rights of individuals. [B]ut as to rights of kings and peoples, it is easier to understand that some condonation has occurred, if only statements, or not improbable inferences, are in evidence. This is above all the case if the right in question was not clear, but had been in dispute. It is, in fact, the part of kindness to believe that the right was suffered to fall into abeyance in order that the seeds of war might be eradicated.

20. Whether things captured after the making of peace must be restored

It is well established that things which have been captured after the conclusion of a treaty of peace must be restored. The right of war had, in fact, already expired.

21. Some rules bearing upon the agreement to restore things captured in war

In treaties which deal with the restitution of things captured in war, first, those provisions which apply equally to both sides ought to be interpreted more broadly than those which are one-sided.[17] Again, the provisions that are concerned with persons are construed more favourably[18] than those that treat of things. Among provisions treating of things, those that deal with land are construed more favourably than those dealing with movables, and those dealing with public property more favourably than those that treat of private property. Also among provisions treating of private possessions, those which order the

---

[16] That is, the right of private individuals to inflict punishment onto wrong-doers (who are their legal equals) is not so widely accepted as the right of private parties to obtain compensation for injuries suffered. The right to punish is more commonly seen as arising 'from inequality' (i.e., as the prerogative of rulers rather than of private parties).

[17] By 'more broadly' is meant that such agreements (applying to both parties equally) should be interpreted to include more types of property than would be the case with agreements that are one-sided.

[18] 'Provisions concerned with persons' presumably refer chiefly to prisoners of war, but could also include hostages.

return of things possessed under a saleable title allow greater latitude than those possessed under a burdensome title.[19]

22. Regarding income

A person to whom a grant of property is made on the conclusion of a peace is entitled to receive the income of it also from the time of the grant, but not before that time.

23. On the names of regions

The names of regions must be accepted according to the usage of the present time, and according to the usage of experts rather than of the common people; for such matters are usually treated by experts.

24. Concerning reference to a former treaty

The following rules also are of frequent application. As often as reference is made to a former or ancient treaty, the qualifications or conditions of the former agreement are in each case considered as repeated. Also the party, who was willing to do an act, must be considered as having done it, if he was hindered from doing it by the other party with whom the dispute occurred.[20]

25. Concerning delay in implementation of a peace treaty

However, the statement of some writers, that delay for a brief period is excusable, is not true unless an unforeseen necessity has proved a hindrance. It is, in fact,

---

[19] By 'a saleable title' is meant title that is not legally encumbered – therefore referring to property to which there is absolute ownership. Such property contrasts with property 'possessed under a burdensome title', in which a plurality of persons have rights of some kind in the property – the most obvious example being property which is mortgaged. Presumably, the difference in treatment is explained by the need to protect the parties with the other interests, such as mortgage holders. An illustrative scenario would be a case in which property was captured in war, and then mortgaged by the captor to a fellow national. If the peace treaty later provided for the return of all property, a question would arise whether the original owner was to be given his property back unencumbered by the mortgage. The dilemma here is unavoidable: either the original owner takes his property back encumbered by the mortgage (and is thereby worse off than he was before the capture); or the mortgage holder loses his security. Grotius's point is that we should be cautious about automatically assuming that the property is to be returned unencumbered. As observed above, there may be factors in a particular peace arrangement which militate against that option.

[20] Suppose, for example, that the 'former or ancient treaty' obligated one state to furnish persons expert in irrigation or mining to another state, to assist in that other state's economic development. Suppose then that a war ensues between the two countries and that the receiving state bars entry to the workers during the course of the conflict. It is held that the obligation to supply the persons should nonetheless be regarded as having been duly discharged.

not strange that some canons favour the excusing of such delay, since it is their duty to influence Christians to that view which is consistent with love for one another. But in this investigation concerning the interpretation of treaties, we are not now inquiring what is the better course, nor what religion and honour demand of each, but to what limit the application of a principle, based wholly on that right, which we have called legal, can be carried.

26. On interpretation in case of doubt

In case the meaning is doubtful, an interpretation is preferably to be adopted contrary to the interest of him who dictated the conditions, because ordinarily he belongs to the stronger party.[21] ... So likewise, an interpretation is adopted against the seller; for he has himself to blame for not speaking more plainly. The other party, however, could rightly accept, to his own advantage, a condition which admitted of several interpretations.

27. The distinction between furnishing a new cause for war and breaking a treaty

Of daily occurrence is the discussion of the question, when should a treaty of peace be considered broken? ... It is, in fact, not the same thing to furnish a new cause for war and to break a treaty [of peace]. [T]here is a great difference as regards both the penalty incurred by the one at fault and the relieving of the innocent party from his pledge in other matters.

A treaty of peace is broken in three ways: by acting either contrary to what is involved in every peace; or against what was expressly stated in the [particular] treaty of peace [at hand]; or against what ought to be understood from the nature of every peace.[22]

28. On breaking a treaty of peace by acting contrary to what is contained in every treaty of peace

A violation of what is involved in every peace will take place if a warlike attack is made, especially when no new cause is presented. If the fact can be alleged with probability, it is better to believe that the wrong was committed without faithlessness than with it. ... Having established this point, we must see by whom, and against whom, the armed attack which breaks the peace is made.

[21] This principle operates in the present-day law of contract, between private parties. It does not, however, operate in modern international law between states.
[22] The first and third of these are not easily distinguished. As later becomes apparent (in Section 40 below), things 'understood from the nature of every peace' refers to things that are characteristic of peaceful relations generally between states. Things 'involved in every peace', in contrast, refers to things that are universally included in peace agreements at the conclusions of wars.

29. If allies have made an attack

I see that there are some who think that, if those who have been allies make such an attack, the treaty of peace is broken. And I do not deny that an agreement can be made on such terms – not, to be sure, that one people should be subject to punishment for another's act, but that peace should not seem to have been finally made, but should remain subject to a condition.[23] . . . We ought not, however, to believe that a peace has been made in this way, unless the fact is perfectly clear. Such an arrangement is irregular, and not in harmony with the common desire of those who are making peace. Therefore, those who made the attack without the aid of others will be responsible for breaking the treaty, and the right to wage war will exist against them and not against the others.

30. If subjects have made an attack

If subjects do anything by armed attack without public orders, it will be necessary to see whether the act of individuals can be said to have been publicly approved. From what we have said above,[24] it can easily be understood that, to show public approval, three requisites are necessary: knowledge of the act, power to punish, and neglect to punish. Knowledge is shown by the fact that the acts are manifest, or have been made subject of complaint. Power is assumed, unless the lack of it is apparent. Neglect is evidenced by the expiration of the period of time ordinarily taken for the punishment of crimes in each state. Such neglect is equivalent to a decree.[25]

31. If subjects should engage in warfare under the command of others

The question is frequently raised, whether the rule just given holds if subjects do not take up arms on their own account but serve under others who are carrying on war. . . . [S]uch service ought not to be permitted.[26]

32. If harm has been done to subjects by the opposing side

Again, a treaty of peace ought to be considered broken, not only if an armed attack is made on the whole body of the state, but also if such an attack is

---

[23] I.e., to a condition that no attacks are made by allied parties. An attack by an ally is therefore not a breach of the treaty. Rather, it is an event which prevents the treaty from entering into force.

[24] See p. 257 above.

[25] I.e., to ratification or approval of the act committed by the subjects.

[26] The clear implication is that, if there is 'public approval' of such service by subjects, in the manner described in the previous section, then the peace treaty will be held to have been breached.

made on its subjects, of course without a new cause. For peace is made in order that all subjects may be safe. Peace, in fact, is an act of the state on behalf of the whole body and on behalf of its parts. Even more, if a new [dispute] arises, . . . it will be permissible [under the peace treaty] for [subjects] to defend themselves and their property. For . . . it is natural to repel arms with arms. Consequently, among equals, it is not to be thought easy to give up this right. But it is not permissible to punish, or to recover stolen property, by force, except after judgement has been refused; for these matters admit of delay, while self-defence does not.[27]

But if subjects commit wrongs so continuously, and in a manner so contrary to the law of nature, as to warrant the belief that they are acting wholly without the approval of their rulers, and if they cannot be brought into court, as in the case of pirates, it will be lawful both to recover property from them and to take vengeance on them, as if on persons who had been surrendered to us. But it is in truth contrary to the conditions of peace on that account to attack others who are innocent.

33. If allies are attacked

Also an armed attack made upon allies breaks a treaty of peace, but only an attack upon those allies who have been included in the terms of peace. . . . Further, if the allies themselves have not made the compact, but others for them, the same rule will nevertheless have to be applied, after it is fully settled that those allies have ratified the treaty of peace. For so long as it is still uncertain whether they wish to ratify it, they are to be considered as enemies.

34. Concerning the breaking of a treaty of peace by acting contrary to the terms of that treaty

[The second way in which] a treaty of peace is broken [is] by acting contrary to what has been stated in the [specific] terms [of the agreement itself]. Under action, moreover, is included the failure to do what one should, and when one should.

35. Whether a discrimination ought to be made between the articles of a treaty of peace

I shall not here admit a differentiation of the terms of peace into those that are of greater and those that are of less importance. For everything that has been included in the treaty of peace ought to seem important enough to be kept. Goodness, nevertheless, and especially Christian goodness, will more easily

---

[27] This emphasises that self-defence action by individuals must be against an *ongoing* attack – so that action taken after a delay cannot qualify as self-defence.

pardon lighter faults, especially if repentance is added. . . . But in order that peace may be still more securely safeguarded, it will be wise to add to the topics of minor importance the provision that the treaty of peace is not to be broken by anything done in violation of these, or that arbitration should be tried before it is permissible to take up arms.[28]

36. Effect of the addition of a penalty

And I am fully of the opinion that this seems to have been the intention, if any special penalty has been added; not because I do not know that a contract can be so made that the one to whom the injury has been done, may have a choice, whether he prefers the penalty or withdrawal from the agreement, but because the nature of the business requires what I have said.[29] [The general] principle indeed is agreed upon, and has both been stated by us above and approved by the authority of history: that a treaty of peace is not broken by the party who fails to stand by it after the other has broken it; for he was only bound conditionally.

37. If necessity has hindered fulfilment

But if necessity is the cause why one party has not fulfilled his promise, as, for example, if the thing has been destroyed or lost, or the act rendered impossible by some chance, the treaty of peace will not be considered as broken; for, as I have said, a treaty is usually not dependent on a chance condition. But the other party will have his choice, whether he prefers to wait, if there is any hope that the promise may be carried out later, or to receive an equivalent in estimated

---

[28] There is a presumption that all provisions of a peace treaty are of equal importance. In practice, however, it is possible that the parties will regard some provisions as being of only minor importance. Grotius advises singling these out explicitly by providing that, in the event of their breach, the peace treaty itself will continue in force. Regarding provisions of major importance, as later explained (at p. 453 below), the rule is that a breach justifies termination of the peace treaty by the non-breaching party.

[29] That is, if a peace treaty attaches a specific penalty to the violation of a specific provision, then a violation subjects the violator to the specified penalty, but leaves the peace treaty itself still in force. In other words, the stipulation of a penalty is a sign that the provision in question is a minor rather than a major element of the settlement. Consequently, the non-breaching party is required to accept the penalty and has no option of terminating the peace treaty. It is conceded that the position is otherwise in private law, where a penalty provision in a contract gives the non-breaching party the option of *either* accepting the penalty (and keeping the contract in force) *or* of terminating the contract. But Grotius insists that 'the nature of the business' of peacemaking between states – meaning the overriding general interest in ensuring that peace treaties remain in force – compels this difference in treatment.

value, or to be freed from mutual engagement corresponding with that item or of equal value.

38. Concerning the options of the injured party in case of breach

Certainly, even after a broken [peace] agreement, it is within the power of the injured party to preserve peace; . . . no one frees himself from an obligation by acting contrary to it.[30] And if the provision has been added, that the treaty of peace should be considered broken by such an act, this provision ought to be considered as added merely for the benefit of the innocent party, in case he wishes to take advantage of it.

39. Concerning the breaking of a peace by acting contrary to what belongs to the special nature of every peace

[The third way in which] a treaty of peace is broken [is] by doing what is contrary to the special nature of the peace.

40. What falls under the term friendship

Accordingly, acts that are contrary to friendship break a treaty of peace which was entered into under the terms of friendship. For whatever the [general] duty of friendship by itself demands of other men[31] ought [also to be performed] by the right of the [peace] agreement. . . . To treaties of friendship, . . . I refer many matters arising out of injuries inflicted [upon subjects of the states parties] without force of arms, and insults, which are frequently discussed by legal experts.[32] . . . [When such injuries are inflicted] the motive of ill-will should as far as possible be [presumed to be absent]. Consequently, if a wrong has been done to a person intimately connected with the party with whom the peace was made, or to a subject, it will not be considered as done to the party himself unless the wrong was done openly as an affront to him.[33]

---

[30] I.e., a breach of a peace treaty – or, for that matter, of any treaty – does not operate, on its own, to terminate the treaty. Termination occurs, if at all, at the option of the innocent party.

[31] Here is an indication of Grotius's support for the Aristotelian principle of the natural sociability of humans – the existence of a general 'duty of friendship'.

[32] Treaties of friendship, in other words, provide for the resolution of disputes that commonly arise between the states, if only by committing each sovereign to administer justice conscientiously to nationals of the other.

[33] If an injury is committed against a subject of one of the states parties to a treaty of friendship, then it will be presumed that that injury was not inflicted against the subject's state – and so will not constitute a cause for resorting to war. The clear implication is that the injury will be duly redressed in the courts of the place in which it was committed. This presumption of non-intent to injure the subject's state

This principle of natural justice is followed by the Roman laws in cases of cruelty in the treatment of slaves [by non-owners].[34] Adultery, also, and violation of chastity, will be referred rather to lust than to rupture of friendly relations, and the seizure of another's property will make the aggressor guilty of a new act of greed rather than of the breaking of faith.[35]

When no new cause is presented, threats that are truly savage are inconsistent with friendly relations. To this head I shall refer also the building of fortresses on the boundaries, not for defence but for the purpose of inflicting harm; and an unwonted levying of troops, if it shall be apparent, from satisfactory indications, that these are being levied against no one else than the party with whom the peace has been made.[36]

41. Whether it is contrary to friendship to receive subjects and exiles

It is not contrary to friendship to admit individual subjects who wish to migrate from one government to another. Such liberty in fact, as I have said elsewhere, is not only natural but also advantageous. Under the same principle I include the granting of asylum to exiles. For over exiles, the state has no right.

As I have said elsewhere,[37] it is clearly not permissible to admit towns or large aggregations, which constitute an integral part of a state. It is equally unpermissible to admit those who, by reason of an oath or in some other way, are under an obligation of service or of slavery [in their home country]. Moreover, we have previously stated[38] that, among certain peoples, the same rule has been introduced by the law of nations concerning those who are slaves by fortune of war. But also we have treated elsewhere of the surrender of those who, though not driven into exile, are seeking to escape a justly deserved penalty.[39]

---

is rebuttable, however – in the marginal case in which the wrong is 'done openly as an affront' to the subject's sovereign, it can be a just cause for war.

[34] *Digest*, 47.10.15.35 (Ulpian). In Roman law, if a non-owner of a slave committed an injury to a slave, then this act could constitute an offence against the owner – but only in the case of aggravated assaults or 'such insulting acts as clearly tend to dishonour the master himself'. Justinian, *Institutes*, 3.4.3.

[35] The point is that these various wrongful acts will not be understood to be complete repudiations of friendly relations in general, but instead will be treated as isolated wrongs to be remedied on a case-by-case basis, within a framework of generally amicable relations. Similarly, in the case of peace treaties, violations which occur should be presumed not to be indicative of a desire on the violator's part to repudiate the peace treaty as such.

[36] Actions of the kind stated may give rise to a right of defensive war – i.e., a fresh cause of war – on the part of the threatened state. This is, of course, on the understanding that there is no justification for these threatening acts (i.e., no 'new cause is presented' which justifies them). On the right of defensive war, see p. 89 above.

[37] See p. 134 above.   [38] See p. 372 above.   [39] See p. 293 above.

42. How war may be ended by drawing lots

The result of a war cannot in all cases be made subject to the chance of drawing lots, but only in those cases in which the issue is one over which we have full power. For the obligation of the state to protect the life, chastity, and other rights of its subjects, and of the king to protect the welfare of the state, is too great to permit the disregard of those considerations which stand in the most natural relation to the defence of themselves and others. Nevertheless, if on a careful estimate, the party attacked in an unjust war is so far inferior that there is no hope of resistance, it is apparent that a decision by lot can be offered, in order that a certain peril may be avoided by recourse to an uncertain one.[40] This, in fact, is the least of the evils.

43. Whether it is lawful to end a war by a set combat

There follows a much disputed question concerning combats which are agreed upon with definite numbers, for the sake of ending a war. . . . If we consider only the law of nations, in a strict sense, there should be no doubt that, according to it alone, such contests are lawful; for this law permits the killing of enemies without distinction. If, again, the opinion of the ancient Greeks and Romans, and of other nations, were true, that each man is the master of his own life without restriction, then such combats would not lack moral justice also. But I have already several times said that this opinion is in conflict with true reason and the precepts of God.[41] Elsewhere I have shown, both by reason and by the authority of the Sacred Writings, that whoever kills a man on account of things which we can do without sins against the law of love for his neighbour.

Let us now add that a man sins also against himself, and against God, who values so cheaply the life which was granted to him by God as a great favour. If the issue at stake, such as the safety of many innocent persons, is worthy of war, we must strive with all our strength to win. To use a set combat as an evidence of a good cause, or as an instrument of divine judgement, is unmeaning, and inconsistent with the true sense of duty.

There is only one condition which can render such a combat just and patriotic, from the point of view of one side merely; that is, if otherwise the expectation is in all respects warranted that the party supporting the unjust cause is [otherwise] going to be the victor with great slaughter of innocent persons. He, in fact, should be subject to no censure who prefers to fight in the way that will

---

[40] It may be open to dispute whether the just side should really be held to lose its rights in the event that it loses the draw. It could be contended that the drawing of lots is best seen as a stratagem of war, to buy time or to lull the unjust aggressor into a sense of false security, with a view to allowing the just side to triumph eventually, as it (by definition) deserves to do. It is unfortunate that Grotius does not discuss this question.

[41] See p. 392 above.

give to him the greatest probability of success. But this also is true, that some acts, which are not done rightly . . . are held permissible [by the law of nations] for the avoidance of more serious evils which cannot otherwise be escaped; as in many places base usurers and prostitutes are tolerated.

Therefore, as I previously said, when it is a question of avoiding war, if two persons, who are striving for the sovereignty, have prepared to contend with arms against each other, the people can allow such a combat in order that a greater calamity, otherwise imminent, may be avoided; so the same thing will have to be said when it is a question of ending a war.[42]

44. Whether the act of kings in such cases binds their peoples

On the other hand, those who thus refer a controversy to the outcome of a combat can indeed deprive themselves of whatever right they themselves possess; but in those kingdoms which are not patrimonial, they cannot also give a right to another who does not possess it. In such cases, therefore, in order that [an agreement to a set combat] may be valid, it is necessary to add the consent both of the people and of those persons, already born, who have the right to the succession.

45. How the victor is determined in a set combat

Often in such combats, the question is raised, which of the two should be considered the victor. Only those can be considered vanquished on whose side all have either fallen or taken to flight. . . . [W]ithdrawal to one's own territory or towns is a sign of defeat. . . . The other evidences – the collecting of spoils, the giving up of dead for burial, and challenging to battle a second time, which . . . you sometimes find mentioned as signs of victory – prove nothing in themselves, excepting in so far as, in connexion with other signs, they bear witness to the flight of the enemy. Surely in case of doubt, the one who has retired from the field of battle may be presumed to have fled. When, however, there are no sure proofs of victory, the issue remains in the same condition as before the battle, and must be referred either to [a new] battle or to new agreements.

46. On ending war by arbitration

[T]here are two kinds of arbitrators. One is of such a sort that we ought to render obedience, whether he is just or unjust; and this kind of arbitration . . . is found when the parties resort to an arbitrator under mutual promises to abide

---

[42] The concern is with the special case in which the disputing parties *themselves* agree to a decision by battle between themselves, rather than by means of using surrogate champions. See p. 309 above.

by his decision. The other deals with matters of such a kind that they ought to be referred to the decision of a just man.[43]

Either [an arbitrator] is charged with the task of reconciliation only, . . . or he serves as one whose decision must be absolutely obeyed. It is the latter class with which we are here dealing, and of which we said something above, when we spoke of the methods of avoiding war.[44]

Although municipal law may make provision for arbitrators to whom resort is had under promises on both sides, and in some places has provided that it shall be lawful to appeal from them and to make complaint of injustice, nevertheless such a procedure cannot become applicable in relation to kings and peoples. For here, there is no higher power, which can either hold fast or loosen the bond of the promise.[45] Under such conditions, therefore, the decision of arbitrators, whether just or unjust, must stand absolutely.

47. How arbitrators are to decide

In respect to the duty of an arbitrator, the point must be considered, whether he has been chosen in the place of a judge, or with somewhat larger powers. . . . Aristotle . . . says that 'it is the part of a fair and kindly man to prefer to have recourse to an arbitrator rather than to go to law'; and he adds as the reason, 'For the arbitrator has regard to what is fair, but the judge follows the law. Indeed the arbitrator was brought into existence for this very purpose, that equity might prevail.'[46] In the passage just quoted, equity does not properly mean, as elsewhere, that division of justice which interprets more narrowly the general import of law according to the intention of the lawgiver, for such interpretation has been committed to the judge also. [R]ather it means everything which is better done than left undone, even outside of the rules of justice properly so called.

[I]n a case of doubt, it ought not to be understood that so great power has been granted [to an arbitrator]; in doubtful cases, in fact, we follow the narrowest interpretation. But this statement is especially in point in respect to those who hold sovereign power; for since they have no common judge, we must consider that they have restricted the arbitrator by those rules by which the office of a judge is usually restricted.

48. Whether arbitrators ought to decide on the basis of possession

Nevertheless this observation should be made, that arbitrators chosen by peoples or by sovereigns ought to render a decision regarding the main point at issue, but not in regard to possession. For decisions regarding possessions

[43] *Digest*, 17.2.76 (Proculus).   [44] See p. 308 above.
[45] I.e., there is no higher authority, such as a court, to which the losing party can appeal if he believes that the arbitral opinion rendered was contrary to justice.
[46] Aristotle, *Rhetoric*, I.13.

belong to municipal law; by the law of nations, the right of possession follows ownership. Consequently, while the case is under advisement, no change ought to be made, not only to avoid prejudice [to the ultimate decision], but also because recovery is difficult.[47]

49. On the effect of surrender pure and simple

The acceptance of an arbitrator is of a different sort when anyone entrusts the decision regarding himself to an enemy; for this is pure surrender, which makes the one who surrenders a subject, and confers the sovereign power on him to whom the surrender is made. . . . But here we ought also to distinguish what the conquered ought to endure; again, what the victor can do lawfully . . . in conformity with the full discharge of duty; and finally, what it is most fitting for [the victor] to do.

After the surrender, there is nothing that the vanquished [is exempt from suffering]. He is, in truth, already a subject; and, if we consider only the strictly legal rights of war, he is in such a position that everything can be taken from him – his life, his personal property, and the property not only of the state but also of individuals. . . . Also, we have shown that the putting to death of those who had surrendered was sometimes lawful.[48]

50. The duty of the victor to those who surrender unconditionally

But in order that the victor may not do anything unjustly, he ought first to see to it that he kill no one, unless this fate is deserved by the prisoner's own act; again, that he take nothing from anyone except as a lawful penalty. Moreover, within this limit, so far as one's own safety allows, it is always the part of honour to incline to clemency and generosity; sometimes, in consideration

---

[47] In saying that decisions on possessions belong to municipal law, Grotius is asserting that municipal law sometimes protects the rights of possessors against owners, for example in cases of usucaption or prescription. Possessory rights are therefore, to some extent, independent of ownership rights. It is contended that, in the law of nations, this is never so, i.e., that the law of nations always regards a right of possession as flowing exclusively from ownership. Consequently, in an international arbitration, the only relevant question will be ownership per se. For this reason, arbitrators should never attempt to order a transfer of property pending their decision, because that eventual decision is the sole and exclusive basis for awarding possession. An interim order for possession therefore would risk prejudicing that eventual decision (and can be very difficult to reverse if the need should arise).

Grotius appears to be speaking too broadly here, however, since there seems to be no reason why a possessory right, independent of ownership, cannot be created by treaty, e.g., by a leasing of territory. The discussion should therefore be understood to be confined to cases in which ownership of the thing in question is actually contested.

[48] See p. 352 above.

of the circumstances, such a course is even made necessary by the rule of custom.[49] As I have said elsewhere, wars are well ended when they terminate with pardoning.

And I do not think that it makes any difference whether the one who surrenders says that he surrenders himself to the wisdom, or to the moderation, or to the mercifulness of the victor. All these words are merely gracious expressions. The fact remains, that the victor becomes absolute master.

51. Concerning conditional surrender

Nevertheless, there are also conditional surrenders. These either safeguard the interests of individuals, [so] that the safety of their lives, or the freedom of their persons, or even certain [of their] property may be reserved; or they make provision for the whole body of the people. Such surrenders in some cases may even introduce a sort of mixed sovereignty, as I have explained elsewhere.[50]

52. Who can, and should, be given as hostages

Hostages and pledges are accessories of treaties. I have said that hostages are given either of their own will, or by him who holds the power and authority.[51] For in the supreme civil authority is included the right over the acts as well as over the property of the subjects. But the state or its ruler will be obligated to compensate the person who suffers, or his relatives, for the inconvenience. If there should be several persons, and it should make no difference to the state which of these should go as a hostage, it seems clear that pains should be taken to have the choice settled by lot.

53. On the rights of hostage-holders

I have said that, according to the strict law of nations, a hostage can be put to death; but that is not . . . in accord with moral justice,[52] unless there is a fault on the part of the hostage meriting such punishment. Hostages, moreover, do not become slaves. Furthermore, by the law of nations they can both hold property and leave it to their heirs; although the Roman law provided that their property should go to the state treasury.[53]

54. Whether a hostage may lawfully escape

Is the question raised whether a hostage may lawfully make his escape? It is agreed that he may not, if at the beginning, or afterward, he gave a pledge, in order that he might have more liberty [during his period as a hostage]. Under

[49] I.e., by the law of nations.   [50] On mixed sovereignty, see p. 62 above.
[51] See p. 353 above.   [52] I.e., of natural law.
[53] *Digest*, 49.14.31 (Marcion). The state treasury, that is, of Rome, which is the holder of the hostages.

other conditions, it seems to have been the intention of the state not to bind its citizen not to try to escape, but to give to the enemy the power to guard him as it might wish.

55. Whether a hostage may be lawfully detained for any other reason

The obligation arising from the use of hostages, moreover, is distasteful, not only because it infringes liberty, but also because it arises from the act of another.[54] Consequently, a narrow interpretation is here in point.[55] Hence it follows that hostages given on one account cannot be detained on another. This is to be understood as applying in case some other promise has been made without the addition of hostages.

If, however, good faith has already been violated in another matter, or a debt contracted, the hostage can then be retained, not as a hostage; but in accordance with the law of nations, according to which subjects can be detained 'by reprisal' (κατ' ἀνδρολη ψίαν) on account of an act of their rulers.[56] Nevertheless, provision may be made that this should not happen, by adding an agreement regarding the return of the hostages when the matter on account of which they were given has been closed up.

56. Whether a hostage is set free at the death of the one for whom he came as hostage

One who has been given as a hostage, merely to take the place of a captive or [other] hostage, is set free at the death of the latter. For Ulpian says that at

---

[54] I.e., it entails subjecting an innocent party (the hostage) to suffering a loss of liberty because of the action of some other party. This thesis is questionable, however, given that the hostage is typically given by agreement by one sovereign to another, and that the hostage acts in the service of his sovereign as a loyal subject. In fact, Grotius concedes, in the next paragraph, that a hostage is not to be compared to a victim of reprisals. He unfortunately does not allude here to the thesis advanced earlier (at p. 338 above) that subjects are to be regarded as sureties for their sovereigns. If that principle were applicable here, then it could not be said that the hostages were suffering for the act of another – they are simply being called upon to perform their suretyship obligation. Perhaps we are simply meant to infer from what Grotius says that the suretyship theory is not applicable to the case of hostage-giving, as it is to the capture of enemy property. But it would be interesting to have his explanation as to why this is not so.

[55] I.e., the rights of hostage-holders should be construed as narrowly as possible.

[56] It appears to be admitted that 'ordinary' hostage-holding is not comparable to a situation of peacetime reprisals. The practice of 'androlepsy' – meaning the capture and holding of persons rather than property as a reprisal – differs from hostage-holding in that, in the androlepsy case, the person is taken against his or her will.

the moment the latter dies, the right of pledge is destroyed, as in the case of a ransomed captive.[57] Therefore, as in Ulpian's inquiry, the ransom, which was to take the place of the person, is not due [if the person to be ransomed dies], so here the person who was made the substitute of another will not remain bound.

57. Whether a hostage may he retained after the death of the king who gave him

The decision whether a hostage may still be held after the death of the king who made the treaty is dependent on the question treated by us elsewhere, whether the treaty should be considered personal or real.[58]

58. On hostages as principal parties

It should be added, in passing, that sometimes hostages are not mere accessories to the obligation, but are in fact the principal party. This would be the case, for example, when anyone has promised under contract [that some other party will perform some act, with the promisor then becoming a hostage pending performance].

On the other hand, the opinion of those who hold that hostages without their consent can be mutually bound for each other's acts is not only severe but also unjust.[59]

59. The obligation arising from pledges of property

Pledges of property have certain points in common with hostages, and certain points peculiar to themselves. . . . It is a characteristic peculiar to pledges of property that an agreement made concerning them is not taken as strictly as one concerning hostages. For the matter is not equally distasteful, since things are made to be held, but men are not.

60. When the right of redemption of pledged property is lost

This also I have mentioned elsewhere, that no length of time can bring it about that a pledge of property should not be redeemable, if that is performed for which the pledge was given.[60] . . . Thus [a delay in payment by] the debtor should [not] be ascribed to . . . the abandonment of ownership [of the object

---

[57] *Digest*, 49.15.15 (Ulpian).
[58] For this discussion, see p. 244 above. If the treaty was a personal one, then the hostage is to be freed upon the death of the monarch. If the treaty was a real one, however, the hostage may continue to be held.
[59] A holder of this opinion is stated to be Gentili, *Law of War*, 2.19.
[60] See p. 123 above.

pledged], unless inferences that are warranted suggest another interpretation; as if a person, prevented at the time when he wished to redeem a pledge, had [then] allowed the matter to pass without mention for so long a time that it might warrant the presumption of [abandonment of the pledged property].[61]

[61] The situation envisaged is one in which the debtor is in default for a very long time – but in which he does eventually pay. In such a situation, the creditor might contend that the long period of time in default could be taken as evidence of the debtor's intention to refuse to pay – and, by that same token, as evidence of the debtor's intention to abandon ownership of the item that was pledged for the debt. The pledged item would then have no owner, and the creditor could obtain title by occupation, in the manner described at p. 106 above. The creditor would thereby become the full owner of the pledged item, from the date at which the abandonment occurred. If, then, the debtor tendered his payment some time *after* that, the creditor could argue that the object was no longer a pledge – and that, in consequence, the creditor had no duty to return it to the debtor when the payment was made. On this reasoning, the creditor ends up with the repayment of the loan by his debtor, *and* title to the pledged item. In opposition to this thesis, Grotius argues that there is a strong presumption against abandonment by the debtor.

21

On good faith during war; herein also concerning a truce, the right of safe-conduct, and the ransom of prisoners

1. What a truce is

Even during a war, the sovereign authorities are accustomed to grant certain rights, which, . . . I may call 'intercourse of war'. . . . Among these are included the truce, the right of safe-conduct and the ransom of prisoners. A truce is an agreement by which warlike acts are for a time abstained from, though the state of war continues. I say, 'though the state of war continues', for . . . there is no middle ground between war and peace. War, furthermore, is the name of a condition which can exist even when it does not carry forward its operations.

This I say that we may know: that, if an agreement has been made which is to be valid in time of war, this will be valid also in a truce, unless it is clearly apparent that the agreement applies not to the state of war but to its acts. On the contrary, if anything has been said in regard to peace, this will not be applicable in time of truce. . . . Nevertheless, if it shall be apparent that the sole and only determining cause of an agreement was the cessation of warlike acts, it may happen that what has been said of a time of peace will in that case apply during the truce, not from the force of the word, but from a sure inference as to the intention [of the parties], regarding which we have spoken elsewhere.[1]

2. Further on truces

A truce . . . is a period of rest in war, not a peace. And so the historians use the term properly in saying, as they frequently do, that a peace was refused, a truce was granted.

3. Whether a new declaration of war after a truce is necessary

In consequence, after a truce there will be no need of a new declaration of war. For when the temporary obstacle is removed, the state of war, which was not

---

[1] See p. 238 above on interpretation of treaties.

dead but sleeping, asserts itself, just as the right of ownership and the power of the father assert themselves in a man who has recovered from insanity.

4. How the period of time fixed for a truce ought to be reckoned

The duration of a truce is commonly . . . either a continuous period, as for one hundred days, or with the designation of a fixed limit, as up to the first of March. In the former case, the calculation must be made exact to the minute. . . . In the other case, doubt is generally raised, whether the day, the month, or the year, which has been fixed for the duration of the truce, should be understood as reckoned inclusively or exclusively.

By nature, at any rate, there are two kinds of boundaries: one within the thing, as the skin is the boundary of the body; and the second outside of the thing, as a river is the boundary of a country. Boundaries which are fixed according to choice can be established by both methods. But it seems more natural that the boundary, which is a part of the thing, should be assumed.[2] . . . Such an assumption, furthermore, is not inconsistent with practice. . . . This interpretation, then, is all the more to be adopted when the extension of time contains an advantage in itself, as in the case of a truce, which spares human bloodshed.

But the day 'from' which a certain measure of time is said to begin will not be included in the measure, for the force of that preposition is to separate, not to unite.

5. When a truce begins to be binding

Incidentally, I may add this, that a truce, and everything else of the kind, is binding on the contracting parties immediately after the agreement is completed. The subjects on both sides, however, begin to be bound as soon as the truce has taken the form of a law; and this requires some sort of publication abroad. As soon as the publication has been made, it begins to have a binding force on the subjects. Nevertheless, if the publication has been made in one place only, that force does not manifest itself at the same moment throughout the whole area under governmental control, but only after a sufficient time for carrying the news to the different places. Therefore if in the meantime, subjects have done anything contrary to the truce, while they will not be liable to punishment, the contracting parties will, nevertheless, be bound to make good the loss.[3]

---

[2] The assertion is that it is more natural to count inclusively when fixing a time period – so that, for example, a truce extending 'to 1 March' should include within it the whole of the first day of March.

[3] In modern parlance, it would be said that, in this case, there would be state responsibility for the breach of the truce (with a consequent duty of reparation), but not criminal responsibility on the part of the individuals committing the breach.

6. What is lawful during a truce

What is lawful, what is not lawful in a period of truce, may be understood from the very definition. For all acts of war are unlawful, whether against persons or against property, that is, whatever is done by force against the enemy. In a period of truce, in fact, all such acts are contrary to the law of nations. . . . Even property of the enemy which has come into our hands by chance will have to be restored, although it had been ours before. For as regards the legal right, according to which such matters have to be judged, the property in question has become theirs.[4]

On both sides it is lawful to go and to return, but with such equipment only as does not suggest peril.

7. Whether during a truce it is lawful to retreat and repair walls, and the like

It is not inconsistent with a truce to withdraw with the army further inland. . . . [A] truce does not prevent the rebuilding of walls, nor the enrolment of soldiers, unless some special agreement has been made.[5]

8. Regarding the seizure of places in time of truce

Without doubt, it is a violation of a truce to bribe garrisons of the enemy and seize places which they were holding. Such an acquisition, in fact, cannot be lawful except by right of war. The same principle must be applied [to assisting] subjects [of the enemy who] wish to revolt.

It is indeed lawful to take possession of ownerless property provided this has been really abandoned, that is, with the intention that it should no longer belong to those to whom it had belonged. But it is not lawful if the property is merely unguarded, whether the guard was removed before the truce was made, or afterward. Continuance of ownership in one renders possession by another unlawful.

---

[4] In this situation, private property belonging to one side is captured by the other during the hostilities. After that, a truce is declared. During the truce period, the property comes 'by chance' into the hands of persons on the side to which it had originally belonged. Ordinarily, the ownership of that property would revert to the original owner, by postliminy. See p. 376 above on postliminy generally. Grotius holds, however, that the property still belongs to the enemy side, on the thesis that the principle of postliminy operates only during a time of active hostilities, not during a truce. For his authority, see *Digest*, 49.15.19.1 (Paul).

[5] The rationale for this is that these acts are not, by their nature, acts of war. Consequently, a truce, which applies only to acts of war, does not cover them.

9. Whether, at the end of the truce, one can return who has been detained by *force majeure*

The question is raised, whether a person, who has been hindered by *force majeure* from returning, and is arrested within the territory of the enemy after the expiration of the truce, has the right to return.[6] If we consider the strict law of nations (*ius externum gentium*), I do not doubt that this person is in the same position as one who, although he had come in time of peace, by his own misfortune is caught among the enemy by a sudden outbreak of war. We have noted above, that such a person remains a captive until the conclusion of peace.[7] Nor is moral justice opposed to this, since the property and acts of the enemy are liable for the debt of the state and are taken in payment. The case in question does not in reality furnish more ground for complaint than that of so many other innocent persons upon whom the misfortunes of war fall.

In this connexion, moreover, no comparison can be made with merchandise in a case of confiscation. . . . In such cases, *force majeure* frees from the penalty.[8] But in the case of the person forcibly detained after a truce, it is not, properly speaking, a question of penalty, but of a right, which was suspended during a certain time only. Nevertheless, there is no doubt that the releasing of such a person is a more kindly, yes, also a nobler, act.

10. Of special agreements during truces

Certain acts are unlawful during a truce on account of the special nature of the agreement; for example, if a truce has been granted only for the purpose of burying the dead, no deviation from that condition ought to be made. So if a truce has been given to those who are besieged, with the provision merely that

---

[6] An example would be a national of one belligerent who was in the territory of the other, and who had the right to return to his home country during the period of truce. Suppose that, during the truce period, inclement weather prevented this right of return from being exercisable. Should the period of the adverse weather condition (i.e., the *force majeure*) be disregarded, with the effect of extending the departure time by a length of time equal to it? Or does the right of return expire with the termination of the truce as an absolute matter, without regard to the misfortune of the weather? As explained in the next paragraph, the voluntary law of nations adopts the latter view.

[7] See p. 377 above.

[8] The situation envisaged is one in which a person's property is subject to confiscation as punishment for some offence, and in which property comes into the jurisdiction of the court by virtue of *force majeure*, such as a ship entering a port in refuge from a storm at sea. In such a case, according to Roman law, the property was safe from seizure because of the *force majeure* feature. See, for example, *Digest*, 39.14.15 (Alfenus Varus); and 39.14.16.8 (Marcion). But this principle only applies, it is contended, to cases in which confiscation is a penalty. Therefore, confiscation could still occur as, say, a measure of requisition to deal with some kind of emergency (although, in that event, compensation might be owed for property taken).

they are not to be attacked, it will not be lawful [for the besieged party] to admit auxiliary forces and supplies. For, while such a truce is advantageous to the one side, it ought not to make the situation harder for the other side which granted it. Sometimes also the agreement is made, that it shall not be lawful to go back and forth. Sometimes, again, provision is made for persons and not for things. In the latter case, if persons are injured while property is being defended, the truce will not be violated. For … it is permissible to defend property [in this circumstance].

11. Effect of violation of the terms of a truce

If the good faith of the truce has been violated by the one party, it should not be doubted that the party injured is free to take up arms even without declaring war. For the main points of the agreement are implied in the manner of a condition in the agreement, as I have said a little above.[9]

12. If a penalty has been included in the terms of the truce

This is established, that if the penalty agreed upon [in the truce terms] is demanded and is paid by the one who has done the wrong, the right [of the non-breaching side] to make war no longer remains. The penalty, in fact, is paid with this in view, that all else may remain in safety. On the contrary, if war is begun [by the non-breaching side], it is necessary to consider that, since the choice was given, the idea of paying the penalty has been abandoned.[10]

13. When the acts of private citizens break the truce

Private acts do not break a truce unless, in addition, there is a public act, that is, through command or approval. Private acts are understood to be in accordance with public command or approval if the guilty parties are neither punished nor surrendered, and if restitution is not made.

[9] On the importance of conditions, see p. 219 above. Note that what is meant here is that, if one side violates the truce, then the other side has the option of recommencing the hostilities. That is to say, the breach of the truce does not *itself* automatically terminate the truce.

[10] This point is not very clearly explained. The position appears to be the same as for peace treaties containing penalty provisions: that the payment of the penalty must be accepted by the non-breaching party if it is tendered, and that the truce then continues in effect. It should apparently be understood that the case is different when the breach consists of a recommencement of hostilities – an act which, by its nature, amounts to a repudiation of the truce agreement. It would seem that, strictly speaking, the non-breaching party should have the right (as with breaches of treaty generally) to elect whether to continue the truce or to rescind it. The assumption, however, seems to be that, once hostilities have recommenced de facto, an option to continue the truce does not realistically exist.

14. Interpretation of the right of safe-conduct outside of the period of truce

The right of safe-conduct outside of the time of truce is a kind of privilege. In its interpretation, therefore, the rules which are laid down in regard to privileges ought to be followed. This privilege, however, is neither harmful to a third party nor very burdensome to the one who grants it. Consequently, within the natural meaning of the words, a loose rather than a strict interpretation ought to be admitted, and so much the more in case the favour has not been granted in response to a request, but has been offered voluntarily; so much the more, also, if a public advantage of some sort is connected with the business outside of private gain. A strict interpretation, therefore, even according to the meaning of the words, ought to be rejected, unless otherwise some absurdity would ensue, or very probable inferences as to intention seem to require it. On the other hand, a freer interpretation than is afforded by the natural meaning of the words will be in point, in order that a like absurdity may be avoided, or because of very cogent inferences.

15. Who are considered as combatants in safe-conduct arrangements

From what has been said, we draw the inference that the right of safe-conduct granted to combatants extends not only to inferior officers but also to officers of the highest rank; for the natural meaning of the word admits of this interpretation, although there is another interpretation that is narrower. Similarly a bishop is included under the term clergy. Sailors also, who are serving in fleets, are understood to be combatants,[11] and in fact all are who have taken the military oath.

16. Interpretation of the terms 'go', 'come', and 'depart'

A provision in regard to going is considered to cover also the return, not from the meaning of the word, but to avoid an absurdity; for a favour ought not to be void of use.[12] And a safe departure should be understood to hold good until the person has reached a place where he is in safety.

However, a person to whom permission has been granted to depart cannot also return. Again, a person who has received permission to come himself will not be able to send another; and the reverse of this also holds. Such, in fact, are different matters; and in such cases, reason does not compel us to go beyond the meaning of the words. Nevertheless, this principle is applicable with the understanding that, though an error confers no right, it at any rate

---

[11] See *Digest*, 37.13.1.1 (Ulpian).
[12] Permission to go somewhere would have no practical effect (i.e., would be 'void of use') if it were not coupled with permission to return.

relieves from the penalty, if a penalty formed a part of the agreement.[13] Also, the person who has received permission to come will [be allowed to] come only once and not a second time, unless the allocation of time supplies a different interpretation.

17. Further on the interpretation of the right of safe-conduct

The son does not follow his father, nor the wife her husband, otherwise than in accordance with the right of residence.[14] For we are accustomed to live with our family, but to travel abroad without it. Nevertheless it will be understood, even if not expressly stated, that one or two servants are included in the case of a person for whom it would be unbecoming to travel without such attendance. For he who grants a favour grants that which of necessity follows. However, in such cases, necessity must be understood in a moral sense.[15]

18. On the extension of safe-conduct to baggage

Similarly, not all kinds of goods will be included in the safe-conduct, but only such as are ordinarily taken on a journey.

19. Who are included under the terms 'attendants' and 'nationality'

If the term 'attendants' is used, those ought not to be understood whose case is more provocative of hatred than that of the one for whom the safe-conduct is arranged. Such are pirates, brigand deserters, and fugitives. The designated nationality of the attendant indicates clearly enough that the right is not extended to others.

20. Whether a right of safe-conduct is annulled by the death of the grantor

Since the right of safe-conduct is derived from the force of authority, in case of doubt it is not annulled by the death of the one who granted it. This is in

---

[13] The concern is with errors on the part of grantors of safe-conducts. For example, a person who was granted only a right to depart might be allowed, by error, also to return. Or the grantor of the safe-conduct might erroneously allow a substitute to be dispatched. The point is that the persons benefiting from these errors will not be subject to punishment, even if the safe-conduct expressly included punitive provisions in the event of breach. More generally, it may be said that acts outside the scope of a safe-conduct will not be treated as breaches if there was effective acquiescence by the grantors.

[14] See *Digest*, 43.26.21 (Venuleius).

[15] That is, necessity must be given an objective, generally agreed meaning, determined according to general moral standards.

accordance with the rules which I have stated elsewhere in regard to favours granted by kings and other rulers.[16]

21. Concerning a safe-conduct granted subject to the pleasure of the grantor

There is usually a discussion regarding a safe-conduct granted with the restriction, 'so long as I wish'. The opinion of those is nearer the truth who think that a favour of this kind continues even if no new act of will occurs.[17] In case of doubt, the presumption is that that remains in force which is sufficient for the validity of the right. But the force of the safe-conduct does not continue when the one who granted it has ceased to be able to wish it, a condition brought about by death.[18] When in fact the [grantor ceases to exist], the assumption of continuance also will cease, just as the accident ends with the destruction of the substance.[19]

22. Whether security outside of the territory also is due

Moreover, safe-conduct is due to the person to whom it has been granted even outside of the territory of the grantor. For it is granted in derogation of the right of war, which in itself is not confined to a territory, as we have said elsewhere.[20]

23. The favour of ransoming captives

The ransoming of captives is in large measure an act of favour, especially among Christians, to whom the divine law especially commends this kind of compassion.

---

[16] See p. 227 above.

[17] The question is whether the safe-conduct is valid only so long as the grantor actively has in his mind the opinion that it should; or whether, once granted, the safe-conduct privilege continues automatically until an explicit decision is made to terminate it.

[18] *Digest*, 39.5.32 (Scaevola). The *Digest* reference concerns a private-law matter: the death of a person who had granted a licence to occupy an apartment, with the licence terminating automatically upon the grantor's death. Grotius contends that the same principle applies to the grant of the right of safe-conduct in wartime.

[19] The 'accident [ending] with the destruction of the substance' is a reference to Aristotelian philosophy. Very broadly, a 'substance' is an entity which has properties; and the 'accidents' are the properties which a given substance has. Grotius is therefore asserting that, once a thing possessing properties ceases to exist, so do the properties of that thing. In the present context, the thing (or substance) disappearing is the grantor of the safe-conduct, as a result of death or insanity. The accident in question is the will to continue the safe-conduct in force.

[20] See p. 351 above, on the rights of war being exercisable everywhere, at least for the belligerents vis-à-vis one another.

24. Whether ransom may be forbidden by law

These considerations lead me not to venture to approve without discrimination the laws which forbid the ransom of captives such as existed, we read, among the ancient Romans.... [I]f we should only have regard for considerations of humanity, it would in many cases be better that a right which is sought in war should be lost, than that a great many men, our relatives, in fact, or fellow countrymen, should be left in the most pitiable condition.[21] Such a law [prohibiting the ransom of prisoners of war], therefore, does not seem just, unless the need of such severity is plain, with the purpose in view that greater evils or the largest possible number of evils, which are otherwise with moral certainty inevitable, may be avoided. In case of such necessity,... the captives themselves, in accordance with the law of love, ought to bear their lot with resignation [and] not... set themselves in opposition. [This is] in accordance with the principles which we have laid down elsewhere in regard to the surrender of a citizen for the public good.[22]

25. Whether the right to a captive can be transferred

According to our customs, it is true, those who are captured in war are not slaves. Yet I do not doubt that the right to collect the price of ransom from a captive can be transferred from the party who holds the captive to another. For nature allows a transfer of ownership, even in things which do not have corporeal existence.

26. Whether a ransom can be owed by one person to several

Further, the same person can owe a ransom to more than one person if he has been let go by the first and captured by another before the first ransom has been paid. Such, in fact, are different debts, arising from different causes.

27. Whether an agreement can be annulled on the ground that the wealth of the captive was unknown

An agreement in regard to the amount of ransom cannot be annulled on the ground that the captive is [later discovered] to be richer than was believed [at the time of the making of the ransom agreement]. By the strict law of nations (*iure gentium externo*), which we are investigating, no one is compelled to make

---

[21] The 'right which is sought in war' refers to the right to enslave captives instead of ransoming them. Grotius holds that, from a humanitarian standpoint, it is good for such a right as this to be 'lost'.

[22] See p. 315 above.

good what he has promised in a contract at less than a fair price, if there has
been no deception. This can be understood from the explanations previously
made concerning contracts.[23]

28. What goods of the captive belong to the captor

From what we have said, that captives are not our slaves, it follows that there is
no room for the complete acquisition which, as we have said elsewhere, is the
essential condition of ownership over the person. No other property, therefore,
will be gained by the captor than what he has actually taken.[24] In consequence,
if the captive has something concealed on his person, it will not be acquired,
since it has not been taken. Just so Paul the Jurist [held] . . . that a man, who has
taken possession of a farm, has not taken into his possession a treasure which
he does not know is on the farm; for a person cannot possess what he does not
know of.[25] The conclusion from this is that property concealed on the person
of a captive can be used in paying the price of the ransom, since ownership has
in effect been retained.

29. Whether the heir owes the price of ransom

This question is also commonly raised, whether a ransom agreed upon, but
not paid before death, is due from the heir. The answer seems to me void of
difficulty. The ransom is not due if the captive died in prison. There was, in fact,
a condition attached to the promise, that the captive should be set free; but a
dead man is not set free. On the contrary, if the captive dies when at liberty, the
ransom is due; for he had already gained that in return for which the ransom
had been promised.[26]

I admit that obviously the agreement can be made also with different conditions, so that the ransom may be unreservedly due from the very moment of
the contract, the captive being retained no longer as a prisoner of war, but as
security for himself. On the contrary, the contract can be so drawn up that the
payment of the price shall only be made if, on the appointed day, the captive is
alive and free. But these conditions, as being less natural, are not to be assumed
without clear proofs.

---

[23] See p. 214 above.

[24] The captor, that is, only acquires title to property that was discovered on the person
of his captive at the time of capture. He does not acquire, say, title to real property
owned by the captive or to the contents of the captive's bank account.

[25] *Digest*, 41.2.3.3 (Paul).

[26] It should be appreciated that captives were typically given their liberty during the
period of time in which the ransom was paid.

30. Whether a person, who has been released in order to free another, ought to return if the other has died

Again, the question is proposed for discussion, whether a return to prison is obligatory for a man who has been released under the agreement that he should cause another to be freed, where the other has anticipated release by dying.[27] I have said elsewhere that [an] act, . . . if fairly promised, is satisfactorily performed if nothing on the part of the promisor [remains to be done],[28] but that in the case of burdensome promises the promisor is obligated only to an equivalent amount.[29] So, in the question under discussion, the one who has been released will not be bound to restore himself to custody; for this was not the agreement, and the presumption in favour of liberty does not allow a tacit agreement to be understood. But the person who has been released ought not to get his freedom as clear profit; he will pay the estimated value of what he cannot furnish.[30]

[27] The situation envisaged is that a combatant has been captured by an enemy soldier. The prisoner gains his release by promising to use his freedom to liberate some third party from imprisonment. In the context, the agreement would be that the prisoner of war would promise to procure the release of a fellow-soldier of his captor, so that the arrangement will amount, in the end, to a prisoner exchange. The problem posed is that the fellow-soldier of the captor dies in custody before the captured (and released) belligerent obtains his freedom.

[28] See p. 201 above.

[29] Something which is 'fairly promised' refers to a promise made in a contract in which there is no inequality between the parties, i.e., in which the promises made by the two parties are of equal value. In that case, the promisor is discharged from liability if he does everything which it is possible for him to do to carry out his promise (even if the anticipated fruits do not materialise). If, however, the promise is a 'burdensome' one (in which the promisor commits himself to provide something in excess of what he himself gains from the arrangement), the position is different. According to natural law, the promisor needs only to do whatever will suffice to make the value of his acts equivalent to the value of what he himself stood to gain from the arrangement. This principle seems, however, not to resolve the problem at hand, which is the disappearance of the thing which has been contracted for. Grotius effectively concedes this by proceeding to resolve the matter on a different basis.

[30] The released prisoner of war, then, does not have to return to the custody of his captor. But he must compensate his captor by furnishing the equivalent of what he promised – and was unable – to deliver.

22

On the good faith of subordinate powers in war

1. The kinds of military leaders

I have said that, after considering the good faith pledged by the highest authorities, I must treat of that which subordinate officials pledge to one another, or to others. Either the subordinate officials are next to the highest authority, such as have properly been called generals; . . . or they are officers of lower rank.

2. Whether an agreement made by military leaders is binding on the supreme authority

In dealing with the promises of military leaders, the subject must be viewed under two aspects; for the question is raised whether such promises impose a binding obligation on the supreme authority, or only on the leaders themselves. The first point should be settled in accordance with the principle which I have elsewhere stated, that an obligation is imposed on us . . . by the person whom we have chosen as agent to execute our wishes, whether our wishes have been stated in express terms or are inferred from the nature of the responsibility.[1] For the one who grants a power grants the means necessary for the exercise of that power, so far as he possesses them. . . . In two ways, therefore, subordinate authorities will be able to bind the supreme authority by their actions: either by doing that which is thought on probable grounds to lie within their field of duty; or [alternatively by acting] even outside their field of duty, in accordance with a special responsibility, known to the public, or to those whose interest in the matter is at stake.

3. Whether such an agreement can become the occasion of an obligation

There are also other ways in which the supreme authority is obligated by a previous act of its agents, but not in such a way that this act should be, properly speaking, a cause, but rather an occasion, of obligation. This may happen in

[1] See p. 194 above.

two ways: either by consent; or by reason of the act itself. Consent is revealed by ratification, not only express but also implied, that is, when the supreme authority knew what had been done and permitted the accomplishment of the acts which cannot with probability be referred to another cause.[2] We have explained elsewhere how this matter proceeds.[3]

By reason of the thing itself, states are bound to this extent: that they should not become richer through another's loss, that is, that they should either carry out the agreement, from which they wish to acquire gain, or renounce the gain.[4] In regard to this principle of equity, also, I have spoken elsewhere.[5] And to this extent, and not beyond, can we accept the maxim, that whatever has been done to our advantage is valid. On the contrary, those cannot be acquitted of injustice who disapprove of the agreement and yet retain what they would not have had without the agreement.

4. When the official acts contrary to instructions

Also, we must repeat what has been said above, that whoever has appointed an agent is bound, even if the agent, while yet within the limits of his public function, has acted contrary to secret instructions.[6] This rule of equity was rightly followed [in Roman law] in an action relating to agents, that not every-thing done by an agent is, in fact, binding on the one who appointed him, but only that which, within the limits of his responsibility, was done in the interest of the principal.[7] If now public notice has been given, that agreements should not be made with him, then he will not be considered as an agent. If, however, the notice has been given, but is not generally known, the one who appointed the agent is bound.[8] Also the conditions of the appointment must be observed. For if anyone has wished that an agreement be made under a certain

---

[2] I.e., the performance of the act is, in the circumstances, explicable only on the thesis that the government had approved of the agent's act.

[3] See p. 473 below.

[4] The situation envisaged is one in which a state official, without authorisation, has concluded an agreement, purportedly on behalf of his state, with another state. Furthermore, that other state, thinking that there is a binding treaty in force, has performed part or all of its part of the bargain and has thereby conferred some advantage onto the official's state. This advantage received is referred to as 'the thing itself', meaning the objective situation which is at hand. The fact that the agent acted without authority means, in principle, that his state is not bound by the agreement. But 'the thing itself' reveals that the state has reaped a benefit from the agent's action and the other state's performance. Consequently, the agent's state would be unjustly enriched if it were allowed to repudiate the agreement at this point. It must either give back what it received, or else proceed to perform its part of the bargain.

[5] For Grotius's strong concern over the principle of unjust enrichment, see p. 178 above.

[6] See p. 195 above.   [7] *Digest*, 14.3.5.11 (Ulpian).   [8] *Digest*, 14.3.11.2–4 (Ulpian).

condition, ... it will be most fair that the conditions under which the agent received his appointment shall be observed.

The consequence of this is, that some kings or peoples are put under greater obligation by the agreements of their military leaders, others under less, [if] their laws and customs are adequately known. But if there is doubt on these points, we must follow the line of inference, in such a way as to understand that that is conceded without which there can be no proper discharge of responsibility on the part of the official.[9]

If a lesser official has exceeded the limit of his instructions, in case he is unable to make good what he has promised, he will himself be liable for the equivalent of the loss, unless such recovery is precluded by some law sufficiently well known. But if, in addition, there is deceit, that is, if the official pretended to have greater power than he did have, he will then both be liable for the loss caused by his fault and also, on account of his criminal conduct, he will be subject to a penalty commensurate with the crime. In the former case, his property is liable, and, if that is not sufficient, also his work, or the liberty of his person.[10] In the second case, his person or his property or both are liable, according to the magnitude of the crime.[11]

Moreover, what we have said regarding deceit will be in point, even if anyone has declared beforehand that he is unwilling to make himself liable, because the debt due both for the loss occasioned and as just penalty is associated with the offence by a natural and not by a voluntary connexion.[12]

5. Whether in such a case the other party will be under obligation

But since either the supreme authority, or its agent, is always bound, this also is certain, that the other party to the agreement is under obligation, and it cannot

---

[9] I.e., subordinate officials should be presumed to possess powers proportionate to the tasks which they are required to discharge.

[10] By 'his work' and 'the liberty of his person' is meant that, if the wrong-doing agent's property is not sufficient to compensate for the wrong which he has committed, then he will be subject to compulsory labour, in the manner of a slave, until he 'works off' the deficiency.

[11] In the first case (involving civil liability for loss caused), the property of the wrong-doing official is primarily liable – and, if sufficient to compensate, discharges the whole of the civil wrong. In the second case (involving criminal liability), both his person and his property are, from the very outset, subject to action by the state, depending on the precise nature of the punishment for the particular offence at hand.

[12] In other words, it is not open to an official simply to disclaim any personal liability for his acts at the outset (on the ground that he is acting on behalf of his state). The reason is that the civil and criminal liability for his wrong-doing arise automatically, by operation of general natural law. And natural law cannot be disclaimed.

be said that the agreement is one-sided.[13] We are done with the relation of lesser officials to their superiors.

6. What generals or magistrates are able to do with regard to those of lower rank

Let us see also what higher officials are able to do with regard to those of lower rank. We ought not, I think, to doubt that a general may place a binding obligation on his soldiers, or magistrates on their fellow townsmen, within the limits of those powers which they are accustomed to exercise; beyond those limits, consent would be necessary. On the other hand, a compact of a commander or of a magistrate will, in general, be advantageous to those of lower rank in respect to matters merely expedient. [S]uch arrangements, in fact, are [therefore] sufficiently understood as in their power. In respect to conditions which have a burden attached, the obligation is absolute within those rights which [the higher officials] are accustomed to exercise, but, beyond those, only if accepted. These provisions are in accord with the principles which we have elsewhere discussed, growing out of the law of nature regarding a stipulation in behalf of a third party.[14] The general statements will now be made clearer by the presentation of particular instances.

7. Whether generals have the power to make peace

It does not fall within the province of the general to conduct negotiations with regard to the causes or the consequences of a war; the terminating of war is, in fact, not a part of the waging of it. Even though the general has been placed in command with absolute power, that must be understood to apply only to the conduct of the war.

8. Whether generals may make a truce

Not only generals in command but also officers of lower rank have the power to make a truce, but only with those against whom they are fighting, or whom they are holding in a state of siege. This applies only to themselves and to their troops; for other officers of equal rank are not bound by such a truce.

---

[13] In other words, it must not be thought that, in this case of wrongful action by the official, no contract is in existence. The reason is that the treaty *does* have to be carried out, on the official's side, by someone – either by the agent personally, or else by his state (if the state is bound, as discussed above). Consequently, the other party to the treaty is obligated to carry out its part of the agreement.

[14] See p. 200 above.

9. What security of persons, and what property, can be given by generals

Likewise, it is not within the province of generals to dispose of men, dominions, and territories taken in war. . . . Over other matters, which fall under the head of booty, we see that some rights are granted to commanders, not so much by reason of the strength of their authority as by the customs of each people. But in regard to that subject we have said enough previously.[15]

However, it is quite within the power of generals to grant things which have not yet been taken,[16] because in many cases, towns and men surrender in war on the condition of preserving their lives, or of keeping also their liberty or even their property. In such matters, circumstances generally do not afford opportunity [for the general to refer the decision to] the decision of the sovereign authority. For a like reason, this right ought to be granted also to commanders not of the highest rank, within the limits of the matters entrusted to their administration.

10. How such agreements should be interpreted

For the rest, in dealing with the agreements made by generals [which] are concerned with a matter outside their field, the interpretation must be restricted so far as the nature of the agreement allows, lest indeed by their act either the sovereign power be obligated to a greater degree than it wishes, or [the generals] themselves suffer injury in the discharge of their duty.[17]

11. How a surrender accepted by a general is to be interpreted

In consequence, one who is received in unconditional surrender by a general is considered to have been received on such terms that the decision in regard to him belongs to the victorious people or king.

12. How to understand the proviso, 'if the king or the people has approved'

Thus the added proviso, 'Let this be valid, in case the Roman people shall have ratified it', which is often found in treaty compacts, will have the effect that, if

---

[15] See p. 362 above.
[16] I.e., to give legally binding assurances to persons that their property will not be taken from them in the future.
[17] The potential 'injury in the discharge of their duty' is the possibility of personal liability, either civil or criminal, for actions taken outside the scope of their authority, as explained at Section 4 above.

the ratification does not follow, the general will himself in no respect be bound, unless in some way he has thereby been made richer.[18]

13. How to understand the promise to surrender a town

Also those who have promised to surrender a town can allow the garrison to withdraw.

[18] The formulation quoted has the effect of making the validity of the agreement conditional upon later ratification by the state whose general concluded it. (The most common type of agreement would be terms of surrender negotiated by a victorious general with a defeated enemy.) If the envisaged ratification does not take place, then the agreement will be entirely without legal effect, i.e., neither the state nor the general himself will be under any legal obligation to carry it out. The only exception to this principle is the marginal case in which the commander who negotiated the agreement benefited personally from it in some way. In that case, he will be liable to carry out the agreement, even in the absence of ratification, to the extent necessary to prevent the occurrence of unjust enrichment.

23

On good faith of private persons in war

1. Whether private persons are bound by a pledge given to the enemy

It is strange that legal authorities have been found who would teach that the obligation was binding when an agreement was made publicly with the enemy, but that agreements made by private persons were not binding in like manner. For since private citizens have private rights, which they can place under obligation, and enemies are capable of acquiring right, what can stand in the way of the obligation? Add that, unless this rule is established, opportunity is given for slaughter [of captives], an impediment is set to liberty. For captives in many cases will not be able to guard against the former, or to obtain the latter, if the good faith of private persons has been done away with.

2. Whether private persons are bound even to a pirate or brigand

Still further, not only is a pledge, which has been given to an enemy, recognised by the law of nations, but also a pledge to a brigand or to a pirate, just as we have said above in regard to public faith.[1] There is this difference, that if an unjust fear inspired by the other has induced the promise, the promisor can demand restitution; or if the other party is unwilling to make restitution, he can take it [by force]; such a procedure [however] has no place in case of a fear arising from a public war, according to the law of nations.

If an oath also has been added to the promise, then what has been promised will have to be made good by the promisor, if he wishes to avoid the crime of perjury. If such a perjury has been committed against a public enemy, men are accustomed to punish it; but if against brigands or pirates, it is overlooked, because of the hatred of those whose interest is at stake.[2]

---

[1] See p. 418 above.
[2] I.e., violation of an oath which is attached to a promise made to pirates or brigands is a violation of natural law; but it generally goes unpunished by human authorities. This is on the understanding that the oath is made to God and not to the pirates or brigands themselves.

3. Whether an exception is here made for a minor

Also in this aspect of the good faith of private persons, we shall make no exception for a minor who has sufficient intelligence to understand his act. For the privileges which favour minors arise from municipal law, but we are treating of the law of nations.

4. Whether an error gives release

Also as regards an error, we have said elsewhere that it gives the right to withdraw from an agreement only if that which was erroneously believed had the force of a condition in the mind of the promisor.[3]

5. Concerning an objection raised from the point of view of public advantage

It is more difficult to decide how far the power of individuals may extend in making an agreement [with enemies of the state]. That public property cannot be alienated by an individual is well established. For if this right is not permitted even to generals in war, as I have just shown, still less will it be permitted to private citizens. But in regard to their own acts and property, the question can [also] be raised because it is evident that these also cannot be put at the service of the enemy without some degree of damage [to the state]. For this reason, such agreements on the part of citizens may seem unlawful on account of the state's right of eminent domain, and on the part of enrolled soldiers on account of their military oath.[4]

It must be understood, however, that agreements which avoid a greater or more certain evil ought to be considered advantageous rather than harmful to the public interest, because a lesser evil assumes the appearance of an advantage.[5] . . . In fact, neither an act of sincere good faith, by which one does not yield absolute power over himself and his possessions, nor the public

---

[3] On conditions and their significance, see p. 219 above.

[4] An example of the sort of agreement spoken of would be an agreement by a private subject to sell food or other supplies to an enemy army. The concern is that such an arrangement might strengthen the enemy and impede the war effort of the subject's state.

[5] An example of this type of arrangement would be an agreement by a private subject, in the face of an enemy takeover of his property, to surrender a portion of his property voluntarily to the enemy in exchange for the exemption of the remainder of his property from pillage. So long as this does not advance the enemy's cause in any way – e.g., by enabling him to move his troops faster than he otherwise would be able to – this kind of agreement is permissible because it simply substitutes a lesser loss for a greater one (i.e., the loss of part of the subject's property for the loss of the whole of it). In practical terms, though, it is difficult to imagine why the enemy would ever enter into such an arrangement unless he received at least some advantage from it – in which case the agreement would not be allowed.

advantage without the authority of law, can render void and deprive of all legal effect that which has been done, even if it is granted that this was done contrary to duty.⁶

A law may indeed deprive either permanent or temporary subjects of such power. But the law does not always do this, because it spares the citizens; and it cannot do this in all cases, for the reason that human laws, as I have said elsewhere, have the power of imposing obligation only if they have been passed in a humane manner, and not if they impose a burden which is plainly inconsistent with reason and nature.⁷ And so special ordinances and orders, which openly claim some such right [i.e., to deprive subjects of the power to conclude contracts] ought not to be considered as laws. Moreover, general laws ought to be received with so benevolent an interpretation as to exclude misfortunes arising from extreme necessity.⁸

But if the act of the private person, which had been forbidden by law or by an order and prevented from becoming valid, could rightly have been forbidden, then the act of the individual would be void. Nevertheless, he could be punished on this account, because he promised what was not within his right; and especially, if he promised it on oath.⁹

6. The previous statements are applied to a pledge given of return to prison¹⁰

The promise of a captive to return to prison is properly allowable; for it does not render the condition of the captive worse. Therefore Marcus Atilius Regulus did not merely act nobly, as some think, but also as his duty required.¹¹

---

⁶ In other words, even if subjects are prohibited by their national law from entering into contracts with the enemy, such contracts will nevertheless not be entirely void if they were entered into 'in sincere good faith'. This is on the assumption that the agreement in question did not give the enemy 'absolute power' over the contracting subject (e.g., allowing the enemy to conscript him into its forces) or prejudice 'the public advantage'. Note that what Grotius is saying is that the agreement itself will not be void, provided that these conditions are met. He is not saying that the subject will not be exposed to personal punishment for violating the national law against concluding such contracts. In effect, then, the contention is that the law should be understood to deprive the subject only of the *right* to conclude contracts with the enemy, but not of the *power* to do so.

⁷ See p. 228 above.

⁸ On the general principle of exceptions to laws in cases of necessity, see p. 70 above.

⁹ In general, laws forbidding contracts with enemies are to be understood as affecting only the right and not the power to contract. Sometimes, however, states can validly remove the power as well as the right – though Grotius fails to explain under what circumstances this would be so. In such a case, a purported contract with the enemy will be void *ab initio*. It is pointed out, though, that in addition, the subject may be subject to criminal punishment for the act of *purporting* to contract with the enemy.

¹⁰ In his Latin text, Grotius inadvertently misnumbered the sections of this chapter, jumping directly from 5 to 7.

¹¹ The case envisaged is one in which a captive is released for some limited, specified purpose, with a promise on the captive's part to return once the task has been

7. The pledge not to return to a certain place, or to serve as a soldier

It is also customary for prisoners to promise not to return to a certain place, and not to take up arms against the one who had them in his power. . . . Some writers declare such an agreement void, because it is contrary to the duty due to the country of allegiance. But whatever is contrary to duty is not at once also void, as I have said just above and elsewhere. Then, too, it is not contrary to duty to obtain liberty for oneself by promising what is already in the hands of the enemy. The cause of one's country is, in fact, none the worse thereby, since he who has been captured must be considered as having already perished, unless he is set free.[12]

8. The pledge not to run away

Some prisoners also promise not to run away. Contrary to the opinion of certain writers, such a pledge is binding on them, even though they made the promise when in chains. For in this way, either lives are ordinarily saved, or milder captivity secured. If, however, the prisoner shall be put in chains afterward,

> performed. The promise is binding because the enemy receives nothing from it beyond his original entitlement as captor. The classic case of this was Regulus, who commanded a Roman army during the First Punic War. In 255 BC, he suffered a devastating defeat by the Carthaginians and was taken prisoner. This much is historical. Of dubious authenticity is the famous story of subsequent events. After being held for five years, Regulus was released on parole and sent to Rome, in the company of Carthaginian peace negotiators, in the belief that he would help persuade the Romans to agree to end the war. In the senate, he maintained a stubborn silence at first, until he was commanded to speak. He then eloquently pleaded *against* concluding peace, successfully urging Rome to fight on. He was aware that death awaited him at the hands of his captors if he returned to captivity. But he gallantly refused to break his parole arrangement. Refusing even to see his family, he returned to captivity, where he was duly tortured to death. The story was a great favourite of the Romans, with Regulus hailed as the embodiment of high-minded duty and devoted faith to one's pledged word. Grotius, however, points out that Regulus was not merely being high-minded – he was actually legally obligated to return to captivity

12 This section concerns what are known as parole agreements, although Grotius does not use that term. The typical parole agreement entailed the release of the prisoner, on the condition that the prisoner not re-join his own forces and continue in the war. Grotius holds these agreements to be valid on the ground that they confer onto the enemy no advantage additional to what was already possessed (i.e., the power to prevent the captured soldier from rejoining his force, by enslaving or imprisoning him). Nor do they involve any additional injury to the soldier's state, since it has lost the soldier's services in any event by virtue of his capture by the enemy. Parole arrangements of this sort were very common in warfare from the seventeenth to the nineteenth centuries in Europe and colonised areas. The last major use of parole arrangements was in the American Civil War (1861–5). Since then, parole arrangements have become uncommon. And some armed forces (such as the US one) expressly forbid their soldiers to conclude them.

then he will be released from the promise, if it was made on the condition that he should not be put in chains.

9. Whether one who has been captured can surrender to another

Rather foolishly the question is raised, whether one who been captured can surrender to another. It is quite certain that no one by his own agreement can take away a right gained by another. But the captor has gained a right, either by the law of war alone, or partly by the law of war and partly by the consent of him who is waging the war, as I have explained above.[13]

10. Whether private persons should be compelled by their rulers to carry out promises

Regarding the effect of agreements, an important question is, whether private persons, in case they are negligent, ought to be compelled by their rulers to fulfil their promises. It is nearer the truth to say that they should be compelled to do so only in regular warfare, on account of the law of nations by which those who wage war are bound to render justice to each other, even in regard to the acts of individuals.[14] [A] a case in point would be if envoys of the enemy should be injured by [breaches of contract made by] private citizens.

11. On the interpretation of agreements of this sort

In the matter of interpretation, the rules should be observed which have already been mentioned several times, to wit: that we should not depart from the natural meanings of the words except in order to avoid an absurdity, or from some quite satisfactory surmise as to the intention; and that in case of doubt we should be more inclined to interpret the words against the one who made the condition.[15]

One who has made an agreement regarding his life does not have the right to liberty also. Arms are not included under the term clothing; for these are different things. Aid is rightly said to have arrived if it is in sight, although it is doing nothing; for its very presence has an influence.

---

[13] See p. 369 above.

[14] By 'regular warfare' is meant war as customarily carried out by European states in conflicts with one another. The most important issue is whether a soldier's state of nationality would enforce a parole agreement which the soldier concluded with the enemy side. At first glance, it would seem odd that a state at war would enforce a contract to which it was not itself a party, and which had the effect of keeping the paroled soldier from performing war service. Nevertheless, the practice that evolved in European warfare was that parole agreements were enforced by the soldiers' home states.

[15] On these general rules of interpretation, see p. 243 above.

13. Who ought to be said to have returned to the enemy

One who has returned secretly, so as to depart immediately, will not be said to have returned to the enemy. For returning ought to be understood as coming a second time under the power of the enemy.

14. What are adequate reinforcements in the case of a surrender made conditionally

In the case of [a conditional] agreement to surrender, which shall not hold if adequate reinforcements have arrived, the reinforcements ought to be understood to be such as will cause the danger to cease.

15. Provisions on the execution of an agreement do not constitute conditions

This also must be noted, that if any covenant has been made regarding the method of execution, this adds no condition to the agreement. The case is as if they said that payment is to be made in a certain place, which afterward changed ownership.[16]

16. Regarding hostages given for such agreements

In regard to hostages, the position must be maintained which we stated above, that in most cases they are merely accessory to the principal act.[17] Nevertheless, the agreement can be so made that the obligation shall present an alternative – that is, either that something shall be done, or that the hostage shall be retained.[18] But in case of doubt, we must maintain what is most natural, that is, that the hostages shall be believed to be only accessory.

---

[16] A condition is something which, if not met, prevents a would-be contract from taking effect in the first place. A provision relating to the means of discharging the contract cannot, in Grotius's opinion, have such an effect and therefore cannot be regarded as a condition.

[17] See p. 447 above.

[18] In general, hostages are 'accessory to the principal act' in that the holding of the hostages is closely tied to the obligation to perform the contractual obligation. This means that the hostages are held pending performance of an act. But it is conceded that there is nothing to prevent an alternate arrangement from being agreed to: that hostages are to be given only after an agreement has been breached.

24

On implied good faith

1. How good faith may be tacitly interposed

[C]ertain things are agreed to by silence; and this is found to be the case in public agreements, in private agreements, and in mixed agreements. The reason is that consent, no matter how indicated and accepted, has the power of transferring a right. But there are also other signs of consent besides spoken and written words, as we have already more than once indicated.[1] And certain signs by nature form a part of the act.

2. The case of a person who desires to be received under the protection of a people or a king

An example may be found in the case of the person who comes either from the enemy or from a foreign country and entrusts himself to the good faith of another people or king. For there ought to be no doubt that such a person tacitly binds himself to do nothing against that government under which he seeks protection.

3. The case of one who asks or grants a parley

Likewise the person who asks or grants a parley tacitly promises that it will be without hurt to those who take part in it.

4. Whether a person who asks or grants a parley is hindered from promoting his own interests

But that implied consent must not be extended beyond what I have said. For, provided that the parties to the conference suffer no harm, it is not treacherous, but reckoned among honourable artifices, to divert the enemy from warlike plans by the pretext of a parley, and in the meantime to promote one's own advantage.

---

[1] See p. 33 above.

5. Of mute signs which by custom have some meaning

There are also certain mute signs which have a significance arising from custom. Such were in ancient times the use of fillets and olive branches; among the Macedonians the raising of spears, among the Romans the placing of shields over the heads, all signs of a suppliant surrender, which in consequence imposed the obligation to lay down arms. But whether one who indicates that he accepts such a surrender is under obligation, and how far, should be inferred from what I have said above.[2] At the present time, white flags are the implied sign of a request for a parley; they will, therefore, be no less binding than if the parley had been requested by word of mouth.

6. On the implied approval of a treaty compact

How far a treaty compact made by generals ought to be considered as impliedly approved by the people or king, I have already stated above, to wit: when both the action was known and something was done or not done for which no other cause could be assigned accept the wish to ratify the treaty.[3]

7. When a punishment is impliedly remitted

The remission of a penalty cannot be inferred from the sole fact of its being disregarded. There is need, besides, of some such act as either in itself may show friendship, as a treaty of friendship, or such as will express so high an opinion of the virtue of the party subject to punishment that his previous deeds ought deservedly to be pardoned; whether that opinion is expressed in words, or through acts, which customarily have such significance.

---

[2] See p. 444 above.   [3] See p. 237 above.

25

Conclusion, with admonitions on behalf of good faith and peace

1. Admonitions to preserve peace

At this point, I think that I can bring my work to an end, not because all has been said that could be said, but because sufficient has been said to lay the foundations. Whoever may wish to build on these foundations a more imposing structure will not only find me free from envy, but will have my sincere gratitude. Yet before I dismiss the reader I shall add a few admonitions which may be of value in war, and after war, for the preservation of good faith and of peace; just as in treating of the commencement of war I added certain admonitions regarding the avoidance of wars, so far as this can be accomplished. And good faith should be preserved, not only for other reasons but also in order that the hope of peace may not be done away with. For not only is every state sustained by good faith, . . . but also that greater society of states.

   [T]his good faith the supreme rulers of men ought so much the more earnestly than others to maintain, as they violate it with greater impunity.[1] [I]f good faith shall be done away with, [rulers] will be like wild beasts, whose violence all men fear. Justice, it is true, in its other aspects often contains elements of obscurity; but the bond of good faith is in itself plain to see, nay more, it is brought into use to so great an extent that it removes all obscurity from business transactions. It is, then, all the more the duty of kings to cherish good faith scrupulously, first for conscience's sake, and then also for the sake of the reputation by which the authority of the royal power is supported. Therefore let them not doubt that those who instil in [rulers] the arts of deception are doing the very thing which they teach.[2] For that teaching cannot long prosper

---

[1] Rulers violate the principles of good faith 'with greater impunity' in the sense that, when they commit violations, they are less likely to be punished than ordinary subjects would be. Precisely because there is no superior power to punish sovereigns for breaches of good faith, it is all the more imperative for rulers to exercise self-discipline of the most exacting kind.

[2] I.e., such wicked advisers (Machiavelli being probably in mind here) deceive themselves, and perhaps the rulers too, if they believe that they do good service by advising rulers to act in bad faith.

which makes a man anti-social with his kind and also hateful in the sight of God.

2. That peace should always be kept in view

Again, during the entire period of administration of a war, the soul cannot be kept serene and trusting in God unless it is always looking forward to peace. . . . Violence is characteristic of wild beasts, and violence is most manifest in war; wherefore the more diligently effort should be put forth that it be tempered with humanity, lest by imitating wild beasts too much we forget to be human.

3. That peace should be accepted even at a loss, especially by Christians

If, then, it is possible to have peace with sufficient safety, it is well established by condonation of offences, damages, and expenses. [T]his holds especially among Christians, on whom the Lord has bestowed His peace. And His best interpreter wishes us, so far as it is possible and within our power, to seek peace with all men. It is characteristic of a good man . . . to be [neither willing] to begin war, [nor] gladly to pursue it to the bitter end.

4. Whether the weaker should sometimes yield to the stronger

This one consideration ought to be sufficient. However, human advantage also often [points] in the same direction. [T]hose who are weaker [should be wary of] a long contest with a stronger opponent. . . . [J]ust as on a ship, a greater misfortune must be avoided at some loss, with complete disregard of anger and hope which . . . are deceitful advisers.[3]

5. On the usefulness of moderation to a conqueror

Again, human advantage [also points] in the same direction [for] the stronger [party]. The reason is . . . that peace is bounteous and creditable to those who grant it while their affairs are prosperous; and it is better and safer than a victory that is hoped for.[4] It must be kept in mind that Mars is on both sides. . . . And especially must the boldness of the desperate be feared; wild beasts bite most fiercely when dying.

---

[3] The point is that, if a ship is in peril at sea, it will often make sense to jettison a part of the cargo in order to save the remainder, along with the ship and crew. In such dire circumstances, emotional considerations such as anger and hope should not be allowed to gain the upper hand.

[4] I.e., a victory that is merely speculative.

6. On treatment for peace when the issue is in doubt

But, if both sides seem to be equal to each other, this in truth . . . is the best time to treat of peace, while each has confidence in himself.

7. On the keeping of peace with the utmost scruple

Moreover peace, whatever the terms on which it is made, ought to be preserved absolutely, on account of the sacredness of good faith, which I have mentioned; and not only should treachery be anxiously avoided, but everything else that may arouse anger. . . . [N]ot only should all friendships be safeguarded with the greatest devotion and good faith, but especially those which have been restored to goodwill after enmity.

8. A prayer, and the end of the work

May God, who alone hath the power, inscribe these teachings on the hearts of those who hold sway over the Christian world. May He grant to them a mind possessing knowledge of divine and human law, and having ever before it the reflection that [rulers] have been chosen as [servants of God] for the rule of man, the living thing most dear to God.

Appendix 1

Note 18 (p. 329): the text of Grotius's note

There has been published in Italian a book called *Consolato del Mare*, in which have been collected the edicts of the emperors of Greece and Germany, and of the kings of France, Spain, Syria, and Cyprus; also those of the Balearic Isles, the Venetians and the Genoese. In title [cclxxvi] of that book, questions of the kind under consideration are discussed, and the following principles stated:

> If both the ship and the cargo belong to the enemy, the case is clear that they become the property of those who take them; if, however, the ship belongs to those who are at peace, but the cargo to the enemy, the belligerents may force the ship to convey the cargo to some port belonging to them, upon condition, however, of paying the cost of the voyage to the owner of the vessel. On the other hand, if the ship belongs to the enemy, but the cargo to others, the latter must bargain for the price of the vessel; or, if the shippers do not wish to bargain, they must be compelled to go with the ship to some port belonging to the side of the captor, and to pay to the captor the price due for the use of the vessel.

In Holland, in the year 1438, when the Dutch were at war with Lübeck and other cities on the Baltic and the Elbe, in a full meeting of the senate it was decided that merchandise clearly belonging to others, even if it were found in vessels of enemies, did not form part of the booty; and since then this has been recognised as the law there. This was also the view of the king of Denmark, when, in 1597, he sent an embassy to the Dutch and their allies to claim for his subjects freedom of navigation and of carrying merchandise to Spain, with which the Dutch were waging a very bitter war.

In France, there has always been granted to those at peace freedom to carry on commerce, even with those who were enemies of the French. So indiscriminately has such freedom been taken advantage of, that the enemy have often concealed their property under the names of others, as appears from an edict of the year 1543, . . . which has been carried over into an edict of the year 1584, and subsequent edicts. In these edicts, it is expressly provided that it is permissible for those on friendly terms with the French to carry on commerce in time of war, provided that this is done in their own ships, and by their own people, ships, and cargoes; it is permissible to carry their goods wherever they may wish, provided that these goods shall not be material serviceable in war, by means of which they wished to help the cause of the enemy; in case material serviceable for war should be transported, the French are permitted to take such material for themselves, paying a fair price for it. Here we must note two things: by these laws material of war did not become legitimate spoil; and innocent merchandise was much farther removed from the same danger.

I should not deny that the northern nations have at times made use of another right, but in different ways, and having in view rather a temporary advantage than the maintenance of permanent justice. For when, making a pretext of their own wars, the English interfered with the commerce of the Danes, for this cause war arose between the peoples with the result that the Danes imposed tribute on the English. Although the cause of the payment was changed, the name of it, *Danegeld*, remained until the time of William [the Conqueror], who founded the dynasty now ruling England; this is recorded by the reliable De Thou, in his history of the year 1589.

Again, Elizabeth, the wisest queen of England, in the year 1575, sent Sir William Winter and Robert Beal, Secretary of the Royal Council, to Holland in order to make it plain that the English could not suffer the Dutch, in the very midst of Holland's war with Spain, to detain English ships which had sailed for Spanish ports. This is reported by Van Reyd for the year 1575 in his *Dutch History*, and by the Englishman Camden for the following year. However, when the English had themselves become enemies of the Spaniards and were interfering with the exercise of the right of navigation to Spain on the part of German cities, from the controversial writings of both peoples, which deserve to be read for an understanding of this controversy, it appears that the English themselves in their writings admit this, when they adduce as the two chief points in support of their case that the things which were being carried by the Germans to Spain were material for war, and that previous treaties had forbidden such transportation.

Such treaties were afterward made by the Dutch and their allies with Lübeck and its allies in 1613, providing that neither the one party nor the other should permit subjects of the enemy to trade within their territory, or aid the enemy with money, soldiers, ships, or provisions. Later, in 1627, it was agreed between the kings of Sweden and Denmark that the king of Denmark should prevent all commerce with the people of Danzig, who were enemies of Sweden, and should not permit any merchandise to pass through the Cimbrian Strait [Baltic Sound] to the other enemies of Sweden; for these services the king of Denmark stipulated certain advantages for himself.

These, however, are all special agreements, from which no inference can be drawn which would be binding upon all. This was in fact said also by the Germans in their writings, that not all merchandise was excluded by the treaties in question but only such merchandise as had been imported into England or manufactured there. The Germans, nevertheless, were not the only ones who opposed the English when the latter forbade commerce with their enemy. Even

Poland sent an embassy and complained that the law of nations was being infringed upon when, because of the war between England and Spain, the Poles were deprived of the freedom of commercial relations with the Spaniards; this is related under the year 1597 by Camden and Van Reyd, whom we have cited already.

Moreover, after the Treaty of [Vervins] had been made with Spain [in 1598], while Elizabeth, queen of England, remained at war, the French refused to accede to the request of the English that the English should be allowed to search French ships that were sailing to Spain, in order that munitions of war might not be secretly conveyed therein; the reason alleged was that this was seeking a pretext for plundering and disturbing commerce. In the treaty which the English made with the Dutch and their allies in 1625, an agreement was reached that other nations, to whose interest it was that the greatness of Spain should be diminished, should be invited voluntarily to forbid commerce with the Spaniards. If, nevertheless, the nations should not do this of their own accord, it was decided that vessels should be searched to see if they carried any war material, but that otherwise neither the ships nor their cargoes should be detained, and that damage should not be done on this pretext to those who remained at peace.

In the same year, it happened that certain men sailed from Hamburg for Spain in a ship laden chiefly with military stores; these stores were seized by the English, but the value of the rest of the merchandise was paid. The French, however, when French ships sailing for Spain were confiscated by the English, made it plain that they would not permit such procedure.

We have, therefore, well stated the case in saying that public proclamations are required. The English themselves came to hold the same opinion. An example of such a proclamation by them is given by Camden under the years 1591 and 1598. However, such proclamations have not always been obeyed, and distinctions have been made between times, causes, and places. In 1458, in fact, the city of Lübeck decided that it would not obey the proclamation made by the city of Danzig, forbidding them to carry on trade with Malmo and Memel, then at war with Danzig. Similarly, the Dutch in 1551 refused to obey when Lübeck notified them that they should refrain from commerce with the Danes, who were then their enemies.

In 1522, when there was war between the Swedes and the Danes, the king of Denmark requested the Hanseatic cities not to carry on commerce with the Swedes. Some of the cities, being in need of his friendship, complied, but the others did not. When war was raging between Sweden and the king of Poland, the Dutch never suffered themselves to be prohibited from commerce with one or the other nation. The Dutch, moreover, always restored to France the French ships which on their way to or from Spain were intercepted by Dutch vessels, Holland and Spain being at war. See the speech of Louis Servin, one time royal advocate, delivered in 1592 in the case of citizens of Hamburg.

But the same Dutch did not permit merchandise to be brought by the English into Dunkirk, off which they kept a fleet; just so the city of Danzig, in 1455, notified the Dutch not to carry anything into the city of Königsberg, as Gaspar Schutz narrates in his *Prussian History*. Add Cabedo, *Decisions*, xlvii, 2, and Seraphinus de Freitas in his book *On the Just Asiatic Empire of the Portuguese*, where he cites various others.

Appendix 2

Alternative outline

Note: The numbers refer, in order, to the book, chapter and section where the subject in question is treated.

I. Political theory

1. Civil power:	I.3.6
2. Sovereignty	
What it consists of:	I.3.7–19, 24
Mixed sovereignty:	I.3.20
Compatibility of sovereignty and lesser political status:	I.3.20–3
Covering: unequal alliances, tributaries, feudal subordinates	
Acquisition:	II.4.11
Loss by usucaption, lapse of time:	II.4.12–13, 15
Whether people can reclaim:	II.4.14
Alienation:	II.6.3–13; III.20.5
Abdication:	II.7.26
3. Sovereign rights	
Eminent domain:	II.14.7–8
Revocability of grants:	II.14.13
4. Sovereigns and duties	
Oaths, promises of sovereigns:	II.14.3–4
Contracts of sovereigns:	II.14.5–6, 9–12
Contracts by usurpers of sovereignty:	II.14.14
5. Sovereign immunity:	II.14.1–2
6. Succession:	II.7.12–25, 27–37
7. Legitimacy	
On obedience to a usurper:	I.4.15–20
8. Right of a state over subjects	
General:	II.5.23
Withdrawal of subjects from state:	II.5.24
Right of state over exiles:	II.5.25

II. Natural law and natural rights

Further reading

Ago, Roberto, 'Le droit international dans la conception de Grotius' (1983) 182 *Receuil des Cours* (Hague Academy of International Law) 375–98

Basdevant, J., 'Hugo Grotius', in A. Pillet (ed.), *Les fondateurs du droit international* (Paris: V. Giard and E. Brière, 1904), at pp. 125–267

Borschberg, Peter, 'Hugo Grotius, East India Trade and the King of Johor' (1999) 30 *Journal of Southeast Asian Studies* 225–48

Brett, Annabel, 'Natural Right and Civil Community: The Civil Philosophy of Hugo Grotius' (2002) 45 *Historical Journal* 31–51

Bull, Hedley, Benedict Kingsbury and Adam Roberts (eds.), *Hugo Grotius and International Relations* (Oxford: Clarendon Press, 1990)

Dumbauld, Edward, *The Life and Legal Writings of Hugo Grotius* (Norman, OK: University of Oklahoma Press, 1969)

Edwards, Charles S., *Hugo Grotius the Miracle of Holland: A Study in Legal and Political Thought* (Chicago, IL: Nelson-Hall, 1981)

'The Law of Nature in the Thought of Hugo Grotius' (1970) 32 *Journal of Politics* 784–807

Forde, Steven, 'Hugo Grotius on Ethics and War' (1998) 92 *American Political Science Review* 639–48

Haakonssen, Knud, 'Hugo Grotius and the History of Political Thought' (1985) 13 *Political Theory* 239–65

Haggenmacher, Peter, *Grotius et la doctrine de la guerre juste* (Paris: Presses Universitaires de France, 1983)

Jeffrey, Renée, *Hugo Grotius in International Thought* (New York: Palgrave Macmillan, 2006)

Kennedy, David, 'Primitive Legal Scholarship' (1986) 27 *Harvard International Law Journal* 1–98, at 76–95

Knight, W. S. M., *The Life and Works of Hugo Grotius* (London: Sweet and Maxwell, 1925)

La Pradelle, A. de, *Maîtres et doctrines du droit des gens* (Paris: Éditions internationales, 2nd edn, 1950), at pp. 71–92

Lee, R. Warden, 'Grotius – The Last Phase, 1635–45' (1945) 31 *Transactions of the Grotius Society* 193–215

Porras, Ileana M., 'Constructing International Law in the East Indian Seas: Property, Sovereignty, Commerce and War in Hugo Grotius' *De Iure Praedae* – The Law of Prize and Booty, or "On How to Distinguish Merchants from Pirates"' (2006) 31 *Brooklyn Journal of International Law* 741–804

Salter, John, 'Hugo Grotius: Property and Consent' (2001) 29 *Political Theory* 537–55

Stumpf, Christoph A., *The Grotian Theology of International Law: Hugo Grotius and the Moral Foundations of International Relations* (Berlin: Walter de Gruyter, 2006)

Thomas, Jeremy, 'The Intertwining of Law and Theology in the Writings of Grotius' (1999) 1 *Journal of the History of International Law* 61–100

Tuck, Richard, 'Grotius and Selden', in J. H. Burns (ed.), *The Cambridge History of Political Thought 1450–1700* (Cambridge University Press, 1991), at pp. 499–529

Natural Rights Theories: Their Origin and Development (Cambridge University Press, 1979), at pp. 58–81

The Rights of War and Peace: Political Thought and the International Order from Grotius to Kant (Oxford University Press, 1999), at pp. 78–108

Van Ittersum, Martine Julia, *Profit and Principle: Hugo Grotius, Natural Rights Theories and the Rise of Dutch Power in the East Indies, 1595–1615* (Leiden: Brill, 2006)

Wight, Martin, *Four Seminal Thinkers in International Theory: Machiavelli, Grotius, Kant, and Mazzini* (Oxford University Press, 2005), at pp. 29–61

Wright, Herbert F., 'Some Less Known Works of Hugo Grotius' (1928) 7 *Bibliotheca Visseriana* 131–238

Zemanek, Karl, 'Was Hugo Grotius Really in Favour of Freedom of the Seas?' (1999) 1 *Journal of the History of International Law* 48–60

Index of names

Abraham (biblical patriarch), 38, 68
Accursius, 17
Africanus, 179
Alciatus (Andrea Alciato), 17
Alexander the Great, 173, 240
Alfenus Varus, 162, 166, 452
Ambrose of Milan, 41
Antiochus IV (Seleucid ruler), 240
Antoninus, 174
Aratus, xiii, 410
Arias de Valderas, Franciscus, 10–11, 12
Aristotle: on alliances, 64; on arbitration, 443;
   on captured property, 359; on civil power,
   50; on *culpa* (negligence), 387–9; on division
   of law into law of nature and volitional law,
   28; on extinguishment, 171; fear, actions
   under influence of, 191; Grotius's use of, xx,
   xxi, 11, 12–14; on insanity of barbarians, 303;
   on justice and equity, 28; on natural law, 30;
   on resistance to sovereignty, 72; on
   restorative and distributive justice, 26, 27; on
   rights and duties, xxv; on slavery, 52, 304,
   403; on sociableness, as human
   characteristic, 85, 439; on sovereignty, 53, 62;
   sovereignty, political theories of, xxvi, xxvii;
   on substances, 456; on uncertainty in moral
   questions, 307; on virtue as mean in
   passions, 13–14; war for crimes against God
   and, 288
Arminius, Jacob, xv
Arps-de Wilde, E., xxxiv
Augustine of Hippo, 44, 81, 281, 285
Ayala, Balthazar de, 11, 12–14, 347

Bacon, Francis, xix–xx
Barclay, William, 71, 73
Bartolus of Sassoferrato, xiv, 17, 304,
   342

Beal, Robert, 478
Belli, Pierini, 318
Bodin, Jean, 18, 222, 245
Brasidas, 240, 241

Cabedo, Jorge de, 480
Callistratus, 163
Calvin, John, xvi
Camden, William, 478, 479
Carneades of Cyrene, 2, 5, 6
Cassius (Gaius Cassius), 48, 49
Cato the Elder (Marcus Porcius Cato the
   Censor), 413, 414
Cato the Younger (Marcus Porcius Cato of
   Utica), 48, 413
Celsus, 109, 180
Charlemagne, 175
Charles V (Holy Roman Emperor), 318
Cicero (Marcus Tullius Cicero): biographical
   information, 23; on contracts, 205; on
   interpretation, 249, 250; on natural law not
   conflicting with just war, 34, 36; on need for
   law, 7; on oaths, 218; obedience, crimes of
   those under obligation of, 319; on
   postliminy, 410; on private or individual acts
   in public war, 413; on promises, 250; on
   property rights, 98, 99; on public war, 48,
   343; on resistance to usurper, 76; on
   self-defence, 7; on sovereignty, 53, 54, 63; war
   defined by, 23; on war's ends, 313
Constantine I (Roman emperor) 40

Dante, Alighieri 304
De Thou, Jacques Auguste, 478
Decimus Brutus, 48
Demosthenes, 340
Descartes, René, xix–xx
Dio Chrysostom, 106

Subject index

abandoned property: acquisition by occupation of, 115; assertion of liberty by subjects following, 123; inundated lands, 163–4; length of time of non-possession, 118–19, 120; presumptions of human intent regarding, 116–18, 119–20; rights not daily exercised, retention of, 123; silence, non-possession, and loss of hope of recovery as grounds for, 117–18; sovereignty acquired by long-standing possession following abandonment, 121; thrown-away things, 117; for time exceeding memory of man, 119, 120; truces, seizure during, 451; unborn children's right to, 120–1; usucaption or prescription following (*see* usucaption or prescription)

abdication: of hereditary kingdom, 155; right of resistance against abdicators of sovereign power, 72

absolute declarations of war, 345–6

absolute sovereignty, xxviii–xxix, 58, 59, 223

accessories to crime, 292

acquisition of property, 105–15: abandoned property, 115; by actual delivery, 169; alienation, secondary or derivative acquisition by, 138–9, 144–5; alluvial lands and deposits, 162–6; another's property, things fashioned out of, 167–8; by civil law, 160; division, through, 105; formation of new property from existing materials, 105; by fraudulent possession, 168; human law on, 161; income from possession, entitlement to, 168; by infants and insane persons, 107–8; inundated lands, 163–4; islands, 162; by law of nations, 159–69; occupation, now only through, 105, 106–7; offspring of animals, 166–7; ownership, possession by, 106–7; persons, acquisition of rights over, 124–37; private ownership, origins and development

of, 92–4; rivers, 108, 113–14; sea, parts of, 108–13; servitude or pledge, not through, 105; by set-off, 144–5; sovereignty, possession by, 106–7; treasure-trove, 161; in war (*see* captured property); wild animals, fish, and birds, 160–1

'Adamus Exul' (Grotius), xiii

adopted children, 134, 135

adrogatio, 135

adulterers, liability of, 256

Aequicolae, 346

aged persons, preventing killing of, 390

agents: promises made through, 194; promises revoked after acceptance by, 198–9; war, auxiliary agents as efficient causes of, 77

agnate lineal succession, 153

Algerian pirates, 383

alienation of property: civil laws regarding, 144–5; secondary or derivative acquisition by, 138–9, 144–5; by set-off, 144–5; wills as form of, 143

alienation of sovereignty, 139–43; absolute sovereignty and power of, 58; for advantage or necessity, 141; infeudation as, 141; intermediate governmental authority, alienation of, 142; part of the whole, over, 139–40; pawning as, 141; peace, for sake of, 427–8; public domain, alienation of, 142–3; right of resistance against alienator, 73; unoccupied lands, over, 140

alliances. *See* treaties and alliances

alluvial lands and deposits, 162–6

ambassadors. *See* legation

American Civil War, 469

American Indians, Grotius's work on, xviii

amnesty clauses, 421

Amphictyonic Council, 173

An Abridgement of All Sea Laws (Welwood), xiv